KONRAD ADENAUER

MEMOIRS 1945–53

KONRAD ADENAUER
MEMOIRS 1945-53

Translated by Beate Ruhm von Oppen

HENRY REGNERY COMPANY
CHICAGO

To My Fatherland

CONTENTS

CONTENTS

9

CONTENTS

ILLUSTRATIONS

Acknowledgments

The publishers wish to thank the following for providing illustrations for this volume: Associated Press, 1; Max Martin Brehm, *Mit dem Bundeskansler in USA,*11; Hermann Claasen, *Gesang in Feuerofen* (Dusseldorf: L. Schwann, 1949), 4; DPA, Hamburg, 3, 5, 6, 9 ; Georg Munker, Bonn, frontispiece; Presse-und Informationsamt der Bundesregierung, 2, 10; Horst Tappe, cover; US Army, 8

TRANSLATOR'S NOTE

WHEN I asked the author of these *Memoirs* whether he had any wishes regarding the translation, he said: 'Wishes? No.' After a moment's reflection he added: 'It should be accurate, of course.'

What is accuracy? Is it – always – possible? Is it desirable? A reader of a translation should be aware of these questions. The translator owes him an implicit or explicit answer to them.

There is the well-known conflict between beauty and fidelity in all translation. It seems to me that – whatever may be said about it in other cases – in a personal and historical document fidelity deserves to win. I have tried to make it prevail, to produce as close an English equivalent to the German original as possible. 'The German original' includes the personal mode of utterance of its author. To 'de-personalize' would have been to traduce.

In a book of this kind there is the additional problem of re-translation or its avoidance. It is obviously invidious to put English *words* into an Englishman's or American's mouth that he may not actually have *said*. Once or twice a risk was taken and very short utterances are 'quoted' in re-translated direct speech. In all cases of longer pronouncements I have sacrificed 'drama' or readability to reliability and put them in indirect speech. I always tried to track down English or American original texts. Where they were available, or made available, they appear as quotations; otherwise I paraphrased or described a re-translation as such.

What appears as quotation can therefore be accepted as original (unless the original was German or French). This applies *a fortiori* to written documents, such as the letter of dismissal by Brigadier Barraclough. Exceptions are clearly marked as re-translations. International agreements or pronouncements of which there is an official English or American version appear in the wording of that version.

B.R.v.O.

INTRODUCTION

RECENTLY I was talking about our times with a professor of modern history at a German university. In the course of our conversation I asked him what he – a historian – thought about coming developments.

He replied that it was not the task of the historian to foresee events. Historians were not prophets. They sought rather to record or to ascertain what happened as truthfully as possible.

I responded that in my view the historian's task was a different one. To my mind historians, especially professors of modern history, must at least make the attempt, by way of analogies between past events and those of our times, even our days, to discern the probable direction in which events seem to be tending, and then to point to developments that may be expected and even, if necessary, to sound warnings.

The historian did not agree with me. He repeated, once more, that historians are not prophets.

Of course I do not demand prophesy of a historian, but I think that his work – especially if he is a modern historian – is not complete until he has tried to predict future developments from present events, as well as possible.

Although I am no historian, I have lived through much, and helped to shape quite a lot of it, in agitated and even tempestuous times. Of course I am not a prophet either and I may well be wrong in what I say about the future. But I shall be content if I make the reader think about affairs at present and whither they may lead.

A long life gives men a chance to acquire experience. Experience can be a guide to thought and action which nothing can replace, not even innate intellect. This is particularly true in the field of politics.

My memories go back a long way. When I was a student in my first semester at the University of Freiburg in 1894, all things seemed to have their firm, appointed place on this earth. Nobody could have imagined the turmoil the next decades were to bring. At the turn of the century the German Reich was the strongest land power and Great Britain the greatest sea power in the world, and Europe was the centre of the world's political and economic power.

15

The United States had no army worth mentioning, no considerable navy, and had not yet entered world politics.

1914 brought the First World War. It brought the United States into world politics. The German Empire came to an end and was succeeded by the Weimar Republic. The year 1933 brought Hitler and National Socialism to power. He wantonly unleashed the Second World War. It finished with the complete destruction of Germany in 1945 and with a fateful weakening of Europe.

This book begins with the events after Germany's collapse in 1945. It is to give my reminiscences of my experiences since 1945, without omissions, without colouring. At the same time, however, it is meant to put the reader in a position to think about the future.

To present the material merely chronologically would not properly convey to the reader the connections between events which alone will allow him to understand what happened and what is happening. The material therefore had to be organized in a way that permitted these connections to be recognized. Hence important developments and issues – the questions of reunification, of those expelled from their homes, of the equalization of burdens, of reconstruction, and of economics – had to be left to the next volume. Another thing that has to be left until then is the appreciation of the great help given me by those who accompanied me on my way.

1

BOWED BUT UNBROKEN

The End of the War; American Occupation

At the end of September 1944 I was arrested again and sent to the Gestapo prison at Brauweiler, near Cologne, after a rather exciting escape from the concentration camp on the Cologne Fair Grounds where I had been taken during the aftermath of the attempt on Hitler's life of 20 July 1944. When I arrived, the commissar in charge of the prison asked me please not to take my own life as this would only cause trouble for him.

I asked him what made him think that I might take my life. He replied that as I was now nearly seventy years old and had nothing more to expect from life, it seemed reasonable to suppose that I would put an end to it.

I told him not to worry: I would not cause him any trouble.

During the following weeks the Americans were approaching the Rhine from the West. All inmates of the prison, myself included of course, were led to a wall in the garden and told that we would be put against that wall and shot as soon as the Americans crossed the Erft, a small tributary of the Rhine about ten or fifteen miles from Brauweiler. No one would make much fuss about our deaths.

At Brauweiler I was kept in solitary confinement and liked it. As I was not being bothered too much with interrogations and the like, I heard no more about proceedings against me, so I asked my son Max, who was an officer serving at the front, to go to the Chief Security Office in the Prinz-Albrecht-Strasse in Berlin as soon as possible and make inquiries about my case. After a short time I heard from Max that he had been to the Security Office. At first the people there knew nothing about my file, but later they found it in the basement. Max was told that it had been taken there in an air raid and then been forgotten. Since there was no further interest in the events leading to my arrest, my case would soon be settled. I would be released at once.

Shortly afterwards – it was on a Sunday, 26 November, my name-day – a Gestapo commissar came round on an inspection of Brauweiler. I asked him about my release, and told him that I had had news from Berlin that I was to be freed. I was anxious to get away from Brauweiler as soon as possible because of the danger in which the American advance put us prisoners. The commissar told me that the order for my release had arrived. I would be set free in the next few days.

I replied that I demanded immediate release

He suggested that I should wait until the next day, a Monday. When I arrived at Brauweiler Gestapo officials had taken my private belongings – braces, tie, bootlaces and other objects with which one could take one's life. The officials were off duty this Sunday afternoon, but they would give me back my things on Monday.

I repeated my demand for immediate release, with or without braces.

The commissar shrugged his shoulders and reluctantly gave his consent. I asked some officials to telephone two friends of mine, brothers called Sinn, to tell them I was coming.

I lost no time and, without braces, bootlaces, tie, or any of the few belongings I had with me when I was arrested, set off for the place a few miles from Brauweiler where they lived. One of the officials even came a little way with me on his bicycle to show me the road.

My two friends – both bachelors – received me royally. There was a festive coffee table, with candles alight in silver candlesticks, and they produced the best cake they had been able to find. After all I had been through, I really appreciated their reception.

The good coffee made me feel stronger and we discussed the quickest way for me to get to my family at Rhöndorf.

I was not allowed into the administrative district of Cologne and I was afraid that if I used the railway I would be recognized and that the Gestapo might arrest me again for entering the banned district.

The Sinn brothers got me a commercial vehicle. With this I drove to Königswinter, where I asked someone to telephone my house to say that I was free and on the way home.

But I was prevented from taking the road along the Rhine which connects Königswinter and Rhöndorf because of floods. To avoid them, I had to drive around the entire Siebengebirge range to reach Rhöndorf via Honnef.

It was late in the evening when I reached home. My family had given up expecting me that day because they had thought there was no way round the high water. Their joy at my arrival was all the greater.

I saw the end of the war at home in Rhöndorf. I had been firmly convinced that there would be no fighting in Rhöndorf and its vicinity. Since the American troops were advancing in the direction of Mainz and the British in the direction of Wesel, I thought that the Americans would cross the Rhine near Mainz and the British near Wesel. Rhöndorf lay almost exactly in the middle, so I thought it highly probable that they would pass us by. My family and I – there were fourteen of us in the house – looked forward to the end of the war with no fears. But things turned out very differently.

It may seem surprising that I was so well-informed about the course of the fighting. The reason was that, apart from the time I spent in concentration camp or in prison, I did not let a day pass without listening to several foreign broadcasts. The stations I listened to most were the BBC German broadcasts from London and the Swiss transmitter at Beromünster. In addition my friend

Herr von Weiss, the Swiss Consul-General in Cologne, who lived in Godesberg after his house in Cologne had been destroyed, kept me informed by
word of mouth and by giving me foreign newspapers. Major Schliebusch, a
member of the High Command of the Armed Forces, also gave me regular
news. From all these sources I was able to form a fair impression of what was
going on. That was how I knew about the American and British troop movements at Mainz and Wesel. Listening to foreign radio broadcasts was made
easier by the fact that our house is in an isolated position on the slope of a
hill and that it was inhabited only by members of my family.

The German troops did not blow up the bridge at Remagen, whose bridge-
head on our side was about seven miles upstream from Honnef. Consequently the Americans changed their deployment completely and used the
weakly defended bridge at Remagen for their first Rhine crossing, with the
result that we got involved in the thick of the fighting at Rhöndorf. Twelve
American shells landed in my garden, three of them hit my house from the
front, while the back of the house was under German mortar fire from the
right bank of the Rhine.

It was a Sunday morning when I made my first direct acquaintance with the
American army. I had, very unwisely, gone into the garden to observe the
movements of the Americans on the left bank of the Rhine from the highest
accessible point. Suddenly, about three hundred yards away, I saw a shell
hurtling towards me. (I could gauge distances fairly well, because I knew the
area intimately.) I flung myself to the ground. We knew from experience that
the Americans usually fired three shells at the same target; so I waited for the
other two. The first shell, the one I had seen, hit the ground about twelve
yards away from me. It was a standard American high-fragmentation shell
and the shrapnel whizzed by above me. The second shell landed seven yards
below me, and the third five yards. Then I ran back into the house. Apart
from the fact that my hearing was badly impaired for quite a while, I was not
injured. In subsequent encounters the American forces proved much more
tractable than on this occasion.

On the morning of 8 March we had a telephone call from my sister, Lilly
Suth. She and her husband had moved to Unkel, a place further up the Rhine
from Rhöndorf, after the destruction of their apartment in Cologne. She was
quite excited, and told me: 'We are free, we have Americans here – quite nice
people, by the way.'

We later found out that we had telephoned across the firing lines; the
telephone office at Honnef served Unkel which was occupied by American
troops, while Honnef – Rhöndorf was still in German hands.

I had prepared an emergency shelter for my family in our wine cellar in the
hillside behind the house. We now spent the greater part of our days there.
The youngest child of my eldest son, Konradin, aged two months, hung in a
basket from the ceiling.

The population in our shelter had now grown to eighteen. Louis, a French

19

prisoner of war, who had helped with the work in our garden, had come to ask for shelter for himself and – as he put it – two friends. He and his friends had escaped from a prisoner of war camp because they were afraid of being taken deeper into Germany by the retreating German troops. They were full of fears for the future. I was glad to let them stay with us. But there turned out to be four of them, not three. We moved closer together in the shelter and awaited the end of the war.

One problem facing us was how to get enough drinking water for so many people. The piped water supply had stopped working. There was a well about two hundred yards away. In the mornings, at about seven o'clock, the Americans paused for an hour in the bombardment of the right bank of the Rhine. Apparently this was their breakfast hour. During this lull two of my daughters had to make their way to the well, finding cover where they could, along the garden walls, to fetch enough water to last us twenty-four hours.

We spent eight days in our cellar before the Americans arrived and the shooting stopped. The German troops withdrew from their trenches in the wood behind our house.

The Americans issued orders that were hard and oppressive, but what mattered to us and gave us comfort was that the fighting, the war, and National Socialism were over and gone. Along the road beside the Rhine the American tanks were rolling in a gigantic column towards Cologne.

Reinstatement as Oberbürgermeister of Cologne by the Americans

A few days later an American officer, a German Jewish emigrant who knew my name, came to see whether I was still alive. Some days after that some American officers arrived and asked me to come to Cologne to see the commandant there and to take over the administration of the city.

An open jeep brought my wife and myself to Cologne. The impressions I received during the drive were dreadful. A ferry took us across the Rhine near Unkel and then we drove to Cologne through a number of localities including Bonn. Everywhere we saw damaged houses, everywhere the evidence of fighting.

I was deeply shaken by the sight of Cologne. The city's population before the war had been roughly 760,000. Now (as a later census revealed), there were about 32,000 inhabitants in the districts on the left bank of the Rhine. The right bank was still occupied by German troops. The fiercest fighting had ceased, but shots were still being exchanged.

Our way led us past the house of some friends. I asked the driver to stop and went inside to look for them. The front door stood open and chairs and books lay about in wild disorder in the various rooms. Nobody was at home. That was the state of affairs nearly everywhere.

The American Commandant of Cologne, Lieutenant Colonel R. L. Hyles, who had sent for me, now asked me to become Oberbürgermeister (Lord

Mayor) of Cologne once more. I told him that I had three sons in the German armed forces, at the front. The Nazis would certainly shoot them if it became known that the Americans had made me Oberbürgermeister of Cologne. But I also told him that I was prepared to give all the help I could. The Commandant took my point. For the time being, I was given the status of an adviser and only became Oberbürgermeister after the cessation of hostilities in Germany.

The Americans with whom I dealt were all intelligent and reasonable men. We soon understood one another.

I still remember very vividly my first meeting with Lieutenant Colonel Hyles. There was another American officer present on that occasion. When Lieutenant Colonel Hyles had finished his discussion with me, the other American pulled a map of North America from his wallet, spread it out in front of me and, pointing to the Southern area of the United States, said: 'That is Texas, the greatest, most beautiful, richest country in the world, and I am a Texan!' He said this with a serious expression and a proud face. I must admit that once I had seen Texas I understood his pride.

After my conversations with the American officers I walked about in the city and found everything empty, desolate, destroyed. I went to the central office of the Gestapo. I wanted to have another look at that thieves' den. It was in a big house on the Appellhofplatz. All the doors from top to bottom of the entire building were open. Papers and files were strewn about the floors. I walked through all the rooms and finally came to one which, to judge by its furniture, must have been the office of a high Gestapo official. Man is a strange creature. This whole house had been a source of torment for so many people, as well as for my wife, myself, and for my daughters. But the thought crossed my mind that I wanted to take away a souvenir of this place for myself and my family. There was a bronze candlestick on the Gestapo official's desk. Its shape was simple and distinguished – which suggested that the Gestapo had taken it away from someone. I took the candlestick. I see it every morning at home and it is a constant reminder of all that happened – the suffering and the injustice.

The task confronting me in a war-ravaged Cologne was a huge and extraordinarily difficult one. The extent of the damage suffered by the city in air raids and from the other effects of war was enormous.

More than half of the houses and public buildings were totally destroyed, nearly all the others had suffered partial damage. Only 300 houses had escaped unscathed.

The damage done to the city by the destruction of streets, tram rails, sewers, water pipes, gas pipes, electrical installations and other public utilities, was no less widespread. It is hard to realize the threat this constituted to the health of the people. There was no gas, no water, no electric current, and no means of transport. The bridges across the Rhine had been destroyed. There were mountains of rubble in the streets. Everywhere there were gigantic areas of debris from bombed and shelled buildings. With its razed churches, many of them almost a thousand years old, its bombed-out cathedral, with the ruins of once beautiful bridges sticking up out of the Rhine, and the vast expanses of derelict houses, Cologne was a ghost city.

People were living as best they could in the cellars of bombed houses. They did their cooking on primitive brick fire-places, using lignite briquettes. They fetched water in pails and tin bowls from the few pumps that had remained intact.

The difficulties facing the municipal administration seemed insurmountable. Its offices were moved into the rooms of a tolerably well preserved building belonging to an insurance company. Cologne's old City Hall lay in ruins.

On the day before the Nazis removed me from my post as Oberbürgermeister – it was a Sunday – I had quite deliberately taken leave of my office and of the City Hall, for I had a premonition that the following day would see me dismissed and hounded out and that I would never see my former place of work again. I took the key of the City Hall home and I still have it in Rhöndorf today.

The great majority of people fled or were evacuated in the last months of the war. Now, after the end of hostilities in Germany, they came back. They came back from all the regions of Germany to which they had fled or been sent during the war. Every day thousands of citizens streamed back into Cologne, on foot or by whatever transport was later available in goods trains. I can still see those open freight cars, jammed with people who wanted to get home again, no matter what hardships were involved. Pale, tired, haggard, they carried the few belongings they still had, and usually found nothing but their destroyed homes. It seemed almost impossible to provide these many thousands of people with accommodation, food, and other necessities.

The difficulties of the city administration started with the most ridiculous trifles. We did not even have enough paper and other office supplies to tell the American Commandant's Office of the needs and wishes of the people of the city. It was extremely difficult to find personnel for the most vital tasks. Many of my former colleagues from the days before 1933 were dead or were living somewhere else in Germany and unable to return.

But life had not died in the destroyed city. Feeding the population was the biggest and most difficult task we had. Barter trade flourished. Monetary value had in practice been almost entirely replaced by the value of goods.

I took some emergency measures to get food supplies for the people of Cologne. I had all the intact vehicles in the city requisitioned and sent them out into the countryside to buy potatoes, grain, vegetables, and livestock, so as to provide at least a small amount of food.

I approached the American military commander and asked him to place food from American army depots at the disposal of the population: again the Americans helped whenever they were in a position to do so. There really was a good human relationship between me and the American officers with whom I had to work. Later I heard that I was No. 1 on the American 'White List' for the whole of Germany. That meant that I was regarded as especially trustworthy. This may partly explain the great consideration I always met with in my dealings with the Americans, shown in this letter, written by Colonel Patterson:

Military Government
Detachment E 1 H 2
Cologne   8th May 1945

Colonel Geary
XXII Corps,
APO 250, U.S. Army

Dear Colonel Geary:
This is to introduce to you Dr. Konrad Adenauer, Oberbürgermeister of the City of Cologne, who will furnish you with any information or advice which you might desire of him with regard to the holiday of the 10th of May 1945.

Dr. Adenauer was Oberbürgermeister of the City of Cologne from 1919 to 1933, when he was removed from office and severely persecuted by the Nazis. Dr. Adenauer's reputation extends far beyond the Cologne area; *his name is Number One on the White List for Germany.*

Before his recent appointment to his old office, Dr. Adenauer acted as Special Adviser to the writer for civilian affairs for the City and the Regierungsbezirk* of Cologne. The writer has a very high regard for Dr. Adenauer's integrity and for the selfless and democratic ideals which he incorporates in his person and in his work.

Sincerely,
(signed) Patterson
Lt. Col. CAC

I owed it to my good relations with the American occupation forces that I was able to bring to a successful conclusion one affair which I still remember especially vividly.

The City of Cologne owned a very rich art collection, of which the most important part was devoted to paintings of the medieval 'School of Cologne'. These pictures were among the most valuable of all German works of art. In order to protect them from destruction they had been removed, during the war, to a bomb-proof basement in a fortress in Southern Germany. I was very anxious to bring these pictures back to Cologne as soon as possible because I feared for their future. On the other hand, it was taking a considerable risk to transport them back: there was the uncertainty of road travel and there was a further great danger in that the Allies had confiscated all works of art in

---

* Regierungsbezirk: subdivision of a province.

23

German possession. I decided to let a municipal hearse fetch the pictures from Burg Hohenzollern, where they were, and bring them back to Cologne. The hearse did indeed bring the precious paintings back safely. I had them stored in the basement of a house in the Hermann Pflaume Strasse which had been rented by a Catholic parish; a chapel had been installed there. I counted on the Americans' respect for church property and hoped that the pictures would be safe. Later a danger did arise in the form of a general American order that all works of art in German possession were to be surrendered. There was to be an investigation to determine whether they included any items stolen by Germans. I thought it best at first to disregard this order: I was afraid that the Allies might retain part of the surrendered pictures as compensation for works stolen from other countries.

But somehow the Americans had learnt of the whereabouts of the Cologne pictures and the American Governor sent an officer with the message that the occupying powers must insist on the order being carried out. They preferred not to have to use force. Oberbürgermeister Adenauer was therefore urgently requested to hand over the pictures belonging to the Cologne Museum. The Governor pledged his word of honour that the pictures would be returned if they could be proved to be German property. I had to obey this order. Later I received back all the paintings of the 'School of Cologne' in accordance with the Governor's word.

The other big problem, apart from food, was housing. The city administration had issued public warnings against returning, but these warnings were not heeded and we had to deal with the consequences. Attempts were made to make the ruins as habitable as possible; we also put up emergency huts in order to relieve the worst pressure.

Soon after starting my work in Cologne, I succeeded in getting the municipal buses released. I sent them to Buchenwald, Dachau, and Theresienstadt to fetch back those inmates of the concentration camps who came from Cologne. I did not subscribe to the idea of the collective guilt of all Germans, but I did consider us all under an obligation to make restitution for the injustice done in the past to our own people too, and I felt an urge to get the poor inmates of the concentration camps taken back to their home town as quickly as possible.

It was clear to me that priority must be given to a revival of commerce and traffic. The Rhine bridges had been destroyed and it was important to restore them. I had obtained purchase permits for iron from the American Governor and bought up great quantities of steel from a factory on the Lower Rhine.

The problem of unemployment played an important role in our situation since nearly all factories, firms, and businesses had been destroyed. The measures I took were intended to revive trade and traffic and so to create employment.

I go into all this detail of the devastation and of life in Cologne because I saw it with my own eyes and because it was my task to cope as best I could with the consequences of the war in the Cologne area. Similar conditions existed all over Germany, although Cologne, because of its situation, had probably suffered most. In the course of the war the Allies had come round to the view that German ability to resist would be hardest hit by the destruction of houses and apartments and that this would paralyse the German economy far more effectively than the destruction of single factories. The Allies further decided that massed attacks by a thousand or more aircraft would be most likely to reduce the German will to resist. This led to the planned destruction of civilian residential areas. The paralysis of the means of transport and communication by the destruction of bridges of all kinds, especially the big Rhine bridges, of railway stations and the like, was part of the same plan.

By the end of the war in 1945, forty per cent of all transport installations in Germany were destroyed. More than fifty per cent of all pre-war dwellings in the big cities – in some cities as much as eighty per cent – were totally destroyed and a large percentage was heavily damaged. The material loss of pre-war property was stupendous. The withdrawal of protection of German patents abroad represented a permanent loss, to which was added the seizure of all German assets abroad.

After the defeat, conditions in most parts of Germany were indescribably hard. Not only was there universal devastation, but the central German administrative bodies had ceased to function or were no longer allowed to function, so that only local communal administrations could slowly begin to deal with the greatest and most immediate hardships – hunger, homelessness, and cold.

In the American and British zones the conquerors had made attempts to revive – at least to some extent – the local institutions. In some places, for instance in Cologne, these efforts were successful. But the Allied Control Council in Berlin did not work. And because the Allied Control Council did not work, all the efforts made in municipalities and even in entire occupation zones were bound to be fruitless. Economic misery continued to grow.

British Occupation in Cologne

My relations with the officers of the American occupation forces were, as I have said, very good. Things changed when, after a while, on 21 June 1945, the Americans left Cologne and were replaced by British troops. Conflicts soon arose between me and the British administrative officers. In my opinion the British were treating the population badly. Their attitude to me was also very negative.

The British installed a tapping device on my line at the telephone exchange at Bad Honnef. My line was the only one in this medium-sized telephone exchange that was being supervised by the British. The postal officials naturally found out very soon that this device had been installed and informed me at once.

The British had very close relations with the German Social Democrats. This was probably due to the fact that after July 1945 Britain had a Labour Government.

In these really very hard months after the end of the war we in Cologne endeavoured to achieve cooperation between all parties. Nevertheless, a report written for the British Secret Service by Town Councillor Görlinger, a leading member of the Social Democratic Party, shows how the Social Democrats were using their connections with the Labour Party. I shall quote some of the more significant portions of this report, which was written in July 1945, and which reached me at once:

When, after an absence of twelve years, I returned to Cologne, the city in which I had played a leading part as a Social Democrat for over two decades, I found a scene of devastation which struck me as hopeless. I went at once to the City Hall of Cologne, to Oberbürgermeister Dr Adenauer, who was very surprised to see me again, as everyone in Cologne had been convinced that I was dead. I asked him for a brief survey of the political situation. He stressed the fact that the Americans had at first appointed Mayor Brisch and his brother-in-law, Herr Suth, to take over the direction of affairs in the city, and that they had offered him the administration of the province. When urged to do so, he had, however, decided for the city of Cologne but with the express proviso that he could resign at any time. He stated the same condition when the British assumed the occupation of the city.

Despite the prohibition of political parties, the former Social Democrats and Communists among the workers are very active and deeply shocked by the policy pursued by Adenauer, Suth and Schwering, supported by the Catholic clergy in Cologne. The trade unions have been given permission to organize. The members of the former Free Trade Unions, Christian Trade Unions, and Communist-oriented trade unions are working together to develop industrial organizations. Their cooperation seems happily free from all tensions and based on complete trust. Of particular interest is the fact that a majority of the leading Catholics in Cologne are strongly opposed to a revival of the *camarilla* of the Centre Party which was formerly such a feature of Cologne politics, and that they stress the value of sincere co-operation among all democratic representatives.

. . . The school problem has always been one of the politically most controversial questions in the Rhineland. The Centre Party, which favoured the denominational schools demanded by the Pope and bishops under Canon Law, was in severe conflict with the Socialist working class and parts of the progressive bourgeoisie who favoured a secular school system and the relegation of religion to a place outside the curriculum. In order to prevent a revival of this old quarrel, my friends had come to an agreement with leading members of the Centre and Catholic clergy to opt for an

26

inter-denominational basis for elementary schools. There must not be another segregation of children into Catholics, Protestants, Jews, and Freethinkers. Religious instruction was to be given separately for different denominations in the school. This solution also recommended itself in view of the extraordinary difficulties confronting any educational organization when elementary school buildings have been destroyed. A few days ago it became known that Oberbürgermeister Dr Adenauer had ordered primary schooling, which begins today, 23 July 1945, to be resumed on a denominational basis. An advisory council of citizens, such as probably exists in most towns and rural districts of the occupation zone, has not been called in Cologne. The Oberbürgermeister merely conferred with the Archbishop, who is bound by Canon Law, and with Superintendent Dr Encke of the Protestant Church before the denominational segregation of the children was ordered. Two days ago I had a discussion with Oberbürgermeister Adenauer and told him that by this action he had revived a fundamental controversy and torpedoed the necessary cooperation. He argued that he wanted to base the new start on the legal position of 1933, which in the case of Prussia admitted denominational schools. This means the negation of all experience gained during twelve years of National Socialist rule and I told him that by this action he had shown his inability to rally a leadership that could bring together those groups prepared to base their cooperation on a new spirit. Our discussion was very heated.

. . . Dr Adenauer has submitted a memorandum, dated 28 June 1945, to the Commandant of Military Government, which is to be passed on to General Eisenhower. In it he expresses the opinion that the moment has come to consider whether the stringent measures for the purge of Nazis should not be relaxed. This document contains the following sentence, verbatim: 'I make this proposal although National Socialist propaganda in Germany – clandestine, of course – has lately increased considerably. I believe that if the screening of Party Members is carried out roughly in the way proposed by me, it will be possible to make proper use of many people who at the moment are excluded from all activity and fall prey to this propaganda, *and thus to remove them from exposure to National Socialist propaganda.*'

. . . There is talk in Cologne of an impending occupation of the District of Cologne and, perhaps, of Aachen by the French. There are separatist tendencies in Aachen, Bonn, and Cologne, but for the time being they are very tentative. I have been unable to establish any connection of leading personalities with these tendencies.

(signed) R. Görlinger
Grafenwerthstr. 8

The Social Democrats tried to represent the Christian Democratic Union as successor party to the Centre and to burden the CDU with the mistakes made by the Centre. These efforts were not without success and explain the initial British mistrust of the CDU. Herr Görlinger tried to represent me as a politician who attempted to take former Nazis back into the administration. His proof was a memorandum I submitted to the Commandant of Military Government with the request to transmit it to General Eisenhower. In this memorandum I had proposed to stop simply excluding former members of the NSDAP* from all work, thus driving them into the arms of Nazi propaganda, and instead to institute a first rough screening process and to admit people to work according to the result of such screening.

Görlinger's report had its effect on the occupying authorities. I was certainly not in favour of allowing National Socialists who had incurred heavy guilt to go scot free; on the other hand I was aware of the weakness of human nature. Anyone who has ever lived in a police state knows how much courage it takes to oppose the state, how much danger is involved for the individual and his family. In my view it was necessary to consider every case on its merits. Heroism is not a common commodity. In this matter the attitude of Cardinal Galen, the Bishop of Münster, was similar to mine.

The First Meeting of the Town Council in Cologne

On 1 October 1945 the first meeting of the Cologne Town Council took place on the orders of the British Military Government, which also appointed the Council's twenty-four members. The Town Council was to support the municipal administration in the execution of its duties. The orders of the Military Government formed the legal basis and defined the scope of its activities and of those of the municipal administration. The Town Council was not a freely elected body. Its members had been selected by the occupation power according to their callings and their political attitudes.

As Oberbürgermeister I was happy to have advice, help and constructive criticism from the townspeople once again. I also welcomed the convening of the Town Council because I hoped that it would be instrumental in letting the public know about the problems and difficulties with which we had to contend and that it would enable us to call on the cooperation of all of the people.

Major Prior, the representative of the British Military Government in Cologne, opened the meeting. He told us that it was the chief aim of the Military Government to 're-educate' Germany in the truest sense of the word. Let me reproduce some extracts from his speech:

All the Germans I meet are eager to express their abhorrence of the National Socialist Party and all for which it stands but the fact remains that for 12 years Germany has apparently supported and willingly shared in the systematic plunder of Europe. The ultimate responsibility for the actions of the government of a country belongs to the people who tolerate the

---

* National Socialist German Workers' Party.

continuance of that government. It is to assist in kindling this flame of democratic responsibility that I today vest in the assembled Town Council for the city of Cologne the powers previously enjoyed under the Weimar Republic, subject of course to my overriding authority as Commander of the Military Government.

The rules of procedure for the new Town Council will be the same as those according to the Rheinische Städteordnung. The public and press will of course be admitted to all meetings of the Council. . . .

The Council today has only 24 members. It is my intention that this Council be increased in numbers at a later date to embrace an even wider section of the population. It is my wish that subcommittees be appointed from among your number to deal with the various aspects of the Civic Administration. It is my further wish that a subcommittee be established within the next few days to consider and direct the emergency measures necessary to meet the problems of the approaching winter:

(a) shelter programme and emergency housing repairs
(b) emergency feeding and fuel
(c) public health including speedy improvisation of emergency hospitals.

The Civic Administration has already been instructed that all else will be subordinated to these overriding necessities to prevent undue suffering of the population.

In conclusion I wish to stress strongly to all persons present that to achieve the re-education mentioned in the first part of my opening address it is essential that all people who possess the desire for a reformed Germany must prove this by making the Denazification of public and industrial life an accomplished fact in both word and spirit.

In opening this Council and in handing over the Chairmanship of this meeting to Dr Adenauer, Oberbürgermeister of Cologne, I do so with the high hope that this rebirth of municipal responsibility will be instrumental in restoring this once so beautiful city to its former state.

The members of the Town Council did not need any special admonition. We were all prepared to give of our best in the rebuilding of our homeland.

One of those present at this first meeting of the Cologne Town Council was Hans Böckler, who later became Chairman of the German League of Trade Unions. I did not know then what a significant role he was to play in a matter of decisive importance for our people.

I tried to express our feelings in a speech I made at this meeting when I said, *inter alia*:

. . . I sincerely welcome the fact that this assembly has been called into existence. The previous state of affairs has made it impossible to call for the participation of representatives of the townspeople in the work of public administration. It is a great step forward that the orders of the Military Government now give us this opportunity.

... It is my hope and my desire that the Military Government's orders will permit the meeting of a freely elected Town Council in the foreseeable future.

... Our tasks, which have just been outlined by the British Military Government Commander of the City of Cologne, present infinite difficulties. Of all the big cities of Germany, Cologne is the one that has suffered the greatest devastation.

... The winter ahead of us will be very hard. We must above all provide food, fuel, and housing. We – you and we – will do everything in our power to create conditions that are at least tolerable. It will not be possible to do this to the extent you and we would like. But – and I am now addressing myself not to this hall alone but to all the citizens of Cologne – I ask all our fellow-citizens always to remember this: the guilty, those responsible for this unspeakable suffering, this indescribable misery, are those accursed men who came to power in the fatal year 1933. It was they who dishonoured the German name throughout the world and covered it with shame, who destroyed our Reich, who, when their own well-deserved perdition was certain, systematically and deliberately plunged our misguided and paralysed people into the deepest misery. They did this not, as is often assumed, so that the German people should perish with them – though that idea may also have influenced them in their decisions and actions; they intended something much more devilish: they wanted and they still want the thought of revenge and retribution to re-animate the German people against its wartime opponents. . . .

Ladies and gentlemen, the tasks awaiting us are so pressing, so heavy, but also so compelling that there will be little time for political discussion. ... Nonetheless I should like to say a few words about a political question which is particularly close to my heart, a few words on the nature of democracy.

The word 'democracy' is used so often nowadays that it is in danger of devaluation. We must not allow it to be so abused. We should not only speak of democracy, always and everywhere, but always and everywhere we should act according to the principles of democracy.

It is in accordance with the principles of democracy that the will of the freely elected majority should decide matters. But, ladies and gentlemen, let me here say a word, let me insert the words 'in the last resort'; it is in the last resort that the will of the freely elected majority should decide. The principles of democracy also demand respect for and confidence in the man of different political views; they demand an effort to enter into his thoughts and his reasoning and to reach an understanding with him; they require that the ultimately coercive act of voting someone down should be resorted to only when all else fails. I hope that the newly created communal committees and our own assembly will become a sanctuary and a nursery of a truly democratic way of thinking.

... Let us, then, go to work together, bent down, bowed low, but – ladies and gentlemen – unbroken.

Dismissed by the British

The British asked us to do our best to overcome our difficulties. But our own strength was insufficient, especially in view of the many rules and regulations laid down by the Military Government.

At the end of September 1945 there was a severe conflict between the British and myself. The British Military Government asked me to cut down the trees in the parks and ring roads of Cologne so that the timber could be given to the population as fuel.

When I was Oberbürgermeister of Cologne before 1933 I had put a Green Belt, a bit more than half a mile wide and more than ten miles in length, around the city area of Cologne. In my judgment this Green Belt was of vital importance to the health of the people of Cologne. In my view the amount of timber gained by the felling of the trees would have made next to no difference to the fuel shortage in Cologne. As this was mainly due to a scarcity of coal, trees from the parks would not seriously have affected the situation. On the other hand the city of Cologne would have suffered incalculable damage by the loss of its trees, a loss that it would take several decades to make good. I refused to cut down the Green Belt and asked the British authorities to release requisitioned stocks of coal. I also requested a supply of coal from the Ruhr for domestic fuel needs.

The reaction to my demand was fairly icy and I scarcely hoped that my request would be granted. I therefore tried to use the Press to give a little publicity to our needs. On 5 October 1945 I received a representative of the *News Chronicle* and one of the Associated Press at my house in Rhöndorf. I made some notes about this conversation:

On 5 October 1945 a representative of the *News Chronicle* and one of the Associated Press (Miss Barbara Page), who had been introduced by Mr Stern-Rubarth, came to see me. I told them very emphatically of my fears that the Allies had no intention of giving the German population coal for cooking. I pointed to the very serious consequences – consequences for which we could be blamed: the death of untold thousands, the debilitation of others, diseases and epidemics. I also told them that de Gaulle had just made a speech at Saarbrücken in which, according to the BBC in London, he had said that Frenchmen and Germans must let bygones be bygones and must cooperate, mindful of the fact that they were Europeans. The journalists said that they had heard this speech and that de Gaulle had even said that Frenchmen and Germans must remember that they are Western

Europeans. I replied that I wished a British statesman might have addressed us as Western Europeans. The representative of the *News Chronicle* asked me for my views on the Rhine-Ruhr state. I replied that after the events of the last hundred years I could understand the French and Belgian insistence on security. But it was wrong to separate a Rhine-Ruhr State from the area of Germany not occupied by the Russians and to detach it from Germany.

The part occupied by Russia was lost to Germany for a period of unforeseeable duration. Both journalists agreed with this. If a Rhine-Ruhr State was formed separate from the other parts of Germany, the question at once arose of what the position of the parts to the North and South of this Rhine-Ruhr State was to be in international and constitutional law. True to her imperialist tendencies, Russia would immediately declare that the part occupied by her, that is half of the old Germany, was the German Reich. The three severed parts of the zones not occupied by the Russians would automatically strive for reunification with the Russian-occupied old Reich, and would thus positively have their faces turned to the East rather than to the West. It was necessary to maintain a constitutional relationship between the three parts of German territory not occupied by the Russians that would remain after the creation of a Rhine-Ruhr State. This relationship might take the form of a federation. Above all, I considered it essential to knit the economy of the Rhine-Ruhr State with those of France and Belgium in order to allow common economic interests to develop.

I considered such interests the safest and best foundation for a rapprochement between peoples and for the safeguarding of peace. The *News Chronicle* representative asked whether in that case Cologne would have to be occupied by the French, and I replied that that would not be necessary in this context. The security demands of France and Belgium could be met as outlined above and by a system of international control; but if it was unavoidable, even this would have to be accepted in the interests of the more important objective. It was a question of secondary importance.
9 October 1945

The day after this interview – it was the 6th of October – I received an order to present myself at Military Government headquarters. On my way there I wondered what kind of an answer I would get to my request for coal, and was considering what further course of action to take should the response be negative.

When I arrived at the office of Brigadier Barraclough, the Military Governor of the North Rhine Province, there were several British officers present. None of these gentlemen stood up when I came into the room. After a few very formal words of welcome I was not offered a chair. I thereupon took one and was about to sit down, when Brigadier Barraclough said rather curtly: 'Don't sit down!' So I listened to the following communication standing up:

Headquarters Military Government
Köln   Regierungsbezirk   6 October 1945

Herrn Oberbürgermeister
Dr. h.c. K. Adenauer
Allianz Buildings,
Cologne

1. I am not satisfied with the progress which has been made in Cologne in connection with the repair of buildings and the clearance of the streets and the general task of preparing for the coming winter.
2. About 2 months ago I personally warned you of your responsibilities in connection with this work. You have not fulfilled those responsibilities to my satisfaction. I am fully aware of the difficulties with which you have had to contend. I know that many of your colleagues have been removed for political reasons. I know the difficulties in connection with the labour situation in Cologne. I am fully alive to the position with regard to communication, shortage of coal, shortage of transport etc., etc.
3. I am however convinced that with proper supervision and energy on your part, more could have been done to deal with these problems than has, in fact, been done.
4. In my opinion you have failed in your duty to the people of Cologne.
5. You are therefore dismissed to-day from your appointment as Oberbürgermeister of Cologne.
6. You will leave Cologne as soon as possible, and in any case not later than 14th October.
7. You will immediately hand over the duties of Oberbürgermeister of Cologne to the Bürgermeister of Cologne Herr Suth.
8. Herr Suth will carry out the duties of Oberbürgermeister of Cologne as a temporary measure pending the appointment of an Oberbürgermeister.
9. After you have handed over to Herr Suth you will take no further part in the administration or public life of Cologne or any other part of the North Rhine Province.
10. You will not indulge either directly or indirectly in any political activity whatever.
11. If you fail in any respect to observe the instructions contained in this letter, you will be brought to trial by the Military Court.
12. You will acknowledge receipt of the letter hereon.

(signed) Barraclough
Brigadier Comd. Military Government
North Rhine Province

I was asked to sign the original of this letter to confirm receipt. Asked whether I had any remarks to make, I said: 'No!' and left the room.

c   33

The decisive passage of this letter of dismissal was point 10: 'You will not indulge either directly or indirectly in any political activity whatever.'

Many years later, when I was already Federal Chancellor, I met Brigadier Barraclough at a state banquet. He asked me: 'What did you really think when you got your letter of dismissal?' I replied: 'I have a file "Dismissal by the Nazis" at home. I will now start a file "Dismissal by the Liberators".'

The economically most valuable part of the three Western occupation zones had gone to the British and the city of Cologne was a significant centre of their zone. Even during the Weimar period I had played a leading role in the Centre Party, although I was not a prominent *party* politician. But the Oberbürgermeister of Cologne was bound to play an important part in German public life; and now this post was occupied by a man who had enjoyed the confidence of the CAC, as Colonel Patterson had explained in the letter quoted above, and this must have influenced the British. Not that this alone would have been sufficient reason to remove me as Oberbürgermeister of Cologne, but the essential point in my dismissal was the prohibition of further political activity. It is in this perspective that one must see Görlinger's letter and the effect of Colonel Patterson's letter on the British. They must have regarded me as inconvenient for their policy, because of the friendliness of the Labour Government towards the SPD and because of the strong ties with the Americans which I was assumed to have in view of Patterson's letter. This explains the fact that I was forbidden to engage in 'any political activity whatever'. The reason for my dismissal was not that I had not done my duty to the people of Cologne; this reason was a ridiculous invention. When I later reread Colonel Patterson's letter I understood the political meaning of the whole operation.

The prohibition on entering Cologne was a personal hardship for me because my wife was suffering severely from the after-effects of her stay in Brauweiler, the Gestapo prison, and was in a Cologne hospital. It took a lot of effort to get permission to visit her twice a week, and the time and route to be taken on these visits were meticulously laid down.

When I was dismissed by the British occupation forces, forbidden to engage in any political activity on pain of court martial, and expelled from Cologne, my friends, who were afraid of the occupation forces, avoided me. When I left Cologne, nobody said goodbye. The atmosphere around me was very similar to what I remembered when the National Socialists had hounded me out.

There was a secretary in my office, Fräulein Goldkuhle. Without my prior knowledge she wrote a letter to Brigadier Barraclough. In it she explained that she did not feel entitled to an opinion on my dismissal as Oberbürgermeister, but if the reason given was that I had not done my duty to the people of Cologne, she could state from her own knowledge of my activities that the allegation was untrue; I had done everything within my power for the people of Cologne.

As a result of this letter my successor was told by the British occupation authorities that Fräulein Goldkuhle was to be immediately dismissed from the service of the City of Cologne and was never to be re-employed. I saw to it that the administration of the University of Cologne employed Fräulein Goldkuhle. Later, when I was Federal Chancellor, I was instrumental in getting her a post in the Foreign Ministry. She was an excellent worker and a good linguist.

All this brought my political activities to an end for the time being and I returned once more to dedicated gardening. But a surprise awaited me. One day a British colonel attached to the headquarters at Bünde came to see me. I had met him before; in civilian life he was an Oxford don. He wanted some political information and advice. I told him that I was very sorry not to be able to oblige him, but the British zone ended about three miles from my house and if we both went to the French zone in his car I could talk politics with him there. He looked at me in amazement and asked what all this meant. I told him what had happened, and stressed the ban on political activity. He could only shake his head, and said that nothing was known of this at Bünde but that we *would* have our conversation. And so we did. A day or two later I was informed by British Headquarters at Bünde that I was allowed to take part in political activities again, except in the *Regierungsbezirk* of Cologne. This was presumably the result of my visitor's intervention. I was even asked by the British to make a public appearance at an important CDU meeting that was to take place at Bad Godesberg in December.

Reflections on the Situation of Germany

Whether my dismissal was a good or a bad thing I was unable to tell at the time. The sudden standstill after the most strenuous activity was a hard blow. I did not at that time know the exact reasons for my dismissal.

Now I had time and leisure to read newspapers thoroughly, to listen to the radio, and most important to hold long and detailed conversations with my old friend von Weiss, the Swiss Consul-General, about world events.

A letter I wrote to the then Oberbürgermeister of Duisburg, Herr Weitz, on 31 October 1945, shows my assessment of the political situation.

Russia holds the Eastern half of Germany, Poland, the Balkans, apparently Hungary, and a part of Austria. Russia is withdrawing more and more from cooperation with the other great powers and directs affairs in the countries dominated by her entirely as she sees fit. The countries ruled by her are already governed by economic and political principles that are totally different from those accepted in the rest of Europe. Thus the division of Europe into Eastern Europe, the Russian territory, and Western Europe is a fact.

Britain and France are the leading great powers in Western Europe. The part of Germany not occupied by Russia is an integral part of Western Europe. If it remains crippled the consequences for the whole of Western Europe, and that includes Britain and France, will be terrible. It is in the real interests not only of that part of Germany but also of Britain and France, to unite Europe under their leadership, and politically and economically to pacify and restore to health the part of Germany not occupied by Russia. The separation of the Rhineland and Westphalia from Germany does not serve this purpose; it would have the opposite effect. It would bring about a political orientation towards the East of the part of Germany not occupied by the Russians.

In the long run the French and Belgian demand for security can only be met by the economic integration of Western Germany, France, Belgium, Luxembourg and Holland. If Britain, too, were to decide to participate in this economic integration, we would be much closer to the ultimate goal of a Union of the States of Western Europe.

As for the constitution of the part of Germany not occupied by Russia: at the moment there is no sensible constitution and a constitutional structure must be found and restored. As the creation of a unitary centralized state will be neither possible nor desirable, the constitutional cohesion can be looser than before; it might take the form of a federal relationship.

I knew the anxieties of Germany's western neighbours. I understood and appreciated them fully in view of their experiences in the past hundred years. I thought it was wrong to try to calm their fears by pointing to the distribution of power in the Europe of 1945. Political history has shown that nothing ever stands still and that political circumstances can change very rapidly.

A solution to the German question had to be found that was organic and natural and that would therefore be durable; a solution which would reassure our western neighbours and give them a feeling of lasting security. I did not, however, regard an amputation of German territory, such as the Allies were planning – with France, for instance, wanting to detach the left bank of the Rhine – as such a solution. Also whoever undertook such a dismembering had to consider what was to become of the rest of Germany and whether it would not thereby become, as Churchill put it, a rotting corpse in the middle of Europe, which would present as deadly a danger to Europe as any victorious National Socialist Germany could have done.

I am a German, but I am also, and always have been, a European and have always felt like a European. I have therefore long advocated an understanding with France; I did so, moreover, in the 1920s, during the severest crises, and also in the face of the Reich Government. I always urged a reasonable understanding that would do justice to the interests of both countries. After the First World War I advocated a plan for an organic integration of the French, Belgian, and German economies for the safeguarding of a durable peace. In my view parallel, unified economic interests are and always will be the healthiest and most lasting foundation for good political relations between peoples. Despite the misery prevailing in Europe I saw great possibilities for the future of Western Europe. The unification of Europed seemed far more feasible now than in the 1920s. The idea of international cooperation between peoples must succeed.

I thought a great deal about the problem of a United States of Europe with Germany as a part. In a future United States of Europe I saw the greatest and most lasting security for Germany's western neighbours. The French fear of German resurgence which caused France to press for a policy of dismemberment of Germany seemed to be altogether exaggerated. After 1945 Germany lay prostrate – militarily, economically and politically – and in my opinion this condition was a sufficient guarantee that Germany could not again threaten France. In the future United States of Europe I saw great hope for Europe and thus for Germany. We had to try to remind France, Holland, Belgium, and the other European countries that they were – as we were – situated in Western Europe, that they are and will forever remain our neighbours, that any violence they do to us must in the end lead to trouble, and that no lasting peace can be established in Europe if it is founded on force alone. General de Gaulle had recognized this in his speech at Saarbrücken in August 1945: 'Frenchmen and Germans must let bygones be bygones, must work together, and must remember that they are Europeans.'

These words gave me great hope for Germany and for the realization of my hopes for a united Europe.

I realized that we Germans could only engage in a very limited foreign policy at first. The aim of our foreign policy had to be to take part, as equals, in peaceful cooperation in the concert of nations. The burdens put on Germany vis-à-vis other countries as a result of a lost war should not exceed what Germany could bear and fulfil. Even the vanquished have a right to live and work. Bitter need without hope is the greatest obstacle to peaceful development. The victor, who has the power, also has obligations towards the vanquished under human and divine law.

I knew that a united Europe would only be possible if a community of the peoples of Europe could be restored in which every people made its irreplaceable and indispensable contribution to the European economy and civilization, to Western thought, writing, and creativeness.

Germany lies at the centre of Europe. Because of its geographic position, a healthy and politically viable Europe can arise only if Germany is fully accepted as an economically and politically sound member. The way to the achievement of this aim would be long and would call for much tenacity and patience. Yet political reason told me that this objective would be reached.

I reflected a good deal on the course of German history. I cast my mind back to the hard years that Germany went through, especially in the Rhineland, from 1918 until 1924. The present position of Germany, the position of every individual, was incomparably worse, and yet it was useful to recall the first post-war years after 1918 and to remember what the German people had achieved in a decade and a half. I was thinking particularly of my hometown, Cologne. Then, too, misery and anxiety about Germany's future weighed us down. There was widespread unemployment, inflation, and uncertainty about political developments. But by combining their efforts the people of Cologne had succeeded in surmounting all these miseries and dangers. In those strenuous years we created in Cologne the Fair, the Mülheim bridge, Niehl harbour, the university, the great urban developments and settlements, and the Green Belt. We also organized the Exhibition of the Rhenish Millennium and held the 'Pressa', the first and so far the only press exhibition in the world.

The thought that we had then been able to do all this gave me the courage to believe that we could overcome our present difficulties. To be sure, these earlier accomplishments could not compare with the great tasks now facing the whole of Germany. But for me, who had been Oberbürgermeister of Cologne in those years, they were concrete evidence, personally experienced, of what can be done with courage, patience and perseverance.

I also pondered why the Weimar Republic that arose after 1918 lasted only fourteen years, why Bismarck's Reich, founded in 1871 and soon one of the most powerful countries in the world, collapsed in 1918, after less than fifty years – this German Reich which seemed easily as strong and as firm as any other European country of the time. I asked myself how the National Socialist Reich had come about, welcomed at first with jubilation by many ordinary people, then feared by so many because of its abysmal meanness and malice – feared, despised and cursed. What made this National Socialist Reich possible among the German people? How was it possible that a war could be started by the National Socialist Government, a war which, despite its initial dazzling successes, was bound to be lost in the end? How was it possible for miracles of bravery and dedication to duty to be performed by the same people who carried out crimes unexampled in number and enormity? How could the war be continued long after defeat had become a certainty, and continued to the point of self-destruction? How did the German people fall into this abyss?

During the National Socialist period I was often ashamed to be a German, ashamed to the depths of my soul. From Consul-General von Weiss, I had learned of the atrocities committed by Germans against Germans, and of the crimes perpetrated against mankind. Yet after the catastrophe, when I saw how the German people bore their terrible fate, endured in hunger, cold, need and death an existence temporarily without hope for the future, in complete political impotence, despised by all the peoples of the earth; when I saw the German people suffering this fate in patient strength that seemed stronger than their misery, then I was proud once more to be a German. I was proud of the fortitude with which the German people bore their fate, proud to see each one suffering without despair, struggling not to go under but, from this present distress, to save himself and his family for the sake of a better future.

The history of Germany in the last hundred years passed before my eyes and I asked myself what had allowed it to take this course. It was a question that had to be asked. If we were to emerge from this misery and to find the right way forward, we had first to understand what had brought us so low. We could find the way to a better future only if we recognized how we had got into this most fatal period in the history of the German people. To find our course we had to search our consciences.

What were the fundamental reasons that brought us so low from such heights, and finally plunged us into the abyss? Details hardly matter in such an examination. Many of them are still unclear. But we have to look for the deeper, the most effective causes of the catastrophe.

It is my conviction that the seminal causes reach far back before the year 1933. National Socialism was the immediate cause of the catastrophe, but it could not have come to power in Germany had it not found fertile soil for its poisonous seed among much of the population. I stress: throughout broad strata of German society. It is wrong to say that the military or the big industrialists alone were responsible. They certainly have their full measure of responsibility, and their personal guilt was commensurate with their power and influence. Nevertheless, had not many of the people – farmers, shop-keepers, professionals, intellectuals, workers – been animated by the wrong spirit, the victorious advance of National Socialism in the years after 1930 would have been impossible.

For many decades the German people suffered from a wrong attitude to the state, to power, to the relationship between the individual and the state. They made an idol of the state and set it upon an altar; the individual's worth and dignity had been sacrificed to this idol.

The belief in the omnipotence of the state, in the primacy of the state and in the power concentrated in the state above all else, even above the eternal human values, was first enthroned in Germany after the victorious war of 1870–1 and the subsequent headlong economic development.

The rapid increase in industrialization, the concentration of large masses of people in the cities, and, a connected phenomenon, the uprooting of many people, cleared the way for the pernicious growth of materialism among the German people. A materialist ideology was bound further to emphasize the importance of power and of the state which gathered and embodied this power, and to lead to the subordination of ethical values and of the dignity of the individual.

Marxist materialism contributed a great deal to this development. Anyone who works for the centralization of political and economic power in the hands of the state or of one class, and who therefore advocates the principle of class war, is an enemy of the freedom of the individual and is bound to prepare the way for dictatorship in the minds of his adherents. That such a result is inevitable is shown by the history of the countries that regard Karl Marx as their Messiah and his teachings as gospel. National Socialism was simply the last logical development – pushed to criminal lengths – of that worship of power and that scorn for the individual which naturally arise from a materialist ideology.

A people prepared first by an exaggerated idea of the state, its nature, its power, and the unconditional obedience owed to it, and further mentally and morally conditioned by the materialist ideology, was ready, as soon as economic circumstances for large parts of the population worsened, for the fairly rapid acceptance of the totalitarian state. The masses were led, without a will of their own. They accepted a doctrine that made their own race the master race and their own people the master people, and which called other peoples inferior, some of them fit only for destruction. It was, moreover, a doctrine that was ready to destroy political opponents at whatever cost, even among its own race and people.

National Socialism found the strongest mental and moral opposition in those parts of Germany which, whether Catholic or Protestant, had been least affected by socialism and the doctrine of Karl Marx.

The preponderance, the omnipotence of the state, the precedence attributed to it before the dignity and liberty of the individual, violate Christian natural law. I believe that the individual is prior to and ranks higher than the state. The dignity, liberty and autonomy of the individual should provide limits and guidance for the state, but the liberty of the individual does not mean licence or caprice. It obliges every man to use his freedom without forgetting his responsibility for others.

I believe that it is the function of the state to serve the individual. Materialist ideology turns the individual into a small, anonymous cog in a huge machine. I regard this ideology as destructive.

The aim of the state must be to awaken, gather, tend and protect the creative powers of a people. In the reconstruction of Germany we had to try to educate the whole population to a sense of responsibility and to independent political thinking. The state had to be a community of destiny founded on the rights and liberties of individuals, and this community had to combine varying interests, ideologies, and opinions. In the Germany of the future we had to educate our young people to become politically responsible human beings, not prepared to be supervised and led, but willing and able to find their own place in the social and political fabric. I was convinced that this education must be imbued with a Christian and democratic spirit and that it must give all young people access to those universally valid human convictions and attitudes from which they had hitherto been debarred.

The homeless, atomized mass that had been pushed about hither and thither, this post-war people of ours, called on us to address ourselves to every single individual and to help him to achieve an awareness of himself and a sense of responsibility. To what extent this would be possible seemed to me to be the decisive question for the destiny of our people.

If this task was undertaken with conviction, with devotion, and with knowledge, I was sure that in due course individuals would emerge whose strength of character and soundness of judgment would make them able and willing to assume political, moral and intellectual leadership.

In the rebuilding of Germany the great task consisted in awakening and strengthening the democratic forces in the population and in allowing them to grow. A feeling of political responsibility on the part of every single individual was a precondition of a politically healthy Germany. Democracy does not mean simply the parliamentary form of government; it must above all have a safe anchorage in the consciousness of the private citizen. The first months after January 1933 showed us how the parliamentary form of government can be used to bring about dictatorship if people are not genuine democrats in their thinking and feeling. Democracy means more than a parliamentary form of government; it is an ideology which has its roots in the recognition of the dignity, the value, and the inalienable rights of every single individual. In its political, economic, and cultural life a real democracy must respect these rights. Truly democratic thinking means being always guided by respect for other men and for the sincerity of their desires and endeavours.

2

THE CHRISTIAN DEMOCRATIC UNION: PRINCIPLES AND AIMS

The Beginnings of Political Life in Germany after the Defeat in 1945

In 1933 the National Socialist Government prohibited all other parties. In the twelve years of National Socialist rule there was only the NSDAP (National Socialist German Workers' Party). But the members of the various old parties continued to maintain a loose coherence.

After the German defeat in the spring of 1945, and even before the Allies had allowed the formation of parties, party-political movements began to stir, mostly among the parties that had existed before 1933.

It was not until the summer of 1945 that the Allies began to concern themselves with the re-establishment of political parties. In Section II, Point 9 of the Potsdam Agreement of 2 August 1945 they laid down the ruling that democratic political parties were to be allowed and encouraged throughout Germany; they were expressly granted the right to call meetings and to conduct public discussions.

Even before any decisions were made at Potsdam, the Russian Military Government had, by a so-called 'order' of 10 June 1945 from the head of the Soviet Military Administration, Marshal Zhukov, announced the admission of anti-fascist parties and trade unions in the Russian occupied part of Germany.

The American Military Government allowed political parties to resume on 13 August 1945. On 27 August 1945, however, this permission was limited to the formation of parties at the *Kreis* or district level. It was November 1945 before political parties were allowed to organize on the *Land* level.

In the British zone political parties were officially allowed on 15 September 1945, and the permission immediately extended to party formation at the zonal level. This fact had far-reaching political results for the CDU: the CDU in the British zone assumed the leading role in the national development of the party.

In the French zone political parties were admitted in December 1945. It was spring 1946 before the parties in the French zone could begin work.

The Social Democrats made the most rapid recovery. They profited from the fact that the trade unions, their traditional basis, had been allowed to re-form soon after the collapse, before the separate parties were allowed to combine in larger areas and to develop their activities accordingly. Dr Kurt Schumacher, an uncommonly gifted man, became the recognized leader of the Social Democrats. Schumacher had great faith in his party and in himself, especially when, after the victory of the British Labour Party in England at the end of July 1945, the British Labour Government gave help to the German Social Democrats.

The Communist Party, whose representatives had suffered severe persecution at the hands of the National Socialists, and most of whom now returned from the concentration camps, was also able to form again very quickly. It benefited greatly from its relations with Soviet Russia. At first it also received help from the British and American occupation authorities. It was soon able to engage in intense activity throughout Germany.

The Centre Party was probably the one whose nucleus had weathered the political storm most successfully. In the last free Reichstag elections in 1933 the districts of Cologne and Aachen, where the Centre had previously had a majority, had the lowest percentage of National Socialist votes compared with the rest of Germany. In my opinion this was clear proof that a party resting on the principles of Christian ethics has a firmer stand in political storms.

After the collapse, when political life resumed, former leading members of the Centre debated whether the Centre should be revived in its old form or whether a new party should be founded, a Christian party relying equally on Protestant and Catholic Christians. The Centre had been founded in the nineteenth century as a defence against the ecclesiastical measures of the Prussian State in its conflict with the Catholic Church. From its inception therefore the Centre had the reputation of being a party of political Catholicism. It had only a tiny number of Protestant members. The new situation in Germany called for a big party that would include Protestants as well as Catholic Christians without discrimination.

The discussions on the problem of a new Christian party which took place among members of the former Centre were often difficult and frequently painful. There were members of the Centre, worthy people with whom I had close personal ties, who could not be convinced that it was necessary to give up the Centre and embark on the founding of a new Christian party. A political divorce became inevitable.

The Need to Found an Ideological Party Based on Ethics

For many years I had believed that we needed a Christian party based on the foundations that both Catholics and Protestants had in common. Only this could, I thought, help us to counter the increasingly materialistic approach to political matters; and only this could lead to a political life in Germany that was not based merely on the interests of separate strata and classes.

In 1922, as President of the Catholic Conference in Munich, I expressed the view that no platform could be too broad for a Christian party that wanted to withstand all internal and external dangers. In a speech I made on that occasion I said:

> In our fight for the recognition of Christian principles in public affairs we must seek allies among non-Catholics and must, as far as possible, disarm the opposition of those that we cannot win over as allies. It is possible, it is almost certain, that we have kept unduly aloof from non-Catholics. By this we have not promoted Christian ideals. As far as we possibly can, we must join the efforts of the people in the Protestant camp who think like us, and we must seek to support and help each other.

Developments since that time had confirmed my conviction. I had seen that the parties of the Weimar Republic were unable to withstand National Socialism. When I speak of the old parties, I mean all of them: the Centre, the SPD, and the many other parties of those days. The failure lay in the behaviour of these parties in the period prior to the so-called seizure of power by the NSDAP. At that time parties with a democratic basis could have successfully opposed National Socialism by legal means. In another volume dealing with the years before 1945, I shall describe in greater detail my experiences and observations as President of the Prussian State Council and my views on the events which led to the development of the German catastrophe. Here I mention the failure of the parties under the Weimar Republic only in order to explain the fact that a large number of people who thought as I did believed that only a new party based on the broadest Christian foundations, on firm ethical principles, and able to draw on all strata of the German electorate, would be in a position to re-animate Germany.

The National Socialists had opened our eyes to the power wielded by a dictatorial state. I had seen the atrocities of National Socialism, the consequences of dictatorship. I had lost the vocation to which I had devoted my life; my wife was hopelessly ill as a result of a stay in the Gestapo prison at Brauweiler. I had seen the consequences of the war. Three of my sons had served at the front and I had suffered constant anxiety for them; one of them had been severely wounded.

I had heard about the crimes committed against Jews and by Germans against their fellow-Germans. I had seen where an atheistic dictatorship could lead. I had seen Germany plunged into chaos.

From the East we were menaced by the atheist, communist dictatorship. The Soviet Union showed us that a dictatorship of the Left is at least as dangerous as one of the Right. As a result of the war the Soviet Union had advanced deep into central Germany, up to the Elbe, and was a great danger to us.

We had seen in the National Socialist state, and we saw again in Communist Russia, the dangers inherent in a party that disregarded ethical principles. This convinced most of the adherents of the former Centre, and many members of the former parties of the Right, of the necessity for us to unite into a new party founded on an ethical basis.

The conviction began to spread that only a great party with its roots in Christian-Western thinking and ethics could educate the German people for their resurgence, and build a strong dyke against the atheist dictatorship of communism. We were not alone in this view. All over Germany, including the Soviet occupied zone, political groups and associations based on these principles sprang up quite spontaneously. They may have differed in some of their political and economic demands, but they were agreed in essentials. The most important feature of these groups was their common adherence to democratic political convictions and Christian loyalties developed over the centuries in our country. The proposition that the dignity of the individual must be the paramount consideration, even above the power of the state, is one that derives naturally from occidental Christianity. During the National Socialist period it seemed to be buried. National Socialism, despite its suppression of individual liberty, had found so large a following because political awareness and responsibility were very poorly developed in a great many people. Moreover, owing to their history, the Germans were all too inclined to submit to the power of the state. To this must be added the pressure of deteriorating material conditions and, in particular, large-scale unemployment. The majority of Germans did not recognize the dangers of National Socialism in its first years. They did not see that it put the power of the state above the claims of the individual. When they did see, it was too late.

Western Christianity denies the dominance of the state, and insists on the dignity and liberty of the individual. Only this traditional Christian principle could now help us to show the German people a new political goal, to recall them to a new political life. This conviction would give our party the strength to raise Germany from the depths. Hence the new party had to be a Christian party, and one that would embrace all denominations. Protestant and Catholic Germans, indeed all who knew and valued the importance of Christianity in Europe, should be able to join – and it goes without saying that this also applied to our Jewish fellow-citizens.

Only a very great party that included all strata of society could rebuild prostrate, broken Germany. It must be a party which could appeal to employers and employed, the middle classes, farmers, civil servants, intellectuals, people from the North and the South, those driven from their homes and those who had simply fled. The ethical foundations adopted by the CDU must be strong and elastic enough to contain and case the tensions that exist in a big party.

It was not easy to found a new party in the sombre situation of post-war Germany. Material misery was great and it was easy to be discouraged by the political indifference then prevalent. For us the present was oppressive and the future without hope. The German people were regarded as the heirs of the crimes of National Socialism and were hated throughout the world. Party politics seemed quite pointless. It took a lot of courage to refound an old party; it took much more to found a new one.

45

When I look back to those dark days it seems to me almost a miracle that everywhere, all over Germany, groups were being formed to demand a new Christian party. They demanded it because of the experience of the National Socialist period. Such groups were formed in all four zones of Germany. Gradually they forged tenuous links amongst themselves. It took years before a tight organization could be developed.

These groups wanted their name to include the word 'Christian': they wanted to indicate their essential aims and their opposition to National Socialism. At the first so-called 'Reich Meeting' of the Christian Democratic party groups which took place at Bad Godesberg in December 1945, it was decided to adopt the name of 'Union'. This was to underline the fact that it was to be a rallying point for all who shared our political principles – whatever their denomination or occupation.

This was the origin of the Christian Democratic Union in the whole of Germany. In Bavaria the same Christian party developed under the name of 'Christian Social Union'.

We were well aware that the creation of a new party was a difficult task; the new edifice could not be built in a day. Inter-denominational tensions in Germany could be overcome only by deliberate and painstaking work. The Social Democrats, based on the trade unions, would strongly oppose the formation of a new great popular Christian party. We knew that very hard work lay ahead of us, work that would require much patience.

The CDU was a new party that drew on old traditions. But it had to begin by drawing up a detailed programme and by creating an organization. This put it at an initial disadvantage compared with the other political parties, which were content to continue where they had left off in 1933. In addition the CDU was at a special disadvantage in the British zone compared with the Social Democrats. In July 1945 the government of Britain had passed to the Labour Party. It was often fairly obvious that the British occupation authorities favoured the Social Democrats. The KPD (Communist Party) and the Centre were also well treated by the British and American occupation forces. At first no one quite trusted the CDU, the new party.

The state of mind of the Germans was very precarious at that time. Not only were the people suffering great material hardships, but much psychological damage had also been done and the education of the younger generation had been neglected.

The framework of family life had cracked under the strain of the flight and expulsion of many millions of people, the evacuation of the big cities, and the large-scale destruction of housing. Another disturbing factor was the uncertainty about the fate of hundreds of thousands of German prisoners of war. The nation was labouring under an enormous burden, and it was necessary to awaken the deepest intellectual and spiritual forces if any resurgence was to be made possible. Such forces were to come especially from the Christian foundation of our party.

There was, too, the danger of atheistic Soviet communism. The Soviets had penetrated deep into central Germany, up to the Elbe. A German party founded on Christian principles would be able to combat this new threat.

That was how we saw the great tasks before us and we went to work full of courage and idealism.

The First Meetings of the CDU in the British Zone

I had worked for the CDU from the moment of the collapse. But when the British Military Government forbade me all political activity following my dismissal as Oberbürgermeister of Cologne, I had to interrupt this work.

Later, when the British amended this prohibition and finally lifted it altogether, I once more dedicated myself to reconstruction and to working for the new party.

The first big meeting of the CDU in which I took part was the 'Reich Meeting' at Bad Godesberg in December 1945. Members from all over Germany had come together there. But Andreas Hermes, one of the chief founders of the CDU in Berlin, had not been allowed by the Russians to go to Bad Godesberg. The main purpose of the meeting was to underline the all-German character of our party and our efforts for unity in a partitioned Germany.

Another very important meeting took place at Herford in Westphalia on 22 and 23 January. It was the first meeting of the Zonal Committee of the CDU in the British Sector. I opened the meeting as the oldest member present and subsequently became its chairman by general request.

Nearly all the twenty-six delegates from the Rhineland, Westphalia, Hanover, Schleswig-Holstein, Hamburg, Bremen, Oldenburg, Brunswick, and Lippe were present, nominated by the different *Land* organizations in accordance with the apportionment agreed at the meeting at Bad Godesberg.

We all knew that our first task was to lead the German people out of their present political apathy. We had to try to convince Germans that it was up to them actively to overcome the misery in which we all found ourselves.

At Herford we made the first attempt to organize the CDU on a broad basis. We decided that this Zonal Committee, which had met here for the first time, was to become the Party Executive for the whole British zone, in conjunction with an executive still to be elected; this body would then have authority over the executives in the *Länder*.

The composition and election of the zonal executive was discussed in detail, but decisions were postponed until the next meeting of the Zonal Committee which took place at the end of February 1946 at Neheim-Hüsten in Westphalia. I was elected chairman, with Dr Holzapfel of Herford vice-chairman *ad interim*. These elections were unanimous.*

* Minutes of the first meeting of the Zonal Committee of the CDU of 22 and 23 January 1946 at Herford.

At the Herford meeting delegates reported on the growth and situation of the *Land* organizations. On the whole these reports gave a very satisfactory picture. One particularly pleasing piece of news was that the younger generation from all strata of society and in surprisingly large numbers were working devotedly for the CDU. We were entitled to be pleased with our success so far, though an inordinate amount of work, especially in organization, remained to be done.

At Herford we again unanimously demanded the unity of Germany in spirit and in political structure.

The most important and most often emphasized principle in our discussions on political, economic, and spiritual reconstruction in Germany was the value of the individual as a corner stone of Christian democracy.

There were intensive discussions about economic reconstruction. We also dealt with a reform of the electoral law and drafted a proposal for it.

An annex to the minutes of the meeting was especially noteworthy:

> Two things were particularly characteristic of the busy proceedings. The first was the strong feeling of harmony among the delegates; this meant that some questions of fundamental importance, which in former days would have led to prolonged disputes, were quickly disposed of in the atmosphere of good will as soon as they had been clearly stated and briefly discussed. We enjoyed a total absence of the usual fights and verbal tournaments of the old style party meetings.
>
> The second striking fact was the common sense of an immediate connection between what we were saying and the real will of the people; none of the resolutions that were passed betrayed anxious electoral calculations.

I was against calling the CDU a political rallying movement and vigorously opposed this view of the party.

Among former members of the Conservative and Liberal parties in North Germany, who no longer had a large following and some of whose prominent representatives had now joined the CDU, the idea had gained ground that the CDU should 'rally' all elements to the right of the Social Democrats. Herr Schlange-Schöningen had sent circular letters to his friends in the North of the British zone in October and December 1945. In these circulars he envisaged the CDU as a 'rallying party'. Herr Schlange-Schöningen intended to have the circulars printed and distributed as a pamphlet. I protested strongly against this step and prevented all further dissemination of these views. The CDU must be a party with a new programme of its own. 'Rallying' is no foundation on which to build a party, because nothing in a 'rallying movement' points to the future.

A new party like ours needed time to develop its ideas into a firm and clearly defined programme. I was hoping that we would see this happen at a meeting of the Zonal Committee at Neheim-Hüsten. I was sure that at that time many statements made during the early stages of the growth of the party would be recognized as unclear or obsolete.

The question of socialization or nationalization of large enterprises was particularly controversial in those days. Strong currents in the CDU favoured far-reaching socialization. But opinions on this question were much divided at first.

The clarification of the CDU's position on socialization was one of the most important tasks that faced us at the meeting of the Zonal Committee at Neheim-Hüsten. Apart from this question, there were a number of other issues to be cleared up. They had arisen from the fact that the CDU had been founded independently in many places. It was now necessary to harmonize ideas and views and to work out a common approach.

We had come together at Neheim-Hüsten to create a party programme even though its validity might not extend beyond the British zone, as no links between parties across zonal borders were yet allowed. We tackled this task seriously and energetically. It was at this meeting that important principles were agreed upon. We also considered the most urgent needs of the initial period of reconstruction. Our proposals were a result of the principles adopted at this meeting and of the general situation of that first part of the occupation.

The general tenets of the programme articulated at Neheim-Hüsten concerned:

(1) The relationship of the individual and the state.
(2) Economic and social life.
(3) Education and intellectual life.

Principles and aims on the first point were agreed upon relatively quickly. The consequences of National Socialism's anti-religious attitudes showed that men needed ethical foundations for their lives. We summed up our basic standpoint as follows:

The Christian foundation of the Democratic Union is the absolutely necessary and decisive factor. We want to replace the materialistic ideology of National Socialism with a Christian view of the world; the principles of materialism must be superseded by those of Christian ethics, which shall be normative in the reconstruction of the state and the delimitation of its power, in the rights and duties of the individual, in economic and social life and in relationships between peoples.

Only Christian precepts guarantee justice, order, and moderation, the dignity and liberty of the individual and thus true and genuine democracy, which must inform not only public life but the life of the individual as well.

We regard the lofty view Christianity takes of human dignity, of the value of each single man, as the foundation and directive of our work in the political, economic and cultural life of our people.

Then followed the basic principles of the relationship between the individual and the state:

(1) The principles of Christian ethics and culture and true democracy must be the foundation and informing spirit of the life of the state. The power of the state is limited by the dignity and inalienable rights of the individual.
(2) The right to political and religious freedom.
(3) Justice, equality and security under the law for everyone.
(4) Recognition and protection of women in their work at home and in the family. Freedom for women to engage in professional and public life.
(5) The majority has no arbitrary and unlimited rights over the minority. The minority too has rights and duties.

Cultural questions were also rapidly agreed upon. Three points from our programme are worth quoting:

Point 1: A return to the foundations of Western Christian culture whose core is a respect for the dignity of the person and the value of every single individual.
Point 4: The schools to have the ideological form desired by those who are entitled to decide about the education of a child, namely the parents.
Point 5: Protection for the Christian churches and religious associations. They are to be free in their activities. Cooperation of the Christian denominations while their independence and separate life are fully preserved; cooperation between state and churches.

Schools and education had been badly neglected and misused during the National Socialist period. We regarded good schools of all kinds, schools that would pay equal attention to learning and character, as extremely important for the recovery of the German people. Due to the spiritual and intellectual aridity of the twelve years of National Socialism and to losses sustained in the war, there was a conspicuous lack of really able and prominent men in all fields. Despite the prevailing economic distress, the state should and must now smooth the path of the more than averagely gifted by material aid. Without this there was a danger that the German people would sink well below their former level.

Trust and cooperation between state and church was another basic demand of our programme. State education was to instil respect for the churches: church education was to foster respect for the state. Christian denominations were to cooperate in public life while maintaining their identity and separate character.

At first there were considerable differences of opinion over the principles guiding the development of economic and social life. In many of the initial appeals issued independently by the CDU in various places in 1945, the question of the socialization of mineral wealth and of large enterprises figured prominently. These early appeals envisaged, for instance, the nationalization of mines and other monopolistic sectors of the economy. The discussion at Neheim-Hüsten showed that many of those present held views that were quite close to those of the Social Democrats. There was a clash of opinion on socialization and discussions lasted until late into the night before any clear outcome could be foreseen.

Many of my party friends shared my dislike of excessive socialization of the economy. In my view what was needed was a just social order that would enable every man to acquire property for himself and his family. I was convinced that it was unnecessary to nationalize in order to inspire greater efforts from the German people. A worker or employee had no greater rights or liberties in a nationalized than in a private enterprise. The concentration of political and economic power in the hands of the state was, I thought, likely to lead to undue dependence on the state. I was not necessarily opposed to certain sectors of the economy being publicly administered, but I thought that too much state power might have a deleterious effect on total production.

The liberty of the individual was a principle that must apply in the economic sphere as elsewhere. I believed in the distribution of power and opposed its too great concentration, whether in the hands of individuals, companies, private or public organizations. Similarly I was against too much power being concentrated in the hands of the state; hence I opposed the socialist economic experiments advocated by some of my party friends. My views were shared by the majority.

At last we agreed to postpone deciding the basic question with the following argument, which became part of the programme published on 1 March 1946:

> There is nothing practical that can be done on the urgent question of a socialization of parts of the economy, because the German economy is not free. At a later date its solution will be found in accordance with economic and political criteria and above all the criterion of the common good.

This compromise was of the utmost importance for the CDU. Had it not been reached I fear that our party would have broken apart. It was largely thanks to Johannes Albers from Cologne, a member of the former Christian Trade Unions, that we reached agreement. He talked to people for hours on end, trying to find common ground among the various viewpoints. He deserves the profound gratitude of the CDU.

Point 10 of the economic programme of Neheim-Hüsten expressed one of my own chief concerns. It ran:

> Property-holding is one of the essential safeguards of the democratic state. The acquisition of a moderate amount of property by all who toil honestly should be facilitated.

I knew from my own experience and from my work as Oberbürgermeister of Cologne what a house and a garden can mean to a family. I also knew how important healthy living conditions are for the life of the family and of the people. I was therefore anxious to stress our special interest in this question. The Neheim-Hüsten programme said:

> The reconstruction of destroyed cities and towns should avoid needlessly over-crowded housing. The land needed for a spacious building policy should be acquired by expropriation if necessary.

In our rebuilding, we wanted to avoid the evils of earlier industrial and urban development. The concentration of great masses of humanity in small spaces was not to be repeated. For many years I had thought that the mistaken land and settlement policy of former times was a principal source of the loss of roots and lack of inner strength in large parts of our population. I therefore saw this task as one of the greatest and most vitally important challenges for the future of the German people.

I consider this meeting at Neheim-Hüsten one of the most decisive meetings of the CDU. We overcame the groups that advocated a strong dose of socialization and so prevented a break-up of the party.

I have already stressed that the liberty of the individual was the crux of the CDU programme. Socialism is not limited to the form of the economy. Excessive socialization of the economic structure concentrates too much power in the hands of the state and we know from our own experience how dangerous this is for a people. Socialism is bound to lead to a subordination of the rights and dignity of the individual to the state or to a collective like the state. It was my conviction that the deification of the state and the unlimited expansion of its rights, which rested on the materialist view of the world and which we had experienced in the past, must never again be allowed to prevail.

3

THE ADVISORY COUNCIL OF THE BRITISH ZONE IN 1946 AND CONDITIONS IN GERMANY

The Gradual Growth of Administration in the British Zone

The decision of the Potsdam Conference to treat Germany as a single econo-mic unit proved impossible to carry out. The victorious powers had made an agreement that required unanimity by the Control Council for every decision. (The Allied Control Council was the four-power body set up to decide questions concerning Germany as a whole.) But the four powers were never agreed on their programme for Germany and the Soviet Union in particular pursued its own policy. At first even the three Western powers disagreed over policy towards Germany.

The four occupation zones were drifting further and further apart economic-ally and the economic chaos grew from the spring of 1945 onwards. Ger-many's economic structure required an exchange of agricultural products from the East, and to a lesser extent the South of the country, with the industrial production of the Ruhr and of other industrial regions. This exchange was stopped by the division of the country into four zones. The zonal com-manders acted on the directives of their respective governments and each pursued his own policy in his own zone. This could only further hinder an economy already largely paralysed by the ravages of war.

The occupying powers had assumed supreme power in Germany by the four declarations issued on 5 June 1945, and their authority extended to the lowest echelons of administration. The Military Government installed offices in the *Gemeinden* (communes) and districts and nominated German administrative councils.

I do not want to go into details of administrative development in the separate occupation zones; the development of political life is described else-where. My domicile and my field of activity were in the British zone of occupation and I prefer to describe my experience there.

In the British zone the Provincial Councils were revived soon after the end of the war. But key functions were kept in the hands of the Military Govern-ment. The British and the other occupying powers were not equal in practice to the extraordinary tasks involved in administering a destroyed country.

In February 1946, the British Military Government announced that it intended to create a German so-called 'Consultative Council' for the British zone. This soon became known as the Zonal Advisory Council. It was to be composed of representatives of the political parties, the trade unions, the administration, and of cultural, social, and economic life. The Advisory Council had, and this was stressed, an advisory function only and would not make decisions. Its thirty-two members included eight representatives of the political parties and six representatives of the administration, namely: the *Oberpräsidenten* of the Provinces of Hanover, Schleswig-Holstein, Westphalia, North Rhine, the Bürgermeister of Hamburg, and a joint representative of the *Länder** of Bremen, Brunswick, Oldenburg, and both parts of Lippe. There were also representatives of the zonal offices set up by the British in the autumn of 1945 for industry and trade, food, justice, health, posts, transport, finance, labour, security, education, and refugees. Finally there were two representatives of the trade unions and two representatives of the cooperatives.

The CDU sent Dr Paul Otto from Osnabrück and myself.

The Work of the Zonal Advisory Council in 1946

I should like to enlarge a little on my work in the Zonal Advisory Council because our problems there so clearly show the conditions then prevailing in Germany.

The opening meeting of the Zonal Advisory Council took place on 6 March 1946 in the building of the old Hamburg General Command. The British Commander-in-Chief and Military Governor, Air Marshal Sir Sholto Douglas, arrived amid a roll of drums and a blare of trumpets. *Oberpräsident* Lehr, the President of the Provincial Council of North Rhine, introduced individual members of the Council to the British officer.

The first to be presented was Dr Kurt Schumacher, chairman of SPD, who was known to have especially close connections with the British Labour Party. He had a rather long and very cordial welcome. My presentation was much cooler and very much shorter. It lasted only one minute and forty-five seconds. Douglas asked me about my political career to date. I said: 'In 1917 I became Oberbürgermeister of Cologne; in 1933 I was removed by the National Socialists because of political unreliability. In March 1945 I was reinstated by the Americans and in October of the same year dismissed by the British for incompetence. That is why I am now on the Zonal Advisory Council.' Douglas looked somewhat surprised and walked on without saying a word.

On the first day of our meeting in Hamburg Hinrich Wilhelm Kopf, one of the most prominent politicians of the SPD in Lower Saxony, who was at that time *Oberpräsident* of the Province of Hanover, brought together Dr Kurt

* There is no exact English equivalent for *Land* (plural: *Länder*): 'State' is the nearest English equivalent.

Schumacher and myself so that we might pursue a common line in the Council.

That evening Schumacher and I sat down for a talk. We discussed the food situation and Schumacher shared the CDU's opinion that the Allies' victory meant they had assumed responsibility for the population under the Hague Convention of 1907 and that we must insist on their fulfilling this responsibility.

We then discussed the dismantling of our industries, which put a great additional obstacle in the way of economic reconstruction. Schumacher agreed that we must make it clear to the Allies that this would make payment of the reparations that were being demanded impossible.

I told Schumacher that the CDU had passed resolutions at the Neheim-Hüsten meeting that expressed exactly what we had just been saying. Schumacher noted this and it really seemed as if there were a possibility of collaboration between the CDU and the SPD.

But then Schumacher went too far. He said that our discussion had shown agreement on the basic question, our attitude to the Allies; but he asked me, as the chairman of a very young party, to agree that it was reasonable that the CDU should recognize the SPD's claim to leadership. It was obvious, he claimed, that the SPD was largest party in Germany and would remain the largest. I demurred and suggested that the decision concerning the relative strength of the parties should be left to future elections. On that note we parted.

As a rule the Zonal Advisory Council met once a month, in Hamburg. The meetings lasted two or three days. The agenda was prepared by a British liaison team and a German secretariat. In practice the British usually told the German secretariat what was to be discussed. The Council was not allowed to object to the agenda. This emerged painfully when the Military Government reduced the daily fat ration for the population to six grammes. Sir Cecil Weir, head of the economic division of the Military Government, rejected our complaint with the laconic remark that fat only served to make food palatable and more digestible and that the food value of fat was greatly exaggerated. If the total food consumption did not exceed three thousand five hundred calories per day fat was not necessary.

I attended the meetings of the Zonal Advisory Council in Hamburg regularly. Getting there was quite a problem. Hans Böckler, a trade union leader on the Council, and I shared a permit from the Military Government to use one vehicle and a modest petrol ration. This naturally caused difficulties at times, for instance if I had to go to Hamburg a day earlier to attend a meeting of a committee of the Council or Böckler had to stay a day or two longer for similar reasons. But we got on very well and always found some solution. I mention it only as an example of the conditions in those days.

Another difficulty was finding accommodation in a city that had suffered so much destruction. I usually stayed at the Pension Prem which did its best to look after the members of the Council who were put up there. One unpleasant memory is of the winter months when I slept in an unheated room, lying in bed in my suit and coat, shaking with cold like most Germans at that time. My driver had to sleep in a hospital bath-tub because it was impossible to get a room. He was very pleased because the bathroom was reasonably warm. I think we should often recall the memory of that time, of which I have given only a sketchy account; it was a period of real need and misery which many Germans now seem to have forgotten.

The work in Hamburg took up much of my time, particularly because of the distance and the poor transport between Cologne and Hamburg. The problems that occupied us in the Zonal Advisory Council were very difficult. We had some outstanding experts there in some fields, such as food and health, who always gave a current analysis of the situation. Twelve committees were formed in the Council. They worked out detailed reports on the most pressing problems for the full assembly.

Discussions in the Advisory Council showed very clearly how difficult it was for the British Military Government to master its work. For reasons we failed to fathom their methods were not always correct. Some of the most important decisions were submitted to the Council without prior consultation or any chance of later modification. The reform of the social insurance system, for instance, only reached the Council when the Allies were nearly agreed among themselves, so that we could bring very little influence to bear on an issue that was of the greatest importance for our people. The de-nazification question was similar. Here too the Council could express its opinion, for instance on the amnesty of the younger people or on the composition of de-nazification tribunals, but the basic decisions had already been taken by the Allies and had to be accepted as presented.

Many very important subjects of the greatest interest to us were not discussed at all in the Council. I tried, for instance, to get some clarification of the position of Germany in international law by asking for the opinions of German and foreign experts. Discussion of my motion was refused. We were told that Germany's status was that of an occupied country. In a way this answer was satisfactory because it enabled us to point to the obligations that an occupying power had towards the occupied population under the Hague Convention of 1907. Later the British told me that the Legal Division of the Control Commission was preparing the exact definition of the status of Germany in international law as I had asked.

Discussion of the dismantling of industry was likewise forbidden in the Zonal Advisory Council; and this was the very question that lay at the core of our economic difficulties. The dismantling policy caused more and more unemployment among Germans and our economy became increasingly paralysed. The economic plan for Germany drawn up in accordance with the Potsdam decisions of July-August 1945 provided for the dismantling of the big iron and steel works in North Rhine-Westphalia and other parts of

Germany. I believed that such action would destroy the future of the German people for many decades. It meant that for a long time Germany would be unable to export, and that the amounts of steel needed for reconstruction would not be available.

The British told us that discussion was forbidden because dismantling was connected with the matter of reparations; and reparations were the concern of the Control Council. They had to be discussed on a four-power basis; that is, with the Soviet Union. This struck me as impossible, and I went to Berlin – as far as I remember it was in April 1946 – to see the British Deputy Military Governor, Lieutenant General Sir Brian Robertson. I told him that the German population would no longer have the slightest respect for the Zonal Advisory Council if it became known that that body was not allowed to talk about the most important of all economic questions: dismantling. Lieutenant General Robertson, whom I came to know and esteem as a very wise and high-minded man, was willing to listen to my arguments and promised me that the matter would be considered. In fact the ruling was changed and we were allowed to discuss the problem of dismantling in particularly hard cases.

It was clear to me that we must try to change the situation in which we were allowed to handle only questions of third- and fourth-rate importance while the decisive issues were settled by the Military Government without consultation with us.

I did not exactly regard the Advisory Council as a powerful instrument for the implementation of German demands; but it did offer the possibility of getting a better hearing and of eventually achieving a little more influence over the course of events.

An important advantage of the Council lay in the fact that it brought us into fairly regular contact with the occupying power and gave us a chance to try to cultivate an objective or functional relationship. I was hoping that the psychological climate between the Military Government and the Germans would gradually change. From the very beginning one of my chief aims was to persuade the occupying powers that we Germans were not as bad or unreliable as we were always being painted in these first months and years after the end of the war. I considered it one of our chief tasks to create confidence in ourselves.

One of the really important points on which we were called to advise after the *Land* of North Rhine-Westphalia had been created by a decree of the British occupation authorities, was the question of division into *Länder* and the internal structure of the Zone. We had to give expert opinions on the number of the new *Länder*, their boundaries, the constitutional rights of these *Länder* and the composition of their governments, as also on the question of whether the *Regierungsbezirke* were to be maintained or abolished.

To understand why the British could not cope with the problems in their Zone, one must bear the prevailing conditions in mind. The food situation was catastrophic and deteriorated visibly during the first few months of our work in the Zonal Advisory Council. For every four-week rationing period we needed 186,000 tons of grain. At the end of May we had no reserves whatever for June. The prospect of imports to tide us over until the new harvest was highly uncertain. All the remedies that were being considered were full of risks or would take too long to come into effect. A severe reduction of livestock, which was considered, would have meant a decisive setback for milk production and that would have further aggravated the shortage of fats. Attempts to improve the food situation without purchases abroad, by fresh fish supplies, foundered on the fact that no fishing vessels were available. There was even a danger that fishing vessels that had been used as minesweepers during the war would have to be destroyed or surrendered. The Council's initiative in this matter did produce results and some fishing vessels were actually released later. I proposed that the surrender of our whaling fleet, which was to go to Great Britain and Norway, should be postponed for a year or two, so that fat supplies might be augmented by fish oils.

The population was entitled to barely more than a thousand calories daily and it is impossible to do any real work on that amount. The consequences of a further reduction of this ration are obvious. The Administration of Food and Agriculture was hoping to increase the ration to 1,540 calories a day, although the minimum requirement for human nutrition is a daily ration of 2,500 calories. Hopes for an improvement in the food situation in 1947 did not materialize.

The worst blow came in the spring of 1946 when the fat ration of 400 grammes per person per four-week rationing period was to be cut in half. The deficiency in fats and albumen led to a huge increase in tuberculosis and hunger oedema. In November 1946 the health authorities estimated the number of oedema cases at several hundred thousand.

Constant malnutrition was bound to cause the greatest harm. Reports to the Advisory Council on the people's state of health gave an alarmingly deteriorating picture. Statistics showed that in March 1946 men weighed on the average seven kilograms below normal. Their weight had sunk to 9.1 kg below normal by June – that is thirteen per cent below normal weight – while the inmates of the old people's homes averaged as much as 12 kg or twenty per cent below normal. We were particularly worried by the fact that children showed even worse effects of malnutrition than adults. More than fifty per cent of the pupils in an elementary school class that was tested in the spring of 1946 had tuberculosis. The average performance of pupils in a cross-section of the Hamburg schools, for instance, was found to be below average in sixty-two per cent of cases, and doctors attributed this to malnutrition. In November 1946 forty-six thousand cases of open and infectious tuberculosis were registered in the British zone. But there were only thirteen thousand hospital beds available to receive the worst cases. In addition there were another hundred thousand cases of tuberculosis in need of treatment. It was estimated that there were really two hundred and sixty thousand cases of TB in the

British zone if one included the unreported cases. Many thousands of these infectious patients had to share a room with other members of their families. It was obvious that we were facing dreadful dangers to the health of the population and the impossibility of securing even a moderate sufficiency of food caused grave anxiety.

In these conditions output kept doing down. Competent authorities estimated that the general capacity to work had sunk to well below half the normal. There was little comfort for the Zonal Advisory Council in being told that there was a world shortage of oil seeds, especially soya beans – which we wanted to import – and that Great Britain too had had to reduce rations of soap and edible fats. Mortality was rising considerably. While there had been 11.8 deaths registered per thousand inhabitants in 1938, the number was already up to 15.1 in April 1946 and had risen to 18 by June 1946.

During the first years after the war of course the food situation was bad all over the world. The destruction of great parts of Europe during the war and the reorganization from a wartime to a peacetime economy could not help creating a general food crisis. But however much we might take into account the worldwide food situation, the fact was that we were suffering severe hunger and we kept coming back to the question of how this could be alleviated.

The cries for help from Germany did not remain unheard. Very soon after the war people in America, England, and many other countries began to organize relief for Germany. This help came first from individuals who sent things to their German relatives, then from small organizations and church institutions. When details of the situation of the German population became more generally known, church representatives of all denominations in America, England, and other countries began to set up large-scale relief operations. As early as July 1945 the Lutheran Churches of America handed over the first big sum of money to Germans in Stuttgart, despite the fact that the military authorities were not yet allowing charitable aid for Germans.

Food and clothing then poured into Germany. They were being sent on grounds of sympathy, humanity, and charity. They were partly organized, partly unorganized, and it is difficult to be sure of the exact amount of this help. The relief consignments increased to such an extent that organizations had to be set up abroad as well as in Germany for channelling and distributing this aid. The big welfare organizations CARE and CRALOG took up the dispatch of important foodstuffs and clothing to Germany in the spring of 1946. During the period from spring 1946 to spring 1949 alone, food to the value of more than 175 million DM was sent to Germany by CRALOG. Between 1946 and 1952 CARE sent parcels to the amount of nearly 295 million DM to needy Germans in the area of the Federal Republic.

No one who was not living in Germany at that time can imagine what this relief, coming from private or church sources, meant to hungry and defeated Germans. The arrival of a CARE parcel made any day into a feast day for a family. As well as material help there were great psychological effects. It was not so much the material assistance that helped us as the connection with the outside world, the hope for reconciliation, a ray of light pointing to a brighter future – all these were awakened in Germany by these actions. All my countrymen would want me to thank the many nameless donors for the helping hand they held out to us in those years of greatest hardship.

In England and America important voices were being raised in public asking for much more help for Germany and for planned distribution. In Great Britain it was above all Lord Beveridge and Victor Gollancz who aroused the public conscience among the victorious nations. Victor Gollancz published a book *In Darkest Germany* in which he described the German conditions in detail. He also published a pamphlet entitled *Leave Them To Their Fate*. It was extraordinarily effectively written. Victor Gollancz gave hard and clear statements of the British views and demands concerning Germany, but then argued that in the final resort the problem of Germany fell under a humanitarian principle of the British conscience for the world. *The Times*, the *Daily Herald*, the *Observer* and the *Manchester Guardian* published letters by Gollancz in which again and again he pointed to the human aspect of the German problem; he also condemned at a very early stage the amount of dismantling demanded by the Allied governments.

In 1947 I met Victor Gollancz personally and found him to be a very intelligent and wise man. He owned a large publishing house and he had great influence on public opinion in Great Britain. Germany owes Victor Gollancz a great debt of gratitude, a debt which is all the greater in view of his Jewish descent.

Oberkirchenrat Cillien from Hanover visited England for two weeks in the summer of 1946 and made a very interesting report on his trip. He met prominent men in political and social life, and was impressed by the readiness of the British as private individuals to help. He also got the impression that government offices were doing everything in their power to alleviate conditions in Germany, and that the British could not understand why there was so little German recognition of all the trouble England was going through to save Germany from catastrophe after her defeat. British occupation policies were indeed being harshly criticized in Germany, especially the dismantling of big industrial plants, and many a hard word was said against the British.

Oberkirchenrat Cillien told me that German appreciation and courtesy, whose absence had been so remarked on in Britain, were in his view a precondition of any later understanding and rapprochement. This door must not be allowed to close – not even if German complaints were justified. He had found a plain and simple readiness to give help the predominant characteristic in all his conversations with leading personalities, especially of the Church of England. His visit to the Bishop of Chichester, Dr George Bell, showed this. Dr Bell, incidentally, had protested strongly against the unlimited bombing of

Germany during the last years of the war. The Dean of St Paul's, the Very Reverend Walter Robert Matthews, had received Cillien with great kindness on the steps of the cathedral. All this Cillien took as a sign of the readiness of British Christians to hold out a hand to a beaten enemy, without resentment. He was most impressed by British respect for the individuality of an alien people.

It was bitter for Cillien, who had rendered outstanding service to the CDU since its inception, to find that in England the SPD was thought to have the greater political prospects. He noticed, however, that the importance of the CDU's work and programme were gradually being recognized and might eventually find support. He stressed that in this matter things should not be forced but that we should simply wait, because in view of the British mentality anything else would only harm the CDU.

I discuss British attitudes as an example of the mood in one of the victorious countries. In America and elsewhere people thought along similar lines: sympathy with their fellow men moved them to help the opponent who had been beaten and lay prostrate.

Public opinion in the victorious countries was being stirred by the pronouncements of important men: I have mentioned only a few of their names. This was of great political importance because it prepared the public understanding for government relief operations, and because it meant that the need to help Europe and especially Germany was being recognized, if only on humanitarian grounds at first.

In order to increase agricultural productivity, and thereby domestic food production, we required sufficient coal to begin making artificial fertilizers. The situation in the coal mines was catastrophic.

Coal mining had always had a key position in the German economy, and its significance was even greater now. Coal was not only the most important source of energy for electricity and gas, but was also needed as domestic fuel for our freezing people. It was also our most important, in fact our only, export. With coal we could pay for imports of food and raw materials. Coal was needed to get the economy going: to start building work in our destroyed cities, to produce artificial fertilizers for the neglected and impoverished soil, for any and every improvement of economic conditions.

The production of this important and precious raw material was terribly low. It stood at a mere sixty per cent of the figure for 1938 and the demand was now very much greater due to reparation claims and industrial needs.

The British Military Government had convoked a German Economic Council and this body drew up a report on measures to solve the economic crisis, especially the crisis in the mining industry. The report, which was ready in April 1946, clearly showed the interconnections between various economic problems, and included proposals for their alleviation.

These proposals concentrated first of all on increasing coal production as the only way to initiate an upward trend in our economy as a whole. It seemed to the members of the Zonal Advisory Council, from the findings of this report, that the best way to reach this goal was to do everything to raise the performance of the individual miner. That this was the most important starting point was shown by the following figures: while a man had produced 1,547 kg per shift during 1938, the last year of peace, the corresponding production figure for March 1946 stood at 711 kg, which was even below the figure of 773 kg for December 1945. This decline was due partly to malnutrition, partly to a lack of will to work that resulted from general bitterness about social conditions, such as cuts in pension claims, and from discontent over the limitations of the rights of factory representatives.

During the first post-war year, the mining industry in the British zone was facing an exceptionally serious crisis. The key men with indispensable experience in mining had been removed from their positions and the British were carrying the responsibility.

On the orders of the British Military Government, men from all parts of the British zone were forced to work in the mines. This proved completely futile. Also, miners were given special food rations which they were supposed to eat alone, away from their families. It is easy to imagine the psychological consequences. The miner was expected to eat his fill at his place of work while his wife and children went hungry at home.

The Economic Council pointed out that one of the causes of the malfunctioning of the mines was that the industry was to a very large extent not in German hands. The Economic Council thought that this was the decisive psychological cause of the declining will to work among the German miners, who felt that they were owned by foreign powers whose aims and intentions they neither knew nor trusted. Thus there were, for example, exaggerated ideas about the volume of coal deliveries to foreign countries. It was said that production was not really as low as the British authorities were claiming, but that the coal was being taken from the mines for immediate shipment abroad and this was why so little remained for the German economy.

It was true that large amounts of coal were being exported, but coal had to be exported to permit imports of food. Even in peacetime German agriculture could feed only between sixty and seventy per cent of the population and now it was in a parlous plight. War had swept over the country. For years farmers had had to do without enough fertilizers or labour. There was no more good seed, tools were worn out and used up. As a result we were in even greater need of food imports from abroad than usual, especially in view of the fact that the important agricultural regions of the East were not sending food to the Western zones. The food situation was steadily getting worse and there seemed to be no escape from disaster. We seemed to be condemned to die of hunger – slowly and surely and, as the *Daily Mail* put it, 'hygienically'.

Under the Potsdam Agreement another eleven to thirteen million people who were expelled from the territories beyond the Oder-Neisse Line were to be squeezed into our zone. At the same time, also under the Potsdam

Agreement, our industrial capacity was to be reduced. All this was bound to lead to catastrophe.

The occupation authorities were not familiar with conditions in Germany and often asked for German advice, including that of the Zonal Advisory Council, too late or not at all. Failures arising from the lack of coordinating activity across the zonal borders can be indicated by one example. It was a case where the Zonal Advisory Council was able to help by sending a proposal to the Control Commission.

The expellees and refugees streaming into our country were being sent to the British zone in particularly large numbers. The province of Schleswig-Holstein, which originally had a population of 1.3 million inhabitants, had received 1.2 million refugees by the middle of 1946 and more than a hundred thousand were announced for the next few months. Refugees came to number nearly one hundred per cent of the original population. The majority of these refugees were in poor health and capable of no more work than the local population. Further, although Schleswig-Holstein was a predominantly agricultural area only thirty per cent of the people sent there could work on the land. One could only shake one's head. Nonetheless the Allies decided that during the summer of 1946 one hundred and seventy thousand people who had been evacuated to South Germany from the British zone during the war were to be forcibly repatriated to the British zone and this at a moment when conditions made their reception quite impossible. We succeeded in getting this decision rescinded.

Another of our worries was the excessive felling of trees in our zone. Not content with the use of trees from the city parks and open spaces as fuel – in Cologne I was able to resist such measures – the local Military Government offices insisted that the woods, far from numerous in the British zone, be cut down regardless of consequences. Even before 1945, during the war, the felling of wood had exceeded the normal amounts in north-west Germany; now four times the normal amount of timber was to be cut for pit props and eight times the normal amount for fuel. The dangers of such measures for the fertility of the soil and for water supplies were especially stressed by Ober-präsidenten Lehr and Kopf, two experts in this field. We tried to impress on the Control Commission the irreparable damage that these orders were bound to cause. Here too some arrangement with zones that had more forests would have been an obvious solution.

The nature of many of our problems simply forced us to look at questions with supra-regional eyes and to act accordingly.

The Military Governments, no matter how well-intentioned, were unable to make sensible decisions for their separate zones, which was one of the chief reasons for the further decline of our economy.

We did, however, meet with understanding and a conciliatory spirit especially from the Deputy Military Governor, Lieutenant General Robertson. From the very beginning he worked with the Zonal Advisory Council with an awareness of the wider connections, the larger picture, and the political necessity of transferring an increasing measure of responsibility to the Germans as quickly as possible.

It was Lieutenant General Robertson, with his American colleague, General Clay, who worked for economic cooperation between the British and American zones.

Another problem was the education and training of the younger generation, those who had grown up entirely or largely under the National Socialist régime. They were not the generation that had brought Hitler to power, but it was they who now had to bear the full measure of the physical and psychological consequences. Their ideals had been shattered overnight. They did not know of the atrocities that Germans had committed against Germans and against other people. The care of these young people was, I thought, one of our most urgent duties. The age groups in question would soon influence political life in Germany. Their attitudes and ways of thinking would set the tone for the country. In the National Socialist years they had heard only official indoctrination. It was impossible to expect political judgment from people who were still children when Hitler came to power. I thought that all who had political responsibility, and especially the CDU, must inform and instruct these young people. We had to show them what National Socialism had meant and to convince them that Germany's present situation was the result of National Socialist policy and leadership. This education must not be left to the victors, but must come from authoritative German quarters. It had to be tackled systematically and calmly or nothing would be achieved. Enlightenment had to be sought with the help of universities and colleges, and of leading men and women of all persuasions. Punishment for the guilty was necessary, but so was instruction and enlightenment for the large groups of people who were not guilty but had been systematically misled.

Vocational training of youth was bad, in most cases, and the prospects for the future were therefore dim. This was due to the war and to the neglect of the schools by National Socialism.

Academic youth was a big problem. The universities were overcrowded and the number of professors and lecture rooms totally inadequate. The Zonal Advisory Council had heard a suggestion for a year of 'practical work', to give young people something to do. It struck me as an interference with personal liberty. The 'practical year' was also supposed to counteract excessive intellectualization. The argument was that it would have a strong influence on the general attitude of the young. I did not see that the 'practical year' was necessary, since post-war conditions forced young people to do just such work in any case. They did their bit wherever they might be, in the fields and in the mines.

This was not the right way to stop the rush to the universities. I suggested that it would be better to find ways of guiding those young people for whom we could not find a university place to other work and training.

The occupation powers were constantly talking about 're-educating' the German people for democracy. Their intentions were good, but the means employed in the British zone were not always the most suitable.

At the meetings of the Zonal Advisory Council of 10 and 11 July we were informed of the Military Government regulations for electoral procedure in the local and *Kreis* elections of 15 September and 13 October 1946 respectively. These plans, in my opinion, failed to take account of conditions then existing in Germany. I pointed out that the gentlemen from England who had elaborated these regulations should remember that no elections had taken place since 1933 and that no party except the NSDAP had existed between 1933 and 1945. The British wanted ballot papers with the names of the candidates for election but without the party to which they belonged. We had to get permission to mention the parties on the ballot papers.

While these questions were being discussed I recalled my earlier motion to hold elections for the diets in the individual *Länder* in the British zone at the same time as the district elections. From newspaper reports I gathered that the British Control Commission did not intend to have *Landtag* elections until the next year, 1947.

We were asked for our opinion on a whole series of very important laws: the plans for the reorganization of the *Länder* in the British zone, plans for land reform, and so forth. These were measures of such far-reaching significance that I thought they ought to be left to a freely elected parliament. The nominated Provincial Councils and *Landtage*, which did not even meet in public, ought to be replaced by better institutions. I did not see why provincial diets could not be elected by proper procedure if we were to have district elections anyway. Understanding and better relations between the population and the occupying power was more likely if freely elected provincial diets provided a public forum for the views of the representatives of the authorities and for frank and open criticism. I was sure that the disturbed atmosphere between the German population and the occupying power before July 1946 was due to the secrecy with which important negotiations were carried out. The more openly things were discussed, and the more calmly and serenely criticism was met, the more moderate, reasonable and constructive this criticism would become.

In the American zone elections had already taken place in April 1946. The British argument for postponement was that there was to be a fundamental reorganization, a reshaping of Germany, in 1947. I did not consider this a compelling argument. It meant waiting for many months, and I thought it urgent that the Germans in the British zone should be made aware that they were responsible for their own fate and that voting was a part of this responsibility.

The Germans were hearing a lot about democracy; I thought a beginning should be made with the simplest democratic procedure.

My demand for *Landtag* elections in the autumn of 1946 was countered by the argument that the electoral campaign would disturb people and create a 'bad atmosphere'. This left me unimpressed, for who could guarantee that next year the atmosphere would be better? Elections had been held in the American zone and the CDU had found the 'atmosphere' excellent. The time had come to remember the principles of democracy. The land reform laws suggested by the occupying power might determine our fate and that of millions of people for decades. I could not see how anyone with democratic sentiments could fail to provide for freely elected bodies to decide such important issues. I announced that my party would ask for a postponement of land reform discussion until a freely elected parliament could make a final decision. I did not consider land reform a task that could be settled in the dark. It had to be done in public so that everyone concerned would be answerable to the people. To be sure, it was for the occupation authorities to decide whether to implement the decisions of a freely elected parliament, that was their affair; but I still thought that we should urge the earliest possible elections in the Zonal Advisory Council.

I urged my fellow members of the Council to appeal with me to the Military Government to hold free *Landtag* elections as soon as possible. I told them that it was our duty to try to enable people to vote freely as soon as possible.

My motion was at first declared unsuitable for discussion by the British Control Commission, but the Control Commission revised its opinion and allowed debate. This showed that they might be prepared to hold elections if the Council voted for them. The Council defeated the motion by the small majority of fifteen votes to eleven. Surprisingly Dr Schumacher, leader of the SPD, was one of those who spoke against me before the vote.

I thought it in the interests of the British Military Government that there should be a forum in which representatives of the people could freely and openly discuss the problems that the autumn and winter would bring. This would give the Military Government a clearer impression of the mood of the people than they had hitherto received. Moreover I believed that discussions in provincial diets would be much more effective than an occasional speech by a party representative at a meeting in opening the eyes of the public outside Germany to conditions there, to the disaster towards which we and with us Europe were drifting.

My ideas did not prevail. The district council elections took place separately on 13 October 1946. The provincial diet for North Rhine-Westphalia was not elected but was nominated.

General Reflections on those Times of Hardship

Conditions in the other three zones of occupation were similar to those in the British zone, perhaps a little better or worse here or there. Taking it all in all, the present in Germany was hardly bearable and the future looked hopeless. It is important to remember those days again and again so as to understand and to appreciate the developments of later years.

I have not tried to give a complete picture of Germany in those days: I am only writing down what I remember, and must therefore limit myself to recording a few facts that strike me as characteristic or worthy of note.

I observed one positive phenomenon at that time. Everywhere there was a magnificent readiness among people to help one another and a will not to despair despite the horrors of the past; there was a search for strength to come to terms with life, a search that led to religion and to art. It was an inspiring sign of the vitality and strength of our people. No one who lived through those times will forget this general and visible turning to the things of the spirit.

4

THE VICTORS AFTER THE DEFEAT OF GERMANY

Unconditional Surrender and the Allied Declaration of 5 June 1945

At the time of its defeat in 1945 Germany was in chaos. Hitler and his men had done everything to implement his statement that the Germans should perish if they could not conquer.

The German armed forces had surrendered unconditionally. But there were many – I was among them – who held that with the surrender Germany did not cease to exist as a subject and object in international law. The unconditional surrender of the Wehrmacht on 7 and 8 May was a military act which did not nullify the status of Germany in international law.

The victorious powers assumed governmental authority in Germany. The collapse of the National Socialist Government had left a political vacuum. Yet we were not without all protection in international law; we could cite the Hague Convention of 1907 which all the victorious powers of 1945 had signed. Under the Hague Convention the victors had certain rights in an occupied country – and Germany had that status, later confirmed by the Zonal Advisory Council. But they also had duties towards the inhabitants of the country they occupied. One of these duties was to ensure adequate food supplies for the occupied population.

The war of 1914–18 had not ended with an unconditional surrender of the armed forces nor had governmental authority lapsed in Germany. The Allies regretted that they had not then assumed governmental control of Germany, as they had subsequently been obliged to negotiate with the representatives of the defeated German government. The Allies believed that this was the reason the Treaty of Versailles had failed so badly, enabling the Germans to evade its provisions, to rearm after a short time and to plunge the world into the Second World War.

This was a mistake they did not want to repeat. At a conference at Casablanca in January 1943 the Allies agreed that the war was to be terminated only by an unconditional surrender, which, it was hoped, would pacify Europe permanently and require no agreement with representatives of the defeated country. The demand for unconditional surrender was to leave the Allies a completely free hand in the shaping of the defeated Germany with which they were to make peace.

Shortly before his suicide on 30 April 1945 Adolf Hitler had designated Grand Admiral Dönitz as his successor. At first the Allies seemed to recognize Dönitz as Head of State, or at any rate the initial British attitude had very much the appearance of recognition. British troops gave the 'Reich Government' and 'High Command of the Armed Forces' an extraterritorial enclave in the vicinity of Flensburg. Grand Admiral Dönitz and his entourage were permitted to keep their arms even after the capitulation had gone into force. The British and American Control Commissions seemed to respect the Dönitz government. But soon there were serious differences among the Allies concerning the position of Dönitz, and finally the British summoned him to a British warship and arrested him. Later, at Nuremberg, he was sentenced to ten years' imprisonment.

Four declarations basic to future Allied policy in Germany were published on 5 June 1945. They had been signed that day at the headquarters of Marshal Zhukov in Berlin. The governments of the United States, Great Britain, the Soviet Union and France were represented by General Eisenhower, Field Marshal Montgomery, Marshal Zhukov and General de Lattre de Tassigny, who signed the documents.

The first declaration regarding the defeat and occupation of Germany provided *inter alia* that the four Allied governments should assume supreme authority with respect to Germany, including all the powers of the German government, the High Command, and any state, municipal or local government or authority. The boundaries of Germany or any part thereof, and the status of Germany or 'of any area at present being part of German territory' were to be determined at a later time.

There followed fifteen articles specifying conditions that were to be immediately carried out. These included the disarming of the German armed forces, the release of Allied prisoners of war, the arrest of Nazi leaders and war criminals and measures concerning the occupation of the country.

The second declaration announced the establishment of a *Control Council* which was to consist of the four commanders-in-chief, each one of whom had supreme authority in his zone. But in matters affecting the whole of Germany they had to make joint decisions. *These had to be taken unanimously*. There followed further details concerning the organization of the Control Council.

The third declaration concerned the division of Germany into four zones of occupation, the distribution of the area of Greater Berlin among the four great powers, and its division into four sectors. The fourth declaration concerned consultation with other Allied nations.

The most significant provision of the second declaration, and the one that proved of the greatest consequence, was the requirement of *unanimity* for Control Council decisions. *This provision was crucial for the future fate of Germany*, because it handed all decisions to the Soviet Union.

The Potsdam Conference of 17 July to 2 August 1945 and What It Meant for Germany

From 17 July until 2 August 1945 the three great powers – the United States, Britain and the Soviet Union – met at Potsdam for a conference of great significance. France was not represented at this conference.

Those assembled at Potsdam dealt in detail with the policy to be pursued toward Germany. Decisions already taken at Teheran and Yalta were made more specific and attempts were made to reach agreement on questions that were still open.

The public at that time heard hardly anything about the Potsdam Conference. I learned of its results only from the published final communiqué.

I shall quote some characteristic and important passages from the official communiqué published by the US State Department.

> The Allied armies are in occupation of the whole of Germany and the German people have begun to atone for the terrible crimes committed under the leadership of those whom, in the hour of their success, they openly approved and blindly obeyed.

> Agreement has been reached at this conference on the political and economic principles of a co-ordinated Allied policy toward defeated Germany during the period of Allied control.

> The purpose of this agreement is to carry out the Crimea declaration on Germany. German militarism and Nazism will be extirpated and the Allies will take in agreement together, now and in the future, the other measures necessary to assure that Germany never again will threaten her neighbours or the peace of the world.

> It is not the intention of the Allies to destroy or enslave the German people. It is the intention of the Allies that the German people be given the opportunity to prepare for the eventual reconstruction of their life on a democratic and peaceful basis. If their own efforts are steadily directed to this end, it will be possible for them in due course to take their place among the free and peaceful peoples of the world.

For the time being no central German government was to be established. The communiqué went on:

> Nothwithstanding this, however, certain essential German administrative departments, headed by State Secretaries, shall be established, particularly in the fields of finance, transport, communications, foreign trade and industry. Such departments will act under the direction of the Control Council.

These German administrative departments never became effective, for the reason that they were put under the direction of the Control Council. The functioning of the Control Council as a coordinating body was closely tied to a common policy of the occupying powers since, as mentioned before, the

70

decisions of the Control Council had to be unanimous. Here and subsequently it became clear that agreement among the four powers could rarely be reached.

At the Potsdam Conference the United States and Great Britain endorsed the Soviet demand for a surrender of the Northern part of East Prussia and declared

that they will support the proposal of the Conference at the forthcoming peace settlement.

It was further agreed

that, pending the final determination of Poland's Western frontier, the former German territories East of a line running from the Baltic Sea immediately West of Swinemunde, and thence along the Oder River to the confluence of the Western Neisse River and along the Western Neisse to the Czechoslovak frontier, including that portion of East Prussia not placed under the administration of the Union of Soviet Socialist Republics in accordance with the understanding reached at this conference and including the area of the former Free City of Danzig, shall be under the administration of the Polish State and for such purposes should not be considered as part of the Soviet Zone of occupation in Germany.

The economic principles for Germany agreed upon at the Potsdam Conference put the emphasis on a development of agriculture and of peaceful domestic industries. The official final communiqué said:

In order to eliminate Germany's war potential the production of arms, ammunition and implements of war as well as all types of aircraft and sea-going ships shall be prohibited and prevented. Production of metals, chemicals, machinery and other items that are directly necessary to a war economy shall be rigidly controlled and restricted to Germany's approved post-war peacetime needs to meet the objectives stated in Paragraph 15. Productive capacity not needed for permitted production shall be removed in accordance with the reparations plan recommended by the Allied Commission on Reparations and approved by the Governments concerned or if not removed shall be destroyed.

At the earliest practicable date the German economy shall be decentralized for the purpose of eliminating the present excessive concentration of economic power as exemplified in particular by cartels, syndicates, trusts and other monopolistic arrangements.

In organizing the German economy primary emphasis shall be given to the development of agriculture and peaceful domestic industries.

During the period of occupation Germany shall be treated as a single economic unit.*

* Foreign Relations of the United States. Diplomatic Papers. The Conference of Berlin (The Potsdam Conference) 1945, Washington, 1960, Volume II, p. 1504.

Reparations, which were to be removed in kind within a period of two years, included assets, gold, ships, industrial installations and current production. War booty was not to be counted as reparations.

A commission was appointed to work out a detailed industrial plan for Germany in accordance with the Potsdam decisions. The resulting plan was approved by the Allied Control and published on 26 March 1946.

The general level of industrial production was to amount to roughly fifty to fifty-five per cent of the production of 1938. The plan was based on the following considerations:

1 Elimination of the German war potential and the industrial disarmament of Germany.
2 Payment of reparations to the countries which had suffered from German aggression.
3 Development of agricultural and peaceful industries.
4 Maintenance in Germany of average living standards not exceeding the average standard of living of European countries (excluding the United Kingdom and the Union of Soviet Socialist Republics).*

A detailed discussion of this plan is necessary to remind Germans of what was once in store for them.

All productive capacity not needed to achieve about fifty to fifty-five per cent of the production of 1938 was to be dismantled and either sent abroad as reparations or destroyed on the spot.

The plan differentiated between totally prohibited industries and industries whose production was to be restricted. Prohibited industries included those producing arms, ammunition, aircraft, sea-going ships, radio transmitting equipment, heavy tractors, numerous chemicals, synthetic fuel, synthetic rubber and oils.

I shall list some of the industries whose production was restricted by the plan: steel to 7.5 million tons per annum (i.e. thirty-three per cent of the raw steel production of 1933), copper to forty-eight per cent, zinc to sixty per cent, lead to fifty-four per cent, tin to fifty per cent, and nickel to eighteen per cent of pre-war production. The basic chemical industries were to retain only forty per cent of the production capacity of 1936. This especially affected nitrogen, phosphate, calcium carbide, sulphuric acid, alkalis, and chlorine. Machine manufacturing and engineering were restricted as follows: the machine tool industry was to retain eleven point four per cent of 1938 capacity; heavy engineering industries were to retain fifty per cent of 1938 capacity. The limitations on production of means of transport were laid down in the minutest detail. Even the number of telephones was prescribed and it was kept extremely low.

* Beate Ruhm von Oppen, ed.: *Documents on Germany under Occupation 1945–1954*, London, Oxford University Press, 1955, p. 113. Hereafter cited as Ruhm von Oppen, *Documents*.

These are only some parts of the industrial plan. The figures speak for themselves. The consequences of these Allied decisions would have come very close to the plans championed by the American Henry Morgenthau.

The economic directives adopted at Potsdam meant that German industry was to be destroyed or reduced to a minimum and that Germany was to become an agricultural country once more. This would have meant a sentence of death for many millions of Germans, for our land can produce at most seventy per cent of the required food. It seemed that the manufacture of goods for export, and hence the ability to pay for food imports, had been made impossible by the Potsdam decisions. If they had really been carried out, they would have led to unrest and to riots. In the end the three Western zones too, and hence all of Germany, would have gone communist.

Tensions Appear among the Allies

At Teheran and Yalta the United States, Great Britain and the Soviet Union had agreed to establish democratic countries in Eastern Europe, in Bulgaria, Rumania and Poland. A democratic order was to be the foundation of the states of Europe and thus of the reshaping and reconstruction of Europe. Consul-General von Weiss, the Swiss representative in Germany, had kept me informed on what had leaked out or had deliberately been made public by the Western Allies concerning the conferences of the big three.

But developments after the conclusion of the war against Germany took a different course.

An arresting declaration was made by the American Secretary of State, Byrnes, on 19 August 1945. According to a Reuters despatch Byrnes stated that present conditions in Bulgaria could not be described as satisfactory. Bulgaria did not have a government that could be regarded as representative of all democratic elements in the country. The forthcoming elections would not be carried out under conditions that were free from fear and intimidation. The American government had sent a message to this effect to the American representative in Sofia asking him to pass it on to the Bulgarian government.

A speech by President Truman in New York on 27 October 1945 on the occasion of the American Navy Day seemed to me a very clear indication of the growing tension between the Soviet Union and the Western Allies. He said:

> We shall approve no territorial changes in any friendly part of the world unless they accord with the freely expressed wishes of the people concerned.
>
> . . . We believe that all peoples who are prepared for self-government should be permitted to choose their own form of government by their own freely expressed choice without any interference from any foreign source.

73

That is true in Europe, in Asia, in Africa, as well as in the Western hemisphere.*

These words suggested distinct displeasure.

In the end it was the Soviet policy toward Poland that decisively affected the attitude of the Western powers vis-à-vis all Soviet policy. After the end of the war in 1945 Poland was the chief cause of growing tensions, especially between Britain and Soviet Russia.

After the conquest of Poland by Germany in September 1939 a Polish government in exile had been formed by General Sikorski in Paris; it later moved to London. This government in exile demanded territorial expansion in the West after the conclusion of the war against Germany, but it also demanded territorial acquisitions in the East, namely the Eastern Galician oil region which Poland had taken from Russia in the war of 1920 and which the Russians had ceded to the Poles in the subsequent Treaty of Riga. The Russians had taken back this area, under an agreement with Hitler, after the Germans had marched into Poland in September 1939.

Soviet Russia had no intention of giving up Eastern Galicia and the British government found itself in a difficult situation when, in the summer of 1941, Russia became Britain's ally. As Herr von Weiss told me more than once, the anti-Soviet tendency of the Polish exile government in London was quite obvious. In the meantime in Moscow a group of Poles friendly to the Soviets had constituted itself as the 'Union of Polish Patriots' on 1 March 1943.

The 'Union of Polish Patriots' did not recognize the Polish government in exile in London and after the rupture of diplomatic relations between the Soviet Union and the London Poles the Moscow group of Polish exiles was the one on which the Soviet Union relied for the formation of the future Polish government. As soon as the German troops had been driven out of Poland in the autumn of 1944 they were followed by members of the 'Union of Polish Patriots' who founded a 'Committee of Liberation'. Soviet Russia wanted to keep the valuable region of Eastern Galicia after the end of the war and therefore prevailed on the Polish politicians sent from Moscow to renounce the Eastern Galician areas ceded to Poland in the Treaty of Riga in 1921.

The Polish politicians sent from Moscow pursued a pro-Russian policy. The Russians were not willing to let the London Poles participate in the Polish government as had been agreed at Yalta. The agreement that the restoration and reconstruction of Poland was to take place on a democratic basis was not kept.

Churchill had gone to very great lengths to get the London Poles on the one hand and Stalin on the other ready for a compromise. He obviously aimed at the creation of an independent Poland that should be as strong as possible. He seemed to think of this strong Poland as an important member of a stable post-war Europe.

* Harry S. Truman, *Memoirs*, Doubleday & Co. Inc., 1955. Volume I, p. 538.

It was clear that the Western powers were very displeased by the Soviet attitude in this matter. They seemed slowly to recognize what aims the Soviet Union was pursuing in Europe and what danger to the Western world, especially to Europe, was represented by communism.

In March 1946 I read in the newspapers of a speech which Churchill had delivered in Fulton, Missouri, in the presence of the American President Truman. This speech is a classic statement of the growing disapproval of Soviet policy by the Anglo-Saxon powers. Churchill's clarity in Fulton left nothing to be desired. The speech seemed to me to mark a turning point in the attitude of the Western powers toward the Soviet Union. Because of its great importance I want to quote some parts of this speech:

A shadow has fallen upon the scenes so lately lighted by the Allied victory. Nobody knows what Soviet Russia and its Communist international organization intends to do in the immediate future, or what are the limits, if any, to their expansive and proselytizing tendencies . . .

From Stettin on the Baltic to Trieste in the Adriatic, an iron curtain has descended across the Continent. Behind that line lie all the capitals of the ancient states of Central and Eastern Europe. Warsaw, Berlin, Prague, Vienna, Budapest, Belgrade, Bucharest and Sofia, all these famous cities and the populations around them lie in what I must call the Soviet sphere, and all are subject in one form or another, not only to Soviet influence but to a very high and, in many cases, increasing measure of control from Moscow. Athens alone – Greece with its immortal glories – is free to decide its future at an election under British, American and French observation. The Russian-dominated Polish government has been encouraged to make enormous and wrongful inroads upon Germany, and mass expulsions of millions of Germans on a scale grievous and undreamed-of are now taking place. The Communist parties, which were very small in all these Eastern States of Europe, have been raised to pre-eminence and power far beyond their numbers and are seeking everywhere to obtain totalitarian control. Police governments are prevailing in nearly every case, and so far, except in Czechoslovakia, there is no true democracy.

Turkey and Persia are both profoundly alarmed and disturbed at the claims which are being made upon them and at the pressure being exerted by the Moscow Government. An attempt is being made by the Russians in Berlin to build up a quasi-Communist party in their zone of Occupied Germany by showing special favours to groups of left-wing German leaders. At the end of the fighting last June, the American and British Armies withdrew westwards, in accordance with an earlier agreement, to a depth at some points of 150 miles upon a front of nearly four hundred miles, in order to allow our Russian allies to occupy this vast expanse of territory which the Western Democracies had conquered.

If now the Soviet Government tries, by separate action, to build up a

75

pro-Communist Germany in their areas, this will cause new serious difficulties in the British and American zones, and will give the defeated Germans the power of putting themselves up to auction between the Soviets and the Western Democracies. Whatever conclusions may be drawn from these facts – and facts they are – this is certainly not the Liberated Europe we fought to build up. Nor is it one which contains the essentials of permanent peace.*

The Foreign Ministers' Conferences in Paris of April 1946 and June–July 1946; Molotov's Speech of 10 July 1946

It was the issue of Poland that had prevented Allied agreement. The Potsdam Agreement had stated explicitly that Germany was to be treated as a single economic unit. This provision proved illusory because the victorious powers did not agree on their political aims. It seemed that France, Great Britain, and the US had believed that, just as the four Allies had been united in the destruction of Germany, they would be equally united in the shaping of whatever was to be put in its place. This was a fundamental mistake. Soviet Russia had her own plans.

On 29 April 1946 the American Secretary of State, Byrnes, announced a plan for occupation policy in Germany at the Foreign Ministers' Conference in Paris. Byrnes proposed that the German question should be put on the agenda and made public the plan for the disarmament and occupation of Germany for twenty-five years which had previously been given to the three great powers confidentially in February 1946. He proposed discussion of this plan at a Foreign Ministers' Conference.

It had been chiefly the French who demanded a guarantee to protect them from a resurgence of Germany and the new dangers they saw in this. The French had also demanded the internationalization of the Ruhr or the complete destruction of its economic potential. In addition they demanded a permanent military occupation of the Rhineland which might eventually be superseded by an autonomous Rhenish state. It was in order to meet France's demands for security against Germany that Byrnes had offered a guarantee that Germany should remain disarmed and occupied for twenty-five years, perhaps even for forty years.

The French Foreign Minister Bidault and the British Foreign Secretary Bevin agreed to a discussion of the plan submitted by the Americans. Molotov indicated that Soviet Russia disapproved of the plan.

The American plans for Germany had appeared in the press and filled me with great anxiety for our future, an anxiety that was only increased by their connection with the levels of industry plan for Germany published in March 1946. These plans were bound to have grave psychological consequences in

* Randolph Spencer Churchill, ed.: *The Sinews of Peace; Post-war Speeches by Winston S. Churchill*, London, Cassell, 1948, pp. 100–1.

Germany. The lack of hope that the present emergency would ever be overcome was already oppressive enough.

There was another Foreign Ministers' Conference in Paris from 15 June to
12 July 1946 at which the plan for Germany submitted by Byrnes was
discussed.

Press reports of the views expressed by the French Foreign Minister Bidault
at this conference indicated that fear of a resurgent Germany seemed to
dominate political thought – especially in France.

Bidault again demanded a political and economic detachment of the Ruhr
from Germany, the political separation of the Rhineland from a centralized
Germany and the establishment of French control in the Saar. He supported
Byrnes's plans for German economic unity which should include the German
territories in the West as a transitional solution; he recognized that this would
make it easier to carry out the reparations programme.

Bevin, the British Foreign Secretary, indicated general assent to Byrnes's
twenty-five-year plan on behalf of Great Britain. Bevin made further statements which, to judge from press reports, led to recriminations among the
Allies over the way the Potsdam Agreement was being implemented. He
accused the Soviet Union of disregarding decisions taken with its own
consent.

Bevin very energetically demanded that the Potsdam Agreement should be
carried out in its entirety and that Germany should be treated as an economic
whole.

If it should prove impossible to cooperate with the other zones on a basis
of reciprocity, Great Britain would be forced to reorganize the British zone
in a way that would spare the British taxpayer additional burdens in connection with the occupation. If the zones continued to be treated as separate
entities it would mean a division of Europe that might endanger the peace.

The tenor of Bevin's speech was encouraging for us and the British soon
showed that he had not uttered empty words.

On 10 July 1946 Molotov made a speech which suddenly struck a new note
regarding Germany. He said he considered it wrong to agrarianize Germany.
He advocated the reconstruction and maintenance of the German industrial
potential. The destruction of what remained of German industry, he said,
would tend to undermine the economy of Europe and lead to a disruption of
the economy of the world.

But Molotov's eloquence at the Foreign Ministers' Conference in Paris on
10 July 1946 and Soviet Russia's actual policy in the Soviet zone were two
different things. The policy actually pursued by the Soviet Union was that
described by Churchill in his Fulton speech.

Soviet Russia made full use of the provision that every commander-in-
chief had supreme authority in his zone and was bound only by the directives
of his own government. The Russians had insisted on this provision at
the Potsdam Conference. Russia subsequently took far-reaching measures

regarding the economic, administrative and political development of her zone in order to make it into a Soviet satellite.

Through pressure on the Social Democratic Party (SPD) the Soviet Union forced it into a merger with the Communist Party (KPD) to form the Socialist Unity Party (SED) which then had to submit to the purposes of the Soviet occupation power. The other parties were suppressed.

From the very beginning the Russians seemed to pursue a clear policy toward Germany. It was their aim to include the whole of Germany in their sphere of power. They acted precisely in accordance with Lenin's watchword: 'Whoever has Germany has Europe.' In a speech on 22 October 1918, Lenin had said: 'Germany is the most important link in this chain [of world revolution]... and it [the German revolution] is decisive for the success of world revolution.'

The policy of the Western Allies towards us showed all too clearly that they had not recognized the Soviet aim. The United States of America had an atomic monopoly and saw in this, rather short-sightedly, an absolute guarantee of superiority to any danger that might threaten from the direction of Soviet Russia.

Our Position between the Two Power Blocs

In my opinion the Western powers were not equal to the Russians politically. As far as I could see they lacked a clear and consistent understanding of the post-war situation. Their countries' people, especially those of the United States, were longing for peace and preferred not to see the growing communist danger. The Western countries had finally prevailed after bitter fighting. Political thought and public opinion were entirely concentrated on punishing Germany for what she had done and on rendering her powerless. There were not many who looked further into the future.

It is a true saying that geography, the geographic situation of a country, constitutes one of the essential factors in its historical development.

Germany lies at the heart of Europe. The Western powers were not clear in their minds about what was to be done with this country whose destiny was in any case bound to be of the greatest importance for the fate of Europe and thus for their own. There was no unity among the Western powers concerning policy towards Germany. This was the case, for instance, in the matter of the Ruhr and of the detachment of the left bank of the Rhine desired by France.

The aim of the Russians was unambiguous. Soviet Russia had, like Tsarist Russia, an urge to acquire or subdue new territories in Europe. The policy of the Western Allies had allowed the Soviet Union to assume governmental power in a very large part of the former German Reich and had furthermore given the Russians a chance to install governments subservient to Moscow in a large part of Eastern Europe.

By our geographic position we found ourselves between two power blocs standing for totally opposed ideals. We had to join the one or the other side if we did not want to be ground up between them. I considered a neutral attitude between the two power groups unrealistic for our people. Sooner or later one or the other bloc was bound to try to get the German potential on its side. Soviet Russia was making it quite clear that for the time being she was not willing to release the German territory she had been allowed to take over, and that moreover she had every intention of gradually drawing the other part of Germany towards her as well.

There was only one way for us to save our political liberty, our personal freedom, our security, the way of life we had formed in many centuries and which was based on the Christian and humanistic ideology: we must form firm links with the peoples and countries that shared our views concerning the state, the individual, liberty and property. We must resolutely and firmly resist all further pressure from the East.

It was our task to dispel the mistrust harboured against us everywhere in the West. We had to try, step by step, to reawaken confidence in Germans. The fundamental precondition for this, in my view, was a clear, steady, unwavering affirmation of identity with the West. The orientation of our foreign policy had to be clear, logical and open.

5

CLARIFICATION

The Creation of the Land *of North Rhine-Westphalia*

The Western powers had to see Soviet policy in action, first in Bulgaria and Rumania and finally in Poland, before they recognized the Soviet design to create satellite countries in Europe. It seemed to me that it was mainly the establishment of a communist government in Poland which at last opened the eyes of the Western Allies. They now realized that they had to build a dam against further encroachment by the Soviet Union in Western Europe and that this must be done by the political and economic consolidation of their zones of occupation in Germany.

The decisive change in the behaviour of the Western powers occurred after the Foreign Ministers' Conference in Paris which ended on 15 July 1946.

Ernest Bevin, the British Foreign Secretary, had already intimated at this conference that Great Britain intended to take independent measures in her zone if no unity could be achieved on the German question.

On 15 July 1946 the British Military Government asked me to fly to Berlin at once. I was told that my stay might last a week or two. I knew nothing definite. I was not told, nor was there even the slightest hint, what the purpose of my visit might be. I was unable to give a Berlin address to my family because I did not know where I was to stay. I was told only that my trip to Berlin had to be treated in the strictest confidence.

On my arrival in Berlin I was asked to come to a talk with the British Deputy Military Governor, Lieutenant General Sir Brian Robertson. Dr Schumacher, the leader of the SPD, was also present as were my secretary Dr Löns and another representative of the SPD, as well as Jakob Kaiser, the well-known leader of the CDU in Berlin.

We were told that the British Military Government had decided to create a new political entity in the British zone, and with immediate effect. We were shown the borders of the region envisaged for North Rhine-Westphalia on a map. This plan was a complete surprise to me. Lieutenant General Robertson explained that it was due to Soviet refusal to agree to the merger of the four zones of occupation. He said that the British and American governments had therefore decided to bring about the quickest possible economic and political consolidation in the parts of Germany occupied by them.

It was clear from what Robertson said that the attitude of the Soviet Union played an essential part in the creation of the *Land* of North Rhine-Westphalia. It was also clear that Britain and America were not willing to give in to France's demand for the neutralization of the industrial area and for the amputation of the left bank of the Rhine.

The creation of this *Land* also showed the clear intention to prevent Prussia being reconstituted as a *Land*. Foreign policy considerations played the chief role here.

Britain and the United States had wanted to await the outcome of the Paris Conference of Foreign Ministers, and had especially wished to observe the behaviour of the Soviet Union at this conference, before deciding on a step which was bound to have a decisive influence on relations between themselves and the Soviets.

Lieutenant General Robertson asked Dr Schumacher and myself what we thought of this new proposal. I said that it was necessary to interlock the former Rhine Province as far as possible with other German regions to the East and West in order to protect the left bank of the Rhine from France's demands. I therefore supported the creation of North Rhine-Westphalia.

Dr Schumacher asked whether any change in the decision was still possible. He was told: 'No, the decision is made.' Whereupon Dr Schumacher declared that he and his party were against the creation of a *Land* of such magnitude as North Rhine-Westphalia in the framework of a Germany with a federal structure. This did not, however, prevent him from later proposing the creation of another *Land*, to include the entire British zone apart from North Rhine-Westphalia, when the Zonal Advisory Council was being asked for its opinion regarding the reorganization of the remaining parts of the British zone. But then the Military Government acted on the advice of the *Oberpräsidenten* Dr Lehr and Hinrich Kopf, who agreed in proposing the establishment of the *Länder* of Lower Saxony and Schleswig-Holstein beside the Hanseatic Town of Hamburg.

The official announcement of the creation of North Rhine-Westphalia was made by the British Military Government on 18 July 1946. The establishment of this *Land* was a step of far-reaching political importance for us Germans and for Europe. The British, obviously acting in agreement with the Americans, aimed at and succeeded in putting an end to all discussions with France concerning the internationalization and neutralization of the Ruhr as well as the detachment of the left bank of the Rhine from Germany.

If these French demands had been met, it would, in my opinion, have meant the economic disintegration not only of Germany but also of Europe. Since economic decay is good soil for the growth of communism, communism and with it the Soviet Union would eventually have become masters of the whole of Germany.

I considered the foundation of North Rhine-Westphalia a wise decision and one of great consequence.

In the creation of a big West German *Land* inside Germany, such as was

F   81

now being formed by the decision of the British Military Government, I saw a reliable guarantee of peace in Europe. In my view such a West German *Land* was the surest guarantee against Germany, even after her recovery, initiating actions that might lead to war. Such a territorial unit must in the nature of things, both because of the views of its inhabitants and because of its economic structure, aim at collaboration with Germany's Western neighbours, with Holland, Belgium, Luxembourg, France and Britain.

I thought it was important that the Ruhr, an industrial district, was now being incorporated into a bigger unit with rural areas and regions with medium and light industries. For if the Ruhr, which already had a large communist vote and where since the collapse of Germany strong communist agitation had developed, had become a *Land* on its own, the CDU would not have had a chance there. In all probability the KPD would have become the decisive party there in the course of time. This would have had harmful consequences for developments in the whole of Germany in that the KPD would have had a good chance to forge links with the Soviet Union. The merger of the Rhineland, whose population was predominantly conservative, with the Ruhr, seemed to me greatly to reduce the danger of connections between left-wing groups of the Ruhr and the Soviet Union.

In the creation of the *Land* of North Rhine-Westphalia I saw grounds for hope that France might gradually be convinced that such a unit would be a surer guarantee of a lasting peace than a permanent occupation or even amputation of German territories. To be sure these were thoughts that reached far into the future, but I considered conditions in Europe and in the world to be such as forced one to plan well beyond the immediate future.

I cannot say with any certainty to what extent talks with the French played a role in the discussions between the United States and Great Britain concerning the creation of North Rhine-Westphalia, but it is very likely that there was some kind of agreement with France regarding the Saar in this connection. As mentioned before, the French had demanded the detachment of the Saar from Germany. On 7 July 1945 the American military authorities had handed over the Saar to the French to be administered by them and the Saar mines were put under the direction of French commissions. Later the Agence France Presse reported the confiscation of the Saar mines by France on 23 December 1945.

I was anxious about these measures and the demands repeatedly voiced by French politicians that the Saar should be annexed to France. I had learned that the French Foreign Minister had handed a Note to the Ambassadors of the United States, Great Britain and the Soviet Union on 12 February 1946, in which these governments were told that the Saar had been taken out of the French zone of occupation. Consul General von Weiss told me that this Note stated that the Saar was removed from the competence of the Berlin Control Council with immediate effect and that it would never again come under German administration. On the other hand the Note also was said to have stated – probably in analogy to the Potsdam agreements regarding the German territories given to the Poles – that the final status of the Saar was to be determined at the moment of the peace settlement.

When I then learned, roughly at the time I was told of the formation of North Rhine-Westphalia, that at the Paris Foreign Ministers' Conference the Foreign Ministers of Great Britain and the United States had given their consent to France's demand for the detachment of the Saar from the German economic system, and that in addition the area administered by the Saar government had been considerably enlarged, I feared that the British had bought the consent of the French to the formation of North Rhine-Westphalia by a concession concerning the Saar. As their reason for their claim to the Saar the French had put forward their economy's vital need of the Saar coal deposits.

This connection between the formation of North Rhine-Westphalia and the Saar question was a negative aspect of the newly created *Land*. But we Germans were powerless and not in a position to influence the actions and decisions of the Allies effectively. I endorsed the creation of North Rhine-Westphalia because I hoped that in the course of time there would emerge a possibility of retaining the Saar for Germany. And that is in fact what happened.

On 6 September 1946 the American Secretary of State, James F. Byrnes, made a speech to leading figures of the American Military Government and the Ministers President of the *Länder* of the American zone in the State Theatre in Stuttgart, in which he said:

> The United States does not feel that it can deny to France, which has been invaded three times by Germany in 70 years, its claim to the Saar territory, whose economy has long been closely linked with France. Of course, if the Saar territory is integrated with France she should readjust her reparation claims against Germany.
>
> Except as here indicated,* the United States will not support any encroachment on territory which is indisputably German or any division of Germany which is not genuinely desired by the people concerned. So far as the United States is aware the people of the Ruhr and the Rhineland desire to remain united with the rest of Germany. And the United States is not going to oppose their desire.
>
> While the people of the Ruhr were the last to succumb to Nazism, without the resources of the Ruhr Nazism could never have threatened the world. Never again must those resources be used for destructive purposes. They must be used to rebuild a free, peaceful Germany and a free, peaceful Europe.
>
> The United States will favour such control over the whole of Germany, including the Ruhr and the Rhineland, as may be necessary for security

---

* Byrnes is here alluding to statements concerning Poland. (Author's footnote.)

purposes. It will help to enforce those controls. But it will not favour any controls that would subject the Ruhr and the Rhineland to political domination or manipulation of outside powers.*

On 22 October 1946 Ernest Bevin, the British Foreign Secretary, made a statement to similar effect in the House of Commons.

These statements by Byrnes and Bevin seemed to confirm my surmise that the United States and Great Britain had agreed to the separation of the Saar from Germany; but on the other hand they also meant a rejection of the French demands for internationalization of the Ruhr and amputation of the left bank of the Rhine. I had the impression that in the whole matter of North Rhine-Westphalia and the Saar there had been a compromise between the French on the one side and the British and Americans on the other, one of whose features must have been the allaying of French fears that Prussia might be restored.

The Economic Fusion of the British and American Zones and the Formation of the Bizone

The four zones of Germany were drifting further and further apart economically and the general misery and economic chaos had grown steadily since 1945. It was obvious that this source of unrest was bound to infect the other countries sooner or later. The Americans seemed to recognize the danger this boded for Europe.

On 20 July 1946 the US Military Governor General McNarney asked the three other occupation powers in Germany to put into effect a uniform economic policy in all zones. The United Kingdom declared itself prepared for this on 1 August 1946. France rejected the plan on 10 August 1946. The Soviet Union did not react to the American proposal in any way. The Russians were not interested in the economic recovery of the three Western zones of Germany. The communists were convinced that the capitalist world was approaching its economic demise. The economic chaos in the Western parts of Germany could only accelerate the process. The Russians are said to be excellent chess players. In their eyes Germany was an important chessman destined to promote the disintegration of the capitalist world. Post-war history has many examples of this Russian strategy.

The Western Allies had handed over large tracts of the German territory they had conquered to the Russians with whom they agreed on quadripartite occupation of Berlin. But the Western Allies had not paid enough attention to the isolation of Berlin in Russian-occupied Germany. They had neglected to secure a land corridor to Berlin. Subsequent years proved this omission to be a serious mistake.

At the sixth session of the Zonal Advisory Council in Hamburg on 14

* Ruhm von Oppen, *Documents*, p. 159.

August 1946 Lieutenant General Robertson gave a detailed account of the advantages and disadvantages of the impending merger of the American and British zones.

Voices in Germany had expressed the fear that these Anglo-American measures – which the French were bound to join sooner or later – would result in a division of Germany into Eastern and Western Germany.

Lieutenant General Robertson assured the members of the Zonal Advisory Council that it was not the intention of the British and American governments to bring about a division of Germany. But something simply had to be done in order to counteract the economic divergence of the zones and the growing economic chaos.

The advantages of a fusion of the British and American zones were great, he said. The British zone had large industrial areas in the Rhineland and Westphalia, the American zone had agricultural regions and a considerable part of the manufacturing industry. If trade between these two zones could proceed unimpeded, the resulting benefit would be mutual.

Lieutenant General Robertson then explained the planned measures in some detail.

The agreement between the British and American Military Governors on the economic fusion of the two zones was concluded on 5 September 1946. It was signed in Washington on 2 December 1946 by the American Secretary of State James F. Byrnes and the British Foreign Secretary Ernest Bevin. A British White Paper giving details of this fusion was published on the day of the signing.

I hoped for an improvement in living conditions in the British zone from this bi-zonal agreement. Economic and food conditions, especially in North Rhine-Westphalia, had been catastrophic up to this point. I hoped that our economy would be set in motion, in part at least, and I found special encouragement in the provision that the costs to the British and American governments were to be defrayed by future German exports insofar as this was 'consistent with the rebuilding of the German economy'.

From the better future coordination and exploitation of the economic resources of the two zones I hoped for a gradual elimination of obstacles to the shipment of food supplies into the British zone. The placing of much administrative responsibility in German hands was another promising development.

The Anglo-American agreement of 2 December 1946 stated that important administrative powers were to be transferred to Germans. The sooner this was done, and in particular the sooner the British reduced their enormous administrative apparatus – which was also extremely expensive for an impoverished country such as ours – and retired from administration to control, the sooner they would also begin to foster liberty and democracy among our people and especially the young. We had heard a lot of preaching about democracy, but there had been little democratic action.

The Speech of the American Secretary of State on
6 September 1946 in Stuttgart

The planned economic fusion of the British and American zones was another step in the general direction of a change in the German policy of the Western powers. This change was clear in the above-mentioned speech given by James F. Byrnes, the American Secretary of State, at Stuttgart on 6 September 1946 before representatives of American Military Government and the Ministers President of three South German *Länder*.

Byrnes spoke of the need to achieve economic unity for Germany and to revive its economic powers as well as strengthening German political responsibility. The American people did not want a hard or soft peace but a lasting peace with Germany. I shall quote verbatim two passages from this speech which sounded a note quite different from that to which we were accustomed from the Allies:

> ... But just because suffering and distress in Germany are inevitable, the American government is unwilling to accept responsibility for the needless aggravation of economic distress caused by the failure of the Allied Control Council to agree to give the German people a chance to solve some of their most urgent economic problems. So far as many vital questions are concerned, the Control Council is neither governing Germany nor allowing Germany to govern itself . . .*

> ... The United States cannot relieve Germany from the hardships inflicted by the war her leaders started. But the United States has no desire to increase those hardships or to deny the German people an opportunity to work their way out of those hardships so long as they respect human freedom and cling to the paths of peace. The American people want to return the government of Germany to the German people. The American people want to help the German people to win their way back to an honourable place among the free and peace-loving nations of the world.†

In his Stuttgart speech Byrnes also spoke, for the first time, of a military power struggle between East and West. In this connection Byrnes said that the United States of America did not consider it in the interest of world peace for Germany to become a pawn between East and West. But he also said that Germany must not be allowed to become a partner of either East or West. I thought this a statement both premature and open to misunderstanding.

Byrnes had obviously not yet recognized the importance of Germany for the Western World. This may have been partly due to the fact that at that time the United States still had its atomic monopoly.

Byrnes said that the American people wished to return the government of Germany to the German people. He said that Europe could not recover if

* Ruhm von Oppen, *Documents*, p. 155.
† Ruhm von Oppen, *Documents*, p. 160.

Germany was turned into a poorhouse, and he made unambiguous statements that the United States would not permit Germany to become the vassal of a foreign power or subject to a domestic or foreign dictatorship.

Report of the Former American President Hoover of Spring 1947 on Conditions in Europe

The economic fusion of the British and American zones and its positive effects on our economy came too late to relieve the prevailing hardship, which had been increased by the especially hard winter of 1946–7. Bizonal administrative offices for single sectors of the economy were set up in the last months of 1946, but their efforts and coordination did not affect the plight of the German population as rapidly as would have been necessary to produce immediate improvement.

In 1946 President Truman commissioned ex-President Hoover, who was given a large staff, to make a report on the food situation in Europe. The results of his investigations were published in the spring of 1947.

According to the Hoover Report the food situation of Italy, France, Belgium, Holland and Great Britain had reached almost pre-war standards. The report stated, however, that the food situation in Germany was dangerously below the average of the other European countries, and it was indeed very alarming. President Hoover made concrete proposals for immediate measures in Germany; for instance, he considered it absolutely necessary that fertilizers and seed be imported into Germany because at present the soil was insufficiently productive.

In this report President Hoover said:

> But our economic interest is far wider than this. We desperately need recovery in all of Europe. We need it not only for economic reasons but as the first necessity to peace ... There is only one path to recovery in Europe. That is production. The whole economy of Europe is inter-linked with the German economy through the exchange of raw materials and manufactured goods. The productivity of Europe cannot be restored without the restoration of Germany as a contributor to that productivity.

President Hoover stated in his report that Germany had, by its territorial losses to Poland and by the economic amputation of the Saar territory, lost twenty-five per cent of its food production, thirty per cent of its coal production and twenty per cent of its production of consumer goods compared with 1936, but that the population of Germany in 1936 had been 68 million whereas by 1949 it would be about 71 million including the Soviet zone.

He described the notion of agrarianizing Germany as illusory. He said that such a step would require 25 million Germans to be either exterminated or resettled.

President Hoover also called it an illusion to think that Germany could be enabled to pay for its necessary imports by light industry alone – especially as competition from other countries had to be reckoned with. Germany could not become economically independent without support from abroad under the present industrial plan of March 1946. But the greatest illusion was to think that Europe could ever recover without Germany's restoration to economic health. Hence, unless it was intended actually to let the Germans starve, Germany would be a heavy burden for the taxpayers of the Allied Western powers under the present industrial plan. If the present policy was to be persisted in, the consequence would be a cesspool of unemployment in the centre of Europe which must, sooner or later, contaminate neighbouring countries. Germany could continue to be kept in chains, but then Europe too would probably remain in rags.

I want to take this opportunity to thank President Hoover on behalf of all Germans and to express my admiration to him for this report on the situation of the defeated and ostracized Germany. The report is a great humanitarian document. It must have been the first time in the history of the last few centuries that a humanitarian spirit animated the victor and that the victor desired to help the vanquished to emerge from their misery.

6

THE TURNING POINT

The Moscow Foreign Ministers' Conference of Spring 1947

Although in those years Germany was as yet unable to exercise an immediate influence on international affairs, there were, nonetheless, certain possibilities of indirect influence. One means, and it was not the least of them, was the general bearing of the Germans. Despite sorrow, anxiety and hunger their attitude was commendable. The attitude of German political agencies toward the occupying powers was equally important; by and large it was correct. Gradually the occupation authorities, including the topmost echelons, became convinced that the Germans were better than had been supposed and that the barbarism of National Socialism had affected only a relatively small percentage of the country.

Conversations with foreign politicians and journalists offered opportunities of letting people abroad know something about conditions and attitudes in Germany. I took every opportunity to talk to them and to give interviews, and, in the event, not without success.

Conversely it was important for every German who came in touch with foreigners to form some idea of what was happening outside Germany, especially concerning the relations among the victorious powers. Gradually foreign newspapers began to come into the country, and finally the occupation authorities gave permission for the issue of German papers. In their very early days these German papers were not very satisfactory. It could hardly be otherwise after twelve years of National Socialism, war and destruction. These papers were not subject to censorship, but their licence could be withdrawn at any time. That was enough.

This first number carried a message from General Eisenhower, the Comdaily paper in German for the whole of Germany. The first issue of the paper, *Die Neue Zeitung*, appeared on 18 October 1945.

This first number carried a message from General Eisenhower, the Commander of the American forces in Germany and Military Governor of the part of Germany occupied by US troops. In his message Eisenhower said, *inter alia:*

> Through its emphasis on the affairs of the world, the 'Neue Zeitung' will broaden the view of the German reader by giving him facts which were suppressed in Germany during the twelve years of National Socialist rule.

General Eisenhower here touched a point of the greatest importance for us Germans. It was a fact that the gagging of the German press by the National Socialist régime from 1933 to 1945 had deprived many of us of any perspective on world events. It was especially necessary for leading German personalities to try to regain some knowledge of world affairs as quickly as possible and as accurately, in order that we should be in a position to make the right decisions when the time came when we could once more make foreign policy.

There were disagreements among the victorious powers which were to be of decisive importance for our future. Attempts were made to settle these differences at conferences. In particular the years 1946 and 1947 were full of more or less unsuccessful conferences of the victorious powers. My *Memoirs* which, after all, are to trace the developments that led to the present state of affairs, would have a conspicuous gap did they not contain some essential points about this period of conferences.

From 10 March to 24 April 1947 there was a Foreign Ministers' Conference in Moscow at which the United States was represented by Marshall, Great Britain by Bevin, France by Bidault and the Soviet Union by Molotov.

Lieutenant General Robertson, who was present at the conference, gave a detailed report before the Zonal Advisory Council on 30 April 1947. We learned further details from newspaper reports and semi-official publications.

Robertson said in his report that this was the first conference to have dealt thoroughly with the future of Germany. He admitted that the conference had brought few decisions and openly confessed that little had been achieved towards the immediate and practical alleviation of Germany's present problems; he thought that the result of the conference must be a great disappointment to us.

Bevin had submitted a plan for Germany in Moscow with which Marshall had agreed in essentials. I shall return to this plan in connection with the London Foreign Ministers' Conference of December 1947.

Bidault repeated the earlier French demands for the amputation of the Ruhr and the Rhineland from the rest of Germany and for the permanent occupation of the left bank of the Rhine by the Allies. The French envisaged the creation of a Rhenish state whose autonomy was to be guaranteed. Bidault demanded the internationalization of the Ruhr, for which he submitted a plan. The coal mines and foundries of the Ruhr were to become the property of the countries that had fought against Germany; their management was to be by the Big Four, in conjunction with Belgium, the Netherlands, and Luxembourg. The Saar was to be incorporated into the area of French economic jurisdiction.

Molotov, who submitted his own plan for Germany, declared that the Soviet Union demanded permanent control of the Ruhr by all four great powers.

Bevin and Marshall opposed the detachment of the Rhineland and the Ruhr from the rest of Germany but agreed to the inclusion of the Saar in the

French economic system. Marshall expressed the opinion that the natural resources of the Ruhr should be regarded as a European asset, but that an international régime should be instituted only if Germany used these resources in ways opposed to the interests of other countries.

Regarding the future political structure of Germany, all agreed that as far as possible all political power was to be given to the *Länder*.

One point of special interest in the Russian proposals is the repetition of the Soviet claim to reparations to the amount of 10,000 million US dollars at 1938 world prices.

One of the positive results of the Moscow conference was the decision that the German prisoners of war who were being held in Russia, France, Britain, and the United States, in camps, and as workers, were to be repatriated in the foreseeable future. The CDU and the other German parties had asked again and again in resolutions and speeches for a discussion of this question. In Moscow it was due to the initiative of the British Minister of Labour that the question was broached. The Foreign Ministers assembled in Moscow passed a unanimous resolution on this point. The German prisoners of war were to be repatriated by 1 December 1948 at the latest. The Soviet Union broke this commitment as it did so many other international obligations.

Another positive result of the Moscow Conference was the announcement that German industrial capacity was to be raised to the extent necessary for it to meet German peacetime requirements. The concept of German peace-time needs seemed very alastic to me. I was afraid that no attention would be paid to exports, which we needed for a healthy economy.

All in all, the Moscow Conference was a complete failure. It showed clearly that there had been unity in the winning of the war but that there were not the slightest vestiges of unity over what was to be done thereafter. As far as could be judged from press reports, the American Secretary of State, Marshall, was very reserved in the course of this long conference – it lasted over six weeks – probably because the United States was coming to realize the dangers of world communism and the importance which a healthy Germany would have for Europe and for the world, and also because he did not consider that the proposals made at the conference were calculated to achieve any desirable goal.

The Truman Doctrine: the Declaration of the President of the United States of America of 12 March 1947

The year 1947 saw further conferences in New York, in London, in Moscow, and again in London in December 1947.

One thing emerged clearly at these conferences: a constant contest between the two Anglo-Saxon powers and a Russia seeking to extend her influence everywhere. France, which had at first seen the European situation in a rather narrow perspective, was coming closer and closer to the views of the United

States and Britain in the course of 1947. It was slowly becoming evident that the Western Allies were determined to offer stronger resistance than heretofore to the ambitions of the Soviet Union.

During these years the difference between the Western Allies and the Soviet Union developed in several parts of the world: in Germany, in Korea, whose occupation posed problems similar to those of the occupation of Germany; in Iran, where the Soviet Union refused to evacuate the Northern part it held occupied, in accordance with an agreement with the Western Allies that stipulated evacuation by 2 March 1946; in Greece, where vigorous communist activity led to a civil war; and in Turkey. The discovery of Soviet atomic espionage in Canada put a further strain on relations between East and West.

The help given by the Soviet Union to communists in Greece prompted the President of the United States, Truman, to issue a very sharp and unambiguous declaration, addressed to the Soviet Union, on 12 March 1947. Truman had become President of the United States after the death of Roosevelt, having occupied the office of Vice-President for only a few months.

He needed very little time to form a clear impression of the political situation in the world, and of the dangers of communism to all free peoples.

The British who, during the first year and a half of the post-war period had supported the Greek Government, saw themselves forced to restrict or even to abandon their obligations in many parts of the world. In the case of Greece this meant complete withdrawal.

The sufferings and poverty of the Greek population gave ample opportunity for successful activity by the communists, and in consequence the Greek Government had urgently appealed to the United States for financial and economic aid.

The precarious world situation prompted President Truman to make a declaration of very far-reaching importance at a joint session of the Senate and the House of Representatives in Washington on 12 March 1947. It has entered history as the Truman Doctrine.

President Truman announced that the United States was prepared to meet the Greek request for economic and financial aid. He further announced that Turkey, which found itself in a similar situation to that of Greece, was to receive American support as well. President Truman then said:

> We are the only country able to provide that help. I am fully aware of the broad implications involved if the United States extends aid to Greece and Turkey . . .
>
> One of the primary objectives of the foreign policy of the United States is the creation of conditions in which we and other nations will be able to work out a way of life free from coercion. This was the fundamental issue in the war with Germany and Japan . . .
>
> We shall not realize our objectives, however, unless we are willing to help free peoples to maintain their free institutions and their national

integrity against aggressive movements that seek to impose upon them totalitarian régimes. This is no more than a frank recognition that the totalitarian régimes imposed upon free peoples, by direct or indirect aggression, undermine the foundations of international peace and hence the security of the United States.

The peoples of a number of countries in the world have recently had totalitarian régimes forced upon them against their will. The Government of the United States has made frequent protests against coercion and intimidation, in violation of the Yalta agreement, in Poland, Rumania, and Bulgaria . . .

I believe that we must assist free peoples to work out their own destinies in their own way . . .

The seeds of totalitarian régimes are nurtured by misery and want. They spread and grow in the evil soil of poverty and strife. They reach their full growth when the hope of a people for a better life has died. We must keep that hope alive. The free peoples of the world look to us for support in maintaining their freedoms. If we falter in our leadership, we may endanger the peace of the world – and we shall surely endanger the welfare of our Nation. Great responsibilities have been placed upon us by the swift movement of events.*

Rarely has the danger of our epoch been seen with such clarity, rarely have the logical consequences resulting from it for the free peoples, and above all the United States of America, been expressed so clearly as President Truman saw and expressed them on this occasion.

The Marshall Plan for the Reconstruction of Europe

The industries of almost all the countries of Europe were destroyed and had to be built up again. The loss of life was tremendous. The general change from a war- to a peacetime economy was attended by the greatest difficulties. Developments in Europe seemed to proceed in an irresistibly downward direction, which everywhere gave to the Communist Party advantageous opportunities for its propaganda. On 8 May 1947 the then Under-Secretary of State in the American Department of State, Dean Acheson, made a speech at Cleveland, Mississippi, in which he spoke openly of the failure of the Moscow Foreign Ministers' Conference and emphasized the determination of the United States to embark on European reconstruction even without unity among the Big Four. Dean Acheson also referred to Germany in this speech, and said that in the circumstances the United States would have to do everything possible to facilitate the reconstruction of the great workshop of Europe. He made similar references to Japan, and said that the final recovery of Europe and Asia depended to a large extent on the recovery of Germany and Japan.

* *Department of State Bulletin*, 23 March 1947, pp. 534–7.

The American economy, he said, needed the European market, and the United States had an interest in Europe's restoration to health for the sake both of security against world communism and of the American economy. In his Cleveland speech of 8 May 1947 Dean Acheson mentioned the fact that the United States had given aid to many countries during the post-war period and pointed out that these measures were taken not only from humanitarian considerations but chiefly as a matter of national self-interest. For unless all the countries in the world had a healthy economy there could be no durable peace for any country. The war would not really be over until the people of the world could again feed and clothe themselves and could face the future with some degree of confidence. World peace was in the interest of the United States. Since world demand, however, exceeded the American ability to supply, the United States would have to concentrate its assistance in areas where it would be effective in strengthening the authority of the United Nations and in fostering liberal trading policies. Free peoples who were seeking to preserve their independence, their democratic institutions and human freedoms against totalitarian pressures, either internal or external, would receive top priority for American reconstruction aid. This is how Dean Acheson outlined the great American aid programme which entered history as the 'Marshall Plan'.

After the conclusion of the Moscow Conference Secretary of State Marshall had called for immediate measures to bring about the recovery of Europe – if necessary without prior agreement among the Great Powers. He said that the entire economy of Europe would have to cooperate as a harmonious whole; and that it was the goal of American foreign policy to restore a healthy and coordinated European economy.

At the Annual Dinner of the Democratic Party on 5 April 1947 President Truman said that it was not enough to say 'we do not want war' but that one had to anticipate developments and to act in such a way as to destroy at the outset any germ of war that might spread across the world. The past had shown that wars were started by aggression by superior armed force or by secret infiltration. President Truman said that it was the duty of the United States and the United Nations to protest wherever the rights of free peoples were threatened. This protest had to be made effective by help given to those peoples whose freedom was endangered by foreign pressure.

One month after Dean Acheson's speech, on 5 June 1947, Marshall made the famous speech at Harvard University that inaugurated the great European recovery programme, probably the greatest assistance programme the world had ever seen.

In his speech at Harvard Secretary of State Marshall described the general situation in the world as serious and pointed in particular to the economic system of Europe which had been disrupted by war. The healthy balance between imports and exports had been dislocated in most European countries. Governments were forced to use foreign currency and credits to buy the food and industrial goods most urgently needed for the reconstruction of their countries. This development, which made any normal exchange of goods in the world impossible, was bound to lead to a catastrophe. The division of labour, a system founded on the exchange of production, was threatened with breakdown. Europe's requirements for the next three or four years of foreign food and other essential products – principally from America – were so much greater than her present ability to pay that she must have substantial help or face economic, social, and political deterioration of a very grave character. The remedy lay in breaking the vicious circle and restoring the confidence of the European people in the economic future of their own countries and of Europe as a whole.

Aside from the demoralizing effect on the world at large and the possibilities of disturbances arising as a result of the desperation of the people concerned, the consequences to the economy of the United States should be apparent to all. It was therefore logical that the United States should do whatever it could to assist in the return of normal economic health in the world, without which there could be no political stability and no assured peace. American policy was directed not against any country or doctrine but against hunger, poverty, desperation, and chaos. Any government that was willing to assist in the task of recovery would find full cooperation on the part of the United States Government. Any government which tried to block the recovery of other countries could expect no help from America. Governments, political parties, or groups which were seeking to perpetuate human misery in order to profit therefrom politically or otherwise would encounter the opposition of the United States. It was evident that, before the United States Government could proceed further in its efforts to alleviate the situation and to help European reconstruction, there must be some agreement among the countries of Europe as to the requirements of the situation and the part those countries themselves would take, in order to give proper effect to whatever action might be undertaken by the American Government.

Marshall stressed that the United States had no intention of undertaking to draw up unilaterally a programme for Europe. That was the business of the Europeans themselves. The role of the United States should consist of friendly assistance in the drafting of a European aid programme and of later support for such a programme, which should be a joint one agreed to by most, if not all, European nations. Marshall emphasized that political passion and prejudice should have no part in the drafting of the programme. With this sentence he indicated, in my opinion, that the future programme of aid was also to apply to Germany.

In a statement made a few days after his Harvard speech Marshall stressed once more that the initiative for the programme would have to come from Europe and that the United States would undertake no steps until the countries of Europe had indicated their attitude to the proposals put forward at Harvard. Marshall emphasized particularly that the European recovery programme was to apply to all countries of Europe, including the Soviet Union and the communist-ruled countries of Eastern Europe.

On 14 June 1947 the British Foreign Office announced that Foreign Secretary Ernest Bevin intended to meet the French Premier Ramadier and Foreign Minister Bidault in Paris during the second half of June in order to discuss the American proposal. I learnt from the press that the President of the French Republic, Auriol, announced France's willingness to cooperate in the common plan for Europe. President Auriol spoke of the need for Europe to unite. Economic and political questions, he said, formed one whole and he thought it wise to make an immediate start on the economic problems in the hope that the alleviation of economic misery would bring a decrease of political mistrust. He described the speech of the American Secretary of State as courageous and stressed France's resolve to take up the plan proposed in it immediately. Bevin, who was in Paris on that day, made a statement of a similar nature.

This was the beginning. There followed the acceptance by many European countries of the American offer of help. The foreign ministers of those countries which had indicated their agreement were invited to a conference in Paris. A number of East European countries had indicated their readiness to discuss this programme, which was now generally called the 'Marshall Plan', as had the Soviet Union, and Molotov appeared at the Foreign Ministers' Conference in Paris which began on 27 June 1947.

Marshall had expressly spoken of a European economic plan that would have to be jointly drawn up by the countries concerned. Any Western agreement with the Soviet Union on a joint reconstruction plan for Europe seemed very unlikely to me. Soviet Russia's economic system and the system introduced in many East European countries on the Soviet model were so closely bound up with their political system that I considered a common plan of reconstruction impossible.

Nonetheless Molotov put in an appearance at the Foreign Ministers' Conference in Paris. I imagine that the positive response to the American invitation in virtually all East European countries forced him to make it appear, at least, as though the Soviet Union were prepared to cooperate with the United States. Or perhaps Molotov hoped to bring some communist influence to bear on the economic reshaping of Europe during the negotiations on the recovery programme. But if such were his intentions he must have found himself confronted by a solid Anglo-French phalanx. Be that as it may, I was not surprised to learn that Molotov left Paris under protest as early as 2 July 1947. It was obviously on Moscow's urgings that Poland, Czechoslovakia, and other East European countries had to retract their announced intention to cooperate. Their representatives left Paris as well.

Before he left the Paris Foreign Ministers' Conference Molotov had accused the United States of pursuing nothing but imperialist designs in Europe and of trying to make Europe politically and economically dependent on America.

As I learned later from the press and from a confidential source, Molotov had demanded during secret talks with the British and French foreign ministers that every country should receive assistance in accordance with its needs. He rejected the plan of a joint European aid programme as constituting interference in the internal affairs of individual European countries.

The British and French proposed an organization that would draw up a detailed European economic plan. This organization was to be above the individual countries. In this proposal Moscow saw a danger to its East European sphere of power. Molotov refused to accept verbal assurances that the organization would not interfere in any country's internal affairs or touch its sovereignty. He said he thought that the amount of American credits for each country was bound to depend on that country's 'obedience' to the central organization and the Soviet Union would have nothing to do with such an arrangement. What the Russians had in mind was that the amount of aid each country received should be determined by that country's contribution to the defeat of Germany. Molotov strongly opposed the possibility of including Germany in the programme; this was a feature of the Anglo-French proposals.

But Bidault and Bevin were not deflected from their course by Russia's resistance. The two foreign ministers issued a joint invitation to twenty-two countries, including the East European countries, to a conference on the Marshall Plan that was to take place in Paris on 12 July 1947. The British and French governments were convinced of the need for speedy action to initiate the reconstruction and economic development of the countries of Europe.

There is no need to describe the course of the negotiations on the Marshall Plan in detail. But I must mention the fact that the East European countries did not accept France's and Britain's invitation to the Paris Conference of 12 July 1947 – and that this was very probably due to pressure from Moscow.

The Revised Level of Industry Plan for the Bizone of 26 August 1947; Industrial Dismantlings; Effects of the Marshall Plan in the Western Zones of Germany

The conference which opened on 12 July 1947 began to work out details for the Marshall Plan. This was the beginning of the reconstruction of Europe. The first British and French proposals had suggested that Germany too should receive aid. Germany was represented in Paris by the Commanders-in-Chief of the three Western zones.

Germany's participation in the Marshall Plan required changes in the existing provisions of the occupation régime. As early as 30 April 1947, Lieutenant General Robertson had told the Zonal Advisory Council that the industrial plan for Germany would have to be revised. From 22–7 August 1947 representatives of the American, French and British Governments conferred on the future production of German industry. Under the existing dispensation it was impossible for Germany to make the contribution to the reconstruction of Europe required by Acheson and Marshall. The American and British delegations submitted plans for a new economic policy in Germany to the representatives of the French Government. These plans, however, could affect only the American and British zones because the French were still not ready to agree to an economic fusion of their zone with the other two. Press reports indicated French reservations to the British and American proposals for the industrial reconstruction of Germany, stemming from France's fear that German reconstruction might change the balance of the volume of industrial production to the disadvantage of other countries; in the eyes of the French this would revive old fears.

On 27 August 1947, as a result of the London Conference, a new plan was published for the levels of industry in the combined Anglo-American zones, which brought us considerable economic relief. The USA and Britain stressed that their invitation to the other two powers to fuse their zones with the Bizone remained open.

The bizonal level of industry was to reach ninety to ninety-five per cent of the level of 1936. The plan stated explicitly that export requirements had been taken into account so as to render the German people self-supporting. A Reuters dispatch of 29 August 1947 said that the experts had agreed that the bizonal area must make good its deficiencies from the rest of Germany or from abroad; that in addition to pre-war foreign trade, the bizonal area must produce a surplus over its internal requirements for trading with the remainder of Germany; and that this particularly affected requirements for the industrial capacity of steel and steel products. These products were those most needed by the rest of Germany and therefore the most dependable as exchange for key products essential to the bizonal economy.

The production in restricted industries would have to be raised above pre-war levels. The plan then dealt in detail with the raised levels of production in restricted industries. Thus permission was granted for steel capacity, which under the March 1946 level of industry plan had been limited to 7.5 million tons annually for all of Germany, to be raised to 10.7 million tons per annum for the bizonal area alone. Heavy machine industry was to be permitted about eighty per cent of pre-war production of which, however, thirty-five per cent was to be removed as reparations.

The plan announced that all plants which had been built for war industries or had been converted to war production should be dismantled and removed from Germany or destroyed. The formulation of this point of the new industrial plan was not very concrete and it was left to the occupation authorities to determine which plants were to be designated as war industries.

On one hand it had to be admitted that the new plan brought great improvements for the Anglo-American zone, but dismantling and destruction of big industrial installations continued. In my opinion this procedure conflicted with the measures of support intended by America for Europe and for us.

The industrial dismantling being demanded struck me as a matter of decisive importance for the life of our people. I was in complete agreement with the removal or demolition of real arms industries. It also went without saying that Germany had to make restitution, but the dictates of humanity and international law equally forbade measures that would deprive the German people of the means of existence. The dismantling programme, which especially in the British zone was being actively continued, deprived hundreds of thousands of Germans of work.

A dismantling list for the British zone was published in the middle of October 1947. When I learnt of it I publicly raised a sharp protest against the measures proposed. I declared that the intended plundering of German industry was incompatible with international law, the Hague Convention, and the provisions of other international agreements.

At a CDU meeting of 17 October 1947 I said:

> The CDU and all other German parties and the trade unions, all who have the welfare of the German people at heart, will be faced by important decisions in the next few days; for a first glance at the list shows, especially to anyone familiar with conditions, that the dismantling of nearly seven hundred plants constitutes a grave interference in German economic life.

I went on to say that the German economy would not survive anything of this kind, let alone be able to contribute to the rehabilitation of the economy of Europe. The Allies obviously held two mutually contradictory sets of ideas. One was reasonable and directed towards the common good of Europe and demanded the Marshall Plan; the other was the well-known notion that one should take as much as possible from the prostrate Germans regardless of what became of the people. We could only hope and wish, and strive for reason to prevail in this matter too and for the dismantling list to be amended. The German people could live only if it retained its economic capability.

In October 1947 the CDU published a resolution asking the Allied authorities to review the list of the plants to be dismantled. It had been drawn up without any German participation and a review should examine to what extent the list would leave Germany with the industrial capacity granted it by the new industrial plan. In particular, it should be ascertained what effect the damage done by the dismantling of key plants and technically indispensable installations would have on the reconstruction of the German and European economies. The list of the plants to be dismantled showed that these incursions into the economy had not been systematically thought out in accordance with the general plan.

I took a public stand against the strong combinations proposed for some branches of industry in connection with the dismantling. This was meant by way of compensation for prohibited industries, in order to make possible any export at all, but it would result in a concentration of economic power and an intolerable pressure on the small and medium-sized industrial plants. It was the intention of the CDU to strengthen small and medium industries because in our opinion this was the only way to real economic democracy. The kind of industrial concentration that would inevitably result from the Allied measures I regarded as a sociological mistake because it would uproot those who worked in the small and medium-sized plants or lived in rural areas and would make them into an industrial proletariat.

The planned dismantling seemed to me incompatible with the Paris talks on the Marshall Plan which ended in late September 1947. On 22 September 1947 the representatives of sixteen European countries had signed a report which included proposals for a four-year programme for European reconstruction. This was the answer to the offer made by Secretary of State Marshall on 5 June 1947.

Since I knew that Germany too was to have a part in this European recovery programme, I was naturally keenly interested in learning details of the European proposals as soon as possible. I was therefore very grateful to the Swiss Consul-General von Weiss when he told me something about the proposals articulated at the Paris Conference not long after its conclusion. As far as he could learn, the programme was based on the following principles: every participating country was to increase its production in agriculture, fuel and power, and transport, and to modernize its industrial plants. The achievement of financial stability within each country was essential for the fullest exploitation of the productive and financial resources of Europe. Economic cooperation between the individual countries was to be encouraged. The recovery programme sought to reach the level of pre-war agricultural production by 1951, and the same was to apply to mining and industrial production. To reach this target the participating countries needed imports of food, raw material, and capital from America.

The Paris talks had expressly emphasized the need to include the German economy in the European economic system, because the German contribution was needed in the reconstruction of Europe. From press reports it emerged that it had been stressed in Paris that an increase in the production and export of Ruhr coal was decisive for European recovery. All imports needed to increase the production of Ruhr coal were to enjoy priority not only in the German but also in the entire European import programme. It was said that as long as the Western zones of Germany were in a state of economic prostration, an economic recovery of the countries of Western Europe was impossible. Western Germany would have to raise its foreign trade beyond the pre-war level. Only then would it be in a position to achieve a proper balance of payments by the end of 1951, i.e. by the end of the four-year programme. It was stressed again and again that all economic measures of the Western zones of occupation would have to fit into the framework of European cooperation.

During the months of October and November 1947 the American Government examined the plan drawn up by the sixteen European nations. President Truman announced that a special session of the relevant committees of the

Senate and House of Representatives was to be convened in order to discuss the plan to aid Europe.

On 10 November 1947 American Secretary of State Marshall announced before the Senate Foreign Relations Committee that the European Recovery Programme would require 16–20,000 million dollars for the four years and asked Congress in the name of the Administration to appropriate this sum. This motion was in the main accepted by Congress.

I had learnt from a speech by the American Secretary of State that 300 million dollars was to be allocated to Western Germany for the first phase of the Marshall Plan. This was the first really convincing sign of a serious intention to help German reconstruction. Without American help the reconstruction of Germany was impossible, but it was equally impossible without our own cooperation, our confidence and our own will to rebuild. The German interest and the European interest were identical and I warmly welcomed the fact that in explaining his propsals Marshall had described the German question as the heart of the European question.

The London Foreign Ministers' Conference of 25 November to 15 December 1947

In the course of 1947 the French Government seemed to be moving increasingly closer to the Anglo-American policy toward Russia. An economic and financial agreement concluded between the United States and France on 28 May 1947 indicated this new direction. Nevertheless public opinion in France was still primarily dominated by fear of Germany and less attention was paid to the dangers to Western Europe, including France, from the intentions of Soviet Russia. The Communist Party emerged as the strongest party from the French elections of autumn 1946.

When the French showed themselves ready to accept American help for France they began to oppose the Soviet views announced by Mr Molotov on 2 July 1947 in Paris, and thereby established the direction of future French policy.

The second half of 1947 brought a further deterioration in the relations between the Western powers and the Soviet Union. The Marshall Plan conference in Paris which met despite Russian protest led to further coolness when representatives of the American, British and French Governments discussed future German industrial production in London from 22–7 August 1947 at a meeting to which the Soviets were not invited. The Soviet Government, in a note of 18 August 1947, sharply protested against a tripartite conference on Germany on the grounds that all decisions regarding Germany were the province of all four occupying powers under the Potsdam Agreement. The three Western powers continued their deliberations notwithstanding, and published the above-mentioned revised industrial plan for the Anglo-American zone.

The Foreign Ministers' Conference anticipated in Moscow in the spring of 1947 met in London on 25 November 1947. It was attended by the foreign ministers of the four victorious powers. The German question was the chief subject of discussion.

The three demands made by the CDU before the London conference were:
1 The abolition of zonal frontiers.
2 The establishment of a control commission which could function for the whole of Germany.
3 The creation of a status for Germany which would delineate the rights of the occupying powers and the duties of the Germans.

On 26 September 1947 a study group of the CDU/CSU published this resolution:

> The study group of the CDU/CSU of all zones urgently appeals to the Allies and to world opinion before the opening of the London conference not to allow Germany to be dismembered or mutilated. The study group knows that it is voicing the opinion of the entire German people.

In a resolution of the zonal committee of the CDU of the British zone, we stated our great anxiety that the various modes of German political, economic and social life were increasingly losing their legal foundation and that the legal foundations lost during the National Socialist period had not been regained. A clear legal basis was the prerequisite of every democratic polity, and it was this that distinguished it from a dictatorship.

The opinion expressed by a well-known British legal expert in a South German legal journal, *Süddeutsche Juristenzeitschrift*, that Germany did not come under hitherto valid international law or under the Hague conventions was untenable and in conflict with the legal principles laid down in the first Nuremberg verdict.

The economic demands and measures which were constantly being imposed on the German people, such as the current plans for dismantlings and decartelizations, were as devoid of any foundation in international or German law as were the alterations recommended for existing social insurance.

When the Zonal Advisory Council met in Hamburg on 24 November 1947 I had a chance to voice our demands and expectations regarding the London conference in some detail. I said:

> The London Conference is meeting tomorrow, on 25 November. It has been called primarily in order to decide questions that affect Germany's fate. Germany is not represented at this conference. We who have met here on the day before the beginning of the conference act in accordance with a duty of our conscience and a duty of the heart if we tell the powers assembled in London that the entire German people are united in desiring the preservation of German unity. I also believe that the entire German people are as one in the conviction that the dismemberment or mutilation of

Germany would be as significant for the fate and future of Europe as for the German question alone.

What we Germans want – and I think we are of one mind in this too – is that the zonal frontiers should disappear, that means that Germany should be put under *one* controlling body, that this body should confine itself to control and should not engage in administration. We also demand that in future German laws should no longer require the consent, that is the unanimous consent, of the powers represented in the controlling body, but that laws should automatically become effective unless there is a unanimous veto of the controlling body within a period to be fixed.

A beginning has lately been made to giving more powers to the Germans. But there should be clarity on the point that what has been conceded so far is by no means sufficient . . .

We also address the urgent request to the London Conference that the reconstruction of Germany should at last be put into the hands of the German people so that they can assume responsibility. In the last few weeks statements have been made in responsible British and American quarters which clearly show that soon – we do not know when exactly – a beginning will be made in giving Germany a new constitutional structure today, and we want to express our opinion on this new structure. Let me make a few prefatory remarks before I put before you the views of the Christian Democratic Union.

In rebuilding Germany we want to learn from the mistakes of the past, including the errors of the Weimar Constitution. We want to keep in mind specific German traits, and finally we want to avoid being unduly influenced by present conditions . . .

As I have already briefly indicated, once this new German state is established the position of the Allies in relation to it must be quite different from that now obtaining in relation to the *Länder* and the zones. It must then be limited to genuine control and a right of veto; apart from these the appropriate German agencies must enjoy complete freedom in the reconstruction of Germany.

There are two other matters that are of decisive importance to us in any future constitution: there must, first, be a constitutional court. We must make this constitutional court independent, as independent as is humanly possible. This constitutional court should have the task of protecting the central power from disobedience or encroachments by the *Länder*; conversely the court should also have the task of protecting the *Länder* from encroachments of the central power.

The constitutional court should further be charged with affording to every inhabitant of Germany the necessary protection against infringement of his basic rights. This too is an absolute necessity. There are not only dictatorships of individuals, there can also be a dictatorship of a parliamentary majority – and it is against this we want to be protected by a constitutional court. In this matter, too, we want to learn from the experience of 1933.

Before a new German constitution sees the light of day we want a Statute that gives to the occupying powers their appropriate rights and duties, and which assigns to the Germans their duties, but also their rights. We find the view intolerable which was expressed in a letter to the *Oberbürgermeister* of Essen. Regarding the rights of the occupying power it said that a case like that of contemporary Germany had not been envisaged by the Hague Convention.

I want to state here, in parenthesis, that it is a general view among lawyers that if a certain case has not been envisaged in a legal agreement, that case should be treated according to the rules of analogy.

This letter further states that the Allies assumed all constitutional authority in Germany and then there is a sentence – a sentence which in our opinion should never be repeated – the sentence that the right of the Allies was limited by their own wishes. That is intolerable; those are words we never expected to hear again. It does not say 'humanitarian limits' or anything like that, but 'limited only by their own will'. I like to think that the author of these lines did not know what he was writing. For this is a kind of absolutism worse than was ever expressed in the worst days of the absolutist régime.

But if such views prevail in high places, this gives us all the more reason to insist on the promulgation of an occupation statute as soon as possible – unless there is to be a peace treaty – an occupation statute that delineates rights and duties of conquerors and conquered: for just as the vanquished have duties, they have rights too . . .

In conclusion I should like to say this: it seems to me that we Germans must now think every day about what is being decided about our fate in London; this really is the most essential and the most important thing at the moment for every German. I therefore think that wherever possible we must bring home to the German public that our destiny is now being decided in London and that the course and results of the conference will lead to decisions which will – despite the fact that we are unable to participate – be of the greatest consequence for us Germans for a long time to come.

I therefore conclude as I began: we Germans are all united in addressing the urgent request to the representatives of the Allied countries assembled in London to do everything in their power to preserve German unity.

At the Foreign Ministers' Conference in London Bevin resubmitted, with some modifications, a plan for Germany on whose main points the three Western Allies were agreed. The essence of this plan lay in the proposal to create in two stages a federal constitution with a bi-cameral system for Germany. The first stage provided for the establishment of German central administrative departments; the second stage was to see the establishment of a German Council to control these administrative departments. Elections were then to be held after the approval of a provisional constitution by the Control Council. The provisional constitution was to be ratified after a trial period, but for this too the permission of the Control Council was required. The last step was to be the election of a government to take over the powers of the central administrative departments. The Control Council was to reserve to itself all decisions regarding demilitarization, denazification, and the foreign relations of the future German state.

Bevin's plan was based on the premise of the existence of Germany as an economic unit. The principle laid down at Potsdam, that no reparations should be taken from current production, was explicitly reiterated. In the economic area Bevin's plan foresaw far-reaching measures of nationalization which I shall go into in greater detail elsewhere.

On 8 December 1947 Molotov submitted the Soviet demands regarding Germany. They included the well-known demand of $10,000 million worth of reparations for the Soviet Union and the demand for four-power control of the Ruhr. Moreover Molotov insisted that the fusion of the British and American zones should be rescinded. The Russian plan called for the immediate creation of a German democratic government which was to speak for Germany when the Allied draft agreement was discussed at the peace conference. The Soviet Union regarded the question of a central German government and the question of the peace treaty as indissolubly linked.

Bevin made a compromise proposal to the effect that representatives of a German government which could be considered a partner of a German peace treaty should be given an opportunity to express their opinion at the peace conference. Molotov rejected this solution and advocated the addition of the words: 'the establishment of a German democratic central government in accordance with the decisions of the Potsdam Conference was recognized to be a matter of urgency.' Bevin thought that the peace conference should not be delayed until after the formation of a German government, but conceded that a German government must be formed before the conclusion of the work of the peace conference. Molotov insisted on his point of view that there must be a German government at the outset of the conference.

The Russians had already taken many preparatory measures for a future German government in their zone and had taken decisive steps to establish central German departments. The administrative machinery established by them was staffed by leading German communists.

On 15 December 1947 Molotov proposed that representatives of the German People's Congress in Berlin should be heard by the London Foreign Ministers' Conference. A so-called German People's Congress had been held in Berlin on 6 December which demanded German unity and a just peace. The SED (Socialist Unity Party) had called this People's Congress with an eye to the London Foreign Ministers' Conference. It had expressed the demand for the formation of a central German government in which all German democratic parties were to be represented. A delegation of the People's Congress consisting of Otto Grotewohl and Wilhelm Pieck were to present the German view in London as representatives of the People's Congress.

The American, British, and French foreign ministers rejected Molotov's proposal by stating that they did not regard this People's Congress as representative of the will of the German people.

In stressing his claims for $10,000 million worth of reparations Molotov had demanded that Great Britain and the United States should state clearly how many industrial installations and how much coal and other goods they had already exported from their zones.

The British and Americans regarded these demands of Molotov's as offensive and resolutely rejected Molotov's allegation that they had derived profits from their zones. The atmosphere was worsening visibly and Bevin said openly that in view of the experiences in Moscow and now in London it was doubtful whether any problems could be solved.

Marshall discussed the basic difference of opinion between the Western Allies and the Soviet Union regarding the settlement of German frontiers and reparations claims. To impose reparations to the tune of $10,000 million would mean to enslave the German people. The United States were ready to grant authority, responsibility, and initiative to the Germans, but a German government of the kind proposed by Molotov could only amount to a façade.

The press reported Marshall as saying that the occupying powers had caused the division of Germany and it was only they that could remove it. The three powers had agreed to German unity, it was only the Soviet Union that refused it. He therefore moved the adjournment of the Conference.

There had been simultaneous negotiations on an Austrian state treaty at the London Conference. They too led to no agreement. Molotov told the press that the three other foreign ministers formed a united front against the Soviet Union; concessions made by him in the Austrian question had not even been discussed. Everything would be possible if the German people were allowed to develop their industry and agriculture under appropriate control. The rejection of the proposal of a central German government proved that the other powers were determined to continue their policy of dividing Germany.

The London Foreign Ministers' Conference was adjourned *sine die* on 15 December 1947. It had broken down completely.

In view of this conclusion of the conference the Western Powers now saw themselves forced to settle the German question without the Soviet Union. They set about this task at conferences, to which they also invited the Benelux countries and which met in London during the first half of 1948.

7

THE LONDON RECOMMENDATIONS

New Proposals for Germany

The London Foreign Ministers' Conference had dispersed without results. The chief reason for this was the disagreement between the Soviet Union and the USA. The Soviet Union was bent on further expansion in Europe. I repeat: it is impossible to draw any other conclusion from Russian actions during the period of occupation than that, from the outset, it was the Soviet purpose to gain control of Germany and after Germany the rest of Western Europe. The USA and the countries of Western Europe had recognized this, although it took them a long time, and were now resisting Soviet endeavours. This recognition also caused France to abandon her original intentions to partition Germany and made her align herself with the policies of America and Britain. I think Winston Churchill was the first to assess Russian aims correctly. It was therefore all the more regrettable that he had to relinquish the premiership after the Labour Party's electoral victory.

The economic decline of Western Europe had proceeded apace as a consequence of Germany's hopeless situation. On 26 November 1947 the governments of Belgium, Luxembourg, and the Netherlands had sent a Note to the four foreign ministers meeting in London, in which they demanded that Germany's political and economic structure should be fixed. The Note stated that an end had to be put to uncertainty and confusion in order to bring about some general stability in Europe. It was necessary to find a means of getting Germany on her feet again in the context of a peaceful and successful organization of Europe and the whole world.

In his statement before the House of Commons of 22 January 1948 Bevin had asked for especially close cooperation between Great Britain, France and the Benelux countries. On an Anglo-American initiative representatives of the United States, Britain, France, and the three Benelux countries were invited to London for the second half of February, in order to discuss the German question. This conference took place from 23 February until 6 March 1948. It was now generally accepted that the Benelux countries must have a part in the determination of future policy toward Germany.

The relationship of occupied Western Germany to the European Recovery Programme, in other words within the Marshall Plan, was a special subject of discussion. Other points on the agenda were the role of the German economy in the European economy; the control of the Ruhr; the question of security vis-à-vis Germany; the political and economic organization of Europe.

The Soviet Government protested against this conference, at which it was not represented. The Americans replied that Moscow had prevented the economic unity of Germany agreed at Potsdam and had thus virtually forced the Western powers to initiate talks on the matter. The invitation to the Soviet Union to participate in four-power talks remained open in all respects. The British told the Russians that they knew of no agreement that precluded discussions of common problems between two or three occupying powers. In fulfilling its duties as occupying power the British Government would endeavour to do all it could to promote the peaceful reconstruction of Germany and of Europe.

At the conclusion of the first phase of the London talks there was already far-reaching agreement on the guiding principle for the reconstruction of Germany and her integration into the community of free nations. Recovery seemed about to begin at last in the three Western zones. Our satisfaction on this score was somewhat impaired by a very painful interlude concerning the Saar.

On 20 February 1948 France, the United States, and Great Britain signed an agreement endorsing the economic absorption, by then an accomplished fact, of the Saar by France. The agreement stated that from 1 April 1948 onward trade between the Bizone and the Saar would be conducted as foreign trade and that German imports from the Saar would have to be paid in dollars.

The agreement was probably the price paid to France for renouncing her plans to partition Germany – to detach the left bank of the Rhine, and to neutralize the Ruhr – and for aligning herself with the American and British plans.

On 7 November 1947 General Robertson had been appointed Military Governor of the British zone. On 7 April 1948 he made an important statement to the diet of North Rhine-Westphalia, in which he stressed that a turning point had been reached in policies toward Germany; Germany would return to the family of nations, and economic relations between the peoples of Western Europe would have to be conducted in a spirit of confidence and of mutual give and take.

Robertson said that great things could be achieved with honest and full cooperation between the occupying powers and the German people. On the other hand there would inevitably be failure if we did not all join in the common effort. He mentioned the Marshall Plan as the factor which made the realization of hopes possible, enumerating the economic advantages it would bring to Europe and to the people of Western Germany, and reminded his listeners that the Marshall Plan did not aim merely at giving economic aid to Germany and other needy countries. The guiding idea of the Marshall Plan was that of self-help, the idea that all countries were to cooperate in order to repair, by combined effort, the damage done to the economic structure of Europe. Every country, the victorious powers no less than our own, was being asked not only to receive but to make its contribution to the reconstruction of Europe in a spirit of magnanimity.

Robertson emphasized that it was the first aim of British policy to bring about peace and prosperity in a united Europe in which, he said, Germany would have to play her full part.

He discussed the importance of the Ruhr for the economy of the whole of Western Europe. He explained that events were moving in the general direction of integration of industry throughout Western Europe.

This development was still in its beginnings, but once the great European recovery programme, the Marshall Plan, had gathered momentum, it would become increasingly clear that every participating member had to make its contribution to the common pool. The proposed control of the Ruhr was consonant with the great design and with the dignified cooperation of Germany in it.

At the end of his speech Robertson again emphasized that the salvation of Germany was in our own hands. We could achieve this goal, but we could also throw away the possibilities we now had. He said:

Germany's salvation is in your hands to win or cast away. Only have the courage and you will win it. Come forward determined to make the best of the largest part of your country which is on the right side of the iron curtain. The rest will come in time. We offer you our good-will and our cooperation. Do not be frightened by the mischief-makers who scream 'collaborators'. The time has come to realize that the interest of all Europeans is converging. Our needs and your needs cannot be dealt with separately for we all form a part of Europe.

General Robertson had already proved himself a man of insight and vision as British Deputy at the Control Council in Berlin. The speech he made before the diet in Düsseldorf contributed mightily to reviving our courage.

Voices were increasingly being raised that demanded economic and political progress in Germany. I want to mention another one of the most significant.

A European congress was being held at The Hague from 7 until 10 May. It had been called by four European organizations including the United Europe Movement founded by Winston Churchill and the Conseil Français pour l'Europe Unie whose president was Edouard Herriot, a man I knew from my days as Oberbürgermeister of Cologne before 1933. It was the first great congress of this kind that I attended.

Winston Churchill was elected Honorary President of the congress. In his speech he expressed an especially cordial welcome to the German delegates. He discussed the German problem and said that in his view it consisted in restoring the economic life and the former good name of the German people and freeing Germany's neighbours from the fear of a revival of German military power.

In his speech Winston Churchill underlined the fact that the aim of European unification was not confined to Western Europe. The congress desired the participation of all peoples of the continent whose way of life accorded with the Charter of Human Rights. All the countries of the East and South-east of Europe were constrained to hold aloof. The United States of America had given a warm welcome to the unification of Europe. The congress at The Hague was intended to help governments to create the new Europe, but all were grieved and perplexed by the discordant attitude and policy of the big Eastern group. President Roosevelt had spoken of the four freedoms. Today the freedom from fear was the freedom that mattered most.

The congress led to the establishment of a permanent council and a joint executive committee of the sponsoring associations for European unity.

The European Congress at The Hague ended on 10 May 1948. Its result was laid down in a solemn declaration. Three resolutions had been adopted which I shall quote, in part verbatim:

1 The Congress:

'. . . Recognizes that it is the urgent duty of the nations of Europe to create an economic and political union . . . Declares that the time has come when the European nations must transfer and merge some portion of their sovereign rights so as to secure common political and economic action . . . Demands the convening, as a matter of real urgency, of a European Assembly chosen by the Parliaments of the participating nations . . .'

The reason for this procedure was that parliaments were the legitimate expression of the will of the peoples, that their electoral machinery could go into action immediately, and that their composition best corresponded with the different constitutional mechanics of the participating countries. The European Assembly was at first to assume a consultative role and to prepare the formation of the future Union. A Charter of Human Rights must be drafted and an international Court of Justice established with adequate sanctions for the implementation of this Charter. The Union would also have to solve the German problem.

2 Economic Resolution:

The new Europe must find a proper balance between private initiative and the new economic necessities. Trade unions would have to be made part of the new system. Steps should be taken to achieve an abolition of tax barriers, a coordination of budgetary policy, a multilateral credit system and the convertibility of currencies. There should be a joint programme for the key industries, transport should be coordinated and labour should be able to circulate freely. The ultimate goal was a customs union and the unification of currencies.

3 Cultural Resolution:

The Congress recommended the establishment of a European Cultural

Centre with branches in different cultural departments as well as a European Centre for children and young people.

The final appeal read:

We desire a United Europe, throughout whose area the free movement of persons, ideas and goods is restored;

We desire a Charter of Human Rights, a Court of Justice with adequate sanctions for the implementation of this Charter, and a European Assembly where the live forces of all our nations shall be represented.

The Congress also pledged itself to give fullest support to all persons and governments working for this lofty cause.

The talks of the six powers who had met from 23 February until 6 March 1948 were resumed on 20 April 1948. The conference lasted until June 1948 and closed with the publication of concrete proposals by the six powers concerning the future development of Germany and the shape they thought political life in Germany should take. These proposals became generally known as the London Recommendations.

I shall here confine myself to mentioning only a few of them very briefly.

The recommendations were submitted as a whole since their main provisions were mutually dependent and formed an indivisible programme. Principal features included the following:

Association of the Benelux countries in policy regarding Germany;
the role of the Germany economy in the European economy and the control of the Ruhr;
the evolution of the political and economic organization of Germany;
security questions.

The Recommendations stated (once more) that there must be a close association of the economic life of the countries of Western Europe and of a democratic Germany. It had been agreed to recommend the establishment of an international authority for the control of the Ruhr in which Great Britain, France, the Benelux countries, and Germany would participate. The establishment of this authority would not involve the political separation of the Ruhr area from Germany. What was contemplated was control of distribution of coal, coke and steel from the Ruhr in order to ensure on the one hand that industrial concentration in that area should not become an instrument of aggression, and on the other hand that all countries participating in a European cooperative economic programme, including Germany itself, should benefit from the production of the Ruhr.

Regarding the evolution of political and economic life in Germany the German people should be given the opportunity eventually to re-establish German unity, at present disrupted, on a free and democratic basis. In these circumstances the delegates thought it desirable that the German people in the different states should henceforth be free to establish for themselves the

111

political organization and institutions by which to assume those governmental responsibilities which were compatible with the minimum requirements of occupation and control and which ultimately would enable them to assume full responsibility. The delegates considered that the people in the *Länder* would wish to establish a constitution with provisions to which *all* the German *Länder* would subscribe as soon as circumstances permitted.

Therefore the delegates agreed to recommend to their governments a joint meeting between the military governors and the Ministers President. At that meeting the Ministers President would be authorized to convene a Constituent Assembly to prepare a constitution for the approval of the participating states. Delegates to this Constituent Assembly were to be chosen in each of the states in accordance with procedure and regulations to be determined by the legislative bodies of the individual *Länder*.

The constitution should be such as to enable the Germans to play their part in bringing to an end the present division of Germany not by the reconstitution of a centralized Reich but by means of a federal form of government which would adequately protect the rights of the respective *Länder*, and which at the same time would provide for adequate central authority and would guarantee the rights and freedoms of the individual.

If the constitution as prepared by the Constituent Assembly did not conflict with these general principles, the military governors would authorize its submission for ratification by the people in the respective *Länder*.

The problem of security was considered under three aspects:

(1) General provisions
(2) Measures during the period in which the occupying powers retained supreme authority in Germany
(3) Measures after this period.

The American, British, and French delegates reiterated the firm views of their governments that there could not be any general withdrawal of their forces from Germany until the peace of Europe was secured and even then not without prior consultation. It was further recommended that the governments concerned should consult together if any of them discerned a danger of resurgence of German military power or of a German policy of aggression.

The prohibitions on the German armed forces and the German General Staff as contained in four-power agreements were reaffirmed as well as the exercise of controls by the military governors with respect to disarmament and demilitarization, level of industry and certain aspects of scientific research. To ensure the maintenance of disarmament and demilitarization in the interests of security, the three military governors were to set up a military security board in the Western zones of Germany to carry out the proper inspections and make the necessary recommendations to the military governors who would then decide the action to be taken.

It was once more affirmed that Germany must not again be permitted to become an aggressive power. Prior to the general withdrawal of the forces of occupation, agreement was to be reached among the governments concerned with respect to necessary measures of demilitarization, disarmament and control of industry, and with respect to key industries. There should be a system of inspection to ensure the maintenance of the agreed provisions on German disarmament and demilitarization.

Regarding the draft agreement on the international control of the Ruhr the Recommendations stated that international security and general economic reconstruction demanded that the resources of the Ruhr should not in future be used for the purpose of aggression but should serve the interests of peace; that access to the coal, coke, and steel of the Ruhr, which was previously subject to the exclusive control of Germany, was in future to be guaranteed without discrimination to the countries of Europe cooperating in the common good; that it was desirable for the political and economic well-being of these countries and of a democratic Germany that there be close association of their economic life.

Attitude of the CDU to the London Recommendations

Immediately after the publication of the London Recommendations the chairmen of the West and South German *Länder* organizations of the CDU met under my chairmanship at Bad Königstein in order to discuss these decisions which were of the utmost gravity for us. On 10 June 1948 we published a declaration which sharply rejected part of the London Recommendations.

The executive committee of the CDU of the British zone had already previously passed a resolution stating that the London Recommendations provided an insufficient basis for peace and liberty. We would gratefully welcome another conference that might develop new principles for the political reconstruction of Germany, this time with the admission of German representatives whose views would be heard.

We asked for an understanding of our desire that three years after the termination of the state of war German representatives should play a responsible part in negotiations concerning the future fate of our people, a people situated in the centre of Europe. We were willing to give the widest security guarantees to our neighbours, notably France, but in our opinion it would be desirable that this should be done with our participation in discussions and should not be a dictated arrangement. In the conclusion of our declaration we said: 'We regard ourselves as in no way beneficiaries of discord between the great powers. We are no less interested in their understanding than they are themselves. We would therefore be grateful for a renewed attempt to include Russia in a new conference.'

The London Recommendations seemed to me to be fraught with such grave consequences for the German people that I felt it necessary to make the attempt to bring about a unanimous declaration of all German parties in the

H   113

three Western zones with the exception of the Communist Party. I first sent a telegram to Dr Schumacher, the chairman of the Social Democrats, in order, if the SPD agreed in principle to a joint declaration, to approach the other parties with the same request. In this telegram to Dr Schumacher of 10 June 1948 I stated that I considered the consequences of the London Recommendations for the German people to be extremely dangerous and that I believed that everything should be tried to achieve a common stand of the German parties. I informed the participants in the meeting of the chairmen of the *Länder* organizations of the CDU in South and West Germany at Königstein of this telegram.

All those present agreed with it unanimously. They asked me to do all I could to bring about a discussion of this matter with the SPD. We decided that if the talks I asked for came about, Herr Süsterhenn from Koblenz and Dr Schroeter from Kiel were to accompany me.

The following day Herr Eichler, a member of the executive committee of the SPD, told me by telephone that on the basis of my telegram he had been asked by the party executive in Hanover to meet me for talks. We met on Sunday, 13 June. Herr Eichler told me that Dr Schumacher was very ill and unable to engage in any activities, but that the gentlemen of the party executive would be very glad if I could nevertheless come to Hanover for discussions. He did not tell me at that time that the party executive of the SPD was already firmly determined not to take part in any joint declaration of the parties.

On 17 June I went to Hanover with Dr Süsterhenn; Dr Schroeter was unable to come with us. At the Party headquarters of the SPD we met Messrs Ollenhauer, Heine, and Henssler of the SPD. I gave a detailed account of the reasons for my telegram. I said that in a phase as decisive as the present it was necessary that the voice of the German people should be heard as one voice abroad. It was therefore my intention that, if we could agree on this point with the SPD, we should then jointly approach the other German parties, the Communists excepted. I also said that a joint declaration of all German parties save the KPD was necessary for the years ahead, because a form of nationalism might arise that might be disastrous for the people; the present German parties should protect themselves against possible later allegations that they had remained silent in the face of an agreement which was simply impossible for Germany.

Erich Ollenhauer stated, on behalf of the gentlemen of the SPD, that their party was about to discuss the London Recommendations in a larger circle in Hamburg in a few days' time. They too were in no way in agreement with their contents. But they believed that it would make a deeper impression abroad if the German parties did not voice their rejection jointly but singly.

I continued my discussion of the consequences of the London Recommendations. So far, I said, Britain had been able to act alone in what was by far the greatest part of Western Germany. Now there was to be an agreement concerning vital German questions between six powers. To amend such an agreement the consent of all six powers would be needed. It would therefore be very hard to change. That was why I regarded the present juncture as decisive for the future fate of the German people. The agreement had not yet been concluded; so far there had only been 'Recommendations'. I pointed out that nationalism was born at the moment the Versailles Treaty was signed. I was afraid that if things went on as heretofore, we might have to reckon with a revival of national socialism, this time with an Eastern orientation, in Germany.

The representatives of the SPD more or less agreed with my analysis, but could not be made to budge from their rejection of my proposal. Dr Süsterhenn made another attempt to persuade them and underlined what I had said. But he was equally unable to convince the representatives of the SPD.

These talks showed that we were largely agreed regarding the actual contents of the London Recommendations, but that the executive committee of the SPD was not prepared for a joint declaration of the German parties. We discussed the consequences of the Recommendations in detail at a meeting of the Zonal Advisory Council on 9 June. The disappointment was quite general.

The Zonal Advisory Council was directly touched by the contents of those Recommendations because all zonal institutions, including the Zonal Advisory Council, were to cease to exist as a result of the London conference.

Much time was bound to pass before the formation of a German government for the three Western zones as envisaged by the London Recommendations – and this fact was in conflict with our view that we should resolve our immediate dissolution. We considered the Zonal Advisory Council necessary for the period pending the establishment of a central German government and therefore agreed, in view of this difficult situation, to adjourn ourselves *sine die*. Certain special committees of experts were, however, to continue their work.

We communicated our decision to the Military Government. General Robertson asked for an opportunity to address a full meeting of the Zonal Advisory Council for the last time.

The last meeting of the Zonal Advisory Council took place on Tuesday, 29 June 1948. General Robertson appeared at this last meeting of the Zonal Advisory Council of the British zone in order to take his leave of us. He thanked us for the work we had done and assured us that we had been of great help to the British Military Government. He said *inter alia*:

The advice you have given the Control Commission has not always been taken. Maybe there have been times when you have thought that your advice has been ignored. Ladies and gentlemen, it has never been ignored, though I will agree that it has not always been followed. In retrospect I do not think that you will bear me a grudge for this . . . The opportunity for a mutual exchange of views and the occasions which Question Time has afforded for public discussion of policy have been of immeasurable value and significance in the revival of popular participation in political decisions in the British zone.

On the London Recommendations Robertson had this to say:

I have heard some criticisms of the London decisions in Germany. I have heard some criticisms outside Germany also – particularly in France, some particularly sharp ones – and the interesting thing is that most of these criticisms that come from Germany have this in common with the criticisms that come from outside Germany, that they are directed towards the same parts of those London decisions. They are directed towards the same points in the decisions but they are directed from the opposite points of view. That perhaps is evidence that the scales have not been balanced without some degree of fairness . . .

This programme is designed to give the German people their own Government, and I repeat what I said before that it is the desire of my Government and indeed of the American and French Governments to join with the fourth occupying power in extending these arrangements, or whatever arrangements may be decided upon, to the whole of Germany. The process by which this stage of Government will be achieved is slower than some of us would have wished, but it is a sure process, and we believe that it does ensure that the Government so created shall have authority and prestige to the full extent that we can accord it.

The extent to which authority will be preserved in the hands of the Occupying Powers will be precisely defined. The manner in which they will preside in the exercise of their authority will be made clear to all. As to the structure of the Government itself, very broad terms of reference will be given to the Constituent Assembly . . .

An aspect of the London decisions to which I think the most attention has been accorded in Germany is the document regarding the establishment of an international authority for the Ruhr. I will be quite frank with you, ladies and gentlemen, and say that I would not expect any document on such a subject to be greeted by the German people other than with a certain reserve; but when the terms of this document are studied dispassionately I do not think that any German need regard this as an intolerable interference with the Government of his country or with his self-respect; although that it might have been something very different from what it is can be judged, I think, from the criticism that has been levelled against it in many quarters in France already . . .

General Robertson had said explicitly that the full content of the London negotiations had not yet been published and that he believed some of the German criticism would cease when it was. I thought that his advice to start our work was right. Once we had begun we would see whether any progress could be made and whether this work was worth while for Germany.

8

THE PARLIAMENTARY COUNCIL

The Events Leading to the Formation of the Parliamentary Council

First steps towards the new policy decided on in London was the convocation of the so-called 'Parliamentary Council' which was to work on a preliminary constitution for the three Western zones of Germany.

The Military Governors of the three Western zones met in Frankfurt am Main on 1 July 1948. They had invited the eleven Ministers President of the Western zones of occupation. They were handed three documents containing the outlines of the Western Allies' ideas concerning future developments in the Western zones and directives regarding the composition and scope of a future German political structure. I shall summarize these documents briefly.

The first document authorized the Ministers President to call an assembly, in accordance with the decision made by the six powers in London on 7 June 1948. The members of the assembly were to be elected by the *Länder* legislatures in accordance with an agreed method of distribution. Its task was to be to draft a democratic constitution for the three zones. This constitution would establish for the participating states a governmental structure of a federal type as being best adapted to the eventual re-establishment of German unity. The constitution would protect the rights of the participating *Länder*, provide adequate central authority, and contain guarantees of individual rights and freedoms.

Document I continued: 'If the constitution as prepared by the constituent assembly does not conflict with these general principles, the Military Governors will authorize the submission for ratification. The constituent assembly will thereupon be dissolved.'

The ratification in each participating *Land* was to take place by means of a referendum requiring a simple majority of the voters in each state under such rules and procedures as it might adopt. When the constitution had been ratified by two-thirds of the states, it was to come into force and was to be binding upon all states. Thereafter any amendment to the constitution would have to be ratified by a like majority of the states. Within thirty days following the coming into force of the constitution, the institutions for which it provided were to be established.

Document II dealt with the territorial reorganization of Germany. The Ministers President were asked to examine the boundaries of the several states in order to determine what modifications they might want to propose.

117

Document III concerned the legal powers of a future constitutional German government and especially the relationship between this government and the Allied authorities. This relationship was to be based on the following general principles: The Military Governors were to grant legislative, executive, and judicial power to German governments and were to reserve to themselves such powers as were necessary to ensure the fulfilment of the basic purposes of the occupation. These powers were for the time being to include those necessary to enable the Military Governors to conduct or direct Germany's foreign relations.

The Military Governors were to exercise the minimum control over German foreign trade and over internal policies and measures which could adversely affect foreign trade, in order to ensure a respect for obligations entered into by the occupying powers in regard to Germany and the proper use of funds made available to Germany.

The Military Governors were to exercise such controls as had been or might be agreed upon, as for example, regarding the international authority for the Ruhr, reparations, the level of industry, decartelization, disarmament and demilitarization, and certain aspects of scientific research. They would be equipped with powers to protect the prestige of the occupation forces and to ensure their security and the satisfaction of their requirements within defined limits agreed upon between the Military Governors. Ensuring the observance of the constitution which they had approved would be one of their important functions. Document III further provided for the resumption by the Military Governors of the exercise of their full powers in any emergency threatening security, or if it should be necessary in order to secure compliance with the constitution and the occupation statute.

The procedures for the exercise of these controls by the Military Governors were precisely laid down in Document III. The Military Governors were to have special responsibility to observe, advise and assist the federal and *Land* governments in regard to the democratization of political life, social relations, and education. But this was not to imply any restriction of the legislative, executive and judicial competence accorded to such governments.

The Military Governors requested the Ministers President to submit their observations on the above principles.

The Ministers President of the *Länder* met at Koblenz from 8–10 July 1948 in order to confer on the documents they had been given by the three Military Governors. They drew up detailed comments on the documents and forwarded them to the Military Governors. In a covering letter they declared themselves prepared to cooperate in the solution of the task set them and 'to reach the goal set in the documents as quickly and effectively as possible'. They were convinced that the difficult conditions prevailing in Germany could only be overcome if the German people were enabled to administer their affairs on the broadest territorial basis possible. They therefore welcomed the Allies' intention to join the German *Länder* in a unified area whose people could elect a government able to look after the interests of Germany as a whole without endangering the rights of the *Länder*.

The accompanying note of the Ministers President stressed their desire to avoid anything that might appear to confer the character of a state on the structure to be created. The procedure to be adopted should express the provisional nature of this structure, 'an *institution* owing its origin solely to the circumstances connected with the present state of the occupation of Germany. In view of the impossibility of reaching an agreement of the four occupying powers concerning Germany, the Ministers President were particularly concerned that the impending reorganization should avoid anything apt to deepen the split between West and East even further.'

The Ministers President opposed the Military Governors' proposal to submit the new law to popular referendum. Such a referendum would confer an importance on the Basic Law which should be reserved only for the constitution ultimately to be adopted. They stressed that 'in their opinion a German constitution could not be created until the entire German people had the opportunity to constitute itself in an act of free self-determination'.

Concerning Document III, the covering note of the Ministers President stated that they were pleased to learn of the intention to establish relations with the occupying powers on a clear legal basis. But the Ministers President pointed out that an occupation statute was a matter of urgency even before the body charged with framing a Basic Law for the area of the three Western zones began its deliberations. They further thought that the occupation statute should make it clear that the planned reorganization ultimately derived from the wishes of the occupying powers, because such derivation had other consequences than an act of free self-determination of the German people. They also thought it advisable to leave the international authority for the Ruhr outside the occupation statute, in view of its particular function. Regarding the resumption of full powers by the Military Governors to deal with emergencies, the Ministers President believed themselves in agreement with the Military Governors in thinking that in the case of mere police emergency it should be the task of the *Länder* governments to take the necessary measures. The Ministers President included in their Note a request to the Military Governors to keep developments under regular review in order to determine whether they did not warrant further extensions of German legal powers and further reduction of controls.

As a result of talks between the three Military Governors and the Ministers President of the *Länder* in Frankfurt on 20 and 26 July 1948, the Ministers President told the Military Governors that they were prepared to convoke a 'Parliamentary Council', as they called it, 'in order to restore, at least in part, the German unity at present disrupted'. The Parliamentary Council was to have the exclusive task of drafting a Basic Law. When the Parliamentary Council had finished its work the Ministers President would submit the result to the Military Governors and would then request authorization to proceed with ratification in the *Länder*. The Ministers President would examine the Parliamentary Council's Basic Law to see whether it proposed a form of government providing on the one hand for an amount of central control and on the other for protection of the rights of the *Länder* and for a guarantee of the rights and freedoms of the individual.

The referendum on the Basic Law stipulated in the documents was the subject of controversy at the meeting of the three Military Governors and the Ministers President of the German *Länder* on 26 July 1948. The reasons adduced by the Ministers President against a referendum have already been mentioned. The Bavarian Minister President, Dr Ehard, repeated the point of view of the Ministers President on this question. The following solution was jointly arrived at: The Military Governors stated that they had taken cognizance of the request of the Ministers President to leave the ratification to the *Länder* diets. Since the Military Governors had different directives from their governments, they would have to report the views of the Ministers President and asked that this should not be taken as rejection of their request. The Allied governments later gave their consent to the German ratification proposal. The meeting of 26 July 1948 led to the following agreement on Document I:

> The Parliamentary Council will meet not later than 1 September 1948. The delegates will be chosen in each of the existing *Länder* according to the procedures and directives adopted by the legislative bodies of each of these *Länder*. The result of the deliberations of the Parliamentary Council, described as 'Constitution' in the London Protocols, as 'Basic Law' according to the Koblenz resolutions, will be called 'Basic Law' (provisional constitution).
>
> The London Resolutions stipulated the ratification of the Basic Law (provisional constitution) by popular referendum. The German Ministers President have protested against this solution and have proposed ratification by the *Länder* parliaments. This solution will come into force unless the governments in Washington, London and Paris raise objections to it.

The Ministers President had stated their wish to define the occupation statute determining the relationship between the Allied powers and the future federal government before the Parliamentary Council began its work. The Military Governors told them that, unfortunately, this could not be done. But they gave an assurance that the Parliamentary Council would be kept informed of all stages of the evolution of the occupation statute and that they would also have opportunities to make representations regarding the statute to the Military Governments.

The Ministers President now convened a committee of experts to collate facts and draw up criteria to facilitate the work of drafting the Basic Law. These experts met at Herrenchiemsee from 10 to 25 August 1948 and made a comprehensive report which was given to the members of the Parliamentary Council at their first meeting. Meanwhile agreement had been reached that

Bonn should be the venue of the Parliamentary Council. Its members had been elected by the *Länder* diets as planned.

The future legal position of Berlin struck me as a special problem. Would the new arrangements intended for Germany by the three Western powers extend to the area of Berlin that they occupied? I shared the general German opinion that after the collapse of four-power administration in Berlin in the spring of 1948 (the result of the London six-power conference), the part of Berlin occupied by the Western powers would also have to come under the new arrangements for Germany. Berlin must be included in the future reorganization of Germany with equal rights and duties.

In order to underline this aim and our ties with Berlin we decided to invite delegates from Berlin to the meetings of the Parliamentary Council. These delegates took part in the meetings as non-voting representatives.

The Parliamentary Council at Work

The Parliamentary Council convened on 1 September 1948 in the Pädagogische Akademie in Bonn. Of its sixty-five members, twenty-seven belonged to the CDU/CSU, twenty-seven to the SPD, five to the FDP, two to the DP (Germany Party), two to the Centre and two to the KPD.

Minister President Stock of Hesse made the opening speech in his capacity as chairman of the conference of Ministers President. He characterized the new phase in German post-war history in eloquent words.

> We act today for the first time in the new era of German history since the capitulation not by *Diktat* but under agreements arrived at between the Military Governors and the Ministers President. The Economic Council was established by a military proclamation of two of the occupying powers; the Parliamentary Council has been formed and called together by German decision.

I had been elected president, Herr Adolf Schönfelder (SPD) and Dr Hermann Schäfer (FDP) first and second vice-president. It fell to me to reply to the opening speech. I said that it was certainly not easy for us, the members of the Parliamentary Council, to accomplish our task under existing conditions; but that we had met mindful of Germany's need and of our duty to our people, in order to create a Basic Law by joint effort. Our work in the Parliamentary Council would be guided by the determination to shape a Basic Law that would permit us to preserve possibilities of unity for the whole of Germany and that would leave a place in the new state that the German territories in the East could fill at any time.

The decisive factor in my election as President of the Parliamentary Council on 1 September 1948 was the fact that during the years from 1920 to 1933 I had been President of the Prussian State Council, a smaller parliament, and therefore had some experience in the direction of such a body. Another reason was the fact that I was the chairman of the CDU/CSU group in the Parliamentary Council and that this group had the same numerical strength as the SPD group.

My chief task as President of the Parliamentary Council was to see to it that the work of that body produced a positive result.

Both the Military Governors and the Ministers President urged speed. But an excessive acceleration of the work of the Parliamentary Council was impossible in view of the great number of difficult matters that had to be settled in connection with the Basic Law and the electoral law. We were well aware of our responsibility and were not willing to yield to the pressure of time and produce a hasty and superficial draft whose shortcomings would then have disastrous consequences in practice.

This is not the place to go into the discussions of the individual articles of the Basic Law. I must limit myself to a description of the broad outlines of the work of the Parliamentary Council and to emphasizing some decisions of particular importance.

As President of the Parliamentary Council I tried to get as large a majority as possible for each article as it was put to the vote. But there were great differences of opinion among the parties on some essential points, and we often required long and time-consuming negotiations before they could be reduced and compromise solutions found.

In the course of our work we also negotiated frequently with the Military Governors or their representatives on a number of points of the Basic Law. We had to meet their wishes on many occasions, but were also able to get them to accept many of our wishes and principles.

Our work was made very much harder by our ignorance of the contents of the occupation statute that was to determine the relations of the future federal republic and the Allied occupying powers. The governments of the occupying powers were working on the occupation statute simultaneously with our labours on the Basic Law. From time to time the Military Governors asked for progress reports on our work but were unable to tell us anything about the contents of the occupation statute which should have been one of the essential bases of our work.

Professor Carlo Schmid was the chairman of the main committee of the Parliamentary Council and exercised much influence on the work on individual articles. We followed the general principle that we must learn the lessons of the mistakes of the Weimar Republic. The position of the future Federal President was not to be endowed with the powers possessed by the President of the Weimar Republic. Another principle was the strengthening of the position of the Federal Chancellor compared with that of the Reich Chancellor of the Weimar Republic. The future Basic Law was to make it impossible to remove individual ministers by a vote of no confidence, thus making it harder for the Federal Chancellor to fulfil his mandate. If the parliament disapproved of the policy of the Federal Chancellor, it was not to be allowed to remove the minister in question, but should have to table a vote of no confidence against the Federal Chancellor himself. However, the Weimar Republic also served as a warning of what happens when it is too easy to bring down a government; to guard against these dangers we included a provision to the effect that parliament could only table a vote of no confidence against a Federal Chancellor if at the same time it could propose a new Chancellor commanding the necessary parliamentary majority to form a government.

Professor Theodor Heuss was a member of the Parliamentary Council as delegate of the FDP. He had a decisive influence on the formulation of the Basic Law, and contributed to peace and serenity by his Suabian humour and good nature when discussion grew heated.

But I can remember an occasion when even he found the speeches of the communist deputy Renner getting on his nerves. He lost his composure to the extent of shouting something about shutting up to Renner, in his Suabian dialect. As President I had the inescapable duty of ringing my bell and asking whether Heuss had intended to insult Renner. Heuss replied that he had intended to give pleasure to Herr Renner. This produced smiles and laughter all round. I now had to ask Renner whether he felt insulted. Renner said he did not. That settled the affair. Generally speaking relations among the members of the Parliamentary Council were amicable during our meetings as well as at other times.

The special committees carried the main burden of work on individual articles of the Basic Law. I always had to keep informed about the activities of the various committees and had to try – by official or by private talks – to remove whatever difficulties emerged. My experience as President of the Prussian State Council from 1920 to 1933 was useful in my work as President of the Parliamentary Council.

The Controversy Concerning the Relationship of Central Government and Länder

As President of the Parliamentary Council I often had to go to Frankfurt to inform the Military Governors of the progress of our deliberations. I got the impression from my talks with the Military Governors that the three Western powers were by no means as united in their ideas as we had at first assumed.

The French urged a very loose connection between the Länder and a weakening of the Central (Federal) Government. General Clay advocated a system corresponding to the American federal constitution. General Robertson, the British spokesman, did not object to somewhat stronger centralization provided it did not conflict with the federal principle.

The views of the CDU/CSU corresponded most closely with those of General Clay. The Länder should be endowed with a great measure of independence vis-à-vis the Federal Government, but this independence should not go so far as to render the future federation impotent.

Inside the Parliamentary Council there were considerable differences of opinion on this central question between the CDU/CSU and the SPD. The SPD advocated more power for the central government than was compatible with the Allied views expressed in the Documents. Above all the SPD stressed the need to equip the Federal Government with greater authority in the field of finance. The SPD programme called for a planned economy and for nationalization and the Social Democrats knew that these plans could only be carried out by a strong central power.

On 19 October 1948 I was handed an Allied document containing directives for an intended declaration to the President of the Parliamentary Council concerning the distribution of power in the field of finance. It was the work of an office subordinated to the Allied Military Governors. I could not regard it as an official communication but was told that it was 'fairly official'.

This document stated that the Military Governors had received a report on the work of the Finance Committee. They were impressed by the committee's speed and thoroughness. It was natural that the Military Governors took a special interest in the work of the Finance Committee because the distribution of financial authority between federal and *Länder* agencies was one of the crucial problems of federalization.

The new communication went on as follows: Document I, which had reached the Parliamentary Council through the Ministers President, had laid down the principles with which the Basic Law now under discussion would have to agree in order to be accepted by the Military Governors. It was obvious that the extent to which the draft Basic Law conformed to these principles could not be assessed until the draft was complete. There was a close connection between the financial authority of the Federal Government and the legislative power of the *Länder* Chamber just as there was a close connection between the powers and the composition of the *Länder* Chamber. Since this last question had not yet been settled, it was still impossible fully to appreciate the significance of the financial proposals.

Naturally, the document continued, the Military Governors were reserving their final judgment until the entire draft was complete. But they wanted to emphasize their view that the authority of the Federal Government in the field of public finance should be limited to the raising of taxes and the disposal of funds. The Federal Government should, of course, be allowed to fix taxes and to issue general directives regarding assessment for other taxes to the extent required to ensure uniformity in the federal area, but the collection and use of such taxes should be left to the *Länder*; and appropriations should only be made for purposes for which the Federal Government was responsible under the constitution.

The document further stated that the Military Governors had directed the liaison officers to communicate these impressions and views to the Parliamentary Council, as a contribution to the discussion that was still in progress and on which it was thus impossible or unnecessary to pronounce a final judgment.

On 17 November 1948 General Robertson invited me to lunch at Bad Homburg. After lunch, in which only his family and his deputy, Mr Steel, had taken part, Robertson, Steel, and I had a talk lasting two-and-a-half hours. The day after I made a note on this conversation for the records.

Among the points stressed by Robertson were these:

1 The three Military Governors and the three governments were, of course, not in agreement on all points, but they were agreed on some very essential points of the future Basic Law. They had already given an outline of these in Document I. They had decided, at their meeting in Frankfurt on 16 November, to send the three liaison staffs to me to add a few points. Of course it was impossible to make a full assessment of the federal character of the Basic Law before that law was available in its entirety. But some points were essential, including the financial status of the *Länder*. They would communicate with me about this.

2 In view of the international situation it was extremely desirable that a West German government should be formed as soon as possible.

3 The communication I would get from the liaison staffs would not mention Berlin for reasons connected with the Berlin elections. But it was unthinkable that they would agree to a constitution that made Berlin part of the federation, if only because there were special agreements on the administration of Berlin between the three Western powers and the Russians.

I requested Robertson to let the heads of the liaison staffs bring an *aide mémoire* when they came because otherwise misunderstandings about what had been said might easily arise. He replied that they were anxious not to give any appearance of putting pressure on the Parliamentary Council. This was the reason why they did not want to leave an *aide mémoire*, but the Note would be read to me slowly enough to have it taken down in shorthand.

Robertson emphasized the decisive importance of constitutional provisions to depoliticize the civil service, which made it imperative to make civil servants ineligible to parliaments.

I stated that we thought it very undesirable, from our own as well as from the Allied point of view, that the Allied governments should raise any objections after the reading of the Basic Law in the Parliamentary Council. Robertson was in complete agreement with this. I proposed that there should be a discussion between some representatives of the Parliamentary Council and such representatives of the Military Governors as could make decisions when the Council approached the end of its deliberations. He welcomed this suggestion and assumed that his colleagues would also welcome it and that, if we so desired, the three Military Governors themselves would be at our disposal for such a discussion.

I then broached the question of the occupation statute. He stated that the occupation statute would be ready in two to three weeks, at which time, if we wished it, there could then be a discussion of it between them and some representatives of the Parliamentary Council. I repeated a suggestion I had already made to the liaison staffs to the effect that the occupation statute should include a clause providing for progressive amendment of the statute in step with general developments. I believed that great store would be set on such an express provision in the occupation statute on the German side. He told me that he had already been informed of my suggestion by the liaison staffs and that it had been decided to include such a provision as the last paragraph of the occupation statute.

I then explained to him that the Basic Law could not be finished before the middle of December at the earliest. Another four weeks would pass before the Allies returned it. He agreed.

It would then have to be voted on in the *Länder*. This would take at least six weeks. That would take us to the end of February or the beginning of March. Then there would be elections to the federal parliament, requiring at least another six weeks, so that the federal parliament could not meet before the end of April or the beginning of May at the earliest and a West German government could not be set up before the middle of May.

Mr Steel said they had thought that the elections to the federal parliament and the voting on the Basic Law in the *Länder* could be conducted at the same time. I told him that I considered this quite impossible, and that I also considered it wrong for tactical reasons. We had surely to try and get as large a majority as possible for the Basic Law when it was voted upon. If simultaneously the political parties starting shooting at each other as they were bound to do in the elections for the federal parliament, the electorate would be utterly confused.

My arguments were accepted, although General Robertson regretted having to postpone the establishment of a West German government for reasons of foreign policy. I suggested that the Parliamentary Council should, for the time being, be left in existence even after it had finished its deliberations on the Basic Law, because the Western Allies too might in certain circumstances be glad to have a body able to speak in the name of the German people. General Robertson saw the justice of this. He said he would back my view in discussions with his colleagues.

Finally we discussed the question of the seat of the federal parliament and the Federal Government. General Robertson advanced some doubts against Bonn, notably because the Allies could not let the officials of the Bizonal administrations, who had done their duty, be suddenly dismissed. He also wondered whether there was proper accommodation for the Allied offices that would need to be in close proximity to the federal offices. I reassured him on both points.

The 'Frankfurt Affair'

On 19 November I informed the Council of Elders of the Parliamentary Council of the content of my talk with General Robertson. I emphasized my view that before there was any final vote in plenary session there should be some accommodation with the Military Governors to avoid a situation where Allied objections were raised after the plenary session had adopted the Basic Law. A demand for changes by the Military Governors at that late stage would be time-consuming and detrimental to the reputation of the Parliamentary Council. This suggestion was universally welcomed. Jean Stock of the SPD suggested that the discussion should take place after the second reading of the draft in the Main Committee. If the Military Governors desired any changes, they could then be taken into account in the third reading in the Main Committee.

On 22 November 1948 the Military Governors sent a memorandum to the Parliamentary Council in which they commented on a number of important points in the Basic Law and demanded changes because they did not think that the decisions made so far by the Parliamentary Council accorded with the stipulations of Document I. They listed eight such points. There were considerable differences of opinion when the Parliamentary Council discussed this memorandum, especially on points that concerned the Bundesrat and financial and cultural questions. These differences reached such a pitch that there was no hope of completing the second reading of the Basic Law by 16 December, the day General Robertson had suggested for a meeting. I did not think it advisable to cancel the meeting to which the Military Governors had promised to come. The members of the inter-party committee and the Council of Elders shared my opinion.

I offered to inquire about details of the coming occupation statute at the conference with the Military Governors. I would also ask the Military Governors whether their governments had meanwhile come to a decision on the question whether the Basic Law should be ratified by plebiscite or by voting in the *Länder* diets. I further suggested that the questions of finance and of Berlin should be broached. None of those present said anything against the procedure I proposed.

On 16 December I travelled to Frankfurt, as had been arranged with the Military Governors. I was accompanied by some members of the Parliamentary Council, including Professor Schmid, Dr Pfeiffer, Dr Menzel, Dr Höpker-Aschoff, and Dr Lehr. General Koenig led the discussions on the Allied side as spokesman of the Military Governors.

At the beginning of the discussion I pointed out that our deliberations on the Basic Law would take longer than had been envisaged, particularly because there were differences of opinion about questions of education and finance and the position of the Bundesrat. I said nothing specific about the nature of these disagreements. I continued that sometime in January was the earliest we would be able to submit the Basic Law to the Military Governors. I then inquired whether the Military Governors could tell us anything about the occupation statute. I reminded them that they had told the Ministers President in a letter of 17 July that they would inform the Parliamentary Council of the guiding principles of the occupation statute. We, the members of the Parliamentary Council, urgently wanted to know the basic outlines of this document because of its importance for our own work.

It was only later in the discussions that General Koenig took up this question and stated that the Military Governors were not in a position to tell us the text because it still had to be examined by the Allied governments. It was possible that this might lead to changes in the occupation statute. In these circumstances the Military Governors unfortunately could not tell us anything about the occupation statute, let alone give a complete text. General Koenig asked me to let him have a list of the points that were holding up our work. The Military Governors would examine it promptly and let us have an answer to our questions as soon as possible.

General Koenig said that I had told the Military Governors how much longer we would need to complete the Basic Law. They, the Military Governors, were hoping that it might be possible to let us have the full and final text of the occupation statute during that period. In the further course of the discussion I broached the question as to whether the Basic Law was to be adopted by referendum or by ratification in the *Landtage*.* This question, too, remained unanswered. Some discussion also took place on the importance of the future *Länder* chamber and on cultural matters such as denominational schools.

At the end of the meeting General Koenig came back to the question of the occupation statute and asked us if we had any special requests that we wanted to express at this juncture. It was agreed that our talks should be continued the next day.

The next day, before our meeting with the Military Governors, we had a discussion among ourselves. In this gathering of members of the Parliamentary Council Dr Höpker-Aschoff complained, in the name of Professor Schmid and Dr Menzel, of my having used the discussion with the Military Governors the day before to call upon the Military Governors to arbitrate between our differences of opinion, especially regarding the question of finance. I was completely taken aback by Dr Höpker-Aschoff's statement because I had said nothing whatsoever of the substance of our differences of opinion when I spoke to the Military Governors. I said that I would gladly read a statement at the afternoon conference with the Military Governors that would make it clear that I was not calling for arbitration from the Military Governors in any way whatsoever. We agreed on the following text:

Press and radio have disseminated a DENA† report to the effect that Dr

* *Länder* parliaments or diets.
† German news agency.

Konrad Adenauer asked the Military Governors for information on three points: the composition of the second chamber, the Military Governors' view on financial jurisdiction, and the question of whether the constitution is to be ratified by referendum or by the *Landtage*.

This report is incorrect. The conclusion has been drawn from it that I asked you, the Military Governors, for arbitration on the differences of opinion on some points among members of the Parliamentary Council. This is quite wrong. Neither have we asked for your arbitration nor have you ever shown any intention to arbitrate. We believe that we must on no account allow the impression to arise that the Parliamentary Council was prepared to renounce the legislative autonomy with which it was endowed, thus forcing on the Military Governors, before negotiations are concluded, a role which corresponds neither with your intentions nor with the view the Parliamentary Council takes of the scope of its mandate. Several passages of the memorandum transmitted to us by your liaison staffs on 22 November are open to different interpretations. We merely asked for a more precise exposition of the views expressed in those passages.

When agreement had been reached on the text of the statement I was to deliver, Professor Schmid said that he also wanted to make a statement on behalf of his party. It would only consist of two sentences and the content would be of no great importance.

The afternoon meeting with the Military Governors passed off very quietly. I made my statement, Professor Schmid made an additional statement as announced, and it seemed to me that all was well. After the meeting with the Military Governors, the members of the Parliamentary Council conferred together for another half hour and nothing critical was said. In the evening we returned to Bonn.

The next day under the chairmanship of Professor Schmid, I gave a full report on the whole substance of our Frankfurt discussions and the events connected with them. When I had finished there was a heated argument during which I was once more accused of having tried to outmanœuvre the Parliamentary Council and persuade the Military Governors to settle questions in dispute among us. I emphatically rejected these accusations. But there were further disagreements concerning the correctness of my conduct of the negotiations with the Military Governors. The SPD expressed its lack of confidence in me; the CDU/CSU rejected this. Gradually tempers cooled off.

The Final Phase of the Negotiations

Meanwhile, during these months, London was the scene of negotiations on uniting the French zone with the Bizone, economically and politically. These negotiations did not lead to a positive result until the Foreign Ministers' Conference in Washington at the beginning of April.

I

The negotiations on the occupation statute were also moving slowly and we of the Parliamentary Council, seeing the need for finishing the Basic Law quickly, informed the Military Governors that we were willing to conclude our work without being in possession of the occupation statute.

On 7 February 1949 the head of the British liaison staff, Chaput de Saint-onge, contacted my office to find out how we thought the draft Basic Law should be treated by the Allied powers. He wanted to inform us that it could already be predicted that the French would object to two points of the Basic Law as it was formulated at that moment, namely the financial provisions and the provisions regarding the federal civil service. Under no circumstances would the French accept a strong federal civil service; they wanted the central functions to be the domain of *Länder* officials.

Chaput de Saintonge pointed out that in view of the present international situation the United States and Great Britain had little chance of circumventing the French demands. Britain and America were afraid that the Schuman Government might not last if they put France under too much pressure over these questions. Britain and America were, moreover, of the opinion that everything should be done to stabilize political conditions in France. If the two great powers were faced with the choice between a politically stable France and a Western Germany without constitution and without federal government, they would at the present juncture undoubtedly opt for political stability in France. If we insisted on our demands, we would have to reckon with the rejection of the constitution and a long postponement of the establishment of a federal government.

Chaput de Saintonge indicated that the British thought it inadvisable for objections to be raised by the Military Governors after the last reading of the draft Basic Law in the Main Committee and its adoption in plenary session. Such a procedure would do great harm to the prestige of the Parliamentary Council and of the future federal government. The British hoped that it would be possible to hold negotiations between representatives of the Parliamentary Council and the Military Governors and their experts after the third reading in the Main Committee and before the second reading in plenary session, so that a timely attempt could be made to settle differences of opinion.

The draft Basic Law was ready on 11 February and I sent it to the Military Governors. In a memorandum of 17 February the Military Governors told me that they would examine the draft in the form adopted in the third reading by the Main Committee, in order to establish to what extent it met the demands laid down in the Allied memorandum. The Military Governors would make their views known to the Parliamentary Council at the appropriate time. They did this in a Note of 2 March 1949 which stated that there were discrepancies between the Basic Law and quite a number of provisions asked for in their memorandum of 22 November. They were willing to disregard minor deviations but were obliged to insist on our reviewing certain articles which, in the opinion of the Military Governors, departed from the given directives to a regrettable extent. Among these was a definition of the authority of the Federal Government which was not sufficiently clear to preserve the position which the *Länder* must have in a federal system. They made concrete suggestions for a reformulation.

The Military Governors also stated that they had noted with concern that the provisions on financial jurisdiction were in marked discrepancy with those agreed upon in London and communicated to us in the memorandum of 22 November. Here too they demanded an amendment of the articles submitted by us.

There were heated debates in the Parliamentary Council The SPD refused to comply with the demands of the Military Governors and insisted on leaving the Basic Law in the form we had reached in our draft.

To Compromise or Not to Compromise?

The question that now arose was whether or not we should aim at a compromise with the occupying powers. I was for agreement with the occupying powers. In my view the question was not: is the Basic Law, if it is adopted in the form desired by the Military Governors, an ideal law? I thought that the advantages accruing to Germany from a basic law, however imperfect it might be, should be weighed against the situation that would arise if there were no basic law at all. I said that we had to be clear on the point – on which the French had been quite explicit – that failing the endorsement of the Basic Law by the Military Governors the whole game would have to start anew: the results of the London six-power conference of June 1948 would be null and void. No man could predict what would happen then.

At that time it was reasonable to assume that the Military Governors would agree to the formulation of the Basic Law given in the third reading of the Main Committee of the Parliamentary Council provided their wishes regarding the financial clauses were met. The big question now was whether a large majority of the Parliamentary Council would be willing to comply with the wishes expressed in the Military Governors' Note of 2 March 1949.

Before accepting or rejecting the desired changes, one had to look at Germany's position from the point of view of domestic as well as of foreign policy. The overwhelming majority of the Parliamentary Council did not consider the financial provisions desired by the Military Governors the best solution. Better solutions were imaginable, but I did not attach enough importance to this question to sacrifice the whole Basic Law to it. There was after all the possibility that if we adopted the financial provisions desired by the Allied powers, and if then, after two or three years it should turn out that these provisions served neither the federal nor the *Länder* interest, an amendment of this point could in all probability be carried through with the consent of the Allies. I could not imagine that the Allies would be so unreasonable as to resist, when the time came, a change desired by the Federal Government and

131

the *Länder*, if practice had meanwhile shown the solution they had desired to be unworkable.

I considered that if the passage of the Basic Law was seen from the point of view of foreign policy, the following reasons were decisive and argued for consent to the changes demanded:

The Allies had gradually split into two power blocs after the end of the war in 1945. Soviet Russia was on one side, the Western powers on the other. Germany was torn apart in four zones. Centrifugal tendencies were noticeable in the separate zones. On 28 December 1948 the Ruhr Statute was adopted in London, resulting in control of the most important German economic area. Germany could not be represented in the Ruhr Authority – the body charged with the implementation of the Ruhr Statute – until a German federal government had been created.

In a statement on the Ruhr Statute as chairman of the CDU in the British zone on 30 December 1948, I said that that document would have very serious consequences, not only for Germany, but also for Europe and especially for Western Europe. To the German people it showed with shattering clarity that we had lost the last shred of our sovereignty and that so far nothing of this sovereignty had been given back to us. Certainly this very voluminous document could only be properly judged after very detailed study. As far as I could tell at that moment everything would depend on the spirit in which the document was used, on whether it was really used 'to secure the peace' and to bring about the political and economic well-being of the countries of Europe, including Germany. This last intention had been clearly and repeatedly expressed in the Statute.

No one could blame us Germans if our attitude towards the Ruhr Statute was very negative. If the Statute were carried out to the letter, similar organizations would be set up for French and Belgian industry and in due course all these organizations would have to be joined together in one unified whole. This lay in the nature of things. It was in the long run impossible to orient only one part, the Ruhr, towards European interests and to leave the other coal and iron areas of Europe untouched. I regarded the Ruhr Statute as a test of vitality of the idea of an economic and political federation of Europe. We Germans had to see this statute as a beginning of European cooperation, but only a beginning. The Ruhr Statute would only stand the test of time, albeit with modifications, if the European federation came about. If the Ruhr Statute were really to be the beginning of a European federation, we Germans should make the sacrifice at first demanded of us alone and do it in the expectation that the European development would bring with it sacrifices but also advantages for all participating countries, including Germany. In my opinion it would have been wise to include a clause providing for the adaptation of the statute to future developments. I repeated that German representatives would only have a voice in the Ruhr Authority *after* the establishment of the federal republic.

132

Preparations for a federation of Europe were proceeding apace. The establishment of the Council of Europe could be predicted for the summer of 1949. The foreign ministers of Britain and France had declared their readiness to include the German Federal Republic about to be established as an equal partner in the European Union.

The North Atlantic Treaty had been signed in Washington on 4 April 1949. Here, too, membership of a future German Federal Republic was seen as a possibility. As soon as we had a Federal Government, it would, after inclusion in the Council of Europe and the North Atlantic Treaty Organization, be the equal of the other countries in decisive respects. This would be bound to affect all questions connected with the occupation. The occupying powers could not then disregard the views of the German Federal Government.

In my opinion there were decisive arguments in favour of setting up a federal parliament and a federal government as quickly as possible. These arguments were so cogent that I could not imagine anyone being able, upon calm reflection, to understand the Parliamentary Council rejecting the chance now offered to the German people, and rejecting it solely because it was unwilling to make the attempt to begin by working with the financial provisions desired by the Allies. As I saw it the essential thing was to keep up the momentum, to create the preconditions for the establishment of the Federal Republic of Germany and the formation of a federal parliament and a federal government capable of action.

The Occupation Statute Is Delivered and the Basic Law Approved

On 25 March the Military Governors had told the Parliamentary Council that they could make a final pronouncement on the Basic Law only after it was adopted by the Parliamentary Council and handed to them. They were, they said, of the opinion that it was now up to the Parliamentary Council, which had been informed of the views of the Military Governors, to exercise its own responsibility in bringing its work to an acceptable conclusion. In other words, it was up to us to meet their demands or to bring about the rejection of the Basic Law.

On 5 April the three Military Governors sent the following message to the Parliamentary Council by their liaison officers in Bonn:

The Foreign Secretaries of the United States, the United Kingdom and France, who during their current meetings in Washington are studying the problems of Western Germany, are gratified to learn that the competent committees of the Parliamentary Council are pressing forward with the work of completing the draft of the Basic Law. The Foreign Secretaries understand that decisions will be taken in Bonn during the next few days on several important issues connected with the Basic Law. They trust that the Parliamentary Council and the responsible German party leaders will

133

give due consideration to the recommendations of the Military Governors, which conform with the provisions of the London Agreement authorizing the establishment of a German democratic federal government. The Foreign Secretaries desire that the decisions of the Parliamentary Council will be taken in a spirit of facilitating a mutually co-operative attitude between the future German federal authorities and the occupying powers, which is one of the important objectives being sought in the current talks in Washington regarding Germany.*

On 10 April 1949 the Military Governors transmitted the Occupation Statute to us together with a note stating that the foreign ministers in Washington had discussed the question of a German federal republic from all points of view and had reached a number of important political decisions regarding it. They had decided that the German authorities were to be free, in general, to take administrative and legislative measures which were to have validity if the Allied authorities did not object to them. In certain limited areas, however, the Allies were to reserve the right of taking direct action themselves. These areas were listed in the Occupation Statute.

With the establishment of the German Federal Republic the Military Governments as such would cease to exist and the work of the Allied authorities would henceforth be divided between a supervising High Commissioner and a commander-in-chief who would carry out the military tasks. The three High Commissioners would together form the Allied High Commission and it was the intention of the three governments to impose stringent limitations on the supervisory staffs attached to the High Commissioners. (It may here be mentioned that the future British High Commissioner had roughly 6,000 officers, civil servants, and employees under him who were all concerned with matters of German administration.)

In the accompanying note the foreign ministers stated that it was one of the guiding purposes of the three Allied governments to promote and to facilitate the closest integration of the German people constituted in a democratic federal state into the framework of a European union in a way beneficial to both sides. Before these far-reaching developments could be initiated, however, it was essential for the Parliamentary Council to reach agreement on the Basic Law for the German Federal Republic.

My first perusal of the Occupation Statute led me to the conclusion that wisely handled it could lead to the gradual evolution of German autonomy. I welcomed the foreign ministers' reference to their dedication to the idea of integrating the German people in a European union. In the Occupation Statute I saw a voluntary and progressive limitation of the authority of the Western occupying powers and I derived special encouragement from the revision clause which expressly referred to the possibility of revision in step

* US Office of Military Government for Germany, Civil Administration Division, *Documents on the Creation of the Federal German Constitution*, September 1949, p. 115.

with general developments. Admittedly my assessment of the Occupation Statute was based on the assumption that the document agreed with the German view concerning the continuing existence of the whole of Germany as a political entity (*staatliche Fortexistenz*) and that it guaranteed the claim of the German people to the restoration of its political and economic unity.

On 14 April 1949 there was a meeting between the three Military Governors and representatives of the Parliamentary Council under my direction. The Military Governors' demands regarding the Basic Law was the main point on the agenda. The representatives of the Social Democrats, notably Carlo Schmid, declared that they had to reject the Military Governors' demands, but would give a final reply after the Annual Conference of the SPD which was to take place in Hanover on 19 and 20 April.

Dr Kurt Schumacher, the chairman of the Social Democratic Party, had prepared the Hanover conference very carefully. Many German and foreign journalists had been invited and a general atmosphere of tense expectation was being created which pointed to the SPD having something important to say at this conference. The climax was obviously to happen at the final meeting. In the presence of a large number of German and foreign press representatives Dr Schumacher proclaimed a kind of ultimatum. He declared that the SPD would give its assent to the Basic Law only if the following demands were met:

Germany must be free to make political decisions and this freedom should not in any way be limited by the occupying powers; the constitution should confine itself to the most essential provisions; there must be adequate sources of revenue for the federal authorities in order to secure the Federal Government's independence from the *Länder*; there must be a guarantee of the legal and economic unity of the federal area.

There was great surprise on 22 April when the Military Governors, acting on the instructions of their governments, informed the Parliamentary Council of the views of their foreign ministers on the Basic Law. This communication met practically all the demands proclaimed by Dr Schumacher at the SPD Conference.

I was amazed at the speed with which the Allies had reacted to Dr Schumacher's demands. Only later did it become known that after the conclusion of the Foreign Ministers' Conference in Washington the Military Governors in Germany got two Notes that were to be transmitted to the Parliamentary Council. In one Note, that of 5 April 1949, the Allies were unyielding in their demands and gave no sign of any readiness to compromise. This Note was given to me as President of the Parliamentary Council. The second Note, which was later given the date of 22 April 1949, was much less hard and uncompromising and was only to be handed over in case the Parliamentary Council refused to enter into a discussion of the Allied demands.

A British officer had informed the SPD of the existence and contents of this second Note, but the SPD did not inform the Parliamentary Council. Instead the SPD, knowing of the second Note, made its far-reaching demands of 20 April 1949. This sequence of events was the cause of much bitterness not only to me as President of the Parliamentary Council but also to all members of the Parliamentary Council who did not belong to the SPD.

The second Note which was now communicated to the Parliamentary Council, having been given the date of 22 April 1949, ran as follows:

A. The Foreign Ministers are not able to agree at this time that Berlin should be included as a *Land* in the initial organization of the German Federal Republic.
B. In the financial field any provisions put forward by the Parliamentary Council in the direction of securing financial independence and adequate strength for both the *Länder* and Federal Governments in operating in their respective fields will receive sympathetic consideration.
C. On the question of Article 36 (Article 95c) they will also give sympathetic consideration to any formula which

1. eliminates from the Federal powers those matters definitely excluded by the London Agreement;
2. assures to the *Länder* sufficient powers to enable them to be independent and vigorous governmental bodies;
3. assures to the Federal Government sufficient powers in the important fields of government to enable it to deal effectively with those fields in which the interests of more than one *Land* are substantially and necessarily involved.

D. Finally the Foreign Ministers are ready to contemplate a suggestion for the right of the Federal state to supplement from its own revenues appropriations made by the *Länder* from revenues from their own taxes levied and collected by them, by grants for educaton, health and welfare purposes, subject in each case to specific approval of the Bundesrat.*

The moment the Foreign Ministers' concessions were made known the Parliamentary Council resumed discussions of the Basic Law on this new basis. We reached agreement on the new formulation after two days' deliberations. I informed the three Military Governors of this agreement when I met them on 25 April 1949. The Military Governors raised no objections and we proceeded to the vote on 8 May 1949. The Basic Law was adopted by 53 votes against 12. Voting on individual articles had led to more debates and I repeatedly had to point out to the members of the Parliamentary Council that voting on the Basic Law did not mean voting on the Ten Commandments but merely on a law intended for a time of transition.

Immediately before the final adoption of the Basic Law, anxiety was once

* US Office of Military Government for Germany, Civil Administration Division, *Documents on the Creation of the Federal German Constitution*, September 1949, p. 135.

more expressed that this Law might constitute an obstacle to the reunification of Germany. We met these last objections against the adoption of the Basic Law by agreeing on a preamble which stated clearly that this Law was a provisional document which was to have validity until the day of reunification. The preamble says

> . . . It [the German people] has also acted on behalf of those Germans to whom participation was denied. The entire German people is called on to achieve by free self-determination the unity and freedom of Germany.

The long procedure of voting was finally concluded toward midnight of 8 May 1949. It was the fourth anniversary of the end of the war. We had completed the tasks the Parliamentary Council was called upon to perform. Despite some discordant notes here and there our work had been inspired throughout by a feeling of love and obligation toward the German people. We all wished that God might bless this people and this work for the benefit of Europe and for the sake of peace in the world.

The Military Governors formally approved the Basic Law in Frankfurt on 12 May 1949. On the same day the Occupation Statute was promulgated. We had previously been informed of its wording on 10 April 1949.

The Basic Law was now forwarded to the Ministers President of the *Länder* in order for it to be adopted in the *Landtage* in accordance with whatever procedures had been decided on there.

The Federal Capital Is Chosen

On 10 May the Parliamentary Council voted on whether Frankfurt or Bonn was to be the provisional federal capital. The parties were very divided on this point. The CDU/CSU favoured Bonn, the SPD Frankfurt.

The SPD pointed out that Frankfurt already housed a number of Bizonal administrative offices and that this would facilitate the development of federal authorities. The SPD's most important reason was, however, that Frankfurt was located in Hesse, a *Land* with a Social Democratic Government, and the city was associated with a Social Democratic tradition and atmosphere. They expected Social Democratic influence to radiate throughout the federal area if Frankfurt was chosen as provisional federal capital.

The CDU/CSU wanted Bonn because we wanted to avoid too close a proximity of the new Federal Government and the seat of Allied Military Government. We wanted to do everything to avoid giving the impression that the new Federal Government was nothing but an executive organ of the Allied occupation powers. I was often charged with advocating Bonn as federal capital because Bonn was close to Rhöndorf where I lived. The charge was very naïve.

What finally proved decisive for the choice of Bonn as federal capital was a declaration by the British that they were prepared to release the Bonn area from the British zone and from British Military Government if it were selected as provisional capital. The Americans were unable to give a similar assurance for Frankfurt because there were many American organizations and very important administrative offices in Frankfurt, for which it would have been very difficult to find accommodation elsewhere.

There was great uncertainty about the outcome of the voting. The procedure was long and tedious and took until nearly midnight. The delegates wrote the name of the city they proposed on slips of paper. It was my task as President to receive these papers and to read out the name of the city written on it, whether it was Bonn or Frankfurt. Other cities were mentioned too. Toward midnight the voting was over and the Parliamentary Council had chosen Bonn by a very narrow margin.

The Electoral Law

The matter of an electoral law was still unclear at the beginning of May. The Military Governors had proposed and in fact demanded that each *Land* should formulate its own law for elections to the Bundestag. The Parliamentary Council opposed this demand almost unanimously and it was thereupon withdrawn by the Military Governors.

A further obstacle to the adoption of an electoral law lay in differences of opinion between the CDU/CSU and the SPD. The law had provided for the election date to be fixed by the Presidium of the Parliamentary Council. It was not clear what was to happen if the Parliamentary Council dissolved itself on 23 May. The SPD wanted a period of at least 90 days between the promulgation of the electoral law and the election. This would have meant that elections could not take place until the end of August or even the beginning of September. For reasons of domestic as well as of foreign policy, however, the elections had to be held as soon as possible. The CDU/CSU wanted to fix a shorter period between adoption of the electoral law and election day. We finally agreed on the middle of August. The Parliamentary Council fixed the number of deputies as 410 and adopted a system of proportional representation.

The Basic Law Is Signed

Bavaria had not endorsed the Basic Law, but it was backed by the ten other *Länder* and thus had its required two-thirds majority. At a solemn ceremony on 23 May 1949 the Basic Law was signed by the Ministers President and the Speakers of the *Landtage* in the presence of representatives of the three Western powers.

I think all the Germans who were present must have been aware of the significance of this day. Anyone who had lived and thought through the years after 1933, the total defeat in 1945 and the assumption of all political authority by the victorious powers, could not help being deeply moved by the events of this May day. It had all started with the decisions of the London Conference of June 1948. The freedom of movement of the Parliamentary Council was, unfortunately, circumscribed by these decisions, and factors on which the will of our people had no influence made it impossible for this Basic Law to be valid for the entire German people.

Although the highest agencies of the Federal Republic of Germany did not as yet exist, the Basic Law had validity as of 23 May 1949 and this put the relations between the occupying powers and ourselves on a new footing. In a speech I made on this occasion I thanked the representatives of the occupying powers for confirming this by their presence.

The parliament about to be elected would face arduous tasks. The Federal Government was not going to find it easy to assert its authority over the *Länder*. If the federal parliament failed, democracy would go under. Federal President, federal government and federal parliament had to show the world that this German republic was the expression of a democratic people of political maturity.

Using the opportunity of the presence of Allied representatives to point to our precarious economic situation and to the dangers entailed in the dismantling policy so far pursued by the Western Allies, I said: 'Economic, social and political reconstruction appear to us endangered by a continuation of the policy of dismantling. We urgently request that no further dismantlings be started in case our political reconstruction should be endangered by them. The fate of German democracy depends, to a large extent, on the dismantling programme.'

After the signing I promulgated the Basic Law in the name of the Parliamentary Council and with the assistance of the delegates from Berlin in accordance with Article 145. It entered into force on 23 May 1949. Thus began a new epoch in the history of our people, so full of dramatic changes. The Federal Republic of Germany entered history on 23 May 1949.

This is what I said in my concluding remarks:

We are firmly convinced that our work constitutes a major contribution to the reunification of the German people and to the return of our prisoners of war and those who have been deported. We desire and hope that the day may come when the entire German people is again united.

In our work we were all guided by the aim expressed in the following words of the Preamble of the Basic Law: 'Conscious of its responsibility before God and Men, animated by the resolve to preserve its national and political unity and to serve the peace of the world as an equal partner in a united Europe, the German people in the *Länder* of Baden, Bavaria, Bremen, Hamburg, Hesse, Lower Saxony, North Rhine-Westphalia, Rhineland-Palatinate, Schleswig-Holstein, Württemberg-Baden, and Württemberg-Hohenzollern, has enacted, by virtue of its constituent power,

139

this Basic Law of the Federal Republic of Germany to give a new order to political life for a transitional period.'

Long may the spirit and the resolve that speak in these sentences continue to live in the German people.

Taking the surrounding circumstances into account, it must be admitted that the Parliamentary Council did very good work. It had to deal with the representatives of the three occupying powers who put close limits on its scope. The Ministers President of the *Länder* had an understandable tendency to put the interests of the *Länder* first. When there were differences of opinion we had to convince the representatives of the occupying powers and the Ministers President of the cogency of the views of the Parliamentary Council. Further, the time at the disposal of the Parliamentary Council was extraordinarily short. The opinions of the parties represented in the Parliamentary Council often diverged and had to be harmonized. When all this is understood it is clear that the members of the Parliamentary Council worked well and earned the gratitude of the German people.

9

BERLIN, BULWARK OF THE WEST

In accordance with their discussions at Teheran in 1943 the victorious powers decided at the Yalta Conference of 1945 to divide Germany into zones for purposes of control and administration. On 5 June 1945 the four Allies published the four Declarations dealt with in Chapter 4 which among other things confirmed the special status of Berlin as capital of a Germany that was to be jointly occupied and administered.

Berlin belonged to none of the four occupation zones, but from the very outset was under the direct joint administration of the four powers. This administration was carried out by a joint institution of the four Allies, the Allied Kommandatura.

At the moment of Germany's military surrender on 7 and 8 May 1945 the military situation did not correspond to the zonal frontiers agreed on for the subsequent occupation. Parts of Saxony, Thuringia, and Mecklenburg were occupied by British and American troops. On the other hand Soviet troops had captured Berlin on 2 May 1945.

Immediately after the occupation of Berlin by Russian troops a City Executive (*Magistrat*) was formed for the city of Berlin. This was done with the help of Russian troops, and the Executive was under Communist influence. The Soviet Military Administration declared its seat to be in Berlin.

In June 1945 Truman and Churchill proposed to Stalin that British and American troops were to withdraw to the areas assigned to them as occupation zones and that the areas thus evacuated were to be occupied by the Russians; in exchange American, British, and French troops were to be sent to Berlin for the joint occupation of that city. Arrangements for free access to Berlin for the Western Allies were to be made by the Military Governors. *No written agreement was made to provide for free access to Berlin for the occupation forces of the Western Allies.*

Stalin accepted the procedure suggested by Truman and Churchill. Troop movements began on 1 July 1945 and the first British and American troops entered Berlin on 4 July 1945. French troops occupied the French sector of Berlin on 12 July 1945.

Allied Control bodies for Berlin were formed in accordance with the governmental agreements of September 1944. Representatives of the Allied High Commands including a representative of the French Republic met on 7 July 1945 and agreed on details concerning the joint administration of

Berlin. The Allied Kommandatura for Berlin was put under the direction of a supreme military commander and the commandant of each of the four sectors was to occupy this office for fifteen days at a time. The Kommandatura was directly subordinated to the Allied Control Council. An order of 21 January 1946 once more confirmed that Berlin did not form part of any of the four zones of occupation. Accordingly decrees and orders of the commanders of any of the four occupation zones were to have no validity in Berlin.

The German administration of Berlin was established under four-power control. The City Executive that had been formed early on under the Soviet Military Administration issued a constitutional statute for the boroughs and on 13 August 1946 the Kommandatura gave its approval to a provisional constitution for Greater Berlin.

The occupation systems for Berlin and for the whole of Germany agreed by the victorious powers presupposed trust and cooperation among the occupying powers. This necessary basis of mutual confidence was lacking in the administration of Berlin as much as in the administration of the zones outside. As a consequence neither was functioning properly. The zones, originally created for purposes of military occupation, began to develop into independent units administered in accordance with the directives of their respective Military Governors. In Berlin a similar state of affairs developed between the Western Allies and the Russians. The more the Allied Control Council, the body responsible for all questions concerning the whole of Germany, lost its ability to act, the greater became the difficulties of Berlin's political, economic, and military situation.

When, in February 1948, the three Western powers met in London for a conference to discuss a joint policy at least for the Western parts of Germany, the Russians protested strongly. On 20 March 1948 the Russian Commander-in-Chief, Marshal Sokolovsky, left the Control Council meeting saying that the Western powers had violated the agreement on four-power control. He protested against the London decisions of the six-power conference of 6 March 1948 concerning the future shape of the three Western zones. The meeting of 20 March 1948 was the last joint meeting of the Control Council. The Soviet attitude was noticeably stiffening. Soviet pressure on Berlin was increased to the point of a complete blockade of access by land and water transport.

The agreements of the occupying powers had been based on an assumption of an unlimited right of access which up to that moment had not been called in question by the Soviets. In fact it was precisely the Soviet representatives in the control bodies that had repeatedly demanded that the inhabitants of the Western sectors of Berlin should be supplied from the occupation zones of the Western powers. The Allies had recognized this responsibility for the population of West Berlin as resulting from the occupation rights in Berlin and had therefore presupposed unrestricted military and civilian traffic for people and goods between Berlin and their zones of occupation. As regards air connections with Berlin, the Control Council had on 30 November 1945 agreed on the establishment of three air corridors to Hamburg, Hanover, and Frankfurt. It had been understood that traffic in these corridors would be limited only by considerations of safety. A Soviet report of 5 February 1947 explicitly mentioned 'unlimited flights by Allied aircraft over the Soviet occupation zone of Germany'.

At the end of March 1948, giving the most various reasons for their action, the Soviets cut off one land connection after the other. On 30 March 1948 the Soviets demanded the right to check the troop trains of the Western Allies. The Western powers rejected this demand. When the obstacles increased, the United States and Great Britain began, on 10 April 1948, to build up the so-called little air lift for their personnel. The currency reform in the Western zones came into force on 20 June 1948. On 18 June inter-zonal traffic was stopped, on 24 June 1948 rail traffic ceased on the last open route from Berlin to Helmstedt, and on 30 June 1948 the Russians stopped traffic to Berlin on the waterways. Simultaneously all supplies from the Soviet zone and Soviet sector to the Western sectors of Berlin were cut off.

Negotiations with the Russians on a joint settlement for Berlin of the question of currency reform led to no result. On 22 June 1948 the Soviet Military Administration tried to enforce the currency reform of the Soviet zone in the whole of Berlin. Thereupon the Western powers introduced the new Western Mark in their sectors of Berlin on 24 June 1948. These events further worsened Berlin's situation. The blockade of Berlin began on 24 June 1948. The Soviets tried to force the Western powers and West Berliners to give in by blocking all access by land and water. They evidently wanted to starve Berlin into their own sphere of power and thereby to remove the Western Allies.

The Western response to this challenge was the airlift to supply Berlin. This most magnificent use of air power in modern history began on 25 June 1948 and it succeeded in preserving the liberty of the people of West Berlin. During the period from 25 June 1948 to the end of the blockade in May 1949, about one and a half million tons of goods of all kinds, such as food, coal, raw materials, and medical supplies, were flown into Berlin by the Western powers.

The attitude of the West Berliners which had already been brave and courageous under the earlier pressures, instead of softening, grew harder. In those months of the greatest psychological and economic pressures it was truly admirable. We Germans owe all the people of Berlin heartfelt gratitude and recognition for their courageous example and for their endurance in long months of extreme difficulty and hardship.

The CDU of the Western zones had maintained the closest links with the Berlin CDU from the beginning. The first central body of the three Western zones, the Parliamentary Council, insisted on the participation of representatives of Berlin. They could have only an advisory voice, but they were present at the meetings and discussions concerning the future German constitution.

143

Since 1945 the Russians have let slip no opportunity in their effort to gain control of the whole of Berlin, just as they had at the very outset used the Red Army to occupy Berlin *de facto*. The people of Berlin suffered great hardships. Their fate was more uncertain than that of the inhabitants of any other part of Germany. The Soviets broke off the Berlin blockade during the night of 12 May 1949. They had failed to break the resistance of the people of Berlin and to force the Western powers to renounce their position in Berlin. Berlin remained the bulwark of the West.

Berliners have the gratitude of all Germans and all people everywhere who love freedom. We all thank them for their courage, their energy, their tenacity, their perseverance and bravery, for the historic feat they performed for all of Germany and for freedom. By the suffering imposed on them and endured so bravely, Berliners have inscribed Berlin all the more deeply in the hearts of all Germans as the capital of Germany.

10

GENERAL DISTRESS CONTINUES

My Speech in Berne of 23 March 1949

At the end of February 1949, Dr de Senarclens, the President of the Swiss Group of the Inter-Parliamentary Union, invited me in my capacity as President of the Parliamentary Council to make a speech on the situation in Germany on the occasion of the meeting of the Inter-Parliamentary Union on 23 March. He wrote that little was known in Switzerland about German conditions and he therefore asked me to give this Swiss group some account of matters of concern in Germany. I was glad to accept the invitation, which gave me the first opportunity of telling a foreign audience about conditions in Germany and of drawing the attention of the world to our plight.

The meeting was held in the parliamentary hall of the Swiss Bundesrat. The speech caused a great stir in a number of countries and made people take an interest in Germany. It gives a clear picture of the German stituation at that time and I shall reproduce extracts from it:

We live in disturbed times. New problems arise every day, developments never stand still. Despite the number and variety of problems, every responsible person must realize that for the present and coming generation there is now only one main problem, and it is this: the world has seen the formation of two power-groups. On one side there is the group of powers led by the United States of America and united in the Atlantic Pact. This group defends the values of Christian and Western civilization, freedom, and true democracy. On the other side there is Soviet Russia with her satellites.

The line dividing these two groups of powers runs right down the centre of Germany. Twenty million Germans live under Soviet rule, about 43 million in the orbit of the Atlantic bloc.

These 43 million Germans in the area of the Atlantic bloc possess the most important mineral deposits and the greatest European industrial potential. But this area, the three Western zones of Germany, is in a state of disorder that is in the long run untenable. Even today a very considerable part of these 43 million live in such abject housing conditions, such a state of legal bondage as may have been imaginable in the Balkans a hundred years ago but would hardly have been thought possible in central Europe for centuries . . .

It is impossible to understand the present condition of Germany without a brief survey of what happened after 1945. The unconditional surrender of the German armed forces in May 1945 was interpreted by the Allies to mean a complete transfer of governmental authority into their hands. This interpretation was wrong from the point of view of international law. By it the Allies in practice assumed a task which it was impossible for them to fulfil. I consider it to have been a grave mistake. They would have been unable to solve this task with the best will in the world. There was bound to be failure and this failure badly affected the prestige of the Allies in Germany. It would have been wiser if the Allies had, after a short intermediate state due to the confusion left by the war, let the Germans order their affairs and had confined themselves to supervision. Their attempt to govern this large disorganized country from outside, often guided by extraneous political and economic criteria of their own, was bound to fail. It brought about a rapid economic, physical, and psychological disintegration of the Germans which might have been avoided. It also seems that intentions such as had once been manifested in the Morgenthau Plan played their part. This continued until the Marshall Plan brought the turning point. The Marshall Plan will remain for all time a glorious page in the history of the United States of America. But the change was very slow and the economic, physical, moral, and political decline of Germany which had begun with the unconditional surrender took great efforts to reverse.

Until June 1948 the economy was planned down to the smallest detail, down to trouser buttons and penny items. Then the Economic Council in Frankfurt resolutely changed course for the Anglo-American zones and gradually introduced a social market economy in the two zones. More and more parts of the economy are now being freed from the quota system. Every economist and every politician who is concerned with questions of the economic order should be urged to study the course of events in the Anglo-American zone since June 1948. Naturally we do not have a completely free economy in the Bizone. There never was such a thing in a modern state. Every trade agreement after all means a certain direction of economic life. But as far as possible we have returned to a free system of supply and demand while observing certain considerations of social policy. The upswing taken by economic life in the Bizone since we went over to a social market economy is astounding. This economic upswing can only to a small extent be attributed to the introduction of the new Mark in 1948, or to the help given by the Marshall Plan. The French zone where the Reichsmark was likewise replaced by the Deutschmark and which also received Marshall aid did not experience anything remotely like the same recovery and the same economic upswing.

The departure from the principles of the rationing and quota system considerably reduced the corruption which had been one of its concomitants. There was also a great reduction in the number of officials. Naturally the transition to the greater freedom of an economy that had so long been in fetters did not take place without some friction. At this moment we are worried by the existing imbalance between prices of some commodities and wages. But prices are sinking and we hope that these difficulties can be mastered without excessive shocks to economic life.

Our economic recovery was and still is badly impeded by the dismantling policy. There is no one in Germany who objected or objects to the complete dismantling of war industries. But the dismantling that is going on now also has other aims in view. The aim seems to be to keep the German economic potential at a level that is incompatible with the aims of the Marshall Plan. There also seems to be a tendency to eliminate German competition in the world market. A well-known example of this is the case of the Kolibri comb factory, a case that caused a great stir in Germany and which was also mentioned in the British House of Commons. It was found that despite all German protests the dismantling of this factory took place at the instance of a British officer who runs a rival business in England...

The Ruhr Statute of 1948 is a decisive factor in German economic life. It established a Ruhr Authority with a membership of fifteen including three Germans. It has the right to regulate the entire coal, iron, and steel production of the Ruhr and its power extends to the fixing of prices. The level of production of coal, steel, and iron, and the prices of these commodities are decisive for the whole economy of a country. There is thus the possibility here of exercising a decisive influence on the economic life of Germany. All will depend on the spirit in which this Ruhr Statute is applied in practice. If it is used as an instrument to hold down the German economy, the Marshall Plan is nonsense. Nor would any nation be able in the long run to tolerate such restrictions on its economy. If, however, the Ruhr Statute is used as an instrument in the German and the European interest, if it means the beginning of a new economic order in Western Europe, then it can become a promising starting point for European cooperation.

Let me mention the question of German patents in this context. You know that all German patents were released. At the end of 1948 the director of the American office for technical services, Mr John Green, gave the press a report on his activities which were concerned with the exploitation of German patents and industrial secrets. What strikes one in this report is the fact that AMTORG was the keenest purchaser. That is Moscow's foreign trade organization. During one month alone the Russians bought more than two thousand Wehrmacht reports on secret German weapons for which they paid six thousand dollars. According to a statement made by an American expert the patents formerly belonging to IG Farben have given the American chemical industry a lead of at least ten years. The damage thus caused to the German economy is huge and cannot be assessed in figures. It is extraordinarily regrettable that new German inventions cannot be protected either, because Germany is not a member of the Patent Union.

147

Britain has declared that it will respect new German inventions regardless of what the peace treaty may say. But America has refused to issue such a declaration. German inventors are therefore not in a position to exploit their inventions. This puts a considerable brake on German economic development.

The German biological or demographic problem is a particularly serious and important chapter, important also for the whole of Europe. In this context I must first of all speak of the problem of expulsion. According to American figures a total of 13.3 million Germans were expelled from the Eastern parts of Germany, from Poland, Czechoslovakia, Hungary, and so on. 7.3 million arrived in the Eastern zone and the three Western zones, most of these in the latter. Six million Germans have vanished from the earth. They are dead, gone. Most of the 7.3 million who stayed alive are women, children, and old people. A large proportion of able-bodied men and women were deported to Soviet Russia to do forced labour. The expulsion of these 13 to 14 million from their homes, partly from regions inhabited for centuries by their forebears, has entailed untold misery. Atrocities were committed that are worthy of being put beside those perpetrated by the German National Socialists. The expulsions resulted from the Potsdam Agreement of 2 August 1945. I am convinced that one day world history will pronounce a very harsh verdict on this document. As a result of these expulsions great masses of people were crammed together into very little space, notably in the British and American zones. The housing situation, which was in any case bad after wartime destruction, became intolerable once 7.3 million refugees were added to the already cramped population.

The demographic structure of the population is terrifying as regards both age and sex. There are 28.9 million men and 36.2 million women. There is a special preponderance of women in the age groups between 20 and 40 where there are about 160 women corresponding to every 100 men. The disproportion between the numbers of single men and single women is particularly striking. For every 100 men of thirty there are more than 300 unmarried women of twenty-six or under. The famine years of 1946–7 have done enormous damage in both the physical and the ethical respect. The food situation has improved considerably within the last year but is still far from satisfactory. Cases of tuberculosis have risen from 53.5 per 10,000 persons in 1938 to 127.5 in 1948. On 31 October 1948 there were 159,055 cases of tuberculosis in North Rhine-Westphalia. 37,273 of these were open, that is infectious cases. For these 37,273 cases of open tuberculosis there were about 14,000 hospital beds available. That means that in about 23,000 cases the source of infection could not be isolated and it is quite common for one member of a family after another to contract tuberculosis. Before 1933 there were 20 to 22 cases of venereal disease for every 10,000 persons. In 1948 the figure was 51.74.

For Berlin we have particularly reliable statistics. In 1947 mortality there was roughly 29 for every thousand of the population. Births amounted to

10 per 1,000. Infant mortality in the second quarter of 1946 exceeded 135 per 1,000. Compare this with New York, for instance, where it is 10.1 per 1,000. The calculations quoted by the American Dr Gustav Stolper in 'German Realities' predict a future birthrate of at most 600,000 per year; in 1915 it was 1.5 million. These facts should, I think, assuage French fears on the question of security.

In looking at the state of mind of the Germans, one immediately has to emphasize the unprecedented change in the social structure. Before the war about forty per cent of the population belonged to a middle stratum; now the proportion is down to twenty-three per cent and is still declining. There is an immediate danger in the excessive proletarianization of the Germans, especially if one takes into account the millions of expellees and the people who were dispossessed by aerial bombardment. The danger of an 'Easternization', as a German writer calls this proletarianization, emerges quite naturally from the present plight of the German nation. I think the Allies failed to appreciate the full importance of the housing problem. The Allied authorities allocate coal and iron. The building industry has never been given enough of these basic materials, and hence it has so far been impossible to make a real impact on the housing problem. And yet the solution of the housing problem must be the foundation of any political, physical, ethical and moral reconstruction.

The behaviour of the Soviet troops in their advance into Germany, and the accounts of prisoners of war returning from Soviet Russia, Yugoslavia, and Poland, have made popular feeling against Soviet Russia so negative that the Communist Party, which is regarded as closely linked with Soviet Russia, is of little numerical importance today. Nonetheless one should not underestimate the influence on important branches of industry and their workers exercised by the Communist Party and by infiltration from the East.

There are probably relatively few adherents of the Hitlerian type of nationalism in Germany. But a renascence of some national feeling is noticeable. One can only welcome the reawakening of a healthy and proper feeling of nationhood, because a people that has lost that surrenders to fate. Nor can the German people be expected to have much spiritual resistance to infiltration from the East if they are not permitted to feel as a nation. But I really think it would be absurd to speak of any significant nationalist tendencies. When recently some French papers started a discussion in the press about raising 20 German divisions, the younger generation, as far as I could tell, were all against it.

There is a general strong desire to restore German unity and to reconstruct Germany. I consider the frontier adjustments that are planned in the German West very unwise. Such dictated border adjustments hurt a people's justified national feelings. Minor, technical rectifications could have been carried through by way of negotiation with the German *Länder* if they were so urgent that they could not wait for the peace treaty.

Public opinion is not free in Germany. The press in particular is subject to an unsatisfactory system. Papers have to be licensed. The licensees, who have to invest considerable amounts, are responsible to the Military Governments for what is said in their papers. Although the distribution of licences has for some time now been the task of German committees, the Military Government reserves the right to withdraw a licence at any time and the owner who loses it can do nothing about it. It is obvious that the owner of a licence for whom considerable property is at stake will see to it, even without pre-censorship, that his papers carry nothing that might arouse too much displeasure in the relevant offices of the Military Government. It might be mentioned, incidentally, that Goebbels adopted a similar procedure in the first years of the National Socialist régime. As regards radio and news agencies there was a rather one-sided political personnel policy at first under the influence of the Military Government. Things are slowly changing for the better. But taking it all in all I do not think that the reports which foreign countries get on the situation in Germany are distinguished by lucidity.

I should perhaps say something about our student population. Our students deserve high praise for their industry. They do very well in their examinations despite extremely adverse conditions. Many of them are married. Their prospects after they have passed their exams are very poor. They therefore study primarily with a view to later employment and take no interest in anything except their subject. That is a great pity.

German science and learning have fallen behind, I was told by a well-known scientist the other day. Some outstanding Germans have emigrated. Young German scientists cannot travel abroad for further studies. Moreover they lost whole years of work and training through the war. But this scientist also told me that intelligent people – of whom there are quite a number among the younger generation – are filling the gaps so that we may expect German science and scholarship to regain their previous level in the foreseeable future.

The establishment of the West German state is a goal we must reach as quickly as possible. Its rapid creation is most important for us Germans, but it is also important for Europe, for reconstruction and for the European federation.

Relations between France and Germany are one of the most important problems, if not the most important one, for France, for Germany, and perhaps for Europe too. On its solution depend the chances of peace for a long time. In view of the past, France's desire for security is perfectly understandable. I think there is now a situation in which France need no longer have the slightest fear: Germany is disarmed, its armed forces have been smashed, its war industries have been dismantled. It is occupied, supervised, divided in two parts, and thus paralysed. I mentioned the biological condition of the German nation which is a security factor of the first order for

France. And to this one can add the psychological attitude of the Germans.

There is a very widespread, deep conviction in Germany that Europe can only be saved by the union of the countries of Western Europe. I believe that any Frenchman examining all these factors calmly and without prejudice must see that as far as is humanly predictable France will never again have cause to fear Germany. If France now shows herself wise and magnanimous in her dealings with Germany, she will render historic service to the cause of Europe. Germans are full of praise of the French attitude to the European question and the attitude of the French Foreign Minister, Monsieur Schuman, was the cause of great satisfaction in Germany. There is hardly an idea that has as much appeal in Germany as the idea of uniting Europe. Germans therefore welcomed the wholehearted backing this cause found in the Benelux countries. Britain's attitude at first was not all a European might have desired. But we are glad to see that the recognition of Europe's position in the world, the recognition that Britain has now become a European power and that a great European task awaits her, is beginning to gain ground in public opinion.

The day after this speech a storm broke loose. Foreign papers, especially English papers, reported statements I had not made or that were completely distorted. The *Daily Herald*, for instance, commented at some length on my speech under the heading 'German accuses Allies'. It was stated that I had made a furious, anti-Allied speech in which I raised the wildest accusations against the Western occupying powers and claimed that Allied measures regarding German patents were sheer robbery.

I had said nothing of the kind. The facts were that in a survey of the present state of the German economy I had mentioned the view of leading foreign politicians that the German patents were extremely valuable. What I was concerned to do in my speech was to point out that German inventors still did not enjoy international protection of their rights and that this constituted a notable obstacle to German recovery.

There was now quite a polemical press campaign about the Berne speech in German papers as well as abroad. I rarely speak from a manuscript. But this time I had done so and was thus able to counter the distortions of the speech.

The battle lasted two weeks. Its highlights were such pronouncements as this: 'The German people must disown such politicians and all the more in this case since the name of Adenauer has repeatedly been mentioned in connection with the office of the future German federal president . . . Not even the nationalists of the Weimar days dared indulge in such language.' This commentary was broadcast by the radio station at Koblenz in the evening of 25 March.

All voices were not critical, however; there was a positive echo too, which came especially in the many letters from all parts of the population praising my courageous pronouncements in Berne and congratulating me on my speech. Among one of these was the father of Hans and Sophie Scholl, the Munich students who had been members of the resistance against Hitler and were executed in 1943 at the ages of 24 and 21. Herr Scholl wrote: 'Your frank words in Berne will earn you recognition and respect in Germany and outside, among all Germans who love truth and clarity, however loudly the hounds may be yapping at the moment . . .' He enclosed a copy of an Open Letter he had written to the *Süddeutsche Zeitung* in protest against an article of 29 March 1949. In this letter Scholl rebutted the attacks made on me for my speech in Berne. He wrote: 'Are the Germans once more, just as in the Third Reich, going to keep silent or even to applaud everything that is done even if it is wrong or unjust? Is this not racism too if the inhabitants of Germany are collectively declared guilty, dishonourable, or politically immature only because they are Germans, no matter whether they were Nazis or spent a whole long life giving an example of democratic and liberal beliefs in action, and this amid greater dangers and sacrifice than any member of the occupation has known?'

11

ON THE ROAD TO RESPONSIBILITY

The CDU

Since 1946 I had given my full attention to work for the CDU, which involved me in a large number of tasks. I had been elected chairman of the zonal executive of the CDU in the British zone and chairman of the party in the zone. Originally I did not want to accept the latter office because I thought that the combination of the two offices would overtax my strength. On further reflection, however, I decided that both functions were best combined, and accepted.

The most significant task was the development of our party in the British zone, which had the largest population of all zones of occupation and a special importance because of its industry and agriculture. We also had to establish close connections with the CDU in the other zones in order to build an organization throughout Germany. The Bavarians founded a sister party, the Christian Social Union. Their desire for a separate party seemed justified by the special conditions prevailing in Bavaria.

More comprehensive forms of organization began to emerge in 1946. As early as 1945 a so-called Reich Association of the CDU, intended to reach across *Land* and zonal borders, had been founded in Berlin. In the American and French zones the *Land* party organizations were not merged but continued to exist separately and were only loosely linked in the so-called *Ellwanger Kreis*.

But the CDU did not have an easy time in the British occupied zone. The British authorities regarded this party, which had been founded after 1945, with great mistrust and seemed to think that its founders were predominantly former Nazis. A Labour Government was in office in Great Britain and had close ties with the German Social Democratic Party. Prominent representatives of the SPD had spent the National Socialist period in exile in Great Britain. The SPD thus had good relations with its party friends in Britain.

The CDU was undoubtedly the strongest party, but it had to work hard to assert its claim to leadership in the face of the attitude of the occupation authorities. The British treated the SPD as the party of the future German Government.

The treatment and assessment of the German Communist Party by the British military authorities was quite incomprehensible to me. They regarded the KPD as no different from the other German parties, and treated it almost as well as they treated the Social Democratic Party, certainly better than the CDU. The British policy-makers did not seem to know or to want to know that the communists got their directions from Moscow; they did not seem to think of the possibility that the Soviet Union might be intending to let Germany share the fate of Poland, Czechoslovakia, and other East European countries.

The British Occupation and the CDU

How difficult it was for us of the CDU to assert ourselves was shown quite clearly in the Provincial Council of the North Rhine Province. At the end of 1945 the British Military Government had called a Provincial Council in the North Rhine Province which was to assist in an advisory capacity in administrative and other problems. In the middle of January Dr Weitz, the Oberbürgermeister of Duisburg, approached me to ask if I might be prepared to serve in the 'Rhenish Provincial Council'. He wrote that the present composition of the 'Rhenish Provincial Council' was in many respects far from satisfactory. I replied that I was prepared to serve.

At the end of March 1946 I was given permission by the Military Government to become a member of this non-executive Provincial Council of the North Rhine Province. I was taken aback to find that its composition bore little relation to the actual proportions of party strength and lodged a complaint about this with Oberpräsident Lehr, the chairman of the Provincial Council. In his reply of 5 April 1946 he gave me the following account of the genesis of the Council:

> The Military Government in the North Rhine Province decided that the Provincial Council, which at first was to consist of only a small number of people, should include not only a certain number of representatives of the political parties, but also a fixed number of nonpolitical representatives. The latter were to be drawn from the trade unions, from business, the universities, the arts, crafts, medicine, etc.

The reason given for this directive was that the structure of party politics had undergone such changes since 1933 – old parties had disappeared and new parties arisen – that the old ratios of party strength could hardly serve as a guide to present relationships. But in a letter to Oberpräsident Lehr of 15 April 1946 I insisted on some consideration of party strengths, arguing that the proportions obtaining in the last provincial diet before 1933 could serve as guidance to some extent. But they had been completely disregarded. I found that seven representatives of the CDU, six of the SPD, and seven of the KPD had been nominated. We considered this a totally unrepresentative composition as far as parties were concerned.

I had been asked by the CDU Executive which discussed this matter on 10 March 1946 to lodge a strong protest against this excessively unfavourable treatment of the CDU and to urge a change as strongly as I could. I argued that if it was believed that the political structure of the population had changed so much in the meantime that the proportions of 1933 could hardly serve as a guide, I would urge some examination of the outcome of the voting on denominational elementary schools. This had resulted in a shattering defeat of the opponents of denominational schools and showed very clearly that in all probability proportions were more favourable for the CDU now than they had formerly been for the Centre Party as compared with the other parties. I said that I did not know how much influence the British Military Government had had on the composition of the Provincial Council, but that I had been asked, in case there had been such influence, to call the attention of the British Military Government to this undemocratic discrimination against the CDU. I pointed out too that there had for some time been lively complaints that our party had been quite obviously discriminated against in appointments to the more important positions in the office of the Ober-präsident. For the time being I did not want to examine the statistical justification of these complaints, but wanted to draw attention to the fact that they were very widespread and very vocal. I therefore asked that this matter should be considered with some care.

My endeavours to get adequate representation for the CDU in the 'Rhenish Provincial Council' despite the relative insignificance of the functions of that body were prompted by my conviction that in view of coming developments one could not begin too soon to oppose the apparent preference given to Social Democrats and Communists by the British. It was known that the British were planning to reorganize this non-executive Provincial Council into a nominated Provincial diet. I also knew that the Military Government intended to establish a proportion of 1:1:1 between the CDU, the SPD, and the KPD in this reorganization. The representatives of the CDU called emphatic attention to the most recent elections that had taken place in the American zone in April 1946. We regarded the proportions planned by the Military Government as quite impossible and fully realized that tough negotiations on this matter lay ahead of us.

Dr Lehr wrote to me on 8 May 1946 that he had had a very serious conversation with Brigadier Barraclough in which he had pointed out that in the Provincial Council of Westphalia a proportion of 55:45 had been established between the Left and the so-called bourgeois parties. He said that he had drawn attention to the fact that this distribution had caused unrest among the population and that a political crisis had to be avoided at all costs in view of the present despondent atmosphere due to the food and economic situation. Dr Lehr passed on Brigadier Barraclough's request that I should write him a strictly personal letter with a brief outline of my suggestions and a precise account of my objections. On 14 May 1946 I wrote to Brigadier Barraclough:

In accordance with the invitation of Oberpräsident Dr Lehr I take the liberty of explaining the views of the Christian Democratic Union of the North Rhine Province concerning its participation in the Provincial diet which is in process of being formed.

We assume that in its nomination of members of this body the British Military Government is guided by the intention of doing justice, to the greatest possible extent, to the relative strengths of the political parties among the population in the distribution of seats. In the nature of things it is difficult to give precise figures for this strength. But there are nevertheless certain pointers that make some conclusions concerning the relative strengths possible. We believe that the following can serve as pointers: the results of the last elections for the Rhenish Provincial diet of 1929, the results of the last free Reichstag elections of 1932, and the elections in the American zone which were held in January and April of this year, as well as – to some extent at least – the outcome of the voting on denominational schools recently conducted in the North Rhine Province.

As regards in particular the elections in the American zone, we think we are justified in saying that conditions in that zone and conditions in the North Rhine Province were and are similar to a significant degree. For the assessment of election results in the American zone I should like to draw particular attention to the fact that in the second election of April 1946, our sister party there had a considerable increase in votes in comparison with the first election, while the Social Democratic Party suffered considerable losses. From the comparison of these successive results one might draw conclusions regarding a certain tendency in the attitudes of the electorate.

While fully aware of the need for caution we believe that one thing can be said with absolute certainty concerning the North Rhine Province: if elections were held now, the KPD and SPD together would not get a majority of votes. There is no doubt that the Christian Democratic Union would emerge as by far the strongest party.

As regards the Centre and the Democratic Party [or its successor(s). *Translator*.] we believe that the strength of the former is being over-estimated considerably. There is no doubt that in the North Rhine Province the Centre is already receding. We do not think that, apart from a few small localities where there are special conditions, the Centre will be able to get any significant number of votes. The Democratic Party never amounted to anything in the North Rhine Province; nor will it in future. One surprising feature of the elections in Württemberg is the fact that the Democratic Party only got a small proportion of votes – eleven per cent – even in a region where it could traditionally count on a convinced body of voters . . .

It was my opinion that the CDU had to have the same number of seats as the two Marxist parties combined.

According to Military Government instructions District elections were to be held on 13 October 1946. I believed that elections for the Rhenish Diet should be held simultaneously and thought that they should be conducted according to the former Prussian rules for elections for Provincial diets, albeit with such modifications as might be called for by present conditions. In the name of the CDU, I made a proposal to this effect in a letter to the Oberpräsident of North Rhine Province of 14 July 1946, after my motion to hold Provincial elections at the same time as the District elections, on 13 October, had been defeated by a small majority at the Zonal Advisory Council in Hamburg on 10 July 1946. After some initial hesitation the Military Government had allowed the motion to be put to the vote. Among those who opposed it, as previously mentioned, was Dr Kurt Schumacher, the Chairman of the Social Democratic Party. The SPD could hardly be interested in seeing its position, which was strong due to the help of the Military Government, weakened by an election. It therefore had no interest in supporting my motion.

Thus the members of the *Landtag* of North Rhine-Westphalia were not chosen in a free election, but were nominated by the occupation authorities in accordance with a British Military Government order of 29 August 1946. The *Land* Government, which was likewise composed of Military Government nominees, did not take part in the selection of members or the distribution of seats to the individual parties. The 200 members of the *Landtag* of North Rhine-Westphalia were composed as follows: seventy-one belonged to the SPD, sixty-six to the CDU, thirty-four to the KPD, eighteen to the Centre, nine to the FDP*, and two were Independents. The *Landtag* met for the first time on 2 October 1946.

District elections took place on 13 October. On 17 October, when the results of these elections were known – and they were very favourable for the CDU – the zonal executive of the CDU for the British zone published a resolution stating that the outcome of these elections should have far-reaching political consequences. The composition of the nominated *Land* governments and of the nominated *Land* diets in the British zone must now be brought into line with the freely expressed will of the people. I must add here that a similar procedure to that described for North Rhine-Westphalia had been used by the Military Government in the *Länder* that had been meanwhile created in the British zone, in Lower Saxony, Schleswig-Holstein, and Hamburg.

After this outcome of the district elections the British Military Government was no longer able to maintain the previous distribution of *Landtag* seats among the parties. The redistribution of December 1946 allocated seats in the North Rhine-Westphalia diet as follows: ninety-two to the CDU, sixty-six to the SPD, nine to the FDP, twelve to the Centre, nineteen to the KPD, two to Independents. The total remained at 200. Our attitude in the face of the British Military Government's attempts to bring the Social Democrats to power subsequently proved decisive for the outcome of the first Bundestag elections of 1949.

* Free Democratic Party.

Relations between the CDU and the Other Parties

Local and district elections had been fixed for 5 September and 13 October 1946 respectively. I was sure that these elections had, for the British zone, an importance far exceeding that of normal local and district elections because they were the first free elections in the British zone and would give the first indication of the political complexion of the population. The election campaign had to be fought on principles and it had to be clear and uncompromising. During the months preceding September and October all echelons of the CDU concentrated on the elections. I considered the prospects good. During these months the shape of the parties became clearly discernible. The common feeling of being in the same boat that we all shared when first the pressure of National Socialism was lifted from us, gave way to a fight between the parties.

At the end of September 1945 there had been a meeting of leading representatives of the CDU and the SPD at Bad Godesberg. Herr Severing led the SPD. The CDU was represented by Herr Lehr, Herr Müller, Herr Schwering, Herr Warsch, and myself. We agreed to respect each other without blurring the differences that divided us on questions of political principle. This mutual respect and cooperation seemed the natural outcome of our conviction that the CDU and SPD, as the biggest parties, had to work together to lead the German people out of its misery. But the SPD did not keep the agreement. They spread insults against the CDU. It was said, for instance, that the CDU was not an ideological party but merely one that defended property and used Christianity as camouflage. The SPD also claimed that it was entitled to leadership in Germany because among all parties it was the only one that for eighty years had held high the principles of peace and democracy. Such statements conflicted with the agreement of September 1945.

The differences dividing the CDU and the SPD emerged clearly at the first Party congress of the SPD which took place in Hanover in May 1946 and was the first post-war party congress of the SPD. Here are some statements made by Dr Schumacher on 10 May 1946:

> If you ask for the real foundations of democracy, it pains me to have to say that today in Germany democracy is not yet much stronger than the Social Democratic Party. All others had to see the war potential and the superiority of Anglo-Saxon arms before they discovered their democratic hearts. We of the SPD did not need this demonstration; we would be democrats even if the British and the Americans were fascists.

He also said:

> As Social Democrats we have no cause to condemn or abandon Marxism wholesale . . . In its two most important aspects, the economic view of history and the concept of class war, Marxism is by no means obsolete.

Schumacher criticized the political parties that were in process of formation, on the grounds that they were too much animated by mere traditionalism.

> ... the leaders of the bourgeois parties that are arising again are still living entirely in the mental world of 1932. The political practices of those days have unfortunately hibernated only too successfully in the chill climate of dictatorship. This can be seen especially clearly in the case of the CDU.

Speeches of this kind obviously called for hard replies from the CDU and contributed not a little to the exacerbation of the election campaign.

On economic policy Schumacher had this to say:

> Planning is the first prerequisite if catastrophe is to be averted in Germany and we already see it being opposed by the bourgeois parties. We shall either succeed in giving Germany a socialist economy and democratic politics or we shall cease to be a German people ... We need a radical land reform, and we need this radical agrarian reform, which will increase production, will have to be promoted by consumer cooperatives, and will settle new farmers – we need this reform *now*.

The man who spoke these words, who claimed that his party was the only democratic party in Germany, was the same man who in the Zonal Advisory Council had prevented the holding of free elections to the *Landtage*. He had the arrogance to present himself and his party as the only representatives of democracy in Germany and yet proposed to carry out such measures as a radical land reform without any chance of freely elected parliaments being able to take part in these important decisions.

Dr Kurt Schumacher thought in terms of class war. Capitalism and socialism belong to the same epoch. Both are expressions of anti-transcendental ways of thinking, of an over-valuation of the economic aspect of society – whether its form is capitalist or socialist. Socialism is founded on the materialist view of history which says that production and the exchange of products is the foundation of all being and all that happens. Marxism is regarded as scientifically disproved, but Dr Schumacher still seemed to regard it as fundamental.

The question whether we were to have a planned or a free economy played a very big part in the political fighting of this first electoral campaign in 1946. But these debates were rather theoretical because ultimately it was the British who made the decisions. Their decrees regulating provisions for war invalids and dependents of the war dead and changing taxation laws are only two examples, but I could list more. These decisions were made without any elected representatives of the population having the least say in them.

In those hard years the question was repeatedly raised whether it was not possible for the two strongest parties, the CDU and the SPD, to put aside the problems that divided them and to act together in the interest of the German people. During the years after the collapse I made the most earnest efforts to

159

achieve some common action with the SPD on important questions. Unfortunately these efforts were unsuccessful.

Such was the distress prevailing in Germany after 1945 that it would have been most valuable if all German parties had taken a common line in their dealings with the Allied powers. During the early post-war years I made repeated attempts to arrive at a common attitude on vital questions in the first instance with the Social Democrats, who were the biggest party beside the CDU. After the district elections of 13 October 1946 I wrote to the central executive of the SPD in my capacity as CDU Chairman in the British zone. I said that the SPD and the CDU were the strongest parties and therefore had the greatest part of the responsibility for the German people. I asked whether the SPD was prepared to cooperate with the CDU on the proportional basis that was now known and whether it would instruct subordinate organizations likewise.

At first the central executive of the SPD did not reply to this letter. After eight or nine days I sent a telegram requesting an answer; it then took another four or five days before there was a reply from Dr Schumacher. It was negative. Dr Schumacher stipulated that in the case of cooperation we should have to acknowledge the socialist programme. I thereupon terminated the correspondence.

The situation in Germany was worsening steadily owing to unemployment, malnutrition, the shortage of coal, and the hopelessness that was becoming quite general. In 1947 the CDU made another attempt, this time on a broader base, to achieve something like a national representation, a united attitude of all German parties on the problems that were weighing us down. Our efforts foundered on Dr Schumacher's refusal to cooperate.

In all its meetings, conferences, and resolutions the CDU had again and again raised the demand for German unity and the abolition of the zonal frontiers. It seemed to us that this demand could be put forward more impressively if it had the support of all German parties. In its endeavour to achieve a national representation the CDU had approached all parties in the Russian zone as well, including the leaders of the SED. It was in particular Heinrich Lemmer and Jakob Kaiser who undertook these steps.

The reason Dr Schumacher gave for his refusal to cooperate in the nationally representative body we were trying to convene was that he could see no possibility of negotiating with the SED on behalf of his own party as long as the conditions for democracy did not exist in the Russian zone, and what he chiefly had in mind was the admission of the SPD. I must here interpolate that under the pressure of the Soviet occupying power the KPD and SPD had been merged to form the SED. Dr Schumacher had opposed this measure very energetically.

In view of the political situation the CDU decided that it would be wrong to give up the attempt to arrive at the formation of a joint representation of the German political parties. We were convinced that nothing should be left untried to prevent the splitting up of Germany into two parts. That our efforts to get all parties to act together came to nothing was entirely Dr Schumacher's fault. As far as I was able to ascertain his attitude had a mixed reception in his own party – but his opinions prevailed.

Later I tried once more to achieve common action with the SPD. Once more I proposed joint discussions to find out whether our two parties could not after all relegate divisive factors to the background and adopt a common line of cooperation. I made this suggestion at the end of 1947. Dr Schumacher replied that my proposal was very interesting and he would come back to it. But I never heard any more from him about it. I repeated my proposal, using the Minister President of Schleswig-Holstein, Lüdemann, as intermediary. Again there was no answer. When I asked Lüdemann what success he had had he said: 'Dr Schumacher is not willing.'

Although the CDU was prepared to cooperate with the SPD in vital questions, it was important, from the point of view of developing the parties, that we should make the differences between us quite clear in all the election campaigns after 1946, be they for district or *Länder* parliaments. This applied particularly to questions of ideology, culture, and education. The strongest differences divided us from the SPD in matters of ideology as well as in the educational and ecclesiastical fields. This was most clearly shown in the school question. The SPD did not recognize the right of parents to send their children to schools they were free to choose. The SPD was against denominational schools even where parents desired them for their children.

The differences between the CDU and the SPD were exacerbated by the claim to leadership in Germany which was perpetually raised by Schumacher and the SPD executive. Dr Schumacher made this claim for the first time in directives he issued in September 1945 on the SPD's relations with other political factors in Germany. After that the claim kept on being made.

The CDU and SPD were, of course, also diametrically opposed in their economic views. But the differences of opinion on the reorganization of the shattered economy were only part of the basic differences between the CDU/CSU and the SPD.

The CDU had decided that in the local and district elections there should be no compromise with the Communists, the Social Democrats, or the Centre Party. The question whether compromise with the Free Democrats was a possibility was left open. Even at that time, in 1946, the FDP wore a different aspect in the different *Länder*, as it continued to do in subsequent years. It had a different face in Hamburg and, say, in North Rhine-Westphalia.

In some respects we agreed with the FDP, as, for instance, in our joint opposition to radical socialization or the nationalization of the key industries. In other respects we were sharply divided. This was especially the case in the question of the parents' right to choose what schools they wanted and the whole related problems of the reorganization of the schools.

In the *Landtag* of North Rhine-Westphalia the CDU and FDP were getting on relatively well and were able to collaborate. I endeavoured to maintain a relationship of understanding with the FDP wherever possible, a relationship that did not, however, mean that we had to abandon our differences in matters of principle.

The KPD also played different parts according to which *Länder* were concerned. Thus the KPD spoke often and loudly of democracy, of national sentiment, and of German unity in the British and also in the American zone. In the Western zones it acted as though it alone among all parties had any national feelings. In the Eastern zone, however, where the KPD had forced the SPD into a shotgun marriage under Soviet pressure its actions were by no means democratic and its cloak of nationalism was full of holes. In all the years after 1945 the KPD showed itself to be one hundred per cent Marxist, and by its nature a totalitarian party devoted to the class struggle. It also demanded from the whole German people a foreign policy that was completely oriented toward Soviet Russia.

A Planned Economy?

During the years 1946, 1947, and 1948 one of the fundamental problems in the economic field was the question of nationalization and of planning. The British Military Government tried to prescribe what it thought right to German administrative and governmental bodies; the prescription consisted of measures akin to those of the socialist Labour Party which governed Britain at that time.

In the beginning of 1947 the great element of danger lay in British plans to carry out large-scale nationalization in the British zone which housed Germany's most important industrial area. The British Foreign Secretary Bevin and the British Minister responsible for occupation matters, Hynd, had expressed this quite clearly. They had declared that the key industries must never again return to the hands of those who had misused them to support Hitler and his aims. They said that the British therefore proposed handing these industries over to the German state that was to be created. If these British intentions had been carried out, and these industries had been put under central agencies of the state, the German state of the future would have had more power over the people than the National Socialist state had in the first years of its existence. The question of nationalization was of the greatest importance for our future development and the measures announced by the British seemed very dangerous to me.

In an interview with a representative of a British newspaper, the *Daily Mail*, in January 1947, I suggested that public opinion in the Allied countries should very seriously examine the question of the consequences for the intended 're-education of the German people' of continual violations of international law such as were happening in Germany. The Germans were witnessing constant demonstrations of the principle of might prevailing over right and must conclude that other nations subscribed to this principle. I told the correspondent that in my opinion the only people entitled to settle the future structure of the German economy were the Germans and they should do it through freely elected representatives. The CDU was resolutely opposed to the concentration of great economic power in the hands of private persons or in the hands of the state and this attitude was the outcome of bitter experience undergone especially after 1933. We had clearly expressed this attitude in our programme of 1 March 1946. Just as we were opposed to excessive concentration of political power and wanted some distribution of it along federal and democratic lines, we were also concerned to prevent undue concentration of economic power and the two were, of course, connected.

I told the correspondent that the CDU favoured agrarian reform, a land reform of the kind that would remove the political dangers arising from excessively large estates. We also advocated a reform of the industrial economy which would disperse economic power in such a way as to prevent its misuse against freedom. But we rejected the nationalization of key industries. Whoever held the key industries controlled – as the very name implied – the entire economy. The state that held the key industries held power such as Hitler required several years to gain after 1933. I was quite unimpressed by the objection that the state could not misuse this power because it was controlled by elected parliaments. We had seen in Germany in 1933 how a democratic constitution could be used to eliminate the control by parliament. We of the CDU did not want a return of such a state of affairs under any circumstances. Many Christian Democrats inclined to the view that a principle of distribution of power should be applied to the key industries: economic power should be shared between public and private hands, without excluding the initiative of enterprises which was indispensable for Germany's recovery.

The British Government had made repeated statements to the effect that the key industries were not to be returned to their former owners. As far as I knew these former owners were all companies. We were of the same opinion as the British Government where shares were concerned that belonged to war criminals, active National Socialists, and war profiteers. But we were not of one mind with the British where the shares belonged to people who were politically blameless. There were over a million shareholders of key industries whose average holdings amounted to between 4,000 and 5,000 Reichsmark. These people as a rule had put their savings into such shares. The CDU did not see why these people should be expropriated and moreover without compensation. When such measures were carried out in the Russian zone, the British public had unanimously and resolutely opposed them. I did not understand why public opinion in Britain did not see that the same attitude should apply in the case of the British zone of Germany.

The question of nationalization was assuming an increasing importance and the CDU had to put its views on it clearly and precisely. The socialism of the Social Democrats was absolutely materialistic. At the Party Congress of the

SPD in Hanover in May 1946 Dr Schumacher had proclaimed his faith in the Marxism of class war and in the economic interpretation of history. National Socialism, war, and defeat had in part destroyed German economic life, and plunged another part into indescribable disorder. To socialize or nationalize everything that could be nationalized was a simple, but a deadly prescription. It would not have allowed the creative powers of the individual to come into play – and without that no reconstruction was possible after such total destruction. Nor would such a system have made good use of the economic potential of the individual person, of which much still remained despite everything. We had confronted a huge mountain made up of shattered fragments, but also of some useful material. Before one established a new order one had to find out what useful elements that mountain contained. We started with the conviction that there must be no all-powerful state as there had been in the days of National Socialism, that the dignity and rights of the individual had to be respected everywhere, and that in the economic life of the people too, the individual and his well-being must be the goal. We believed that only a free people could carry out the gigantic task of building up a new economy. We had had many discussions and investigations for the purpose of mastering these problems.

The chief milestones of all our deliberations were the meetings of the British Zone CEU at Neheim-Hüsten at the end of February 1946 and at Ahlen in early February 1947. In the Federal election campaign of 1949 we took our stand as far as economic questions were concerned on the economic, agricultural, social, and housing policy embodied in the principles announced by the study group of the CDU/CSU in Düsseldorf in July 1949.

A Bizonal Economic Council had been set up in Frankfurt, on the orders of the American and British Military Governments in February 1947. A majority of this Council, in which the CDU/CSU played a leading role, had accepted the responsibility, against the votes of the SPD, of introducing a radical change from the economic policy followed up to that time and initiating the so-called 'social market economy'. Everyone could see the success of this change and if one remembered that the economy had been controlled and planned ever since 1934/5 there was no reason to expect that all the harm would be undone in a short while and all would now be well. This needed time and patience. But even the results of the first few months were amazing.

The SPD's response was to say: That there has been a change is undeniable, but the change is not due to the social market economy, but firstly to the currency reform, secondly to the Marshall Plan, and thirdly to the mild winter. All this success is illusory. Professor Nölting, the Minister of Economic Affairs in North Rhine-Westphalia and the SPD's candidate for the Federal Ministry of Economic Affairs in the event of the SPD forming a government, had said in a speech that the collapse of our economy was simply camouflaged by seasonal appearances. But this temporary blossoming would be over in the autumn and then the German people were in for a terrific shock. Our currency would probably collapse.

But the rapid economic recovery in the Bizone was in fact not only due to the currency reform, Marshall aid and the mild winter of 1948–9. The example of the French zone showed this clearly. It had the currency reform at the same time as the British and American zones, and it also partook of Marshall aid, but it did not change over to a new economic system. The result was that the French zone continued to stagnate as it had done before the currency reform. Professor Erhard, the director of the Economic Council in Frankfurt, mentioned a fact that needs emphasizing when he said: 'Imports of raw materials under the Marshall Plan did not start until the end of 1948, but the economy experienced a sudden acceleration the moment competition started again and the social market economy was introduced.' As for the mild winter, it may indeed have contributed somewhat, but one cannot live on a mild winter alone.

Let me summarize the main features of the social market economy from a CDU/CSU pamphlet issued in July 1949 where the system is explained in detail. The 'Social Market Economy' produces the maximum economic benefit and social justice for all by letting free individuals make an efficient contribution to an order that embodies a social conscience. It combines freedom and obligation, genuine competition and an independent control of monopolies. Genuine competition is possible where there is a system that rewards the better performance in a framework of equal chances and fair conditions of competition. The proper market price gives the right direction to the cooperation of all concerned.

The Social Market Economy stands in sharp contrast to the system of a planned economy which we reject no matter whether the planning is done by centralized agencies or by way of decentralization, whether it is self-administered or administered by the state.

The Social Market Economy also contrasts with the so-called free economy of liberalism. We need an independent control of monopolies to insure against a relapse into the 'free economy' and to safeguard genuine competition. Private persons or associations or combines should not be allowed to direct the economy any more than the state or semi-official authorities. The Social Market Economy renounces the planning and direction of production, labour, or sales. But it favours the organic means of a comprehensive economic policy based on elastic adaptation to market research. This comprehensive policy combines monetary, trade, tariff, tax, investment, and social policies as well as other measures designed to ensure the welfare of the whole people and the supplying of their requirements, including, obviously, appropriate provision for the needy parts of the population.

Europe

The two world wars, the war of 1914–18 and the war of 1939–45, had begun in Europe. Their destructive effects were felt all over the world. But the greatest and most far-reaching devastation had taken place in the countries of Europe.

Europe's situation had changed fundamentally in the last fifty years. Since the beginning of the century the countries of Europe had lost much of their political and economic importance owing to the rise of the United States and the results of warfare in Europe. Moreover no country had emerged from the Second World War with so much gain in territory, population, and political power as Soviet Russia which now stood on the Elbe, in the middle of Germany. To preserve the traditions and the very existence of the countries of Europe, especially in face of the big communist power bloc in the East, it was more necessary than ever to create a united Europe.

In 1929 the French statesman Aristide Briand had advocated a federal union of Europe, but unfortunately his proposals and arguments had found no political realization. They were taken up again after the Second World War, by General de Gaulle among others. But it was not until Winston Churchill made a speech on the United States of Europe at Zürich on 19 September 1946 that the world once more began to take a real interest in the question. This interest in creating a united Europe has never died down since then although the idea has still not found concrete political embodiment.

The European Congress at The Hague dealt with the problem of uniting Europe very thoroughly in March 1948. This congress was also attended by Germans and I was present as chairman of the CDU. At The Hague I met Winston Churchill who was most charming and friendly to me. I have mentioned this encounter before.

Since its inception the CDU had always, from deep conviction, backed a European federation. In the creation of such a federation we saw and we still see the only possibility of saving the existence, the tradition, and the influence of Europe. The United States, too, emphatically desired a European federation. At the Amsterdam assembly of the World Council of Churches conference of 1948 John Foster Dulles, who was later to play a decisive role in American foreign policy, stressed the need for Europe to unite in order to preserve its Christian tradition.

A great step forward in the direction of economic and above all political unification of Europe was taken when the European Coal and Steel Community was set up. Its members included France, Italy, Belgium, Holland, Luxembourg, and the German Federal Republic. It came into existence in 1951, after difficult negotiations initiated by a proposal of the French Foreign Minister Robert Schuman. I shall return to this subject in greater detail. In my capacity as chairman of my party and later as Federal Chancellor I put all my strength and all my influence into the effort to bring about the unification of Europe.

The Election Campaign of 1949

When countries or régimes collapse, there is nearly always a government that can take over in some way from its predecessor. But in Germany after the collapse of National Socialist rule there was a political vacuum. This meant that the first elections for a federal parliament after the collapse were of truly historic importance. It also meant that every individual German had a very significant decision to make. It was ultimately for the voters to decide how the vacuum would be filled, whether with a parliament and government that would try to hand us over to socialism and the supremacy of the state, or with a federal parliament and government that would put the freedom of the individual first and foremost, his economic freedom included.

The federal parliament and government were going to be confronted by tasks that had either just been neglected for years or else had been dealt with by *Länder* parliaments or Bizonal para-governmental institutions that were dependent on the occupying powers – without much regard for the central needs of Germany as a whole. So far there existed no common parliament or executive for the three Western zones of occupation. All this was now to change. Eleven, counting Berlin twelve, *Länder* were to form one federal state, the Federal Republic of Germany.

In the federal election campaign of 1949 the CDU/CSU concentrated on the questions it regarded as most urgent for the alleviation of distress. Here housing had pride of place because the rights and freedom of the individual are not worth much if he and his family continue to suffer the effects of a housing shortage that threatens to shake the foundations of the community and especially of the family. If it is remembered that in the area of the Federal Republic there was a shortage of roughly 6 million housing units, it is clear that it would only be met by the mobilization of all private and public energies. The CDU was determined to tackle the task and to bring it to a successful conclusion. It struck me as quite impossible for the German people to recover morally, politically, and economically as long as a large proportion of it was without housing. I was convinced that the new Federal Government and parliament would have to devote quite a new kind of attention to the housing question, an attention that would differ markedly from that bestowed on the problem so far by the *Länder* – which, perhaps, had not been able to do much more than they did. The encouragement of building activity was also the best means toward the elimination of unemployment.

This question was, of course, very closely connected with the problem of looking after returning prisoners and expellees. It seemed to me that the problem of expellees, in particular, was one that could not be solved by the Germans out of their own resources alone. I saw this problem as one that would need foreign capital for its solution.

As far as self-help was concerned, there had to be an equalization of burdens, that is a tolerable adjustment between the expellees who had lost

167

everything and those who had been able to save at least some of their property when Germany collapsed. We had to provide some legislation for emergency help and for settlement aimed at the absorption of the expellees in the German economy. But it was not only a question of creating new livelihoods but also of preserving those that existed. That was the reason for the CDU's demand for a reasonable and social system of taxation, for we realized that the severity of taxes in those days was bound to act as a disincentive to work and saving.

It went without saying that there also had to be measures to relieve the distress of all the groups that were living in intolerable conditions due to the war and its consequences, particularly such groups as invalids and people who had lost their homes in the bombing. The CDU was of the opinion that this programme of social aid and welfare could only be carried out if the social market economy continued, which the representatives of the CDU and CSU had carried in conjunction with the FDP in the Frankfurt Economic Council, and which had been recognized as the right system.

The CDU intended to take a special interest in youth. The younger generation was to sustain and shape the new state and had to grow in such a way as would enable it to assume responsibility in public life. The first requirement for this, in the eyes of the CDU, was a body of social legislation that facilitated comprehensive professional and vocational training and enabled members of the economically weaker sections of the population to rise as well. In order to foster the idea of international reconciliation in the hearts of the young, the CDU/CSU advocated an increase in the exchange programmes between nations.

In the field of foreign relations the Federal Government would at first have to operate within strict limitations because German foreign policy was going to be the domain of the Allied High Commission. But the CDU/CSU argued that the future Federal Government must always endeavour, by frank and open discussion with the High Commissioners and the occupation powers, to work for the gradual abolition of the provisions of the Occupation Statute that limited our sovereignty. We were determined to make our contribution to the European community of nations and hoped that Germany would soon be allowed to take part in the federation of Europe that was in process of creation.

But this federation could only be realized if it was based on sound economic foundations. This meant that Western Europe's basic industries had to be put at its service. This was the only angle that made the Ruhr Statute acceptable to us – which seemed tolerable if it was treated as Germany's contribution to the re-ordering of the whole European economy. The European federation could only gain the momentum it needed if the status of the Ruhr was extended to the Saar, to Lorraine, and the productive areas of Belgium and Luxembourg.

If the nations of Europe were to find each other and if, as the CDU ardently desired, the Germans too learned to think as Europeans, they had to be made to feel that Europe was not going to leave the Germans in the lurch. The future Federal Government would therefore have to impress on the Allies most emphatically that they had to fulfil the obligations that devolved on them, as a result of occupation and demilitarization, for the defence of the German state. The CDU wanted the citizens of the new Germany to become Europeans determined to make their contribution to the European community in the spirit of Christianity and Western civilization. This alone could ensure peace for Germany and for the world.

Many small parties took part in the federal election campaign. The Germans have a tendency to split up into many parties and this tendency found support in the relaxation of the licensing system for political parties decreed by the Allies. The reason for this action was the desire to make it possible for all shades of democratic groupings to express themselves freely and to be represented in these first federal elections.

The CDU tried to counteract this splintering process. We were convinced that we needed a strong parliament and government for the tasks that lay ahead of us. We tried to convince the electorate that in practice splinter parties are not able to carry out their special programmes, simply because they are splinter parties and unable to assert themselves. On the other hand they prevent the formation of large majorities which alone enable governments to act and they also prevent the formation of a large and constructive opposition party. The CDU/CSU appealed to all Germans to make a clear decision for one of the big parties.

In the course of the election campaign the real fighting took place between the big parties that had already been formed in the preceding *Landtag* and local elections. In essence the election campaign was a battle between the CDU/CSU and the SPD.

The SPD had a great advantage over the CDU/CSU. It could base itself on a tradition and on a very thoroughgoing organization and a body of trained party personnel. In addition the SPD decidedly had the sympathy of the occupying power in the British zone. The CDU/CSU, a young party which had only been founded in 1945, worked very hard to get votes. The SPD manifested considerable arrogance and a somewhat excessive consciousness of its own value, witness the epithets Dr Schumacher, the leader of the Social Democratic Party of Germany, applied to the CDU, calling it, for instance, a 'rabble of political minors' or the 'most heathen of all parties, a party of Mammon.'

The objective differences in the aims of the big parties emerged more and more clearly in the course of the election campaign. The CDU/CSU advocated the continuation of the social market economy which it saw not only as the practical application of the recognition of an economic truth, but also as the basic affirmation of its belief in the liberty of the citizen, a view which gives not the state and its might, but the human individual, the central place in all thinking and action.

169

The SPD demanded a departure from the economic system introduced by the Frankfurt Economic Council and demanded the nationalization of important sectors of the economy, including among them not only the industries concerned with basic materials but also the insurance and credit business. Their goal was a directed economy and the extension of control to all the heavy industries of Europe.

The election campaign also showed clearly how great our differences were in the field of ideology and education. One of the chief bones of contention was the right of parents to choose how they wanted their children to be educated. The SPD claimed that this meant church domination in the schools, while we explained that it meant no more than the parents' right to choose. It also meant that the state had no right to take children away from their parents, a postulate to which we attributed particular significance after the experience of the National Socialist era and the events in the Russian zone.

A letter by Dr Kurt Schumacher, dated 14 February 1949 and published in *Neuer Vorwärts* on 2 July 1949, is illuminating on the SPD's attitude to the church: '. . . The great contest between the CDU and Social Democracy concerning political priorities has begun and will come to its first climax in the elections to the first West German federal parliament: such subjects as the equalization of burdens, socialization, and the totalitarian claims of the episcopate in all questions affecting culture, church, and education, show how broad the battlefront will be and how violent the clash must be. There can only be one watchword: to fight and not to capitulate! . . .'

On 23 June 1949 the *Kölner Rundschau* reported a speech Dr Schumacher had made in Gelsenkirchen. According to this report he said 'we shall not knuckle under, neither to a French general nor to a Roman Cardinal'. The *Kölner Rundschau* commented that the following sentences showed even more clearly how occupation power and church were being equated: 'We respect the church, but we are determined not to subject the German people to a fifth occupying power.'

The *Süddeutsche Zeitung* of 7 June 1949 reported the SPD deputy Marx on the subject of the church as saying that:

> The SPD should not incline to compromise in the field of cultural and educational policy. It would only harm the party. It was a matter for regret that the party had not taken steps to initiate a *Kulturkampf* in the Parliamentary Council. What was needed was to ward off political catholicism which committed unconditional treachery in its social policy for the sake of gains for its cultural policy.

The first issue in 1949 of the periodical of the socialist student association *Die Fackel* carried an article by Hans Jürgen Laves which threw much light on the SPD's attitude to the church. It said that '. . . it was therefore quite natural for socialism to see its first task in the economic field and quite rightly it still treats the economic system as the primary question. But we must not stop there. Man still needs to be liberated in another field, in the realm of the spirit. And here the Christian church is the oppressor which in essentials still plays the same role as it did a hundred years ago in the days of Marx. Socialism wants to educate men for freedom, the church educates them for its opposite . . . To force some dogma or doctrine on them, to give them blinkers, may make people obedient subjects, be it of the teacher or of God; but this is not the way to raise them to a higher level, one that is compatible with human dignity . . . The problems of today will not be solved by any clinging to so-called absolute values which prevent the living, active, and rational revitalization and perpetual recreation of all values. Only in development is there life; rigidity is death. The church, however, is rigid, it has not kept in step with the times and thus there is no living, sustaining, or directive strength left in Christianity, as the failure of all Christians in two worldwide catastrophes in the space of thirty years has shown. The revolution needed to overcome this rigidity is too great and comprehensive for the church to be able to rise to it. It is therefore useless to try to revive this moribund institution. What has to fall will fall and we should not attempt to save it for another few decades.'

We had also had heated controversies with the Social Democrats in the Parliamentary Council in another field, that of legislation affecting marriage and the family. Mindful of these struggles we had to tell the electorate that the SPD held such views as were expressed by a lady deputy, Dr Selbert, when, speaking in favour of an SPD motion to put illegitimate children on an equal footing with children born in wedlock, she said on 18 January 1949 that it meant disregarding the realities of life if one failed to recognize that nowadays there were new forms beside marriage, forms that were by no means immoral or to be condemned. The principles of family and marriage had been fractured by life. Life was creating its own law.

Her arguments were followed by those of Dr Greve, another member of the SPD, who said that the sentence that marriage is the legal form of the community of man and woman could never be valid law because it did not help those who did not recognize its validity to find it written in the constitution. The same objection applied to the second sentence calling marriage the foundation of the family.

During the last weeks before election day foreign policy began to dominate the election campaign. As previously mentioned the CDU/CSU advocated German membership of a European federation and explained its stand to the electorate. The cessation of dismantling was a very important demand addressed by us to the occupying powers and we were not afraid to voice sharp criticism of occupation policy in this respect.

The SPD's criticism of the measures taken by the occupying powers far exceeded ours, certainly as regards acerbity of tone. Dr Schumacher's exaggerated accusations and challenges gave rise to some anxious commentary in the press, especially in American periodicals. The attacks of the SPD were, however, directed not only against the occupying powers, including, incidentally, the British, but above all against the CDU/CSU which was described as pro-French and charged with un-German conduct. The SPD was attempting to give itself the air of being the national party *par excellence*, the only party that had maintained the German point of view in the deliberations about the Basic Law. The Note of the High Commissioners of 22 April 1949 thus assumed a special importance in the election campaign.

My personal secretary, Herr Blankenhorn, had found out that the SPD had learnt the contents of this Note from the British High Commission as early as 14 April. The files contained a note by Blankenhorn, dated 30 April 1949, saying:

> In the morning of Saturday 30 April the head of the British liaison team, Mr Chaput de Saintonge, asked me to come for a discussion of the state of the work on the constitution and the political situation connected therewith. During this conversation Mr Chaput de Saintonge told me confidentially that after the discussion between the Military Governors and the members of the Parliamentary Council of Thursday, 14 April, General Robertson had asked Professor Carlo Schmid and Dr Menzel over and had given them a rough outline of the contents of the second Note of the Foreign Ministers which the liaison officers in Bonn only communicated to the President of the Parliamentary Council on 22 April. This [earlier] communication to Professor Schmid and Dr Menzel had taken place with the consent of General Clay. It was intended to inform the SPD of possible concessions of the Foreign Ministers before 20 April, the day their party executive was to meet in Hamburg.
>
> I have reported this confidential information to the President [of the Parliamentary Council] Dr Adenauer with the consent of Mr Chaput de Saintonge.

In their election manifesto of 9 July 1949 the Social Democrats had declared:

> In the fight for the Basic Law it was again the Social Democrats who took the decisive step in the direction of German self-determination. If it had been left to the desires for power of the Allies and their German assistants, a viable German state would have been made impossible. Its place would have been taken by eleven West German fatherlands. Under Allied protection clericalism, particularism, and the material egotism of those who have something, would have established the dominance of their interests over the German people. Legal, economic, social, and cultural unity would have ceased. Nationalist communism from the East would have grown into a gigantic danger in a fragmented Germany, a new breeding ground for crises and unrest in Europe.
>
> By their intervention on 20 April the Social Democrats averted this danger.

It was now an absolute necessity to put the record right regarding the second Allied Note. I informed the public of what had really happened in a speech I made in Heidelberg on 21 July 1949. There was a storm of indignation among the Social Democrats and they denied the truth of my statement. On 25 July I had the following telegram from the executive of the SPD:

> Contrary to the truth you claimed in Heidelberg that the SPD's rejection of exaggerated Allied wishes was based on prior knowledge of their intention to yield. This is not the first time that your claim has been rejected as utterly baseless. We leave it to the German electorate to pronounce their verdict on you.
>
> Fritz Heine, SPD Executive.

I wired the following reply to the SPD Executive:

> The head of the British Liaison team with the Parliamentary Council in Bonn has told my personal secretary Herr Blankenhorn for the purpose of passing it on to me that the contents of the second Note of the Foreign Ministers in Washington were communicated to the Chairman of the SPD group in the Parliamentary Council, Professor Schmid, and Dr Menzel. This took place on 14 April in the IG Farben building after the earlier discussion with representatives of the Parliamentary Council in a separate conversation by a high-ranking British official, and with a view to the impending meeting of the Party Executive of the SPD that was to formulate an attitude to the question of the Basic Law. According to the British liaison team this communication took place on 14 April. The liaison teams communicated the Note to the Presidium of the Parliamentary Council on 22 April.

Dr Schumacher called me *Lügenauer* or a liar and the SPD refused to give up the fight. They demanded that I name the 'high-ranking Briton'.

I gave the desired information in a telegram to the SPD on 28 July 1949:

> In your telegram to me of 27 July you maintain that the chairmen of the SPD group in the Parliamentary Council, Schmid and Menzel, were not informed on 14 April by one of the highest British representatives in Germany. May I point out that according to a Foreign Office statement in London of the same day the two gentlemen were informed by General Robertson and his political adviser, Mr Steel, of the furthest extent to which the British Government thought the Allies might go with concessions on the Basic Law if the Washington conversations were taken as base. I never claimed more than that.

On 27 July 1949 the British Foreign Office had confirmed, in a comment on the controversy, that during a conversation of 14 April 'the British spokesman intimated to the representatives of the SPD to what kind of constitution the Allies could, in the British view, at the very outside give their consent. This advice was based on what the British representatives themselves knew of the Washington decisions'.

Thus the second Allied Note of 22 April 1949 still supplied headlines after the event. The contents and tenor of the controversy may be gathered from such headlines as 'What really happened in Bonn and Hanover', 'Dr Adenauer's revelations', 'Cold shower for the SPD', 'Who is the liar now?', 'New SPD telegram to Adenauer', and 'The end of a lie'.

The following incident of which I was told by a high Catholic dignitary in February 1954 is of great interest in this context: a few months before the Federal elections of 1949 he had been invited by General Robertson to the house of Governor Lingham in Hanover, where he met a high Protestant dignitary and Dr Schumacher. In the course of the conversation Robertson said that Schumacher would soon have to form a cabinet and it was very desirable that he should have the cooperation of the churches rather than their obstruction. The Protestant dignitary declared that he was quite prepared for cooperation. He only wished that some subordinate organs of the SPD would not make difficulties for the churches. The Catholic dignitary said he was not ready to cooperate. What mattered was not whether subordinate organs of the SPD caused difficulties for the churches. Those could be surmounted. What mattered was that he found the principles of the Social Democrats incompatible with his conscience. Robertson tried very hard to persuade him, but he could not change his point of view. Schumacher sat through all this with an immobile face and said nothing.

We had to destroy yet another halo the SPD tried to wear. In its election manifesto the SPD had tried to explain that alone and unaided by other parties it had succeeded in refusing to merge with the Russian-directed communists. The party claimed that it was still carrying the burden of the fight for Berlin and even today the burden of resistance in the Eastern zone. Against this we had to point out that in the Soviet zone and in Berlin the SPD had assumed a historic guilt by breaking up the uniform resistance of the German parties in that zone against communism and against the Russians. We pointed out that at the foundation of the SED twelve members of the leading body of the Social Democrats, which numbered fourteen, went over to the SED. Of the SED Ministers President of the Russian zone five were former Social Democrats. On the other hand we were able to point to the example given by Jakob Kaiser and Ferdinand Friedensburg who had stayed on in the Berlin Town Hall when the fight of the Russians and the Eastern police against the town hall was raging.

We had to oppose the systematic attempts of the SPD to present history as though there had only been one patrotic party in Germany, the SPD, both in the struggle for the Basic Law and in the fight for the Soviet-occupied zone.

The election campaign had produced clear fronts. The CDU/CSU championed the freedom and welfare of the individual. On this foundation we announced measures to relieve distress, first of all in housing, measures for expellees and returned prisoners. We announced a taxation policy to benefit people with middle incomes, and invalids, and a plan for the reduction of unemployment – measures that could only be carried out on the basis of the social market economy.

On the other side there was the SPD with its principles of the all-powerful state, the planned economy, nationalization and the fight against the parents' rights to decide the education of their children, principles opposed to our view of marriage and the family.

On 14 August the German people was to decide whether it wanted to be ruled in accordance with obsolete socialist principles or whether it preferred to entrust its destiny to a new party that championed the freedom of the individual against the dominance of mere numbers or class, which had set itself the task of securing for our country its appropriate place in a Christian Europe and of making its contribution to the building of an effective dam against the flood of Bolshevist Marxism.

12

THE ESTABLISHMENT OF THE FEDERAL REPUBLIC

The Conference at Rhöndorf on 21 August 1949

The CDU/CSU emerged as the strongest party from the first German federal elections of 14 August 1949. It polled 7·36 million votes against the SPD's 6·93 million. This lead was not great, but the very fact that we had emerged as the strongest party from the election campaign filled us with satisfaction and hopes for the future. The Social Democrats had entered the campaign with a large and experienced organization and full of confidence, and we had defeated them. We felt ourselves equal to the task that lay before us, that of assuming leadership in the government. We were a young party, a people's party counting members of all strata of the population among its voters, a party which, standing on the foundations of Christian principles, included members of both Christian denominations.

Ten parties in all were represented in the Bundestag. The distribution of the 402 seats was as follows:

> 139 CDU/CSU (plus 2 members from Berlin)
> 131 SPD   (plus 5 members from Berlin)
> 52 FDP   (plus 1 member from Berlin)
> 17 DP (Germany Party)
> 17 Bavarian Party
> 15 KDP
> 12 WAV (Association for Economic Reconstruction)
> 10 Centre Party
>   5 Representatives of the National Right
>   1 Slesvig League
>   3 Independents

The eight members from Berlin had no vote.

The CDU/CSU now considered with which party it would form the government. Was it to be a grand coalition with the SPD or a so-called little coalition with the FDP and another party? I knew that many members of the CDU/CSU regarded a coalition with the SPD as the best solution. It was also evident that the occupying powers, notably the British, would welcome this solution. However, they refrained from all interference. The SPD had intimated after the election that it would be prepared to work with the CDU/CSU on condition that it got the Ministry of Economic Affairs in the first cabinet.

The election campaign had largely been fought on economic issues, especially that of whether there was to be a planned economy on Social Democratic principles or the social market economy. If the SPD got the Ministry of Economic Affairs it would have been tantamount to the surrender of one of the essential points in the CDU/CSU programme. In my opinion the voters who had opted for the CDU/CSU would feel betrayed, and that might in turn have dealt an annihilating blow to our young party.

We still had no uniform party organization in the three zones and therefore had no party institution entitled to make pronouncements that were binding for all three zones. In these circumstances I thought it best not to wait for the formation of the parliamentary group of the CDU/CSU before discussing the question of a grand or little coalition, but to collect a suitable group for such a discussion even beforehand. If there was overall agreement, we would communicate this to the public, while not prejudging any decision the parliamentary group of the party might make.

As chairman of the CDU in the British zone and chairman of the strongest party committee I therefore invited a number of leading members of the entire CDU and of the CSU, with which we had close relations, to a discussion of this question on 21 August 1949 at my house at Rhöndorf. I chose this meeting place as affording maximum privacy.

The group that assembled on Sunday, 21 August 1949 included members of the Frankfurt Economic Council and the Economic Administration because the work done at Frankfurt had played a not insignificant role in the election campaign and because the SPD in its post-election statements had stressed the decisive importance of their demand that the Ministry of Economic Affairs must have a Social Democrat as its head if the Social Democrats were to join a grand coalition. There were also some representatives of the former Parliamentary Council whom I had invited because they had helped to formulate the Basic Law and were therefore best qualified to judge matters connected with the outcome of the election. I also asked representatives of the CDU and CSU in different *Länder* of the Trizone to give us as complete a picture as possible of the opinions prevailing in all zones. I regarded this meeting as very decisive for the future of Germany.

As host I spoke first and declared that I would consider a coalition with the SPD a mistake. I said that I knew that quite a number of those present did not share this opinion. I explained that the election results showed quite unambiguously that the overwhelming majority of the German people did not want to have anything to do with socialism of any shade. The elections had produced an impressive affirmation of the basic ideas of the Christian and democratic view of the state and society.

The election campaign had been fought primarily on ideological questions but there was no doubt that economic questions had also played a decisive role. I realized, I said, that since the electorate had voted as it had, the policy of the Frankfurt Economic Council simply must be continued. In the votes polled by the Social Democrats and the Communists about eight million voters had expressed themselves in favour of a socialist economy, while thirteen million (adding the votes of the FDP and of other non-socialist parties to those of the CDU and CSU) chose the social market economy. One had to respect the clear will of the electorate; any other course of action would be undemocratic. I was convinced that even these general considerations forced us to draw the necessary conclusions from the election. I was sure that in the economic field, which for a long time to come would remain of the greatest importance, any collaboration with the Social Democrats was impossible, as activities in the Economic Council had shown. The logical consequence of the election was that we would have to follow in the composition of the government the road we had taken in Frankfurt.

The CDU/CSU, I continued, had not achieved an overall majority. We were the strongest party group, but would have to form a coalition with one or more parties in order to get a working majority. As I saw it the FDP, with whom we had already collaborated in the Economic Council, and the German Party were eligible as coalition partners.

I realized that our future government would require social policies. We knew the chairman of the FDP, Blücher, to be a man with a very open mind on social questions. I knew that on the other hand there were groups that, to put it mildly, had strong tendencies in the direction of aggressive enterprise. But I was convinced that our views would prevail on the most important questions of social policy.

Apart from the question of economic policy there was another reason for rejecting the idea of a coalition with the SPD. If the CDU and SPD were to form the government after these first elections of the year 1949, there would not be a forceful opposition in parliament. I was afraid of the development of an extra-parliamentary opposition on a nationalist basis, with nationalist demagogues endangering the young state. I did not consider that we ran the risk of a nationalist opposition in the case of the SPD.

The effects abroad of an extreme or nationalist opposition would be very harmful. Only four years had passed since the end of the war and the nations were still very mistrustful of us. Our economic situation was not such as to deprive radical tendencies of fertile soil, especially if nationalist tendencies were added. It was therefore important in my view that the SPD should have the role of the opposition.

I admitted that there might be times of emergency in the life of a people, especially in war, when everything had to be subordinated to one aim, when all differences of party were relatively insignificant, and when a cabinet representing all parties was the right solution. But I did not think that we had this kind of emergency in Germany. The German situation was difficult and the coming months and years would bring us very big problems indeed. This state of affairs would go on for a long time, but was not desperate.

I told my listeners that I thought that we had not applied the basic principles of democratic parliamentarianism correctly in Germany between 1918 and 1933. It had been our constant aim then just to form coalitions. Less attention had been paid to the question of whether these coalitions were strong enough to do fruitful work. If a coalition was made up of elements that diametrically disagreed in the most important respects, and especially if these elements were about equally strong, there was a danger that such a coalition government would be paralysed and remain sterile. The Germans would have to get used to the strongest party assuming the leadership and the other great party opposing – opposing in a responsible way that was compatible with the interests of the country as a whole. If then the leading party was unsuccessful, the electorate could present the bill at the next election. If the opposition party opposed well, it had the chance to gain power at the next election. That was the nature of parliamentary democracy.

I spoke as persuasively as possible to those assembled. When I had finished the applause was none too strong. Most of those present maintained a cautious silence.

Minister President Altmeier of the Rhineland-Palatinate spoke next and spoke in favour of a coalition with the SPD. He argued that we had to tie the SPD to our government as with a rope, for if we did not, we had to expect a strong opposition that would use nationalist arguments to attack every attempt at an understanding with the occupying powers. He thought that whenever we got concessions, even big concessions from the Allies, the SPD would always declare that we had achieved too little and the Social Democrats would have done better. Since in view of the conditions in which the Germans had to live at present it could be predicted that there would be much discontent for a long time to come, he was afraid that the SPD would have much success with this method. We, on the other hand, would find it hard to defend ourselves against their charges and it was therefore to be feared that by the end of the first legislature the SPD would have made such gains that it would emerge victorious from the second federal election. Altmeier's speech was received with strong applause.

There then ensued a passionate debate on the pros and cons of the basic arguments advanced by Altmeier on the one side and by myself on the other. In the course of this debate I tried to convince those present that if we stuck to our line and carried out our party platform step by step, we would certainly succeed and our success would be such as to make all criticism on the part of the SPD appear as mean and petty-minded grumbling. I said:

It is my opinion, in contrast to the gentlemen who advocate a coalition with the SPD, that at the end of our four-year term of office we shall be in a stronger position than before and that we shall have still less to fear from the opposition than we have today. The voters have decided for the principles of the CDU and we are committed to their decision.

I persistently returned to these arguments in the course of the debate and had the impression that the other side was gradually losing heart. But there was still a small group that tenaciously advocated collaboration with the SPD. Even to reduce the opposition to this had taken at least four hours. We needed some refreshments and I judged the moment right for a short break.

The atmosphere seemed to be getting less tense. During the eating interval I engaged some of the toughest fighters for a coalition with the SPD in further conversations. After an hour's break I could risk starting the discussion of the question of the grand or the little coalition once more.

Again I spoke first and immediately went to the heart of the matter. I spoke as though an agreement on a coalition with the FDP and the German Party was a *fait accompli*. Such a coalition gave us 208 seats; 139 belonged to the CDU/CSU, 52 to the FDP, and 17 to the DP. We thus had a solid majority to govern with.

I next broached the question of the distribution of the offices of Federal President and Federal Chancellor. I was surprised when someone interrupted me and proposed me as Federal Chancellor. I had a look at their faces and said: 'If all those present agree, I accept. I have talked to Professor Martini, my doctor, and asked him if at my age I could accept this office at least for a year. He has no objections. He even thinks I can carry on for two years.' There was no protest. That settled the matter.

Next came the question of who was to be Federal President. Being our strongest partner in the coalition, the FDP should supply the President, and I proposed Professor Heuss. Someone asked if Professor Heuss knew about this. I had to admit that unfortunately I had not yet had a chance to talk to him. He told me later that the first he knew about it was from the press. Someone objected that it was well known that Professor Heuss's attitude to the church was not exactly friendly. I told this gentleman: 'His wife is a good Christian. That is enough.'

Seeing how readily the group had already entered into discussions of the staffing of offices, I had the impression that my views had carried the day against those of Herr Altmeier. Summing up I once more took the opportunity to explain my attitude to the question of coalition and said:

There is a great difference between ourselves and the Social Democrats regarding the principles of Christian conviction. Moreover there is an unbridgeable gap between ourselves and the Social Democrats in the matter of economic structure. There can only be either a planned economy or a social market economy. The two will not mix. In view of these differences it would not even be possible to have a Christian Democrat as Minister of Economics and a Social Democrat as Under-Secretary of State. We could never get things moving. We have got to steer a steady course. Only then can there be a good parliamentary opposition.

There were hardly any objectors left and it was now only a question of composing a final communiqué to inform the public of our decision. A great number of journalists had waited patiently and probably tensely for the outcome of this conference at the foot of the hill by the path to my house. We agreed on the following press release:

> The conference of CDU/CSU politicians at the house of Dr Adenauer at Rhöndorf came to the conclusion on Sunday afternoon that the elections have resulted not only in an impressive affirmation of the basic tenets of the Christian Democratic view of society, but also an unambiguous endorsement of the social market economy as opposed to a socialist planned economy. There is therefore an obligation to continue this general policy and to draw clear conclusions from it for the formation of the federal government.

I was very satisfied with the result of this hot summer day. The CDU/CSU was ready to accept full responsibility for the political developments of the next four years.

The members of the CDU and CSU who had met at Rhöndorf were not an official party committee. Unlike the SPD and the FDP, the CDU/CSU of the three Western zones had not yet constituted itself as one party at that time. This meant that the Rhöndorf decision could not yet be regarded as absolutely binding, a fact we had to take into consideration in the wording of the communiqué, which therefore had to sound rather less specific than I would have liked.

A group of CDU/CSU politicians who favoured the grand coalition with the SPD had formed round Karl Arnold, the Minister President of North Rhine-Westphalia. The Rhöndorf communiqué was bound to come as a great surprise to the members of that faction who had not been present at the meeting and only learned its result from the press. This created a situation that made it necessary for me to repeat and explain the Rhöndorf decisions quite clearly at a press conference. This took place on 23 August 1949 in the building of the Bundestag in Bonn. On the same day the CDU group in the *Landtag* of North Rhine-Westphalia passed a resolution to the effect that the outcome of the elections put the CDU under an obligation to carry out its mandate and there was a unanimous expression of confidence in me. The Rhöndorf decision had thus been approved by the strongest CDU group of all the *Länder*.

After the Rhöndorf conference a legend had sprung up that 'an emissary of the Vatican' had been present. I used the press conference of 23 August 1949 to shed some light on this affair. Let me quote from the minutes:

> I saw a very interesting piece of information in today's *Rheinecho* to the

effect that 'quite accidentally the Papal Counsel-General Gündel turned up in the house where the conference was taking place in order, as he later explained, to ask Dr Pünder a number of questions. He left the conference less than half an hour later. To judge from the expression on his face he was very satisfied. We do not know what he learnt there'. I should like to comment as follows: I never saw nor do I know this gentleman. My family told me that he was not wearing any socks. I could hardly imagine that a representative of the Vatican would turn up without socks. Further investigations produced the following facts: this gentleman is a member of the General Council of the Steyl Fathers who have monasteries in Holland and in Western Germany. He has no connections with the Vatican – I am very sorry, but that is how it is. This cleared up the matter of the socks to my satisfaction. The gentleman merely wanted to see Dr Pünder. In any case I want to state quite explicitly that so far the Vatican has not been bothered in any way with the question of creating a federal cabinet.

The Federal Republic

The Federal Parliament first had to elect a Speaker. On 7 September 1949 the former chairman of the Frankfurt Economic Council, the CDU deputy Dr Erich Köhler, was elected the first Speaker of the Bundestag. He had done well as chairman of the Economic Council. My opinion that Professor Heuss was the right person for the office of Federal President found general acceptance and on 12 September he was elected by the votes of the CDU/CSU, the FDP, and the DP.

The election of the Federal Chancellor was scheduled for 15 September 1949. I was elected in the first vote, by an absolute majority of all members of the Bundestag, a majority of one. When I was later asked whether I had voted for myself I replied: 'Naturally – anything else would have been hypocrisy.'

My election as Federal Chancellor and the formation of a coalition composed of the CDU/CSU, FDP, and DP groups, were the logical outcome of the political state of affairs. I did not think that the interests of the entire population, the interests of Germany, would have been better served by a coalition between the CDU/CSU and the Social Democrats. I was and still am of the opinion that the opposition is a necessity of state, that it has a political task to perform in the state, and that real progress and the habit of democratic thinking can only be achieved if a government majority and an opposition face each other. I was further of the opinion that in view of the unsettled state of affairs prevailing in Germany, it was far better for the opposition – which, of course, always exists – to show itself clearly in parliament.

The representatives of the parties concerned concurred in the upshot of the Rhöndorf conference and agreed with the arguments in favour of the coalition of CDU/CSU, FDP, and DP.

The Bundestag and Bundesrat had constituted themselves on 7 September 1949. The Bundesrat Speaker was chosen on the same day, the Federal President on 12 September, the Federal Chancellor on the 15th. The cabinet was formed on 20 September and the following federal ministers were nominated:

Herr Franz Blücher as Federal Minister for the Marshall Plan
Dr Gustav Heinemann as Minister of the Interior
Dr Thomas Dehler as Minister of Justice
Herr Fritz Schäffer as Minister of Finance
Professor Ludwig Erhard as Minister of Economic Affairs
Herr Wilhelm Niklas as Minister of Food and Agriculture
Herr Anton Storch as Minister of Labour
Dr Hans Christoph Seebohm as Minister of Transport
Herr Hans Schuberth as Minister of Postal Affairs
Herr Eberhard Wildermuth as Minister of Housing
Dr Hans Lukaschek as Minister for Refugee Affairs
Herr Jakob Kaiser as Minister for All-German Affairs
Herr Heinrich Hellwege as Minister for Bundesrat Affairs

The Federal Government was now established and the Occupation Statute entered into force on the same day. It was the beginning of a new epoch in post-war history.

During the four years after the catastrophe of 1945, legislative and executive power had largely been in the hands of the occupying powers. It was only step by step that executive and legislative functions were redelegated to German authorities at various levels and with a limited power to make decisions.

With the establishment of the constituent organs of the Federal Republic of Germany a large portion of responsibility and authority to make decisions now passed into our hands. Admittedly we were still not completely free, because the Occupation Statute contained significant restrictions. We had to do our part to create conditions that would enable the Allied powers to apply the Statute with generosity and restraint. It was the only way for the German people to regain full freedom. It was my hope that the Allied powers would help, by appropriate use of the revision clause of the Occupation Statute, to accelerate the further political development of our country.

The Cabinet Introduced to the High Commissioners; The Occupation Statute Comes into Force

The High Commissioners had let me know through Blankenhorn that they intended to present the Occupation Statute in a solemn ceremony. I might introduce the cabinet on the same occasion.

I did not like this plan. An Occupation Statute remains a disagreeable thing for a conquered nation and its presentation is no cause for celebrations.

Through Blankenhorn I requested the High Commissioners to see the matter from my point of view and to desist from such a ceremony. The High Commissioners thereupon decided merely to announce the entry into force of the Occupation Statute by an address of their chairman. The act was, however, to be endowed with a ceremonial character by the High Commissioners' receiving me standing on a carpet, while I stood in front of it. Their chairman was to make a speech and proclaim the entry into force of the Occupation Statute. Then I was to step on the carpet. I declared myself agreeable.

On the appointed day, 21 September 1949, I went up to the Petersberg in the company of a few Federal Ministers – I had not taken the whole cabinet with me. We were led into a room where we were received by the three High Commissioners standing on a carpet. François-Poncet was chairman that day. While I stopped in front of the carpet he took one step forward to greet me. I saw my opportunity, went towards him and thus stood on the carpet as well. None of the High Commissioners objected. François-Poncet gave his address.

After introducing the members of my cabinet I made a speech in which I told the High Commissioners that it was the clear desire of the Federal Government first and foremost to tackle the great social problems. I was convinced that a healthy polity could develop only when each individual was assured a minimum of economic opportunity to earn a livelihood. Not until we succeeded in providing adequate housing and appropriate opportunities for work would we be able to enjoy inner stability in Germany.

Disorder and crises in this part of Europe would, however, constitute a serious threat to the security of the entire continent. For this reason the social programme of the Federal Government should at the same time help to ensure a peaceful development in Europe. We would, of course, do everything in our power to master these problems with the forces at our own command. I felt, however, that the problem of expellees was not only a national, but an international one, and needed the help of the world to solve it.

If we wanted to establish peace in Europe, we could, in the view of the Federal Government, achieve this only by working along entirely new lines. I saw such an opportunity in the efforts for a European federation which had just borne its first fruits at Strasbourg. I believed, though, that such a federation would have vitality only if it was built on close economic cooperation among the nations. The organization created by the Marshall Plan represented a good start in this direction. Germany was fully ready to cooperate responsibly.

I saw another opening for creating a positive and viable European federation in the hope that the control of the Ruhr would cease to be a unilateral arrangement and that it would gradually grow into an organism which would embrace the basic industries of other European countries as well. I was certain that the narrow nationalistic conception of the states that prevailed in the nineteenth and early twentieth centuries must now be regarded as obsolete.

This conception had given birth to nationalism with its attendant fragmentation of life in Europe. If we now returned to the sources of our European civilization, born of Christianity, we could not fail to succeed in restoring the unity of Europe in all fields of endeavour. This was the sole effective guarantee for the preservation of peace.

Champagne was served and I soon took my leave. As Blankenhorn, who was accompanying me, and I put our coats on in the cloakroom, an official of the High Commission stepped up to Blankenhorn and gave him a book wrapped in packing paper.

When we were seated in the car I asked Blankenhorn to have a look to see what he had been handed. He took from the parcel an Occupation Statute that was bound in parchment and set in beautiful type. But it was unsigned.

This document had a strange fate. When I asked the Foreign Ministry for it in 1962 it turned out that Herr Blankenhorn still had it. I asked for it to be put in the files and this was done.

The Occupation Statute

The Occupation Statute represented a big step forward compared with our previous state. Of course everything depended on the spirit in which it was applied and whether it was the spirit expressed in the covering Note of the Foreign Ministers of Britain, France, and the United States of April 1949 when they wrote to the President of the Parliamentary Council: 'that a major objective of the three Allied governments is to encourage and facilitate the closest integration, on a mutually beneficial basis, of the German people under a democratic federal state within the framework of a European association.'

I was convinced that, if the Occupation Statute was applied in this spirit, it would facilitate a vigorous life of our own and further progress. The Statute was to be reviewed after twelve months or at the latest after eighteen months in the light of experiences gathered by the High Commissioners in its implementation. I was convinced that they would then conclude that it was possible to extend still further the German authorities' scope in the legislative, executive, and juridical fields.

The Federal Government therefore had to endeavour to observe the provisions of the Occupation Statute. In so doing it had to be led by the hope that the extension of its powers would come as soon as possible when the Statute was reviewed. It was my conviction that the only way for our country and people to regain their freedom lay in close agreement and cooperation with the High Commissioners.

The Programme of the Government; Parliament Begins its Work

Although the competence of the Bundestag and the Federal Government was still circumscribed by the Occupation Statute, the progress made in comparison with the state of affairs we had known since 1933 filled me with satisfaction. We had, of course, to admit that Germany and the German people were not yet free, that we did not enjoy equal rights with other nations, that we were, and this was especially painful, torn in two – and yet we enjoyed at least a relative measure of political freedom. Our economy was recovering slowly. The protection of the individual had once more become a valid principle. No one among us could be deprived of liberty and life by a secret state police or similar institution as had been the case in the National Socialist Reich and was still the case in large parts of Germany. These gains – the protection of the law, the protection of personal freedom so long denied us – were so precious that despite everything we still lacked we must rejoice in what had been achieved.

I had proposed the appointment of thirteen federal ministers to the Federal President. I realized that many must consider this number too large and these critics included the budgetary authorities. I had to fight for this number of ministers. To be sure we were still at the beginning of the reconstruction process, but the tasks confronting us were exceptionally great. They called for dedicated, creative, and forceful people in parliament and in the government. There was a large number of new tasks requiring the attention of government departments and of parliament, among them the question of expellees. Tasks which had existed before had now assumed such proportions that the traditionally established ministries could not cope with them. This was true of housing and building.

Several of the newly created ministries would be only temporary. When they had fulfilled their tasks or when their tasks had once more been reduced to normal proportions, they would disappear again.

There was one ministry among these thirteen that had the special task of looking after close relations with the Bundesrat. I wanted this ministry to show that we had the earnest desire to guarantee the federal character of the Basic Law, to safeguard the rights of the *Länder*, and to so harmonize the work of the Bundesrat with that of the Bundestag and the Federal Government that close cooperation was guaranteed.

There was one ministry lacking among the thirteen: a ministry of foreign affairs. I had not acceded to the request to establish a ministry for international relations. I had refrained from establishing such a ministry because under the terms of the Occupation Statute foreign affairs, including international agreements concluded by Germany or on her behalf, were the province of the Allied High Commission for the three zones.

But the fact that we had as yet no ministry of foreign affairs did not mean that we renounced all activity in this field. It was the paradox of our situation that although Germany's foreign affairs were being looked after by the Allied High Commission, every activity of the Federal Government or the Federal Parliament, even in domestic affairs, was in some way or other bound to involve foreign relations. As a result of the occupation, the Ruhr Statute, the

Marshall Plan and so forth, Germany was more closely connected with foreign countries than ever before. All these affairs were to be combined in a State Secretariat to be established in the office of the Federal Chancellor. Quite apart from this I believed that, as a consequence of the great responsibility resting upon them, the High Commissioners would not make any important decisions in foreign affairs without first communicating with the Federal Government.

The work awaiting the Federal Government and parliament was unimaginable. In the fields in which the federal authorities were now competent they had to examine the laws already passed in the eleven *Länder* in order to see whether they agreed and were equivalent. Laws and decrees that had hitherto only been valid in the Bizone had to be extended to the French zone. Laws and decrees issued by the various Military Governments in fields for which federal authorities now had competence had to be reviewed and where necessary had to be adapted to the new conditions with the consent of the High Commission. Laws had to be passed that the Basic Law provided for. Laws which the Frankfurt Economic Council had been unable to finish had to be completed and passed. All this work, whose volume was all the greater because the time factor had sometimes led to some lack of precision, could not be done too fast because we wanted at last to return to something we had lost during the National Socialist epoch and after: clarity, security, and unity of the law.

The coalition negotiations had shown quite clearly that there was agreement among the coalition parties on the need for all their work to be guided by a determination to act in accordance with a true social conscience. The guiding light of all our work was to be the endeavour to alleviate distress and to bring about social justice.

It is impossible to give even an approximate account of all the tasks awaiting the Federal Government. But I should like to give a brief outline of some of the most important among those I mentioned before.

The refugees and expellees had to be distributed more evenly over the *Länder* of the Federal Republic. This was in the interest both of the overcrowded *Länder* and the refugees themselves. The fate of those who had been expelled from their homes was especially hard. The question of their future was one that Germany could not solve by herself. It was a question which required an international approach, but a solution had to be found if Western Germany was not to become a centre of political and economic unrest for a long time to come.

The housing situation, which not only put insurmountable obstacles in the way of the social and ethical recovery of the German people but also made the life of the expelled and the bombed-out intolerably hard, had to be improved with all the means at our disposal. We had to do everything to promote building in the most energetic way, by making federal funds available and by urging the *Länder* to exhaust all possibilities of getting houses built. I was

187

determined to go over to a policy of cautiously and deliberately relaxing planning regulations and the fixing of rents to get private capital once more interested in the construction of residential housing. I was convinced that the energetic promotion of building activity would revitalize the labour market.

With respect to economic policy the Federal Government was determined to continue in the direction taken in Frankfurt with such success. In applying the principle of the social market economy we had, of course, to guard against rigid dogmatism and to adapt to changing conditions. State controls were to be abolished wherever this could be done without undue risk. What I had in mind was to use the means of competition and the increasing integration of the German into the world economy to provide a systematic corrective against the structural defects of the German economy, the result of many years of state controls and war economy.

In the past the German economy had become strong not least by the application of science. As far as its financial resources would permit, the Federal Government would sponsor scientific research and would urge business to do likewise. Only by outstanding achievements could we hold our own in the world's markets.

The question of the dismantling of our industrial installations was one of the greatest importance for our people. There was hardly anyone in Germany who would object to the dismantling of genuine war industries. But the wholesale destruction of great economic assets was a matter which should not be dismissed abroad as having been decided once and for all. There was a psychological aspect of great significance in this matter of dismantling. The majority of Germans simply could not understand how they could be given economic help with one hand, while the other destroyed economic assets. Also the people thought that such action was incompatible with the repeated statements of foreign statesmen that Germany was needed for the reconstruction of Europe.

The Federal Government also thought it necessary to pay special attention to helping and consolidating the middle class.

The tasks of the ministry for food and agriculture were to have a new character. Agricultural production was to be increased quantitatively and qualitatively to a greater degree than had been possible hitherto. We still had to import fifty per cent of our food requirements. If the German economy was to achieve a satisfactory trade balance by 1952, it was necessary to increase agricultural production considerably in order to reduce the expenditure of foreign currency on food imports as much as possible.

The accumulation of capital must be our foremost goal and this applied to savings as well as to investment. Only if we did everything in our power to increase the accumulation of capital in Germany could we expect that foreign capital would be made available for the reconstruction of our economy. This reconstruction was the vital basis of any foreign policy and for the integration of the refugees and expellees in the life of the country. Only a flourishing economy could in the long run sustain the stress of the equalization of burdens.*

I wanted to pass the final legislation for the equalization of burdens as soon as possible in order to do away with the uncertainty that afflicted both those who were to receive help and those who were to be called upon to provide it. The most lowly sufferers would have to be treated with special solicitude.

The dangers of deflation were as great as those of inflation. The state of our economy at that time demanded an active development policy to advance funds for undertakings that could rely on future financing from domestic or foreign sources.

The Federal Government had a very special concern for Berlin. Since the currency reform and up to September 1949, that is during approximately fifteen months, the budget of the combined economic area of the British and American zones had channelled DM 414 million to the city government of Berlin. In addition Berlin had received DM 688 million from GARIOA† funds by 13 September 1949. I was determined to continue with this help.

The coalition partners who formed the Government saw their noblest duty in being guided by a social conscience in all their actions. This applied particularly in the narrower field of social policy. The Federal Government would endeavour to develop its social policy in tune with the changing conditions of the time. Although a healthy economic policy that gave work and bread to the largest number was the best social policy, after this war and this distress in Germany there would always be a large percentage of people in need of special help. Among these were war invalids who could not earn their livelihood and the dependants of the war dead. They should have a guarantee of adequate means to live on. Uniform legislation for assistance had to be drawn up from the entire federal area.

While the Federal Government would be resolved to let bygones be bygones wherever this was a defensible view, for many had already atoned enough for guilt, the government was on the other hand quite determined to act upon the lessons learnt from the past in its dealings with all those who endangered the existence of our state, whether they belonged to the radicals of the Right or the radicals of the Left.

The most important task facing the Federal Government, however, was to do everything to undo the division of our fatherland. In the Soviet zone the German population had no free will of its own. What was done there did not have the support of a free population and thus had no legitimacy. The Federal Republic, on the other hand, was based on the freely expressed will

---

* The 'equalization of burdens' (*Lastenausgleich*) was intended to adjust the economic and social inequalities that had arisen out of the Second World War by spreading monetary and other social obligations according to the individual citizen's ability to meet them.

† GARIOA – Government Appropriation and Relief for Imports in Occupied Areas. Imports put at the disposal of the population by the occupying powers for the prevention of famine, disease, and unrest.

of about 23 million Germans who were entitled to vote. The Federal Republic was therefore the only legitimate political organization of the German people until German unity was achieved. From this there followed far-reaching consequences in domestic and foreign policy. The Federal Republic also felt and still feels a responsibility for the fate of the 18 million Germans who live in the Soviet zone. The Federal Republic alone was and is entitled to speak for the German people. It did not and does not recognize statements by the Soviet zone government as binding for the German people.

The position of Berlin became especially critical as a result of developments in the Soviet zone. Berlin stands out in that zone as outpost and bulwark of the democracies of Western Europe. Thanks to the admirable strength and tenacity of its inhabitants and thanks to the help given by the Western Allies, Berlin had survived the blockade.

Article 23 of the Basic Law stated that Greater Berlin was to belong to the Federal Republic as a twelfth *Land*. At the time of the adoption of the Basic Law the international situation was such as to render the implementation of this clause impossible, and continuing international tensions still stand in the way of carrying out Article 23; but the decision of the Parliamentary Council as embodied in that article is only suspended. The article was to enter into force the moment the international situation permitted it. Until then Berlin was to adapt its laws to federal laws in order to bring about the *de facto* connection between Berlin and the Federal Republic that now exists.

For decades mankind had lived in an epoch of political and social unrest. Owing to its rapid and uneven development and its central position in Europe, the German people had become a centre of this unrest. The German Federal Republic was recovering slowly but steadily thanks to the help given by the Western Allies, thanks also to the industry and steadfastness of its inhabitants. All the more did the Federal Government feel the obligation to help the inhabitants of the Soviet zone and of Berlin. It was prepared to fulfil this duty and had and still has as its foremost aim the restoration of unity in peace and freedom.

I was and am convinced that our epoch, which often looks so hopeless, will eventually lead to fruitful new ventures in the field of national and supranational organization, new ways of ordering things that must be based on the principle of equal rights for all. Our foremost aim was to unite Germany on a basis of law and liberty and to lead her into a European system.

There was no doubt in my mind that by our antecedents and our convictions we formed part of the world of Western Europe. We desired good relations with all countries, but especially with the countries of Western Europe, the Benelux countries, France, Italy, and Great Britain. The hostility between Germany and France which dominated centuries of European politics and led to so many wars, destructions, and bloodlettings must be finally removed from the earth.

I wanted the Federal Republic to be accepted into the European Union as soon as possible. We would be willing and happy collaborators in the great task of uniting Europe. Article 24 of the Basic Law provided for the possibility of transferring sovereign powers to international institutions and of joining a system of mutual collective security for the maintenance of peace. The article says: 'In so doing [the Federation] will consent to limitations upon its sovereign powers apt to bring about and secure a peaceful and lasting order in Europe and among the nations of the world.'

The Federal Government was determined to do everything in its power to walk along the path shown in this article to the maintenance of peace in Europe and the world. All our work would be animated by the spirit of the civilization of Western Christianity and by respect of the rights and dignity of the individual. I hoped that with God's help it would be possible to unite the German people and to contribute to peace in Europe and in the world.

13

THE BEGINNINGS OF FOREIGN POLICY

German Foreign Policy

Soviet power grew greatly during the war and during the first post-war years. Russia brought the countries of Eastern Europe under communist rule by revolutions directed from Moscow. It conquered the eastern parts of Germany. With a correctness dangerous to itself the United States Government handed over parts of central Germany conquered by American troops to the Soviets. Soviet Russia stood in the middle of Germany, on the Elbe. The European balance of power was destroyed; therefore Western Europe, including the part of Germany not handed over to the Soviets, was in constant serious peril. Nor could the United States be indifferent to such a shift of power in Europe.

It took the three Western powers some time fully to appraise this danger. Churchill was the first to see that Western Europe including Germany had to be understood as a single power factor posed against the Soviet Union which continued to have further Western aspirations, and that a dismemberment of Germany, such as France was seeking, was wrong.

The United States became only gradually aware that disorder and misery in Western and Eastern Europe and the considerable increase in Russian power constituted a potential danger to itself. Marshall then made his famous proposal of providing means, on a large scale, for the economic reconstruction of Western Europe including Germany and of Eastern Europe including the Soviet Union. Russia rejected the proposal and forced her satellites to do the same. The countries of Western Europe accepted it. France too agreed, although French policy during the first years after the war had not always been close to that of the United States and Great Britain but had been solely dictated by the fear of a resurgent Germany and aimed at nothing but a permanent weakening of Germany.

The dismantling plan, which primarily affected the British zone, was a reminder of the fear and hatred of Germany during the first post-war years. It was an anachronism in the new era. The British zone contained the industrial area of the Rhineland and Westphalia, with its mines, iron foundries, steel plants, and its big chemical factories. If these had been dismantled as planned any economic and political recovery of Germany and Western Europe would have been impossible. Since the industries of Western Europe were inter-connected, the dismantling of the Rhenish-Westphalian industrial area would have made the realization of the Marshall Plan impossible. It was my firm conviction that if the dismantling plan had been carried out, Germany would have gone communist from misery and hopelessness. I considered it the first and paramount aim of the Federal Government to reverse the dismantling plan at any cost.

All the countries that had been at war with Germany had a very strong desire for security. We had to find a way that would on the one hand satisfy this desire for security and on the other permit the reconstruction of Western Europe including Germany. This way would also, I realized, allow us to regain our equality among the free peoples of the world step by step.

In my eyes the various regulations, agreements, and statutes of the first post-war years – the Ruhr Statute, for instance – were transitional arrangements. They were merely stages along our road to the re-establishment of equality. I judged all such agreements primarily by their potential for further development.

Disagreement between Soviet Russia and the free peoples was, I felt, bound to grow. America too had a vital interest in the creation of a strong Western Europe. For this Germany was indispensable. A country in shackles is not a real, full partner. I therefore thought that our fetters would gradually fall away.

As John Foster Dulles once put it: America was not pursuing a German or a French policy in Europe, but an American policy. That was a very true saying. The foreign policy of a country is always inspired by its own real or imagined interests. It was in the interest of the United States that Germany should become strong once more. Therefore the many examples of discrimination, such as the Ruhr Statute, the Occupation Statute and the provisions regarding the rearming of Germany, could only be of a transitory nature. In the long run the German people could not be a perfect partner of the peoples whose interests were parallel to ours unless there was equality. These were the guiding principles of my policy toward the Western powers during all the years when, as Federal Chancellor, I had to determine the guidelines of our policy.

The most important prerequisite for partnership is trust. To make us trusted was the first commandment, as I have repeatedly stressed earlier in this book. The faster and more firmly confidence in us grew, the sooner the goal of partnership would be reached.

I had no doubt about the method for attaining partnership and equality. It was only natural for us Germans (on the one hand) and the Allies (on the other) to see the same set of facts from two different points of view. We had always to remember what had passed among us during the years from 1933 to 1945, we had to remember what disaster the National Socialist Government had brought upon the whole world. We had to remember that years after the end of the war almost all nations of the world, especially the European countries, were still suffering severely from the consequences of that war. We also had to recognize that after the defeat we were without power.

We therefore had to start from the assumption that in all our negotiations with the Allies for greater political power the psychological element would play a very great part. We could neither demand nor expect full confidence at the outset. We had to be fully aware of the fact that confidence could only be regained slowly, step by step, and that we had to be careful to avoid everything that might reawaken mistrust. It would have been undignified and wrong to follow a policy of slavish submissiveness. Yet it would have been stupid, unwise, and futile for us to harp on our indispensability.

We had particularly to guard against speculations that we might profit from disunity among the great powers. The methods of German foreign policy must be absolutely honest and straightforward. We should try to advance slowly, bit by bit, and never to lose patience, one of the strongest factors in politics.

I regarded the nearest Western neighbours' demand for security as of primary psychological importance. This desire for security had deep roots. To some extent one could meet it by rational arguments, but it seemed to me impossible to rely solely on an appeal by and to reason – just as one cannot deal with love or hate by rational argumentation alone. This was a matter, I thought, that required special patience and care; we had to try to meet our neighbours' need for security by gaining their confidence. I hope that this exposition will contribute to an understanding of our policy in those difficult years.

The Dismantlings

I want to return to the question of dismantling. On Friday 30 September 1949, there was a thorough discussion in the Bundestag of Allied dismantling policy in Germany. By the dismantling of large installations such as the Thyssen-Hütte or the Dortmund-Hörder-Hütten-Werk the numbers of unemployed in the Federal Republic were further increased. Moreover such dismantling was in violent contradiction to the reconstruction demanded by the Marshall Plan which proposed to utilize Western Germany's industrial capacity. It really appeared as though the Marshall Plan programme on the one hand, and the industrial plan for Germany on the other with its programme of dismantling, had been drawn up quite independently and in pursuit of diametrically opposed purposes.

In this Bundestag debate I stated that the treatment of the question of dismantling by the Allies was a great disappointment for us all and especially for the Federal Government. I seized the opportunity of the debate to try to draw the attention of the Western Allies to the psychological significance of this question. I said:

I know that the Western Allies sometimes think that we Germans want to make some kind of propaganda when we keep coming back to the question of dismantlings. And then there arises a feeling that one cannot give way to German demands for reasons of prestige. It has rightly been stressed – and I want to underline this – that it is neither a German desire to score a point nor an urge to make propaganda, but rather compelling economic logic and in addition psychological reasons of the utmost importance that occasion these demands. If the German people is to be integrated into the cultural and economic life of Europe, the majority of Germans must be convinced that the three Western powers really want this.

But I think it must be said that it is precisely the unjustified destruction of German assets that causes doubts among large parts of the German population as to whether those who tell us from abroad that they want to lead us back into the European community are really in earnest.

Those among you, ladies and gentlemen, who lived through the days of the Versailles Treaty will bear me out when I say that that treaty, concerning the possibility of whose fulfilment there were the gravest doubts at the very moment of its signing, subsequently proved the best propaganda for unbounded nationalism.

I think we have to prevent the dismantlings becoming a slogan, in later years, such as the signing of the Versailles Treaty became.

I therefore want to address an urgent request to the Western Allies from the platform of this house to regard the question of dismantling primarily from this point of view, not to delay its settlement unduly, but to confront it resolutely. It seems to me that with some good will it should be possible to find a solution that satisfies the Allied demand for reparations without causing these feelings of bitterness among us.

The further course of the debate showed clearly that all parties in the house were agreed that a reduction or better still the complete cessation of dismantling – real war industries excepted, of course – could be asked of the Allies and must be achieved. The dismantlings that had taken place were bound to have increased the number of unemployed and the misery among the population.

The Ruhr Authority

On 29 December 1948 the three Western Allies and the three smaller neighbours, Belgium, Holland, and Luxembourg, issued the Ruhr Statute, a special system of ordering the workings of the Ruhr industry. The Ruhr Authority envisaged by the Statute, a body consisting of representatives of the six powers, was established on 28 April 1949. There was also provision for representatives of the Federal Republic as members of the Ruhr Authority.

There was a clash of opinions between the Government and, above all, the Social Democratic opposition on a question closely connected with the problem of dismantling, namely that of recognizing the Ruhr Authority by sending it a German representative. In practice the function of this Authority amounted to control of the entire German economy because of the overwhelming importance of the industrial area of the Ruhr for all economic life in Germany. I have discussed my own views on the Ruhr Statute elsewhere.*

Undoubtedly the Ruhr Statute meant the control of the German economy. The great question was in what spirit it would be applied. It could represent the beginning of a European federation, and in that case I was gladly prepared to advocate German membership as an advance contribution to such a development. But the Statute could also be applied in a spirit of outright control of the German economy – and this possibility was full of dangers.

In Germany a storm had been let loose against the Ruhr Statute and German membership in the Ruhr Authority primarily by the SPD, but also by leading personalities of the industrial area. Now, after the establishment of the German Federal Republic, the question of sending German representatives to the Ruhr Authority had become acute. The Allies expected us to meet their wish, but to do so meant the recognition of the Ruhr Statute and the Ruhr Authority. It was a difficult situation for the Federal Government.

We discussed the question thoroughly at a meeting of the cabinet on 25 October 1949. I explained that, from the point of view of foreign policy, participation in the Ruhr Statute would have favourable consequences. If we refused to send representatives it would amount to 'obstruction' which in turn would lead to a stiffening of Allied attitudes. I therefore thought that significant considerations of foreign policy made it important for us to assent to membership of the Ruhr Authority. Moreover the Ruhr urgently needed American loans. We would certainly not get these if we took up a negative attitude in the face of Allied wishes.

It was objected that membership would entail great difficulties in domestic policy which would be particularly serious in view of the *Landtag* elections, due in spring 1950, in North Rhine-Westphalia which contained a third of the population of the Federal Republic. Dr Erhard, the Minister of Economic Affairs, pointed out that the Ruhr Authority was an institution independent of the British High Commission. Beside the Ruhr Authority there were other bodies, dominated by the British High Commission, for the control of the coal and steel industries. He thought that if we joined the Ruhr Authority, British control of the economy of the Ruhr would pass to the Authority, and the dominating British influence would be reduced. He therefore favoured German participation.

The overwhelming majority of the cabinet was agreed on the point that any German influence on the policy of the High Commission was hardly possible in the foreseeable future – and the same applied to the Security Board of the Allies – but that German membership of the Ruhr Authority might offer some chance of influencing policies there. Difficulties inside Germany might be circumvented by trying to send a trade union leader as German delegate. It

* See Chapter VIII.

was known that Dr Böckler, the leader of the German Trade Union League, had a positive attitude in this matter and was by no means of one mind with the leadership of the SPD.

I thought it necessary to establish contact in this important question with the strongest opposition party, the SPD, and wanted to explain the point of view of the government to Dr Schumacher and see whether we could not agree on a common line before the Government took any further steps. However, discussions with the SPD did not take place until 4 November 1949.

In my talks with the High Commissioners I had refrained from giving the slightest indication that the Government might be ready to agree to membership of the Ruhr Authority. In all my talks with the High Commissioners I kept demanding a reduction of dismantling, which I always mentioned in connection with the question of reparations. The High Commissioners remained negative and adamant.

The present Ambassador Blankenhorn, who always accompanied me on my visits to the Petersberg, made a note on 30 November 1949 which I shall quote in part:

> At every meeting between Federal Chancellor Adenauer and the High Commissioners, the Chancellor invariably raised the question of dismantling, but met always with an absolutely negative response. During a conference on 27 October 1949 this attitude was so pronounced that the Chancellor made a very energetic statement to the effect that he felt they believed that he was trying to use the fact that a state had been created in the Eastern zone as a means to blackmail. Nothing was further from his mind and he would consider such tactics below the dignity of the High Commissioners and his own. Nor did he want to see the Occupation Statute abolished now, for he was convinced that it was bound to disappear today or tomorrow or the day after. What oppressed and terrified him, though, was the lack of any understanding of the psychological effects of this matter on the German people. He was always afraid that if there was a strong movement to the right one day, the word dismantling would have the same effect in propaganda as the Treaty of Versailles had in its day. He really was deeply shocked by the lack of understanding of the German mind.
>
> The chairman McCloy answered that he should transmit his demands [author's note: he meant the revised dismantling list] to the High Commissioners by 31 October at the latest. The conversation ended on a very cool note.

After this conversation with the High Commissioners I set up a committee of members of the Bundestag parties to examine and endorse an overall proposal on dismantling that had already been prepared by the Ministry of Economic Affairs. This plan proposed the substitution of other works for some that were on the dismantling list. The committee set to work and I got this proposal to the High Commissioners in the evening of 30 October.

It was my intention not to give any indication that we might be willing to send a representative to the Ruhr Authority until it was absolutely clear that Britain and France were going to agree to the economic alleviations for Germany that America had already demanded, that is, not until all three High Commissioners were ready to make concessions on dismantling. I could not risk telling the German public that we were prepared to join the Ruhr Authority until I was sure of correspondingly large concessions from the Allies. The difficulty for France, I must admit, lay in the fact that the French Government would be faced with domestic difficulties if the concessions it made were too great and that at a time when it was in danger of being overthrown.

The Attempt 'To Break Out of the Ring'

There was intense diplomatic activity during the last days of October 1949. Sir Brian Robertson was in London for talks on 27 and 28 October. On 31 October the American High Commissioner likewise went to London for discussions with Bevin.

On this 31 October I was just examining the document on dismantlings which the Bundestag party committee was going to send to the High Commissioners when I got a telephone message that General Robertson wanted to see me that evening and that the matter was very urgent. He had just come from a discussion with the British Foreign Secretary, Bevin, and had some very important things to tell me. Since I assumed that this most probably concerned the dismantling problem, I kept back the Bundestag document for which the High Commissioners had set this day as time limit on 27 October.

I saw General Robertson alone and we had a long discussion. He told me that he now knew Bevin's plans exactly. He knew that Bevin would make no concessions whatsoever regarding a reduction of the dismantling lists. A proposal to strike works off the dismantling list or to make substitutions, as a proposal of the Ministry of Economic Affairs suggested with the approval of the parties in the Bundestag, had not the slightest chance of success. It would be rejected out of hand. He therefore advised me not even to make the proposal. He did say that he saw a possibility of 'breaking through the ring' and this lay in treating dismantling not as an economic problem, nor as a question of reparations, but from the point of view of the security needs of the Western Allies. The Federal Republic must recognize this need by withdrawing its previous refusal to cooperate in the Military Security Board and by sending a member to the Ruhr Authority.

I replied to Robertson that the Federal Government was quite ready for cooperation in the Military Security Board. But I could not state that the Federal Government would send a member to the Ruhr Authority until I had talked with the parties concerned in the Bundestag. Discussion with the parties was indispensable, all the more since the Social Democrats had officially declared a while ago, as General Robertson doubtless knew, that they were opposed to such a step. I could only send the High Commissioners a Note couched in general terms which could be interpreted in the sense desired by General Robertson.

General Robertson thought this would do for the time being. He asked me to maintain absolute discretion about our conversation because the Paris conference of the three Western foreign ministers was due to take place from 9–12 November. As he, Robertson, was due to take over the chairmanship in the council of the High Commission on 1 November, he asked me to address the Note to him.

As a result of this conversation I sent a letter to General Robertson in his capacity as chairman of the High Commissioners on the following day. It ran as follows:

> During the negotiations on dismantling it was stressed that although this question is also related to reparations it is primarily a question of security. The matter of the German war potential was repeatedly raised in this context.
>
> The German Federal Government now declares that it takes account of this desire for security vis-à-vis the Federal Republic as a fact and is prepared to do what it can to meet it.
>
> It is therefore in principle prepared for cooperation in any body serving the purpose of controlling the German war potential. The Federal Government is aware that the productive capacity for steel forms part of the question of security.
>
> The Federal Government proposes the immediate convening of a committee, including German members, for the purpose of examining the question of security and the questions of international economics that are connected with it. It requests that pending the report of this committee dismantlings should not continue or should in any case be slowed down.
>
> The Federal Government expects the work of this committee to lead to a significant improvement in European cooperation.

America was prepared to help Germany in her reconstruction and was surely ready, too, to make concessions to our wishes in the matter of dismantlings, which, after all, were in violent conflict with the help given under the Marshall Plan. England, too, seemed to be prepared for concessions in certain circumstances according to what I had heard from Robertson. To convert France to a new policy toward Germany presented the greatest difficulty. As I saw it, it was now a question of helping the Americans to dispel French mistrust of Germany. It seemed to me that great harm was done by public insinuations against the occupying powers as voiced by the SPD when it said 'that the Western Allies want to perpetuate their position as occupying powers by way of the policy of integration'. As I saw it the SPD's mistrust of the United States was completely unfounded.

The American, British, and French Governments had certainly recognized the necessity of helping Germany in her reconstruction. But that alone was not enough. These governments depended on public opinion in their countries and on the verdict of their voters. I fully recognized the difficulties which the French Government especially had in this respect. There seemed to me to be nothing ambiguous in the American attitude toward us.

I put the greatest hopes in the policy pursued by Secretary of State Acheson to bring about a merger of the economies of the countries of Western Europe. I too had a special interest in the Europeanization of the coal and steel industries.

Fear of Germany had to be taken into account when judging French policy. I used an interview I gave the paper *Die Zeit* on 3 November 1949 for an attempt to break the ice and to explain our attitude to the French and to world opinion. The interview concerned Franco-German relations. I said I was aware:

> that much historical undergrowth is blocking the view for both nations and is making it hard for them to find the way to each other. But in the present state of Europe 'arch-enmities' are an anachronism. I am therefore resolved to make German-French relations a cardinal point of my policy. A Federal Chancellor must simultaneously be a good German and a good European. Because I desire to be both, I must work for Franco-German understanding. Such a policy should not be misinterpreted as being pro-French, let alone anti-British. It is certainly not a question for us of playing one foreign power against the other. Friendship with Britain is just as essential as friendship with France. But friendship with France requires greater efforts because it has so far laboured under inhibitions. It becomes the cardinal point of our policy because it is its sore point . . .

> I think I can say that reconciliation with France is more popular today in Germany than at any moment before 1945. Perhaps it was even more popular immediately after the collapse. Much has happened in the last four and a half years that was apt to create new obstacles, new misunderstandings, but the basic tendency in Germany has remained the same. The younger generation in particular, here as elsewhere, has grasped the need for uniting Europe so clearly that one can only rejoice. It is precisely these young Germans who know that European unification is impossible unless France and Germany understand each other. I am therefore convinced that a constructive policy of the Federal Government toward France can count on a favourable response among the Germans.

On 4 November 1949 I asked the chairman of the Foreign Affairs Committee of the Bundestag, the SPD deputy Professor Carlo Schmid, to come and see me so that I could inform him of the content of my talk with General Robertson and of the Note I had written to Robertson. Professor Schmid took cognizance of the Note and said I surely knew that his party opposed

German membership of the Ruhr Authority. He added that he would try to get the SPD to give such expression to its opposition as might meet my intentions.

On 5 November 1949 I tried to inform the chairmen of the various party groups in the Bundestag of the events of the last few days, but it was a Saturday and all the chairmen had left Bonn.

On Monday 7 November François-Poncet's deputy – François-Poncet himself having already gone to Paris for the Foreign Ministers' Conference – asked Ministerialdirigent Blankenhorn to call on him at noon. He told Blankenhorn that in the view of the French Government my Note to General Robertson of 1 November 1949 was couched in terms that were too general. He asked us to examine whether it would not be possible to be more specific and added that our more concrete proposals must be in his possession by 7 p.m. so that he could instantly forward them to his government.

When Blankenhorn reported this to me, I was just in the middle of a conference with the Minister of Economic Affairs, Erhard, and the Minister of Finance, Schäffer. I knew that during a conversation between Schumacher, Ollenhauer, Schmid and Baade on the one hand and McCloy on the other, the Social Democrats had proposed to McCloy that the August-Thyssen-Hütte combine be made part of a new company and that international groups, consisting of the countries that had been given parts of August-Thyssen-Hütte as reparations, be made stockholders to the value of their reparation allocations. I also knew that the Vereinigte Stahlwerke, which estimated their capital needs for reconstruction to amount to DM 300 million, had drawn up a plan that proposed to raise DM 250 million from abroad and DM 50 million from the cities that housed the principal works of the Vereinigte Stahlwerke. All this was in a document in my possession.

I then wrote the memorandum the French Government had asked for and deliberately left it unsigned. I gave it to Blankenhorn to take to the French High Commission, and hoped in this way to show clearly that my memorandum and its enclosure were merely for information. The text of the memorandum was as follows:

The Franco-German problem is first and foremost a psychological problem. It was this recognition that was in the Federal Government's mind when it declared in its letter to the chairman of the Allied High Commission of 1 November 1949 that it would take into account the desire for security vis-à-vis the German Federal Republic and would be prepared to do what it could to meet it. In order to create the necessary preconditions among the French as well as among the German people for a final and lasting settlement of the Franco-German problem, the Federal Republic is prepared to discuss the following questions with the committee proposed in the letter of 1 November 1949:
1. German adoption of the Ruhr Statute;

2. Close cooperation with the existing security board;
3. Participation of foreign capital in German enterprises;
4. German participation in closer economic association between France, Italy, and the Benelux countries as soon as possible;
5. Termination of the state of war.

In order for the necessary psychological conditions to be created among the German people, too, there must be an announcement of a deceleration of dismantlings already begun and of a renunciation of new dismantlings before the committee starts its discussions . . .

Bonn, 7 November 1949

In the enclosure I elaborated the proposals concerning foreign capital participation in the listed German firms in the conversation between McCloy and the representatives of the SPD and wrote, *inter alia*: 'The security demands of the Allies are to be met by a veto right of the foreign board members.'

In order to make my views on the whole complex of questions headed 'Security Demands of the French' known to the American public and especially to President Truman, I took the opportunity on 7 November 1949 of giving an extensive interview to a representative of the *Baltimore Sun*, an American paper of which, as I knew, President Truman was a regular reader. I said I knew that the French regarded German steel production as war potential. My government held the view that French demands for security in Germany could be met by allowing the French to invest up to forty per cent in German industries, especially the steel industry. According to our plan the United States would provide the means for these French investments. I did not mention the precise amount. I did not object to American capital finding its way to Germany via France or to France participating in German economic enterprises in this fashion. It could only contribute to closer relations between the two nations and to removing a good deal of French anxiety about security.

In this interview I stressed again that I was determined to make the improvement of Franco-German relations the core of my policy. Without a basic understanding between France and Germany it would be impossible to achieve European cooperation. The problem was one of psychology – France really sought security. It was immaterial whether this psychological need struck us as anachronistic or whether it was in fact anachronistic.

I pointed out in the interview that it was simply a fact that French public opinion was dominated by the desire for security from Germany and that this public opinion in its turn exerted significant influence on French policy. 'We as Germans must pursue a policy that respects this feeling of insecurity in France. We are therefore prepared to put no obstacles in the path of the security board that has been set up.'

I was also concerned to acquaint the American public with the importance of dismantling in the context of the German economy. I said in the interview that Germans saw dismantling as a very decisive obstacle to the development of a real European unity. Dismantlings would have to be stopped for economic and for psychological reasons. I also interpolated this sentence: 'We shall soon be prepared to join the Ruhr Commission', without naming a date, but intimating that it would come when conditions were 'favourable'. I also gave some indication that I regarded the end of dismantling as a favourable moment.

The conversations I had wanted to hold with the party representatives in the Bundestag took place on 9 November 1949. I informed the gentlemen of the course of negotiations with the High Commissioners and of recent events. The representatives of the SPD were in absolute disagreement with the way I had chosen. That same evening a spokesman of the Social Democratic Party announced that the SPD would ask for a foreign policy debate to be held at once.

In the evening of 9 November Dr Schumacher held a press conference in Hanover in which he declared that consenting to the admission of the Saar to the European Assembly and the simultaneous admission of the German Federal Republic must be described as an attempt to mislead the German people. By this statement he raised the question of a connection between the membership of the Federal Republic and of the Saar in the Council of Europe – the very connection I was trying to do away with in my negotiations with the High Commissioners, as I shall show later. Dr Schumacher started from non-existent facts. He declared that the Federal Government, and I in particular, were trying to dress up as a great political success what in reality would constitute a heavy burden for the Germans. The Federal Government, he said, was devoid of any conception of foreign policy. It gave in to the demands of the Allies without offering the slightest resistance. The inclusion of the Ruhr question in the security problem was really a victory for the big capitalists. Dr Schumacher attacked 'the unilateral representation of the interests of heavy industry' in the Ruhr Authority and pointed out that the interests of the workers were unrepresented. Dr Schumacher did not seem to see that by linking the two questions we might achieve a reduction of dismantling and preserve the livelihood of hundreds of thousands of workers. He said a little later that the SPD would oppose a policy that put an Allied policeman in Germany in front of the coffers of the rich.

The next day, 10 November, Dr Schumacher held another press conference at which he said that concerning the problem of French security from Germany he had to stress that the German Federal Government could not satisfy this need for security without expecting a *quid pro quo*. The constant mention of the concept of 'security' should not deceive anybody about the fact that the Paris conference was dealing mainly with economic matters, namely the quotas for steel and iron. German industry welcomed the Ruhr Authority only because it would prevent a socialization of Ruhr industries.

The French were pursuing an entirely rigid policy while the Federal Government was trying by *a priori* concessions to maintain a positive position. But this meant maintaining a French and not a German position.

While Dr Schumacher was indulging in such descriptions of myself and my policies, the Foreign Ministers' Conference of the United States, France and Great Britain had begun in Paris on 10 November 1949. The advance concessions towards an auspicious course of this conference which I had mentioned in my Note to Robertson of 1 November, the memorandum of 7 November, and the newspaper interviews, contributed to the assurance that the Germans were prepared to subject themselves voluntarily to limitations to meet the security demands of our Western neighbours.

My statements had found a favourable echo in the French press. The French paper *Parisien libéré* asked if the French Government was aware of the gravity of the hour and of the chance for France that lay in such a German attempt at understanding. There was general agreement in the French press that the German position I had outlined facilitated the solution of the problem of dismantling. Even the left-socialist paper *Franctireur* advocated French agreement to the cessation of dismantling and a revision of the Occupation Statute. Generally the French press gave the impression of a French public opinion ready for compromise. How the foreign ministers in Paris would interpret my offer was still an open question.

Various statements by prominent American politicians had shown that American foreign policy regarded an understanding between Germany and France as desirable. The Americans seemed to share my view of Franco-German reconciliation as the starting point, if not the key, to a political and economic unification of Europe. The French negotiator was Robert Schuman who knew conditions in Germany well. To what extent the British foreign secretary was prepared to yield in the question of dismantlings I had learnt from Robertson.

I now had to wait and see whether the steps I had taken, and which admittedly were not without risks, would lead to success or not. Situations offering chances for the solution of the most difficult problems are rare in political life. Once such situations do arise, the next question is whether the chances are used or missed. The communiqué published at the end of the short two-day conference of foreign ministers was very vague.

It spoke of the three foreign ministers' awareness of the heavy responsibility placed upon them to conserve and consolidate the peace of Europe and of the world. They asserted their determination to meet this responsibility with both firmness and humanity; firmness in their resolve that no country should be permitted to menace the peace and security of its neighbours, humanity in the recognition that a lasting peace could only be found in a close association of the peoples of the world. Since both world wars sprang from a militaristic spirit emanating from Germany, and since the countries represented by the foreign ministers were in occupation of German territory, it was natural that their consideration of the problem of peace in Europe should have been directed largely towards Germany's relations with Europe, the situation in Germany, and their policy in respect to Germany.

The foreign ministers reaffirmed their policy as expressed in the Occupation Statute of giving the Federal Republic a wide area of free determination in the conduct of German affairs, an area which under the Statute would grow wider as the administration of the Federal Republic gave evidence that it was proceeding towards the establishment of a free, democratic, and peaceful Germany. At the same time, the ministers considered it appropriate to support and foster the progressive integration of the German people into the European community. These decisions were based on the expectation that the government of the German Federal Republic would give further evidence of its pacific intentions and of its sincere desire to associate itself with those nations devoted to the cause of democracy, justice under law, and peace. Consequently the three foreign ministers had given their High Commissioners certain instructions and powers, which would permit them to achieve these aims.

The German Press Agency (DPA) reported on 10 November that according to reliable sources Acheson, Bevin, and Schuman were well disposed toward my suggestion of a mixed committee of experts to work on a system of security guarantees against the misuse of German heavy industry. What actually had been discussed at the Paris conference of foreign ministers I hoped to learn during the visit of the American Secretary of State Dean Acheson which was to take place on 13 November and which had been publicly announced before that conference.

In the meantime the SPD made known through the press its negative assessment of the Paris conference. On 12 November 1949 Dr Schumacher told a correspondent of the United Press that the Paris conference of foreign ministers had foundered on the 'blockheadedness and primitiveness of French national policy'. The outcome of the conference would lead to a deterioration of conditions in Germany. 'The policy of making offers is a bad one and I have demanded a foreign policy debate in parliament in Bonn in order to let the French know what we do not want.' On the subject of Secretary of State Dean Acheson's forthcoming visit he said that Acheson was 'coming to see the wrong man' in Germany, a man 'whose heart belonged to France'. Dr Schumacher seemed to enjoy his press agitation. About me he said: 'Despite unambiguous statements of principle by the opposition, the Federal Chancellor has not understood that this is not the way to bring about international reconciliation, but that such inadequate and hopeless antics, which border on political charlatanism, can be clearly recognized as expressions of big business policy. Big business is wrong in thinking that it can get into international deals by servile submissiveness where more arrogant tactics are of no avail.' In another statement, he said:

Next Tuesday, 15 November, the Federal Chancellor will face the Federal

Parliament, miserable and empty-handed, not as a representative of the interests of the people and of many of his own voters, but as advocate of his capitalist friends in the CDU, FDP, and DP. He has not represented a German policy, he has not pursued a European policy, he has merely taken the first faltering steps in an impossible kind of foreign policy . . . It does not take much to see that the Federal Chancellor was not backed by the people, not the democratically elected parliament, but a political insecurity which exhausts itself in mere tactics and is the expression of an authoritarian arrogance that he thinks he can also use in his dealings with parliament.

A telegram received by the SPD from Morgan Philips, the Secretary General of the Labour Party, in reply to a memorandum the SPD had given the Labour Party in August 1949, was interesting in the context of the SPD's attitude. This telegram, of which I knew, was dated 13 November 1949 and said:

The Executive Committee of the Labour Party came to the unanimous view that a suspension of dismantling was to be welcomed as soon as the Allied governments were convinced that the measures to be taken are sufficient to safeguard their future security. These include the recognition of the Security Board and of the Ruhr Authority by the German Government.*

I can imagine that Dr Schumacher was none too happy when he received this telegram.

While he poured the stream of invective over me and my political abilities, I continued my efforts in tenacious negotiations with the High Commissioners to wrest concessions from them in the dismantling question.

Acheson in Bonn: First Visit of a Foreign Minister

I was looking forward to the visit of the American Secretary of State Dean Acheson with the greatest interest. It was the first visit by a Foreign Minister to the newly created German Federal Republic. Dean Acheson was the first great statesman who visited me as Federal Chancellor. Incidentally, Dean Acheson was also the first great statesman who visited me three days after I laid down the office of Chancellor of the German Federal Republic.

Other participants in our conversations were the High Commissioner, McCloy, on the American side, and on the German side Blankenhorn and von Herwarth. Dean Acheson made an excellent impression on me. I found him most likeable from the very first day of our meeting. At first I tried, at some length, to explain to him the present psychological situation in Germany, so as to make our demands for a revision of the dismantling lists more understandable. I pointed to the refugee problem, to unemployment, and to the prostrate economy.

* Retranslated from the German.

First of all, however, I expressed to him the gratitude of the German people for the political help the United States had given, and also for the material help which awakened and sustained the hope of many people in Germany for a better future. I expressed my hope that the United States would continue to lend its political and economic assistance to Europe.

Acheson thanked me for what I had said. He acknowledged the great progress made in Germany in recent times, but said he wanted to point to an important factor, to the great importance of avoiding a situation in which the parties in Germany vied with each other in criticism of the occupying powers with consequent tensions for the cooperation between the German authorities and the High Commissioners. American public opinion was quite ready to give economic and political aid to Europe and especially to Germany. He was always glad to see that there was a widespread conviction in Congress and all over the country that Europe was uniting and that America had to help this process on. But if now the German political parties and public opinion increasingly developed a critical attitude toward the occupying powers, one had to reckon with a sudden swing away from this positive mood in America. There was a danger of the conviction gaining ground among many Americans that Europe simply could not be helped and that it was not worth investing further millions or even billions of US dollars. Similarly, too much criticism inside Germany would, of course, also decide the fate of the Schuman Government in France which on its part was doing everything toward an understanding with Germany and the gradual integration of Germany in the European community. I must mention here that during the years after 1946 the Communist Party in France was the strongest party in the National Assembly and that government in France was far from stable.

Dean Acheson then mentioned another point which he said was very close to his heart. The Germans had often voiced the wish for a termination of the state of war by America. In principle there was no objection to this at all. On the other hand one had to consider the fact that it was on the basis of the state of war that Congress had passed legislation conferring considerable powers on the administration which alone enabled it to maintain, for instance, the occupation and the High Commission and to take other important measures. The termination of the state of war with Germany would mean the relinquishing of the powers that Congress had granted the administration. New powers would have to be created. That would mean that a new legal basis would have to be found for the occupation, the maintenance of the High Commission, and a number of other measures, for which Congress alone would be competent. This would project all problems and the treatment of the question of Germany on to the plane of American domestic politics and would make them much harder to solve.

I told Acheson that I fully appreciated all this and that I had asked a group of experts to ascertain which parts of the war legislation of the Allies were exercising pressure on German economic, political, and cultural life. As soon as these experts had finished their survey, I would submit it to the High Commissioners.

Dean Acheson spoke briefly about the Foreign Ministers' Conference of the three Western powers on 9 and 10 November and said he thought it could be described as having been peaceful and that the High Commission had been equipped with far-reaching powers to enable it to discuss new possibilities with the Federal Government.

We owe a great deal to Dean Acheson. He was a man of great wisdom and vision. He recognized the importance of Europe and the importance of Germany for Europe.

I mentioned before that the final communiqué of the conference of the three foreign ministers in Paris of 10 November 1949 was couched in very general terms. It was therefore with great interest that I looked forward to the conversation with the three High Commissioners which took place on the Petersberg on 15 November.

The Results of the Paris Foreign Ministers' Conference of 9–10 November 1949

General Robertson, who was in the chair that day, opened the conversations on the Petersberg on 15 November. He first spoke about the Paris Foreign Ministers' Conference, saying that it had dealt with a far larger number of questions than I had raised in my Note of 1 November. He now wanted to talk about those questions as well as the additional ones that had been discussed in Paris.

The three foreign ministers had given the three High Commissioners certain instructions representing a programme, a whole, which was to form the basis of a reordering of Allied policy in Germany. The great aim of this policy was the integration of Germany in the community of European nations. The narrower aim was the establishment of more normal conditions inside Germany and of more normal relations between Germany and her neighbours, naturally keeping in mind that under the Occupation Statute certain fields, such as questions connected with the problem of security, were to remain the province of the occupying powers.

The programme drawn up in Paris was to apply during the time pending the revision of the Occupation Statute. There were to be no amendments of the Statute before the term for revision provided for in that document.

According to Robertson's report the following points were among those settled in Paris:

1 German admission to the Council of Europe as Associate Member was to be the subject of a formal decision by the Council of Ministers at its forthcoming meeting. The measures then to be taken would have to be discussed after that.

2 There were certain constitutional obstacles to German participation in a large number of international organizations. A study group was to make a report that would provide directives for the High Commissioners. Individual cases would then be examined and discussed with the Federal Government on the basis of these directives.

3 The question of terminating the state of war would have to be discussed thoroughly at a later point, being a very complicated technical and legal problem. The American Secretary of State Dean Acheson had already informed me of the American view on the problem on 13 November. There had been no decision made on it in Paris.

4 The present four-power agreement regarding the control of German shipbuilding was still valid; it forbade or restricted shipbuilding. It had been laid down in the agreement that Germany was to begin by rebuilding her coastal shipping before any ocean-going ships were built. Germany had fulfilled the first condition and was now to be allowed to build a limited number of ships whose size and speed would enable them to compete with those of other countries.

5 The Paris three-power conference had decided to give Germany the chance to establish consular and economic representation in foreign countries.

Robertson emphasized that the Allied Governments had made very generous concessions. These concessions must, however, not be allowed to trigger off German demands for further concessions.

At today's meeting I was expected to make known the views of the Federal Government on the question of decartelization, exclusively from the point of view of security. In view of the change in the programme of revision so far in use, decartelization had assumed an even greater importance than before. Today responsibility for it was shared by German and Allied authorities. The High Commissioners set great store by an explicit confirmation of the Federal Government's willingness to cooperate in this question.

Regarding the reparation programme and dismantling Robertson mentioned several points which would in all circumstances have to remain unchanged and he expressed the hope that there would be no difficulties made on the German side. They included:

1 Industries of war production. There could be no change in this area.

2 There could also be no change regarding decartelization measures.

3 No agreement for any change in reparation and dismantling measures that were already in force would be given. Where dismantlings had started no retroactive cancellation would be granted. In certain cases where some installations had already been dismantled rendering the works unable to function, the High Commissioners had some margin for decisions of their own.

o   209

The American High Commissioner McCloy spoke next. The concessions that had been made to Germany demanded readiness for cooperation on the German side. The future attitude of the German Government would determine the timing of concessions within the framework of the programme laid down by the foreign ministers and would also influence the Allied attitude regarding a revision of the Occupation Statute. It was clear that this decision did not aim at increasing the German economic potential. But neither was it intended to fix the present state of affairs for all eternity. Every increase of the industrial potential would have to be examined for its justification in the light of existing facts.

The foreign ministers hoped that the Federal Government would be able to carry out a far-reaching liberalization of administrative institutions, above all regarding their personnel, a liberalization which would get away from a certain authoritarian character that had been a feature of German democracy even before 1933.

As I had to make a statement to the Bundestag on the Paris Foreign Ministers' Conference that afternoon, I was anxious to discuss the *modus procedendi*. Robertson acceded to my request and declared that the policy of the Allied Governments, which would in future be based on the Paris decisions, meant a change in their previous attitude. Such a change was always difficult, but especially so for the French Government at this moment because Schuman would have to account for it in the impending debate in the French parliament. Schuman would have trouble if details of the Paris agreements were represented as big concessions. For this reason a large number of points that had been discussed must not be published but must be reserved for further discussion. In a week's time one might consider publishing the results of the deliberations. He advised me to declare in the Bundestag that discussions had begun with the High Commissioners and that they were developing well from the German point of view.

In reply I welcomed the Allied intention, as expressed by Robertson and McCloy, to lead Germany back into the European community. I had on various occasions made a special point of initiating decisive steps to bring about an understanding between France and Germany. This had brought upon me a number of attacks by the Social Democrats. I was anxious to discuss these questions in the forthcoming Bundestag debate in order to put a stop to further corrosion by the poison the Social Democrats were spreading.

In the French Chamber, as I knew, great trouble might arise. As far as I was informed there was to be a vote in the French Chamber on the question of whether or not Germany was to be admitted to the Council of Europe. I had so far not touched on this question in my correspondence with the High Commissioners. I now had to ask the French High Commissioner, François-Poncet, whether it was not better to leave this question untouched before the Bundestag debate. Once the question was broached I was afraid of major attacks from the SPD. In any case, things were bound to be said by opposition speakers in connection with the Saar question that ran counter to French views.

François-Poncet replied that the French Foreign Minister would announce the views of the French Government regarding future policy toward Germany in the French National Assembly on 22 November. This would be followed by a debate and a vote on French policy toward Germany. If this vote was favourable, it would mean French consent to German membership of the Council of Europe. He stressed that conditions were auspicious. It was, of course, another question whether Germany wanted to apply or would rather wait to be invited to the Strasbourg Assembly. If Germany made an application, it would be accepted at once.

Furthermore the Saar had applied for membership of the Council of Europe. This application was being examined under the provisions of the constitution of the Council. This was not a purely French problem, but the French Government hoped that the Saar would become a member in the coming year.

I interjected that there must be a misunderstanding regarding the membership of Germany and the Saar in the Council of Europe. According to my information so far the main subject of the French debate on 22 November was German membership and this was to be voted on. My information was that this was arranged between the parties so as to ensure a propitious course for the debate in the Chamber.

I feared that if I spoke about German membership of the Council of Europe to the German Bundestag it would lead to a discussion of the question of the Saar. Earlier resolutions made me certain that the Social Democrats would table a motion that Germany was only to join the Council of Europe if the Saar did not join simultaneously. I therefore thought it better to leave the subject unmentioned in the Bundestag and to return to it after the French Chamber had had its debate.

Robertson agreed that it was better to await the outcome of parliamentary debates in Paris and London – where there was also to be a debate in the Commons on this complex of questions – before the Federal Government applied for membership in the Strasbourg Council.

McCloy also spoke and said he could not judge whether the procedure I proposed was good or not. Undoubtedly German membership in the Council of Europe had played a great part in Paris. German membership in the Council of Europe was the key to the integration of Germany in Western Europe. The three foreign ministers had declared that they would welcome it. This declaration had not touched on the question of the membership of the Saar.

François-Poncet returned to the question once more. If I wished not to speak about the Council of Europe, he had no objection. The path to German membership had been prepared. On 22 November the French Chamber would deliberate on this question, but not on this point alone. The Saar question would certainly play a great part. He, François-Poncet, was afraid that it would play a role that might not be at all agreeable to me. He knew that a certain number of French deputies would only agree to German membership of the Council of Europe if the Saar became a member at the same time. In any case the French Government had to know right at the beginning of this debate in the Chamber what the attitude of the Federal Government was on German membership of the Ruhr Authority and of the Military Security Board.

I then stated that the Federal Government was in favour of cooperation with the Military Security Board. Regarding the membership of the Federal Republic in the Ruhr Authority, I pointed out that I had some reservations concerning Article 31 of the Ruhr Statute. It had a rather intricate provision which could be read to mean that Germany would by joining the Ruhr Authority issue a blank cheque for all decisions taken by the six countries who had drawn up the Ruhr Statute in London in 1948. The three High Commissioners told me unanimously that they considered this interpretation of Article 31 wrong. No one was thinking of demanding a blank cheque from Germany, let alone of laying a trap. The article was merely intended to state that when Germany had joined the Ruhr Authority she would have to abide by majority decisions. I requested further confirmation of this point in view of the fact that the Ruhr Statute had not only been signed by the three Western Allies but also by the three Benelux countries. I was assured this would be done. I said that if this confirmation proved satisfactory I was prepared for cooperation with the Ruhr Authority.

Regarding the declaration on decartelization of the German economy asked for by Robertson at the beginning, I stated that the Federal Government was prepared to meet the wishes of the Allies. A special decartelization law was already in process of preparation.

My endeavours had to be directed towards winning the support of parliament and the German people for my policy. This would certainly be very difficult as Dr Schumacher was speaking in very negative terms about my policy. To start with I would confine myself to general observations in parliament today. I would, however, be very grateful to General Robertson as chairman of the three High Commissioners if he gave me the opportunity of saying something general to the Bundestag about dismantling.

Robertson replied that he would meet this request. First, however, he wanted to say regarding the statements on the Ruhr Statute, the Military Security Board, and decartelization that I had just made in my capacity as Federal Chancellor that these statements constituted essential elements of a satisfactory settlement. It went without saying that I could only speak for my government. If the German parliament rejected my statements, the settlement would naturally be reduced in scope. But he thought it unlikely that parliament would do this.

Robertson then turned to the dismantling question. He remarked that where dismantling had begun the former state of affairs could not be restored. The dismantling of docks and of the machine industry was about to be completed. The installations on the reparations list had already been allocated and were about to be sent away. The situation was different in the synthetics and steel industries because here dismantling had only just begun. These industries would have special treatment. They were the subject of the special powers granted the High Commissioners at the Paris Foreign Minister's Conference. In accordance with the foreign ministers' instructions these matters were to be discussed with the German Government. I was free to use this statement on dismantling in the Bundestag this afternoon.

What he was going to say now, however, was not meant for publication: In my letter of 1 November to the chairman of the High Commission I had requested a stoppage of dismantling until the negotiations of the proposed commission were completed. The dismantling of certain key industries would be slowed down during the negotiations. This gave rise to two questions: (1) which firms were to be affected by this? and (2) how was 'deceleration' to be interpreted?

The firms affected were:

1 Gelsenberg Benzin
2 Chemische Werke Hüls
3 August-Thyssen-Hütte Hamborn
4 Ruhrstahl Hattingen
5 Charlottenhütte
6 Borsig Berlin

In many plants dismantling would be slowed down so much that practically nothing of importance would happen while the negotiations were proceeding, in other words, nothing was to be done that would prejudge the final result of the negotiations. For the sake of the French parliament, however, these measures must not be represented as final decisions.

I thanked General Robertson and told him that he had rendered the Federal Government a great service. My policy of understanding and cooperation would undoubtedly be greatly facilitated by my being in a position this afternoon to use the statements he had given me for publication.

On the afternoon of the same day I made a statement on behalf of the Government to the German Bundestag. It was couched in the agreed terms. I gave a detailed account of events since 31 October 1949 and pointed to the negotiations that had begun with the High Commissioners. I urgently appealed to the members of the Bundestag and to the German public not to disturb these negotiations by inappropriate criticism lest fears of a resurgent German nationalism be aroused abroad.

With a view to the impending debate in the French National Assembly I addressed these words to the French people at the end of my speech:

213

The question of Germany and France is in reality one of the cardinal questions of the destiny of Europe. I am told by many visitors to France and by many foreign journalists that in France too there exists an honest and wide-spread desire to do away with Franco-German differences once and for all. I beg the French people and the people of the world to be assured that the overwhelming majority of Germans is animated by the same desire.

The Petersberg Agreement

There was another meeting between the High Commissioners and myself on the Petersberg on 17 November. The High Commissioners asked me to give them a description of the Bundestag debate after my statement for the Government. This is what I told them: The Bundestag debate had taken a course that changed the political roles of the 'twenties. This time the nationalists were sitting on the left and the deputies on the right were reasonable. I was fairly sure that the Social Democratic Party was inwardly divided. The High Commissioners undoubtedly knew of Senatspräsident Kaisen's speech to officials of the SPD in Berlin in which he said that I should be given a chance. With this, I knew, he had not just spoken for himself, but for a whole group of Social Democrats of whom I particularly wanted to name Mayor Brauer of Hamburg. I had learnt from a fairly reliable source that the SPD group in the Bundestag struck a few sentences from Dr Schumacher's speech before he gave it. It was, incidentally, a rather weak speech, a fact that caused general comment. The only speech that struck me as especially significant was Professor Schmid's. He claimed that in the 1920s the Germans signed agreements with mental reservations. I thought this was in fact not so. I knew all the leading German politicians at that time and did not think them capable of such deceit. Secondly I found it deplorable that Professor Schmid made this suggestion just before the beginning of the debate in the French Chamber where it might have disastrous consequences. I therefore rebutted this charge very sharply and was applauded by almost all deputies with the exception, naturally, of the SPD and the KPD. With a view to the forthcoming debates in London on 17 November and in Paris on 22 November I made an explicit statement that if I signed a document I did it from conviction and that I would stand by my signature and do everything to see it carried out. I had put great emphasis on this statement, especially for the benefit of the German public. In the end the Social Democrats did not dare table any motion because, I was sure, they were afraid that it would split their party.

It would undoubtedly be possible for by far the largest part of German public opinion to be kept reasonable. All in all I felt I could say that the Bundestag meeting of 15 November received my report well and that the debate was a success for the Federal Government.

The Ruhr Statute was the chief subject of questions, but I thought it could be better discussed in the Bundeshaus after 22 November. As the Ruhr Statute was drawn up before there was an Occupation Statute, it had certain features that it would not have had if the Occupation Statute had been in existence. I realized that now was not the time to discuss an amendment of the Ruhr Statute; it could not be done in conjunction with our present negotiations. I would, however, welcome it – although I wanted to say so only privately at this moment because of the forthcoming French debate and would not say it more loudly until after 22 November – if there could be a declaration to the effect that, as was the case with the Occupation Statute, the Ruhr Statute was to be subject to review in accordance with changing circumstances. I asked leave to raise this matter again at a later point.

Robertson spoke after me and said the time had come when we must agree on a method of documenting our joint decisions to date. The High Commissioners did not yet have any very clear ideas about it, but they were agreed that the document must embody what we had agreed on. He gave me an assurance that neither the contents nor the wording of the document would be decided without me or my representative. 22 November 1949 was suggested as the date of publication of the agreements. It was the date of the debate in the French Chamber. In point of fact the agreements were published on 24 November.

Robertson then spoke on the Ruhr Statute. At our last meeting of 15 November we had discussed it with special reference to Article 31 concerning German accession and assumption of responsibilities. I had drawn attention to the inclusion of responsibility for 'such other dispositions as may be agreed by the signatory Governments', arguing that I could not issue a blank cheque for future 'dispositions' on which the the six signatory powers might agree in future. He said he wanted to tell me of an unofficial conference with representatives of the International Ruhr Authority at which this question was discussed. He could tell me as a result of these talks that no further 'dispositions' were to be expected of the signatory powers.

He continued that the question of amending the Ruhr Statute at a later date was, however, one to which only the participating governments knew the answer, adding that he frankly did not know what his own government's attitude would be. He was afraid that it would not be possible to reach agreement on this question between the various governments by 22 November. It was, however, for me to decide whether I wanted to state before my parliament that I thought some points in need of revision and that I would urge such revision. The High Commissioners would not object.

François-Poncet endorsed Robertson's remarks.

I replied that after Robertson's statement on Article 31 I could now agree to German accession to the Ruhr Authority, adding that I was convinced that, once cooperation had started, the redundancy of certain provisions of the Statute would soon be seen quite clearly. I did not want to make further public statements on this whole business before 22 November.

215

I told the High Commissioners that I had asked the trade union leaders to a conference next Monday to give us a chance of having an unhurried and quiet conversation about it all. I had no doubt whatsoever that they would show understanding of the whole situation.

Robertson called my declaration of accession to the Ruhr Authority satisfactory. All that was needed now was that I should make a public and official declaration, after the protocol on the results of the negotiations had been drafted, to the effect that the German Federal Government was now prepared to accede to the Ruhr Statute. He added that if it came to a vote of confidence in the Bundestag and this vote should go against the declaration, this would clearly mean that the vote had gone against the entire settlement, not only against this one point, and that therefore the entire settlement was null and void. But he thought it unlikely that this would happen.

We then discussed the revision of reparation demands and dismantling plans. Robertson explained in detail how far the Allies were prepared to go in the question of revising reparations, starting with the industries producing synthetic oil and synthetic rubber. The Allied Governments had always attributed the greatest importance to these industries from the point of view of security since they had really only been developed with a view to a war economy. Nevertheless the Allied Governments were prepared to adopt a more liberal policy towards these two industries because of the general settlement and the assurances they hoped to get: he did not want to go into detail beyond saying that their dismantling had not yet gone very far.

In this field there were two points the Allied Governments considered important. The first was that if these plants took up production again, they must not produce things that were on the list of prohibited goods. Regarding the steel industry he said that it was a difficult problem to which the foreign ministers had given much attention in Paris. They were not prepared to raise the production level of 11·2 million tons for the area of the West German Federal Republic. On the other hand they were convinced that present capacity could easily produce that amount. In fact German industry had not yet reached this production level, but this was probably due to the marketing situation. Nor was it to be expected that the figure would be reached in future. There was therefore no economic logic in changing the reparation plan as far as the steel industry was concerned.

The ministers, Robertson continued, had had a very thorough discussion of the point raised by the Chancellor, that this was not an economic but a psychological question. This was the sole reason for authorizing the High Commissioners to discuss the deletion of a number of steel plants with me. They wanted to stress, however, that plants already dismantled must not be rebuilt or re-equipped. Under the regulations of the Military Security Board the situation now was that in restricted industries such as the steel industry intended alterations or the installation of new equipment would require a licence. In view of the fact that the present capacity of the steel producing industry was well above the present limit of 11·2 million tons the Security Board would in principle refuse licences calculated to increase the production of an individual plant. Robertson added that he thought all this went without saying and that he was convinced that I would agree with him. He only thought these things should be spelt out in order to prevent all misunderstandings. Equipment already dismantled would be available for reparation deliveries. There might be cases, and he personally knew of one, where a small part was dismantled in a plant, paralysing the entire plant. In such cases the High Commissioners would naturally use their new powers.

They had received special instructions regarding the plants to be deleted from the list. The gist of these instructions was that the High Commissioners should keep a special eye on these plants and keep informed on production there. As soon as we observed that the steel production limit for the whole of West Germany was being exceeded, we were to intervene in these plants at once. From this we could see that the deletion of the steel plants from the list was conditional on the maintenance of the production limit. McCloy, he added, had already explained that none of this was meant for eternity. But for the present steel production figures were fixed.

Robertson finally dealt with two points of my Note. I had proposed a committee which should, with German participation, examine steel production and steel requirements in Western Europe including West Germany. The foreign ministers appreciated the motive behind the proposal, but came to the conclusion that at the moment such a committee could not do any useful work. He added that this very question was also being studied by the OEEC. One of the foreign ministers' reasons against setting up such a special committee now was that it would interfere with the work currently being done at the OEEC.

With regard to my proposal that foreign capital should be invested in the German steel industry, again the foreign ministers appreciated the motive behind it. But quite frankly the foreign ministers could not deal with the question because there was not time. The High Commissioners were hoping to get instructions from their governments in the foreseeable future which would enable them to lift the prohibition on the investment of foreign capital in West Germany. The High Commissioners were convinced – and thought I would agree with them – that this would be a measure of the greatest importance for the German economy and from which many industries, including, probably, the steel industry, would benefit. As for my specific proposal on this he could only add that the Allied Governments were giving it the most careful attention.

Robertson now asked me to comment on the proposals made by the Allied Governments. He also asked me for a declaration on the democratization of public life in Germany. Finally he asked me if the Federal Government was prepared to use its influence and power in order to assure smooth dismantling operations where they still remained to be carried out.

I began by answering the last question. Once the question of dismantling had been disinfected I thought I could guarantee that the dismantling still to be done would take place without friction or harmful psychological consequences among the people. As for the second question, I declared that Germany had passed all the laws and decrees needed for the implementation of democratic principles. The Federal Government was determined to see to it that they were carried into practice.

It seemed to me that the relatively greatest effect of the National Socialist tradition was to be seen in the Jewish question. I could here give an assurance that I was firmly resolved to do everything humanly possible in this respect. I had decided to establish a special department for Jewish affairs in the Federal Ministry of the Interior and to put a German Jew in charge of it who was to be nominated by the representatives of German Jewry. This department was to ensure that nothing happening in the area of the Federal Republic was counter to Jewish interests. It was at the same time to give Jews living in Germany confidence that they were protected. The body representing the German Jews had warmly welcomed the establishment of such a department and was going to suggest a suitable candidate for it.

Coming last to the first question, cooperation with the Security Board, I wanted to say that the Board would have our unreserved cooperation – not from a feeling of coercion, but because we ourselves wanted to be absolutely sure that no military preparations were taking place in Germany that we objected to ourselves, and also in order to strengthen the feeling of community in Western Europe by our cooperation.

When I had finished McCloy added a few remarks on the question of democratization. It was probably very difficult to find words for a country's progress on the path of democracy. He thought we were all agreed that the foundation of the present German Federal Government was democratic and had turned resolutely away from the leadership principle of the Nazi days. He was glad of what I had said about the application of the principle of racial tolerance. Then he added that the Allies had from time to time had occasion to be disturbed by the return of leading personalities of the former Nazi period to important positions. He was not one of those who said that Nazis should forever be excluded from the normal life of the German people. On the contrary, he had said more than once that he felt it was important to take mere hangers-on and not very active Nazis back into the normal stream of the life of the nation. It was much better to include these people in the normal life of the nation than to keep them in a special group beyond the pale. He felt that the moment had come when it was more important to look at the present attitude of these people than to limit oneself to a scrutiny of their former attitudes and weaknesses. However, one could now observe the tendency of certain groups and certain very highly-placed individuals to displace others who had resisted during the Nazi period when it was very difficult to resist. Moreover, the latter had manifested a strength of character that was probably worth more than mere efficiency. He thought that this tendency was more noticeable in the *Länder* than at the Federal level. At the moment he did not know of any case in the Federal Government that gave cause for complaint, but he would be glad if some attention were paid to the matter, and if the Federal Government were to initiate the appropriate measures at its own level and via the *Länder* governments so that the High Commission need not become active in this regard. He thought that that would in any case make a much less favourable impression in the Allied countries than spontaneous measures taken by the Federal Government. He did not want to limit his remarks to the influence of former Nazis but thought it might be as well to go further back in history to examine the influence of the Bismarckian attitude. It would be eloquent proof of German intentions to turn away from the authoritarian principle, a principle which not only during the Nazi era, but even earlier, had made the German people somehow susceptible to such excesses. He could imagine that such measures might for instance be concerned with more intensive education for public responsibility and a reform of the civil service. It was indeed a matter that it was hard to put into words.

I replied: 'I understand these anxieties and I must say that sometimes I myself get very annoyed about certain things. When I see, for instance, that the founder of the Gestapo, the former Regierungspräsident Diels of Cologne, is having his memoirs published in Düsseldorf and when I read that these are said to make a most interesting book, I am very sorry that the Federal Government does not have more power to intervene. On the other hand I was very surprised when I heard that this gentleman, Herr Diels, was the guest of the Allied Governments for many months at Nuremberg, was allowed to go hunting and lived a life of ease and splendour.' McCloy asked me to let him know in time if I ever heard again that the Allies were indulging in festivities with a representative of the Gestapo. I told him that it would give me the greatest pleasure.

After this interlude I asked the High Commissioners to remember when assessing the situation in Germany that there was still great confusion in the political thinking of the Germans. How great this confusion was could best be seen from the fact that in the Bundestag debate of 15 November the extreme right advocated reconciliation with France. While in the 1920s Strasser, von Reventlow, and many others always spoke of France's desire for hegemony, it was now Dr Schumacher who spoke in that vein. The roles of right and left seemed to have been exchanged. But I felt that all this would settle down once we had a little peace and quiet.

After these exchanges the amendments of the reparation list were once more discussed thoroughly and in great detail. The High Commissioners' treatment of the matter was generous and at the end of the discussions I thanked them and expressed the hope that the German people would acknowledge this Allied generosity.

Robertson drew attention to the fact that the revised dismantling list was not yet ready for publication. He urged me to make absolutely sure that the list did not become known before the debate in the French Chamber on 22 November because publication might affect that debate very badly.

In our discussion of 15 November six plants had been mentioned that were to be struck from the dismantling list. On 22 November I would be able to name twelve plants that had been deleted from the list. So far my negotiations with the High Commissioners had resulted in eighty per cent of our demands being met.

Now that the question of the dismantling list seemed to be settled, Robertson once more raised the question of shipping and suggested that it should be made part of the general settlement. The same should be done with the question of German membership in international organizations and the question of terminating the state of war. The question of German representation abroad would also have to be cleared up and should perhaps likewise be included in the agreement.

A final report and communiqué was to be drawn up at a conference scheduled for Tuesday, 22 November 1949. That conference lasted over eleven hours. It took tough negotiations to formulate the communiqués on the agreements and the texts of the agreements themselves. The most difficult passage was the one concerning the accession of the Federal Republic to the Ruhr Authority. What made this point so difficult was the fact that as chairman of the CDU in the British zone I had very strongly criticized the Ruhr agreement when it became known in December 1948. To be sure I had said in essence that the question was in what spirit the agreement would be applied. In order to remain true to this basic line, I needed a passage in the communiqué on the new Petersberg Agreement to the effect that the Federal Government considered some provisions of the Ruhr agreement to have been rendered obsolete by developments and that the Federal Government, desiring a review of the agreement, wished to participate in the negotiations on it.

I knew that there would be a very hard debate with the Social Democrats in the Bundestag after the agreement and the government statement on it had been read. During those eleven hours of negotiation on 22 November I tried to remove as many targets of critical attack as possible. The High Commissioners did not accept my proposal. They stressed that the Federal Government could not be allowed to make its accession to the Ruhr Authority dependent on conditions; but there was no objection to my saying something along the lines I had suggested in my exposition in the Bundestag.

It had been my endeavour in the negotiations on the wording of the communiqué and on the wording of the agreement to get a clear expression of the agreement's aim to integrate Germany into the orbit of Western Europe. What I was concerned about was to show the German people clearly that this was a highly political matter.

Not all German wishes and proposals had been met; nonetheless, the Petersberg Agreement represented a very great success. For the first time since the collapse we were officially recognized as equal and for the first time we re-entered the international sphere.

The atmosphere of these negotiations with the High Commissioners was very good. The Agreement itself said: 'The discussions were animated throughout by the desire and the determination of both parties that their relations should develop progressively upon a basis of mutual confidence.' This 'cooperation in a spirit of mutual confidence' had repeatedly been referred to and was a matter of actual fact; after all our power had been destroyed we Germans could only rise again by cooperation based on mutual trust. The Petersberg Agreement was a great step forward. I was convinced that this was the way to ensuring Germany's future and the salvation and future of Western Europe – for which Germany was indispensable – and that it was the way also to the highest goal, ensuring the peace of the world.

The Petersberg Agreement stated that the integration of the Federal Republic as a peaceful member of the European community was a primary objective. To this end German association with the countries of Western Europe in all fields was to be diligently pursued by means of her entry into the appropriate international bodies and the exchange of commercial and consular representation with other countries. The Agreement said: 'Both the High Commissioners and the Chancellor appreciate that progress towards this objective must depend upon the re-establishment of a true sense of security in Western Europe and they have addressed themselves particularly to this end. In all these matters they have been encouraged to find a wide community of ideas and intention.'

The Petersberg Agreement laid down the results of our negotiations in altogether ten points. These included the agreement to promote the participation of Germany in all those international organizations through which German experience and support could contribute to the general welfare. The Western Allies, it said, 'record their satisfaction at the various steps already achieved in this direction, including German participation in the Organization for European Economic Cooperation (OEEC), and at the desire expressed on both sides that the Federal Republic should be promptly admitted to the Council of Europe as an associate member and finally at the proposed signature of a bilateral agreement with the United States of America covering Economic Cooperation Administration assistance'.

It had been agreed that the Federal Government could now initiate the re-establishment of consular and commercial relations with those countries where such relations appeared advantageous.

The decisive importance of the Petersberg Agreement was in the economic field. The deletion of many plants from the dismantling list and further relief in economic matters smoothed the path to the reconstruction of German economic life. The reprieve of important industrial installations was significant; but what mattered just as much was the psychological effect of these concessions on the initiative and daring of our entrepreneurs and other leaders of economic life, and on the will to work of our labour force, the indispensable condition of success. The contents of the Agreement embodied the points discussed with the High Commissioners.*

The Stormy Bundestag Debate of 24–25 November 1949

On 24 November, speaking for the Government I informed the German Bundestag and with it the German public of the contents of the Petersberg Agreement.

I have been reproached for not submitting a resolution for the adoption of the Petersberg Agreement. But it must be remembered that the Bundestag was a very young parliament and many of its members were apt to try meddling in the executive where they had no business. We were convinced that the Federal Government had to see to it that the executive and the legislative arms remained separate. This was especially important in all matters affecting relations with the High Commission or with the Allied powers. The SPD tried to exercise a decisive influence on foreign policy by way of the foreign affairs committee whose chairman was a Social Democrat. The KPD tried to create trouble wherever they could, by all kinds of questions. That was the reason why the governmental coalition, which had the parliamentary majority, explicitly declared that the Petersberg Agreement did not fall within the competence of the Bundestag and was not to be made the subject of a Bundestag resolution. Incidentally, the Petersberg Agreement was not ratified by the French Chamber of Deputies or by the British House of Commons or by the American Congress.

After the government statement which was made at 5 p.m. according to an arrangement made with the governments of France, Great Britain, and the United States – the text of the Petersberg Agreement was to be made public simultaneously in Paris, London, Washington, and Bonn – the meeting was interrupted until 9.30 p.m. when the debate on the statement was to proceed.

The SPD's rejection was very violent. I had not expected it to be otherwise. The debate became heated and dramatic. Dr Arndt was the first SPD speaker. In the course of his very long speech he tried to suggest that in signing the Petersberg Agreement I had tried to eliminate parliament. It was an attempt 'to win constitutional battles by an authoritarian *coup de main*'. I did not have the right to agree to Germany's participation in the International Ruhr Authority, nor did I have the right to oblige the Federal Republic to join the Council of Europe. Arndt said:

> I am afraid that the Western Allies, instead of pursuing a European policy, are getting into a policy of interests which tends rather to prop up an authoritarian Adenauer régime than to allow it to be replaced by a democratic régime . . . What we have to debate and to vote on today is nothing

* The text can be found in Ruhm von Oppen, *Documents*, pp 439–42.

but a test of whether the Basic Law is a scrap of paper and whether the majority can continue in its endeavours to ride roughshod over it, as has already happened several times in this house, or whether we here respect the Basic Law.

(Social Democrats: Very good!)

We thought we were on the way to a parliamentary democracy and find ourselves on the way to a monarchy without a constitution.

(Loud laughter and interjections in the centre and on the right.)

Ladies and gentlemen, I am afraid you won't laugh much longer.

(SPD: Very true! Unrest and laughter on the right and in the centre.)

You may rest assured that we shall at all times direct the brightest searchlight into this darkness and you may rest assured that we remember that the Federal Chancellor took an oath on the Basic Law when he assumed his office here and by God, Mr Chancellor, we shall not let you forget this oath! . . .

The KPD described my policy as a 'policy of adventures'. To counter this adventurous policy the representatives of the KPD demanded the creation of a 'national front of all Germans who desire the unity and independence of the fatherland'.

While especially the KPD and the SPD were sharply rejecting my policy, several telegrams arrived from the workers of the plants that had been reprieved from the dismantling list endorsing my actions. It all became very exciting when I read the text of a UP report which reproduced the reaction of the executive of the League of German Trade Unions to the agreement between the Germans and the Allies. This report was handed to me when I was in the middle of replying to a speech by the SPD deputy Dr Schäfer. This is what the official record of the Bundestag says about this part of the debate:

Now I must, ladies and gentlemen, inform you of a despatch that has just reached me. From this despatch you will see that, thank heavens, there are even in Germany great and influential organizations that think differently from the representatives of the opposition. I have just received the following telegram from Düsseldorf, which is the reaction of the League of German Trade Unions to the German-Allied agreement:

'In the German-Allied Protocol which had just been published one could recognize the earnest endeavour of the Allies to meet German needs' says a first reaction of the League of German Trade Unions.

(Hear, hear! on the government side.)
(Interjection from the SPD: Who says that? – Deputy Dr Schumacher: So what?)

A number of problems, however, remain. It will therefore be the noblest task of all the authorities concerned to dispel the worries about their livelihood of those working people who continue to be threatened by the dismantlings.

(Very true! on the left. Deputy Dr Schumacher: So what?)
    – One moment! It is very much a question whether you will continue to say 'Very true!' when you hear what follows, the chief point.
(Hilarity.)

Although the German-Allied Agreement was not satisfactory in all respects, it was the opinion of the Trade Unions that it was right for the Federal Government to cooperate in the Ruhr Authority.

(Sustained and lively applause on the right and in the centre.)
(Deputy Dr Schumacher: That is not right! Unrest.)
    – I shall read you the sentence once more.
(Deputy Dr Schumacher: Who signed that?)

Although the German-Allied Agreement was not satisfactory in all respects, it was the opinion of the Trade Unions that it was right for the Federal Government to cooperate in the Ruhr Authority. Above all because it seemed that the apprehensions concerning Article 31 had been disposed of. The Trade Unions hoped that the Federal Government's step would eventually lead to the inclusion of the heavy industries of Europe in the competence of the Ruhr Authority.

(Applause in the centre and on the right.)
(Deputy Dr Schumacher: Who signed the telegram?)
(Interjection from the left: Signed 'Adenauer'!)
(Hilarity in the SPD and KPD.)
(Deputy Dr Schumacher: A telegram in indirect speech! You will get the answer tomorrow!)
(Deputy Dr Wuermeling: The dictatorship of the SPD over the trade unions!)
(Further interjections. Unrest. Speaker rings his bell.)

This telegram is a despatch of the United Press from Düsseldorf.

(Laughter on the left. Interjections on the left: Aha! Commissioned! By Adenauer! Deputy Dr Schumacher: In indirect speech! Unrest. Speaker rings his bell.)

    – I cannot understand all this excitement.

(Unrest. Speaker rings his bell.)

I read you a telegram of the United Press.

(But you said you had received a telegram from the trade unions!)

224

1　Sir Winston Churchill in conversation with Dr Adenauer

2 Dr Adenauer *(extreme left)* and officials of the British Military
Government in Cologne in 1945. General Barraclough is in the center

3 Dr Adenauer with Kurt Schumacher, leader of the SPD, at left, and
Professor Carlo Schmid

4 Cologne in 1945. Ruins of the Church of St. Columba, with the destroyed City Hall in the background

5   Chancellor Adenauer being greeted in the White House by President Eisenhower in April, 1953

6   Vice-President Nixon and Secretary of State Dulles receiving Chancellor Adenauer at the airport in Washington, 7 April, 1953

Clg, den 5.8.49.

Sehr geehrter Herr Präsident!

Ihr Schreiben vom 26.7. ist mir hier mit einiger Verspätung gefolgt.

Leider kann ich Ihnen keine Zusicherung betreffend eine Abänderung der ergangenen Beschlüsse geben. Wie so oft handelt es sich um eine Mittellösung, die niemanden zufriedenstellt.

In Potsdam — wo Frankreich nicht zugegen war — wurde, unter Ablehnung der Reparationen durch Leistungen auf die laufende Produktion, die Demontage als Hauptquelle der Reparationen angesehen. Die Russen haben beide Verfahren gleichzeitig durchgeführt, abgesehen von der Enteignung der Betriebe als Ganzes.

Die Westalliierten würden durch den Verzicht auf die Demontagen jeden Anspruch auf Reparationen verlieren. Sie verstehen unzweifelhaft, die innerfranzösischen Widerstände gegen einen solchen Verzicht.

Meinerseits verhehle ich mir

keineswegs, wie sehr der Wahlkampf hierdurch belastet ist. Meine dreissigjährige parlamentarische Erfahrung belehrt mich, übrigens, dass unter allen Umständen die Okkupationsmächte die Kosten der Kampagne zu tragen haben würden, selbst wenn die Demontage-Frage nicht im Vordergrund stünde (wie dies z. B. in der französischen Zone der Fall ist). Der Wähler sieht und fühlt nur was besteht, vergisst leichter was besser geworden oder in fester Aussicht steht.

Der Ausgang der Wahlen wird bestimmend sein für die weitere Entwicklung der Beziehungen zwischen Westdeutschland und den Alliierten. Jeder Radikalismus würde die angestrebte und durchaus mögliche Entspannung ernstlich in Frage stellen. Seit Juni 1948 wurde Wesentliches erreicht, ohne Zwang und Drohung. In diesem Sinne bleibt jede Möglichkeit offen; nur muss sie beiderseits verstanden werden.

Mein Wunsch, sehr verehrter Herr Präsident, und meine Hoffnung gehen darauf hinaus, von ganzem Herzen.

In freundlichster Erinnerung

Ihr ergebener

Schuman

7 Letter from the French Foreign Minister, Robert Schuman, to Dr Adenauer

8   Dr Adenauer and his cabinet being received at the Petersberg, in Bonn, 21 September, 1949, by the Allied High Commissioners, Robertson, François-Poncet and McCloy

9   During the Pleven Plan Conference in Paris in December, 1951
(from left to right): Hallstein, Bech, Van Zeeland, Adenauer, De Gasperi,
Schuman, Stikker

10   The signers of the Allied-German Agreement on May 26, 1952, in
Bonn *(from left to right):* Sir Anthony Eden, Dr Adenauer, Dean
Acheson and Robert Schuman

11 The high point of the visit to the United States—Dr Adenauer at
Arlington Cemetery

– I read the telegram verbatim, Dr Schumacher.

(Interjections from the SPD: That is no telegram, that is an agency report!)
(Further interjections. Unrest. Speaker rings his bell.)

Speaker Dr Köhler: Dr Schumacher, may I say something. As far as I remember the Chancellor said he had received the following telegram.

(Quite so!)

He did not say from whom.

(Deputy Dr Schumacher: Tomorrow I shall read you the text of the telegram!)
(Further interjections. Unrest. Speaker rings his bell.)

Please let the Chancellor continue.
Dr Adenauer: Ladies and gentlemen, I repeat that this telegram has been generally disseminated by the United Press.

(Deputy Dr Schumacher: So?)
(Further interjection: A lot of forgeries have been disseminated.)

I would like to ask Dr Schumacher to ask not me but Dr Böckler.

(Deputy Dr Schumacher: No, this United Press report is an objective and subjective untruth!)
(Laughter and objections among the government parties.)
(Deputy Dr Wuermeling: How do you know? Are the trade unions under your tutelage?)
(Deputy Strauss: There one sees the true principles!)
(Unrest. Speaker rings his bell.)
I was very grateful to Dr Böckler for this telegram in a political matter that I considered of the utmost importance for us. That the SPD was none too pleased about the attitude of the League of German Trade Unions was understandable.

Incidentally I should like to add here that I did not use the word 'telegram' with malice aforethought in order to mislead Dr Schumacher. During my years as Chancellor I sometimes caused the greatest worries and embarrassments to my staff by asking to be shown a certain 'telegram' by which I often meant agency despatches that reached us on the ticker.

After this incident – it was now after midnight – it was moved that the continuation of the debate on the Petersberg Agreement be adjourned to a later hour of the day that had already started. The majority of the house rejected this motion, however, and the debate continued. It brought another climax in this Bundestag marathon.

The press release of the executive of the League of German Trade Unions continued to be called in question. In order to prove its authenticity I had caused inquiries to be made at the office of the chairman of the League, Dr Böckler. A lady secretary by name of Klein confirmed that the text, as I had read it in the debate, had been given to the press by telephone as a statement by the executive of the League of German Trade Unions. It was about three in the morning of 25 November when I spoke once more in order to discuss the SPD's doubts regarding the correctness of the UP report and to inform the Bundestag of the confirmation by the executive of the League of German Trade Unions. I said:

It is not the task of an opposition to see everything as a matter for opposition.

(Very good! on the government side.)

I regard that as an erroneous view.

(CDU: So do we!)

Furthermore: All of us, I think, in this room who have had any office or function in political or public life have spent years now trying to get dismantling stopped.

(Very true! on the government side.)

I can say it of myself, I can say it of my party, I can say it of the Federal Government.

(Deputy Kaiser: And of the whole people!)

All tried as hard as they could and explored every possibility to try to get the dismantling stopped.
But now I should like to recall what I said in this room when we met last. On 31 October, when we had prepared a big new proposal in agreement with the parties, I was told by the most authoritative British source: 'Don't bother. It is no use. All these proposals will be rejected out of hand.'

(Lively shouts of Hear, hear!)

Then I was told: 'The only way you can get anywhere is by looking at the whole question from the point of view of security. In order to meet the security needs of the West European Allies you must declare that you are prepared to cooperate in the Military Security Board and that you are prepared to send a representative instead of an observer to the Ruhr Authority.' Ladies and gentlemen, I do not understand what it is that always clouds the vision of the speakers of the SPD. It is not in any way the question whether we, the Federal Government, or whether you give your assent to the establishment of the Ruhr Authority!

(Very true! on the government side.)

Everyone knows that the Ruhr Authority exists.

(Very true! on the government side.)
(Objections on the left.)

You know perfectly well that the General Secretariat exists and you know that the whole organization already numbers more than one hundred. You know all that! And you know as well as everybody in the room that the only question is this: shall we send a representative who will cast the three German votes or shall we let the whole dismantling programme unroll relentlessly to the very end?

(Very good! on the government side.)
(SPD objections.)

That is the question we have to decide . . .

(SPD interjections: NO!)

. . . and, ladies and gentlemen, I must conclude – after Herr Ollenhauer's last speeches I must unfortunately draw this conclusion – that the Social Democrats here prefer to let all the dismantling continue to its end.

(Cries of Very good! and Hear, hear! and lively applause on the government side.)
(Interjection from the left: Really shocking!)
(Reply from the right: Your English friends are letting you down!)
(Interjection from the SPD: What political tactlessness!)
(Deputy Schoettle: That is what we are used to from them.)
(Unrest.)

This is the question on which the opposition must take a stand.

(Lively assent from the government side.)
(Interjections from the left.)

– that is the question at issue and nothing else: Is the opposition prepared to send a representative to the Ruhr Authority or not? And if the answer is: 'No', then the opposition knows from the statements made to me by General Robertson that dismantling will continue to the end.

(Deputy Dr Schumacher: That is not true!)
(Hear, hear! and interjections from the government side.)
(Further agitated interjections from the SPD and KPD. The Speaker rings his bell.)
(Deputy Renner: How do you make that up?)
(Interjections from the left: Are you still a German? Do you speak as a German Chancellor?)
(Deputy Dr Schumacher: The Chancellor of the Allies!)

Speaker Dr Köhler: Dr Schumacher . . .

(Shouts of protest in the centre and on the right. Much noise and banging of desk-lids. SPD and CDU/CSU deputies rise from their seats and engage in vehement altercation. Speaker continuously rings his bell. Noise continues.)

Dr Schumacher . . .

(Noise continues as do cries of 'Shame!' and shouts of 'Shocking! Out! Out!' in the centre and on the right.)

Dr Schumacher . . .

(Continuing noise. Continuing bell. Noise continues.)

Dr Schumacher! I must call you to order for calling the Chancellor 'Chancellor of the Allies!'

(Continuing commotion.)

Dr Adenauer, please continue!

(Continuing uproar.)
(Deputy Ollenhauer: Herr Adenauer himself provoked him and no one else!)
(Further shouting and arguments between deputies.)
(Speaker rings his bell. Noise continues. Speaker rings his bell.)
(Deputy Dr Oellers: I move that the Council of Elders be convened.)
(Continued commotion and shouting.)

I have called Deputy Dr Schumacher to order.

(Interjection from the centre: That is not enough!)
(Deputy Dr Oellers: Mr Speaker, I move that the Council of Elders be convened immediately and ask for a vote on the motion.)
(The Federal Chancellor leaves the rostrum.)
(Continued violent commotion. Speaker rings his bell.)

Ladies and Gentlemen . . .

(Continuing noise. Deputy Strauss: You must apologize or we leave the Chamber! Speaker continues to ring his bell.)

Ladies and gentlemen, please be quiet for a moment so that this matter can be dealt with! I have before me a motion to interrupt the meeting and to convene the Council of Elders immediately in view of the gravity of the terms used by Deputy Dr Schumacher.

(Lively assent on the government side and objections on the left. Renewed uproar.)
I note that the majority is for a pause. I suspend the meeting and shall call the Council of Elders at once.

(Vigorous shouts of 'Bravo!' and applause on the government side. Continuing unrest on the left.)
(The session is interrupted: Friday 25 November, 3.21 a.m.)
So much for the Record of the Bundestag. Dr Köhler resumed the meeting shortly after 6 a.m. I continue with the parliamentary minutes:

> Speaker Dr Köhler: Ladies and gentlemen, I resume the meeting which was suspended a short while ago.
> We have had a thorough discussion in the Council of Elders of Deputy Dr Schumacher's interruption in which he called the Federal Chancellor 'Chancellor of the Allies'. Repeated attempts were made to persuade Deputy Dr Schumacher to retract this grave insult to the Chancellor,

(CDU interruption: And to us! Deputy Mrs Weber: To us all!)

> and thus, I add, to this Chamber, the Bundestag, and thus to the Federal Republic.

(Very true! from the CDU.)

> For the Federal Chancellor represents the State, that is what we must remember.

(Laughter in the KPD. Deputy Rische: Don't be so dramatic!)

> That, surely, Mr Deputy, is my affair. I shall thank you for not telling me how I am to carry out my duties!

(Lively applause and clapping in the centre and on the right.)
(Deputy Renner: But it can be overdone!)

> Ladies and gentlemen: after consultations with the parties we transmitted the following proposal to the SPD representatives as mediators: Dr Schumacher should retract his grave insult to the Federal Chancellor in due form and I added – that was at twenty to six by my watch as I should like to stress – that the Chancellor, when this apology has been received, will be glad to see Dr Schumacher in the course of the day. I added that the plenary session will be resumed at six o'clock. I sent up a messenger. What can you tell me? I hear that the message is that discussions have not yet been concluded.

(Unrest. Interruption from the right: This is going too far!)

> Ladies and gentlemen, permit me to continue. I was quite explicit on the resumption of the session at six o'clock and see no reason for allowing another interruption.
> I have ascertained in discussions with the parties that the overwhelming majority of this house regards the terms of Dr Schumacher's interruption of the Chancellor as a violation of paragraph 91 of the Standing Orders, in

229

other words a flagrant violation of order. I regret that the attempts to get Dr Schumacher to retract his interruption have been in vain.

Therefore, by virtue of my office and of my duty to the Chancellor

(Interruption from the centre: And to ourselves!)

and to this Chamber I rule that under paragraph 91 of the Standing Orders Deputy Dr Schumacher be suspended from participation in the deliberations of the Bundestag for twenty parliamentary days for a flagrant violation of order.

At first the SPD had decided to react to this decision of the Speaker's by staying away for twenty parliamentary days as a group. But press reports showed that Dr Schumacher had given the contrary advice 'to abandon the intention to stay away from all parliamentary work for the duration of his suspension. The parliamentary party group decided to comply with this request because it sees in the Federal Government's conduct of affairs an increasing threat to the social fate of large parts of the population and because the group is filled with deep concern about vital national problems. In view of these considerations it has decided not to forego the parliamentary control of this Federal Government'.

Incidentally, I had a written apology from Dr Schumacher a few days after this debate. I accepted it and that was the end of it.

This acrimonious debate in the Bundestag caused the Allied High Commission to declare in a big press conference on 25 November that the Protocol on the Petersberg Agreement published on 24 November was not to be regarded as a stepping stone to further German demands. General Robertson pointed out that the Petersberg Agreement of 22 November was valid until the autumn of 1950 and that the Occupation Statute was due for review at that time. About the possibility of further Allied concessions he said that they were out of the question; the negotiations were concluded. He further stated in the course of the press conference that to promote the prestige and authority of the structure of government, Germany must be introduced into the international political community and causes of friction between the occupation powers and the German people must be removed.

The negotiations were over, Robertson had said in this press conference, and further Allied concessions were out of the question. In fact, however, I succeeded step by step in further conversations on the Petersberg during December and the subsequent months, in achieving further concessions.

This is what the London *Times* of 25 November wrote about the Petersberg Agreement:

Though Dr Adenauer has made many wise and far-reaching concessions it would be a mistake to think that Germany has lost by the bargain. If she has not yet gained full equality she has established her position as a nation with which the Allies must negotiate and to which they can no longer dictate . . . More important than this, however, a way has been found to bring Germany back into the European family without increasing the tensions between East and West. A statement by Britain, France, and the United States alone that they did not intend to rearm Germany would have hardly convinced the Soviet Union and Poland that they meant it . . . A statement by the Federal Government, on the other hand, should carry more weight.

After the Petersberg Agreement it was indeed possible to repeat General Robertson's words, that we had broken out of the ring. I am convinced that the German people would have fallen to communism from sheer misery and despair if unemployment and distress had continued to mount, if the glimmering of hope in a better future to which they still held had been extinguished by failure over the Petersberg Agreement.

14

NEW DIRECTIONS IN EUROPE

Encounter with Robert Schuman in Bonn, January 1950

Ever since the 1920s I had worked for reconciliation and understanding between Germany and France. Good relations between France and Germany were the fundamental precondition for a better future not only of our two countries, but of Europe and of a great part of the world. I knew that lasting understanding could be achieved only by constant purposeful endeavour.

I was also aware that the past cast many shadows across this common endeavour. On the other hand the recognition was growing in both nations that the goal must be reached for the sake of the interests of both countries and their intellectual, cultural, and human ideals. I was sure that neither ruins nor memories would prevail over this clear recognition and the necessities created by general developments; the goal would be reached.

One of the chief obstacles in the way of German-French understanding after 1945 was the Saar question. France wanted to attach the Saar territory to herself; we resisted as best we could. I was in constant personal contact with the representatives of the three (as yet unofficial) parties in the Saar who led the resistance to these French aspirations.

Since 1945 the Saar had been part of the French zone of occupation, but France wanted to attach the territory to herself politically and economically. The Potsdam Agreement, however, and a number of later declarations had made it quite explicit that there was to be no change in the German frontiers of 1937 until the Peace Treaty.

In 1947 – finally and explicitly at the Foreign Ministers' Conference in December 1947 – the United States and Great Britain conceded to France the economic annexation of the Saar. This economic annexation had already been virtually achieved by the introduction of a customs union and by currency measures. But the United States and Great Britain had repeatedly stressed that the final settlement of the Saar question must be reserved to the peace treaty with Germany.

A memorandum of the American State Department of October 1948 expressly declared that legally the Saar, which after the end of the war had been put under French supervision as part of the French zone of occupation, remained under the jurisdiction of the Allied Control Council for Germany as long as this body maintained its authority over the Saar. It was a declaration of the greatest significance in international law. The Saar was part of

French occupation territory under the jurisdiction and sovereign authority of the Western Allies, and this legal state of affairs could not be in any way affected by any assurance given to France concerning support of her claims at the conclusion of a peace treaty.

In October 1948 I had met Robert Schuman, then French Foreign Minister, for the first time. We had a very frank and confidential conversation at Baffenheim, dealing chiefly with the Saar question. Schuman intimated that France regarded the return of the Saar to Germany as possible. France's main concern was the securing of her economic interests. Robert Schuman's views on this nerve-point of Franco-German relations had put my mind at rest. After our conversation I observed the greatest reticence on the Saar in my speeches and was under constant attack for it from Dr Schumacher, the chairman of the SPD.

At the beginning of 1950 the Saar question threatened to develop into an acutely dangerous political issue. During the first half of January 1950 there had been unofficial negotiations between France and the Saar Government (formed in 1947) aimed at the conclusion of 'State Treaties'. According to my information these treaties concerned the autonomy of the Saar and the lease of the railways and Saar mines to France for the duration of fifty years. I did not know the contents of the draft treaty on the autonomy of the Saar. If it was merely intended to consolidate the position of the Saar Government vis-à-vis the occupation power, if the treaty was to create an 'occupation statute', as it were, there would hardly have been any ground for objection. But the use of the term 'autonomy' and certain utterances of the Saar Government pointed to rather different plans. There must be no final settlement of the Saar question that prejudged the peace treaty. The Federal Government must not permit itself to be deprived of the right to be a partner in the negotiations on this question at a future peace conference.

It seemed to me that the development of the Saar question was once more putting the relationship between Germany and France under great strain. This was all the more regrettable at a moment when the German Bundestag was to decide whether it wanted the Federal Republic to join the Council of Europe. My conversations with the chairmen of the party groups in the Bundestag left me with the impression that in case of unfavourable developments in the Saar question they would not accept responsibility for accession to the Council of Europe before their parties and the German public.

On 13 January 1950 the French Foreign Minister Robert Schuman paid his first visit to the Federal capital Bonn. I had taken the occasion of Schuman's impending visit for thorough talks with the party leaders in the Bundestag in order to harmonize the attitude of the Federal Government on the Saar question with that of the parliamentary party groups. I regarded this first visit of the French Foreign Minister to the Federal Republic as very important because I hoped that it might yield the beginnings of a solution of the Saar problem.

On 14 January I gave a luncheon for Schuman at which he said some very encouraging things.

I have the great pleasure of standing before you today not as an individual, but as representative of a nation and a government animated by the same feelings. If now and then we are tempted to hesitate or to be shaken in our faith, we must think back to times when we had not yet come so far, to the years 1923 and 1924, for instance, four and five years after the First World War. If we compare the situation in our relations then with what is possible today, we have more than one cause for hope.

What is most important is the creation of an atmosphere, a climate for our future cooperation. That is the main purpose of this first personal encounter in Bonn. As soon as we broach concrete questions, we naturally feel much more the obstacles and the difficulties still to be overcome; at such times there are means we can employ, certain principles that we must follow. First of all we need frankness in our exchanges, and then a lot of patience. I think the politician of today must above all have strong nerves. It is not always easy to remain calm because what happened on both sides was not always calculated to promote cool judgment. We must on both sides also be aware of the psychological difficulties: you of ours and we of yours. Only when we overcome these obstacles will the road be clear for our work.

This work also requires courage and perseverance. You, Mr Chancellor, have given us the example. All who are here and who in the past suffered so much for their ideas and especially for the idea of liberty and never lost hope, all of them I include in my high regard, in the respect I express to you, and which is due to you, because only the experiences and sufferings of the past create once more a foundation for positive and constructive work.

We shall have to look for solutions from the national point of view in both countries so that problems can be settled. We are not guided by ideological prejudices. We know that despite all justified particular attitudes our nations must stress what we have in common. Only thus can we succeed. We know from history that, especially during the past century, many conflicts arose between Germany and France. It used to be thought that these conflicts are unavoidable. History teaches the contrary. Over long periods we had peaceful relations. That is the very thing we must stress; we must not think only of the events that led to conflict.

In this context I recall my personal experience as a student in Bonn. In those days, when I could not foresee what was in store for us during this half century, I laid the foundations of new spiritual and intellectual insight. I experienced in my own person how much common good can be gained in our cooperation.

That is why I welcome this opportunity for an encounter and share your conviction, Mr Chancellor, that we shall thereby dispel whatever may still lie like a kind of miasma over our political activity and that we shall see more clearly what the fulfilment of our mutual duties demands; for it is a duty we are fulfilling toward our countries. We do it not only for them; what we do will have effects far beyond our frontiers and we shall be guided by what humanity expects of us.

When I now, in conclusion, raise my glass to drink to the health, the future and prosperity of the young German Republic, I do it not only with a sincere wish, but with the conviction that we are already engaged in laying the foundations for this common future and that when one day the history of our time and its problems is written, it will be recognized that we attempted an important piece of work here on the Rhine, our Rhine, the German and French Rhine, this river that is one entity despite all national frontiers. I am convinced that our work will succeed.

On Sunday, the last day of Schuman's visit to Bonn, I had a conversation with him at Castle Ernich, the seat of the French High Commissioner. It lasted two hours and was characterized by mutual trust. Schuman spoke German fluently. We were alone during this conversation.

I gave Schuman a full description of developments in Germany, psychological as well as political. I stressed the fact that rumours had been spread about the French Government's intentions concerning the negotiations and the conclusion of agreements with the Saar Government and that they had caused much agitation in Germany which seemed to me to endanger the accession of the Federal Republic to the Council of Europe. In the main there were two questions: the question of autonomy for the Saar and the question of the lease of the Saar mines to France for fifty or ninety-nine years.

I told Schuman that I saw the legal position as follows: any change of the frontiers of the German Reich could only be made at the peace treaty; that was expressly stated in the declarations of the four Allies of 5 June 1945 in which they had assumed supreme authority. Germany's frontiers could only be changed by the peace treaty. France too had recognized this in the declaration of 5 June 1945. The contents of the agreement on autonomy would therefore have to be examined to see whether or not it was admissible. If it meant the detachment of the Saar from Germany, it was inadmissible. If the three Western Allies tolerated anything of the sort, it was impossible to assert the inadmissibility of the Russians' measures in the East.

We discussed the legal aspects of the Saar mines in detail. I made a note on my conversation with Schuman, from which I shall quote.

I told Schuman that the legal position regarding the Saar mines was as follows: in 1918 the Saar mines were the property of the Prussian State. They had then passed into French ownership. After the Saar plebiscite the German Reich purchased the Saar mines from France and they thus became the property of the German Reich.

Schuman asked whether they had not gone back to Prussian ownership. I said this was not the case. Later I ascertained that after the Saar mines had been bought back, they were made part of the Reich-owned Saargruben A.G.

Since the Federal Republic of Germany was the legal successor of the former German Reich, the property of the former German Reich was now the property of the Federal Republic of Germany. When Schuman doubted this and said that this surely did not apply to property of the former German Reich outside the area of the Federal Republic of Germany, I referred him to the relevant article of the Basic Law that had been approved by the Allies, and told him that Switzerland too, for instance, regarded the Federal Republic as legal successor to the property of the former German Reich located in Switzerland. Obviously this entire argument was new and surprising to Schuman. I then added that for this reason too we, the Federal Republic of Germany, had an interest in what happened about the Saar mines.

Schuman showed himself very surprised at the German excitement. He told me that when he decided to come to Germany he knew nothing of this excitement.

In his view the facts concerning any agreements that might be concluded between France and the Saar were these: the legal situation in the Saar was very complicated; he had not created it, but he had found it so when he took over as foreign minister in 1948. There was a Saar diet, a Saar Government, and a Saar constitution. That the frontiers of the former German Reich must not be changed except by the peace treaty was a principle that France recognized too. But there was a special arrangement for the Saar that distinguished it from the three Western zones, inasmuch as the Saar had not been made part of the French zone of occupation and the Western Allies had conceded its economic unity and customs union with France. The Saar railways were under the administration of the French railways and were joined with them. The Saar mines were also under French administration. All profits were being invested in the mines themselves. None of these things was settled. Moreover the Saar Government demanded more influence than it had so far had under the military régime, and finally it demanded profits from the mines. It was therefore at the request of the Saar Government that the Quai d'Orsay had drafted three agreements with the Saar. These drafts had so far only gone to the ministries concerned and to Bidault for their information. They had not yet been discussed in the French cabinet. Nor had they been communicated to the Saar Government.

When I objected that my informant had seen them there, Schuman said that in that case the French military plenipotentiary Grandval must have given the drafts to the Saar Government. It had been agreed with Hoffmann, the head of the Saar Government, that that government was to receive these drafts on 25 January. They were then to be discussed in Paris on 7 February. When I asked why this whole matter had suddenly become so urgent, and if it would not be better to let it rest, Schuman replied that the negotiations would take half a year at least.

The preamble of the three agreements explicitly stressed that all arrangements were subject to the peace settlement. If, for example, the Saar Government were to be abolished by the peace treaty, or if ownership of the Saar mines were allotted to anyone other than the Saar Government, the agreement would then be void. Incidentally, no ninety-nine-year lease had ever been mentioned, but only a fifty-year lease.

I urged Schuman to consider the situation in Germany and asked him whether it was not possible to have tripartite discussions of all these questions between the French Government, the Government of the Federal Republic of Germany, and the Saar Government. Schuman avoided answering this question. He said that when the draft agreements were discussed, Germany would be able to comment. The statute on autonomy was being demanded by the Saar Government to give it greater freedom than it had under the present military administration. The Saar Government also wanted the Saar mines to be leased so as to get the revenue from the tonnage tax.

Schuman stated that if, as a result of one of the accidents that were always possible in France, he were eliminated and Bidault got the foreign ministry, the situation concerning Franco-German relations would become much more difficult. Bidault was, and especially on the Saar question, much less favourably inclined towards the German point of view than himself.

I suggested issuing a joint communiqué on the whole question. He answered that this was impossible because he had not come to negotiate, only to inform himself. He would say everything that was required in the press conference he was going to hold and he hoped that this would dispel all the anxiety for which there was no cause. At the end of our conversation I once more underlined the unusual political importance of the Saar question. I repeated that if it developed in a certain way, German accession to the Council of Europe was doubtful. I therefore pleaded for everything to be done to avoid such complications.

Other subjects dealt with were prisoners of war, the question of France's diplomatic representation, and the security question. I told Schuman that we must get an Allied declaration that they would protect our security. I told him that I saw some danger in the possibility that the Russians might one day propose that all four occupying powers should leave Germany. If such a proposal was accepted, the Russians would be very close. The army in the Eastern zone was already in existence. Schuman said that he would see this as a great danger too, but he did not think that the United States would accept such a proposal.

No joint communiqué was issued on the visit of Foreign Minister Schuman in Bonn. Each of us held a separate press conference.

Schuman gave the journalists a written statement on the Saar question. It read:

> Concerning the Saar, the French Government is determined to follow the policy laid down in the Saar Statute. The basis of the Saar Statute is the Saar constitution, which, with only one communist vote against it, was unanimously accepted by the Saar Parliament.
>
> The technical discussions which are to take place with the Saar Government are designed to take account of practical necessities. Insofar as they bring about modifications, these will be in favour of the government and population of the Saar. These, like the Statute as a whole, will have to be confirmed at the time of the treaty of peace.

Thoughts on a Solution of the Saar Question

On 18 January the American Secretary of State, Dean Acheson, stated at a press conference that the United States would continue to support the French point of view, that the Saar territory should be detached from Germany and the Saar economy be merged with that of France. The United States would also advocate a certain degree of autonomy for the Saar.

On Thursday 19 January 1950 I had lunch with the American High Commissioner McCloy at Bad Homburg. We talked about the Saar question. In the course of our conversation I suggested the possibility of a settlement for the Saar akin to the Ruhr Statute. I returned to this idea in greater detail in a 'Memorandum of the Federal Government on the Saar Question' in March 1950 and described the solution I had in mind. In the memorandum I stressed the conviction of the Federal Government that the economic questions regarding the Saar which were always adduced by the French Government as basis of its demands there might be resolved within the framework of European cooperation. The core of such a solution might be an 'International Saar Authority' which would further develop the fundamental concept of the International Ruhr Authority. Account could also be taken of the economic nexus of the Saar territory, Lorraine and Southern Germany by a special customs system that might resemble the transition arrangements established in the Saar by the Treaty of Versailles for the years 1920 to 1925. Such a régime might be impossible without the granting to the Saar as part of the French zone of occupation some economic autonomy. Such a measure would have to be enacted by legislation of the Federal Republic making it clear that in international law the Saar belonged to Germany. It could well be imagined that this would bring about a state of affairs which, while meeting the economic aims hitherto pursued by France in the Saar, would obviate the necessity of a political detachment of the Saar from Germany.

The Federal Government had to insist in principle that any special régime created in the Saar and particularly any possible political detachment of the

Saar from the rest of Germany must be made the subject of a genuine plebiscite conducted under the same conditions as the referendum of the year 1935. I told McCloy that he had demanded free elections for the whole of Germany. This justified demand must not exclude the Saar.

The Saar Conventions of 3 March 1950

The official negotiations on the Saar Conventions between the French and the Saar Governments had begun on 7 February 1950. Although Foreign Minister Schuman had told me at our meeting in January that they would occupy several months, there were now rumours predicting their conclusion by the beginning of March.

On Thursday 2 March 1950 I had one of the usual conferences with the three High Commissioners on the Petersberg. We discussed the German economy, financial questions, the refugee problem, and civil service regulations. Some points were somewhat unclear and the French High Commissioner, François-Poncet, asked me if I wished to meet the High Commissioners in about a week for a further conference. I replied: 'I do not know how the Paris negotiations on the Saar are developing.'

François-Poncet gave the surprising answer: 'They are concluded. The four Conventions have been initialled and will be signed at 11 a.m. tomorrow. The text of the Conventions is couched in terms that will give you deep satisfaction, especially the Convention on the Saar mines. This Convention is valid only until the peace treaty. If the peace treaty sanctions the present agreements on the Saar mines, the Convention will simply continue. But in no case would its validity exceed fifty years. As regards the administration of the Saar railways, the present agreement differs from the original project. A kind of Saar Board or Council will be established which will however have no French representative; this means that the Saar railways will not, as originally intended, be under the administration of the French railways. These are some of the main points that might interest you. I would ask you to treat this information as confidential and not to talk about it until it is published by the two contracting parties tomorrow afternoon.'

I answered François-Poncet that I had heard some time before that an agreement such as he had just outlined was intended for the mines. I had then confidentially informed the representatives of the parties in the Bundestag of this. The reaction was very unpleasant, and I had been told that in such circumstances we could not advocate the accession of the Federal Republic to the Council of Europe. I therefore thought it highly unlikely that we would now get a Bundestag majority for accession to the Council of Europe. I felt I had to point out that this fact was a consequence of the way the Saar question had developed. I felt obliged to say that I was convinced the Bundestag would unanimously oppose accession to the Council of Europe and that this would naturally lead to great complications in the European situation.

We then discussed what we should say about this meeting in the press. We agreed on the following press release: 'At the end of the evening the High Commissioners had a meeting with the Chancellor. As usual, they discussed current questions with him, especially the question of refugees, the decree on the civil service, and the question of the embargo on steel deliveries to the East.'

Before the meeting was closed, François-Poncet said: 'Mr Chancellor, you have not yet answered the question whether you want to meet us again in a a week's time.' I replied that after the announcement of the Saar Conventions the parliamentary parties would meet at the beginning of next week. The original plan had been that the Bundestag was not to meet during the next two weeks, but if the Saar agreements were now published in the form he had described to me, we must expect a demand for an immediate meeting of the Bundestag. I would, however, plead that a decision of such enormous importance as would then confront the Bundestag should not be taken in a hurry. Whether I would succeed was another question.

François-Poncet said: 'I agree that it would be wise not to discuss this problem too soon. The first impulse is not always the best. Especially in a country as nervous and excitable as yours it would be advisable to let some time pass and also to look round to see what the general international atmosphere is like.'

We parted without settling the date of a new meeting. The Saar Conventions were signed on the next day, 3 March. The following day – it was a Saturday, 4 March 1950 – I called a press conference in order to make a statement on behalf of the Federal Government on the situation created by the conclusion of the Saar Conventions.

An immediate comment from the Federal Government was urgently required because there was great confusion in the German press. Some headlines may indicate it: *Frankfurter Rundschau:* 'France leases Saar Mines'; *Frankfurter Neue Presse:* 'France drops her claims to ownership'; *Frankfurter Allgemeine Zeitung:* 'The Saar Decision: Against Europe'. This last headline seemed to me to sum up precisely what could be said about the whole matter.

The text of the Saar Conventions had only reached me on 4 March, shortly after eleven o'clock. It was voluminous. The Conventions were very important indeed. Roughly one million Germans living in the Saar were to be detached from Germany. It was also a case of coalmines being taken away which we needed for an economic balance inside the Federal Republic.

The Federal Government had to act as representative of the entire German people because the Western powers at least had always treated us as responsible also for those Germans who did not belong to the Federal Republic, such as the people of Berlin, the Eastern zone, and the Saar. This responsibility forced the Federal Government to state its position in the matter of the Saar.

The whole essence and development of the Saar question were of the greatest importance for another reason: there was a danger of the German people losing faith in the declarations of the Western Allies. The Saar Conventions that had been initialled in Paris were in direct conflict with a series of declarations made by the Government of the United States as well as the British and French Governments. The Allies had so far always maintained the position that a change in the frontiers of Germany could only be made by the peace treaty. In the press conference I stressed the fact that the governments of the Western Allies had repeatedly underlined this premise. They declared it too in 1949 when the cession of border territories to Belgium and Holland was in question. At that time there was an explicit statement by the Western Allies that these were temporary measures and that the final settlement of frontier questions would be made in the peace treaty.

As recently as January of this year the American Secretary of State had told me that although the United States would support French wishes regarding the autonomy of the Saar and its economic unity with France when the peace treaty should be concluded, this did not mean that France had *carte blanche* until then.

At the Paris conference of November 1949 France had, as I learned, proposed that the Saar should be represented in the Council of Europe. At first the Anglo-Saxon powers had opposed the proposal. In the end, however, they had yielded to French insistence, but with the proviso, which was however not made public, that the accession of the Saar to the Council of Europe was to be dealt with in the context of a peace treaty for Germany. At the Paris Foreign Ministers' Conference of 9 and 10 November 1949 the three Western Allied governments had expressly declared that the status of the Saar was not to be finally settled until the peace treaty with Germany.

I saw a great psychological danger for us Germans and for the situation of Europe in the conclusion of the Saar Conventions. I was afraid that the conclusion of these Conventions might cause a revival of nationalist tendencies among the Germans. I was aware of the fact that the Saar question could become a dangerous explosive, a focus of agitation for nationalist circles. At the press conference I therefore urgently pleaded with all Germans, and especially the war generation, not to heed nationalist urgings and insinuations.

During Foreign Minister Schuman's visit in the middle of January 1950 I had begged him to let the Saar problem rest for a while. There was, as I told him, no compelling reason at the moment to settle the Saar question in such a rigid form. I had drawn his attention to the extraordinary difficulties that would result from the conclusion of such Conventions for a moderate, a non-nationalist Federal Government. I had explicitly stated my conviction that it would do grave damage to the attempts at Franco-German understanding that had started so well. I had also told him that it seemed to me to endanger the development of the Council of Europe and the European Union. As a friend of reconciliation between France and Germany, as a friend of the European idea, I had begged him not to let France treat the Saar question now, but to let it wait until Germany had joined the European Union. Evidently Schuman had not been able to prevail in the French cabinet.

Robert Schuman held a press conference on 6 March 1950. He explained that the Saar Conventions were merely a consequence of the Saar constitution of 1947. It was this constitution which really had already brought about the political detachment of the Saar from Germany. He, Schuman, did not understand, he said, why there were these sudden protests in Germany because as he saw it what had happened now was only the logical consequence of the Saar constitution. In the course of the press conference Schuman also said that a European solution was in no way endangered, that France had a genuine desire for reconciliation with Germany. This passage gave me hope.

The Bundestag parties decided to call a special meeting of parliament for 10 March 1950. I was to make a statement for the Government and then the Saar problem was to be debated. I asked all members of the cabinet to take part in this plenary session. We could not underline clearly enough that the Saar question was of the greatest imaginable importance for us: for one thing because it prejudiced the question of Germany's Eastern frontiers, for another because there was a danger that the Saar issue would now considerably reinforce nationalist tendencies which in the end could only benefit the Soviet Union.

There were four Saar Conventions: a 'General Convention', a 'Convention between the French Republic and the Saar on Economic Union', the 'Agreement on the Exploitation of the Saar Mines', and the 'Agreement on the Saar Railways'.

The two first referred to the Saar constitution promulgated in 1947. The two last agreements stated explicitly that their validity after the conclusion of the peace treaty with Germany depended on the contents of that treaty. No such connection was mentioned in the first two agreements. This difference in the formulation of the agreements led the Federal Government and, after discussions of the foreign affairs committee of the Bundestag, that body too, to conclude that the two first-mentioned agreements, especially the politically fundamental 'General Convention', were intended by the two contracting governments to be understood as independent of the coming peace treaty.

On 8 and 9 March declarations were issued making it unambiguously clear that the 'General Convention' was likewise subject to the peace settlement. On 8 March 1950 Lord Henderson made a statement in the House of Lords on behalf of the British Government repeating that the final status of the Saar could be determined only by the peace treaty. In the late evening of 9 March 1950 the representative of the French High Commissioner gave the press an official statement which, translated, read as follows:

Some German political circles have interpreted the absence of explicit references to the peace settlement in some of the agreements made between France and the Saar to mean that these agreements unjustifiably prejudge the provisions of the future peace treaty.

Official French circles declare that there is no foundation for such an interpretation. As Minister Schuman clearly stated at his press conference of 6 March 1950, all the agreements recently concluded between France and the Saar are subject to confirmation in the context of the final peace settlement.

On 9 March I also had a letter from the British High Commissioner General Sir Brian Robertson, saying *inter alia*:*

In Lord Henderson's declaration my Government clearly stated that it is explicitly laid down that the final status of the Saar can only be settled by a treaty of peace. In this sense the Conventions have only a temporary character and are only valid until the peace treaty. That seems to me to be a quite unambiguous statement by my Government concerning its attitude to these Conventions and you will see that it applies to all the agreements and that in this respect no difference is being made between them.

It is quite certain that my Government will maintain this interpretation at the conclusion of the peace treaty.

After these declarations there could be no doubt that the first two agreements made between France and the Saar on 3 March 1950, especially the 'General Convention', also needed confirmation by the peace treaty, despite statements to the contrary by the Saar Government.

This had an important logical consequence: since the settlement of the Saar problem was to be part of the peace treaty, it also concerned the Federal Republic of Germany; the German Federal Republic was thus also entitled to take part in the determination of the final status of the Saar.

In my parliamentary statement I demanded with all the emphasis and the seriousness at my command that the basic rights and freedoms, whose protection the Allies so solemnly promised, should be established. I said I could not imagine that the French people and the French Government knew the conditions actually existing in the Saar territory. I was convinced that if they did they would in no circumstances tolerate their continuance. It was possible that French public opinion might receive what I was saying unfavourably. But I felt an obligation of conscience to speak as I did and believed that if a man like myself who for decades had championed Franco-German understanding said these things, they should at least be examined by public opinion in France. I asked the French public to note that the removal of differences between Germany and France was the necessary precondition for any European recovery, something I had been saying in public for more than twenty-five years, a thesis I had also, constantly and with undiminished resolve, put forward as Federal Chancellor.

* Retranslated.

I summed up what I had to say as follows:

1 The governments of France, Britain, the United States and the Federal Republic of Germany are agreed that the final settlement of the Saar problem should be part of a peace treaty to be concluded with us. This means that we have a right to take part in the settlement.

2 It also means that before the conclusion of the peace treaty no conditions should be brought about in the Saar territory that were not susceptible to change by the peace treaty.

3 The four agreements concluded between the French and the Saar Governments on 3 March 1950 would, taken together, create conditions in the Saar that could no longer be changed by the peace treaty.

4 Under international law France is the trustee for the Saar and the sequestrator of the railways and mines there. Neither under international nor under civil law could France conclude agreements like those of 3 March 1950.

5 The Saar Government has no rights in the railways or mines and is therefore not authorized to conclude the agreements.

6 The German Federal Republic urgently desires that the principles of liberty and democracy be realized in the Saar.

7 The German Federal Republic desires a settlement of the Saar problem that does justice to the interests of all parties concerned, including France. It is convinced that such a solution can be found.

At the end of my statement I made an urgent appeal that the Saar question should in no circumstances be allowed to lead to a disturbance of relations between France and Germany and thus to obstacles in the way of building up Western Europe.

My Proposal to Form a European Political Union

The Saar agreements had caused widespread doubt in Germany as to whether the German desire and hope for good relations with France were reciprocated. Doubts had arisen in Germany about whether France really and seriously wanted to lead Germany back as an equal member into the society of nations and to let her participate in the reconstruction of Europe and the world. It was no good ignoring these doubts, either inside Germany or outside. They had, rather, to be overcome.

In order to overcome the prevailing state of paralysis and mistrust by a visible and decisive step, I proposed a European Union. I did this in an interview with the American journalist Kingsbury-Smith on 7 March. I knew that the idea was bold, I also knew that it would be difficult to put into practice. But that must not be allowed to stand in the way of a bold beginning. The new economic order in Europe under the Marshall Plan had already done a great deal in the desired direction. The same could be said for the Council of Europe. Europe was in great danger and only bold ideas and rapid action could promote her consolidation.

In the interview with Kingsbury-Smith I made the offer of a complete Union of France and Germany and described it as a remedy against all our differences over the Saar and other problems. The Union was to be a foundation stone for the United States of Europe. I made the proposal at a moment when political tension in West Germany threatened to reach a climax as a result of the Saar Conventions which France had just concluded. Something had to be done.

This is what I told Kingsbury-Smith:

A union between France and Germany would give new life and vigour to a Europe that is seriously ill. It would have an immense psychological and material influence and would liberate powers that are sure to save Europe. I believe this is the only possible way of achieving the unity of Europe. It would cause the rivalry between the two countries to disappear.

I stated that I was prepared to support a Franco-German Union provided Britain, Italy, Belgium, Luxembourg, and the Netherlands were free to join as well. I mentioned these countries to prevent giving the impression that a Franco-German bloc would be formed to force its will upon others. I stressed in the interview that the return of the Saar to Germany would be an essential condition for such a union. I also pointed out that I expected the Saar problem to solve itself if the question of Franco-German relations could be answered on a higher plane and from the bold perspective of the union of the two countries.

I was deeply disturbed by the measures France had taken which were tantamount to an annexation of the Saar coal mines for fifty years. I told Kingsbury-Smith of my fears that annoyance at this step would give a boost to nationalism in Germany and might cause extreme nationalists to turn to Russia for support.

On 21 March 1950 I gave Kingsbury-Smith another interview. The Federal Government was still without a foreign minister and it was therefore very difficult to take any steps in foreign affairs. Interviews were a means of reaching a foreign audience. Kingsbury-Smith had come to me for amplification of my offer of union between Germany and France which, as he said, had aroused worldwide interest. I was glad to tell him more.

One of the main reasons for my proposal had been the constantly growing political tension. The general political situation was causing me intense anxiety. It ought to cause all the other statesmen equal anxiety. Some European politicians, however, seemed to be blind to the existing danger. I sometimes asked myself whether the world would ever profit from the lessons of the past. If it meant to do so, it would have to make up its mind to bold decisions. But the will seemed to be lacking in our time. That was why the world was trying to escape into the unknown. I sometimes found a widespread view that the West had time, because Soviet Russia did not want war and would therefore not bring it about. But I regarded it as a great mistake for the world to allow itself to be lulled to sleep by a false feeling of security and to take hopes for certainties.

I continued:

> The United States and Soviet Russia have rearmed. American rearmament has developed so far that there is no great immediate danger of the United States being conquered. But I doubt whether the Soviet rulers are so convinced of the state of American rearmament that war is not worth while for Soviet Russia. It is my conviction that any war would be worth while for Soviet Russia which left Europe in her hands. That can happen in many ways, for instance by military conquest. If Western Europe were occupied by Soviet armies, many millions of people would come under Russian rule. Russia would thereby not only have brought Western Europe under her power geographically, but at the same time the mind and working potential of Europe would be enslaved. All who might form the heart of resistance or the starting point of a rebirth of Western democracy would be liquidated. It appears to me not only questionable but improbable that the United States would fight for the liberation of a Europe that has been 'purged' in this sense. Hence, I believe that the incentive to make war is greater for Soviet Russia than is generally assumed. In these circumstances peace can only be secured if the Soviet leaders are convinced of the hopelessness of conquering Europe.

Kingsbury-Smith asked me to tell him my views on the present situation in Western Europe. I replied that I did not see it as promising. As a result of the last elections Great Britain was not in a position to make really bold decisions. That could already be seen quite clearly in her foreign policy. In contrast to the usual English traditions, government and opposition had very different ideas about the defence of Western Europe. In Italy there were very serious internal tensions. France had one strike after another. The Council of Europe was as yet unable to show any notable results.

In view of this state of affairs the old world did not have much genuine faith in the future of Europe. I was, however, convinced that all this could change overnight once the world had real proof that there was still strength left in Europe for a new life. The cold war was a matter of psychological warfare. If Soviet Russia could really be convinced of the firm determination of Western Europe to take a new and decisive step it was bound to have a profound influence on Soviet policy towards Europe and the world.

Kingsbury-Smith asked me what I thought could be done immediately to bring about the union between Germany and France which I had described as the foundation stone of a united Europe and as the first step in a new direction.

I invited him to remember Germany's political situation at the end of the Napoleonic wars. There were then countless small, independent German states. Every state had its customs borders, its own currency, and its own army. This condition was remedied by the formation of a German customs union

246

and the establishment of a customs parliament which ensured the free exchange of goods between those many states. The customs union and the customs parliament were the beginnings of German unification. What I had in mind was a similar procedure to bring about union between France and Germany. A start could be made with the gradual merger of the two countries with regard to tariffs and the economy. The instrument for such a union might be a common economic parliament to be formed by members of the two countries' legislative bodies. Both governments could decide on a body that would hold joint responsibility with the economic parliament. The scope of the economic parliament and the governmental representation could be enlarged in the course of time so as to bring about the gradual unification of the two countries. The Saar Conventions were an example of how two countries could be merged.

It would doubtless be a big step forward if Frenchmen and Germans sat in one house and at one table in order to work together and to carry joint responsibility. The psychological consequences would be inestimable. French security demands could be satisfied in this fashion and the growth of German nationalism could be prevented. I felt that the understanding that would grow between Germany and France on this basis would be even more significant than all the economic advantages that would undoubtedly accrue.

Kingsbury-Smith asked me what I imagined the general effects in Europe would be and I said:

A union such as I am suggesting is already coming into effect in the Benelux countries. The Scandinavian countries, as well as France and Italy, are contemplating similar measures. I therefore believe that these countries will welcome the union between France and Germany that I am proposing. They will surely be prepared to join such a union. If Great Britain really sees herself as a European power, she could occupy the place inside the framework of the United Nations of Europe that corresponds to her position and strength.

The union I am proposing would also provide an incentive to the Marshall Plan. France and Germany would be the first countries to reach the goals envisaged by the fathers of the Marshall Plan and would smooth a path for the other participants. In this way the American people would see some real returns for the billions of dollars they have given to Europe, because there would be a genuine and significant contribution from within to the reconstruction and unification of Europe.

The Council of Europe would likewise benefit from a union between France and Germany. The Council's effectiveness has been limited by the absence of a real understanding between France and Germany. It seems to me that no sensible person can fail to recognize that the union here proposed will give new strength and new life to the idea of European unification.

I am firmly convinced that the union of the two nations will considerably raise the standard of living of both parts. The bigger an economic area is, the better it can be developed. The United States of America proves that.

As I see it, this union could save the civilization of the West from decline. The cross-fertilization between France and Germany would undoubtedly give an extraordinary impetus to the cultural achievements of the two peoples. It would be another respect in which a Franco-German union would prove a signpost of our epoch.

I concluded the interview by stressing the more certain chances of success of a bold 'flight forward' in the present serious situation. 'Europe must not close its eyes to the danger of the hour. Blindness means capitulation, because it cripples the power of action. The time for action has come. May Europe make the right decisions to face a better and more secure future.'

On 16 March 1950 de Gaulle endorsed the proposal of a Franco-German union. He recalled that Franks, Gauls, and Romans had united to defeat Attila. A union between France and Germany would continue the work of Charlemagne. One could imagine a vast field for joint activity of the two neighbouring nations and he was deeply impressed by the thought of the strength that would be generated by such a union. The future fate of Europe depended in large measure on the development of Franco-German relations. De Gaulle welcomed the Saar Conventions. Economic union between France and the Saar was necessary; and the autonomy of the Saar was the proper foundation for it. He understood perfectly that the Germans regretted this solution, but thought that the Saar was not very important compared with the European interests at stake. If a union between France and Germany, such as I had outlined, were to come about, it was possible that the quarrel about the Saar would lose its importance altogether.

Should We Join the Council of Europe?

The question of the accession of the German Federal Republic to the Council of Europe had to be decided.

The Council of Europe was the first combination of the countries of Europe in a permanent political institution. The Statute of the Council of Europe, which had been signed by ten European countries – Belgium, Denmark, France, Great Britain, Ireland, Italy, Luxembourg, the Netherlands, Norway, and Sweden – had come into force on 3 August 1949. This document describes the goal of the Council of Europe as being the achievement of greater political unity to make possible the realization of the ideals and principles of the common European heritage and the promotion of economic and social progress. The Council of Europe consists of:

1 the Council of Ministers
2 the Consultative Assembly of members delegated by the parliaments of the individual countries, as representatives
3 a Secretariat that deals with the business of both bodies and is headed by a Secretary General.

There was full membership, but also a possibility of Associate Membership. The Petersberg Agreement had envisaged accession as associate member for the Federal Republic.

The accession of the Federal Republic to the Council of Europe was made extremely difficult by the Saar Conventions. There was a danger that there would not be a Bundestag majority in favour of joining.

After a relatively long interruption I had another meeting with the High Commissioners on 22 March 1950. General Hays was acting as substitute for McCloy. In the course of this conversation I brought up the subject of the accession of the Federal Republic to the Council of Europe. I had received a communication from François-Poncet saying that the Federal Republic should apply in writing to the Council of Europe, requesting admission. I told the High Commissioners at our meeting that as far as I knew Article 5 of the Ten-Power Treaty of 5 May 1949 provided for invitations to associate membership to be issued by the Committee of Ministers. François-Poncet had let me know that the foreign ministers of the United States, Great Britain, and France had decided at their conference in Paris on 9 and 10 November that Germany must first file a request for admission. The German public was not yet aware of this condition, which was not based on the European Statute but on a special decision of the three Western foreign ministers. I had so far told nobody of this message from François-Poncet. It was my intention to talk it over first with the High Commissioners because I did not want to create needless excitement among the German public.

I told the High Commissioners that if I were to table a motion in the Bundestag on the question of our joining the Council of Europe, there would probably be no majority for joining. The Social Democratic Party had repeatedly and explicitly declared that if the Saar were to be admitted to the Council of Europe simultaneously with Germany, the SPD would unanimously vote against accession of the Federal Republic to the Council of Europe. The unfortunate development of the Saar question had resulted in the other parties, which had so far not shared the SPD's opinion, now being divided. I was convinced that the majority of the Bundestag would come down against joining the Council of Europe. Whether this was sensible was not the question. In matters that were open to psychological influence, we must take things as they were.

When I had finished François-Poncet explained how he and his colleagues saw the question of the procedure for German accession to the Council of Europe. He admitted that a country wishing to join the Council of Europe had

249

to be invited by the Council. Before a country received this invitation, it was, however, necessary to let the Council of Europe know that the country wished to join, so that the invitation should not be exposed to the danger of rejection. On the other hand the country desiring an invitation must be sure that the Council of Europe was prepared to issue this invitation. This was the reason why the three ministers had informed me that if I expressed my wish to be invited they would advocate an invitation to the Federal Republic. This procedure would prevent surprises on both sides.

What was lacking at the moment to set the mechanism in motion was my expression of the wish of the Federal Republic to be invited. François-Poncet finished with the question: 'You understand that if this invitation were rejected, it would create a very vexed situation. May I hope that I have expressed myself clearly enough?' I replied: 'But not convincingly.' By way of explanation I said that it went without saying that an invitation was only issued if the issuer knew that it would be accepted.

I read the passage concerning the admission of the Federal Republic to the Council of Europe from the Petersberg Agreement. The Agreement said:

> The High Commission and the Federal Government are agreed to promote the participation of Germany in all those international organizations through which German experience and support can contribute to the general welfare. They record their satisfaction at the various steps already achieved in this direction, including German participation in the Organization for European Economic Cooperation (OEEC), the desire expressed on both sides that the Federal Republic should be promptly admitted to the Council of Europe as an associate member . . .

Concerning the statement 'They record their satisfaction at the various steps already achieved in this direction' I said that these 'steps' included the desire expressed on both sides that the Federal Republic should be admitted to the Council of Europe as associate member. This declaration in the Petersberg Agreement fully satisfied the decision of the three foreign ministers of 9 and 10 November, all the more since I had so far not been officially informed of this decision. German public opinion would see a desire to make Germany's accession to the Council of Europe more difficult in the demand to apply, that was now being underlined, while the Petersberg Agreement already fulfilled the stipulated conditions. I was concerned, I stressed, to prevent a further stiffening of public opinion in Germany.

Since the Petersberg Agreement, I continued, the whole situation had changed in a regrettable way. The Saar affair had finally been added to this entire development and it had a worse effect in Germany – I was bound to stress this – than the High Commissioners could imagine. How much I was nevertheless trying to work for the integration of Germany with Europe was proved by the interviews I had given. To be sure I had been given to understand, very courteously, that an interview was not a diplomatic act. Despite this I felt I wanted to say that the plan of a customs union between France and Germany had been suggested by me as far back as 1925 to the government of the then chancellor Marx and had been approved by it. Various adverse circumstances had prevented progress at that time. In conclusion I said that I was afraid that if some gesture was not made toward Germany, I could not submit the question of the accession of the Federal Republic to the Council of Europe to the Bundestag, because I was convinced that the majority would vote against it.

François-Poncet repeated his earlier position. He said: 'This question seems to me quite clear. You have many excellent qualities, Mr Chancellor, but once you have taken your stand on an issue, it is extraordinarily difficult to lead you out of it again. I beg you to think about it. This question contains neither a trap nor a demand. It is based on nothing but good intentions. Every time we try to do you a service, we get a box on the ear. Every time a definite issue is to be decided, you express the wish for a gesture by the other side. What is the gesture you desire?'

I replied that I did not want to comment on the expression 'box on the ear'. François-Poncet said he had been mistranslated and that he had said 'we get rapped over the knuckles'. To which I replied: 'I think an objective listener to our negotiations would not share the view that I am the teacher with a cane.'

Then I once more explained my attitude to the High Commissioners in a few sentences. If the Saar Conventions had not been made, I would have submitted the appropriate application to the Bundestag without further ado. I was pretty sure that I would then have got a majority. As recently as the middle of February I had asked M Spaak whether or not he wanted to invite Germany to join the Council of Europe. I asked him whether, as far as the Council was concerned, any steps were expected from the German side, and he answered: 'No.'

François-Poncet emphasized once more that the Federal Republic could receive no invitation to join the Council of Europe unless I indicated that this invitation would be accepted, and he also pointed out that if the Federal Republic received an invitation and refused it, there would not be another.

I replied to François-Poncet that the significance of the whole matter had been quite clear to me for weeks. In order to prevent this material becoming explosive in the hands of nationalist groups, I had quite consciously used harsher language at my press conference of 4 March than later in parliament. When I discussed the Saar Conventions in the Bundestag I had not spoken about the European Council but had mentioned instead the responsibility of the three Western Allied occupation powers for the German Federal Republic. I said that we were not yet a sovereign state and the High Commissioners were co-responsible for what happened in Germany. I intended, by giving the High Commissioners a frank description of the entire situation, to give them a chance to do something that was in the interest of Europe and of Germany. I had said that what was needed was a gesture to save the situation. I was sorry to have to say that at this moment François-Poncet's news about the procedure for accession to the Council of Europe struck me as the opposite of such a gesture. François-Poncet had just asked me what I meant by a gesture. That seemed obvious to me. It would not take much to win over the Germans even at this last moment. I regretted that I was unable to be more specific because I did not want to lay myself open to being told by Germans: 'You made another proposal and that was rejected too.'

François-Poncet asked me again what I meant by an Allied gesture and whether I wanted the entry of the Saar into the Council of Europe to be given up. I answered that I knew that the foreign ministers of Britain and the United States had, despite their initial protests, finally yielded to Schuman's demands in Paris to invite the Saar to join the Council of Europe. But there had been a limitation: that this was provisional until the peace treaty. I also knew that the publication of this proviso had been prevented. I felt that it would have a beneficial effect if this Paris agreement, by which the Saar as well was to be invited to the Council of Europe, were now published in full. François-Poncet seemed very surprised at my information. He admitted that if a future peace treaty abrogated the agreement with the Saar and if it were decided that the Saar was no longer an autonomous state, it went without saying that this would cancel the Saar's membership in the Council of Europe as an independent country.

I replied that he had made a true observation from the point of view of international law: if the peace treaty abolished the autonomy of the Saar, membership in the Council of Europe was also terminated. I said that I would like to ask, however, for the subject of our conversation not to be shifted. I had said that the Paris conference had explicitly decided that the Saar was to join the Council of Europe 'until the peace treaty', and that this addition had not been published. I wanted to lodge a complaint about the failure to publish this addition although it was an explicit decision.

François-Poncet said the reason was the belief that no one could be so deeply mistrustful. I rejoined: 'Do you mean me, Mr Ambassador?' François-Poncet admitted it. Whereupon I declared that I was still much too trusting.

I then answered François-Poncet's question about whether I expected the Saar not to be admitted to the Council of Europe by saying: 'You gave an assurance on that and you must stand by that assurance.' As I saw it the situation could still be saved by a gesture. I could not make a definite suggestion because I did not want to expose myself to a rebuff.

Robertson now entered the conversation. It was quite clear, he said, that two preparatory steps were required to make Germany's entry into the Council of Europe possible. The first prerequisite was that the invitation to Germany be sent. This was fulfilled by the three Allied foreign ministers' assurance of support for such an invitation. The other prerequisite was the assurance that an invitation of the Council of Europe would be accepted. He,

Robertson, thought that my signature under the Petersberg Agreement represented an obligation on the part of my Government. This signature did not, however, represent an obligation that the Bundestag must accept accession to the Council of Europe. I had made that quite clear when I described the mood in the Bundestag. This really meant that there was no certainty of acceptance. He, Robertson, believed that the three foreign ministers would see such certainty in an application for admission. He wanted to stress, however, that such an application was not the indispensable prerequisite for admission.

He had drawn two conclusions from today's conversation. The first was that there was at the moment no hope that Germany would apply for admission to the Council of Europe on the basis of a vote in the Bundestag. The second was that I believed the situation could still be changed if some new element were introduced. At the moment he could not imagine whether there was a possibility of this. But he knew one thing and that was that the accession of the Federal Republic to the Council of Europe was of the utmost importance for Germany as well as for Europe. François-Poncet commented that he was not sure that a magic formula could be found to solve this difficult problem, but he assured us of his readiness to help.

Since the Council of Europe was due to assemble on 30 March a way out absolutely had to be found before then. We decided that a committee of political advisers should be formed to prepare a proposal. Time was pressing. As François-Poncet stressed, formulations had to be found the very next day to be submitted to the several governments for their approval. François-Poncet thought the problem consisted in putting the right question to the Bundestag. The question had to be put in a form that did not shock. The question would have to have my assent and that of Dr Schumacher.

I said that Dr Schumacher's assent could not be got in any case because he had already fixed his position in public and could no longer depart from it. The Bundestag was meeting on this day, the next day, and the day after. To put the question publicly to the Bundestag was totally inopportune at the present moment. I suggested that communications from the High Commissioners should put me in a position to tell the representatives of the Bundestag parties in a confidential conference – and I would of course invite the Social Democrats too even if they refused – something that would make them declare: If an invitation comes, we shall try to get a Bundestag majority for acceptance. This would also give the Allies the assurance that the invitation was going to be accepted.

François-Poncet asked whether it would be enough for me to tell the party chairmen in the Bundestag that the admission of the Saar could be subject to revision in the same way as the whole Saar Statute. I replied that something more was needed to convince the representatives in the Bundestag that the Federal Republic was really welcome in the Council of Europe. I said: 'Perhaps I may add this quite openly: many of our people are convinced that France does not want to have us in the Council of Europe at all because she has now concluded these Saar Conventions which, as the French Government well knows and as I told Foreign Minister Schuman myself, erect the greatest possible barrier to the entry of Germany into the Council of Europe and for which, furthermore, there was no discernible reason. I asked Foreign Minister Schuman: 'Why do you want to do that now? You have everything you want already.' His answer was: 'We have all we want, but there is no legal foundation under it and that we want to provide now.'

François-Poncet stated that I was one hundred per cent wrong if I assumed that France did not desire Germany's entry into the Council of Europe. He assured me that France wished it as much as the United States and Great Britain.

On the following day, 23 March, I received the parliamentary chairmen of the coalition parties and discussed the situation with them. After fairly long deliberations they agreed to my sending the following letter to the three High Commissioners, one to each:

Bonn, 23 March 1950

Mr High Commissioner,

With reference to our negotiations yesterday I have the honour to inform you of this:

I would make the attempt, and I am convinced that it would be successful, to achieve a majority of the Bundestag for accession to the Council of Europe, if I were first to receive a letter from the three High Commissioners or their deputies covering roughly these points:

1. The three Western Allies – Britain, France, and the USA – hold the entry of the Federal Republic of Germany to be urgently desirable.

2. The Saar's membership in the Council of Europe is provisional until the final settlement of the status of the Saar by the peace treaty with Germany.

3. The Federal Republic of Germany will become a full member of the European Council as soon as possible. Pending full membership she can be represented on the Committee of Ministers by an observer.

If, owing to the shortness of the available time, it is impossible to give a plain assent to point 3, it would be sufficient if the High Commissioners or their deputies wrote that this was so and that the governments of the three High Commissioners would advocate this assurance.

To ensure against the possibility of the High Commissioners sending me such a letter in vain, I suggest they write saying they would send me a Note with the contents outlined above if a Bundestag majority is to be expected. On the basis of this letter I would begin my endeavours among the leaders of the parliamentary party groups and would inform the High Commissioners of the success of my discussions. If a majority seems assured, I would then receive the Note outlined above.

I imagine that subsequent procedure might consist in my letting the Committee of Ministers of the Council of Europe know, through the High

Commissioners, that an invitation would be accepted and that thereupon Germany would be invited. I would then bring the matter before the plenary session of the Bundestag.

Since the Bundestag will still be sitting tomorrow, Friday, I would very much appreciate being in possession of the communications by the morning of Friday 24 March that enable me to begin negotiations with the parliamentary party leaders. In order to avoid even the semblance of an official step toward the High Commission as such on my part, I am taking the liberty of addressing this communication separately to each of the three High Commissioners.

(signed) Adenauer

The answer* came on the same day.

Bonn-Petersberg, 23 March 1950

His Excellency
The Chancellor of the
Federal Republic of Germany

Palais Schaumburg
Bonn
Koblenzer Strasse 141

Dear Mr Chancellor,

I have the honour to acknowledge receipt of your letter of 23 March which is engaging our earnest attention.

In the Petersberg Agreement both sides expressed the desire that the Federal Republic should immediately be admitted as Associate Member to the Council of Europe. Yesterday's discussion between you and ourselves will have confirmed your awareness that our views on the matter have not changed and that we maintain the conviction that this kind of membership would also go furthest to meet the interests of Germany.

We also explained that a separate membership of the Saar in the Council would be subject to confirmation at the time of the conclusion of a peace treaty.

As regards your request for an assurance that the Federal Republic will become a full member of the Council as soon as possible and that meanwhile a German observer should participate in the meetings of the Committee of Ministers, we must say that these are questions exceeding our competence. We must therefore refer back to our governments in order to ascertain whether and to what extent they can support your proposals in practice.

We must also let our governments see the part of your letter that concerns questions of procedure. We therefore sent the text of your letter to our governments at once.

* Translated from the German.

I regret that I am unable to give you an answer tomorrow or in the next few days.

(signature)

My action found the full approval of the cabinet. The ministers thought that my position should be maintained even if it meant a delay in the Ministerial Committee's decision on the accession of the Federal Republic.

The Council of Europe met on 30 March. It adopted a resolution to invite the Federal Republic and the Saar to join the Council of Europe as Associate Members. I received a letter from the Secretary General of the Council, Camille Paris, dated 31 March 1950, in which he informed me of this resolution.

The first two points of my letter of 23 March 1950 had been taken into account, but not the third, for the Statutes of the Council of Europe had not provided for the admission of observers. I was satisfied with the first two points and was prepared, in these circumstances, to advocate the accession of the Federal Republic to the Council of Europe in the Bundestag.

I sent a memorandum to the members of the cabinet in which my reasons for joining were explained. It read:

It should be clear that the Saar question, which has been handled without free and frank exchanges of views on the basis of mutual readiness to come to an understanding, must not be allowed to serve as an excuse for withdrawal from European cooperation which transcends it in importance. It is a fateful question for the German people to decide whether it wishes to see Europe split up between the great power blocs of the United States and the Soviet Union and divided up into nation states warring with each other politically and working against each other economically, or whether Europe is to achieve political and economic unification which will endow it with a weight of its own as well as inner stability. Although the Council of Europe has some faults it is as yet the only way. I must warn against saddling Germany with the odium of having brought the European negotiations to nothing.

The Schuman Plan

On Tuesday 9 May 1950 we held the cabinet meeting on entry into the Council of Europe. I had asked the chairmen of the parliamentary party groups, Dr von Bretano, Dr Schäfer, and Dr Mühlenfeld to join us as well. The conference began at 9.30 a.m. It was very important that the cabinet should come to a decision. A conference of the three Western foreign ministers was due to start in London on 11 May 1950 and it was to deal with the German question. It was a matter of paramount importance that the German Government should make known its readiness for European cooperation before this

256

conference began. I regarded the cabinet decision of 9 May as of great importance and had therefore called a press conference for 8 p.m. in order to
announce it to the German and international public. In the morning I did
not know that the day was to bring a significant turn in the fortunes of
Europe.

While the cabinet was conferring I was informed that an emissary of the
French Foreign Minister Schuman had an urgent communication for me.
Ministerialdirigent Blankenhorn received the gentleman who gave him two
letters from Schuman for me. He said that their contents were of the utmost
urgency and I should see the letters immediately. The Frenchman, whose
name I do not know, pointed out to Blankenhorn that the Council of Ministers
was meeting in Paris at this very moment and was discussing the contents of
the letters. Foreign Minister Schuman would be very grateful to know my
reaction to the letters at once.

Blankenhorn handed me the letters in the cabinet room. One was a hand-
written, personal letter by Robert Schuman. The other was an official covering
letter for the project laid down in a memorandum which later became known
as the Schuman Plan.

In essence Robert Schuman proposed to place the entire French and German production of coal and steel under a common High Authority within the
framework of an organization that should be open to other European
countries as well. Schuman explained that the pooling of coal and steel production would immediately provide for the first stage of a European federation, the immediate creation of a common basis for economic development,
and for a comprehensive change in their development. The merger of the basic
production of coal and steel and the establishment of an authority whose
decisions would be binding for France, Germany, and the other member
countries, would create the first firm foundations for the European federation
which was indispensable for the preservation of peace.

In his personal letter to me Schuman wrote that the purpose of his proposal was not economic, but eminently political. In France there was a fear
that once Germany had recovered, she would attack France. He could
imagine that the corresponding fears might be present in Germany. Rearmament always showed first in an increased production of coal, iron, and
steel. If an organization such as he was proposing were to be set up, it would
enable each country to detect the first signs of rearmament, and would have
an extraordinarily calming effect in France.

Schuman's plan corresponded entirely with the ideas I had been advocating
for a long time concerning the integration of the key industries of Europe. I
informed Robert Schuman at once that I accepted his proposal whole-
heartedly.

The gesture for which I had asked at the conference with the High Commissioners on 22 March had come in an unexpected and very positive form.
The plan outlined by Schuman was going to ease considerably the problem of

the Saar Conventions and the question of the entry of the Federal Republic into the Council of Europe when these were discussed in the Bundestag.

At the evening's press conference I commented on the Schuman Plan and on the Federal Government's decision to join the Council of Europe. I had asked all members of the cabinet to be present because I wanted to underline the great importance of what I had to say. I explained that the two decisions, that of the French cabinet on the Schuman Plan and that of the German cabinet on entry into the Council of Europe, coincided in time quite accidentally. There had been no prior negotiations.

I explained that during the past weeks I had made great efforts to get some assurances from the Allied Governments concerning our accession to the Council because I hoped that a conciliatory gesture from their side would enable us to achieve as large a majority as possible in the Bundestag in favour of accepting the invitation to the Council of Europe. I had intended to wait until the middle of June before asking the Bundestag to vote on this question, hoping that the passage of time or some unforeseen event might produce general agreement in Germany on accepting the invitation. This unexpected event had now happened in the shape of the plan propounded by Schuman.

The international situation had deteriorated and the Western Allies considered a foreign ministers' conference necessary. Implicitly the German question would play a very great part in the conference. Essentially the forthcoming conference would be concerned with examining the situation all over the world in the cold war between the two great power groups and with an effort to consolidate the Western position. European developments would, of course, form only part of the London agenda, but they would be prominent in the deliberations. The Council of Europe was not yet an ideal instrument, but it was a beginning that promised well. The Western powers were agreed that there could be no favourable development for the Council of Europe without German membership. The question of entry into the Council of Europe must not be viewed too narrowly. We must always look for the great and decisive political developments. As the cabinet saw it there could only be one goal for the development of the Council of Europe: to create a federated Europe which would be an eminently pacific factor in the world.

One had to look at the world situation. Two great power groups, Soviet Russia on one side, the United States of America on the other, divided by their ideologies, developments, and general views, were engaged in a cold war which we all hoped would never turn into a hot war. No other country in the world was strong enough, after the two wars we had lived through, to compete with these two. Even after the acute tensions of the cold war that we were experiencing at the moment had passed, there would continue to be latent tension as long as the world was really only being ruled by these two countries.

It must be our aim to create a third force in a united Europe, a force that could not measure up to these two great powers, but which would at least have enough political and economic strength to put its weight into the scales for the preservation of peace when latent differences threatened to develop into acute tensions. That was how I understood the aim of any European policy, an eminently pacific aim intended to ensure lasting peace for the nations of the world.

There was general agreement in the Western world that the Council of Europe could develop no further without Germany. We Germans had to ask ourselves this question: could we accept the responsibility before our consciences and before our people and before Europe of thwarting the development of a federated Europe at the outset by refusing to enter the Council of Europe? Did we Germans not rather have the duty, after the great guilt we had incurred by the war, to devote all our intellectual, moral and economic strength to the bringing about of this Europe and to making it a force for peace? If the question was put in this way, there could be but one answer to it. Developments in the world had taken such a turn that the Saar Conventions and the representation of the Saar in the Council of Europe paled into insignificance and must not be an obstacle to our entry into the Council. We must keep the great goal before our eyes.

I stressed that the cabinet had discussed the possible repercussions of such an entry in Berlin, in the Soviet zone, and in Soviet Russia. If Soviet Russia looked at the Council of Europe calmly, and really desired peace, she would have to recognize in it a component of peace. Soviet reaction might, of course, be different and we had carefully considered it – we had had a discussion that vividly reminded me of discussions of about two years before when it was a question of calling the Parliamentary Council, adopting the Basic Law, and establishing the Federal Republic. At that time, too, it had been considered whether such steps would not discourage the Germans in the East, whether the iron curtain would not become more impenetrable, whether Berlin would not be put in jeopardy. Those who argued then that Berlin and the German East could only be saved if the German West became strong economically and politically, had been proved right. We would otherwise never have been able to give Berlin the help that enabled it to survive. I felt that our experience of the last few years could be applied to the new problem. The principle seemed to be that the stronger the Federal Republic of Germany became politically and economically, the better it would be for Berlin and the German East.

I expressed the hope that our membership in the Council of Europe would very soon produce appreciable alleviations in the whole field of the occupation régime. I was convinced that the revision of the Occupation Statute, which was soon due, would be much more generous if we were members of the Council of Europe.

I then spoke about the decision of the French Council of Ministers of this morning, 9 May 1950. I stated very emphatically that I regarded it as a magnanimous step toward Germany and Europe on the part of France and her Foreign Minister Schuman. It was undoubtedly of the greatest imaginable importance for relations between Germany and France and for the entire future development of Europe. The decision was not a matter of fine phrases but of concrete and precise proposals for a pooling of French and German production of coal, iron, and steel, with the explicit provision that all other countries could join the agreement. I stressed that the French proposal was based on the principle of equality. There was a provision that where the Germans and French could not agree, an arbiter, elected by both sides, would decide moot questions. I regarded Schuman's proposal as a very important step forward in Franco-German relations, a step whose significance could not be underlined emphatically enough. I added that the production of the Saar also fell under this plan and that thus an essential element of estrangement between us was being removed. I declared that the pooling of the basic production of coal and steel created the genuine foundation for the elimination of all future conflict between France and Germany. It was in this that I saw the extreme importance of the decision of the French Government. I was convinced that the negotiations proposed by the French Government would lead to great progress for the future of our two countries and the future of Europe.

The London Foreign Ministers' Conference of May 1950

The Foreign Ministers' Conference met in London from 11 until 13 May. The final communiqué, which also dealt with the German question, struck me as satisfactory for Germany in every respect. Its contents, form and tone showed considerable progress compared with the former treatment of the Federal Republic by the Western Allies, and I was fairly sure that the near future would bring appreciable alleviations for the Federal Republic. I derived special encouragement from the passage in the communiqué in which the Western powers stated that they were as resolved as before to pursue their aim, laid down in the Washington Agreement of April 1949, of gradual German re-entry into the community of free peoples of Europe. When that process was complete, Germany would be liberated from controls to which she was still subject and accorded her sovereignty to the maximum extent compatible with the basis of the occupation régime. The Western powers desired to reach this goal as speedily as possible. The communiqué said, verbatim:

> The Western powers desire to see the pace of progress towards this end as rapid as possible. Progress will depend upon the degree of confident and frank cooperation displayed by the government and the people of the Federal Republic. In the first place the pace will be determined by the extent to which the Allies can be satisfied that their own security is safeguarded by the development in Germany of a desire for peace and friendly association with themselves.

Clearly the Allies were quite prepared to meet our wishes quickly and to a considerable extent. My expectations seemed to be justified. My quick reaction to the Schuman Plan and the cabinet decision on entry into the Council of

Europe seemed to have had a favourable effect on the Foreign Ministers' Conference in London.

There was to be a meeting with the High Commissioners on the Petersberg on 16 May 1950 at which I was to learn more details about the London Conference. McCloy made it clear at the very outset that our discussion that day was to be chiefly about the London Conference. The High Commissioners gave me a summary of the conference and some additional comment with a document I was given.

McCloy said the foreign ministers had been primarily concerned with the question of how a balance of strength could be established between the communist and the anticommunist world. It was found that there was inequality between the military strength of the communist world and that of the anticommunist world. They had discussed possibilities of remedying this state of affairs. There had been agreement on the point that beside military strength what was needed was a balancing of economic strength. The standard of living in the West would have to rise. It was believed that such a rise would be an answer to the East. The strength and vitality of the West would have to be increased at all costs. There had also been discussion of the situation in the Far East, especially in South East Asia, and there had been agreement on the paramount need to hold the position in South East Asia.

The question of West European integration had played a very important role. Dean Acheson, the American Secretary of State, had explained that the termination of Marshall aid at the end of 1952 would not mean the end of America's interest in Europe.

Foreign Minister Schuman's proposal which, as McCloy put it, had had the effect of a little atom bomb, had also been discussed in detail. McCloy observed that all had welcomed the speed with which I had taken up the plan of Foreign Minister Schuman and declared that I was in agreement with the plan and its underlying principles.

McCloy then turned to the contents of the declarations of the London Conference regarding Germany. He said that it was intended to give Germany more and more independence and to interfere as little as possible in the actions of the Federal Government. Germany was to be made a partner of the Western world as quickly as possible, a world that had a great desire for peace and freedom. The declarations had stressed the importance of a democratic polity and the significance of the freedom of the individual in such a democratic polity. The Allies thought that the realization of these democratic principles in Germany was the best guarantee of a kind of security that could never be achieved by artificial measures of control. McCloy thought that I would surely find it significant that the foreign ministers had been agreed that the presence of occupation troops in Germany served less the usual purposes of an occupation than those of defence against attacks by foreign powers that could harm the young German republic during its awakening and growth.

261

He then handed me some documents that dealt with the German question. The first document concerned the establishment of a study group that was not only to work out proposals for a revision of the Occupation Statute, but was also to deal with a number of different factors that might impede further German developments pending the conclusion of a peace treaty. There had been negotiations on the termination of the state of war with Germany, but a number of technical difficulties had been encountered which complicated the solution of the question. It would not be the task of the study group to bring about the termination of the state of war directly or to prepare a peace treaty, but it was to make recommendations for eliminating the major practical inconveniences arising from the continuing state of war and to prevent even graver consequences that might arise therefrom. The establishment of the study group certainly represented progress. Among the questions it would deal with was that of German pre-war contractual obligations and the question of German claims.

One of the documents given me, Document No. 3, concerned Declarations made by the three foreign ministers on Berlin. The High Commissioners told me that the representatives of the Benelux countries had agreed at once to make more purchases in Berlin than hitherto. Mr Harriman also gave an assurance that more purchases would be made in Berlin through the OEEC.

Robertson, commenting on the results of the London Foreign Ministers' Conference, noted that the documents I had been given were by no means propaganda documents. Nothing had been concealed, nothing was hidden behind a smokescreen. What was thought had been said, and nothing had been said that was not meant. If it was stated in the document that the Allies were resolved to pursue their aim that Germany should progressively re-enter the community of free peoples of Europe, then this was precisely what the foreign ministers meant to say. If the document stated that the Western powers desired the pace of progress towards this end to be as rapid as possible, that had not been put there 'because they wanted to say something nice', but because they really meant it. He continued somewhat as follows: 'If the document says that the pace of progress will depend on the degree of frank cooperation displayed by the German Government and the German people, that is, again, exactly what the ministers wanted to say. It is therefore my own opinion that this document closes the period in which there was talk of Allied concessions to the Germans. A concession is something that is extorted by importuning or by pressure and is not something given voluntarily. In my view this document makes it quite clear that from now on there can be no talk of concessions, but that there is a definite plan to accept Germany progressively into the society of the free nations.'

In my reply I welcomed the setting up of the study group. With regard to the Schuman Plan I said that I had been able to react so quickly to it because it was precisely the plan proposed to the then Reich Government by two friends and myself in 1925, after the termination of passive resistance, when relations between France and Germany had reached a nadir. Our first consideration had been political. I said that the Federal Government saw in the Schuman Plan the instrument that would lay really durable foundations for a European federation and the Federal Government would dedicate itself to this plan with all its strength.

I underlined that I found the tone and form of the foreign ministers' decisions most gratifying. I felt that a new chapter was about to start in the relations between the Federal Republic and the three Western powers and I was very happy to gather from what General Robertson had said that my impression was right.

François-Poncet said with regard to the Schuman Plan that the French Government was intending to ask the governments interested in the Schuman Plan whether they would take part in a study commission to be called by the French Government. It went without saying that the German Government would also be invited to be represented on this commission. So far there were only very general outlines of the Schuman Plan. Details would now have to be defined. Monnet was coming to Bonn during the next week in order to discuss the basic features of the Schuman Plan with me.

The Meeting with Jean Monnet

On Tuesday, 23 May 1950 Jean Monnet visited me with the deputy High Commissioner Bérard. We had a very thorough discussion of the Schuman Plan. Jean Monnet was the Plan's economic organizer and its chief mover. He is a man endowed with a very great talent for economic organization, a real man of peace, and a charming negotiator. I continued to enjoy his friendship in later years.

Monnet expounded the French Foreign Minister's ideas for the plan of an economic merger of the coal and steel industry. I was in complete agreement with the project he described to me. According to Monnet the French Government envisaged the following procedure for the negotiations. There was agreement on the point that once the technical experts of six countries sat down together, the technical difficulties and differences of opinion would seem enormous to them and they would then proceed to discuss them in such detail that the whole plan was in danger of being talked to pieces. Monnet therefore proposed that the countries participating in the conference called in Paris on 20 June 1950 should send no technical experts.

He suggested that countries should be represented by persons with a wide economic horizon and European convictions. The last aspect was the most important. It was also necessary that these representatives be in a position to draft and to discuss agreements in constitutional and international law. Monnet thought, and I agreed with him, that only after the conference in Paris – which was to work as fast as possible – had reached a basic understanding on the scope of the High Authority of the Schuman Plan and on the outlines of the treaties to be concluded, and after the parliaments of the six countries had given their approval, should the field be open to technical experts.

Very soon after the publication of the Schuman Plan Italy and the Benelux countries had declared their readiness to cooperate. Britain, unfortunately, was being very reserved. It was agreed that there should be a first meeting of experts nominated by the individual countries on 20 June. At Professor Röpke's suggestion I had nominated Professor Hallstein of the University of Frankfurt for the Federal Republic. Professor Hallstein had not engaged in any political activities before and soon proved his great worth. I shall come back to his work in another context.

The Bundestag Decision on Entry into the Council of Europe

On 13 June 1950 the Bundestag was to hear a Government statement on the entry of the Federal Republic into the Council of Europe. It was to be followed by a debate and by a vote. I began my statement with the changed international situation that had followed the Schuman Plan and the London Foreign Ministers' Conference. In my statement after the Saar Conventions on 10 March 1950 I had said that doubts had arisen in Germany as to whether it was really seriously intended to include us in the work for the reconstruction of Europe. I had added later that this mistrust must be overcome by a resolute step forward and had proposed a union between France and Germany which other European countries could join. This clearly visible step that was needed to dispel the doubts among Germans after the developments in the Saar question, doubts whether France really wanted an understanding, had now been taken for all to see: it was the Schuman Plan. The SPD had called my interviews with Kingsbury-Smith of 7 and 21 March 'confusing'. I pointed out to my critics that the proposal of a political union that I had made in these interviews had been brought a good deal nearer realization by the Schuman Plan. I thought that this Plan deprived the Saar problem of much of its importance because the Saar mines and foundries would fall under the new agreement. I was convinced that if the Schuman Plan was put into practice the Saar question would solve itself.

I then discussed the Schuman Plan more thoroughly. I reported that the Italian Government, the Luxembourg Government, the Belgian Government, and the Dutch Government had already publicly declared their readiness to enter into negotiations on the basis of the programme drawn up by the French cabinet. I was extremely sorry that the government of Great Britain had up to now found no way of accepting the invitation of the French Government. I expressed my profound regret over this and said that I would not cease to hope that in the course of discussions Great Britain would come to a more favourable view of the Plan.

I was in full agreement with the French Government that the significance of the Schuman proposal was first and foremost political and not economic. A careful perusal of the declarations by the French cabinet of 9 May 1950 showed that the intention that this Plan was to be the beginning of a federal structure of Europe was mentioned explicitly in several places. The political importance had been underlined as strongly as possible and I could confirm from personal conversations with Monnet that the political element carried the most weight in the balance of French considerations. There was good reason for projecting such a scheme for iron, steel and coal if the goal was to do away with the differences that had for centuries existed between the French people and the German people. There was no better way of dispelling French doubts about the German people's love of peace than to bring together the two countries' production of coal, iron and steel, which were always the mainstay of rearmament, so that each partner in this pact would know everything that was happening in this important sphere. I declared my conviction that the whole German people desired for the future a removal of all psychological inhibitions between France and Germany so that at long last peace should prevail in Europe.

Not to enter the Council of Europe and to refuse the invitation would be a repudiation of this French proposal, for the political purpose of the French proposal was the creation of a federated Europe. We all knew that the Council of Europe, imperfect instrument though it might still be, tended in the same direction. It was impossible to turn down the invitation to the Council of Europe and at the same time to say: I want to take the other road to a federated Europe. Whoever refused the invitation to the Council of Europe prejudged the Schuman Plan as well.

I then discussed the Saar question in the context of the Schuman Plan and stated that the High Commissioners expressly declared that the invitation to the Saar Government in no way anticipated a decision of the peace treaty. The Saar problem would lose much of its significance in the light of the Schuman Plan. I held that the Saar Government's entry and Germany's refusal of the invitation were not of comparable importance.

I drew the deputies' attention to my exchange of letters with the High Commissioners which had had the purpose of obtaining further concessions. I had taken these steps in order to make it possible for the Social Democrats to give their assent to the Federal Republic's entry into the Council of Europe. As head of government I had been concerned for the Federal Government's motion to be adopted by a very large majority.

At its Hamburg party conference in May 1950 the SPD had shown its opposition to the Federal Republic's entry into the Council of Europe. I was concerned to win over the SPD as well for the Government's motion. I mentioned a speech Henri Spaak had made in Dortmund on 11 June, stressing that Spaak, as surely all members of the Bundestag knew, was a socialist.

Spaak had addressed a mass meeting in Dortmund on 11 June. He had said that for years Europe had lived on American charity. That was no way of conducting a European policy. The remark was not directed against the Americans, but against the Europeans. In the long run the countries of Europe were approaching complete national autarky and hence perdition, unless Europe seized the only chance, European cooperation. Germany, he said, must play a part in the 'concert of Europe'. Her entry into the Council of Europe would benefit not only the Council, but Germany herself. It would be a heavy blow for the European idea if Germany did not join. He put this question to the German Social Democrats: 'How do you intend to solve the European problem and above all the question of the German East if you stand outside Europe?' The thought put forward by the opponents of the German entry into the Council of Europe that a German entry would mean the abandoning of the Saar and of the territories East of the Oder and Neisse was quite wrong. At Strasbourg the Federal Republic would find allies not enemies in its demand for the return of the Eastern provinces and the desire for German unity. Other German problems too, above all the refugee problem, could be solved only by European cooperation and not in an isolated Germany. Should 'Associate Membership' cause difficulties, this would only be a strong argument to convince all member countries of the necessity of accepting the Federal Republic not only into the Consultative Assembly but also into the Council of Ministers, as an equal partner. As soon as the Federal Republic had a foreign minister it would in any case, Spaak thought, have the chance of membership in the Council of Ministers.

I concluded my statement by once more emphasizing the importance of the decision facing the Bundestag. The goal of the Federal Government in foreign affairs had been from the outset to lead Germany into the community of nations as a member with equal rights and equal duties. This path was especially hard because there had so far been no peace settlement owing to the tensions between the two great groups of powers. It had nevertheless been possible to make some considerable progress. I stated that I would not go so far as to say that whoever rejected the invitation was for the East; but he would certainly be making a declaration against the West. The Council of Europe was a first attempt to federate Europe. All were convinced that if the Federal Republic did not participate in it, the Council was finished and the attempt to bring about a European federation had foundered. We must realize that in the face of the pressure from the East it was absolutely necessary to gather the countries of Europe together; by this alone would Western Europe be able to withstand the pressure from the East. The decision that the Bundestag had to take was of great historic significance and each of its members called upon to take part in this decision would one day have to account to his conscience and the German people for this decision.

The voting on the bill for the entry of the Federal Republic into the Council of Europe took place on 15 June. The deputies of the CDU/CSU, the FDP, and the DP were in favour; the members of the SPD and the KPD voted against. The bill was passed by 220 votes against 152.

15

ON THE ROAD TO FULL SOVEREIGNTY

Interview with the Cleveland Plain Dealer

In November 1949 the foreign press suddenly began to discuss the question of the rearmament of Germany. In France much disquiet was caused by this discussion. The French Minister of Information, Teitgen, stated on behalf of the French Government that France would in no circumstances agree to German rearmament or to German membership in the Atlantic Pact. He said: 'The world should realize that France cannot remain a member of a security system that endorses German rearmament.' If one recalls such statements and then remembers that as early as October 1950 the French National Assembly approved a proposal of the then Prime Minister Pleven for a European Defence Community that was to include a German contingent, one can only marvel at these developments.

At the beginning of December 1949 the discussion of the question of German rearmament revived because of an interview I gave the representative of the American paper the *Cleveland Plain Dealer* on 3 December 1949. The Federal Republic at that time was still not allowed to have a foreign ministry and its foreign policy interests were looked after by the three High Commissioners. I therefore tried to use interviews as a means of explaining our views on foreign affairs to public opinion abroad.

The correspondent of this American paper had broached the question of German security and the significance of the Atlantic Pact and asked for my views on the possibility of German rearmament. I told him that I was against German rearmament. I gave as reason the heavy losses Germany had suffered in the last world war. The correspondent then asked what I thought about a German contribution to the defence of the continent of Europe. He pointed out with some emphasis that some rather important foreign circles were dicussing the necessity of a German contribution, perhaps in the shape of Germans serving in other armies.

I replied that we could in no circumstances give our assent to Germans joining foreign armies as mercenaries. Even if the Allies put forward a demand for a German contribution to the security of Europe, I would refuse to establish German armed forces. At the very outside I would be prepared to consider the question of a German contingent in the framework of the army of a European federation.

The next day – it was a Sunday – I was inundated by telephone calls from journalists asking me for the contents of the interview I had given the correspondent of the *Cleveland Plain Dealer*. Evidently the interview had appeared in a garbled version in the United States. In this garbled version it was now causing great excitement in the world press. I was asked whether it was true that I had changed my previous position on rearmament and was now advocating the creation of a German army. I assured all callers that this was not the case. I was still of the opinion that Germany should not be rearmed. We had lost enough blood. But if there was no way out, I was in favour of creating a European army with a German contingent. I emphasized most strongly that the security of Western Germany was a matter for the Allied forces of occupation.

I denied reports according to which I had described the creation of an autonomous German army corps as necessary or had pleaded for German rearmament. I declared once more that I recognized the desire for security on the part of countries that had suffered from German aggression during the last war. But on this very hectic Sunday I also put the question in my conversations with journalists – which danger was greater in Europe today, the Soviet or the German?

The next day I found it necessary to make a statement to the press to counter all the misleading reports that had been published all over the world on Sunday. I gave the following statement to the press.

During the interview that Chancellor Dr Adenauer gave the correspondent of the *Cleveland Plain Dealer*, Mr Leacacos, on 3 December 1949, in the presence of the deputy Chief of Press Affairs Dr Böx, Chancellor Dr Adenauer explained that he was against all German rearmament in principle. He emphasized that Germany had to devote its entire strength to reconstruction, especially after the heavy loss of life during the last war.

When the correspondent asked what the German Government's attitude would be to an Allied demand to participate in the defence of Europe, Dr Adenauer said: If they insist on German participation in the defence of Western Europe, this could only be given in an extreme case and in the form of the creation of a German contingent inside a European army and under European command. The Chancellor rejected the suggestion that volunteers might be recruited in Germany – there was to be no system of mercenaries.

Asked whether German industry could produce arms, Chancellor Dr Adenauer replied that it was not able to do so because the industrial installations that would be needed for such production had been destroyed. If there had to be any rearmament at all, it would have to be with American arms.

This statement had a largely positive reception at home and abroad. But again there were some very critical voices. I found a report in the *Daily Telegraph* of 5 December 1949 very interesting. According to this report Field-Marshal Sir William Slim, Chief of the Imperial General Staff, had said at the American Military Academy at West Point that Germany was 'the most valuable and the most dangerous nation in continental Europe'. The question of rearming Germany was a matter for the politicians and statesmen. If he were instructed to carry out such a plan, he could make an effective job of it.

What one learned about American attitudes from the press indicated fairly general agreement that the present burden on the American budget, resulting from military aid already assigned to the signatory countries of the North Atlantic Treaty Organization, excluded the possibility of any further expenditure for German rearmament. The opinion was also being expressed in some quarters that Germany could look after her own rearmament. This was reported by the Washington correspondent of *Le Monde* who continued that it had been pointed out to him that the German level of production that had once more been limited at the Paris conference was quite insufficient to permit of any manufacture of war material. Moreover Truman and other responsible American politicians were constantly criticizing the high military appropriations. This put effective material obstacles in the way of German rearmament. From any point of view, however, it belonged to the realm of fantasy.

In an editorial of 5 December 1949 the *Journal de Genève* expressed the opinion which I shared, that in the final resort the question of German rearmament depended on France and on Europe and that the French attitude would decisively influence Washington:

> In the end it will be French opinion that will decide Washington's attitude. If France is willing to hold out her hand to Germany, understanding will be easy. The French will then be the first to understand that it is better to let a possible attack be held by the Germans on the Elbe rather than to bear the full brunt of it on the Rhine. That is the explanation of the successive trips and contradictory statements by statesmen, generals, and American journalists in Germany and France. Are the Germans to be rearmed? The nations of Europe are asking the question anxiously, for they remember the horrors of the last war against Germany. Moscow does not give an answer, but rearms. Washington is pushing the question aside and regards it as 'not topical'. The only real answer must be given by Europe or more precisely by France which must accelerate Germany's integration within Europe, for then it will not be Germany that is rearmed, but Europe that is decisively strengthened. A nationalist Germany that is excluded from Europe will always remain a danger. Just as surely a Germany that forms part of Europe is a factor for peace.

But public and official attitudes in France left little hope for such a development.

The Rhenish conference of the CDU took place in Düsseldorf on 7 and 8 December 1949. Because of the controversies going on at home and abroad on a future German rearmament, a question of the utmost importance for us Germans, I dealt with it there and said:

> After all that has happened in recent years the German people are absolutely opposed to war. We all hope that there will not be another war. Nevertheless tensions between East and West have been growing recently and if both sides take military precautions it is, of course, possible that something may happen. In that case Germany would face the situation disarmed and unprotected. Although Germans cannot be expected to serve as mercenaries in foreign armies, if a European federation were to ask for a West German contribution to the defence of Europe, Germans could in certain circumstances take part in the same way as Englishmen, Frenchmen, and other nationalities.

My precondition for German participation in European defence was complete equality between Germany and the other European nations. Equal duties presupposed equal rights. I thought that rearmament would have far-reaching consequences for the political position of our people in the world. Rearmament might be the way to gaining full sovereignty for the Federal Republic. This made it the essential question of our political future. The Western Allies, especially France, had to be made to face and to answer the question of which danger was the greater: the Russian threat or a German contribution to a European defence community.

I was anxious about the security of the Federal Republic in view of the way the police in the Eastern zone was being armed. The Russians were stepping up the rearmament of the armed police in Eastern Germany. This constituted a threat to our security. The London *Times* wrote on 19 December 1949:

> The more [the Russians] expand and strengthen the People's Police, the more likely will they make the formation of a similar force in the West. Since the Russian danger is at present greater than the German danger, it is quite certain that if forced to choose the Western powers will rearm Germany rather than submit to threats.

In the interview with the *Cleveland Plain Dealer* I had said that the Federal Republic was prepared, if that case arose, to make a contribution only in the context of a European army or, to put it differently, to the army of a European federation. There could be no European army without a European federation. Inside this federated Europe Germany would have her place as an equal member.

There were three factors that determined my attitude to the question of German rearmament:

1 the achievement of sovereignty as a consequence of rearmament;
2 security against the rearmament of the Eastern zone by Soviet Russia;
3 the establishment of a European federation.

The Effects of Events in Korea on the German Situation

At the Cairo Conference of November 1943 the American President Roosevelt and the British Prime Minister Churchill on the one side and the Chinese Minister President Chiang Kai-shek on the other had come to an agreement that Korea was to become independent after the defeat of Japan. The Soviets later endorsed this agreement. For the first period an occupation of the country was envisaged. In accordance with the Cairo decisions Korea was occupied in the course of August and September 1945. North Korea was occupied by the Soviet Union and South Korea by the United States. The 38th parallel formed the demarcation line. There were negotiations between the occupying powers on free and democratic elections which were to result in a government. These negotiations broke down in May 1946. In May 1948 elections were held in South Korea under United Nations supervision. In the course of the same year the United States withdrew its occupation forces from South Korea. Settled conditions were not established in South Korea because gangs were disrupting normal life. These gangs were largely supported by North Korean communists. On 25 June 1950 North Korean troops crossed the demarcation line. Their watchword was liberation of South Korea from the imperialists. This was the moment when the Korean crisis, which had hitherto been merely smouldering, became open war. There was a meeting of the Security Council of the United Nations. As the Soviet representative did not take part, the Security Council was able to vote a resolution by which the United Nations assured South Korea of its support. On 7 July 1950 the supporting troops of the United Nations were put under United States command, and many countries were promising economic aid.

Owing to the late arrival of military support, South Korea was almost entirely overrun by the communists. By August 1950 only Pusan could be held. The United Nations forces began a counter-offensive in September 1950. After the fighting had gone back and forth for some time it was finally possible, in May 1951, to stabilize the front between North and South Korea near the 38th parallel.

The North Korean attack on South Korea and the fighting there caused much disquiet in Germany. The German situation was not unlike that of Korea. Germany too was divided into two parts: one half was under communist dictatorship and the other characterized by free and democratic political institutions. Strong Soviet forces were stationed in the Soviet occupied part of Germany. Moreover the Soviet zone 'People's Police' was a force that had military training. In the German West there were only the relatively weak forces of the occupying powers. The steadfastness and courage of the free German population had been clearly manifested in Berlin and the same qualities could be seen in the Federal Republic. Yet there was a danger that the West German will to resist a threatened attack from the East might flag if the conviction were to become widespread that a defence of the free West

271

German territory had no chance of success. From the military point of view we Germans were quite defenceless. We had to rely on the help and support of the occupying powers. What was absolutely necessary now was a declaration by these powers showing their readiness and firm resolve to defend the Federal Republic including Berlin. There had to be a visible sign of this readiness.

So far, whenever the subject of a security guarantee had been mentioned, the Western Governments had always pointed out that for the duration of the occupation the protection of the Atlantic Alliance also applied to the German areas occupied by the Western powers. But this did not impress me as sufficient.

I thought it was necessary to reinforce the German police in the *Länder*, to create an auxiliary police force on a local basis, and to strengthen the frontier police as well as the railway police. What I was aiming at was the creation of a federal police force. After the outbreak of the Korean crisis I asked for a memorandum to be prepared on the question which was given to the High Commissioners at the end of June 1950. I pointed to the increased need for security in the Federal Republic.

The first official response to this memorandum was another reference by the High Commissioners to past declarations which had created an unambiguous situation from the point of view of international law. There was at first hardly any reaction to my expressed desire for the creation of a federal police force.

In Korea there was open military conflict. In other parts of the world there was a continuing war of nerves. The communists tried to cause unrest among the people of the West by a whispering campaign and the dissemination of wild rumours.

I had learned that the Soviets had stationed more than thirty divisions in the Russian zone, and according to my information these divisions were fully equipped for war. Jet planes had been brought west from the Russian interior. Apart from this build-up of the Soviet military forces, which had an offensive character, there was the militarization of the eastern People's Police, a force that had been detached from the general police and was given special training. According to reliable reports about 60,000 men had been trained by August 1950. Fifteen weapons training centres had been established for the training of officers and noncommissioned officers, and more were in preparation. At this time the People's Police were not yet in a proper condition for real military action, but their development clearly pointed to the creation of an East German army.

I had become more and more firmly convinced that Stalin had always intended to get hold of West Germany with as little destruction as possible. His policy of the first post-war years had not brought the result he wished, but I was convinced that the Soviet Union had not given it up. If Stalin were to succeed in gaining control in the Federal Republic without too much destruction, he would then be able to exercise a decisive influence on France and Italy, countries whose political order was not very firm and where there were strong communist parties. Soviet dominance in the Federal Republic, France, and Italy would make Soviet Russia into the strongest economic, military, and political power on earth. It would mean the victory of communism in the world, including the United States. My policy has always been informed by the conviction that this is the goal of Soviet Russia.

If Russia should succeed in including Western Germany in the Soviet system, it would mean such an access of economic and war potential that Russia would gain a preponderance over the United States. Russia would certainly respect the American atomic striking force until she herself possessed enough atom bombs. In January 1949 the Soviets had for the first time succeeded in exploding an atom bomb. Soviet Russia would probably refrain from an attack until a balance had been reached in atomic production. Then, however, it might happen that neither Russia nor the United States would use that weapon, as was the case with poison gas which both sides in the last war possessed in equal measure so that both sides were careful not to use it. Once an atomic balance had been reached, land armies and air forces might become the decisive factors.

I was firmly convinced that Stalin was planning the same procedure for Western Germany as had been used in Korea. I assumed that in the course of the next few months Russia would detach herself somewhat more from the Russian zone government in order to endow that government with the semblance of an increased freedom of action. I feared that once that stage was reached Stalin would consider the time ripe for using the Russian zone police for a so-called 'liberation' of the West German territories. I considered it extremely doubtful that in such a contingency, in which not the Soviet Union but the Soviet zone government was the aggressor, the United States would use atomic weapons against Russia.

The Federal Republic was in a very dangerous situation indeed. We were totally unarmed, we had no defence forces of our own. The forces of the Western Allies in Germany were not strong enough as far as I could judge. The Soviet zone, on the other hand, had its People's Police and was strongly armed. The Federal Republic would be quite defenceless against an attack from the Russian zone.

If the Russian zone army were to attack with tanks, as had happened in Korea, the consequences of their advance were easy to foresee. The population of West Germany would stay neutral in the face of this advancing Russian zone army, first and foremost for psychological reasons, because the advancing troops would be Germans. But the people would also stay neutral because events in Korea had taken away much of their faith in the strength of the United States. I mentioned before that North Korean troops occupied the bulk of South Korea in a very short time.

In conversations with people from all walks of life I was shocked by the degree to which their psychological power to resist had been sapped. There seemed to be no faith left in the possibility of successful resistance. An incident in Munich illustrated the situation. The police had tried to take streamers with slogans from a group of demonstrators of the Free German Youth and were repeatedly routed. I had talked to police officials and came away with the impression that the morale and fighting spirit of our police were very low.

The Conference with the High Commissioners on 17 August 1950

The security of the Federal Republic was now the question of paramount importance. It will be recalled that I had proposed the creation of a federal police force to the High Commissioners at the end of June 1950. Owing to the developments in Korea and the nervousness that was spreading all over the world as a result of the Korean crisis, objections to my proposal, which were mainly raised by the French, seemed to be on the wane. By the middle of August I was convinced, on the basis of confidential information, that French resistance might now be overcome if I made another attempt to do so.

I raised the subject of security at a conference with the High Commissioners of 17 August 1950. I must here pause to say that to my great regret Sir Brian Robertson was no longer British High Commissioner. He had been in Germany for nearly five years. He had come at a time when we Germans were in an extremely difficult situation. By his personality, the honesty of his convictions, his humanity and sincerity he had made a tremendous contribution to changes which none of us would have dreamed of in 1946 or 1947. His successor, Sir Ivone Kirkpatrick, soon showed himself as another extremely intelligent man whom I learned to value as a person with an open mind for the problems of Germany.

All three High Commissioners were present at this conference: McCloy, Kirkpatrick, and François-Poncet. I gave a thorough exegesis of the situation in the Federal Republic and begged the High Commissioners to intercede with their governments for some demonstration of military strength that might restore people's confidence in the possibility of resistance. This psychological problem was of the greatest importance and could not be taken too seriously. The situation could hardly be worse and something had to be done.

My second request was that the Federal Government should be enabled to build up a defence force that would be ready by the spring of 1951 to offer effective resistance to an attack by the People's Police, if such an attack should occur. For this arms were needed. It would, of course, be better if the Allies themselves were to take over the protection of West German territory at the Elbe frontier. But I doubted whether this was feasible. I explained to the High Commissioners that I was thinking in terms of a German defence force made up of volunteer units to a total strength of 150,000 men. Under Article 3 of the Occupation Statute the Allies had the right to take measures for the defence of the democratic order. They could at any time use this right as a basis for authorizing the appropriate measures to be taken by the Federal Government.

I noted that Pieck and Ulbricht had repeatedly declared their intention of 'liberating' West Germany, and if these statements were taken in conjunction with the military preparations currently being carried out by the Soviet zone police, there could be no doubt about their purpose. In the face of all this the Federal Government was quite helpless. It had nothing but an enormous responsibility without the means of fulfilling the duties arising from it. The Allied concession of a reinforcement of the *Länder* police forces by a total of 10,000 men was no solution. The whole question was very urgent. A foreign ministers' conference of the three Western powers was due to take place in September and I requested that they should discuss this question. For this it was necessary for the Allied High Commission to make specific proposals to the foreign ministers to avoid further delay.

I continued: there could be no question but that France, Britain, and the United States would fight for themselves and not for Germany. After all that had happened Germany could not expect other nations to defend her. While seeing this point quite clearly, however, it was also necessary to recall the fact that he who held West Germany and its steel production would probably be in a position to decide the third world war in his favour. The Russians were pursuing their intentions with extraordinary skill. An army was being built up in the Soviet zone. At the decisive moment the Russians would stand back and leave the United States and the Western Allies to decide whether they wanted to respond to the Eastern army's invasion of West Germany with war on Russia. A short while ago I had asked an important American politician whether the United States could in such a case be expected to use atomic weapons. His answer was: No. To my mind the only thing that redeemed this gloomy picture was the fact that the Russian zone's army was still short of the necessary number of officers. That gave us a last period of grace.

McCloy was the first to reply. He thought my analysis of the situation was impressive and sombre. The preponderance of the Russian armed forces had long been known. He admitted that the developments of the last few months called for urgent action. The High Commissioners also knew of the great tension that prevailed in West Germany. He thought action must be twofold: strong fighting forces would have to be sent to Western Europe in order to restore the military balance; and in the political field the will to resist would have to be strengthened. It would be a good thing if faith in democracy were emphasized more strongly in the utterances of West German politicians. To be sure one could not fight tanks with words, but it was a proved fact that a courageous spirit could achieve a great deal. In this context he recalled the attitude of the people of Berlin at the beginning of the blockade. The Russians hoped that propaganda might produce weakness in the attitude of the people in West Germany and thus make them ripe for conquest. In order to counter

275

this possible despair effectively it was an absolute necessity that leading politicians in West Germany should speak out against it.

Another and a decisive question was how the West German population would behave if there really were an attack by the People's Police and Allied troops opened fire. Would the West German population back the Allies? Would a West German defence force resist the invading Eastern police? The answer to these questions would shape the decisions to be made by the foreign ministers at the beginning of September.

François-Poncet spoke next and stated that according to information in the possession of the French High Commission one had indeed to reckon with the likelihood of the People's Police being used as a cat's paw by the Soviets. Moreover the assumption must be that the time of attack was not far away. He felt there was no further need to convince the Allied Governments of the danger of the situation. All were agreed that something had to be done as rapidly as possible. But he, too, asked: would a West German police force fight against the Soviet zone police? He, François-Poncet, was not sure whether he ought to answer this question with a Yes or a No. He asked me to expound my views on how German rearmament might proceed.

I first addressed myself to McCloy's points. I said that the parallel between Berlin and West Germany was misleading because if the airlift had not started immediately, Berlin could not have resisted. The display of power had been the signal for resistance. In those days, at the time of the Berlin blockade, there had been great faith – in West Germany as well – in the military might of the United States. This faith had been severely shaken by Korea. Allied military might must now be manifested. There must be understanding of the psychological situation of the Germans whose salient feature was still apathy; this apathy was understandable if one recalled developments since 1914. The Federal Republic was only eleven months old. It had been created out of nothing, as there had had to be an entirely new beginning. This meant that the whole structure was still unstable – and this instability was a factor to be considered when criticizing the attitude of government and people.

I said that I was assuming that the Russians themselves would not invade, for if they did, there was no point in further talk. An attack by the People's Police would confront the Allied Governments with political decisions of the gravest consequence. The relations between Soviet Russia and the government of the Russian zone would ostensibly be changed from the point of view of international law. If the Soviet zone police proceeded to an invasion, the Western Allies would have to decide whether they were to take this as cause for unleashing the third world war. That was why I asked for the creation of a German defence force that could fight when the Allies had to keep aloof. As for the question put by McCloy and François-Poncet whether the West German police would fight against the Soviet zone police, I was fully convinced I could answer in the affirmative. The West German defence forces would fight if they had arms that guaranteed success.

276

McCloy's second question, whether, in a clash between Allied and Soviet zone troops the West German population would back the Allied troops, I answered by saying that the West Germans would undoubtedly do this if the Allied troops were strong enough to halt the invading East German forces at the Elbe. For the people of West Germany would see in them nothing but an instrument of Soviet Russia.

I had to confess that I found François-Poncet's question concerning my idea on the mode of German rearmament very difficult to answer – for foreign as well as domestic reasons. Since the defeat military service had been the object of obloquy. I would rather manage without German rearmament and I had hopes that the volunteer units I had in mind would form a sufficient counter-weight against Russian intentions. I had still not given up hope that an agreement might be reached between Russia and the United States at a later date. If this should not come about, I hoped for an understanding with France which would provide an alternative to the volunteer units, with the help of the United States. I was most emphatic on the seriousness of my intention to spare the German people rearmament.

Kirkpatrick shared my opinion that a good deal of the effectiveness of propaganda depended on the display of power. He said that the Allies would not be able to put thirty divisions into Germany in the foreseeable future, but he thought that a reinforcement of the Allied troops in Germany could contribute considerably to the raising of morale.

McCloy stressed once more that something had to be done in the field of propaganda; above all, however, German criticism of the Allies would have to stop. He asked me whether I would be able to recruit 150,000 volunteers even if the opposition was against it. I answered that I would only do it with the consent of the SPD. I had already discussed the question with Dr Schumacher and we were going to have further discussions about it. In a number of conversations I had acquired great respect for Dr Schumacher's judgment.

In order to decide whether I would be in a position to call for 150,000 reliable recruits, I would be most grateful if I could be given access to the material collected by the Western Allies on all former officers and soldiers in West Germany during the past years. I was convinced that I would then be able, in the course of a few months, to collect quite a number of efficient personnel.

On 11 August Churchill had proposed to the Council of Europe in Strasbourg the creation of a European army with German participation. McCloy asked me what the Government's attitude to Churchill's plan was. It had been warmly welcomed in the United States. He also asked me whether I thought it possible to contribute a German contingent to this European army. I endorsed the plan of a European army and stated my readiness to work for the contribution of a German contingent to this army.

In order to underline the precariousness of our position I once more returned to the situation in Korea. North Korean troops had, with the support

277

of the Soviet Union and Red China, overrun South Korea with the exception of the city of Pusan in the space of a few weeks. Although the United Nations had agreed at the beginning of July to put troops at the disposal of South Korea, the situation at this moment still was that South Korea was entirely in the hands of the communists. We were in danger of a similar fate.

In winding up the conference of 17 August McCloy admitted that the United States had underestimated Russian intentions in Korea, had neglected to take sufficient precautions for defence, and had left much undone in the field of rearmament. America had lost many battles but won all its wars. Rearmament was now proceeding with full speed. Europe would not be forgotten if it showed the courage to defend itself.

The Memoranda of the Federal Government to the Western Powers of 29 August 1950 Concerning the Security Question and the Question of Reshaping the Relationship between the Federal Republic and the Occupying Powers

At the meeting with the High Commissioners of 17 August 1950 François-Poncet had asked me how I envisaged German rearmament and I had given him a brief impromptu answer. But I did not want to leave it at that and drew up a memorandum with concrete proposals. I had to do it very quickly because the foreign ministers' conference of the three Western powers was to meet in New York at the beginning of September and the German question was to be one of the main points on the agenda.

I was and still am convinced that a third world war can be prevented only if every side knows not only that there can be no easy victory but also that a third world war also means the devastation of the victorious country. This was the unfortunate way things had developed, partly through new technological progress, partly from the old habit of thinking that war was the only way to settle points of conflict. One must never lose faith that it must and will be possible to settle difficulties between countries peacefully. I was and still am firmly convinced that the inclination to settle differences of opinion peacefully – and such a settlement always means renouncing some wishes and aims – is all the stronger the more clearly all concerned are aware of the huge risks that war holds for them too. It was because of these considerations that I thought the present state of affairs in Western Europe totally unsatisfactory despite the Atlantic Treaty, despite all agreements, and despite all the international institutions that had been established or planned since the war. For this reason we Germans, and especially the Federal Government, had to keep demanding the build-up of the appropriate military protection in West Germany. I realized that only the United States of America could afford this protection. Europe, and that includes us, had and still has to rely on the help of America. The United States is the strongest country economically. Its economic potential is tremendous. Destiny had allotted a role to the United

States in this period of post-war history such as the Roman Empire may have played in some earlier periods. It goes without saying that in the face of this the countries of Western Europe could not remain inactive or content to say: 'Please, dear Americans, shed your blood, spend your money!'

The decision about the role eventually to be played by the Federal Republic in the defence system did not lie in our hands. But it was certainly to be expected that this was exactly the subject that would occupy the Foreign Ministers' Conference in New York. In the Federal Republic, however, the situation was such that the overwhelming majority of Germans were entirely hostile towards the notion of re-establishing German armed forces, a German Wehrmacht.

The time was gone when one of the relatively small nations of Western Europe could believe that it could manage by itself. If the Germans were to be given a role to play in a Western defence system, we had to examine the matter and, if it looked reasonable, do our part. Europe was and still is the decisive point in all international tensions. Neither Korea nor any other area where a state of war might develop would be of decisive importance. What happened in Europe was and remains decisive. I was hoping that the people who made decisions in America were convinced of this truth and would not be distracted by some fire that might be fanned into flame here or there.

In order to tell the three Western foreign ministers my views on a possible German defence contribution, I wrote a memorandum and sent it with a covering letter of 29 August 1950 to McCloy the chairman of the Allied High Commission that month. In the memorandum I pointed out that developments in the Far East had caused unrest and a feeling of insecurity among the German people. The confidence that the Western world would be able to counter attacks in Western Europe quickly and effectively had been shaken to an alarming extent and had led to a dangerous lethargy among Germans. How serious the whole situation was could be measured by the Soviet forces assembled in the Soviet zone as well as the accelerated build-up of the People's Police. Against these very strong troop concentrations in East Germany, which I listed in detail, there were in West Germany only two American and two British divisions and some French contingents. Apart from some weak forces of the customs police the Federal Republic had no defence units. In the British zone there was a police force organized on a local basis but whose training and equipment were not standardized and who did not have adequate arms at their disposal.

Against an attack by the People's Police from the Eastern zone the police forces of the Federal Republic were totally inadequate because they were numerically weak, and had not had the appropriate weapons or formation training. Nor were they in a position to give effective protection at the zonal frontier which made special demands on account of its extraordinary length. The defence of the Federal Republic against aggression from outside was first and foremost in the hands of the occupying troops. I had repeatedly

279

asked for these troops to be reinforced and was now renewing these requests in the most urgent form, for it was only the reinforcement of Allied occupation forces in Western Europe that could visibly demonstrate the Western powers' serious intention of defending Western Germany in case of need.

In the memorandum I also stated that we were prepared, should an international European army be formed, to contribute a German contingent. The actual words of the memorandum on this point were: 'This shows unambiguously that the Federal Chancellor rejects the remilitarization of Germany by a separate national military force.' I proposed the immediate creation of a Federal security police force strong enough to guarantee internal security. The Federal Government realized that the formation of such a security police force would require a constitutional amendment. It was prepared to take immediate steps toward sending an appropriate draft to the legislative bodies.

At the same time as this memorandum on the security of the Federal Republic I sent another memorandum to the High Commission, asking that this document, too, should be submitted to the forthcoming Foreign Ministers' Conference in New York. It was concerned with the question of reshaping the relationship between the Federal Republic and the occupying powers. Because of its importance I shall give it verbatim:

Memorandum
on the question of reshaping the relationship between the
Federal Republic and the occupying powers

I

The present occupation régime rests on a Statute created a year and a half ago in conditions which to a large extent have ceased to apply today. Since its inception the Federal Republic has consolidated its position in the political and economic fields. It has given a democratic and liberal aspect to public life and has taken its place as a partner in European economic cooperation.

The foreign ministers of the occupying powers in their London communiqué of 14 May 1950 acknowledged 'the natural desire of the German people to secure relaxation of controls and the restoration of sovereignty'.

Since then the reintegration of Germany into the European community has made further progress by accession to the Council of Europe and the negotiations on the Schuman Plan. Furthermore the participation of the Federal Republic in the common defence of Western Europe has recently been under discussion in increasing measure.

II

If the German population is to fulfil, within the framework of the European community, the duties arising from the present situation and its own special peril, it must be put in the appropriate internal state. It must have enough freedom of action and responsibility for the fulfilment of duties to appear meaningful. If Germans are to make all kinds of sacrifice, they must find the way to freedom just as open to them as to any other people of Western Europe.

III

The Federal Government therefore deems it necessary that the relationship between Germany and the occupying powers should be put on a new basis. The Federal Government communicates its request to the Allied foreign ministers for a declaration like the following to be issued at their forthcoming conference in New York:

1 The state of war between the Allied powers and Germany will be terminated.
2 The future purpose of occupation will be protection against external danger.
3 Relations between the occupying powers and the Federal Republic will be progressively replaced by a system of contractual agreements.

Such declarations would find a particularly favourable response among the German people at this moment.

IV

The implementation of these principles requires a comprehensive reshaping of the present legal state of affairs. The Federal Government proposes the establishment of a commission. It should be composed of Allied and German experts, to prepare a review of the situation.

Bonn, 29 August 1950.

Conversation with the High Commissioners on 31 August 1950

At the request of the Allied High Commission we had a meeting on the Petersberg on 31 August 1950 to discuss the contents of the memoranda referred to above. McCloy was represented by General Hays who spoke first and stated that the High Commissioners warmly welcomed my readiness to provide a German contingent for a West European army. General Hays thought that the sombre picture I had drawn would appear much brighter if one took into account the atomic capability of the United States.

He then turned to the subject of the Federal police force. The decisive question here was whether the envisaged Federal police force would, if necessary, be used against the People's Police and whether its organization, equipment, and training was to correspond to that of the People's Police or not. If the foreign ministers were to make any decision on this point at their conference in New York, they would need a clear and unambiguous answer from me which did not fully emerge from my memorandum. The High

Commissioners had also been wondering whether the political parties in the Federal Republic and the *Länder* would agree to such a Federal police force. There was a question whether it would be possible to get the requisite majority in the Bundestag for the constitutional amendment that would be needed.

I emphasized in my reply that the Federal police force would in any case have to be big enough to be capable of effective resistance to the People's Police. There were certain indications that an agreement was being planned between the Soviet Government and the government of the Soviet zone whereby the former would legally detach itself from the latter. This would create the possibility of the independent Russian zone trying to attack West Germany in the coming year. Action by Allied forces would in that case call forth action by Soviet troops and would thus unleash the third world war. It remained to be seen whether the United States would then consider such a decision opportune. This implied great peril for the Germans.

Regarding the attitudes of the political parties to the Federal Government's intention to establish a Federal police force, I could only state that the three coalition parties and the SPD had expressed themselves in favour of such a force. The Ministers President of the *Länder* had not yet pronounced on the question. One had to reckon with an unfavourable response on the part of some of the *Länder*, but the attitude of the Ministers President could be affected by appropriate action by the big parties.

I continued that I could understand it if some countries thought the Federal Government was intending to use the establishment of a Federal police force as a step toward the creation of a national army. But I had repeatedly and unambiguously stated that this was far from being the purpose of the Federal Government.

In the subsequent discussion I asked the High Commissioners whether their respective governments would regard an incursion of the Russian zone police into their own zone as an attack on themselves. There had not yet been a clear statement on this point. There had been declarations that an attack by Soviet Russia upon the territory of the Federal Republic would be regarded as an attack on themselves, but as Russia was going to make the Russian zone into an independent state in the foreseeable future, a further definition of the attitudes of the Allied Governments was needed. I regarded a clarification of this point as of the greatest importance. I thought that an official declaration was needed above all for its effect on the Soviet zone. It must be made clear that an attack on the territory of the Federal Republic would constitute the *casus belli*.

In an earlier conversation with the High Commissioners I had already expressed my hope that the activities of the study group then meeting in London and working on the revision of the Occupation Statute would produce visible results. In this conversation François-Poncet had uttered a warning against excessive hopes, saying that one must avoid creating the impression among the German public that as a result of the London talks all control would cease in the Federal Republic and the High Commissioners would 'die'. I had retorted that there was no need to speak of the death of the High Commissioners; if a caterpillar was metamorphosed into a butterfly it did not mean death. François-Poncet had replied: 'So you want my colleagues and myself to turn into butterflies; but please do not then pursue us with a butterfly net.'

This metamorphosis of the caterpillars into butterflies, that is the transformation of the High Commissioners into ambassadors, was one of the aims of my second memorandum. I explained point 3 of that memorandum as implying a wish for development and not an expectation of a sudden change. The reason for desiring some development was this: it was necessary to obtain more freedom for the fifty million Germans living in the Western zones. The Federal Government had to get the German people used to the idea that great burdens would have to be shared in future in the German and the European interest. One could only make this plausible to the Germans if they were going to enjoy equal rights in the company of other nations in the foreseeable future. If the situation in the world had developed steadily, it would have been possible to proceed to a slow and gradual revision of the Occupation Statute. But in view of the present situation something more impressive had to be done. That was why the three declarations I had requested were needed.

At the end of the meeting Kirkpatrick told me that the Allied High Commission was fully aware of the great difficulties of the present situation of the Federal Republic. The three High Commissioners would use all their influence in New York to bring about a result that would amount to an appeal to the people themselves.

The New York Foreign Ministers' Conference of September 1950

The deliberations of the Foreign Ministers Dean Acheson, Ernest Bevin, and Robert Schuman began in New York on 12 September 1950. The final communiqué of the conference, which was published on 19 September, was very voluminous. The situation in Germany and the relations between the Allies and the Federal Republic in the light of developments since the last foreign ministers' conference of May 1950 had been among the chief subjects discussed. The communiqué began by stating that in their deliberations the foreign ministers had taken into account the views which had been expressed by the government of the Federal Republic on recent occasions. The communiqué stressed that the three foreign ministers and their governments shared the desire of the German people for reunification in freedom and on a basis which respected the fundamental liberties. Despite all efforts to achieve this end, it would obviously not be realized as long as the Soviet Union continued to ignore proposals for democratic all-German elections and to stage controlled elections such as the one to be held in the Soviet zone on 15 October. The communiqué continued:

Pending the unification of Germany, the three Governments consider the Government of the Federal Republic as the only German Government freely and legitimately constituted and therefore entitled to speak for Germany as the representative of the German people in international affairs.

They reaffirm their desire, of which they have already given many proofs, to integrate the Federal Republic into the community of free nations. They are convinced that the overwhelming majority of the German people want to take part in building the European community and strengthening its common civilization. It appears to them that the time has now come to take a new step towards the attainment of these goals.

To judge from the text of the communiqué the three foreign ministers gave serious consideration to the problem of both the internal and external security of the Federal Republic. They recognized the fact that outright military units had been created in the Soviet zone of occupation. This fact together with recent events in Germany and elsewhere had given rise to a situation of great concern. The Allied Governments considered that their forces in Germany had in addition to their occupation duties the further important function of acting as security forces for the protection and defence of the free world, including the German Federal Republic and the Western sectors of Berlin. To make this protection more effective the Allied governments were going to increase their forces in Germany. The communiqué at this point read:

They will treat any attack against the Federal Republic or Berlin from any quarter as an attack upon themselves.

The second part of the communiqué was concerned with the demands I had made in my memorandum of 29 August 1950 on the question of the reshaping of relations between the Federal Republic and the occupying powers. The communiqué stated that the new phase in the relations between the Allies and the Federal Republic would be marked by major extensions of the authority of the Federal Government. To make this possible, the occupying powers were prepared to amend the Occupation Statute while maintaining the legal basis of the occupation, and the Federal Republic would be expected to undertake certain commitments and other actions consonant with its new responsibilities.

At the end of the communiqué the three governments paid tribute to the continued steadfastness of the people of Berlin in their struggle to preserve their freedom. They would continue to oppose aggression in any form against the people of Berlin and were taking steps to strengthen Allied forces there. The Allied Governments were going to continue their efforts to alleviate the economic situation of Berlin. The High Commission had been directed to review the statement of principles governing the relationship between the

Allied Kommandatura and Berlin, and to liberalize controls in the city to the maximum extent practicable.

The New York decisions of the foreign ministers seemed to prepare a new phase in the relations between the Federal Republic and the Western powers. The communiqué read:

> These decisions mark an important stage in the normalization of relations, and should contribute towards the creation of an atmosphere of mutual confidence and understanding. They represent a major advance toward the progressive return of Germany to partnership in Western Europe and the consolidation of the Western nations in their efforts to establish a firm basis for the future peace of Europe and the world.

The demands and wishes expressed in my memorandum of 29 August 1950 appeared to have been met to a great extent. Even if the New York decisions did not fulfil all our desires, I saw in the three foreign ministers' declaration a welcome step along the Federal Republic's way from being an occupied country to become a free nation. This path would require as much patience, good will, and readiness on our side as on that of the Allies.

On 23 September the three High Commissioners gave me a detailed report on the result of the New York Foreign Ministers' Conference. Foreign Secretary Bevin had expressly asked Kirkpatrick to convey his thoughts to me. As Bevin saw it relations between the Allied Western powers and the Federal Republic had entered a critical stage. He felt that the final communiqué of the New York conference represented a big step forward both in content and in tone. He therefore put particular emphasis on the need for all men of good will to try to guide developments forward in the right direction. Foreign Secretary Bevin would therefore welcome every effort by the German Federal Government to ensure good will, patience and resolve along those lines. By such efforts, he was convinced, we would soon reach our desired goal.

McCloy explained that those assembled in New York had tried to find a formula for peace in Europe within a free community. Although there had been much discussion of military matters and much deliberation about what steps could be taken to increase military forces and how and with whom guarantees should be entered into – a measure, incidentally, that would be, at any rate for the United States, quite revolutionary – yet it must not be forgotten that the entire atmosphere of the work there had been peaceful. There had never been any thought of aggression. He hoped that the measures that had been announced would dispel the atmosphere of fear.

The New York decisions had been taken not only to protect Germany against attacks, but also in order to serve the aim of German unity. He thought that in both respects, that of security as well as that of unity, there would now be a period of potentially greater confidence than before. McCloy said that he hoped I saw that my proposals had had the most careful consideration in New York and that the method suggested by me had been examined in all its aspects. And I would hardly fail to notice what conclusions had been reached in New York, namely that the aims I had outlined in my memoranda could be reached by the methods the Allies were now proposing.

The High Commissioners gave me a document in which the foreign ministers' wishes regarding the undertakings expected of the Federal Republic of Germany were made more explicit. This document had two parts. The first dealt with the topics discussed in my memoranda of 29 August 1950; the second part dealt with the revision of the Occupation Statute.

My first demand concerned the termination of the state of war. McCloy explained that agreement had been reached in New York that this wish should be considered; however, constitutional law and procedures varied in the individual Allied countries and they would therefore have to take different measures according to their own legal and constitutional systems. An effort would be made to let the decisions come into force concurrently.

The decision announced in the communiqué had been taken at the highest level in New York notwithstanding the difficulties of which those who made it were well aware. McCloy was hoping that all domestic legal obstacles in America could be overcome no matter how complicated and difficult they might be.

My second demand concerned the gradual replacement of the Occupation Statute by agreements. On this point the document stated that the three powers thought that the bases on which their presence in the Federal Republic and especially in Berlin rested should not be changed for the time being. The powers would, however, use the procedure I had proposed in all cases open to free exchange of opinion and common agreement.

In my memoranda I had raised the problem of the internal and external security of the Federal Republic. Regarding external security the Western Allies had given a complete guarantee for the territory of the Federal Republic and Berlin. It was announced that the Western powers would increase and reinforce troops they had stationed in the Federal Republic in order to make this guarantee more effective.

These military reinforcements would be distributed over the entire Federal area according to strategic considerations. They would form part of the combined European defence army under a joint supreme command. The organization of this army was under discussion by the three powers and the signatory powers of the North Atlantic Treaty in New York. The suggestion that an independent German army might be formed in this context had been rejected. Rather, the question was when and how the Federal Republic could take part in the efforts of the Western nations if she was empowered to contribute military contingents. This matter was being examined at the moment. I would be given an opportunity to discuss it with the High Commissioners.

As for the internal security of the Federal Republic, the foreign ministers had been unable to accede to my request for permission to create a federal police force in the form in which I had proposed it. This form would require a

German constitutional amendment which would take too long. Efforts were being made to work out a system based on the *Länder* but which would have the uniformity, inner cohesion, mobility, speed and ease of deployment of the federal police force I had proposed. The initial strength of this police formation could be 30,000 and might be increased at a later date. It would be equipped with light arms to be agreed in detail.

The second part of the document dealt with the alleviations granted the Federal Republic and with the revision of the Occupation Statute. There would be a far-reaching reduction of controls in many fields, especially that of economic affairs inside Germany, and the present system of reviewing German legislation was to be changed. In some cases Allied powers would lapse as soon as the Federal Republic had assumed the corresponding obligations and had taken the appropriate measures. The High Commission would immediately begin talks with the Federal Government in order to arrive at the necessary agreements on these obligations.

Provisions regarding prohibited and restricted industries were also to be reviewed. The High Commission had received instructions to lift all restrictions regarding the size, speed, and number of commercial freighters that were built for export. Moreover efforts should be made to increase steel production beyond the limits fixed at present, if this benefited the defensive measures of the West.

At the time the Occupation Statute came into force it had been announced that it was to be reviewed after a certain period of time. I was told that if there was surprise in the Federal Republic at the fact that the Occupation Statute was not simply repealed with immediate effect, it should be remembered that the termination of the state of war was not synonymous with the abolition of the occupation régime. If the Occupation Statute were abolished the presence of Allied forces in Germany and Berlin would no longer have a legal basis. But occupation provisions could be lightened and the alleviations that were envisaged would constitute a new phase. It would certainly not be the last phase; another phase would follow later and was already under discussion.

Before, however, the modification decided on in New York could be put into effect, the three foreign ministers expected the Federal Republic to assume two obligations:

1 With respect to the termination of the state of war as well as to the new legal status granted the Federal Republic, the foreign ministers thought the time had come for the Federal Republic to acknowledge German prewar debts as well as the debts arising from economic assistance given after the war and to declare its readiness to cooperate in the elaboration of a plan for the settlement of these debts. There was no reason whatsoever to assume that the Federal Republic was going to be asked for astronomical sums. It was more a matter of recognizing a principle that had always obtained in international law and which maintained the continuity between

287

a political régime and its successor. With the recognition of this general principle there would naturally be an adaptation of the settlement plan to actual conditions and possibilities.

2 A further commitment demanded of the Federal Republic consisted of an assurance of cooperation with the Allies in the equitable apportionment of materials and products required for the common defence that were or might later be in short supply.

McCloy gave me a document on this point and said that I would see from it that the first demand regarding the acknowledgment of debts required confirmation by the Bundestag. However, the High Commission would for the time being content itself with acknowledgment by the Federal Government for the purpose of granting the alleviations that were envisaged. There were two categories of such alleviations. The first would become effective as soon as the two above-mentioned commitments had been assumed. The second category was to come into force when certain conditions which McCloy then explained in greater detail had been fulfilled.

The alleviations of the first category included foreign affairs, economic matters, and the control of legislation. Regarding foreign affairs McCloy explained that the Federal Government was to be authorized to establish a Ministry of Foreign Affairs and to conduct its own foreign policy subject to the Allied right to disapproval, especially regarding West German relations with the countries of the Soviet orbit or with other countries which, for reasons of security, would be communicated to me separately. The Federal Government could send ambassadors abroad but until further notice not to the capitals of the three Allied powers in order to prevent the confusion that might arise from the simultaneous existence of ambassadors and High Commissioners. The Consuls General already representing the Federal Republic in the United Kingdom, the United States, and France could, by mutual agreement, acquire the status of diplomatic representatives.

The diplomatic missions in the Federal area would be accredited with the Federal Government and if necessary with the High Commission as well. The conclusion of trade agreements would continue to be subject to certain reservations. In the field of foreign trade and currency regulations the powers of the High Commissioners were to be exercised only to the extent required for the implementation of certain clearly designated purposes, such as the control of trade in certain products for security reasons, and to guarantee that the conduct of German trade policy accorded with the principles of the General Agreement on Tariffs and Trade (GATT).

Further progress was constituted in the fact that from now on laws of the federation and the *Länder* were to come into force immediately upon their promulgation by the competent German bodies. The procedure of prior examination by the High Commission was abolished. The High Commission merely reserved the right to repeal or declare void laws and decrees that were incompatible with Allied legislation or constituted a grave threat to the basic purposes of the occupation.

McCloy then turned to the category of alleviations to be granted the Federal Government as soon as certain conditions were fulfilled. These included the provision of the Occupation Statute giving the High Commission authority to enforce the Basic Law and the *Länder* constitutions. This provision was to lapse upon creation of a Federal constitutional court charged with effective protection of the rights of individuals and the provisions of the constitutions. Further, the powers of the High Commission in the field of economic deconcentration and of decartelization were to lapse as soon as the Federal Government had promulgated satisfactory legislation preventing the formation of new economic concentrations. In my reply I declared that the document I had just received in conjunction with the explanations given me did indeed mean a step forward in Germany's return to the community of the free and peace-loving nations of the world. I was particularly happy about the security guarantee given for the Federal Republic of Germany and for Berlin which I regarded as one of the foremost gains of the New York negotiations. The assurances on security and the successes achieved in the last few weeks by United Nations troops led by the United States of America in Korea had considerably strengthened the feeling of security in the Federal Republic. I also expressed my special gratitude for what had been said concerning the unity of Germany. I thanked the High Commissioners for their efforts in New York and expressed my conviction that the success of our work would soon be evident and would fill us all with great satisfaction.

In conclusion François-Poncet said that the High Commissioners and I surely agreed that the reorganization of Western Europe which depended on a feeling of community required above all a change in the atmosphere of Franco-German relations. The Schuman Plan was one of the means intended to contribute to the renewal of this atmosphere.

On 24 September 1950 the American High Commissioner McCloy visited me at my house in Rhöndorf to give me some additional information on the course of the New York Foreign Ministers' Conference. A strong interest in the establishment of an international armed force had been shown not only among the three foreign ministers but also in the deliberations of the foreign ministers of the member states of NATO. The Americans had introduced the subject of the participation of the Federal Republic, but the French had declared that they were not authorized to discuss this problem. Among the Socialists in France there was strong opposition to a remilitarization of Germany. If the matter had won support in New York, Schuman said, he was afraid of the Socialists leaving the French cabinet, which entailed the risk of a very grave governmental crisis. In the end it had nevertheless proved possible to convince the French of the necessity of discussing the problem. McCloy had been very much impressed by the manner in which the question of German participation in a European force had been treated at the conference of the NATO powers which was being held simultaneously. It was especially the smaller member states that had most emphatically demanded the inclusion of Germany in such an armed force. There had been general agreement on the point that Germany should not be forced to cooperate but that such cooperation should be voluntary. The inclusion in the international armed force must in no case be allowed to become the subject of a deal. The Federal Republic must not make political conditions for membership.

A leading American military personage had been envisaged as Supreme Commander to be charged with training in peace and operations in war. There were to be no national armies in addition to the proposed international force, with the exception that France was to be able to keep her army in Indochina under her own command.

The German contingent was to participate with equal rights in the planned international force. The Federal Republic was to be represented in the international general staff in exactly the same way as the other nations.

McCloy then commented on the resolution of the New York Foreign Ministers' Conference expressly recognizing the Federal Government as the only legitimate government in Germany. According to McCloy it followed from this that the Federal Government had the exclusive right to assume the rights and obligations of the former German Reich. It also meant, however, that, pending final settlement in the peace treaty, the federation must assume the debts of the Reich. The declaration demanded by the governments of the Western powers by which the Federal Government assumed the previous debts and obligations of the Reich would be necessary in order to introduce a certain order into the extraordinarily complicated and intricate debtor relationship between Germany and other countries, for only if Germany declared her willingness in principle to assume the former debts could there be new investments. McCloy asked me to regard this demand as a positive step. The declaration concerning the assumption of the debts of the former Reich and of the obligations resulting from assistance given by the Allies had nothing to do with ECA assistance given to Germany through the Marshall Plan. It must be treated in the context of the group of Allied demands in order to set in motion the entire programme agreed upon in New York.

The question of Berlin had been one of the chief points on the agenda of the conference. The Allied troops stationed in Berlin were to be considerably reinforced and alert squads of the police were to be organized. Fuel and food stocks for a year were to be assembled. It had not been possible to meet my suggestions about a Federal police force. A strong desire to avoid amendment of the German constitution at all costs had precluded the Federal police force I had asked for being granted.

The reinforcement of Allied troops had also been thoroughly considered. These reinforcements would not be on a zonal basis, nor would the present troops remain in the zones separately, but they would be stationed in accordance with strategic requirements in the Federal area. It must be realized however that these reinforcements would mean an additional burden for the Federal Government and for the population of the Federal Republic. The building of barracks would have to be begun as quickly as possible.

I expressed my great satisfaction with the intention to reinforce Allied troops in Germany. Such reinforcements should be as prompt and as numerous as possible without regard to the burdens they might impose. I would give my full attention at once to the question of the police force. The SPD was insisting strongly on a constitutional amendment, apparently from a desire to use this opportunity to enlarge Federal prerogatives in the long run. I agreed with the foreign ministers' demand for an acknowledgment of earlier foreign debts, but thought the subject called for detailed examination.

Regarding the German contingent in an international armed force, I completely agreed that the German readiness to contribute such a contingent should not be tied to political demands. I had been pleased to hear of the Allied intention to give it equal rights in training, equipment, and participation in the work of the central staffs.

McCloy thought that it was very important to prepare a favourable atmosphere in German public opinion for the creation of a German contingent. People in the United States would not understand any German criticism of the idea, for if the United States assumed an extremely far-reaching security guarantee for Germany in Berlin, it was an absolute necessity that Germany should cooperate in the fulfilment of that guarantee.

I told McCloy of a talk I had had the day before with François-Poncet on the subject of German participation in an international army. François-Poncet had told me that French public opinion still had to be got used to the notion of German participation. Things had happened somewhat too suddenly. I had to say the same for the people of the Federal Republic. The psychological situation in Germany was not the best for the plans we had just discussed. The total defeat of 1945 and the public defamation of military institutions had left strong effects. I believed however that an overwhelming part of the German people would favour participation in the framework of a European army if they were given a thorough enough explanation of the situation. There were special difficulties among a small part of the Protestant Church, above all in the circle around Niemöller to which Heinemann also belonged.

I must interject here that the former Minister of the Interior, Gustav Heinemann, had tendered his resignation because of my willingness to make a German contribution to a European army. I told McCloy that I was determined to accept this resignation, but I had now to be very careful to avoid a situation in which Niemöller and Heinemann were publicly represented as the friends of peace and the Federal Government as tending toward warlike solutions.

Some opposition between Minister Heinemann on the one hand and the other members of the cabinet and myself on the other had already appeared

291

during the discussions concerning the entry of the Federal Republic into the Council of Europe. Heinemann opposed entry because he thought that it would deepen the division between the West and the East of Germany. For the same reason Heinemann had assumed a very passive or even negative attitude toward protection of the constitution, establishment of the police force and the question of a possible participation of Germany in a European-American fighting force. In his own words, Heinemann was of the opinion that after God had twice dashed the weapons from the hands of the Germans they should not reach for them a third time; that one must have patience to discern the will of God in the governance of the world and await developments peacefully and quietly. The will of God was not as yet discernible, but he was convinced that the situation would be clear in a year or eighteen months.

I do not want to say anything here about trusting God and general piety, but I had replied to Heinemann, when he entreated me to do nothing in the matter of defending the Federal Republic, that in my opinion God had given us our heads to think with and our arms and hands to act with. Heinemann maintained his position and tendered his resignation in a moment of agitation. I accepted it because in this important matter the Federal cabinet had to take a united stand.

Heinemann's resignation caused a great stir in Germany, especially because Heinemann was *Präses* of the Synod of the Protestant Churches in Germany and had very close connections in high Protestant places; he had especially close connections with Church President Niemöller who shared his antipathy to a possible German contribution to a European army. Heinemann later joined the SPD and has to this day remained a member of the SPD group in the German Bundestag.

The attitude of the Federal Government was this: the United States of America were at present making the greatest efforts to save Europe and the peace. Peace could be preserved only if an appropriate fighting force was established that made it clear to an attacker that he was endangering himself by any attack. It seemed to me perfectly clear that one could not expect mothers and fathers in the United States to be prepared to sacrifice their sons unless we too made our contribution to defence.

The communiqué published on the meeting of the NATO Council ending on 26 September 1950 stated the Council's unanimous opinion that Germany must be put in a position to contribute to the defence of Western Europe. The members of the NATO Council had taken cognizance of the fact that the occupying powers were examining this matter. They asked the Defence Committee to draw up recommendations as soon as possible on the manner in which Germany could most appropriately contribute.

The Situation in the Late Autumn of 1950

Three questions occupied the centre of political debate in November 1950:

first there was the proposal of the Soviet Government of 3 November 1950 to call a foreign ministers' conference of the United States of America, Great Britain, France, and Soviet Russia for the purpose of fulfilling the decisions of the Potsdam conference regarding the demilitarization of Germany; second, there was a proposal by Prime Minister Pleven for a common European army with German participation, the so-called Pleven Plan, which had been approved in principle by the French National Assembly on 24 October 1950; and third, there was the question of a contribution by the Federal Republic of Germany to the defence of the West which was discussed at the New York Foreign Ministers' Conference and several connected conferences.

There was an inner connection between these three questions which was impossible to appreciate unless one kept in mind the policy of Soviet Russia since 1940 and especially since 1944–5. During these years Russia had subjugated enormous territories, partly by direct annexation, partly by transforming the country in question into a Russian satellite. The procedure had always been the same: first came the creation of a fifth column in the country in question consisting of people blindly obedient to the Soviet Union and capable of any violent action; the concomitant was the intimidation and paralysis of those opposed to Soviet Russia by every kind of terror, single-list elections, and finally formation of a government obedient to Russia by a parliament created by such elections.

By this method Soviet Russia had, in 1940, absorbed Lithuania, Latvia and Estonia; it had subjugated as satellites Albania and Yugoslavia in 1945, Rumania, Czechoslovakia and North Korea in 1948, Bulgaria, Poland and Hungary in 1949, and Manchuria in 1950. In the Soviet zone of Germany the Soviet Union was creating a satellite in accordance with the usual method. In two countries Soviet Russia had used the same procedure but met implacable resistance: Greece and Azerbadjan, where the advance had to be called off. Where it seemed necessary to the Soviet Union not even a semblance of independence in the satellite concerned had been preserved, but even the army of the country had been taken under Russian command, as in Poland and in Czechoslovakia.

The trend of Russian policy toward Germany and Western Europe emerged from the following facts: considerable Soviet troops were concentrated in the Soviet zone of Germany, namely thirty divisions according to a statement by the British Minister of Defence, Shinwell, of July 1950. These divisions were fully equipped with ammunition, fuel, and field rations so as to be able to march at short notice. There were tank divisions and motorized divisions in the Soviet zone and the air force was being continually reinforced. In the Soviet zone itself, as mentioned before, the build-up of an army of Germans started in the beginning of 1950, and was expected to number roughly 150,000 men by 1951 and roughly 300,000 by 1952. The troops of this Soviet zone police were told by their propaganda officers that their purpose was the liberation of the Federal Republic from the Western Allies and its unification with the Russian zone.

Until the summer of 1950 all encroachments by Soviet Russia had been answered only by protest notes by the Western Allies. Only the events in Korea, the invasion of South Korea by North Korean troops, led to a decision by the Western Allies to oppose the communist advance by arms.

In order to complete the picture of the situation in the late autumn of 1950 I must mention that the Communist Party and the SED were diligently increasing their subversive work against the very existence of the Federal Republic. In September 1950 I had received reports on Politburo directives regarding detailed measures to be adopted by the People's Police after an occupation of the Western sectors of Berlin. All organizations were to put themselves at the disposal of the People's Police when it marched in. All motor vehicles were to be tested by that date so that they could be used without delay. Once Berlin was occupied it was to be 'purged' at once.

Conversations with leading officials of the SED and the People's Police showed that they were firmly convinced that West Germany would still be 'liberated' in 1950. All measures could be interpreted in that way. It was pointed out that when it came to the point they could dispose of excellent cadres of approximately 100,000 in West Germany to whom the Federal Republic could in practice oppose nothing. The organization was said to be particularly good in Hamburg and in the Ruhr.

On 3 November 1950 the Soviet Union sent a Note to the United States, Great Britain, and France demanding a foreign ministers' conference. It was characteristic that in this Note the strongest exception was taken to the intended remilitarization of West Germany, while there was no mention at all of the Soviet zone army.

It was equally characteristic that the Note was conveyed at a moment when the discussion of a German contribution to the defensive front against aggression by Soviet Russia had entered the acute stage. It was also characteristic that the Note came at a time when Soviet Russia was supplying more war material to North Korea. The Note demanded that the Prague Resolutions of 21 October 1950 should be taken as basis for the foreign ministers' conference.

The Prague Resolutions had been taken by the foreign ministers of the Soviet Union, Albania, Bulgaria, Czechoslovakia, Poland, Rumania, Hungary and the Soviet zone. Their demands included the 'formation of an All-German Constituent Council, on a parity basis, consisting of representatives of East and West Germany, which is to prepare the formation of a provisional democratic peace-loving all-German sovereign government and to submit corresponding proposals for joint approval by the governments of the USSR, the USA, Great Britain and France and which, until the formation of an all-German government, is to be drawn into consultation on the working out of the peace treaty'.

This basic and decisive component of the Prague agreement was totally un-acceptable to the Federal Republic of Germany. There was no representation in the Soviet zone that was based on free, equal, and secret elections. It was out of the question for us to enter into any negotiations with the Soviet zone on the creation of a joint body until our repeated demands for the holding of free elections in the Soviet zone had been met. As far as I could tell from the first reactions, the Soviet Note produced a negative response in the United States. In Britain it encountered scepticism. Only in France were there voices urging a more favourable response.

The decisions of a conference based on the Prague Resolutions would have been intolerable for us. I had the justified hope that before there was any Allied reply to the Note we would be asked for our opinion and that, as the proposed conference was to deal with our fate, the destiny of the German people and thus of Europe, this opinion would not be disregarded. Develop-ments since 1945, and especially since the creation of the Federal Republic, had reached a point when the voice of the Federal Republic had to be heard and noted. In this connection the express declaration of the New York Foreign Ministers' Conference of September 1950 in which the Western Allies called the government of the Federal Republic of Germany the only legitimate representative of the German people was of the utmost importance.

In my opinion the Soviet Note was nothing but an attempt to prevent or at any rate considerably to delay the consolidation of a defensive front against Soviet aggression which looked like being in process of formation in a Euro-pean defence community.

On 6 September 1950 the American Secretary of State Dean Acheson had made a statement on German participation in the defence of the West. He said it was important to find the appropriate means to enable Germany to take her place in the defence of Western Europe. He referred to a declaration by the American High Commissioner McCloy to the effect that if the Germans wished to defend their own country they should be able to do so. Acheson said that McCloy was quite right. It must be the aim of troop reinforcements in Western Europe to protect the entire Atlantic area against an attack. Since the German people were in this area it was highly desirable that the right way should be found for them to take part in the defence efforts.

From numerous statements by the British Foreign Secretary and the French Foreign Minister it was evident that they did not fully share the American attitude. I had learned that Bevin had gone to the New York Foreign Min-isters' Conference of September 1950 with directives which, similar to those of the French, were negative on the point of a German defence contribution.

On arriving in New York on 12 September 1950 Bevin declared that Germany must be led back into the community of nations, but that he did not believe the incorporation of German military units into the armed forces of Western Europe to be the right way. He made it very clear to the press that he was opposed to the idea of raising German units as part of a Western

European defence force. He was, however, in favour of reinforcing the police forces in West Germany.

The American view that the Federal Republic must be included in a West European defence organization prevailed.

As I have said, another event of great political weight in November 1950 was the French plan for the defence of the West announced by Prime Minister René Pleven on behalf of his government on 24 October 1950. Pleven declared that the nations allied in the North Atlantic Treaty had recognized the need to defend the Atlantic community against all possible aggression along a line that was as far East as possible. They had therefore decided to strengthen the forces stationed in Europe and had agreed to put all these forces, no matter of what nationality, under a single supreme commander. Germany, which was not a member of NATO, was nonetheless being asked to take part in the necessary defence system. It was only just that Germany should make its contribution to a West European defence force. For this reason the French Government had decided to take the initiative for a declaration whose salient passages read as follows:

> The solution of the problem of a German contribution to the common defence is to be sought without compromise and without such evasions as cause delay, among the possibilities of immediate action and with a view to the future of a united Europe.

> The framework in which the European problems are discussed has been established, in the largest manner, by the countries united in the Council of Europe. But the initiatives of successive French cabinets were accompanied by the hope that obligations and institutions would soon strengthen the bold design that had been accepted by all.

> It was in this spirit that on 9 May 1950 the French Government proposed that all European countries should put their coal and steel production together. It said at that time: 'Thus will be brought about, simply and quickly, the fusion of interests which is indispensable to the establishment of a European community, and the ferment of a wider and deeper community will be introduced among countries long divided by bloody feuds.'

> The French Government believed that the realization of the coal and steel plan would help to accustom people to think in terms of European unity before such a delicate question as that of common defence was broached. World events give it no respite. Confident in the peaceful destiny of Europe and imbued with a sense of the need to give all the peoples of Europe a feeling of collective security, the French Government proposes that this question should be regulated by the same methods and in the same spirit.

> It proposes the creation, for the purposes of common defence, of a

296

European Army linked to the political institutions of a United Europe. This suggestion stems directly from the recommendations adopted by the Council of Europe on 11 August 1950, calling for the immediate creation of a unified European Army, which would cooperate for the defence of peace with American and Canadian forces.

The creation of a European Army must not result merely in a bracketing together of national military units, which would in fact be nothing more than a coalition of the old type. Inescapable common duties can be fulfilled only if there exist common organisms. An army of a united Europe, composed of men of different European nations, must involve, to the greatest possible degree, a complete fusion of all its human and material elements under a single European political and military authority.

On 7 November 1950 the French High Commissioner François-Poncet had conveyed to me some amplifications of Prime Minister Pleven's Plan of 24 October 1950. M Pleven particularly wanted me to know that any discrimination against Germany was out of the question and that under the Pleven Plan Germany was to be completely equal with the other partners. This communication gave me great satisfaction.

According to François-Poncet the French Government still held that the problems of Europe could only be solved on the basis of Franco-German understanding. The French Government, he said, was endeavouring to get the Schuman Plan signed as soon as possible. The act of signing, which was to take place in Paris, should be a great demonstration of solidarity. Prime Minister Pleven sent me a message to say that he hoped that I would come to Paris for the occasion.

I took the occasion of my conversation with François-Poncet to remark that the Schuman Plan negotiations were making good progress in general but that the question of abolishing the Ruhr Authority and certain other restrictions on the Federal Republic that were incompatible with the Schuman Plan had not yet been cleared up. At the the beginning of the discussions on the Schuman Plan I had repeatedly pointed out that the Federal Government demanded the dissolution of the Ruhr Authority as a precondition of its signature of the Schuman Plan. I had repeatedly spoken with Jean Monnet, the head of the French delegation, about this subject and he had assured me that he would work for a solution that would satisfy all parties concerned. I now stated once more to François-Poncet that the removal of the Ruhr Authority was the *conditio sine qua non* of our adherence to the Schuman Plan.

With reference to the question of European defence I pointed to the psychological situation in the Federal Republic and to the growing sense of insecurity of the people. I considered further delay dangerous. I told François-Poncet of my regret that the Pleven Plan had not made sufficient provision for measures to be taken immediately.

However, I was fully aware of the positive significance of the Pleven Plan

297

despite its many shortcomings. It seemed to be in process of becoming a significant contribution to the integration of Europe. European integration was and is one of the chief aims of German policy. I believed that the creation of a European army, if possible with British participation, would constitute a very important step forward on the way to the final goal, the integration of Europe, and it was for this reason that I was gladly prepared to cooperate in the Pleven Plan.

Many understandable reservations had been expressed about the Pleven Plan on the German side. It was obvious that the settlement of a matter so difficult and important could not at once and on all points satisfy all interested countries and that much careful deliberation was needed. But the world situation was such that we had to find ways to guarantee peace as soon as possible. The continuation of existing tensions struck me as intolerable in the long run.

Only if Europe gave itself a shape, and one that included a free Germany, could it be a dam against the red flood. Only with a strong Europe had we any prospect of regaining the Soviet zone and the territories beyond the Oder and Neisse for freedom. It was also for the sake of promoting the integration of Europe that I had advocated the Schuman Plan. If coal and steel were administered in common and if in addition a European army was formed, the essential foundations of Europe, it seemed to me, were laid. Then, in any case, a war between France and Germany would seem impossible even to the most sceptical Frenchman. German and French officers would be trained at the same schools to regard each other no longer as opponents but as brothers in arms.

The Attitude of the German People to the Defence Problem

After the experience we Germans had undergone with the totalitarian régime of the Nazi period, after the experience the world had accumulated with totalitarian Soviet Russia since 1944 and which I have sketched in detail above, it seemed to me that the common conviction of all Germans was bound to be this: totalitarian countries, especially Soviet Russia, do not, unlike democratic countries, know law and freedom of the individual as essential factors of the common life of people and nations. Totalitarian countries know only one factor that counts and that is power. With a totalitarian country and especially with Soviet Russia negotiations for the settlement of international questions could succeed only if those engaged in them were just as strong or stronger than Russia. The actions of Soviet Russia since 1945 especially in Greece and Azerbadjan had shown that she was not necessarily willing to take risks.

I was firmly convinced that the Western powers led by the United States of America would be in a position to form a firm defensive front against Soviet Russia. Speeches and other comments by American politicians clearly indicated that the United States recognized the great and heavy task imposed upon it by its tremendous economic and political power and showed that it was ready to fulfil this task for the sake of peace and freedom in the world.

The question of whether the Federal Republic would, if it was asked, participate in a defensive front, was the subject of lively discussion in the Federal Republic. It was a question, really, of saving peace, and the formation of such a defensive front was the only possibility of preventing war and preserving peace. Russian actions since 1945 made plain both the tendency of Russian policy and the possibility of reaching peace with Russia despite that tendency. We Germans had to be clear on the point that we could not possibly expect the United States and the countries of Western Europe to accept the sacrifice involved in mounting such a defensive front while we contributed nothing. A compelling command to defend his homeland and his freedom must be felt by every honest man.

But two conditions must precede German participation: the defensive front had to be strong enough to make any Russian aggression impossible and, second, the Federal Republic of Germany must have the same duties but also the same rights as all other participating countries. Prime Minister Pleven had conveyed to me an assurance on this last point through François-Poncet.

The Social Democrats declared that any military contribution the Federal Republic might make to any defence system would change the constitution and would therefore require a two-thirds majority. They denied the present Bundestag the right to decide the question in the affirmative because when the Bundestag was elected the problem of a defence contribution had not yet been apparent. The Social Democrats therefore thought that a decision for a German military contribution could only be taken on the basis of new Federal elections.

I considered these objections by the Social Democrats legally untenable. Every Bundestag has the right and the duty for the duration of that legislature to deal with all tasks confronting it during that period regardless of whether these tasks were discernible at the time of the elections or not.

The Social Democrats were already talking of a necessary self-dissolution of the Bundestag. But our Basic Law does not give parliament the right to dissolve itself. After mature reflection and with the consent of the Social Democrats the Parliamentary Council had given only the Federal Chancellor the right, should political necessities require new elections, to force such elections by tabling a vote of confidence. What prompted the Parliamentary Council to adopt this rule was the desire to avoid situations in which hetero-geneous political elements that were incapable of joint political work might get together for purely destructive reasons and paralyse political work. In the deliberations about the Basic Law in the Parliamentary Council there had been very detailed discussion of questions of a military nature and of the possibility of war. Article 26, paragraph 1, to which the Social Democrats had given their assent, merely declared the preparation of aggressive war unconstitutional. Article 4, paragraph 3, stated that no one could be compelled against his conscience to render military service as an armed combatant. Another article stated that for the maintenance of peace the Federation may join a system of mutual collective security. All these provisions made it clear that the decision concerning a military contribution did not 'basically change the nature of the Federal Republic of Germany' as the Social Democrats were claiming in the Bundestag.

The Western world was in great danger. The Federal Republic of Germany was part of this Western world. Because of its geographic situation it was even more palpably exposed to this danger than other countries. This common danger created a community of fate, for wherever aggression would strike, it would hit this community in all its members. The danger could be averted and the Germans must never be allowed to lose hope that peace could be preserved. We had to make every effort to preserve it. The experience of the past few years showed that in a position like the present one negotiations aiming at a normalization of relations had prospects of success only if the Soviet Union knew that the partner in the negotiations was strong enough for aggression to entail a genuine risk. The strength of the Western world would be guaranteed only if the Western world organized its defence as a unified defence.

Several kinds of opposition to German rearmament had to be expected: political opposition from the opposition parties; psychological opposition from pacifist-minded, nationalist and certain church circles; former Wehrmacht groups who, for various reasons, could not be given a part in the raising of a German contingent. The more rapidly and visibly the Western occupying powers created the psychological conditions for the creation of a German contingent for a European army, the easier it would be to overcome the opposition. The necessary conditions were: adequate and timely military protection of the build-up of the German contingent by the Western powers, complete political and military equality of the Federal Republic, cessation of the defamation of the German soldier and a satisfactory settlement of sentences for war crimes, some of them just, some of them not.

A German defence contribution was certainly unpopular in the Federal Republic. I was very disturbed by the attitude of the people. The Germans had got into a state of mind as a result of the war and the post-war period in which they valued freedom, but did not seem prepared to make any sacrifice for it. This was an attitude that was understandable in human terms. The communists attempted to use it for their purposes. I had learned, for instance, that Molotov had given a directive for the Foreign Ministers' Conference in Prague in October 1950 that there were to be no polemical attacks on Western Germany by the participants, on either objective or personal grounds, but that everything should be done to achieve closer touch with the Federal Republic. The attempt was to be made to catch the Germans with the watchword of 'National Unity'. The communist Renner made a speech in the

Bundestag on 16 November 1950 that was so redolent of nationalism that I was amazed.

There was no point in shutting one's eyes to the effects of such communist agitation. The pretext that rearmament or a participation of the Federal Republic in a European-American army would deepen the division of Germany served as a welcome self-justification when refusal to participate looked like entailing dangerous consequences.

The agitation of the Social Democrats provided further pretexts for escaping obligations for those who wanted to do so. Their agitation was based on two main propositions, one of which was: admittedly it is a good thing to sacrifice everything for freedom, but you are not free nor are you going to be free; therefore there is no point in doing anything for Europe. The second line of argument ran like this: the Western Allies are not really in earnest about the defence of Western Germany; they only want German troops for delaying actions to protect their own countries. A leading Bundestag member of the SPD had, for instance, said in Munich: It is better for Germans to sit at home with sound limbs, albeit under Bolshevist rule, than with broken bones in dug-outs.

It was now an absolute necessity that, if not all, at least the overwhelming majority of Germans should support a defence contribution. Until the end of the year 1950 the parties that shared the Federal Government's point of view were hamstrung because they did not know whether the Allies would put such a question to the German people. I had no doubt that once they had we would be able to convince most Germans of the correctness of our view, but the Western Allied Governments had to help us by putting the question. Something had to be done to bring about a psychological change in the majority of the German people. The state of twilight, that is the state in which we did not know definitely what the Western Allies would ask of us, the state in which there was merely discussion of a 'possible' German defence contribution, could not go on.

During the month of November a number of *Landtag* elections had taken place, for instance in Hesse, Baden-Württemberg, and in Bavaria. The election campaigns had done a great deal to exacerbate the political situation inside Germany. The results of the *Landtag* elections were not favourable for the government coalition and there were several reasons for this. The decisive factor was the agitation against a German defence contribution which was developed by the Social Democrats with the support of Niemöller. This agitation was quite incompatible with German interests. In effect they were saying: 'Whoever wants war should vote for the government coalition, whoever wants peace should vote for the SPD.' Confronted with this sort of campaign the coalition parties were in a difficult position. We could make no positive statements about our defence contribution. The representatives of the government coalition could not stand up day after day to say: 'We do not know whether we shall be asked. If we are asked, we shall be prepared to make a contribution.' It would have sounded ridiculous. The coalition parties therefore had to be very reticent in what they said and in their replies to the electoral agitation of the SPD.

At the New York Foreign Ministers' Conference of September 1950 and at some subsequent conferences the subject of the German contribution to the defence of the West had then been raised, but both inside Germany and outside there was still very little clarity about it. The Federal Government got hardly any official information concerning the course of these deliberations and had to rely to a large extent on what was published in the newspapers. This created a quite impossible situation for the Federal Government. It was very awkward for government representatives to have to give evasive answers to questions that were put to them. The authority of the Federal Government suffered considerably both among the German public and inside the coalition.

The entire delay of the decision and the developments resulting from it were generally attributed to the attitude of the French Government. The very widespread German good will for an understanding with France suffered a bad shock because of the mistrust that we kept encountering despite all our protestations. For me it was very painful to have to keep more or less silent when I was told that all my efforts in the direction of France had been unsuccessful.

Despite all endeavours of the Federal Government and the coalition parties the notion of making a contribution to and assuming obligations for the defence of Europe remained very unpopular among the Germans. This was due largely to the agitation of the Communist Party and to radio commentaries and newspaper items even in allegedly neutral papers. In order to overcome the negative attitude of the German people it seemed to me necessary to convince them that we were free or that at least there were prospects that the Federal Republic would soon be completely free and that it was therefore worth making sacrifices for this freedom. I believed that generous gestures by the Western Allies toward the Federal Republic were urgently needed. Otherwise I could not see how we could win over the German people to cooperate voluntarily in the defence of Europe.

Conversation with the High Commissioners of 16 November 1950

In my memorandum of 29 August 1950 I had told the governments of the Western Allies that I thought relations between Germany and the occupying powers must be placed on new foundations which should increasingly be embodied in a system of contractual agreements. The Foreign Ministers' Conference of September 1950 in New York had, however, decided merely to improve the Occupation Statute on a number of points. Since the New York conference the situation in the world and in Europe had deteriorated to such an extent that I felt compelled to renew my request to the Western Governments to re-examine my demands in the light of these new circumstances.

I made this request at a meeting with the High Commissioners on 16 November 1950. I asked if it were possible to let the expression 'Occupation Statute' disappear as it had an ugly sound in German ears.

I reminded the High Commissioners of my memorandum of 29 August 1950 in which I had referred to the need to 'place the relationship between Germany and the occupying powers on new foundations and to embody them increasingly in a system of contractual agreements'. I made it clear to the High Commissioners that I considered a quick response to this proposal urgently necessary.

Regarding the question of increasing occupation costs and of a possible German contribution to the cost of joint Western defence, I stated that the total amount of the German contribution must not be fixed without consideration of Germany's special social burdens. The presence of the people expelled from the East and the problem of repairing the remaining war damage must be taken into account. In a speech in San Francisco on 17 October 1950, President Truman had pointed to the special connection between external strength and internal social welfare. He said of the United States: we are strong because of our system of social welfare. External and internal strength and security were in fact inseparable. If the Federal Government, as a result of occupation and defence costs, were forced, despite tax increases, to lower its social benefits, the internal security of the Federal Republic would be endangered and the will to defend it would decrease. I told the High Commissioners that I was prepared to let independent neutral experts examine the Federal Republic's ability to pay, taking into account its social commitments.

In this context I asked for all dismantling still in progress to be stopped. Some of the plants listed for dismantling were, for instance, supplying iron for Canada and enriched ores to Belgium for arms production. If dismantling were to proceed nonetheless people would simply be unable to understand it. I also requested an examination of whether considerable relief could not be granted in the field of prohibited and restricted industries. The currency situation would benefit greatly from such relief. A further request concerned facilities for scientific research which at this time was still restricted in many fields in no way connected with war industries.

The world situation and especially the European situation were more critical and dangerous for the Federal Republic than for any other European country. I was very much concerned, especially with a view to Soviet Russia, to counteract the impression that there was no strong will to resist in the Federal Republic. It was easy to understand that people in Russia and in the SED, who might assess German attitudes on the basis of pronouncements of a small part of the Protestant Church led by Niemöller and on the opposition of the Social Democrats to a contribution to European defence, might think the will to resist in the Federal Republic negligible. I asked the High Commissioners to persuade their governments to enable the Federal Government to enlighten the German people and to engage in an effective campaign for the protection of European freedom.

There were a number of points of detail on which I requested relief from the High Commissioners. I asked for participation of the Federal Government in all questions of deconcentration and decartelization and for an early settlement of the question of restitution. In the field of jurisdiction, I stated that the extradition of Germans to foreign countries, which was being demanded by some countries, was incompatible with Article 16, Paragraph 2, of the Basic Law, and I asked for these demands to cease. I furthermore asked for the quickest possible conclusion of all war crimes trials and for all death sentences that had not yet been carried out to be transmuted into prison sentences because Article 102 of the Basic Law had abolished capital punishment. I also demanded the complete restoration of German jurisdiction. Persons resident in Germany should in principle be subject to German jurisdiction and exceptions must be kept to a minimum. My last request was for a return to the legal situation existing until about 1933 in the field of broadcasting. In view of possible critical developments in foreign and domestic politics, it struck me as inadvisable to leave the monopoly of radio propaganda in the hands of persons who were not responsible to parliament or government.

The High Commissioners assured me that they would transmit my requests to their governments and would inform me of the results in due course.

The Discussion of a German Defence Contribution Continues

In the late autumn of 1950 the United Nations troops in Korea suffered a serious setback after much fighting back and forth. This fact played an important part in the development of the psychological situation in Germany. The Russian danger at this moment appeared even more menacing to most Germans than it had in the first weeks of the conflict in Korea. Broad sections of the population were seized by paralysing fear.

Three chief elements characterized the psychological situation in Germany: the fear of Soviet Russia, which had grown as a result of Red China's successes in Asia; the protracted negotiations between the Western Allies on the establishment of a West European defence front; and the agitation of the Social Democratic Party which tried to explain to the German masses that peace could be preserved for Germany by doing nothing. The situation in Germany could now be saved only if the governments of the Western Allies made a statement that the man in the street could understand to the effect that the Federal Republic of Germany would soon enjoy equal rights with other nations.

The alleviations proposed for Germany by the New York Foreign Ministers' Conference had not yet come into force; as I have said, they were tied to certain conditions. I had to concentrate all my efforts on eliciting from the Allies a declaration that the Occupation Statute would be replaced by agreements at the earliest possible moment. This declaration must not be limited by any conditions if it was to have the desired effect on the German people. Sooner or later the Occupation Statute was bound to be replaced by agreements. If, however, this happened only after prolonged entreaties I was afraid that it would no longer be appreciated by the Germans; whereas, if it were given quickly it would enable the Federal Government to counter the wave of defeatism that was sweeping across Germany for the reasons I have mentioned. On 21 November 1950 the British High Commissioner Kirkpatrick gave me an interim report on the attitude of the British Government to my demands of 16 November. The British Government was not opposed to my demand for the replacement of the Occupation Statute by a system of agreements and was prepared to examine the question. In the view of British lawyers, a considerable difficulty lay in the fact, as they saw it, that the Allied right to keep troops in Berlin rested on the Occupation Statute and that the Federal Government could not accept any commitments for Berlin in the event of the abrogation of the Occupation Statute and its replacement by agreements. In such a case it would therefore be necessary to find a new legal basis for the occupation of Berlin by Allied troops.

The discussion concerning a German defence contribution to a European-American army went on. I heard of a statement by the French Foreign Minister Schuman, of 16 November 1950, in which he admitted that in the course of the present arms negotiations between the Atlantic powers there would naturally be differences of opinion, but that they should not be regarded as lasting disagreements. Schuman assured the members of the American Club in Paris that close collaboration with the United States of America and Great Britain would remain the cornerstone of French foreign policy and that he had no doubt that the Western powers would eventually come to an agreement on their present differences.

These differences referred to the inclusion of the Federal Republic in a European defence community. Schuman declared, and it was an obvious allusion to German rearmament, that feelings had no place in politics, although they had to be taken into account in the psychology of a people.

The French Chamber debated the foreign policy of the Pleven cabinet on 16 November 1950. After a seven-hour debate this policy was adopted by 171 votes to 142. In an earlier debate Foreign Minister Schuman had stated that prospects were good that the West would adopt the French plan for integration of German units into a European army. France would have preferred to treat economic problems before military problems but the latter had been pushed to the foreground by events. A so-called rearmament of Germany outside an American-European framework would serve the interests neither of the desired Franco-German rapprochement nor of the creation of a united Europe. Under the Pleven Plan the French Government would not agree to an independent German army but would accept German groups in a European army.

Russian Notes of 15 December 1950

On 15 December 1950 the French ambassador in Moscow received a Soviet Note for the French Government in which the Russians renewed the protests against the participation of the Federal Republic in a European army voiced previously in their Note of 3 November 1950. Once more they proposed to call a foreign ministers' conference to deal with the question of implementing the Potsdam Agreement on the demilitarization of Germany. The Soviet Government referred to current negotiations on details of an agreement under which West Germany was to be included in the West European and in the North Atlantic groupings. Among other questions under discussion was that of the total strength of the army in West Germany. The Note referred to press reports according to which the Chiefs of the General Staffs of the North Atlantic Alliance were proceeding on the assumption that in the beginning the West German army would comprise one-fifth of all the armed forces of the North Atlantic grouping of powers. This would give a predominant place in the future to the West German army among the armed forces of the West European powers.

The Note stated further that I was in a hurry with regard to the building of a so-called European army because this would mean a strengthening of the Western powers at the proposed four-power conference with the Soviet Union.

The actions of the French Government had shown that it was ready, together with the governments of the other powers, to prepare a direct military alliance with the 'Adenauer government' and West Germany, a circumstance creating a direct threat to peace. The Soviet Government deemed it necessary to state that such a position of the French Government was not only contrary to the Potsdam Agreement regarding the demilitarization of Germany to which France had subscribed but was also in manifest contradiction to the Franco-Soviet Treaty of 10 December 1944. Article 3 of this treaty provided that 'the high contracting parties will after the termination of hostilities against Germany take all the measures in their power to render impossible a repetition of any new German threat and to prevent any action that would permit a repetition of German acts of aggression'.

The Note also made reference to Article 5 of the Franco-Soviet Treaty which read: 'Each high contracting party undertakes not to conclude any alliance and not to take part in any coalition directed against the other high contracting party.' Contrary to the spirit of the Franco-Soviet Treaty, France had joined the so-called Western Union and the North Atlantic Treaty directed against the USSR.

On the same day the Soviet Deputy Foreign Minister Gromyko handed a Note to the British Chargé d'Affaires Nichols in which the British Government was accused of violations of the Anglo-Soviet Treaty of 1942. The purpose of these Russian Notes was easy to see. The NATO Council of Ministers was to meet in Brussels in the second half of December. This conference was to engage in a thorough discussion of German participation in European defence. By their Notes the Russians were trying to torpedo or at least to delay the discussion of this question.

The wording of the Note to the French Government was extremely clever and was bound to have its effect on French public opinion.

Talks before the Brussels Conference

On 7 December 1950 a decision of the NATO Council of Deputies under the chairmanship of the American, Spofford, was announced which represented a compromise between an American plan for the defence of Europe and the Pleven Plan. The French Council of Ministers announced publicly that although it assented to the Spofford compromise it was regarding it merely as an interim solution pending the conclusion of negotiations on a European army. Under this compromise France no longer demanded, as hitherto envisaged in the Pleven Plan, that the Schuman Plan should be signed and a European army created before the formation of German contingents. The United States, on its part, had given assurances of support for the earliest possible realization of the Schuman Plan and for a conference on the European army at the beginning of 1951. Instead of the German battalions stipulated in the Pleven Plan, there were now to be units that were not to be equipped with heavy arms. These units were called 'combat teams'. They were to be combined into larger units only in conjunction with other Allied troops. The numbers of the German contingent were not to exceed twenty per cent of the total of Allied armed forces. With fifty divisions this meant about 150,000 German soldiers. There was to be no German general staff or German defence minister.

On 11 December 1950 I had a fairly long conversation on the Spofford Plan with the American journalist Kingsbury-Smith. I rejected this plan. I told Kingsbury-Smith that I was prepared to leave the question of integrating German troops into the NATO army to the discretion of an American command only if the Western Allies accepted the principle of complete equality for the German military forces, especially with regard to arms and command authority. Stressing my desire not to assume a negative attitude in principle, I continued that Germany was not insisting on numerical equality in the Atlantic army. Numbers were not decisive. It would be all right with me if our contribution of soldiers were fixed at one-tenth of the total number of soldiers in the Atlantic community, but I had to insist on complete equality with the others with regard to weapons and command authority. Our troops must definitely not be intended merely as cannon fodder. Without their own heavy weapons German troops would have no chance of defending themselves effectively and they would therefore regard themselves as expendable. Without decisive German representation in a high command German soldiers would feel like second-class soldiers. In all probability this would achieve the opposite of what France desired. Discontented combat troops were hard to control.

The so-called Spofford Plan would be rejected by the German public, the German Federal Government, and the German parliament. Although I had no desire to disturb the negotiations of the NATO powers, I urgently wished to prevent such a plan from being formally submitted to us. I also included in the interview a warning that if the Spofford Plan were carried out it would interfere with German support of the Schuman Plan. I could not imagine that France was afraid of 150,000 German soldiers. It was foolish to imagine that this small fighting force would invade France if it had Russia at its rear and Western Europe and the United States ranged against it with France.

As for the German contribution to an Atlantic army, I believed that it would be easy to achieve agreement if the three Allied High Commissioners were authorized to negotiate with the Federal Government. It was a psychological mistake to conduct negotiations on the fate of the German people in Washington, Paris or London in which they had no part. I continued that a beginning could be made with the creation of a Franco-German army by the establishment of joint military academies in which young Frenchmen and Germans could receive their training together and from which they could finally be accepted into a European army in equal units. In this way Frenchmen and Germans would stand together and if necessary would fight shoulder to shoulder, like brothers, for the defence of Europe and Western civilization.

The NATO Council met in Brussels on 18 December 1950, and its deliberations were shared by the three High Commissioners. It had been intimated to me that there was a possibility of my being included in the discussions that concerned Germany. As I was too uncertain of their result I did not accept this offer. On 14 December 1950 there had been a detailed discussion with the High Commissioners in preparation for the Brussels Conference. I was asked to give a clear indication of the attitude of the Federal Government to the New York decisions concerning German pre-war debts and the apportionment of raw materials and defence production.

I told the High Commissioners that our Basic Law required a declaration concerning German pre-war debts to be approved by the Bundestag. The foreign affairs committee was already working on the subject.

I was urged to get a Bundestag declaration as soon as possible, preferably before Christmas. At the moment the people and governments of the three Western Allies were very agitated by SPD talk to the effect that the New York decisions were worthless and that it would be better to delay the German response and to see whether all German demands would not be promptly fulfilled after a short period of time. McCloy told me that this kind of talk killed the good will towards Germany which, for instance, existed in America. The reaction to such pronouncements in the United States was severe. The same could be said for Britain and France. There was a genuine desire in the United States to make progress in the direction of the independence of the

Federal Republic, but such progress could be completely blocked if it turned out that the German Government and the bulk of public opinion in the Federal Republic did not wish to carry out the New York decisions.

I replied that I did not consider the statements of the Social Democratic Party identical with the opinion of the Social Democratic electorate. One could scarcely say that the majority of the German people shared the view proclaimed by the Social Democrats.

At this meeting McCloy brought up another matter which had caused him concern and asked for my opinion. He thought that there were many indications that the Russians were going to start a new offensive, not, perhaps, comparable to the blockade of Berlin, but the attempt would be made to separate Germany from the West and dislodge her from her secure position vis-à-vis the East by holding out the bait of German unity. In the East, of course, the concept of German unity implied a totally defenceless Germany. McCloy thought that the Russians had recognized that if Germany allied with the West and participated in a European army or a European defence effort, the fulfilment of the Russian wish to bolshevize Germany would be frustrated. McCloy was afraid that the Russians were prepared to promise anything provided that in the meantime there was a halt in plans for a German contribution to European defence.

McCloy's prediction came true. I shall discuss it in detail in connection with the well-known Russian Note on the reunification of Germany of the year 1952.

16

GERMAN REARMAMENT

The Brussels Conference of the NATO Council, December 1950

Just before the beginning of the Brussels Conference of the NATO Council McCloy had told me in a confidential conversation at his house at Bad Homburg that we should not expect too much from the conference. The question of the German defence contribution was only one of many points on the agenda and there would be correspondingly little time for it. According to McCloy, what it was hoped to achieve in Brussels was a basis for discussion that could then be submitted to the Federal Government for its opinion. In a matter of such vital interest to the Germans as the contribution to European defence, the German point of view should be heard and considered.

It was not to be expected in any case that I would be somehow dictated to. There was the definite intention to provide us with sufficient opportunity for negotiations and for a thorough exchange of views.

McCloy said that the basic point of departure for the Allies and for the Federal Government was the need to create a European defence community to which national interests must be subordinated. There would certainly be discussions on this subject. He, McCloy, would try to take part in or to bring about a declaration by the Allies, with both a political and a military dimension, on the German contribution. In the course of the conversation I once again raised the demand I had repeatedly submitted to the High Commissioners for a contractual reshaping of the relations between the Federal Republic and the Western Allies. McCloy told me that this point was already the subject of discussions and that there were already a number of relevant drafts.

The Brussels negotiations concluded on 19 December 1950 and it was announced that the NATO Council had authorized the High Commissioners to explore the problem of associating Germany with the European defence effort in further discussions with the Federal Government.

At a meeting with the High Commissioners on 21 December 1950 François-Poncet outlined the results of the Brussels Conference. He gave a detailed report on the discussions regarding the creation of a European army. It had been decided to create a supreme command for the European defence forces. President Truman had nominated General Eisenhower for the post of Supreme Commander. He would have a General Staff composed of representatives of all national contingents. If there was a future German contingent,

German officers would also belong to this General Staff. It was further decided to create a joint office to organize the necessary defence production.

The twelve ministers of the NATO Council had expressed a desire for a contribution of German contingents to this common army. The High Commissioners were asked to give the basic outlines of the form the German contribution might take.

The plan for a German association with the joint defence effort had in no way the character of a forced alternative or of an imposed demand. It represented a combination of proposals leaving the German Federal Government complete freedom to study and evaluate it and, if necessary, to make counter-proposals. The High Commissioners had been asked to work out an appropriate agreement. As to both content and form the agreement had an absolutely voluntary character. In general, and with the exception of one proviso to which François-Poncet returned later in the conversation, all solutions were to rest on a contractual basis. François-Poncet said that the idea of an army for the European defence system on a basis of complete equality of all participants had not been lost sight of. The French Government was going to invite all European countries concerned to a conference in January 1951 at which the various modalities of the system of a united European army were to be laid down. The Federal Republic was also to be invited to this conference and would take part in it with the same rights and in the same way as all other participating European countries.

François-Poncet explained that a German military contribution to the joint European defence effort would create a new political situation. The present Occupation Statute would have to be adapted to this new development. I had requested the replacement of the Occupation Statute by a contractual settlement. The Allies were prepared for such contracts provided that the essential legal basis of the presence of the occupying powers in Germany was not changed at this moment. They were, however, prepared to receive and consider all proposals the Federal Government might make in this respect in the most liberal spirit.

François-Poncet concluded by saying that this was the essence of the Brussels discussions regarding the Federal Republic of Germany and he asked me for my opinion on it. I expressed my great satisfaction with the statement that the Federal Republic was to be left completely free to accept the plan elaborated at Brussels, to reject it, or to make counter-proposals. I said that I regarded the coordination of the production of basic materials as envisaged in the coal and steel community and the creation of a joint European army the most essential foundations of European unity and a European federation. I hoped that at the appropriate moment Great Britain too would assume the attitude that seemed logical in view of the community of interests between Great Britain and Europe.

The High Commissioners were undoubtedly aware of the two conditions publicly mentioned in Germany as prerequisites for the participation of the

Federal Republic in the common defence effort. The first was that the entire area of the Federal Republic of Germany must be included in the defence of Europe. Units of the future European army would therefore have to be stationed in the Federal Republic. This would show a serious intention to defend the Federal Republic of Germany too against possible Russian invasion, and that it was not merely a question of covering the retreat of Allied forces. I myself considered the condition fulfilled and for this reason: I was convinced that *Great Britain and France realized that if the Federal Republic of Germany were under Russian domination there would be no security for Britain or for France*. The second condition was the demand for equal status for German forces, i.e. that German contingents should not have to fight under less favourable conditions than those of other nationalities. I therefore proposed that German and Allied military experts should discuss these problems.

From the political point of view I welcomed the declaration of the three Western Allies that they would receive German proposals. There was, however, one sentence in what François-Poncet had said which I had not quite understood – his statement that they were prepared to accept proposals to replace the Occupation Statute by agreements provided that the principle affording the legal basis for the continued presence of the armies of the Western Allies in the area of the Federal Republic was not changed. The principle on which the occupation rested at present was unconditional surrender. If the declaration of the three foreign ministers should be understood to mean that this principle was to be preserved, this would under international law give the Western Allies the possibility of abrogating unilaterally any agreement made with the German Federal Government at any time and withdrawing any sovereign rights that had been granted to the Federal Republic of Germany. François-Poncet's phrase 'at this moment' had however reassured me. I hoped the High Commissioners would understand me if I considered this 'pour ce moment' as short a period of time as possible. It went without saying that several months would be needed for new contractual settlements of all our relations. I urgently requested the High Commissioners to refrain from telling the public that this principle was to be maintained even if there was the emphatic addition of 'pour ce moment', because the German public would either fail to read or would forget these words, but would all the more point to the fact that the principle of occupation was being retained.

I expressed my great hope that rapid progress would be made towards European unification, which was necessary for the preservation of peace in the face of the danger that threatened from the East. I hoped that the Brussels decisions would soon come to a fruitful conclusion.

François-Poncet at once took up my questions on the reservation regarding the legal basis of the Allied presence in the Federal Republic. I had been quite correct in saying that it was unconditional surrender. 'This principle (he said) is like a root in the ground from which the tree of occupation has grown with its many branches. We think we must begin by first attending to the branches, that is, by solving the problems that concern these branches, before we proceed to the removal of the root itself. That is the meaning of the words "pour ce moment". We therefore want to begin with the branches. Once we have converted these branches into contracts we can descend to the root.'

McCloy spoke next. Regarding the legal basis of the occupation in Germany he said that he too had understood the Brussels decisions to mean that the Allies were prepared to create a contractual basis for the modalities, but that they were not prepared to put the Allied right to be in the Federal Republic on a contractual basis for the reason that this was connected with a large number of other questions that still awaited clarification. Further, it was not possible to agree to a contractual basis because a contract could be terminated by either side. Thus it was conceivable that the Federal Republic would give notice of termination and the Allies were not willing to expose themselves to that, as it would remove the legal basis for the presence of Allied troops in the Federal Republic.

I was aghast at what François-Poncet and McCloy had said, and replied that I wanted to employ the same imagery that François-Poncet had used, and point out that if one cut branches off a tree with strong roots it had the strength to put out new branches.

With respect to the position in international law, I said that an unconditional surrender did not give the conqueror the right to occupy the conquered country for ever. The defeated country was entitled to a peace treaty at some stage. I most urgently requested the High Commissioners to take this entire complex of questions under review.

McCloy answered that it was quite plain from the final communiqué issued by the foreign ministers after the Brussels Conference that they were prepared to discuss all political and military problems with the German Federal Government. As for the right of the Allies to remain in Germany, it was a matter that had to be treated with the greatest caution. We found ourselves in a critical situation at this moment. When I said it looked as if it was intended to maintain the occupation of the Fededral Republic for ever, this was nonsense. He could not quite understand how one could speak of eternity in this respect.

We next discussed the answer of the three Western powers to the Soviet Note of 3 November 1950 in which the Soviet Union had called for a joint conference of foreign ministers. The Western powers had assented to the Soviet suggestion for a foreign ministers' conference although the West probably realized fairly clearly that the suggestion was a Russian delaying tactic. Immediately after the delivery of the Russian Note I had received confidential information to the effect that the American Government was prepared to attend a foreign ministers' conference only if preliminary negotiations on the agenda showed the Russians to be in earnest.

313

I was now to be informed of the Note of reply before it was dispatched. It seemed that the Western powers were accepting the Soviet proposal because the Russians had shown a satisfactory attitude in the discussions on the agenda. I was convinced that there was a danger of a negative outcome of the four-power negotiations and of a further deterioration of the world situation. But the Western powers were obviously willing to accept the risk.

We next discussed the equality of status of the German military units. François-Poncet represented it as a matter of course that all units would enjoy equal status. McCloy also underlined the complete agreement on the basic principle of equality: the arms would have to be the same, and German soldiers would have to be equipped just as well as the soldiers of other nations.

After our conversation, François-Poncet sent me at my request the notes he had used at the conversation of 21 December 1950. He pointed out to me that they were only personal notes and not a diplomatic document. He had made them so as not to have to rely on improvization but to have something to refer to when he spoke.

These notes contained supplementary material for what François-Poncet and McCloy had said about equal status of German troops. They struck me as satisfactory, and I shall reproduce them:

> . . . The idea of the creation of an army and a European defensive system on the basis of complete equality of all participants remains the basis of the solution envisaged . . .
>
> The preparatory work for the creation of such army which pursues no other goal than the safeguarding of the security of Europe and the defence of peace requires time for it concerns not only military questions but also the political and financial aspects of the problem of common defence.
>
> Accordingly the Atlantic powers assembled in Brussels held the view that it was necessary to examine the possibilities of immediate measures which would, without anticipating future developments, permit Germany to make preparations for its military contribution to the defence of the West.
>
> During this interim period certain controls would be required. It was however recognized that these controls would be relaxed as soon as the permanent institutions were established into which Germany was to be integrated.
>
> The framework of the possible German contribution was outlined by the member countries of the Atlantic Council on the basis of the reports of the Council of Deputies, in conjunction with the Military Committee of the NATO Council.
>
> The plan envisages that German units can be raised from now on. They would be formed on the model of the most modern fighting units and consist of infantry equipped with high firing power to which tanks, artillery,

engineers and a tactical air force would be added. These units would be trained in Germany with the effective support of the Allied troops in Germany. Their officers and noncommissioned officers could receive this training together with Allied officers and noncommissioned officers at joint schools or academies.

The modalities of the recruitment, equipment, and organization of these German units could be examined and laid down by the Federal Government and the Allied High Commission by mutual agreement.

The equipment of German units with arms would, according to requirements, be supplied either by the Allies or by German industry in accordance with the programmes to be decided.

The future employment of the units concerned would be determined with regard to circumstances at the time and after due consideration of the opinion of the Supreme Command. During the interim period they would be assigned to the Allied forces stationed in Germany.

The German military contribution to the common effort would create a new political situation. It would be expedient to adapt the occupation régime at present in force to this situation.

I was, however, not satisfied with François-Poncet's notes concerning the basic principle of occupation. I conveyed my criticism to the High Commission, which again assured me that no decisions had been taken in Brussels that would maintain the Occupation Statute for all time. On the contrary, the view had prevailed in Brussels that the possibilities of replacing the Statute by contractual agreements were to be examined as quickly as possible. There had, however, also been agreement on the impossibility of naming a date for the termination of the Occupation Statute, particularly since negotiations were in progress with the Soviet Union on a conference of the four-powers and it was thought undesirable to anticipate four-power talks. I was not by any means to understand this last reservation concerning the four-power talks as an attempt to 'sell' Germany. But one had to avoid getting into a bad tactical position.

I was informed that if world events had taken a normal course the idea of a security pact would undoubtedly have been taken up earlier on the American side and that today a new contractual alliance between the Western Allies and the Federal Republic would be in process of being worked out. The Russian danger had caused inhibitions among all the great powers concerned which were certainly regrettable and erroneous but which had to be understood as a result of the uncertainty of the general situation.

The Situation in the USA; Isolationist Trends

The American High Commission told me that the American Government was very concerned about the increasing tendency to neutralism in West Germany.

If this tendency were to prevail, I was told, a revision of American policy regarding this part of Western Europe would become inevitable.

This communication from the American High Commission was corroborated by the reports of Consul General Krekeler on the situation in America. Since the middle of 1950 the Federal Republic had been represented by a Consulate General. Heinz Krekeler, an FDP deputy, was the first German Consul General. At the end of December 1950 he gave me a report on a speech by the former American President, Hoover, of 20 December 1950 arguing that the United States of America should, apart from a few island outposts, retire to the western hemisphere. This meant withdrawal from Europe.

A member of the German Consulate General in New York had a long conversation with Hoover at the beginning of 1951. This official mentioned Hoover's speech and told him that it had caused great consternation and anxiety in Germany. In August 1950 Hoover had told the same person that Germany must rearm or the United States would withdraw from Europe. In his speech of 20 December he had gone a step further by intimating that Europe, and that included Germany, should be left to its fate.

Hoover replied to our official that he had merely said that the United States was in a position to help Europe only with its navy, with food and with arms. America could make no efforts beyond these and anything further would ruin her. The value of the dollar had already declined considerably. The official told Hoover that the German military contribution, as demanded by the Allies, was very small. There was no longer an armaments industry. It was therefore quite impossible to demand that Germany should defend herself against a Russian invasion in the way Hoover seemed to imagine.

Hoover replied that for five years he had unceasingly described the demilitarization of Germany and Japan as 'the greatest folly of history', for these were the only two countries in a position to resist Russia. It seemed however that the stupidity of all governments was going to prevent this.

The official confined himself to the retort that it was a misfortune if a man like Hoover, who more than any other had alleviated the material distress of Europe, now pursued a policy which led to the eventual destruction of Europe by the Russians. Europe was an idea one should not disregard; it was not a mere continent.

Hoover replied with some agitation that the dispatch of American troops and the raising of only sixty divisions in Europe was tantamount to a challenge to Russia. If Europe could not manage to oppose an army of at least equal strength, as was quite feasible, to the three hundred Russian divisions, it would have to be left to its fate. When it was pointed out to him that Germany was neither able nor authorized to create an army capable of defending itself without American help albeit in alliance with other European states, Hoover merely shrugged his shoulders to indicate that in that case nothing could be done.

Hoover's astonishing sally may be explained by the Quaker thesis of the possibility of coexistence between the Western sphere of civilization and communism. Hoover was a Quaker. I must, however, add that this view was not shared by all Quakers. There have always been isolationist trends in America of greater or lesser strength. The burden the American taxpayer had to accept of protecting wide areas of the world against the advance of communism could explain the desire of many Americans to retire to their own continent and to withdraw as far as possible from the growing difficulties outside America. Hoover's speech must have reinforced these trends considerably. Europe had to watch these tendencies in America carefully and had to try to counter them as far as possible.

Notwithstanding a great number of mutually contradictory trends and tendencies in the United States of America it could be said that the bulk of responsible opinion in the administration, as well as the bulk of public opinion, supported President Truman's decision to meet the communist challenge and to restore the lost balance of military strength in favour of the United States by resolutely promoting rearmament. In a report of 28 December 1950 on the political situation in the United States, Consul General Krekeler argued that the American people would continue the line indicated by President Truman despite the material sacrifice this would necessitate: 'The injury inflicted on American self-respect by communist conduct on international occasions provided the basis for the whole-hearted popular support of the President's decision to intervene in Korea. The course of events in Korea and the course of negotiations in the United Nations have inflicted further wounds on this self-respect. So far this has only had the effect of confirming public opinion in its attitude towards rearmament.'

According to Krekeler's report President Truman's foreign policy was meeting with very sharp criticism in the United States; but Truman was a personality apt to stick tenaciously to a decision once taken and unlikely to be deflected from it by criticism or advice from among his collaborators. Truman's character justified the expectation that he would not give up his fundamental decision to meet communism by comprehensive rearmament during his tenure of office, which would last until January 1953, unless events intervened that invalidated the grounds of this decision. As Krekeler said, 'The decision to restore the balance derives not only from the view that it is necessary to be militarily armed for a conflict, but also from the political will to put an end to the state of insecurity hitherto prevailing. It derives from the view that in the long run it is intolerable to live under the constant threat of war and that the continuance of this threat would in the end suffice to destroy the democratic foundation of the United States.'

Regarding the relationship of strength with the Soviet Union, opinion in the United States was undivided: that leeway could and would be made up. Krekeler wrote: 'Everything we have learned here points in the direction of the American Government's being considerably less prepared to make

317

concessions than, for instance, the next strongest partner in the Western coalition, the British. I would like to sum up by saying that the Americans are united not only on the question of military rearmament but also on the political readiness to accept the extreme consequences should the actions of the communist group make this inevitable.'

According to Krekeler's report the public debate concerned above all the question of whether the United States was to continue to make decisive efforts to maintain the position on the continent of Europe. Krekeler wrote:

> In this context it is very interesting to find that the Washington correspondent of the *New York Times*, James Reston, in an article of 23 December 1950, interpreted the views of Hoover and Kennedy, the former American Ambassador in London,* to mean that they considered war with the Soviet Union absolutely unavoidable, and therefore demanded a timely withdrawal to moderately tenable positions. I consider this improbable because Kennedy's utterances in particular show that he does not reckon with a global conflict but believes, although contrary to every experience of past decades, that in its expansion over the whole of Western continental Europe the communist system will eventually founder on its own difficulties. In Hoover's case, too, an essential element undoubtedly lies in the Quaker thesis of the possibility of coexistence of the two systems.
>
> The decision as to whether continental Europe is to continue to receive economic support from the United States, as is still very necessary, will undoubtedly depend largely on overall military thinking. If this area continues to be seen as an essential component of the Western defensive area – as is certainly the policy of the administration so far unshaken by the public debate – the consequence must be that economic help must continue.

From the American point of view it was evident that the fate of the countries of Western Europe was interconnected. Although there were political trends in the United States that attempted to discriminate in Germany's disfavour, they were counteracted by the military whose influence was very considerable. Let me quote Krekeler once again:

> I do not have the impression that United States opinion sees the inclusion of Germany in the Western defence system as decisive in case of war. On the other hand, I believe that it is considered by all the military a precondition for holding the European continental position south of Scandinavia and north of the Alps and the Pyrenees. They probably assume too that a loss of these positions could be made good again only by extraordinary American sacrifice. The awareness of this logic has, however, not yet penetrated the American public consciousness in sufficient measure.

At a meeting we had on 2 January 1951 McCloy confirmed the danger of an American isolationism.

* Father of the late President John F. Kennedy.

McCloy referred to the American conviction that a new great propaganda operation of the Soviets was impending. However determined the United States might be to resist it, a comprehensive review of the whole of American foreign policy would have to be undertaken in American public opinion, above all in Congress in connection with the necessary appropriations. In order to avoid a loss of ground, during this review, to those who were convinced of the need to give up the exposed position of the United States in the Far East and in central Europe, a resolute defensive spirit would have to be manifested much more strongly in Germany than had been the case heretofore. However much confusion might have arisen in certain parts of the world as a result of events in East Asia and of the ever-growing Russian threat, this must not be allowed to seize the Federal Republic as it could have dangerous repercussions on developments in America. It was important that government and parties should not speak two languages. Also, the population of the Federal Republic as a whole should be encouraged to adopt an energetic attitude

McCloy said that if there was any country that had a European task it was Germany, which disposed of more strength and energy than other European countries. In this connection the clarification of Franco-German relations and the progressive integration of Europe, the goal of the Schuman Plan, were of very special significance. The importance of European integration could not be exaggerated. It was the only counterpoise to Russian endeavours to Sovietize Europe. He had to stress again and again that American help for the free nations of Europe depended exclusively on whether or not the spirit of determination asserted itself in Europe. America would shortly be strong enough to make a greater contribution of the kind that Europe so urgently needed in several fields.

I agreed with McCloy's assessment of the political situation. I too regarded the new phase as extraordinarily dangerous. The conditions in which the Soviet Government was conducting its political operations had, from the Soviet point of view, improved from month to month. The atmosphere in Western Germany was very depressed as a result of the unfortunate development in Korea. The example of China showed that even the satellite states, given modern equipment by Soviet Russia, could threaten peace and achieve military successes, without any need for Russian intervention. The United States had placed too much reliance on its atomic weapons and measures of economic assistance. South Korea demonstrated that these were not enough to halt communism.

In Europe so far no defences worth mentioning had been organized. I told McCloy that a visible display of American power was indispensable, for it alone could induce the Germans to show their attitude towards Soviet Russia more clearly. In recent times the propaganda of the SED within the territory of the Federal Republic had become especially active and successful. I pointed out to McCloy that the Federal Government was quite unable to take any effective steps against this because the police were the exclusive responsibility of the *Länder*. The Federal Government, with no power whatsoever at its disposal, did not have the authority it needed for making West Germany a real factor in the defence of Western Europe. The fault lay in the excessive decentralization provided for in the Basic Law.

Turning to the impending four-power conference which was primarily to deal with the fate of West Germany, I said that all were aware of the weakness of the Federal Republic. The Federal Republic would not be represented at this conference. It could be said fairly certainly that the Western Allies were not agreed on the German problem. I knew for instance that there were trends at the Quai d'Orsay that strongly favoured a neutralization of West Germany or Germany as a whole. The attitude of Great Britain was not yet definitely known. I supposed I could assume that the United States did not share the views of the Quai d'Orsay to which I referred.

Germany must regain its sovereignty if it was to accept what the four powers might decide at the conference. Neutralization on a contractual basis was impracticable. Should the notion of neutralization prevail Germany must be granted enough defensive strength to defend its neutrality. In other words, it would need a defensive power that could not be misused for aggressive purposes. I thought that the Federal Republic must be given a chance to discuss this question directly with the separate Western powers.

I then turned to McCloy's main point, the possibility of a revision of the foreign policy of the United States by Congress and by American public opinion and said that I had thought that after Truman's and Acheson's answers to the statements by Taft and Hoover this problem had been settled. The United States must not forget that if Soviet Russia possessed Europe it would then have at its command nearly two-thirds of the arms and military potential of the world. A world thus controlled by Soviet Russia would sooner or later turn against the United States. It was therefore in Europe that the fate of the United States too would be decided. I very much hoped that despite the present lull the United States would continue its active defence policy.

Turning to the subject of rapprochement between France and Germany I said that this was very much hampered by the domestic situation in France. The United States remained Germany's greatest hope.

McCloy replied that the United States administration had often considered renewing the Marshall Plan, but using it at the same time as a means of coercing hesitant West European governments. There was however agreement that America could not work by coercion as the Soviets did. Europe must develop its own strength. The United States had no inclination to use compulsion. Unfortunately the illusion harboured for years in America, that Europe would regain its spirit of resistance after its economic reconstruction, had been destroyed.

I interjected that Europe's spirit of resistance was paralysed by the pressure from the East. One had to remember that Western Europe was still suffering severely from the psychological consequences of the past wars.

McCloy continued that the leading men in the United States were perfectly clear about the Russian danger. Nevertheless, statements such as those of Truman and Acheson were not enough to settle the possibility of a revival of isolationism. Congress would have to discuss the American contribution to the defence of the Western world and he very much hoped that in the end all members of Congress would recognize their international responsibility. But for this it was necessary that Europe should give the appropriate signals. Every one of my utterances and every speech by Dr Schumacher were noted with the greatest attention. American public opinion registered communist propaganda just as it noted the critical attitude of Western Europeans to American economic, political, and military measures. Quite generally Germany was being equated with Korea. The average American asked himself: shall we send our boys to Germany if Germany or Western Europe confine themselves to criticism and show no readiness to take a positive part in the defence of the free world?

I told McCloy that I could well understand this tendency. I too was very annoyed at statements by leading politicians in the Federal Republic opposing a German defence contribution and undermining the people's readiness to defend themselves. I was considering letting a number of refugees and former prisoners from the Russian zone speak in public meetings all over the country to let the German population see something of the true face of Soviet Russians.

McCloy thought that such a propaganda campaign would undoubtedly be extremely useful. No time should be lost and all efforts should be made in the next three months to mould German public opinion.

The conversation returned once more to the forthcoming four-power conference. I asked McCloy how he visualized the outcome of this conference and its effects on the German psychological situation. I pointed out to him that it would be hard to make any useful agreement without asking Germany. Although the Germans had simply accepted certain decisions during the years 1946-8 it would be different in 1951. The failure to let Germany participate in the shaping of its destiny was a very important factor in the paralysis of the younger generation's political interest.

McCloy replied that if the Soviets agreed to free elections and an absolute guarantee for the freedom of movement of all parties there would soon be general agreement. He stressed the need for talks between Allied and German military experts to be taken up as quickly as possible in order to enter the four-power conference from a strong position.

The Attitude of the SPD on the Question of German Rearmament

The best way to counteract the isolationist tendencies in the United States was to keep underlining our allegiance to Western civilization, to the democratic view of life and politics, and the ideals of Christianity, and to stress our community with America. It was absolutely necessary that we should unambiguously declare for the West. Consul General Krekeler emphasized this point to me. He knew American conditions very well and studied and analysed American public opinion thoroughly. At the end of December 1950 he said that it was urgently necessary for us to confirm the flagging American faith in us and that we should make it unmistakably clear that the Federal Republic of Germany identified itself uncompromisingly with the Western cause. American faith in us had been badly shaken by such goings on in the Federal Republic as the violent polemics of the SPD against the Schuman Plan and against a German defence contribution.

The SPD's position on German participation in a European defence community was indeed hostile. President Heuss tried to enter the debate on this question and to exercise a moderating influence on the SPD but his efforts proved unsuccessful. During one of my regular visits he told me of a conversation he had had with Dr Schumacher.

Dr Schumacher thought the offer of a German contribution that I had made in my memorandum of 29 August 1950 had been premature. According to his information on the plans of the Western Allies, West Germany was to be defended so weakly that the Russians could be in Bonn within thirty-six hours. West Germany would be plunged into infinite misery. He said that McCloy had told him that the Americans were convinced of the inevitability of their withdrawal. They would not however let the Ruhr fall into the hands of the Russians intact; they would first destroy it.

In mid-October 1950 General (retired) Hermann Foertsch, a brother of the later Inspector General, had told me of a conversation with Dr Schumacher in which the latter had stipulated an adequate screen of American and British tank forces and corresponding air protection as the prerequisite of a possible German contribution to the defence of Europe. This defence should be conducted as an 'offensive-defensive'. A total plan of defence was absolutely essential. The Allies should not only defend but were to join with us in our defence, and not on our soil alone. Dr Schumacher was afraid that the Americans were anxious to reach a quick agreement with the Federal Republic in order to forestall possible French objections, and he was afraid that this would lead the Americans to make offers to the Federal Republic which they could not keep.

Dr Schumacher favoured the strategy of an offensive defence. He wanted the Americans to have very strong motorized forces in the Federal Republic that would enable them to reach Berlin as quickly as the Russians could reach the Rhine. In case of a military conflict the attack must immediately be carried East so that the issue would be decided outside German territory. A future conflict would be decided by the first battle.

The accounts of Heuss and Foertsch were corroborated by McCloy who told me of a conversation with Dr Schumacher in which he had demanded that the Americans deploy at least sixty divisions on the Elbe. Heuss reported that Schumacher had the impression that the Americans were dominated by pure materialism and had an idea that the Germans should, as it were, make restitution for the last war by sacrificing their people in the glacis of Europe. Dr Schumacher quoted a remark by an American who when asked why the Americans did not train roughly a million soldiers in the Federal Republic instead of in the United States said that that would expose them to the danger of becoming prisoners of the Russians.

Dr Schumacher was convinced that, in the event of a Russian attack, if the Allied plan of campaign were followed West German officers would certainly lead their soldiers over to the Russian side rather than take responsibility for the useless destruction of their troops to cover an Allied retreat.

Heuss said he had pointed out to Dr Schumacher that the United States had widespread military commitments all over the world. In the Republican as well as in the Democratic Party there were strong isolationist tendencies as could be seen from the electoral success of Senator Taft. One had to show understanding for the American Government's inability to rouse its people to a great effort for the defence of Germany if the Germans did not at least express some readiness to take part. Dr Schumacher was not to be moved from his position, nor was he impressed by Heuss's remark that it was not material interests alone that weighed in American thinking but that the Americans were animated by an ethical mission, and, as a result of the two world wars, felt that they had a great responsibility.

Notwithstanding Dr Schumacher's inflexibility I continued my efforts to win over the Social Democratic Party to my policy of making a German defence contribution. I wrote the following memorandum which I sent to Dr Schumacher with a letter on 31 January 1951 in the hope of persuading the Social Democrats to change their minds:

1. The Federal Republic is threatened by the aggressive imperialism of Soviet Russia as is proved by the systematic expansion of Soviet power in all parts of the world since 1945. The increasingly active policies of the Russian zone government in the last few months lead to the inescapable conclusion that we cannot expect this Soviet imperialist expansionism to stop at the Elbe. If Soviet Russia succeeds in forcing the Federal Republic of Germany, with a minimum of damage, into the Soviet sphere of influence, Russian war potential would be equal to that of the United States. At the same time Russia would prevent the unification of Western Europe for the defence of the Western world. In all probability Soviet policy would thereby also succeed in increasing American isolationism sufficiently to make the United States withdraw from the continent of Europe.

2. Despite administration statements there is at this time in the United

States a latent isolationism. Its spokesmen are Hoover and Taft. Mr McCloy stressed this very much, in a conversation with me after Hoover's speech and before Taft's, saying that American policy would be decided in Congress during the first three months of 1951.

On 26 January McCloy told me in the presence of the former Senator Cooper, one of the two Republican advisers given Acheson by Truman, that the attitude of the Federal Republic on a contribution to the common defence would be decisive for American policy, more decisive than the French attitude.

3. For the strategic planning of the common defence and for its organization it matters vitally whether or not the Federal Republic can be regarded as a *safe* area, i.e. as a country reliably on the side of the Western world. The Western world will consider Germany 'safe' in this sense only if the Federal Republic decides to make an appropriate defence contribution.

4. The four-power conference will in all probability take place. France wants it in any case, Britain wants it too, and the United States will not prevent it. At this conference Soviet Russia will propose a package deal consisting of the restoration of German unity, its neutralization, demilitarization, and evacuation. Powerful political groups in France are prepared to accept such a proposal. The British attitude is not quite clear. Official circles in the United States oppose such a neutralization of Germany because it would surrender Germany to the Eastern bloc; to the isolationist on the other hand, such a proposal might appear acceptable.

I see in such a Russian proposal at the conference the greatest imaginable danger for the German people and for Europe.

5. In view of the situation described above and of the weakening of the inner steadfastness of the German people by the continuance of present uncertainty, it appears to me necessary to bring about a decision of the Bundestag as soon as Eisenhower's report has clarified the situation in America.

6. In my opinion the Federal Republic of Germany must declare its readiness to make a contribution befitting its circumstances. The following essential foundations must be postulated:

(a) The military measures of the Western powers must be such as to give certainty, according to expert judgment, that they will use their entire strength to beat back aggression and to prevent the territory of the Federal Republic from becoming a fighting area.

(b) In view of the extraordinary burdens of the Federal Republic in the social field, financial support is urgently required. This support should meet the obligations of social policy, maintain the stability of the currency, ensure a balanced budget and the maintenance of a proper standard of living, as these are all essential factors in the defence potential.

(c) If the Federal Republic of Germany takes an active part in the common defence, the principle of occupation must be replaced by the principle of agreements. The scope of the Occupation Statute is so broad that all its provisions cannot be altered at one time, nor can all Allied orders and decrees be simultaneously superseded; this process must, however, be as rapid as practicable. A beginning must be made by a binding declaration of the Western Allies acknowledging this principle. In certain areas requirements deriving from the presence of Allied troops on German soil must be considered and they must be made the subject of contractual agreements.

The policy of the Federal Republic and the Western Allies toward the Eastern bloc must be parallel. Here it will be necessary to find a mechanism in agreement with the Allies that guarantees harmony in methods and aims.

(d) The German defence contingent must enjoy equal status with the Allied contingents regarding organization, equipment and leadership.

7. Consequences of participation and consequences of non-participation.

(A) Consequences of participation:

(i) The first question that arises is whether such a contribution will bring about Russian aggression.

Soviet Russia's aim is the inclusion of the Federal Republic of Germany in the Soviet sphere with as little damage as possible. Therefore Soviet Russia will prefer the cold war, which has been so successful and whose present results in the Federal Republic have also been profitable for Soviet Russia, to a hot war in the Federal Republic as elsewhere.

For Russia a hot war would at best weaken the war potential of the Western Allies by devastating Germany and preventing the rearmament of France and Italy, but on the other hand it would endanger the existence of Soviet Russia itself through the intervention of the industrially superior United States.

It is therefore improbable that Soviet Russia's answer to a German contribution will be hot war.

(ii) In the unlikely case of aggression a united defence force would stand ready to prevent the Federal Republic becoming a theatre of war. Supplies of raw material and above all of vital food supplies would remain assured.

(iii) The danger latent in the four-power conference of a United States retreat from Europe and thus a handing over of Germany

325

to the Soviet sphere can only or at any rate more certainly be averted by a timely clarification of the attitude of the Federal Republic regarding a defence contribution.

(iv) We would once more become a sovereign state.

(v) There would then be a prospect of developments leading to German unity in freedom.

(vi) A participation of the Federal Republic of Germany gives the only possible chance of exercising any influence on the decisions of the Western Allies vis-à-vis Soviet Russia.

(B) Consequences of non-participation:

(i) If the Federal Republic refuses to make a contribution or evades a declaration – and such an evasion comes to a refusal – it is extremely probable that the Federal Republic of Germany would be swept into the Eastern bloc, perhaps as soon as the forthcoming four-power conference.

(ii) Even if the US were not in this case to renounce its European plans altogether, the strategic planning of the Western Allies would be based on a defensive line in the West and on the assumption that the territory of the Federal Republic is a theatre of war.

(iii) We would get no raw material.

(iv) We would get no sovereignty, and no unity of Germany in freedom.

(v) It is probable that all of Europe would come under Soviet influence.

8. Soviet Russia's posture constitutes a deadly danger to Europe and above all to Germany. The only way to increase the likelihood of avoiding a war, of making the Federal Republic free again and of restoring Germany's unity in freedom, of realizing the various plans for Europe in some form and of preserving Europe, lies in an unprovocative but determined association of the Federal Republic of Germany with the grouping of Western Allied states.

Dr Schumacher replied in a letter of 6 February in which he outlined the views of the Social Democrats. He agreed with me that the former and present state of affairs were in every respect unsatisfactory and dangerous for the security of the Federal Republic of Germany. He thought however that the dangers threatening us from the East could not be removed or even reduced by a German military contribution. He said in his memorandum:

Any German rearmament, even if it proceeds undisturbed, can only meet future dangers . . . The training of the first larger tactical formations requires at least one and a half years. A military contribution of any significance for war could not be made in less than three or four years. During this period Germany would be unprotected. It could neither defend itself by its own strength nor be successfully preserved from a possible Soviet Russian intervention by such Allied forces as are at present available or have so far been promised for the foreseeable future.

Dr Schumacher thought that the effects of a German military contribution on Soviet Russian policy were not predictable. He did not think that one could safely assume that the Russians would avoid a hot war in case of German rearmament. He told me what he had repeatedly said in public that the Social Democratic Party emphatically denied the present Bundestag the right to make such a decision because the SPD maintained that it had been elected in different circumstances.

Furthermore certain conditions would have to be fulfilled by the Allies before a German defence contribution could be endorsed. These conditions must at all events be fixed before any binding declarations were made on the German side. Dr Schumacher wrote:

> The essence of these conditions is their stability and immutability. Their value lies in their factualness. Prerequisites cannot be replaced by promises. There is a difference in kind between them and negotiable conditions or reservations. The actual conduct of the Allies since the days of the Petersberg Agreement forbids the hope that a German earnest of good will can create the necessary preconditions for a just arrangement. The Germans ask no one for anything they are not willing to give themselves. Conversely, however, they must not assume any obligations which others do not expect of themselves.

There was no difference between Dr Schumacher and myself on the point that a German defence contribution must be based on equality. He said:

> There is much talk of what we have in common, but everyone means something different by it. The Germans are being asked to regard their equal rights as something they already enjoy and to behave accordingly. In fact, however, the Allies themselves regard German equality of status only as a future possibility. Any policy that tries to buy equality with military contributions is condemned to failure. The result will always be an actual inequality in favour of the other party. Political equality of status is the precondition of a military contribution and not its result . . . The Petersberg Agreement, the treatment of the Saar question, the inequality in the European Council at Strasbourg, the Ruhr Authority and the Schuman Plan are examples of the extent to which community is used to camouflage selfishness and how far we are from the actual equality of the peoples of Europe.

Dr Schumacher could see nothing positive in the probable consequences of participation in the military rearmament of the Western world given the conditions of that time. He did not consider the consequences of non-participation dangerous. He called my appeal for a German declaration for the West 'extraordinarily provocative', saying:

> The political parties in Germany made such a declaration by proclamations and by deeds without regard for the possible consequences at a time when the Western Allies had still not unambiguously opposed the Soviets. The constant demand for new affirmation means disrespect for what has gone before.

He stated that there was no American policy that would be in a position to relinquish Europe. America's prestige in the world and its position vis-à-vis communism forbade it. He said:

> Today the USA and even its hitherto isolationist elements are interested in the subsidized export of agrarian products. Industry must do everything to maintain the productive superiority of the USA. . . . Even Hoover no longer speaks the language of old-fashioned isolationism.

I cannot in this context discuss all the points mentioned in Dr Schumacher's memorandum. In general I must say that there were a number of points on which there appeared to be agreement with the view of the Federal Government. The essential difference lay in Dr Schumacher's insistence on all the wishes of the Federal Government being fulfilled by the Allies without exception or reservation. His standpoint was very theoretical. He did not seem to have the experience in international negotiations that teaches one to be prepared for compromise if one wants to achieve a result. How could we in this case force the preconditions for a German defence contribution if nothing was done on the German side? How were the free nations that were making considerable sacrifice in the fight against communism to be convinced that a country deserved to be defended if that country insisted on performances on the other side without itself at the same time giving a clear indication of what it would be prepared to do? In the opinion of the Federal Government, the indication that was required was a declaration in principle that we would be willing to make a contribution to the defence of the Western world if the well-known conditions were met. It went without saying that this contribution was to be made for the creation of a defence force for the preservation of peace. Soviet Russia would renounce her intentions of Western expansion only if she was convinced that it would be dangerous to do otherwise.

17

MY FIRST VISIT AS FEDERAL CHANCELLOR AND FOREIGN MINISTER OF THE FEDERAL REPUBLIC OF GERMANY TO PARIS IN APRIL 1951

The Significance of the Schuman Plan

After nearly nine months of discussions the draft Treaty constituting the European Coal and Steel Community had been finished by the negotiators of the six countries intending to form the community. On 11 April 1951 I went to Paris in my capacity as Foreign Minister of the Federal Republic of Germany for the last discussions and the act of signature, which took place on 18 April 1951.

Dr Schumacher had made a speech in which he described the Schuman Plan as economic nonsense. He had issued a warning not to misuse the word 'European' in connection with a plan embracing only the corner of Europe which 'is the breeding ground of capitalism, clericalism, and cartels'.

The Schuman Plan was the *beginning* of European unification. I saw the signing of the ECSC treaty as the opening of a new epoch in the history of Europe.

The recognition that the peoples of Europe must meet each other if they wanted to maintain their freedom and prosperity had dawned after the First World War, but had not yet led to practical results because in all camps traditional thinking and mistrust were still too strong. And then we all had to live through a period in which an exaggerated nationalism brought Europe to the edge of the abyss.

Nearly all the peoples of Europe had drawn conclusions from this catastrophe. They were aware that the reconstruction of European life in peace and freedom was possible only if the people's energies could be enlisted in the service of practical cooperation. They knew that the old forms of international cooperation must be examined and new institutions created where these were inadequate.

With a view to this reshaping of relations between countries, which was already in evidence in 1948 at the Congress of European Associations at The Hague, the Parliamentary Council had, when it created the Basic Law, made a unanimous declaration in favour of European cooperation and had written a provision into the Basic Law enabling the Federal Republic to transfer sovereign rights to supranational institutions and to agree to a limitation on its rights by simple law, if such limitations were calculated to construct a peaceful and lasting order in Europe and between the nations of the world.

Since their inception the German Federal parliament and the German Federal Government had seen one of their noblest tasks in repeated appeals for the creation of a European community and in attempts to bring it about. On 26 July 1950 the Bundestag passed a resolution which read:

> Convinced that the present fragmentation of Europe into sovereign states must lead the peoples of Europe further into distress and bondage every day, the Bundestag of the Federal Republic of Germany, duly constituted after free elections, appeals for a European pact of federation as envisaged by the Preamble and Article 24 of the Basic Law for the Federal Republic of Germany.
>
> This European pact is to:
>
> 1 create a supranational federal authority founded on universal, direct and free elections and endowed with legislative, executive and judicial powers;
> 2 equip this authority with all prerogatives needed to bring about economic unity on a basis of social justice, to facilitate a common European foreign policy serving the peace of the world, to define and safeguard equal rights for all European nations, to guarantee and put under legal protection the basic rights and human freedoms of the citizens of Europe.

By the same token the Federal Republic had worked for an active European policy and had done all in its power to support similar endeavours abroad whenever an opportunity offered.

When Robert Schuman, the French Foreign Minister, appealed for a discussion of his proposal of a European coal and steel community on 9 May 1950 the Federal Government had been unhesitatingly and fully prepared to cooperate. Schuman had demanded 'the creation of concrete facts as precondition of a solidarity of action for the overcoming of the old hostility between France and Germany'. The signature of the ECSC treaty was the first step along the course whose deepest meaning for France and Germany lay in making any war between them not only unthinkable but materially impossible by establishing the joint production of coal and steel. First and foremost the conclusion of this treaty put a solemn and irrevocable end to a past in which two peoples had again and again confronted each other with arms as a result of mistrust, rivalry and egotism.

The final rectification of the relationship between France and Germany made possible by the ECSC was not intended as an end in itself but rather as the core of a solution that should embrace the whole of Europe. I was therefore very glad that from the outset, in addition to France and Germany, Italy, Belgium, The Netherlands and Luxembourg had declared their readiness to cooperate in this great work.

In drawing up the treaty our intention had not been solely to create a union for coal, iron, and steel but we also wanted to shape a model for possible further international institutions in Europe in the future. I was firmly convinced that once a beginning had been made with the coal and steel community, once six European countries had voluntarily and without coercion transferred a part of their sovereignty to a superior body in this treaty, there was hope that similar developments would occur in other fields and that nationalism, the cancer of Europe, would thereby be dealt a fatal blow.

All signatories of the ECSC treaty were agreed that the establishment of the coal and steel community was the first step toward European unification. Similar projects were becoming discernible in the fields of agriculture and transport. I was prepared to work vigorously in these areas as well, as also in the current negotiations on the organization of a European military defence.

It went without saying that the coal and steel community was not to be confined to the six countries participating so far. I hoped that the circle of participating nations would continue to grow, for the meaning of this union could not be truly fulfilled until all the peoples of Europe had a part in it. Even if some European countries were not yet prepared to come to a decision to cooperate on this basis, ways and means should be found to permit them to work with the coal and steel community for their own and the common benefit. I was thinking of Great Britain in particular.

Those who took part in this European work of unification were fully aware of the part the administration and public opinion of the United States had played in all phases of the negotiations preceding the conclusion of the treaty. The efforts of the peoples of Europe would have been and would still be in vain if they could not be sure that the United States of America would give its active support in the future as well. The coal and steel community was not created to shut off Europe from the rest of the world, thus, as it were, transferring national egotism to a continental plane; it was rather to be the goal of the coal and steel community to form the closest links with the entire Atlantic world because only in this way could it truly fulfil its economic and political objectives.

I was convinced that the effects of the coal and steel community would change not only economic conditions on our continent but all of the thinking and political feeling of European man as well. It would lead Europeans out of the straits of their national lives into the broad field of Europe which would bring to the life of the individual a greater and richer meaning.

The youth of all European nations was longing to travel, to learn and to work in other countries. The common economic area in process of formation and the great possibilities it would afford of exchange in all fields would preserve the younger generation from falling prey to false prophets. Human beings whose emotions at this time were still largely characterized by mistrust, rivalry, and resentment would become neighbours and friends.

The signing of the agreement on the Schuman Plan on 18 April 1951 marked the success of the first attempt in modern history to create a great unified economic area for basic products like coal and steel in Europe. Only the future could enable us fully to appraise the economic consequences of this treaty. We could, however, safely expect that the great free common market for coal and steel about to be established, unencumbered by political obstacles and private monopolistic barriers, would perfect the international division of labour, increase the ability of the Western European economy to attract credit, and in the long run enlarge export chances and lower costs of production and distribution.

I was sure that every European, not least the European worker, would draw great benefit from a development which would doubtless very soon enable him to buy more goods than before at cheaper prices and thus to improve his standard of living. The greater significance of the Schuman Plan however consisted in the growth of confidence, the corollary of common effort in supranational work, that would fundamentally change our European life.

The Schuman Plan was a beginning. Just as there were efforts to create a European organization for defence, there were also to be combinations in other fields as soon as possible. The unified economic area for more than a hundred and fifty million people for which we were striving would resemble the economic area of the United States whose astonishing prosperity and strength was made possible by the absence of political obstacles to the free exchange of goods.

Last Discussions of the Schuman Plan; The Saar Question; Abolition of the Ruhr Authority; The Seat of the High Authority

There was little ceremony at Orly airport when I arrived. I was the first member of the German Federal Government to visit Paris since the end of the war. Jean Monnet had come to welcome me at the airport, but there was no member of the French Government because an important meeting of the French cabinet was in session at the time of my arrival.

It was my first official trip abroad as Federal Chancellor and Foreign Minister. I had deliberately chosen to pay my first official visit to the French capital, to underline my conviction that the Franco-German relationship lay at the heart of any European solution.

Since the summer of 1950 the Federal Republic of Germany had been represented in Paris by a Consul General. As first representative of the Federal Republic I had chosen the art historian Professor Wilhelm Hausenstein, who was known as a man of great learning who had always shown a special interest in French culture. I thought it advisable not to send a career diplomat to France as Germany's first representative. The tasks awaiting a German representative in Paris were first and foremost psychological. I considered Hausenstein just the person to master these very difficult tasks and he proved outstandingly successful. He was an important promoter of Franco-German reconciliation. His house in Paris became, as I had expected, an intellectual magnet.

On the day after my arrival in Paris, Vincent Auriol, the President of the French Republic, gave a luncheon in my honour at the Elysée Palace. Our conversation was very friendly and a promising prelude to this very important visit to Paris.

The final discussions of the Schuman Plan in which the six foreign ministers of the countries concerned took part began in the French foreign ministry on the Quai d'Orsay on 12 April 1950. Belgium was represented by Foreign Minister van Zeeland, Luxembourg by Foreign Minister Bech, France by Foreign Minister Schuman, Italy by Foreign Minister Count Sforza, The Netherlands by Foreign Minister Stikker.

Several decisions still remained to be taken: the location of the seat of the coal and steel community; membership, composition and competences of the High Authority; the powers of the Council of Ministers and the Common Assembly; voting methods; the language of discussion, and the powers of the Chairman of the High Authority.

An important question I had to settle with Schuman privately was the Saar problem. France maintained, and the Federal Government denied, that the present status of the Saar had legal legitimacy. Both governments were however agreed that a final settlement of conditions in the Saar must be reserved to a peace treaty with Germany or to a treaty which some day would fulfil the function of a peace treaty.

Both governments, as well as the governments of the other four ECSC countries, shared the conviction that the coal as well as the steel production of the Saar must come under the Schuman Plan. We needed a settlement that respected both points of view, the French as well as that of the Federal Government. We succeeded in finding the right way.

When countries make treaties it is in the nature of things that they must always remember that their partners too have an opposition; therefore, negotiations must be conducted in such a way as to reach a conclusion that both governments can defend before their own parties as well as against their opposition.

The solution found by Schuman and myself was very satisfactory. The following passage was written into the treaty concerning the application of the Schuman Plan to the production of the Saar territory:

The treaty applies to the European territories of the high contracting powers. It is likewise applicable to the European territories whose foreign relations are taken over by a contracting party. As regards the Saar, an exchange of letters between the government of the Federal Republic of Germany and the government of the French Republic is attached to this treaty.

The French Government conducted the foreign relations of diverse territories as, for instance, those of the principality of Monaco. Similarly, it conducted the foreign relations of the Saar territory, a fact we could do nothing about at that time. I needed a declaration that would be a clear answer to the claim of the SPD that signing the Schuman Plan meant the passive recognition of the permanent detachment and political independence of the Saar. A way had to be found that was acceptable to both parliaments, the French as well as the German. Schuman too had to reckon with strong opposition in parliament.

Schuman and I agreed to exchange the following letters on 18 April which were appended to the agreements on the European Coal and Steel Community.

His Excellency,   Paris,
President Robert Schuman,   18 April 1951
Minister of the Exterior

Mr President:

During the negotiations on the European Coal and Steel Community the representatives of the Federal Government repeatedly declared that the final settlement of the status of the Saar can be made only by the peace treaty or a similar agreement. They have furthermore declared during the negotiations that by signing the agreement the Federal Government does not express recognition of the present status of the Saar.

I repeat this declaration and request confirmation that the French Government agrees with the Federal Government that the final settlement of the status of the Saar will take place only by the peace treaty or similar agreement, and that the French Government does not regard the Federal Government's signing of the Agreement on the European Coal and Steel Community as constituting recognition of the present status of the Saar by the Federal Government.

Permit me, Mr President, the expression of my highest esteem.

(signed) Adenauer

Dr Konrad Adenauer,   Paris,
Federal Chancellor and Minister of   18 April 1951
Foreign Affairs of the Federal
Republic of Germany

Mr Chancellor:

In reply to your letter of 18 April 1951, the French Government note

334

that the Federal Government does not regard signature of the Agreement on the European Coal and Steel Community as constituting recognition of the present status of the Saar.

For its own part the French Government declares that it acts in the name of the Saar on the basis of its present status but that it does not regard the signing of the Agreement by the Federal Government as a recognition of the present status of the Saar by the Federal Government. It does not consider that the Agreement on the European Coal and Steel Community anticipates the final status of the Saar which is to be settled by a peace treaty or by an agreement concluded in place of a peace treaty.

Permit me, Mr Chancellor, the expression of my highest esteem.

(signed) Schuman

We were on the way to a united Europe in which frontiers were to disappear. It struck me as a complete anachronism that anyone should want to create another European dwarf state, as was the endeavour of the Saar Government, in this phase of European development.

After the Allied declarations of 5 June 1945 Germany had not ceased to exist as a state, within the borders of 31 December 1937. Although the Basic Law of the Federal Republic of Germany had not been created by the whole German people but only by the German people in eleven *Länder*, with the participation of the representatives of Berlin, they had acted for the Germans who were denied participation. The Federal Government, which derived from free democratic elections, was therefore entitled and obliged to maintain German rights and interests in their entirety. By the Potsdam Agreement and other Allied declarations it had been laid down in principle that Germany's territorial status could be changed only by a peace treaty. Therefore the Federal Government regarded the Saar as legally a part of Germany. The right we claim to represent the interests of the whole of Germany internationally was expressly acknowledged in the declaration of the Allied foreign ministers on the German question in New York in September 1950.

The Franco-Saar Conventions of 3 March 1950 had given the impression that the last word had been spoken that the French Government meant to say regarding the Saar. These Saar Conventions had a strange fate. While the diet of the Saar summarily ratified them at a single meeting a few days after signature, the French Government deliberated until October 1950, that is a full seven months, before it submitted the Saar Conventions to the French legislative bodies for their endorsement. They came into force on 31 December 1950 but with a very significant difference from their original conception. The political Conventions, that is the agreement concerning the detachment from the rest of Germany, had been put into force by the French Government without parliamentary ratification. When the Conventions were discussed in the French National Assembly on 21 October 1950, Foreign Minister Schuman said: 'The agreements that do not require ratification can be changed without

335

participation of parliament. It may be necessary to adapt these agreements easily and quickly to requirements in constant process of development without the intervention of parliament.'

I took these words of Schuman to mean that my fear of the French Government regarding the finality of the Saar Conventions was unjustified and that the French Government shared our opinion that the last word on the Saar remained to be spoken.

The Saar Government had precipitately interpreted the acceptance of the Saar as Associate Member in the Council of Europe and the admission of an observer from the Saar Government to the meetings of the Committee of Ministers of the Council of Europe to mean that the Saar Government was being put on an equal footing with the Federal Government and that an independent state of the Saar had been recognized. The Saar Government would have done well to remember the resolution of the Committee of Ministers of 3 November 1949 which said 'that the situation in the zones of occupation of Western Germany has led to the Saar at present not being represented in the Council of Europe and that it is regarded as desirable that the population of the Saar should be represented in it pending the final settlement of the status of the Saar in a peace treaty'. This resolution of the Committee of Ministers of the Council of Europe clearly showed that the population of the Saar was to be represented in the Council of Europe, but not, however, a Saar state.

On 20 February 1951 Foreign Minister Schuman had countered the urgings of his parliament to engage in discussion on the Saar question with the Federal Government by the remark that he did not want to conduct any sterile debates with the Federal Government on that question and that in politics he would eventually be found to be right who had the stronger nerves. Schuman had spoken from my heart. In the treatment of the Saar question what mattered was to keep one's nerves steady.

This was why I had simply allowed the question of the Saar to run its course in the Council of Europe. The Federal Government did not evade it.

At the signing of the Schuman Plan we were faced with the attempt to introduce the Saar as treaty partner into the circle of European states on the occasion of the conclusion of a multilateral international agreement. The Saar Government had demanded of the French Government that the Saar be admitted as the seventh country and thus as equal partner in the Schuman Plan. After the experience we had had with the claims of the Saar Government in the Council of Europe in Strasbourg our reaction to this tactic was appropriately explicit. Had the Saar Government been admitted as a signatory of the Schuman Plan, the Plan would have been wrecked. The Federal Government would not have signed the Agreement. I had made this clear to the French Government. Difficulties of equal magnitude would have arisen if the French Government had claimed the right to sign the Agreement in its own name and in the name of the Saar Government because such a procedure would have meant the recognition of the Saar as a political entity represented by the French Government in international law. Once the Saar Government knew that it could not expect admission as seventh treaty member, it concentrated its efforts on this last solution, which the French Government also rejected in order not to endanger the Schuman Plan. In the exchange of letters of 18 April the German and French Governments, while both maintaining their own positions, had agreed that the final settlement of the Saar question could be made only by a peace treaty or similar agreement. Such an agreement had not existed between the German and French Governments before that date. The present arrangement meant that until the final settlement by a peace treaty neither side would engage in actions or create conditions which would anticipate a final settlement by the peace treaty.

In the spring of 1950 a cabinet resolution had expressly laid down that the Federal Government would not recognize a Saar state. The Saar Government had not been recognized by any other country than France and the French Government's recognition, as the exchange of letters of 18 April 1951 made explicit, was subject to the final settlement in the peace treaty or a similar agreement. In the exchange of letters of 18 April 1951 it had been possible for the first time to get our legal position accepted in connection with an international agreement. It seemed to me to be of particular importance that it created a legal foundation between the German and the French Governments for the future settlement of conditions in the Saar. Since the exchange of letters formed an integral part of the Agreement on the European Coal and Steel Community, the legal interpretation embodied in it had also been acknowledged by the other signatory powers of this Agreement. This success seemed to me all the greater for having been achieved without much fuss.

If we continued on this path, if, to use the words of Schuman once more, we kept our nerves steady, we could come to an equally calm agreement with the French Government on the Saar question. This agreement could be based on the principle I had stated from the outset, that France had economic interests and that we had economic and national interests in this area. Between these interests one had to find some balance in the spirit of sincere European cooperation that was prepared for compromises, a balance that did justice to all and in particular to the wishes of the people of the Saar. In no event must the question of the Saar be allowed to lead to a disturbance of the efforts to bring about good relations between Germany and France and thus to obstruct the building of Western Europe. Any incidents and difficulties connected with this question must not be allowed to occasion any deviation from the line of policy – decisive for Germany, France, Europe, and world peace – of integrating Europe and creating the accord between France and Germany which is the foundation of an integrated Europe. I was firmly determined to pursue unwaveringly my European policy and the policy of bringing about good relations between Germany and France despite any possible incidents.

When the Schuman Plan came into force the coal and iron of the Saar became European coal and European iron just as the coal and iron ore of the other ECSC countries had done. This disposed of a very essential and not unjustified economic criterion of French policy in the Saar. I believed that the Agreement on the Schuman Plan would one day foster a reasonable settlement of the Saar problem and one that accorded with the will of the people of the territory. My hope was not disappointed.

Another point that had to be cleared up in the negotiations leading to the signing of the Schuman Plan and which in part had been cleared up, although at the last moment it acquired a sudden and somewhat disturbing importance, was the question of the Ruhr Statute. The Ruhr Statute and the Schuman Plan were mutually incompatible. It would have been nonsensical for a Ruhr Authority to control production in the Ruhr, and the High Authority of the Schuman Plan, which was to include representatives of all ECSC countries, to share the same work. The solution of this problem was made more difficult by the fact that Great Britain was a member of the Ruhr Authority but not of the Schuman Plan organization.

Kirkpatrick had acquainted me with the views of the British Foreign Secretary Bevin regarding the Ruhr Authority and the Ruhr Statute. In a long political conversation at the end of November 1950 Kirkpatrick had informed me of Bevin's views, which were quite sympathetic towards the Schuman Plan: Bevin welcomed an early conclusion of negotiations. He intended to make agreements between Britain and the member countries of the Schuman Plan on the basis of the ECSC treaty immediately after the latter was signed. Kirkpatrick responded to the demand I had voiced since the very beginning of the negotiations on the Schuman Plan that the Ruhr Authority and the Ruhr Statute must be abolished by saying that Bevin too was convinced that with the conclusion of the Schuman Plan the Ruhr Authority lost its *raison d'être* and that Bevin favoured the abolition of the Ruhr Authority and the Ruhr Statute. I was very pleased at this attitude of the British Government on the Ruhr question.

During the last conversations before the signing of the Schuman Plan in Paris difficulties had once more arisen in this matter. However, my wishes prevailed and I elicited a written confirmation in response to my demands. On 18 April 1951 Schuman wrote the following letter to me in his capacity as President of the European Coal and Steel Community:

Paris,
18 April 1951

Mr Chancellor:

At the moment of the conclusion of the negotiations on the Schuman Plan, I feel impelled to tell you how much the French Government appreciates the particularly friendly atmosphere in which the negotiations took place and came to a happy conclusion.

338

The agreements signed today create a European community of supra-national character.

They effect a merger of the productive potential for coal and steel in the six countries under the authority of the community and in the interests of all participating countries on the basis of complete equality of status. They thereby open a new era in the relations between the participating countries and represent a decisive phase on the way to European integration. *In the view of the French Government the special obligations imposed on Germany in the field of coal and steel – that is, the Ruhr Statute – are no longer compatible with the common rules to which all signatory states of the Agreement are equally subject.* Accordingly the French Government holds that, provided the participating governments agree, the following measures should be taken:

(1) The functions at present performed by the Ruhr Authority must lapse in the measure to which the High Authority assumes its powers for the exercise of its competence under the agreement concerning the transition period. The Ruhr Authority and the London Agreement of 28 April 1947 by which it was instituted would then have to lapse at the latest with the establishment of the common market for coal, by agreement with the signatory states.

(2) As regards steel production and the productive capacity for steel, Germany should then only be subject to the rules applying to all signatory states. The limitations on Germany's production and productive capacity for steel would accordingly have to be lifted when the Agreement enters into force.

(3) The High Commission would have to renounce on its own behalf and for its affiliated bodies including the control groups such of its functions in the field of coal and steel as fall within the competence of the High Authority, to the degree to which the latter is authorized to exercise this competence in accordance with the Convention of the transition period.

All the measures envisaged in this letter would enter into force at the latest upon the establishment of the common market. Once the Agreement has been signed the French Government intends to take the steps needed to get the required assent to the above-mentioned measures from the signatory powers of the London Agreement as well as from the other occupying powers.

(signed) Robert Schuman

The British Government was in full agreement with the contents of this letter. The Ruhr Statute lapsed with effect as of 21 December 1951.

The Schuman Plan was certainly of great economic importance but its underlying ideals were of even greater significance. A community of European countries was to be created on the basis of complete equality, the only basis of a genuine community. This fundamental idea was of the greatest consequence for the political life of Germany, for France, Europe and the world.

I was convinced that the signing of the Schuman Plan would have effects in the most diverse political fields. On the last day of the negotiations the underlying ideal of the Schuman Plan had made possible a joint decision of the six participating countries which was of the greatest political importance. In a joint resolution signed by all six countries it was agreed that the idea underlying the Schuman Plan was to be promoted by these countries with all their strength in other fields as well, by frequent consultations and personal contact. The word 'consultations' was very important. It means something quite specific in international law and in diplomatic language. For us Germans this promise of more frequent consultations among the Schuman Plan countries on important political matters was a great political achievement.

The negotiations on the seat of the High Authority had produced violent disagreement. The meeting at which this subject was discussed, among others, lasted until five in the morning. Almost every one of the participating foreign ministers wanted to have the seat of the ECSC Authority in his country. Finally Foreign Minister Bech of Luxembourg offered, as a way out, to establish the seat in Luxembourg provisionally. Since the foreign ministers were exhausted by the hard and tiring negotiations and since nobody objected that the little country of Luxembourg might, by housing the seat of this important European organization, acquire an increased political importance within the ECSC, final agreement was reached and his proposal accepted.

Bech's proposal was a generous gesture on the part of Luxembourg in that initially it meant a great burden because space had to be created for the ECSC Authority and accommodation to be found for its servants. Luxembourg did not suffer any harm as a result of the offer, however, and I think that Minister Bech, a very wise man, saw from the very beginning that this would be so.

Although there were a number of difficulties and disagreeable differences at the last negotiations, there was nonetheless in all these discussions a strong undercurrent of readiness to compromise because all present were resolved from the outset to sign the treaty at this conference.

General Impressions; The Signing of the Schuman Plan; The Croix de Guerre

My first official visit to Paris was the subject of lively comment in the French press whose articles, with a few exceptions, were written in a friendly and objective vein and stressed my efforts for Franco-German understanding. The conservative *Figaro* wrote that whoever maintained that I was a friend of France was using a misleading phrase. The truth was that I was a man of good will, a German who wanted understanding with France, and that was why Frenchmen should receive me with due respect. Maurice Schumann declared in *L'Aube*, the paper of the Christian Socialist MRP, 'It required courage for Dr Adenauer to come to Paris despite weeks of snarling from his opponents, but the overdose of provocation also indicates the remedy. To respond with mere mistrust to the rebirth of Pan-Germanism would only be a way of repeating the mistakes of the past. Adenauer is not Brüning and 1951 is not 1931.'

It was left to the communist papers to indulge in agitation against the Federal Republic and myself. They described me as the 'straw man of the American arms manufacturers' and the 'puppet chancellor of the Allies'.

I had flown to Paris a day before the beginning of the Schuman Plan negotiations and used the first day of my stay for a long walk through the Bois de Boulogne along the boulevards and along the Champs Elysées. François-Poncet accompanied me. He had taken my arm and we walked, arm in arm, along the famous shopping street of Paris.

François-Poncet led me to the Arc de Triomphe. We went up by elevator and had a glorious view of Paris.

We had the protection of numerous guardian angels in the shape of security officials and were therefore easy to spot for most of the passers-by. Among those who stopped, looked at our group and recognized me as Federal Chancellor of the Federal Republic of Germany I never noticed any sign of unfriendliness. At first there was obviously a certain feeling of curiosity. The longer I stayed in Paris the friendlier became the faces of the people I met. The atmosphere during this first stay in France as Chancellor became very amicable and I felt decidedly happy at the success for our fatherland.

On the day after my arrival in Paris, Thursday 12 April, the conference of foreign ministers of the six countries participating in the Schuman Plan began in the French Ministry of the Exterior at 4 p.m. It was the first time for nineteen years that the representative of a democratic Germany once more took part in the deliberations of an international conference of foreign ministers. The Beauvais Salon of the Quai d'Orsay, which is hung with precious tapestries and in which in 1946 Byrnes, Molotov, Bevin and Bidault had met, served as conference room. I was seated between the representatives of France and Belgium. Schuman was the chairman of the conference. The official languages were French and German. The first meeting lasted for two and a half hours. That same evening I had a conversation with Schuman alone that lasted four hours. We had a completely frank discussion of the Saar question and of other points where there were still differences between the German and the French views. We talked about further possibilities of strengthening Europe, of the European defence community that was being planned and about joint European plans for agriculture, fuel and power, and transport.

The atmosphere at the conference was informed by a spirit of friendly warmth. It was possible to take all decisions unanimously. No country was voted down on any point. The endeavour to achieve unanimity was invariably crowned with luck and success. Schuman directed the negotiations with inimitable impartiality, with an extraordinary feeling of responsibility, and with kindness and sympathy for all participating countries and especially for Germany.

The delegations had done outstanding work to prepare the conference. Thanks are above all due to Jean Monnet who strove with indefatigable energy during the nearly nine months of preliminary negotiations for a fruitful outcome.

This foreign ministers' conference in which we Germans had been included for the first time was imbued with an atmosphere of rising warmth and growing friendship among the members. It is precisely the relationship of personal trust of the statesmen of different countries amongst each other that is of the greatest importance for the solution of political questions. When one trusts the other man, when one has sympathy for him, when one understands and recognizes his endeavours, one can work in a way which is impossible in an atmosphere of mistrust. Several participants in the conference who had attended numerous conferences at which Germany was represented during the years after 1918 told me unanimously that it was impossible to overestimate the difference in the spirit of this conference compared with the atmosphere of those days.

The signing of the ECSC treaty took place by a solemn act in the Salon de l'Horloge of the Quai d'Orsay in the afternoon of 18 April. So many changes had been made in the treaty of 17 and 18 April that the French Government Printing Office could not finish the treaties in the short time at its disposal. The treaty was therefore signed on blank sheets. Signatures were affixed in alphabetical order. I signed first for Germany – Allemagne.

When I returned to my hotel that day (I was staying at the Hotel Crillon with my entourage) I found an envelope addressed to me personally. It contained a Croix de Guerre from the First World War and was accompanied by a long letter from a young girl, Simone Patrouilles, a Paris student. She wrote:

Mr Chancellor:

I have the great honour to write to you as a Frenchwoman from Paris who, in common with many others in our old city, has been immensely happy at your excellency's visit to our ancient capital, short though your stay may be.

I see in your visit the symbol of a first genuine step on the road to peace and salvation not only for Germany, your fatherland, but also for France and for all nations who are conscious of the joint heritage we have the duty and the mission to defend.

My father died of the consequences of the war of 1914–18 in which he took part from beginning to end. I ask you, Mr Chancellor, to accept this Croix de Guerre of a French soldier which belonged to my father and which

I enclose in this letter and to keep it as a modest token of remembrance of your significant visit to Paris in April 1951. It is a modest gesture of hope for a pure and genuine reconciliation of the two peoples who have suffered so much at one another's hands.

I was deeply moved by the letter. For me this gift, presented to me in Paris at my first official visit as representative of the German people, stood as a sign that it is above all the youth of our two peoples that want to find each other. During all my years as Chancellor this Croix de Guerre was a symbol for me of the genuine desire of the French people to live in friendship with the German people. It is very precious to me.

18

DISCUSSIONS ON THE EUROPEAN DEFENCE COMMUNITY

The Beginning of the Discussions on a European Defence Community in Paris on 15 February 1951

The higher the defence costs of the three Allies rose the more they discussed the question of letting the Federal Republic of Germany help in some way to pay for these defence costs. Because of proposals I had made earlier they understood that the Federal Republic would insist on arms if it were to share in defence costs.

At the New York Foreign Ministers' Conference of September 1950 the French and British delegations had been surprised by the insistence of the American demand for a German defence contribution. After tough negotiations agreement had finally been reached in New York to hand over the problem of Western European defence to a committee of military experts. This committee assembled in New York in October 1950. It had been charged by the foreign ministers with the task of ascertaining whether the defence of Western Europe was feasible without a German contribution and what form a possible German contribution should take. The public was not told the result of the discussions of this committee, but the final communiqué of the Brussels Foreign Ministers' Conference of December 1950 showed clearly that the experts had come to the conclusion that a German contribution was indispensable. The Brussels meeting agreed that a German contribution was wanted, but that its importance should be limited by certain reservations and by restriction to smaller fighting units. The question of whether a German defence contribution was to be set in the framework of the Pleven Plan or in the NATO framework had apparently been left open in Brussels. It may help to say something about the tasks of NATO: during the years after the German defeat Soviet Russia had enlarged its area of domination so brutally and so extensively that the Western Allies finally could not help seeing what danger Soviet Russia posed for the whole of Europe. As a result the following countries had combined in the North Atlantic Treaty on 4 April 1949: Belgium, Denmark, France, Great Britain, Iceland, Italy, Luxembourg, The Netherlands, Norway, Portugal, The United States of America, and Canada. In its essential provisions the North Atlantic Treaty is an agreement for consultation and mutual help resting above all on the natural right of countries, confirmed in Article 51 of the Charter of the United Nations, to individual and collective self-defence against any armed attack.

Under the treaty an attack on one member constitutes an attack against all. Therefore every member will assist the member that has been attacked individually or in conjunction with others by taking measures including the use of arms which it considers necessary to maintain the security of the Atlantic area. This area also includes the occupation troops of the members of NATO in Europe. The obligation to assist is not automatic; the kind and extent of assistance is left to the judgment of the members.

The North Atlantic Treaty is not a purely military document; it also obliges its members to promote stability and welfare in economic cooperation and to eliminate conflict in their international economic policies.

The discussions held in Washington by the French Prime Minister Pleven at the end of 1950 had apparently led to the following compromise solution regarding the German defence contribution: while the need for it was recognized in principle the German defence contribution was to be delayed in order to secure a clear lead in armament to the French. The negotiations on a European defence army scheduled to take place in Paris at the beginning of 1951 were to be given a chance. Moreover, there was a desire not to condemn the four-power conference, which was the subject of a lively exchange of Notes with Soviet Russia during the first half of 1951, to failure at the outset.

The Americans seemed to prefer the inclusion of a German contingent in NATO. Statements of leading American politicians implied that they judged NATO to be the only practical form of Western defence organization against Soviet Russia. On the other hand, the Americans had welcomed the idea of a European army. The British were very reticent in their statements but seemed to support the American preference for NATO over a European army. My talks with the High Commissioners on the Petersberg had given me the distinct impression that the United States and Britain were disinclined to break off the negotiations on a possible German defence contribution in the framework of NATO.

On 24 January 1951 the French Government announced the decision to convene a conference in Paris to discuss the creation of a European army. The Federal Republic was invited in the same manner and at the same time as all European countries that were members of NATO. The German delegation was to be on an entirely equal footing with the other delegations at this conference. The American and Canadian Governments were invited to send observers.

On 26 January 1951 the French Deputy High Commissioner Bérard held a press conference at Bad Godesberg in which he gave a thorough account of the purposes of the Pleven Plan. This plan, which had first been published on 24 October 1950, had the same basis and the same intention as the Schuman Plan, he said, adding that a connection between the idea of a common economy and a common army was natural and self-evident. It was further evident that political and military cooperation could become a reality only on the basis of economic cooperation. There was a connection between the two plans, but they did not depend upon each other.

Bérard explained that the French Government wished to await the signing of the Schuman Plan before proceeding to the second stage of European unification, the creation of a common army. The French Government did not know exactly when the Schuman Plan would be signed, and it was possible that there might be a delay of a few weeks.

The Pleven Plan was not an improvisation. It was the desire of the French Government that the European Governments should achieve agreement on a permanent and lasting institution in the course of the conference. France's supreme goal, the unification of Europe, was a constant element in French policy. If there were now thoughts of creating a European army, the reason was that Europe should possess the requisite armed forces to defend itself against the dangers threatened from the East.

In this press conference Bérard pointed out that the plan of a European army had this great advantage for the Federal Republic: any German rearmament carried the risk of being regarded as provocative by Russia and of being used for propaganda purposes; this danger was removed, the French thought, if German rearmament took place in the framework of a European army.

Hitherto a country's rearmament had meant that the government in question had complete freedom to use its armed forces as an instrument of its policy. The creation of a common European defence force would mean that the armed forces were no longer directly at the disposal of the individual countries. The French Government advocated an integrated army with joint organization and under a single command. At the head of this common European defence organization there must be a common minister of defence. This minister of defence was to be responsible to a council of ministers to be formed by all participating countries. It was the desire of the French Government that the European defence organization should be controlled by a European assembly, be it by the Council of Europe at Strasbourg, or by another assembly created for the purpose. A common budget would be drawn up to finance the European army.

These were the proposals the French delegation would make at the impending conference. It went without saying that all proposals made by other countries would be examined. The final organization of a European army would be determined by the decisions made at the conference.

Regarding the position of the Federal Republic in the proposed defence organization Bérard said it was the view of the French Government that the Federal Republic must take part on a basis of complete equality, which meant that the Federal Republic must be represented in the council of ministers as well as in the interparliamentary assembly and would take part in the administration of the joint budget. Certainly all soldiers and officers would have the same status and enjoy the same rights and privileges. Only such armed forces as were designated for the defence of overseas territories were to maintain their national character, and even they only for an interim period. There would be some differentiation during the transition period arising from the exigencies faced by some European countries in areas situated outside Europe, as for instance France in Indochina.

The conference was to begin on 15 February 1951. The United States warmly welcomed the initiative of the French Government in calling together the interested European powers to discuss the creation of a European army, and accepted the invitation to send an observer. The Canadian Government also announced that it intended to send an observer.

I was informed of a letter addressed to the French Foreign Minister, Schuman, by the American Secretary of State, Acheson, emphatically underlining the positive American attitude. The United States, he wrote, had given numerous proofs in declarations, measures and agreements, of the extent of its interest in Europe as well as of its support for European unity and of its desire for cooperation with Europe. Acheson said that he was convinced of the desire of the American people for this development to continue. If the French Government, in the spirit which spoke so distinctly from the Schuman Plan, worked out the main outlines of a plan to promote the further rapprochement of the free peoples of Europe in close contact with the governments of Germany and the other European countries prepared to participate in the common work, one was justified in the hopes that long-term solutions for many of the present political, economic and military problems might be found.

Acheson stressed in his letter that the United States administration gave its full and whole-hearted support to European integration. If the European countries succeeded in uniting, this unity would provide a solid foundation for the building up of military and economic power. A centre of gravity would be created from which a free Europe could unfold its strength in order to defend its faith in its historic tradition successfully. A strong Europe was indispensable for the development of the free world and the realization of general security in the framework of the Atlantic community.

I chose Professor Hallstein as head of the German delegation to the Pleven Plan conference. He also headed the German Schuman Plan delegation.

On 15 February 1951 the conference on the European army was opened by the French Foreign Minister, Robert Schuman, in the name of the French Government. Belgium, France, Italy, Luxembourg and the Federal Republic had sent representatives as full members of the conference. Denmark, Great Britain, The Netherlands, Norway, Portugal, The United States, and Canada were represented by observers.

The Dutch Foreign Minister, Stikker, told me later that The Netherlands had made their own proposal. The Dutch Government did not consider the Pleven Plan to have much chance of acceptance by the French parliament and therefore merely sent an observer to this conference as a clear manifestation of

347

their scepticism. In the late autumn of 1951 The Netherlands took part as full member in the negotiations on the European defence community because the progress of the negotiations seemed to them to justify a more favourable view of the chances of success.

Schuman said in his opening speech that during a period of nine months the French Government had taken two initiatives toward the creation of European institutions of a completely novel character. The goal of one had been the merger of coal and steel production. The second initiative, the demand for the creation of a European army, was however not a French invention. This idea had first emerged in the Consultative Assembly of the Council of Europe in August 1950 and had repeatedly been put on the list of the institutions generally considered to be inseparable from the concept of a united Europe. Referring to criticism levelled against the French initiative, he said that it was not the idea as such that frightened people; the criticism derived less from a hostile attitude toward the supranational organization itself than from a feeling that the French initiative was untimely and premature. The French proposal had been made at a time when the nations of the North Atlantic Treaty were painstakingly organizing their defence. The question arose whether this effort, which had been all too long delayed, would be impeded and a tremendous and inherently difficult undertaking made harder by further complications. The question needed an answer.

Schuman said that if the French initiative could be proved to endanger or even delay Atlantic defence, the French Government would shelve its proposal until a later date. On the Atlantic defence system Schuman said:

> The Atlantic system may answer and satisfy urgent yet passing needs; the problem of Europe persists. We hold the view that regardless of the situation of the moment and of any intercontinental or global solutions found elsewhere, a Europe must be organized, a Europe that must be redeemed from an anachronistic and absurd dismemberment, a Europe that must overcome an obsolete nationalism. We have recognized and we proclaim this truth in the field of economics and of politics. It holds as well for the organization of defence if one speaks of a military system intended to last.
>
> Atlantic defence and European defence thus do not exclude each other and do not cut across each other. They occupy different planes.

Schuman answered the objection that a European army could not be formed and maintained before a European political authority, a European government, and a European parliament were in existence by saying:

> We are convinced that Europe cannot be brought to life at once like a Utopia. It will come about slowly. It is already in process of evolution piece by piece and step by step, which means for a time that the old and the new will move side by side but that a more or less rapid development has

begun. The measures taken in this process will be constantly tested by experience and adapted to practical needs.

Schuman announced in his opening speech that the French Government had prepared a memorandum setting forth its views on the European army. He quoted from some of its basic ideas:

Within the framework of Atlantic armed forces there will be a European army as a permanent instrument of the security of our continent and as an essential element of European integration. My government has proposed that the establishment of political institutions should proceed simultaneously with the formation of this army.

It would first be necessary to appoint a European defence commissioner who was to work with the Council of Ministers under the control of an interparliamentary assembly. Schuman explained that this commissioner must be obliged to carry out the directives of the European body. He would be responsible for the combat readiness of the contingents provided by each country and for the creation of European units. He would have to be able to rely on the support of the governments that had appointed him and that would have to transfer their authority to him in constantly increasing measure. Schuman emphasized that the European army was not directed against any country, nor was it designed to serve the interests of individual countries.

It would be necessary to recruit contingents in the participating countries in accordance with principles still to be defined. These contingents would have to be under similar legal and disciplinary regulations and equipped with the same arms. They would have to be integrated in larger units comprising contingents of different nationalities. The raising and training of these contingents and the creation of a firm administrative framework would develop progressively through the various phases and would determine the limits of the authority of the Commissioner, his relation to the Council of Ministers, the increase in effective strength, and the increasing integration of contingents. Schuman said:

We must not forget in our work that our immediate aim is the creation of a military instrument whose effectiveness convinces not only our technicians but also our peoples that the army of a united Europe is capable of repelling a possible aggressor by virtue of an inner cohesion and strength equal to those of national armies. For this reason above all we must look for concrete and valid solutions even if they are limited in scope.

At the end of his speech Schuman stressed once more the endeavour of the French Government to convey an awareness of their solidarity to the peoples of Europe while at the same time providing the institution and means to make possible the implementation of this solidarity:

We started on this road five years after the end of the Second World

War. In their concern about their common future, nations which a moment ago were still separated by an abyss have forgotten the struggles of the past and met at the same negotiating table in order to try to replace the tool of just these struggles, the national army, by a common army which must no longer serve anything but the defence of our common civilization.

These, he said, were the guiding ideas submitted for discussion by the French Government. During the conference and in the execution of its decisions all countries would cooperate on a basis of complete equality, an equality of rights and duties toward the community.

To us Germans, Schuman said that we had been invited to this conference of Atlantic nations as a country of which the French Government had repeatedly stated that it could not imagine Europe without its participation. Today it was being proposed to us Germans that we should assume our part in the work of the common defence with the same rights and obligations as all other countries which faced the same dangers and the same problems as a result of their geographic position and their fate.

In conclusion Schuman repeated again:

What we want is not an improvization imposed on us by immediate necessity. The work we seek to create will not be limited in time. It must become a durable structure, the expression of a European community that has at last been founded.

Conversation with the High Commissioners on 5 April 1951

The Paris discussions on the Pleven Plan were very difficult and slow. Something, however, had urgently to be done for the security of the Federal Republic. I broached the subject anew during a conversation with the High Commissioners on 5 April 1951. I reminded the High Commissioners that at the New York Foreign Ministers' Conference of September 1950 the Western foreign ministers had guaranteed the security of the Federal Republic and of the City of Berlin. Shortly after this conference the High Commission, that is François-Poncet, had told me that it was planned, in order to give this guarantee greater effectiveness, to increase the strength of the armed forces of the Western Allies stationed on Federal territory within the shortest time possible. Since the New York Foreign Ministers' Conference nearly seven months had gone by, and I believed it would be hard to say that the world had since become a calmer place; despite the prospect of a four-power conference, the opposite was the case. The war in Korea was demanding ever greater efforts and events in Persia would in all probability necessitate a greater concentration of forces in the Near East. The danger represented by the Soviet troops in the Russian zone remained unchanged. The anxiety of the German people that despite the New York guarantee the Russians might be able to break into Western Europe and especially into West Germany had grown in the meantime. One of the chief tactics of the Soviet Union was to arouse and disseminate fear by the subversive activities of a fifth column.

The negotiations on raising German units, which had begun after the New York conference, had come to a complete standstill. The discussions taking place between military experts of the Western Allies and the Federal Government since January 1951 on the Petersberg were more or less unilateral and theoretical. On the German side they were being continued only because breaking them off could not be kept from the public and would have a deleterious effect on the general atmosphere in the Federal Republic.

The whole development of the situation was causing me, as responsible head of government, the greatest anxiety. I asked the High Commissioners to submit to their governments my request that the NATO Supreme Command inform the Federal Government, or the Federal Chancellor through suitable German military experts, of the military intentions regarding the implementation of the New York security guarantee.

If I were the leader of the opposition in the Federal Republic I would, instead of raging against the Schuman Plan, address a question to the Federal Chancellor pointing to the promise of security made at the New York Foreign Ministers' Conference. I would ask the Federal Chancellor what he had to say now after the lapse of seven months on the measures taken to fulfil the guarantee by the powers who had promised us security.

I would only be in a position to answer as follows: in the budget the sum of so and so many billion DM has been asked for, and air fields are being built. But I would not be able to say anything about the date when the troop reinforcements would arrive in the Federal Republic. Above all I would be unable to say anything about the strategic planning of the Atlantic army, notably whether it was intended to adopt the method which, in the view of our German military experts, alone afforded the possible and certain prospect of success. According to the experience of our military experts in the war with Soviet Russia, the Russians had extremely vulnerable flanks. In the view of these German experts it would certainly be possible to forestall a Russian attack from the outset if appropriate troops were held in readiness on the northern flank and the southern flank, on the zonal frontier or behind it. The German experts believed that with ten to twelve divisions in the north and the same number of divisions in the south and a lesser number in the middle, a Russian attack would not be mounted at all. The High Commissioners pointed out that contrary to my account a reinforcement of Allied troops had in fact taken place. There were now four divisions in the Federal Republic instead of two, and I was told that considerably greater reinforcements were planned for the remainder of 1951.

I resumed where I had left off, and asked the High Commissioners to put themselves in the place of the German who carried the responsibility. Although millions of Germans were involved, we were merely an object of other peoples' actions. The High Commissioners would surely understand that a man who can do something himself in dangerous situations is much less pessimistic than the one who can do nothing but wait for what others will do. I reminded the High Commissioners of my request for security for the Federal Republic which I had expressed as early as two months after the establishment of the Federal Republic. I had been listened to courteously but my request had not been taken quite seriously. I further reminded the High Commissioners of what McCloy had said about a year ago, namely that the presence of one American soldier was the greatest security we could get. I was far from saying that nothing had been done. I fully acknowledged what the American people, the French people, and the British had done.

In two years at the latest the Federal Republic would be plunged into the electoral campaign for the new Bundestag. If within the next twelve months the strength of the Western Allies were not visibly demonstrated to the Germans I was afraid that radicalism would become very prominent in the new Bundestag. The campaign currently going on in Lower Saxony for the *Landtag* elections showed that numerous groups of the radical Right were active there. The decisive factor was that according to very reliable reports there was an extremely close connection between the radical Right and the SED. The instigators of the radical groups of the Right, who in themselves were not at all numerous, were now getting bold because people, being anxious and afraid, were offering no resistance. I feared that there were therefore more people taking out political reinsurance than we thought. The great danger lay in the belief being very widely spread that nothing could be done against the East. It was not my duty to attend only to my daily tasks; I also had to think of future developments, and things were moving very fast. I did not think I was being too pessimistic.

Kirkpatrick replied that he did not want to accuse me of undue pessimism regarding the world situation or the internal situation in Germany but only of pessimism regarding the efforts being made to achieve the strength of which I spoke. He understood very well that a man who had to look on relatively inactive was more anxious than the other man who could tackle a problem himself. The trouble was, however, that with modern arms some time was bound to elapse from the moment when one put the penny into the machine and the moment when one could fetch something out. He was convinced that I would live to see the day when the machine would produce enough to cause me serious embarrassment.

I told Kirkpatrick that I was glad to take that risk. At the end of our conversation I asked the High Commissioners to consider this: every army had its own methods and this was especially true of the Russians. It was a fact that so far neither an American nor a French nor a British general had fought with the Russians. The German generals had relevant experience. I asked them to consider whether it might not be advisable for the military of the Western Allies to make some use of these experts.

The High Commissioners assured me that this proposal would be examined.

They would pass it on to General Eisenhower, the Supreme Commander of NATO Forces in Europe.

Talks with McCloy in April and June 1951

McCloy was intending to go to Washington at the beginning of May in order to address various committees of the Senate on economic and political developments in Germany. The occasion of his trip was the Senate discussion on the appropriation of new funds for use in Germany. Before his trip he asked me to inform him of the most recent German developments and tell him what arguments he could use in his discussions with the Senate committees.

In our talk, which took place on 26 April 1951, McCloy told me that the general situation in Western Europe was causing him great disquiet. Conditions in the French and British parliaments were unsatisfactory. He was afraid that neither country would produce a viable government and that therefore one might expect stagnation in political conditions in central Europe. This would also adversely affect the situation in the Federal Republic. As things stood it would certainly be very difficult for France and also for England to continue work on the evolution of the status of Germany and to put relations with the Federal Republic on a contractual basis.

I gave a detailed account of the present situation in the Federal Republic. I mentioned my endeavours during my visit to Paris to create some clarity concerning the definitive integration of Germany in Western Europe not only among the foreign ministers but also in public. I stressed that the Federal Government was continuing to take an effective part in the negotiations on the Pleven Plan which began in February 1951. I had given the German delegations a directive to this effect but with the proviso that nothing must be allowed to happen in Paris that might disturb the development of NATO.

The problem of a German defence contribution could, however, be solved only if certain indispensable preconditions were met including primarily the effective reinforcement of Allied troops in West Germany. After what Kirkpatrick and he, McCloy, had told me one could probably expect this condition to be fulfilled by the end of the year. The other condition was that the defence contribution of the Federal Government must not impair the fulfilment of our huge social obligations, the consequence of millions of refugees and war damage. The occupation costs that had so far been fixed unilaterally by the Allies exceeded our ability. The Federal Government was engaged in a conscientious examination of the German ability to pay while giving due attention to these great social burdens and hoped to arrive at a figure which would be a feasible contribution toward defence. A last condition was the early publication of a declaration of principles to affirm the new status of the Federal Republic and the guarantee of its equality.

If these conditions were met I believed that the question of a defence contribution would be answered in the affirmative by German public opinion and by parliament. The mood of '*Ohne-mich*' was on the wane.

McCloy replied that, regarding the declaration of principle I had asked for, it seemed to him doubtful that the French and British Governments would soon be prepared to commit themselves. He believed that both Governments first wanted to await a fundamental clarification of relations with the Soviet Union at a possible four-power conference.

Since the Soviet appeal for a four-power conference at the beginning of November 1950 the Western powers had been engaged in an exchange of Notes with the Soviets without any concrete outcome being yet discernible.

McCloy continued that General Eisenhower favoured a German defence contribution. On the occasion of a meeting in Luxembourg, Eisenhower had told him that Western Europe, including West Germany, could only be effectively defended with the help of German troops. Eisenhower had asked him to urge the Federal Government to expand the German police and the frontier police as quickly as possible.

McCloy returned from the United States at the end of June and got in touch with me immediately after his return in order to give me a detailed account of the attitude of the American administration to the most important German problems and of the talks he had had in the United States.

He reported that there was far-reaching bi-partisan agreement on the policy to be pursued towards Germany. The leading men in Congress were chiefly preoccupied by two questions: what progress has Germany made on the road to true democracy? where does Germany stand in the conflict between East and West – does it instinctively incline to the Western world or is the matter still subject to special decisions? These questions had been the subject of discussions he had had with Truman, Acheson and Marshall.

McCloy told me that the American administration would make a hundred and seventy-five million dollars available from ECA funds for the coming year. According to McCloy a special willingness to help was indicated by the inclusion of the Federal Republic in the group of countries who, like Greece and Turkey, received further funds beyond military aid.

War production in the United States was making good progress. He, McCloy, had been assured by competent quarters that although equipment would be insufficient in case of a war there were enough arms available to avoid any delay in the training of troops. Arms production would increase very rapidly from month to month. In certain fields of arms technology extraordinary developments were to be expected.

According to McCloy the Schuman Plan played a decisive role in the thinking of American leaders. It was generally regarded in the United States as a glorious affair. Nobody knew what it really meant, but the general notion connected with it that it would combine Germany and France in a way that would exclude warlike conflict for all time was enough.

The conviction was growing in the United States that Germany could be trusted again. He, McCloy, had talked to larger groups about the Schuman Plan and about German readiness to cooperate in all these fields.

Regarding the German military contribution, McCloy said that in matters of rearmament the time factor played a decisive role in all American thinking which was concerned with finding a way of making progress in the next few months. There was some chagrin at the little progress that had been made in the Paris negotiations on the Pleven Plan. Everyone in America was convinced that if Europe were seriously intending to defend itself, a German contribution would be indispensable politically as well as militarily. The talks on the Petersberg of December 1950 had shown a sufficient basis of agreement, although not on all points, so that one could hope for eventual unity. The United States still maintained the position of the Brussels Conference regarding the creation of a European army. It was needed all the more because no European country had sufficient means to finance its own armament. If, however, the European nations worked together they would probably be in a position to bear the necessary financial burdens. All these questions would be the subject of further negotiations. The road to a European army could, however, only be taken if an actual military force were created and that within the shortest possible time.

American military leaders were very sceptical about the French plans. As a first step it was important for the interim report of the Pleven Plan conference to be expedited so that we could get a picture of requirements and difficulties. A few weeks ago the Joint Chiefs of Staff had circulated questions to the American commanders in Europe on the problem of how a European army could be best and most effectively organized. These reports would, together with the results of the Petersberg conference and the Pleven Plan conference, be submitted to a conference of the foreign ministers of the NATO powers scheduled for September at which these reports were to serve as the basis for the decisions to be taken on the political and military questions.

On the status of the Federal Republic, McCloy said the Americans were prepared to go very far, further than the other Allies. However, some questions remained with which the American administration too was very concerned. Acheson, for instance, had asked him what would happen if the SRP (Socialist Reich Party) made a coup d'état or if other internal unrest were to break out with which the Federal Government could not cope. In this connection the reawakening of nationalism in Germany was being watched with some concern.

Replying to McCloy I said that the issue of a German defence contribution must at all costs be settled soon. It was the chief goal of Soviet policy to bring about a neutralization and complete demilitarization of Germany because without them Russia could not regard the ground as sufficiently prepared for its expansionist policy in the West. Once the question of the defence contribution had been settled positively, any demilitarization and neutralization of

355

Germany would be out of the question. It would mean that the Soviets had failed in the pursuit of one of their essential goals.

An additional consideration was the fact that all rearmament would be set in motion if Germany at least made a start and the other countries could count on a certain protection being afforded by Western Germany vis-à-vis the Soviet threat. The psychological situation in Western Germany on the matter of a defence contribution had taken a turn for the better. Today a majority of Germans were in favour of the defence contribution and such opposition as was still to be found in the Social Democratic Party was limited to a few prominent members of the leadership. The discussions at the International Congress of Socialists in Frankfurt am Main, the positive attitude taken by the trade unions, and the discussions at the International Trades Union Congress in Milan had all given evidence that we in Western Germany were witnessing a change of attitude.

As for the nature of the contribution, it should be decided entirely by military considerations. It would be nonsensical to do something for political reasons that was not feasible militarily. There had almost been unity at the Petersberg talks despite French resistance. At the negotiations in Paris the most important aspects of the problem had not yet been tackled. There was no doubt that in the long run the European army would be absolutely necessary because even if present tensions were overcome, the pressure of the overpowering Soviet empire on Western Europe would always lead to new crises.

The NATO army had been a response to present tensions; the European army was intended for a longer period. The time would certainly come when America would withdraw from Europe. European formations would then be needed. An attempt should be made to bring the Paris negotiations up to the level of the Petersberg discussions. German practice in Paris had been to avoid too much conflict with France by relative reticence as such conflict could only adversely affect the Petersberg discussions.

The negotiations must now be stepped up to show whether the French in Paris had other views from the representatives of France at the Petersberg. It was very much to be desired that the United States should show its approval of the course of the Petersberg negotiations.

In explanation of the Petersberg negotiations it should be said that since January 1951 talks had been taking place on the Petersberg between German military experts and military representatives of the three Allied High Commissioners. These negotiations had taken a very satisfactory course. In addition there had been negotiations between German and Allied representatives since September 1950 on the Petersberg on questions connected with the revision of the Occupation Statute.

I argued to McCloy that the Americans should use their influence to accelerate negotiations in Paris. And if these did not proceed fast enough the decision on the German defence contribution should nevertheless not be delayed, for if Germany were overrun by Soviet Russia the rest of Europe could not be held. This would mean an immediate peril for the United States.

The Interim Report of the Pleven Plan Conference

By the end of June 1951 the deliberations of the Pleven Plan conference had entered a decisive stage. The French delegation was urging the drafting of an interim report and the Americans supported their wish. I instructed the German delegation not to oppose this demand but to see to it that the interim report should be correct and complete and should in particular mention the problems that were still open, some of which had not yet been discussed at all, and should point out their importance.

Under-Secretary of State Hallstein, the leader of the German delegation, said in his talks with the other delegations that an interim report represented merely a cross-section of the state of the negotiations and that no final conclusions could be drawn. Important questions that had not yet been cleared up such as the position of the Commissioner, especially the delimitation of his functions from those of the NATO Supreme Command and from those of the national ministers of defence, must be described as open and important questions in the interim report. In addition the state of the discussion on the transition period, which was particularly important for Germany, must be made clear. There had so far been no satisfactory reply in the negotiations to our demand that all discrimination against the Federal Republic must have ceased by the time of the transition period. Hallstein made it unmistakably clear in Paris that the German Federal Government would sign no agreement that left a number of essential questions open: nondiscrimination, which was connected with the formation of effective nationally homogeneous fighting units, German participation in the Supreme Command, and the raising of German contingents by German authorities, were matters which must first have found a satisfactory solution.

In the deliberations on the Schuman Plan, all negotiating partners had clearly recognized the indissoluble interconnection between particular points of negotiation and general political problems arising from the Occupation Statute, for example the function of the Ruhr Authority, and this recognition found expression in the political decisions taken in the context of the Schuman Plan. The political importance of the idea of a European army was much more weighty than some aspects of the Schuman Plan, and if we were to get a majority in the German Bundestag for the Pleven Plan the treaty on the creation of a European army must do away with all discrimination against the Federal Republic.

In a conversation Hallstein had with Bruce, the American Ambassador in Paris, Bruce told him that it was he who had suggested an interim report, in order to inform the several governments of the progress that had been made since negotiations began. Hallstein told me that he drew Bruce's attention to the difference between the genuinely European Schuman Plan and the Pleven Plan, a largely French concept in origin. Also Hallstein underlined most emphatically to Bruce the German demand for the complete rejection of all discrimination.

During this conversation Bruce told Hallstein that nothing must be planned or done that would hinder combining the Atlantic forces under a unified command.

I had given the German delegation clear instructions at the beginning of the Pleven Plan negotiations that the armed forces whose creation was to be discussed must on no account be allowed to conflict with NATO considerations. Hallstein informed Bruce of these directives and told me that this information visibly reassured Bruce. The leader of the French delegation, Alphand, pointed out to Hallstein that the demands the Federal Government had made at the Petersberg talks went very much further than the concessions granted the Federal Republic on the basis of the Brussels decisions of the three foreign ministers.

In the Pleven Plan the French had originally asked for the formation of very small units or, to use their term, 'combat teams'. In the course of the negotiations on the Pleven Plan they seemed to have departed from this basic idea. Now the formula of 'small divisions' was current which had been launched by the Germans.

On 24 July 1951 the Pleven Plan conference met in Paris and approved an interim report on its activities. The five delegations agreed that the armed forces of a European defence community, with the exception of overseas forces and police troops, should be subject to a common supranational authority. At a press conference on 24 July Alphand, the chairman of the Pleven Plan conference, spoke as follows on the result reached in the interim report concerning the creation of a European army:

> This integration must be as complete as possible as regards men and material to the extent compatible with military requirements. At the same time as it is to develop and not reduce their value and effectiveness, it is also to represent, in conjunction with the European Coal and Steel Community, a very important stage on the road to the creation of a united Europe. As Robert Schuman said in the Council of Europe at Strasbourg, the treaty is to contain no discrimination against any member country.

At this point in the negotiations it was planned that a common defence finance pool should be established to defray all expenditure of the integrated European armed forces. A standardized supply system and a common arms programme were to be instituted to direct standardization of armament and the specialization of arms production which would achieve a considerable saving. The report stressed the fact that the European Defence Community was to serve peaceful purposes. The fact that the forces integrated in the European Defence Community would no longer be under the command of the single national states provided a guarantee that the common interest would take precedence over the goals of the single nations.

The relations between the European Defence Community and NATO were to be very close. The integrated European force was to be put at the disposal of the Atlantic command and to be guided by its directives.

The interim report stated that the delegations had achieved agreement on the number and scope of the various institutions that were to be created. These were:

1 a European defence authority whose task should be that of a European ministry of defence;

2 a Committee of Ministers whose consent would be required for important decisions of the authority;

3 a parliamentary assembly consisting of the same delegates as the assembly envisaged for the European Coal and Steel Community. This parliamentary assembly would be charged with controlling the actions of the authority mentioned under (1) as well as, to some extent, the credits to be granted it;

4 a court of law to adjudicate possible legal questions.

The formations composing the European army were intended to integrate European arrangements for leadership, equipment and supplies. There were to be integrated staffs, integrated air forces, general regulations for standardization, and European schools for training cadres. The size of the basic unit was a question on which there were still differences of opinion and it would have to be decided by the governments.

The treaty was to be concluded for fifty years like the Schuman Plan.

During the transition period, before the supranational authority had the necessary powers, the recruitment of the armed forces was to be conducted by national authorities.

19

PROGRESS

*Revision of the Occupation Statute of 6 March 1951; The
Federal Republic Becomes a Full Member of the Council of
Europe; Termination of the State of War*

Since the establishment of the Federal Republic it had been my constant
endeavour to attain sovereignty for the Federal Republic step by step. A big
step forward was the revision of the Occupation Statute which came into
effect in March 1951.

When the Western Allies presented the Occupation Statute in September
1949 they had announced that it was to be reviewed after an appropriate
period of time. After the Foreign Ministers' Conference of the three Western
powers in London of May 1950 a committee of experts was charged with
working out proposals for amendments. The Foreign Ministers' Conference of
the three Western powers in New York in September 1950 had brought agreement on substantial modifications in favour of the Federal Republic, the most
important of which, however, depended upon the fulfilment of two conditions: the acknowledgment of the foreign debts of the German Reich, and a
declaration that the Federal Republic would be willing to take part in the
joint distribution of raw materials required for defence industries.

As mentioned before, the consent of the Bundestag was required for the
first demand. Agreement between the parties in the Bundestag was reached at
the beginning of March 1951 and accordingly I was able to write to the High
Commissioners on 6 March 1951 that the Federal Republic confirmed its
liability for the external pre-war debts of the German Reich and also for
those arising from the economic assistance received since the end of the war.
I wrote that it was 'in the interest of the re-establishment of normal economic
relations between the Federal Republic and other countries to work out as
soon as possible a settlement plan which will govern the settlement of public
and private claims against Germany and German nationals'.

The High Commissioners had submitted proposals on the distribution of
raw materials to the Federal Government. Under the same date of 6 March
1951 I announced the Federal Government's acceptance thereof: the Federal
Government would cooperate in the apportionment of materials, products
and services which were or might be in short supply or required for the
common defence. This fulfilled the conditions for the entry into force of very
considerable alleviations for the Federal Republic of Germany.

On the very day my letters were received, the Allied High Commission promulgated the entry into force of the amendments of the Occupation Statute decided in New York. I welcomed the announcement of this first revision of the Occupation Statute, which was to be followed by further revisions, as a step on the road to the full sovereignty of the Federal Republic and as a complete abolition of the Occupation Statute. This revision was an important stage in the progressive normalization of German-Allied relations. To be sure, the scope of the relaxations granted did not correspond to my hopes and demands, but it was a good beginning.

A great step forward was the transfer of powers for a regular foreign service from the occupation powers to the Federal Republic. The economic relaxations and the new regulations in the field of legislation were also very important.

The relevant passage of Article III of the amended Occupation Statute reads:

> The occupation authorities, however, reserve the right, acting under instructions of their governments, to resume, in whole or in part, the exercise of full authority if they consider that to do so is essential to security or to preserve democratic government in Germany or in pursuance of the international obligations of their governments. Before so doing, they will formally advise the appropriate German authorities of their decision and of the reasons therefor.

There was some criticism in Germany of the continuation of this Allied power. It was in order to disarm this criticism that I pointed out in a press statement that Germany was threatened by quite special dangers which might make it necessary for the Allies to fall back on this reservation. I added that one should not forget the mentality of other nations and should recognize that development of full sovereignty could take place only gradually.

The transformation of the former office for foreign affairs into a Foreign Ministry represented considerable progress because we were now in a position to enter directly into negotiations and discussions with the governments of other countries. At a meeting of the Federal cabinet of 13 March 1951 it was decided that until further notice I was to carry out the duties of a Federal Minister of the Exterior as well as the duties of Federal Chancellor. I received the certificate of appointment as Foreign Minister from Federal President Heuss on 15 March 1951.

It was not my intention to initiate intense activity in the field of foreign policy immediately after the creation of the Foreign Ministry. Mindful of the psychological situation in other nations and their attitude toward Germany it seemed wiser to begin by maintaining some reserve.

About this time another very important step was taken along the road to the attainment of sovereignty: a resolution of the Committee of Ministers of the Council of Europe of 2 May 1951 accepted the Federal Republic as full member. The Federal Republic thus took part in the spring session of the Consultative Assembly of the Council of Europe for the first time as a full member.

The Dutch Foreign Minister Stikker was the chairman of the Committee of Ministers and made a speech of welcome. He said:

> This is the third international organization in which I have seen Germany take its legitimate place. The first was the OEEC and the European Payments Union, the second the Schuman Plan, and now the Council of Europe. I say 'its legitimate place' because Western Europe has realized that Europe cannot exist without Germany nor Germany without Europe. I am aware of the importance attributed in Germany and especially by the younger generation to the principles of the Council of Europe: the preservation of peace and the striving for greater unity among its member states.

I thanked Stikker for his words and stated that acceptance into membership in the Council of Europe was an event of great significance for the Federal Republic and for the whole German people. I took up Stikker's words that Europe cannot exist without Germany nor Germany without Europe and added that the Germans would dedicate all their strength to Europe and to peace.

In the short space of eighteen months the Federal Republic had covered much ground from complete dependence to equality in the European community. The Federal Republic's membership in the ECSC and the Council of Europe were decisive stages on the road to the European community. These achievements were only possible in such a short time because by its industry, its energy, and its ability the German people had given the Federal Government the prerequisites for its work.

A little more than one and a half years after the German Federal Republic had first seen the light of day it was accepted as a member enjoying equal status in the Council of Europe and thus in the most representative body of the nations of Europe, an event which filled me with great joy and satisfaction. When considering the relatively short time taken to attain this success one must not forget how difficult it was to reopen the door to Europe. In my first statement for the newly established Federal Government in the autumn of 1949 I had emphatically pointed to the patience that would be required to remove the psychological obstacles around us. From the time of this first stage of our re-entry into the European community I did not tire of repeating that the psychological trauma inflicted by National Socialism on all our neighbours would heal only if we did not regard the equality granted us as restoration of an obsolete sovereignty in the style of the nationalist nineteenth century but as our chance to live in and with Europe.

In the resolution of the Committee of Ministers of the Council of Europe of 2 May 1951 I saw confirmation of my policy of tenacious patience. It was not the policy of banging a non-existent negotiating table but the indefatigable manifestation of our will to cooperate in the safeguarding of peace and social progress in Europe which had brought back to us – by way of the Petersberg, accession to the OEEC and cooperation in the Schuman Plan – that measure of sovereignty corresponding to our situation which we could maintain and enlarge only if we contributed it as peaceful capital to the coming European federation.

It could not be said often and clearly enough that a new epoch had started in European politics, characterized by the fact that the leading politicians of the European nations that were still free had clearly recognized that the age of mutually hostile complexes of sovereignty in Europe must be speedily terminated if our continent was not to fall prey to barbarism. One of the most energetic champions of this policy of European federation, the French Foreign Minister Robert Schuman, had expressed this recognition, the innermost motive of his policy toward Germany, when he said, 'The fragmentation of Europe has become an anachronism, a nonsense and an anarchy.'

I was concerned to impress these words on the consciousness of all Germans as emphatically as possible and added that the dismantling of anachronisms was among the most necessary but also the most difficult things in politics.

The resistance encountered by the Schuman Plan as the basis of a European federation among a part of the German people proved how difficult it was to liberate this part of the German people from their earlier nationalist habits of thought. The suicidal dreams of national autarky kept on being dreamed although the facts were abundantly clear by which there had been created, not only for us but more or less for all the peoples of Europe, the completely new situation of interdependence and the inescapable community of fate.

The reproach, voiced more or less openly by the opposition, that I had sold the sovereignty of Germany with my signature to the Schuman Plan had disturbing echoes abroad. Such irresponsible nationalist excesses showed quite clearly how carefully and sensitively our neighbours registered everything that looked like nationalist longing. But the damage done to our position in Europe by the slander of the honest intentions of our partners in the Schuman Plan, especially its French initiators, was virtually incalculable. These irresponsibilities kept opening old wounds and aggravated the mistrust of Germany. For Germany and for Europe everything depended on overcoming the mistrust that had fed on three Franco-German wars. The removal of this root of all the political misfortunes of Europe was a task not only for politicians but a truly national and European task for all who laboured to strengthen our bonds with our neighbours in the light of the new equality of status. One must never forget that between Bonn and Paris lie the gigantic graveyards of Verdun, and that it required a common and continuous effort of the good will of all at last to put an end to one of the most tragic chapters in the history of Europe and to begin a new one.

We had once more, as Stikker had said in Strasbourg, our 'legitimate place in Europe because Western Europe has realized that Europe cannot exist without Germany nor Germany without Europe'. To achieve this legitimate place and to make full use of it for Germany, because it was and is the forum for solving problems we cannot solve alone, therein lay and lies the real task for a German policy of 'Germany in Europe'. We needed more than ever to fill this place in a spirit of truly European cooperation once the ice that surrounded Germany had cracked.

A further important step towards German equality was the declaration of the three Western powers transmitted to me in a letter by the three High Commissioners of 9 July 1951 that the state of war with Germany was to be terminated. A little earlier thirty-seven countries had made similar declarations. This meant that at this time altogether forty-six countries had either terminated the state of war with Germany or introduced legal procedures to this end. These declarations did not mean that a peace treaty had been made; they merely expressed the fact that the disabilities the countries at war with each other had reciprocally imposed on nationals of the other country had now been removed. It was nonetheless a great step forward.

Three-Power Declaration and Final Communiqué of the Foreign Ministers' Conference of September 1951

During the first months of the summer of 1951 the American High Commissioner McCloy was in the United States for discussions with the administration. On 23 June 1951 I learned of an interview McCloy had given in America in which he advocated the fulfilment of the three essential conditions on which the German Federal Government would be ready to make a contribution to the European Defence Community. He enumerated complete equality of status with the other countries that were to form the European Defence Community, the stationing of adequate Allied forces in Germany in order to give the German people a feeling of security, and third, an assurance that within the European defence army no distinction would be made between Germans and nationals of other countries. McCloy announced that these conditions, insofar as they had not yet been met, would soon be considered because the Western Allies were sincerely interested in making Germany once more a free, independent and equal member of the family of nations.

This public statement by McCloy was an encouraging sign for the probable position of the American administration at the forthcoming Foreign Ministers' Conference which was due to take place in September 1951.

Popular attitudes in the Federal Republic on the question of a German defence contribution had become more favourable. To a question circulated by the Emnid institute of public opinion in June 1951, 'do you think that Germany has obligations in the framework of European defence?', forty-five per cent answered in the affirmative and twenty-six per cent said 'No', while twenty-nine per cent had no opinion.

The Washington conference of the foreign ministers of the three Western powers convened on 10 September 1951. Dean Acheson represented the United States, Herbert Morrison Great Britain and Robert Schuman France. This conference was to make an attempt to find new ways to integrate Germany in the community of free nations. The discussions ended on 14 September 1951 and the results were published in a three-power declaration and a press communiqué. These decisions were of the greatest imaginable importance for us Germans, and not only for us but for the whole of Europe and the world as well.

The material published on the conference stressed in the first place the readiness to let Germany participate in the defence of the West and the will to bring about the unity of Europe. The hope was expressed that agreement between the four governments would result from negotiations with the Federal Government and that such agreements would bring about the inclusion of Germany in the European Defence Community, then in process of preparation.

It was further stated that the entry of the Federal Republic into a European Defence Community on a basis of equality and the participation of the Federal Republic in the measures intended was impossible without a complete change in the nature of the relations between the three powers and the Federal Republic. The High Commissioners were charged by their governments to enter into negotiations with the Federal Government as soon as possible with the aim of replacing the Occupation Statute by a system of agreements to be concluded on a basis of equality for Germany. It was to be the goal of the negotiations to restore the sovereignty of the Federal Republic with such reservations, resulting essentially from the division of Germany and the dangers of the general political situation in the world, as might be required for the security of Allied troops in the Federal area, the position of Berlin, and the reunification of Germany. The Allied High Commission was to be dissolved. In future the three Western powers were to be represented by ambassadors. The Federal Government and the High Commissioners were to discuss ways and means of effecting the cooperation of the Federal Republic in the defence of Europe in the framework of a European army which in its turn was to be subordinated to NATO. These discussions were to begin on 24 September after the return of the High Commissioners who had taken part in the Washington Foreign Ministers' Conference.

Everything that was published about the Foreign Ministers' Conference of the three Western powers clearly expressed the firm intention of the Western Allies to offer us a full and equal partnership. We Germans could only note this with great satisfaction and beware of speculations at this time about the detailed directives that were still unknown and of which the High Commissioners were to inform me. What mattered was that there were to be genuine negotiations. I was determined to adhere to the large perspectives that must be the criteria of our decisions. I entered these negotiations with optimism and confidence.

Analysis of the World Situation

It is impossible to appreciate the significance of the impending negotiations without considering the political history of the years since the defeat in 1945, the growing tension in the world, and the tendencies of developments of the preceding months. In the course of events since 1945 one must distinguish between the period from 1945 to the outbreak of the conflict in Korea, that is until the summer of 1950, and the period after. During the first five years after the defeat of Germany the Western Allies, unlike Soviet Russia, had disarmed, and had in part neglected their defensive industries. They had acted as though eternal peace had descended on the world. One country had acted differently, Soviet Russia. Since 1945 Soviet Russia had continued to arm unceasingly and with all her strength while neglecting the most urgent domestic tasks. She had used the time since 1945 for an enormous territorial aggrandizement by means of the cold war without a single Russian soldier being used. Since 1944 Russia had destroyed the sovereignty of many countries.

Soviet Russia had, since 1944, annexed the three Baltic states and had made Poland, Rumania, Bulgaria, Albania, Hungary, Czechoslovakia, and the so-called German Democratic Republic into satellite states. In France and in Italy Russia had built up large communist parties and had waged the cold war, in the Federal Republic, as well, to make it ripe for communism.

The events in Korea had opened the eyes of the Western Allies to the direction of Russian policy. Since Korea the United States of America was arming with all its might. This was a reaction that had not been included in Russian calculations. I think that the Russians believed the rest of the world would swallow Korea too, but the rest of the world had not swallowed Korea.

Since Korea America realized that it was not enough to support Europe economically and that there is only one thing that speaks to a country like Soviet Russia, the language of power. I do not know whether there is any precedent in the history of the world for a country emerging victorious from a war, and thus endowed with enormous power, becoming aware of the obligations such power imposed on itself. I do not know whether there is any example in history of a country after such a terrible war coming to the aid of its prostrate enemy as the United States did to ours.

Our situation was this: on the one side a highly armed Soviet Russia with its satellites, on the other the Western world beginning to rearm and to take shape; we, the Federal Republic, lying between them demilitarized, not sovereign, over-populated, weighed down with burdensome social problems, with a population that in many respects was suffering severe distress. Thus we lay between these magnetic poles. We found ourselves in a vacuum between the Eastern bloc and the Western Allies, unable to defend or protect ourselves with our own strength. In the long run such a state of affairs was untenable. It was this condition of vacuum that we had to remember when attempting to shape a proper perspective on coming developments.

366

The Soviet Russians calculate coolly. Unlike the leaders of German National Socialism, they will not beat their heads against a brick wall. Russia calculates the changes of loss or gain quite coolly and calmly. So far Russia had, by the cold war, made tremendous gains at a very cheap price. She would surely try to continue on this course, in pursuit of what must beckon as the highest prize, the neutralization and eventual incorporation of the Federal Republic into the Soviet Russian sphere of power. A neutralized and demilitarized Federal Republic would become a satellite state in a relatively short time, like the countries of Eastern Europe. If Soviet Russia attained this goal she would increase her war potential in material and manpower to such an extent as to become superior to the United States, for France and Italy, with their communist parties, would then fall into the Russian lap like ripe apples.

The conclusion of such agreements with the Western Allies as were envisaged in announcements of the Foreign Ministers' Conference of the three Western powers of 14 September 1951 would put an end to the Federal Republic's being a political and military no-man's-land, a condition which was impossible and intolerable in the long run. The Federal Republic would become a contractual partner of the Western Allies for mutual defence against any attack on Germany or Europe. At the same time it would regain its full sovereignty. This would inflict an annihilating defeat on Soviet Russia's policy in Western Europe.

The goal of that policy was crystal clear: to maintain Germany's political and military state of suspense and thus make it impossible for Western Europe to grow together. Without unification and integration Western Europe was bound to crumble and the countries of Western Europe were more or less powerless. Soviet Russia calculated that the United States would lose interest in a crumbling Western Europe and withdraw from the continent. Russia would then draw not only the Federal Republic but also the other countries of Western Europe into its sphere of influence, without any war, and finally be master of all Europe. What would then be our lot was clear. One had only to think of Czechoslovakia, Hungary, Poland and the other satellite states. The decline of Germany would be certain. The civilization of the Christian West, Christianity itself, would be destroyed. If Germany remained a no-man's-land and if there were an armed conflict in Europe after all, Germany would become the battlefield of the contending powers. The unhappy fate of Korea would then be ours. By August 1951 the battle had raged back and forth across Korea seven times.

The foreign ministers' declarations and the results of the subsequent negotiations with the Federal Republic would bring decisions of historic magnitude. We would either remain a political and military no-man's-land or we would become, as a free and equal country, partners of the European and with it of the North Atlantic system of defence against any Soviet aggression.

Those were the essential considerations in my conduct of the negotiations and my assessment of their results. If anyone in the Federal Republic or in France or elsewhere in the world were to take exception to this or that point in these negotiations, express this or that concern or anxiety, let this or that look back into the past be decisive for the choices to be made, it would show a completely erroneous sense of proportion in a historic hour. What mattered was that the attempt should be made again and again to take facts and situations as they were and to see them clearly and simply. This was no time to be confused by considerations that had fundamentally ceased to be important. Above all the situation of Germany had to be viewed dispassionately and rationally, with a calm judgment of the entire world situation, detached from all considerations and objectives of party politics and from all backward glances.

In the Federal Republic and in other countries of Western Europe many people were asking whether the policy of European integration, the policy of including the Federal Republic in the European Defence Community which in its turn was to be joined with the North Atlantic Treaty Organization, would not be the very thing to provoke a war with Soviet Russia. It was my firm conviction that that would not be the case. By its whole internal structure the European Defence Community had an unambiguously defensive character and it was out of the question that it would pursue any offensive intentions. The pronouncements of 14 September 1951 expressly stated that:

> The three Ministers reaffirm that this policy, which will be undertaken in concert with the other free nations, is directed towards the establishment and the maintenance of a durable peace founded on justice and law. Their aim is to reinforce the security and the prosperity of Europe without changing in any way the purely defensive character of the North Atlantic Treaty Organization. They reaffirm their determination that in no circumstances shall the above arrangements be made use of in furtherance of any aggressive action.

Since 1945 the Soviet Union had always talked of peace and freedom. Yet she was the only great power which since 1945 had taken peace and freedom from many nations and had constantly threatened us. Although Soviet Russia is consistent and purposeful in her foreign policy, she is cautious as well. She would not accept great risks. If Europe and the United States were to combine for the common defence it would be more than dangerous for Soviet Russia to start a war with this power. I was hoping that once this combination of the strength of Western Europe and the United States had become an accomplished fact, it might become possible to negotiate with Soviet Russia to try to give the world a durable peace.

The Meeting with the High Commissioners on 24 September 1951

As previously arranged, I met the Allied High Commissioners at Schloss

Ernich, the residence of the French High Commissioner, on 24 September 1951 to begin the negotiations on the agreements envisaged in the Washington decisions.

François-Poncet gave me a written report on the results of the Washington Foreign Ministers' Conference and the draft of a General Agreement with the Federal Republic as basis for our discussions.

I glanced through these papers and noticed that the draft Agreement did not contain a clause on mutual consultations on relations with the Eastern bloc. I pointed this out to the High Commissioners and asked what I was to make of it.

François-Poncet replied that in the past the Federal Republic had been given several assurances that she would be kept informed. In the case of the recent international agreements such consultation had in fact occurred on several occasions. A new assurance was possible. He referred me to the draft provisions on consultation in connection with the whole of Germany and Berlin.

I also failed to find a provision for a security guarantee and reciprocal military commitments of the Allies in the event of a German defence contribution.

McCloy replied that the question that I had raised would have to be cleared up in the negotiations.

Kirkpatrick also addressed himself to my objections and thought one should not treat matters too pessimistically and should avoid giving the impression that one did not believe in a peace treaty. As he saw it the impending stage was that of an interim solution which might be expanded into a contractual settlement.

I said that the German people could understand that a peace treaty was impossible at the moment. An agreement that could be presented as a substitute for a peace settlement would be accepted. The German people would not, however, be able to understand the intervention of an interim stage between the Occupation Statute and the peace treaty. I urgently requested that everything should be done to prevent the proposals reaching the public in the form in which they had been presented to me.

We had a recess to give me a chance to study the documents closely. Upon resuming the discussion I said that I found myself in a very difficult situation. I felt that I owed it to the High Commissioners to be completely frank with them. I had all the more right to expect mutual frankness since I had proved how very concerned I was for rapid European integration. My point of departure for the present negotiations was the idea that the abolition of the Occupation Statute must go hand in hand with the German defence contribution. A German defence contribution, i.e. entry into a European army, demanded preconditions different from those contained in the draft I had seen and the explanations of it. A nation could only make a defence contribution on a basis of equality and reciprocity. I had thought that the agreements would be based on these two conditions. I asked the High Commissioners not to think that I had forgotten how much misery Germany had caused the world. All the same, in view of the great dangers threatening us we had to think of the future quite coolly. We Germans could not demand that the world should forget, but the future must not be built on the emotions of the past.

There were legal facts and legislative measures initiated by the High Commission which had to be continued by the Federal Republic. As Federal Chancellor I understood entirely that these measures could not simply be repealed from one day to the next. These things had to be discussed.

The principle of equality proclaimed in the Washington declarations had, however, not been maintained in decisive respects in the documents I had seen. Thus it was, for instance, impossible to speak of freedom in foreign affairs if a Council of Ambassadors was instituted, as envisaged in the draft, with power to intervene in German foreign policy by majority decision and to which an inspectorate was to be attached. This would create the impression in the Federal Republic that the High Commission was continuing in a new guise. I also said that those who composed the draft I had seen seemed to have put aside the idea of a European army. The Federal Republic was not to produce any aircraft or heavy weapons and not to engage in atomic research. If one was going to create a European army with the participation of several countries it was impossible to impose prohibitions on one participant and not on another. These questions must be made the subject of negotiations on the European army and the Western Defence Community. If it was intended to create a European community then all members must enjoy equal trust. It was impossible to have a community with a partner who was trusted as little as we were.

If the Federal Government were to sign the Allied draft agreement as now submitted, it would recognize as justified the mistrust harboured against us. I had to declare that no German Federal Government could ever affix its signature to such an agreement.

It was impossible to explain to the German people that it should be prepared to make sacrifice of lives and material goods without there being at the same time on the other side a corresponding contractual commitment to the defence of the Federal territory. The New York security guarantee of September 1950 was a unilateral declaration; unilateral declarations could also be taken back unilaterally.

It was of the essence of a mutual defence arrangement that it should contain binding obligations regarding possible negotiations with the putative opponent. I must therefore urge the insertion of a consultation clause in the treaty.

In essence the new proposals were nothing but a reduction of the Occupation Statute, although the Federal Government was striving for an entirely new basis of agreement resting on reciprocity. I therefore deemed it necessary to give the High Commissioners an outline of the psychological difficulties implicit in the present German situation.

To assess the state of mind of the German people one had to remember what they had lived through in the last forty years. At this moment most of them were indulging in an ostrich policy by which they thought to remove all dangers from the world.

Yet in this state of mind the German people had now to make a definitive decision for or against integration in Western Europe. If integration did not take place now the moment would be irrevocably lost and the plan would have to be given up. I begged the High Commissioners to look at the situation in this light.

On 15 September 1951 Grotewohl had made a proposal on reunification which I will discuss in detail in another context. Referring to Grotewohl's letter I said that it was a foray into this present situation and that it needed countering. I repeated a remark of one of my colleagues who, after glancing through the documents, had described them as the best assistance Grotewohl could have, if they became known.

It was imperative to be aware of the feelings of the German people. What was needed now was the integration of Germany into the Western European community, failing which it would certainly be sucked into the East. I found myself in an extremely difficult situation. What was I to tell the opposition? What was I to tell the Foreign Affairs Committee about these documents? I honestly did not know what was the right thing to do.

Before the Washington Conference I had made informal suggestions on an agreement with the Federal Republic in individual conversations with the High Commissioners. I had written down these suggestions and at this meeting gave them to the High Commissioners with a request that they should be made the basis of our present negotiations. The chief points were these:

The Occupation Statute must be replaced by a contractual agreement between the Federal Government and the three Western Governments explicitly guaranteeing the security of the Federal territory and Berlin against attacks from outside. The agreement must contain a formulation of the security guarantees for the Federal territory and Berlin, similar to those contained in the New York decisions, against all attacks from whatever quarter.

In the obligations arising apart from these guarantees the Federal Republic might be included by special clauses.

The joint protection of the Federal territory and of Berlin must be afforded:

1 by Allied troops, i.e. land, sea and air forces of the United States, Great Britain and France and

2 by German troops.

These two groups must participate on a basis of complete equality in organization, structure, equipment and command. The supreme command must be composed internationally and its highest office should rotate periodically, perhaps every two years.

All countries participating in this security pact must undertake to avoid in their policy everything that might result in a danger to the security of the Federal territory or Berlin. This applied to special agreements of the one or the other partner with countries of the Eastern bloc.

It must be made clear that the safeguarding of the Federal territory was a matter concerning the Federal Government as much as the three Western Allied Governments participating in the treaty. All questions relating to the political consequences of the pact should be subject to the deliberations and decisions of a consultative council to which representatives of the three Western powers and of the Federal Republic should belong on a basis of complete equality. This might take the form of a permanent conference of ambassadors that would discuss all questions of principle and would control the observation of the obligations arising from the security pact.

I demanded a commitment of the Allies to support us in the overcoming of economic crises, pointing to the exceptional social burdens confronting the Federal Republic because of the problem of refugees and expellees.

I drew the High Commissioners' attention to the internal situation of the Federal Republic. The High Commissioners were undoubtedly aware of the provisions of the Basic Law concerning the vote of no confidence against the Federal Chancellor and new elections. If present negotiations did not lead to a positive result a considerable effect on our domestic policy would follow. If at this stage there were new elections on the issue of the defence contribution, I had no doubt that the people in favour of a defence contribution would be in the minority, because in an election campaign on this subject the opinion of the German people would be confused by emotional arguments of the opposition.

Under-Secretary of State Hallstein who was present at this conference with the High Commissioners had pointed out to me after studying the documents that the proposals made to the German Federal Government conflicted with the Schuman Plan. I told the High Commissioners that in these circumstances even a Bundestag majority for the ratification of the Schuman Plan could no longer be counted on. This subject was so important that I wanted once more to underline our point of departure. This had been – and the Schuman Plan negotiations seemed to justify the assumption – that Germany was in the future to be treated with trust and as an equal partner. Although the present draft agreement assumed that we were to be regarded as a partner in the contribution to be made, it showed that in the final resort we were not being trusted, certain concessions notwithstanding. There could however be no community except one founded on mutual trust.

François-Poncet thanked me for being so frank. There were, however, certain faulty interpretations in some of my statements. I had said that Germany would not be free in its foreign policy if a council of ambassadors were instituted in accordance with the Allied draft. My interpretation of the function of this institution was erroneous. The ambassadors would only meet in cases concerning the rights reserved in the three-power decisions; they would not interfere with questions of foreign policy. The council of ambassadors was in no case to act as a supervisory body; it was on the contrary to be a mixed commission in which Germany was to participate. Its task would be solely to safeguard the observation of contractual undertakings in certain areas.

The Allied draft, he continued, also aimed at settling the question of mutual security. Some of the German proposals had been accepted, but in certain fields there were constitutional difficulties.

It was not possible to adopt the suggestion of the Federal Government that the general Convention should contain an Allied undertaking on economic assistance to alleviate economic crises and unemployment.

The abolition of the High Commission, the termination of control as such – a control that might have lasted much longer than two and a half years – did not appear to strike Germany as a prize, whereas in the eyes of the Allies its renunciation was a great concession.

I replied to François-Poncet that what he had said on the constitutional difficulties of the Agreements was doubly valid for the security guarantee. What he had said showed that the Allies and the Germans were approaching problems from entirely different starting points. For Germany it was not decisive whether the High Commission ceased to be active in 1952 or later; the decisive question was whether a European Defence Community could be created that would work, and this was only possible between partners that trusted each other. If the three foreign ministers began with this proposition it would be easy to come to reasonable solutions. An Agreement of the kind represented by the Allied draft would never be submitted to the Bundestag by a Federal Government and would never be ratified by a German parliament. It attacked the idea of European integration at its core. In saying this I was speaking not primarily as a German but as a Western European.

Kirkpatrick and McCloy had been following the dialogue between François-Poncet and myself with close attention. Kirkpatrick said that he had taken part in many negotiations but never seen one that had started with greater difficulties than this. It was a fact, he said, that the three foreign ministers were seeking a place for Germany founded in freedom and equality. This intention had perhaps not been clearly expressed in every respect and that was a matter on which we would have to negotiate. He was convinced that the difficulties before us were not insuperable. On the issue of the council of ambassadors he could imagine Allied concessions. The limitation of production in the field of heavy weapons and aircraft and the prohibition of collaboration in atomic research in a European framework must be discussed with the governments. As for the security guarantee, there were serious constitutional difficulties because, as far as Britain was concerned, the safety of all her troops was at stake, it being intended to transfer virtually the entire British army to West Germany.

McCloy spoke next, and said that no one should doubt the foreign ministers' sincere commitment to this integration as a decisive element of peace, but the integration of Europe must include Germany, if it was to have the importance for which the Allies hoped.

He continued that I had just given the High Commissioners a draft; and he had looked at it and was bound to say that none of the Allied countries would be in a position to sign it. It would however be one of the bases for further discussion.

If the suggestions on a security guarantee and the strength of Allied troops in West Germany developed in my draft were to find expression in an Agreement, such an Agreement would have to be approved by the appropriate American constitutional bodies. The New York security guarantees of September 1950 had been concerted with the two foreign affairs committees of the Congress. It had been agreed at the time that these declarations were not to be ratified because they were mere statements of an actual situation. The question whether this security guarantee could be confirmed was still being examined. Talks were in progress with the Secretary of State and the Joint Chiefs of Staff. A final formula had not yet been found. There would also have to be consultation with the other nations concerned. One solution might be to make the NATO undertakings as expressed in Article V of the North Atlantic Treaty apply to Germany as well. An undertaking on the NATO model would, however, be less favourable for Germany than the contents of the New York security declaration because under Article V of the North Atlantic Treaty every member of NATO was free to decide how and in what way it would give assistance in case of aggression.

It was extraordinarily difficult to find a formula for an undertaking to station troops in Germany. The difficulties were manifold and the questions of duration and numerical strength were problematical. Never in the history of the United States had such obligations been assumed, apart from certain obligations assumed during the two last world wars.

McCloy continued that on the question of the council of ambassadors, Kirkpatrick and François-Poncet had said what needed saying, as also on the control of production of heavy weapons and atomic energy. These matters would have to be examined to determine whether this control could be shifted to the European plane. In any case it would be wise for Germans to avoid the line of argument of Dr Schumacher who had recently made a nasty crack about a 'horse trade' on Germany. Schumacher's thesis 'we're bound to get everything in any case; the Western Allies must defend us against the East or we go communist', on the basis of which higher claims were made, was ruinous and harmful to German prestige. McCloy recognized the extremely difficult situation in which I found myself, and said that he often pitied me but, he continued, one must rid oneself of emotional disturbances. As an adult person one should not be influenced by the fickle feelings of the mob and the street. It was necessary to withstand certain tempests to reach a common goal. With that the meeting ended and we decided to continue our conversations on Monday, 1 October 1951 at Schloss Röttgen, the residence of the British High Commissioner.

The Course of the Negotiations with the High Commissioners

On the next day, 25 September 1951, I received Dr Schumacher, the chairman of the Social Democratic Party, and Herr Ollenhauer, the chairman of the parliamentary group of the Social Democrats. I informed these gentlemen of the result of my talks with the High Commissioners and was greatly surprised that they were already thoroughly informed on what François-Poncet had said to me, as well as on the contents of the documents on the draft Agreement with the Federal Republic that I had been given. Dr Schumacher showed himself strongly opposed to the negotiations with the High Commissioners and after his talk with me told the press that neither he nor the SPD would change their attitude on a defence contribution. The Schuman Plan was putting the economic strength of Germany, the Agreement on the European Defence Community, the German human potential, in the service of French diplomacy.

On 26 September I informed the Foreign Affairs Committee of the Bundestag about the beginning of the negotiations with the Western Allies, and again was surprised at the extent to which deputies had already been informed.

The draft treaty given me by the High Commissioners contained many provisions I found unacceptable and in the coming negotiations I must try to eliminate them. It was, however, an impossible state of affairs that provisions in the Allied draft that were in conflict with an equal status for the Federal Republic were communicated to a larger group or even to the public at the present stage. In my conversation with the High Commissioners on 24 September I had pointed out to them that it would be made impossible for me to continue negotiations on this draft Agreement if the public got wind of it.

I had learned that there had been negotiations between the High Commissioners and members of the cabinet and of the Bundestag, for example between McCloy and Vice-Chancellor Blücher and Deputy Schäfer. Such discussions as McCloy had engaged in with Blücher and Schäfer, which entailed the risk of discrepancies between the information I gave on the state of negotiations and that given by the High Commissioners, could only breed mistrust. I immediately informed the High Commissioners of my attitude and added that the Allies would surely regard it as equally unusual if I, for instance, had an intimate conversation with de Gaulle who was in opposition to the French Government of the day, a conversation that had been suggested to me several times from various quarters.

The talks with the High Commissioners of 24 September 1951 were the first of several dealing with the political directives of a future Agreement between the Federal Republic of Germany and the three Western powers. Among the chief questions discussed were the security declaration I wanted for the Federal Republic of Germany, the problem of supreme authority and the clauses on retained rights and the declaration of a state of emergency, the question of mutual consultations in the event of negotiations with Soviet Russia, the question of the legal position of Berlin, and the question of the execution of special 'programmes', such as for instance the decartelization of big concerns, especially in the coal and iron industry.

At the beginning of the negotiations I had the impression that the High Commissioners thought the Federal Government was now demanding more than originally, before the beginning of the Washington Foreign Ministers' Conference. To correct this misconception I firmly stressed to the High Commissioners that neither François-Poncet's account of 24 September 1951 nor the Allied draft Agreement with Germany accorded with the declarations of the Foreign Ministers in Washington. The communiqué of 14 September 1951 said

> The foreign ministers have reviewed the relationship of their countries to the German Federal Republic, and have agreed on instructions to the Allied High Commission for negotiation of mutually acceptable agreements with the Federal Government, the effect of which will be to transform that relationship completely . . .
>
> As stated in the Tripartite Declaration issued today the guiding principle of their policy continues to be the integration of the Federal Republic on a basis of equality within a European community itself included in a developing Atlantic Community . . .
>
> The division of Germany, however, prevents the conclusion of such a settlement at this time. This division and the security problem confronting the Federal Republic obliges the Allies to retain, in the common interest, certain special rights but only in relation to the stationing of armed forces in Germany and the protection of the security of those forces, as well as to questions affecting Berlin and Germany as a whole, including the eventual peace settlement and the peaceful reunification of Germany . . .

The Washington declarations were founded on the idea of partnership whereas the documents I had been given were in essentials merely a revision of the Occupation Statute.

François-Poncet had told me that the three foreign ministers in Washington had acknowledged that the participation of the Federal Republic in the defence of the West would allow them to relinquish the exercise of supreme authority in those fields in which it had been the result of Germany's complete defeat.

The Allied renunciation of the exercise of supreme power in the Federal Republic was one of my chief goals in the negotiations. I had to admit that certain reserved powers were justified but it was my aim to embody these retained powers in special contractual agreements not so much for substantive reasons as for the sake of appearances. In the Preamble of the draft Agreement I had given the High Commissioners on 24 September there was an emphatic demand for relations between the three Western powers and the Federal Republic to be founded on 'freely agreed contracts'. I also demanded in my draft Agreement that the relations of the Federal Republic and the three Western powers should in the future be exclusively determined by agreements made between them and the general rules of international law.

The negotiations with the High Commissioners on the question of the renunciation of supreme power were very hard.

It was not clear in the Allied draft Agreement whether the Federal Republic was allowed to act independently on the restoration of German unity or whether it had to comply with what the Allies decided. In this context the Allied draft had an Article that read:*

> At the request of the Federal Government and in all cases where the Federal Republic is not in a position to do so itself, the three powers will arrange to represent the interests of the Federal Republic in relation with other states and in certain international organizations or conferences.

This wording was very indefinite and detailed explanations were urgently required.

Another problem was posed by the demand of the Western Allies that Law No. 27 of the Allied High Commission should continue to be implemented. This Law which concerned the decartelization of big concerns, especially in the coal and iron industry, had been issued before the Schuman Plan. There had subsequently been agreement that it should not be executed as rigidly as originally conceived once the Schuman Plan was in force. Its execution was now being described as one of the basic prerequisites for the creation of the European Coal and Steel Community.

At the beginning of the negotiations François-Poncet had underlined the demand for the execution of this Law, thus creating a very embarrassing situation. I had assumed that the original demand for decartelization had been prompted by the general economic and political views of the Allies. If it was now declared to be a precondition for the realization of the Schuman Plan it meant support for the thesis of the SPD that the only object of deconcentration was the weakening of the German economy in the Schuman Plan. McCloy had repeatedly assured me that the contents of Law No. 27 would be toned down for the sake of overcoming opposition to the Schuman Plan in Germany, but after his latest statements it seemed that the opponents of the Schuman Plan had been right when they said that the intention was to weaken German economic power. This interpretation was further supported

---

* Translated from the German.

by an editorial in *Le Monde* at the end of September 1951 stating that the Schuman Plan was adequately securing the West German economic potential for France and for Western Europe. This was much more important than securing the German human potential and there was therefore no difficulty in envisaging a possible neutralization of Germany.

I was aware of the extraordinary strength of the tradition of the Quai d'Orsay. I had myself experienced and observed how difficult it was, especially in the first years after the war, to work against this tradition, particularly the tradition advocating ties between France and Soviet Russia which I was afraid was still very much alive. I had made a close study of a Note from the French Government to the Soviet Government of 26 September 1951. Its guiding idea was to avoid offending Russia. It was not very encouraging for us to read in this Note that the inclusion of Germany in the Western defence community meant nothing other than a demilitarization of Germany. I asked myself how this could be seen as compatible with the higher aims of the European Defence Community.

A remark made by the French Deputy High Commissioner Bérard to Blankenhorn on the significance of the Franco-Soviet treaty of December 1944 pointed in the same direction as the French Note of 26 September 1951. France seemed to be very concerned to maintain this treaty. Bérard said *inter alia* that France could not relinquish the legal right contained in the Allied decision of 5 June 1945 to station her troops in Germany because to do so would conflict with Article III of the treaty. This made it reasonably clear that Paris was pursuing two kinds of policy: one had the aim of European integration; the other sought to maintain the pact with Soviet Russia. I asked myself how France's Russian policy harmonized with her obligations in a European partnership. I could not but regard it as extremely regrettable and dangerous if France should be prepared to work with Germany only conditionally and for the rest maintained close ties with Soviet Russia.

From my conversations with the French Foreign Minister Robert Schuman I knew that his policy was different. The policy described above was, however, by no means a thing of the past.

The text of the Allied draft Agreement on the deconcentration of German industry justified the opponents of the Schuman Plan. It stipulated the maintenance of controls for coal and steel despite the fact that all parties in the Bundestag had declared their removal to be a precondition for ratification of the Schuman Plan.

In reply to my protest against the Allied draft McCloy had told me that one should recall the historic development of the question. Originally there had been much more far-reaching plans for deconcentration. The Law on deconcentration had been toned down considerably in connection with the Schuman Plan. Deconcentration of the big concerns had however required a great deal of time. There had been many obstacles and delays so that today we were still far from the end of the programme. What should be done was, as it were, to proceed from a certain uniform line and to control not only German but also other industries accordingly. There was a practical solution which was to carry out deconcentration as quickly as possible so that the controls could be removed.

The French too were advocating acceleration of the deconcentration programme because the further continuance of controls must not be brought into connection with the Schuman Plan or other contractual agreements. I agreed with these views of McCloy and of the French High Commission. It would indeed be the best solution to carry out deconcentration before the Schuman Plan was ratified. If it had not been done by then the question would arise how execution was to be guaranteed. There would be great difficulties regarding the ratification of the Schuman Plan. I recalled the exchange of letters with the French Foreign Minister Schuman of 18 April 1951 which excluded any parallelism of the Ruhr control groups and the High Authority and provided for the assumption of the functions of the control groups by the High Authority and in part by the Federal Government.

A question that also caused long and heated discussions was my demand for a security guarantee for the Federal Republic. I was told that the foreign ministers had great understanding for the position of the Federal Government and were prepared to investigate once more how I could be helped despite the difficulties they were having themselves. I must however consider the parliamentary difficulties in other countries. The security guarantee had been a crucial point of the Atlantic Pact. Weeks and months had passed before the settlement of this question. At that time Denmark had been one of the big problems. Her situation in many respects resembled Germany's both as regards geography and because of the immediate threat from the East. At that time the Danish Government had maintained the same attitude as I was maintaining today. In the event Denmark had nonetheless joined the Atlantic Pact and with it Article V of the treaty, and that at a time when the power of the Allies was very much smaller and the threat very much greater than today. It was especially Kirkpatrick who pointed out to me that trouble was to be expected in the British parliament if Germany now got bigger guarantees than Denmark. In order to meet the Federal Government half-way, the Allies had in September 1950 made a declaration on security which required no ratification because it had the form of recognition of a given state of affairs.

McCloy also pointed to the strong opposition against a security guarantee in the Senate and in the State Department. This attitude was understandable in view of the history of the United States which had no precedent for a security guarantee in the sense I desired. Such obligations had hitherto been assumed only in case of war, for example the undertakings to end the war together and to conclude no peace except jointly. The only instance of a declaration of guarantee was the Monroe Doctrine but it had been a declaration

379

and not a treaty. Public opinion was very much opposed to any guarantees, especially in Europe. The United States had joined NATO in a form which he thought would not give me the relief I needed. The declaration in which the government of the United States had taken part in September 1950 was unambiguous. He could imagine its unilateral retraction albeit only after consultation. It had not been easy to get this declaration. It was the recognition of an existing situation. Although it had not been ratified by the Senate, it had been agreed to by Acheson and Truman in consultation with the Foreign Relations Committee of the Senate. All concerned recognized the importance of this declaration. Public opinion and the Senate had increasingly got used to regarding it as a solemn obligation. During his last visit to the United States he had discussed it with Secretary of State Acheson and the Joint Chiefs of Staff. They had said they were ready to reaffirm the declaration if desired. Such a declaration could also extend to the stationing of troops and stress the fact that this would not be a mere matter of appearances. It was, however, not possible to enter into a commitment to send a fixed number of troops for an unlimited period. In order to underline the strength of the forces, the Joint Chiefs of Staff were prepared to word the declaration in such a way as to make clear that the forces sent would not be military missions but combat troops. If the General Agreement were ratified by the Senate the declaration on the security guarantee would be parallel to it. There were indications that this declaration too would be submitted to the Senate. If Germany so desired a NATO assurance could also be extended to her.

McCloy summed up by saying that he saw that the situation was not satisfactory for me. On the other hand it had to be remembered that the United States and Great Britain were offering something they had not even offered to their traditional allies. It could be a dangerous step to issue a security declaration going beyond what had been offered to other countries who had been just as exposed as Germany at a time when military possibilities were very much smaller than today.

I expressed my gratitude for the recognition of the problems of the German Government and said that I too quite understood the difficulties the Allies found themselves in. But I believed a solution possible. The German problems, incidentally, were not altogether comparable to those of the Danes.

The questions concerning mutual consultation in the event of negotiations with the Soviet Union and the problem posed by the intended establishment of a council of ambassadors were solved to my satisfaction. The Allies assured me of consultations and the idea of creating the council of ambassadors as originally envisaged was dropped.

By 10 October 1951 my negotiations with the High Commissioners on the political directives for the future General Agreement had been sufficiently clarified for the experts to begin with the work in special committees on details of the contractual provisions.

Meanwhile the work of the so-called Pleven Plan Conference had progressed rapidly and was to be concluded at the beginning of November. The work of the experts' committees for the General Agreement also progressed very swiftly.

GREAT BRITAIN AND DEVELOPMENTS IN EUROPE

The Situation of Great Britain in the World

Great Britain was in an exceedingly difficult situation after the war. The war had inflicted damage on two of Britain's main nerves. British power in the world rested on two closely connected factors – domination of the seas and the power position in overseas territories that depended on this domination. Dominion of the seas which Britain had held for centuries had been wrested from her by developments in the field of aviation. The aeroplane had become an instrument of power of the first order. England had been the only country to build the great ships and especially the great warships on which British power had been based. The other powers could not do it – not the United States, not France, not Russia, nor Germany. As late as the beginning of the twentieth century the British navy was bigger than the two next biggest navies in the world together. All this had been changed by the development of aviation, and changed for ever. A further change in the wake of this development was a gradual loosening of the ties between the motherland and the overseas possessions which went hand in hand with the dwindling of British preponderance at sea.

In my view this basic change in her position in the world should have influenced Britain's attitude toward the continent of Europe.

In this serious situation the elimination of Winston Churchill as Prime Minister as a result of the loss of the parliamentary elections by the Conservative Party in the summer of 1945 was a further heavy blow. Churchill had recognized the important outlines of the future position of the continent of Europe by the end of the war as early as any other British or non-British statesman. Owing to the prestige he enjoyed in his country and in the world, it might have been possible for him to convince Britain of the need of a close association with Europe. No other British politician had the necessary influence in his country.

What were the consequences? In the face of the new European possibilities Great Britain assumed an attitude of hesitation, irresolution and indecision. She was both willing and unwilling.

When, in November 1951, Churchill became Prime Minister once more, Great Britain's attitude toward Europe had been fixed: wait and see.

Meanwhile, Robert Schuman, supported by Jean Monnet, had made a serious advance toward the unification of Europe by proposing a European coal and steel community. As Schuman wrote me at the time, he had first made his proposal to Great Britain. Great Britain turned it down. He then, on 9 May 1950, made it to the Federal Republic and all interested European countries. I instantly gave my consent.

In a debate in the House of Commons on the Schuman Plan on 26 June 1950 Prime Minister Attlee said that Great Britain could not adopt the principle of subordinating vital parts of the British economy to a European authority. He regarded such a measure as absolutely undemocratic and incompatible with the principles of British democracy. In the same debate Eden, speaking for the Conservative Party which was then in opposition, declared that the success of the Schuman Plan was in the British interest. Yet the Conservative Party did not advocate British participation in the Schuman Plan.

On 18 April 1951 the ECSC treaty was signed in Paris by France, the Federal Republic, Italy and the Benelux countries.

When, in November 1951, Churchill returned to Downing Street, the great moment for England and continental Europe to begin the work of unifying Europe jointly had been wasted. So much was Britain's negative attitude toward the creation of European institutions a matter of principle that, in my opinion, there was no reason to expect a more positive attitude in the future. I felt that the door should be kept open for Britain, but that we should not let the British refusal prevent us from acting. It was and it is necessary to create Europe.

Conversation with Under-Secretary of State Lord Henderson on 29 March 1951

On 29 March 1951 I had a very interesting conversation with the Parliamentary Under-Secretary for Foreign Affairs in the British Foreign Office, Lord Henderson, on Great Britain's relationship with Europe. There had been a change at the British Foreign Office. Morrison had succeeded Bevin.

In the spring of 1949 I had had a long conversation with Bevin on the subject of Europe. We were agreed in essentials, and the Schuman Plan and the Pleven Plan which had become the subject of discussions among the countries of continental Europe accorded with this basic outline. Kirkpatrick had intimated to me that by the time the Schuman Plan was ready Great Britain would be moving closer to it. I took this statement by Kirkpatrick as a starting point for asking Lord Henderson what Great Britain's attitude was on this question now.

Lord Henderson answered that the British attitude toward the Schuman Plan and the problems raised by it was unchanged. For the time being Great Britain was standing aside. By not intervening in the negotiations she had wished to avoid prejudicing them, let alone exercising a harmful influence. Great Britain was waiting to see what the outcome of the Schuman Plan would be. It was possible that the government might later find it necessary to adapt itself to the new situation. First, however, the Schuman Plan would have to be examined, and it was not until this examination had been concluded that his government could say to what extent it would associate itself with the plan.

I replied that it was my conviction that Great Britain must not stand aside from the unification that was now beginning but must from the very outset urge her own views in the general discussion.

Lord Henderson thereupon gave me a detailed account of the reasons for which British membership in the Schuman Plan and similar agreements was impossible. Great Britain was not in a position to accept a supranational authority. She publicly proclaimed this position on all occasions and stood by it now as before. However, once the system of the Schuman Plan had been subjected to a thorough examination some form of loose association might be considered. Great Britain had at any rate remained firm during the negotiations in her determination not to intervene. She had encouraged the partners as far as possible and endeavoured always to stress the common values of the peoples of Europe. Britain had her own views on European integration which ought to be achieved not by way of a supranational authority but by maximum collaboration between the peoples of Europe in the service of the preservation of our common democratic way of life. To this purpose Britain would hold unshakeably, and I must believe him that nothing would deflect Great Britain from this course.

I thanked Lord Henderson for his frankness, saying that I knew the attitude he had just described to be that of the British Government and also of the opposition. I had, however, to emphasize my great concern at Britain's standing apart from the developments that were now in the making in Western Europe. The Schuman Plan had led to a community in the field of iron, steel and coal. The Pleven Plan was to create a community in the field of defence. Thus a common basis had been established in two essential areas, in basic industries and in defence, which must surely also be acceptable for Great Britain. I felt that Great Britain must at all costs try to find a way to change her previous attitude.

Lord Henderson said that Bevin had always sympathized with the idea of a European federation. The overwhelming majority in England, however, preferred the functional method of European integration. Neither the Schuman Plan nor the Pleven Plan represented a functional solution. Both plans would depend upon the establishment of a supranational authority. Great Britain was, however, not prepared to give up her national sovereignty. If other nations wanted to draw up their own Schuman or Pleven Plans Great Britain would not withhold her sympathy as long as these plans were practicable.

I remarked that if you want to make an omelette you must break eggs, but actually had not Britain by recognizing the International Court at The Hague and international arbitration for Egypt also given up part of its sovereignty?

Lord Henderson denied this, saying that an international court of law could not be compared with a supranational political authority. Although he knew that he could not convince me, any more than I could move him from his basic position, it might be worth looking at the premises because they led to the different views. I believed in a federal solution in the matter of European integration; Great Britain, on the other hand, considered the functional method the right one and believed in the cooperation of governments as the first step. Great Britain was already engaged in such cooperation in the framework of OEEC and the North Atlantic Treaty. My example of the omelette was probably very relevant to many aspects of life. In this case, however, what mattered most was to look facts in the face. Thus I too had clearly recognized that in Great Britain the government and the opposition both opposed the renunciation of sovereign rights. Government and opposition were united in rejecting the principle underlying the Schuman Plan. What the future would bring was uncertain. But to judge from the present state of things Great Britain would never take part in such institutions as were being created by the Schuman Plan.

I repeated my deep regret at Britain's standing aside from the integration that had begun with the Schuman Plan and the Pleven Plan. I told Lord Henderson that without British participation an important factor was missing. I was not giving up hope that Great Britain might yet throw a few principles overboard in order to be able to join in the common great plan.

Lord Henderson thanked me for my candour and asked me not to believe that Great Britain was indifferent to the fate and the prospects of a united Europe. He recalled the role Bevin had repeatedly played in the integration of Europe. The quick implementation of the Marshall Plan was due to an initiative of Bevin's. It had also been Bevin who had initiated the Brussels Conference, the Brussels Treaty, and the North Atlantic Treaty Organization in quick succession. It was not sufficient to think only of Western Europe. One had to think of the Atlantic community as well. These two, Western Europe and the Atlantic community, must interpenetrate each other. In all fields where England was pursuing cooperation in Western Europe and in NATO she had always held firm to the high goal of consolidating the democratic way of life in Europe. The cooperation of the nations of Europe was certainly an important instrument for promoting political and economic development in the direction of integration. Seen in this light there was no real difference either in spirit or in objectives between the British and the continental methods. The final aim of Britain too was a fully integrated Western Europe.

I stressed that I had never had a doubt that Britain also had this goal. I only considered it quite essential that Britain should from the outset play the role in the European development which was due to her by virtue of her importance, her way of life, her policy, her thinking, and her experience.

AA   385

Henderson thought that many different paths could lead to the same objective. It was Britain's firm intention to make the fullest contribution to the development of a democratic Europe. In so doing she would not, however, want to put herself under the umbrella – he used the word umbrella – of a supranational authority.

I had met Lord Henderson for the first time two years before in a political conversation, when our chief subject was the entry of the Federal Republic into the Council of Europe. Lord Henderson had told me that he thought the Federal Republic would be a full member in the Committee of Ministers before a year had elapsed after her entry as associate member. This prophecy of Lord Henderson's seemed to be coming true for in March 1951 this step was imminent. Lord Henderson reminded me of this conversation and was glad about the fulfilment of his prophecy. He said that what had then been only a plan and an idea had now born fruit and this made him very happy. He reminded me of his words then when he had said that one should set a goal but could not draw up an exact timetable for the separate stages of getting there. I had told him then that I knew how to exercise patience.

Conversation with the British Foreign Secretary Morrison on 19 May 1951

On 19 May 1951 the British Foreign Secretary, Morrison, was visiting the Federal Republic and I had a chance for an extensive exchange of ideas with him. He had succeeded Bevin at the Foreign Office in March 1951.

I spoke with Morrison about Russia's relations with Europe in connection with the question of whether Russia was really a danger to Western Europe and especially to Germany. In my reflections on this subject which I presented in great detail to Morrison I began with the following historical facts.

For many decades the relations between Tsarism and the Prussian royal court had been very close, if only on a basis of family relationships between the Prussian royal house and the Tsars. After 1918, relations between the Red Army and the Reichswehr were possibly even more intimate than was generally known. At a time when the Rhineland was occupied by French troops the anniversary of the Red revolution was regularly celebrated in a very intimate circle in the Russian embassy in Berlin by the leaders of the Red Army who had come over for this purpose and the leaders of the German army.

These reminiscences, I told Morrison, might well be important in view of the fact that Russia had for a very long time been trying to establish close connections between Germany, German industry as well as the people, and Russia. Regarding the Federal Republic, Soviet Russia was in my view pursuing a dual aim: an immediate objective and a distant goal. The immediate objective was to prevent at all costs the war potential of the Federal Republic being used in a war against Soviet Russia. Russia could prevent this in three ways.

The first possibility was a sudden attack and the destruction of the Federal Republic, but I thought Soviet Russia would adopt this only in an extreme case, especially since the Russians had a different concept of time from ours, and because such basic destruction would conflict with the ultimate goals of Russian policy in regard to Germany.

The second and third methods coincided to a large extent. Russia wanted to increase her influence in the Federal Republic and eventually wanted to be able to utilize the Federal Republic. The expression 'to utilize' had been chosen with care. If it could not be achieved by way of creating a satellite state, Russia would try another method. This might be the neutralization of Germany, which was undoubtedly being very seriously considered by Soviet Russia. I had been deeply gratified by the declaration of the French Foreign Minister Schuman that France would under no circumstances accept this.

A neutralization of Germany, I continued, would result in Russian influence in Germany becoming dominant in a very short time. This would give a great impetus to the Communist Parties in France and Italy and the idea of a united non-communist Western Europe would be finished. It was one of Soviet Russia's aims to do everything to prevent the creation of such a united Western Europe.

The third way was that of the cold war, or, put concretely in the case of the Federal Republic, the way of the fifth column. I told Morrison that a foreigner could hardly imagine the scope of the activities of the fifth column in Germany. I had the justified conviction that in many offices there were people who were so afraid of coming developments as to accommodate themselves in advance to the power of Soviet Russia and who in any case did not oppose the activities of the fifth column.

For the safety of our country it was extremely important that people, especially the younger generation, should be given a feeling of security in the face of the East.

We then talked about German rearmament and Morrison asked me for my opinion of the argument that rearming Germany might provoke the Russians to war.

I told Morrison that I considered such an argument ridiculous. I could not imagine that the Russians would unleash a war on account of at most 250,000 German soldiers. The Russians were attempting to prevent the final integration of Germany into Western Europe because it would conflict with their ultimate purpose of somehow drawing Germany into the Russian sphere of influence. The integration of Germany into Western Europe would undoubtedly be much advanced by participation in European defence.

This brought me to the subject of Europe and I wanted to say something about it that Morrison would perhaps not like to hear, but very great concern made me do it nonetheless. I had the impression that the British public did not yet sufficiently perceive the consequence in Europe first of the destruction of the Austro-Hungarian monarchy and now, after the end of the Second

World War, of the collapse and division of the German Reich. These events had such tremendous and far-reaching consequences that I felt the British public should realize that after the break-up of Austria-Hungary and the break-up of the German Reich, Western Europe could not stand up to the pressure from the East which would always be renewed even if there were periods of standstill unless Britain felt herself to be a part of Europe and not merely a neighbour. It was necessary to understand that the structure of Europe as it had existed throughout the last century and into our own had been thrown askew after the disappearance of Austria-Hungary and the German Reich.

I told Morrison that in my opinion the Federal Republic, France, Italy, and the Benelux countries had not enough inner strength firmly to resist communist pressure from the East in the long run, unless the internal structure of Europe was consolidated once more and strengthened by the accession of Great Britain. If one day Soviet Russia called the tune in Western Europe it would also mean that England's strength had been weakened so much as to be no longer sufficient for commitments in the Commonwealth. It might be somewhat daring to say such a thing to a British Foreign Minister, but I felt that Great Britain had to stand on two legs, in Western Europe and in the rest of the world, and that if she was not firmly rooted in Western Europe she would in the long run be unable to fulfil her tasks in the rest of the world.

Morrison thought that it should be noted that Britain's present attitude to Europe represented an enormous step forward compared with past centuries, perhaps as great as that taken by the United States in its cooperation with other countries and continents. In the nineteenth century Great Britain did not feel herself a part of Europe. She had pursued a policy of the European balance of power, but had reserved the right to keep out of military conflicts or to intervene on either of two sides in a war that broke out in Europe, guided by the British interest and not that of the well-being of Europe. It was one of the consequences of this policy that in 1914 the Kaiser did not know until the last moment how Britain would behave in a conflict.

Today on the other hand Great Britain was in the Western Union, a member of the North Atlantic Treaty Organization, a member of the Organization for European Economic Cooperation and of numerous other organizations. The defence contribution made by Great Britain at very great cost, not only for her own sake or for the defence of the Commonwealth but above all for the defence of Europe, could certainly stand comparison with that of any other Western European country. Great Britain was committed to the defence of Western Europe and had the full intention of meeting her obligations. On the other hand, it was a fact that Britain was an island and that was not the fault of the British; that was the way God had arranged things and the British had to make the best of it. Beyond this there were certain constitutional traditions in Great Britain that perhaps were not always understood on the continent of Europe.

In England the people elected the parliament. From it derived the government and the government was responsible to parliament and in the final resort to the people. The position of parliament was stronger here than in other European countries. Morrison said that it was very hard for the British to think of transferring the prerogatives of parliament which are superior to everything else – and that is the decisive thing in Great Britain – to a kind of supranational organization. That was a lump the British would find it very hard to swallow. They would always be ready to offer their cooperation *ad hoc*. This was not only a possibility, it was something on which one could count. Nonetheless, Europe must remember – and this was no argument, it was simply a fact – that Britain was not prepared and would in the future find it very difficult to be prepared to subordinate herself to a supranational organization that might in some way be above the British Government and give it some kind of orders. He mentioned the Schuman Plan which would be studied quite fairly and open-mindedly and without prejudice. The British would, if it was necessary or justified, gladly give their help in some way. They were always prepared to do this, but it was very difficult to allow the supremacy of parliament to be depleted in any way. Morrison continued that one had to await developments. From various organizations, such as OEEC, that were working very well, a European organization acceptable to all the countries of Europe might slowly develop in the course of time. The British believed that this should happen slowly, by trial and error and constant improvement. In the British view this would be much better than subjecting oneself immediately to a constitution derived from a blueprint which might later not function satisfactorily. It was better to have a slow evolution.

Morrison said he felt that the nations of continental Europe did not always understand the British people. Sometimes the British were taken for wicked and malicious when they were really being sincere and well-meaning. There were some difficulties there. The British on their side also did not always understand the actions of the peoples of continental Europe. Therefore, it was quite a good thing to realize that other countries did not always understand the British.

My Visit to London in December 1951

While in the Federal Republic Morrison had invited me to come to Great Britain. I accepted this invitation. My visit had originally been planned for October 1951 but had to be postponed until December on account of the parliamentary elections that had become necessary in Great Britain.

These elections were held on 25 October 1951 and the Conservatives emerged victorious. Churchill became Prime Minister once more and Anthony Eden was made Foreign Secretary.

My visit to Great Britain was the first official visit of a German head of government since the visit of Chancellor Brüning in 1931.

Before my trip I addressed a press conference on Anglo-German relations. I said that England and Germany had common goals: the preservation of peace and the defence of the democratic order. I gave an assurance that in the pursuit of these aims Germany would prove herself a steadfast and dependable partner.

I stressed that the purpose of my visit to Great Britain was the development and implementation of the policy of friendly cooperation between the Federal Republic and Great Britain. England was the core of the British Commonwealth, I said, and moreover an important member of numerous international groupings, such as the Brussels Treaty. The Federal Republic for its part felt itself to be a member of a European community in process of formation. Both countries, Great Britain and the Federal Republic, would increasingly encounter each other in international bodies because they would be called upon jointly to make responsible decisions. It was therefore necessary and of significance f or the whole free world hat Great Britain and the Federal Republic were trying to define common political goals and to seek agreement concerning the methods for their realization. Apart from possible Anglo-German cooperation in international organizations there were also opportunities for cooperation in traditional bilateral agreements in the interests of both countries. This applied particularly to economic relations. In the sphere of economics a promising spirit of cooperation had been developing.

I knew that there was considerable concern in Great Britain about German economic competition.

Referring to British reticence in the face of the plans for Europe, I said that I well understood that up to a point this attitude was the outcome of Britain's position in the Commonwealth, but the welfare and security of Britain were indissolubly connected with the fate of the European continent. Great Britain and the European combinations in process of formation must have permanent liaison bodies to coordinate their efforts. For the continental Europeans a dose of British moderation and political realism was certainly very valuable.

Fears had been expressed in Great Britain concerning a revival of German nationalism. I gave numerous assurances before and during my visit to England that the overwhelming majority of the German people had left nationalism behind them. I underlined the resolve of the Federal Government and of parliament to prevent a resurgence of possible nationalist movements and drew attention to the fact that the percentage of radical voters in the Federal Republic was uncommonly low. Radical tendencies in Germany would collapse and become an insignificant fraction of public opinion once a free and sovereign Germany, following the present policy of the Federal Government, had re-entered the comity of peoples. The anxiety lest German defence forces should introduce an unhealthy nationalism into the security system of the West was completely unfounded.

Radicalism was to a large extent the bitter fruit of post-war distress. The radicalism of the Right would disappear to the extent to which the policy of the Federal Government and the help and understanding of other countries brought Germany back to an honourable place in the family of free peoples.

Regarding the anxiety that the Federal Republic might, as soon as it had any army, use it as a lever for a Rapallo policy vis-à-vis Moscow, I said that Germany had unambiguously opted for the West. The Germans had learned from experience to seek the fulfilment of their wishes and aspirations in the community of free peoples. By its whole structure a German military contribution in the framework of the European defence community made any Rapallo policy impossible.

The subjects of my talks with members of the British Government were to be the question of Europe and the German defence contribution. My conversations with Churchill especially acquired special significance from the impending meeting of the foreign ministers of the leading countries of Western Europe in Strasbourg. There were to be discussions at Strasbourg of the possibility of the early formation of a European political authority as 'superstructure' for the Schuman and Pleven Plans. The Strasbourg talks were expected to be very important especially because the Gaullists had hinted in the Council of Europe that they were ready to agree to the European army if it were possible to put foundations under the defence plan by the beginnings at least of a political federation. The Americans were getting very impatient and were urging a decision on the political unity of Europe even if at first it was only 'a very little Europe'. I wanted to get a clear impression in London of the attitude of the new British Government towards Europe and I wanted to try to get Churchill to take an active part in the work of uniting Europe. I wanted to familiarize myself, by personal contact with the leading British statesmen, with the atmosphere in which problems were being judged there, problems which were decisive for Great Britain's attitude toward the great issues of our time.

In retrospect I still recall quite distinctly how agreeable I found the open-mindedness and spirit of friendliness with which I was received by all the people I met and especially Churchill and Eden. I had met representatives of British political and cultural life and everywhere had the strong feeling that this visit could and should put an end to the past. This conviction was the most valuable part of the results I was allowed to take back to Germany.

I had come to Great Britain as representative of a country which after a history full of vicissitudes and errors had found the path to a democratic and liberal polity, and which was firmly resolved to link its fate with that of the Western democracies.

British parliamentarism had had a slow and steady development over the centuries and I could not help making a comparison with the fate of Germany. Since the beginning of her history Germany too has known democratic and parliamentary forms. In many communities, be they corporate or municipal, the responsibility of the leaders to the elected representatives of the people had always been essential. It was the tragedy of the development of German democracy that the democratic idea, although always deeply rooted in the people and among the educated classes, found it hard to achieve shape and form on a national level.

In 1848 it seemed as though success might be in sight but the anti-democratic forces then proved the stronger. Imperial Germany was denied the opportunity and the time for a quiet evolution in the direction of genuine democracy. The Weimar Republic, all of whose politicians and statesmen were animated by a lively democratic spirit, was weakened by the effects of the First World War and its extraordinary economic burdens and was finally overwhelmed by National Socialism that led Germany into the fatal period of dictatorship.

On the new attempt to make Germany finally into a democracy there lay the mortgage of the terrible consequences of the collapse of 1945. In the Russian occupied zone of Germany the attempt to establish a democratic order was forcibly prevented and a régime was instituted that shows all the features of totalitarianism. The new foundation of a democratic state was confined to the three zones of Germany controlled by the Western Allies and the free part of Berlin. In view of the general situation one can take satisfaction in the fact that the German people in their overwhelming majority have declared for those parties that stand for democratic principles. It was certainly not easy for the German people, after the destruction of all the illusions of a dark epoch, after the deliberate destruction of all values by their seducers, to regain reason and a sense of proportion and to reinstate the freedom of the individual in the place it deserves.

The democratic principles under which Great Britain and the other countries of Western Europe had been living, protection of human dignity, equality before the law, freedom of the individual and of faith, have found their place in the basic rights of the Basic Law of the Federal Republic of Germany. They have the immediate force of law.

During my visit to Great Britain I had to endeavour to awaken and enlarge understanding for Germany. An opportunity for this was offered me by the Foreign Press Association in London which organized a meeting on 8 December 1951 at which I spoke. I pointed to the necessity of Federal expenditure to stabilize internal order and to achieve healthy social conditions, and emphasized the importance and value of these measures for the defence of democratic freedom against the threat from the East. If part of the German people were at first maintaining a reserve regarding a defence contribution, one should not forget that a people whose trust had twice been betrayed, a people which had only barely escaped complete annihilation, was anxious at the thought of having once more to face a situation in which arms had to be used to defend itself.

I pointed out that every German knew from the bitter experience of the past that only the integration of Germany in the community of free nations could give welfare and security. It was not only fear of Bolshevism that made it so, but a recognition gained independently of it that the problems of the present, the maintenance of peace and the defence of freedom, could only be solved in a larger community. This conviction was shared by the broad majority of the German people, a fact that had given the Federal Government and the freely elected representatives of the German people the chance to join the vanguard of the European movement and to give vigorous support to every action serving the unification and integration of Europe. It was the desire of the Federal Republic to take the process of European integration as far as possible, calmly and without haste but steadily and effectively. The policy of integrating Germany in the community of free peoples was the guideline of German foreign policy. The process of integration and of the formation of larger communities of nations served the preservation of those Christian-Western values that gave meaning to our lives. It also served the social progress and material welfare which can be realized in the democratic world not in opposition to but in harmony with the freedom of the individual and of the peoples.

It was in this context that I had put such high value on the results of the Paris conference of the three Allied foreign ministers in November. The peculiar political state of suspension between East and West in which Germany found herself as a consequence of unconditional surrender and the tensions that had arisen since 1945 between the Western Allies and Soviet Russia had been ended. The Federal Republic now belonged finally and irrevocably to the Western community. This decision did not preclude a relaxation of the tension between East and West, on the contrary it would promote it. One of the reasons for this tension had been the uncertainty of the situation.

As for Anglo-German relations in the context of the future German partnership with the West, I said that we were aware of the impossibility of solving the majority of problems that mattered to the Federal Republic and the United Kingdom in a bilateral dialogue between Germany and Britain. The preservation of peace, the efforts for economic welfare, and defence were tasks of such magnitude, due to the world situation, that their solution could be found only in the framework of comprehensive communities. The same applied to the economic sphere. Here too many phenomena of modern economic processes could only be managed in larger international or supranational communities. In the existing European organizations, notwithstanding the fact that individual countries voiced their concerns quite frankly, a spirit of solidarity had developed.

Great Britain and the British Commonwealth had shown a certain reserve toward plans of European unification. Englishmen had spoken of a benevolent lack of interest. We on the continent could well understand that Britain's position at the heart of the British Commonwealth imposed special obligations, but we were also convinced that the destiny of the continent was closely connected with that of Great Britain. I was happy in the knowledge that this view was shared by the leading men of the United Kingdom not only in the government but also among the opposition.

Conversation with the British Prime Minister Winston Churchill on 4 December 1951

On the second day of my sojourn in London, Prime Minister Churchill and I had a long conversation on Europe after a luncheon he had given for me.

In a speech during the luncheon Churchill had already touched on the subject of Europe when he remarked that it was wrong to say that he had spent his entire life fighting Germany. It was really only five years; on the other hand, he said, he had all his life felt a deep affection for France. How glorious it would be if Germany were now added, if a wide feeling of loyalty could embrace Great Britain, France and Germany and lead our peoples in a broad stream toward a bright future. If we could all combine our efforts, means and strength to found an unshakeable free democracy in which the peoples had the right to decide their own destiny, we would escape the fateful war and be able to live on in a comprehensive true harmony of peace.

At the beginning of the conversation with Churchill in which Foreign Secretary Eden took part on the British side I stated my conviction that the Soviet Union was opposed to the integration of the Federal Republic in Western Europe. To prevent this integration the Soviets were engaging in various strategems. An integration of Europe without Germany was impossible. I was for Western Europe and for the integration of the Federal Republic in Western Europe. Hence I had warmly welcomed the Schuman Plan. This plan did not at first give Germany any special advantages, on the contrary Germany had to undertake to perform in advance of possible returns in many respects. The same applied to the Pleven Plan. But the decisive onsideration was that Germany and France should combine.

In his famous speech in Zürich in the autumn of 1946 Churchill had said that Europe could only come about if Germany and France came to an understanding. I knew Churchill to be an advocate of a special Franco-German understanding.

Referring to the Pleven Plan I repeated the declaration I had made at various times in public and in talks with leading foreign politicians that I did not want a national German army. I told Churchill that the German forces must be integrated in a European army. I was aware of Britain's special position. In France there was anxiety in certain circles at the thought of having to deal with the Germans alone. Therefore these circles insisted on British participation in a European defence community. I told Churchill that it would even be enough if Britain showed strong sympathy for European unification. The West simply must be strong. This was the prerequisite of relaxation without war. We could, however, never be quite sure and had to be appropriately prepared.

Churchill agreed with my last point and said that a détente could be reached only gradually. Pressure from the East would continue to persist for years.

I returned to the subject of Europe and said that Europe must benefit from Great Britain's experience. I repeated that it would even be enough if Britain said where her sympathies lay.

Churchill replied that Britain must maintain the balance. Germany was stronger than France and France was haunted by fear of a German attack. In such an event Britain would stand on the side of France. He did not however anticipate that such an event would occur.

I said, 'One must not even utter such a thought. I beg of you to trust Germany. Sometimes it is difficult to assess Germany correctly. The Germans incline to extremes and are often too theoretical, but we have paid dearly for our lessons. The Germans are no longer caught up in the old habits of thought. Germany and France must unite and this must be done in the next two years. Germany is a shapeless mass that must be formed. What matters is whether this is done by good hands or bad.'

Churchill replied that it was impossible to eradicate all national sentiments. France and Germany must work together. Their troops must march to the strains of the 'Marseillaise' and the 'Wacht am Rhein'.

Eden interjected that Britain was hoping for a European army and would stand at its side accompanying it without being entirely identified with it. Churchill was the father of the united Europe.

Churchill added that his basic belief, the reason he favoured a united Europe, was his conviction that Germany and France must be friends. Great Britain would contribute to this German-French friendship. Germany was stronger than France. Britain would help to establish the balance.

I said Churchill should not overestimate Germany. We too had our weaknesses.

Churchill replied that he knew we had nine million refugees and what we had done was admirable.

I turned to the subject of Soviet Russia and said that the greatest danger came from the Soviet Union. No one outside Germany could imagine how the Soviet Union was attempting to undermine the Federal Republic. The German Communist Party had an income of twenty million marks every month.

Eden said that Germany need not fear being sold to the Soviet Union. England would only act in concert with the Federal Republic and would not surrender the Federal Republic for peace with the Soviet Union. There would be no understanding with Soviet Russia except with German agreement.

Churchill underlined this by saying that Britain would not betray Germany.

If the West was stronger the Soviet Union might perhaps withdraw and permit the reunification of Germany. There would be no understanding at the expense of Germany. Only a false friendship could spring from such a betrayal.

I asked: 'We can, then, count on the support of Britain?'

Churchill replied that the British would stand by their word. Why, he asked, had the Soviet Union acted so foolishly, why on earth? The Soviets were more afraid of British friendship than of British hostility. Contact with Britain would cause the Soviet system to collapse. Any contact of the inhabitants of the Soviet Union with the West would mean the end of the accursed system.

I agreed with this. Communism would be finished once its people came into contact with the free world. The Soviet Union was surrounded by a Chinese wall. They knew why they were cutting off their people.

Churchill next spoke about the Oder-Neisse line, saying that it would be a mistake for Germany to speak of it now. He could give an assurance that it would be cleared up at the future peace settlement. The question should not be raised now.

Churchill inquired whether there was a possibility of good relations between Germany and Poland. I answered in the affirmative. Eden remarked that if Germany terrified her neighbours, she was playing into the hands of the Soviet Union. It was fear of Germany that welded the satellite countries together. I pointed to a meeting of young Germans and Poles that had been very successful. Eden advocated the fostering of relations with Poland and the satellites in the United Nations.

Churchill said again that we should have full confidence in the British who would not conclude any deals behind our backs. I thanked him for this declaration.

Churchill continued that I should depend upon it that all men were longing for peace, but that there was also great fear of the Soviet Union. The door must be left open to an understanding with the Soviet Union, but not at the expense of Germany. If the Federal Republic stood by the West, the United States and Great Britain would reciprocate.

The conversation turned to the internal situation of the Federal Republic. I said there was no need to worry about neo-fascists. The Federal Government was in firm control of the situation and would not tolerate a repetition of the events of 1930-3. Nor should one take Schumacher too seriously. He was a nationalist on a Marxist basis. The greatest danger for the Federal Republic was the refugee problem.

Churchill asked what could be done about it.

I replied that the building of houses and the expansion of industrial production were the best remedies. There was always a danger of the refugees turning to radical extremism while their most urgent and justified demands could not be satisfied. Another danger was the attitude of the young people under thirty-five toward the state. They refused to commit themselves because they had been through too much. The more firmly the Federal Republic was integrated in Europe as an equal partner, the more attractive it would become for the younger generation.

Churchill agreed, saying that youth needed a symbol. Suddenly he asked me whether I was a Prussian. The Prussians were villains and he was afraid of them.

I laughed and replied that I was no Prussian.

Churchill rejoined that the Prussians, on the other hand, had a good fighting spirit.

I returned to the subject of youth. The imagination of the young must be focused on Europe. I stressed the importance of an Anglo-German youth exchange. Far more British visitors should come to Germany. So far hardly any British students were in Germany. Eden concurred with me on the desirability of exchange programmes for the young.

Finally Churchill returned once again to the European development. He said that we would all be destroyed if we failed to agree. If we stuck together, we would, God willing, endure. If we were nevertheless to perish it would at least not be our fault.

Another high point of my five-day visit to Great Britain was my visit to King George VI at Buckingham Palace. The King had just recovered from a long illness and I was the first foreign visitor he received in an official audience after his illness. He had come from his castle at Sandringham to see me.

We had a conversation of about half an hour. I liked him very much. We talked about the whole European situation. The King was very well informed about the problems of the Federal Republic and showed great interest in Germany. His information clearly covered the political situation in general.

I was staying at Claridge's in London. During my stay there were small demonstrations against the Federal Republic and myself, for instance in front of No. 10 Downing Street, in the House of Commons, and during my visit to Oxford.

The welcome of the British press was cool but not unfriendly. A great liberal paper wrote:

> The truth is that both Dr Adenauer and British official opinion have greatly changed since the dark days of 1945. He is not, as he was, acutely distrustful of British policy and disinclined to cooperate. The British on their side see that he has not moved so far towards autocratic conservatism as they once expected and they admire his achievements . . . But it would be wrong to conceal the doubts and differences which still exist . . . Probably the greatest among them is Dr Adenauer's continuing suspicion of Mr Churchill, and especially of Mr Churchill's policy towards Russia . . . Dr Adenauer is said to be obsessed with the fear of a new 'Yalta'. It is as well that he and Mr Churchill should clear their minds on the matter.

The paper was not altogether wrong about my fears and I used several occasions during my stay in Britain to tell pressmen that a neutralization of Germany was unacceptable for Germany and the entire West. A return to Potsdam harboured great dangers for the Federal Republic and for Europe.

A very extensive programme had been drawn up for me. I had to make many speeches, for instance to the British group of the Inter-Parliamentary Union, before the Royal Institute of International Affairs, and, as already mentioned, before the Foreign Press Association in London. Official luncheons, receptions and dinners interspersed with political talks left me little time to enjoy the beauties of London. Nonetheless I took the time for a visit to Westminster Abbey. I greatly valued a visit to the National Gallery and visited the British Museum as well.

I took deep impressions home from my stay in England, impressions that were particularly reinforced by a visit to Oxford. I envy every student who can pursue his studies in the quiet atmosphere of Oxford. At Balliol College I was shown a memorial tablet for the students who had died in the Second World War containing the name of one of my nephews, the second eldest son of my brother August, who had studied there during the years 1928 and 1929.

During these eventful five days I had everywhere found understanding and benevolence towards us Germans. I felt that there were very strong links of a common Western-Christian civilization and tradition between us. I was sincerely grateful for the way I had been received in England. It was not the purpose of my visit to make written agreements or to conclude treaties. Agreements and treaties are not always the most valuable thing. Much more valuable is the mutual understanding of the peoples and of their leaders. This understanding I found in Great Britain in truly surprising measure. In the talks I had people tried to understand the way we thought and I found understanding for the peculiarity of German conditions at that time. I had been able on my part to acquaint myself with British problems in frank discussions and I had sought to understand the trends of thought of my British partners in their historic context.

I regarded my visit to England as very useful and hoped that it would produce greater ease in dealing with various especially urgent questions and would facilitate a solution to the common tasks awaiting all nations of the world.

Churchill too seemed to have found the meeting with me useful. His reply to a telegram I addressed to him on leaving Great Britain was:

> Your visit came at an important stage in the development of a new and happier relationship between our two countries. I share your view that our meeting has been of great service to our common work for the consolidation of Europe and the strengthening of world peace. In this great work you can count upon the cooperation and good will of the British Government and people.

One and a half years later, on 14 May 1953, I had another talk with Churchill on Great Britain and its relationship with Europe. It was a memorable conversation. Churchill summed up his ideas in a metaphor: The United States, Great Britain with the Commonwealth, and the united Europe must be connected like three circles that touch. He illustrated his idea with a drawing he made on a card at table. Nothing had changed in this British attitude.

21

GENERAL AGREEMENT
AND THE TREATY OF THE EUROPEAN
DEFENCE COMMUNITY

General Agreement Initialled in Paris on 22 November 1951

On Tuesday 20 November 1951 I flew to Paris for a meeting with the foreign ministers of the United States, Great Britain and France. Negotiations on the General Agreement had progressed far enough for the chief Convention, the lynch-pin of the whole set of agreements, to be signed.

On Wednesday 21 November I had a long conversation with the American Secretary of State Dean Acheson after a luncheon given by Bruce, the American Ambassador in Paris, for Acheson and myself.

Acheson thought that the next ninety days would be of truly fateful significance. During this time the agreement on the new relationship between the Federal Republic and the Allies and the treaty on the European Defence Community must be concluded. That they should be finished in this period was important because the presidential election would take place in the United States in autumn 1952 and there was a danger that as early as spring 1952 the agreements would be drawn into the agitation of the American election campaign. If this was to be avoided, haste was indicated. He, Acheson, was intending to submit a whole bundle of treaties to Congress for ratification at the beginning of 1952, he hoped before the preliminaries of the election campaign got going. These included the Japanese Peace Treaty, the Security Pact with the Philippines, the treaty on the entry of Greece and Turkey into NATO, and finally the system of treaties with the Federal Republic as soon as they were ready.

I expressed to Acheson my grateful satisfaction at the energy and sense of purpose with which the United States was meeting its responsibilities in the area of world policy and especially in Europe. This firm course was not being pursued in the same way by all the Allied powers. There were some whom I might describe as 'shaky'. I was above all concerned to find out in my talks with the three foreign ministers in Paris whether there were any attempts to make Germany the object of an understanding with Russia of which fears had been here and there expressed in public. Acheson replied that my impression of one or the other of the Western Allies as 'shaky' might be due to the strong reaction against rearmament among peoples suffering the consequences on domestic production and standards of living of the financial burden for defence. No one had, however, dared to approach him with a plan to make Germany the object of an East-West understanding, i.e. of an understanding between the Western Allies and Soviet Russia. None of the great powers of the West had any such thought nor had there been any beginnings of attempts in this direction; on the contrary a number of smaller countries had approached him to point out emphatically what catastrophic consequences any such overtures would have.

We talked in some detail about Article VII of the General Agreement relating to a peace settlement and the reunification of Germany. I said that the Federal Government expected that the Allies would enter into no comitments whatsoever on the territories east of the Oder-Neisse line with third parties, e.g. Poland. This problem must be reserved to the peace settlement. Hallstein, who was present during this conversation, added that the Federal Government was concerned that the peace settlement should cite certain principles, such as those of the Atlantic Charter, which might among other things show the Poles that what was intended was not a unilateral solution serving only German interests, but a sensible and just solution of the entire territorial problem that would therefore respect Polish wishes. This was necessary in order to counter the vigorous Soviet propaganda which conjured up for the Poles the horrors of a returning conqueror who had no other intent than to drive the Poles out of the Eastern territories once more.

In the course of the conversation I gave Acheson an account of developments in German politics and described it as my chief task to arouse a sense of political responsibility among the young. For this to be possible the German state would have to have more authority than heretofore. For this reason alone it was very necessary for the General Agreement to be concluded as rapidly as possible.

In taking my leave I expressed the hope that the United States would continue intensively to participate in the fate of the European world. Acheson on his part reassured me of his determination to continue previous policies. Europe could rest assured that America would remain conscious of her responsibility.

On the next day, 22 November, there was a joint session of the four foreign ministers at the Quai d'Orsay at which the main contractual agreement was initialed. At the beginning of the meeting Foreign Minister Schuman welcomed me with extraordinary cordiality into the circle of foreign ministers and said that this was the first time that the Chancellor and Foreign Minister of the Federal Republic of Germany had been among the foreign ministers of the Western powers. He was using the opportunity to express to me his sincere wishes and those of his colleagues for successful cooperation.

Thanking Schuman for his words I said that I was expecting today's Foreign Ministers' Conference in which Germany was taking part for the first time to have beneficial effects on the consolidation of political conditions in Germany.

So far the Federal Republic had, as it were, been suspended in mid-air between East and West. On this day the Federal Government was beginning to speak with its own authority in association with the Western world. The decisions of the Foreign Ministers' Conference made the Federal Republic into a strong factor in the security of Europe and into a magnet for the Russian zone. Soviet Russia would recognize that she had failed to prevent the integration of Germany with the West by the instruments of the cold war. All this meant a big step toward the consolidation of European conditions.

Acheson, who spoke next, referred to the great changes that had taken place in Germany's relations with the world around her. Even a few years ago it would have been impossible for a German foreign minister to join in the work in Paris. The cooperation begun today must be continued. He wholeheartedly endorsed the welcome Foreign Minister Schuman had given me. Speaking next, Eden said that although he had not been one of the originators of the Basic Law, he had – and this might have been the more difficult thing – supported the endeavours of the Allied foreign ministers from the opposition benches. He very much hoped that this meeting would be followed by others. Great Britain was happy to take a part in Franco-German friendship for which there was a strong desire in Britain in view of the tragic events of the past.

After these words of welcome Foreign Minister Schuman spoke of the significance of the Agreement, which consisted not only in putting an end to a painful past but also in the attempt jointly to construct a world armed against the dangers of the future. For this France and Germany needed sponsors. The governments of the United States and Great Britain were the sponsors of this great enterprise, perhaps the greatest undertaking for centuries. Our nations would understand us. The great goal could be reached only by stages, and this was such a stage.

The connection between the European Defence Community – an expression that had acquired general currency – and NATO took up a great part of the discussions of the foreign ministers. The need for such a link was stressed.

We were agreed to give our assent in principle to the General Agreement before us. Final agreement had not yet been reached on some of the so-called related Conventions. We decided to initial the General Agreement which established the main principles of the future relationship between the Federal Republic and the Western Allies, at this meeting, but not to publish the text until after the conclusion of the related agreements. In the final communiqué on this meeting there was accordingly only a statement that 'certain outstanding points in the General Agreement were settled and . . . the ministers have approved the draft of this Agreement'.

Foreign Policy Difficulties; The Saar Question; NATO

All political questions had been settled in the General Agreement. The related agreements only referred to technical and financial matters, the stationing of large troop units of other countries on German soil giving rise to a number of technical questions that needed contractual settlement; and points concerning the amount of the European defence costs to be borne by each country having to be settled on the financial side.

The purely military negotiations necessitated by the entry of the Federal Republic into the European Defence Community took place in a surprisingly pleasant atmosphere.

It was the express desire of the American Secretary of State that the expert committees dealing with the related agreements should proceed swiftly. When we initialed the General Agreement we counted on the related agreements being ready for signature by January 1952 at the latest, but numerous complications arose in the course of the negotiations and the whole complex of agreements was not available for signature by the foreign ministers until May 1952.

In February 1952 tensions had suddenly appeared between France and Germany during the negotiations on the European Defence Community. They related to the Saar question and to the North Atlantic Treaty. On 25 January 1952 the French Government appointed Gilbert Grandval, the former French High Commissioner at Saarbrücken, Ambassador there. In the spring of 1950, when the Federal Republic was about to decide whether to join the Council of Europe, the decision had been made much more difficult by the Saar Conventions. Now that we were about to conclude the negotiations on the European Defence Community, Grandval's appointment as Ambassador had a similar effect.

Under-Secretary of State Hallstein was in Paris for a foreign ministers' conference in which I was not taking part; he was standing in for me. I directed Hallstein to request from the French Government an explanation for the sudden appointment of Grandval as Ambassador. Schuman's answer was that Grandval had been given the personal title of Ambassador; that his office was henceforth called a diplomatic mission; but that its functions would remain the same as previously exercised by the French High Commissioner in the Saar.

On the same day that Hallstein had this answer from Schuman, the French Deputy High Commissioner in Germany, Bérard, announced at a press conference that in the future the Saar would be represented in Paris by a diplomatic mission and that various French diplomatic missions in other countries would have representatives of the Saar attached to them.

I sent Hallstein a telegram saying that Schuman's answer was unsatisfactory and asked Hallstein to request further clarification. I also instructed him to abstain until further notice in case any resolutions should be passed by the conference on the creation of the European Defence Community.

The Bundestag was to have a debate on the German defence contribution on 7 and 8 February. In view of the surprising appointment of Grandval as Ambassador, I issued a statement to the press on 27 January that it was

403

doubtful whether the Bundestag debate could take place at the present moment.

Acheson had told me in Paris that the American Government was most concerned that the Agreements should be concluded as soon as possible. The Americans appeared to be very irritated at the new difficulties. I received a letter from McCloy of 28 January 1952 saying *inter alia* that it seemed to be fate that at every important juncture of European developments the Saar question came up again. He wished it were possible to tackle this question again at once and to settle it now rather than wait for the peace conference. He felt that it was going to plague all our endeavours until it had been effectively settled. On the other hand, despite its annoying concomitants, it was not sufficiently important to affect the main objectives. Mr Reber had told him that I had written to Sir Ivone Kirkpatrick about the delays in the negotiations saying that too much emphasis was being given to points of minor importance.

I had indeed sent a letter to Kirkpatrick for it seemed to me that the negotiations were becoming a typical example of secondary questions obstructing the achievement of primary goals. In my letter to Kirkpatrick of 24 January 1952 I had said:

> Permit me to state frankly that I see a great obstacle in the way of a timely final result in the weight attributed to many subsidiary questions on the Allied side which they do not deserve when compared with the great tasks we have to solve together.
>
> If the goal we are striving for in these negotiations – the safeguarding of the free world against the threat from the East and the building of a peaceably cooperating European-Atlantic community, including Germany – is to be attained, magnanimous and far-sighted decisions must be taken. The psychological impression our Agreement must make on the German people which is absolutely necessary to make the Germans into full and reliable members of the Western defence community, can equally be impaired by encumbering the related agreements with too many oppressive and basically unnecessary provisions which are bound to cause resentment. . . .

At the time I wrote this letter it was the related agreements that caused me concern. The new complication due to the French action in the Saar was incomparably more dangerous and was apt to make my fears come true.

At that time McCloy was in an American military hospital in Munich, having injured himself on a skiing holiday. I asked the Under-Secretaries of State Hallstein and Lenz and Ministerialdirigent Blankenhorn to go to Munich in order to ask the State Department through the good offices of McCloy to intervene in Paris and to propose that the French Government recall the exchange of letters of 18 April 1951 and re-endorse it to manifest their intention to create no *faits accomplis* in the Saar that might in any way prejudice a future peace settlement. I asked that the State Department be requested to suggest that the French Government concede free elections, with all necessary conditions, for the Saar.

The conversation with McCloy in Munich took place on 30 January 1952. McCloy sent me the reply that he did not think Grandval's appointment was exclusively a Saar affair. The interpreter's minutes on the conversation read:

He (McCloy) believed rather that it was a volley of certain anti-European French circles against the European idea and certainly against the European Defence Community. He knew very well that there were powerful groups in the French Foreign Ministry who had jealously watched this European policy and had always sought an opportunity to torpedo it.

He had always agreed with Monnet that it was wrong to put back the solution of the Saar question until the peace treaty, for such an open wound on the body of Europe would certainly always lead to new complications and would endanger the whole foundation of the European structure. He added that François-Poncet shared this opinion.

McCloy warned against a postponement of the Bundestag debate because it might endanger the other deadlines. He suggested announcing a conference on the Saar question. Hallstein and Lenz pointed out that such a conference would not be opportune; if no agreement was reached at this conference my position would become even more difficult. The debate in the Bundestag on the German defence contribution would become very difficult unless the French gave assurances on free elections in the Saar. McCloy replied that an American step in this direction would hardly have any prospect of succeeding with the French Government because of the American unwillingness to meet far-reaching French demands for help in Indochina. He did, however, say that he would submit my request to ask the French Government to reaffirm the exchange of letters of 18 April 1951 to the American State Department.

Recent events in the Saar had to be seen in the context of the impending signature of the treaty on the creation of a European Defence Community. The connection was this: on 18 April 1951 Schuman had exchanged letters with me stating explicitly that the final status of the Saar was not to be prejudiced by either side. It was, however, being prejudiced by the measures now taken in the Saar. I thought it very dangerous if such actions should disturb confidence in the sincerity of the other party at a moment when negotiations on the European Defence Community were to create a lasting partnership in Europe and between France and Germany.

The debate in the Bundestag on the German defence contribution did after all take place as originally planned on 7 and 8 February 1952.

More excitement had been caused by statements made by Under-Secretary of State Hallstein at the Foreign Ministers' Conference in Paris at the end of January 1952 in connection with the North Atlantic Treaty. The French press reported them as though Germany were suddenly raising the demand of NATO membership in order to exert pressure on France.

The existence of a connection between the European Defence Community and the North Atlantic Treaty had found its first expression in the Preamble of the draft for the General Agreement with the consent of the United States, Great Britain and France. This preamble stated expressly that it was the common aim of the signatory powers to integrate the Federal Republic on a basis of equality into the European community 'itself included in a developing Atlantic Community'. At the deliberations of the Paris Foreign Ministers' Conference in November 1951 the necessary and natural connection between the European Defence Community and the North Atlantic Treaty had been affirmed by all. The obvious reasons for such a link being in the nature of things was this: if we entered the European Defence Community, Germans would be integrated into the European army. As long as present tensions persisted in the world the European army would be put under the Supreme Allied Commander in Europe (SACEUR), at that time Eisenhower, who was in his turn subordinate to other bodies of the Atlantic pact. It went without saying that we simply could not put Germans under a body on whose functioning and work we had no influence. We were the only member country of the European Defence Community that was not at the same time a member of NATO. I personally was sure that if we entered the European Defence Community the march of events would quite naturally make us into members of NATO one day.

Before we entered the European Defence Community and thereby acquired certain obligations, a connection with NATO had to be established to enable us to influence it in some way. To my mind it was self-evident; it was a matter of equity and required by the responsibility of the Federal Government to the German people.

Washington and London were considering these questions much more calmly and logically than Paris where they had stirred up great excitement.

On 4 February 1952 I had given a fairly long account to the CDU/CSU group in the Bundestag on the state of the negotiations on the General Agreement and the European Defence Treaty. In the course of this account I had said that the Saar question and the relationship of the Federal Republic to the North Atlantic Treaty would have to be cleared up satisfactorily. On the next day my remarks appeared in the German press in a rather distorted form. I was reported to have said that the Federal Government could not see itself in a position to sign the General Agreement, the related agreements and the treaty on the European Defence Community until German wishes regarding the Saar and the Federal Republic's accession to NATO were settled. The report caused a storm in the National Assembly in Paris.

French mistrust of the Federal Republic was still very strong and the French Government and Foreign Minister Schuman had great difficulties in getting a majority for their plan.

On 11 February 1952 a debate on the European Defence Community had begun in the National Assembly. On 16 February 1952 the French Prime

Minister, Edgar Faure, put the question of confidence by submitting for a vote a motion which among other things said:

> The National Assembly approves that Germany should not be subjected to discrimination in the integrated organization. It demands that the contractual agreements which are to replace the occupation régime when the European Defence Community has entered into force must contain the necessary guarantees with respect to arms production, the police force, and the distribution of financial burdens. It further demands that the admission of Germany to the European Defence Community should in no case be connected with her entry into the Atlantic organization . . .
>
> The National Assembly enjoins the government . . . to request the British and American Governments to guarantee the commitments entered into towards the European Defence Community in the event of a breach or a violation of the Agreement by a member country and to substantiate this guarantee by an appropriately prolonged stay of sufficiently strong American and British troops on the continent of Europe.

I could only hope that it would be possible to remove the tension between France and ourselves very soon. We had a common goal. We wanted not only to save the peace for ourselves and for Europe at this moment; we wanted to make sure that a war in Europe – a war between Germany and France – would be made impossible once and for all. This was one of the main objectives of my policy, an objective that must not be lost sight of amidst the tensions of the moment. That was why I regarded the creation of a European Defence Community in conjunction with the Schuman Plan as a quite essential element of a lasting pacification of Europe. The great long-range objective, the prevention of European wars, must not be disregarded because of present tensions and difficulties. Every birth is accompanied by labour, and I was aware that the birth of the new Europe would bring labour and critical phases. But if any one thing was necessary, if we were to learn anything from all that had happened since 1914, it was that all men of good will must do their utmost to bring about the unification of Europe.

Visit to London in February 1952; Difficulties Overcome

King George VI died on 6 February 1952. I was invited to the funeral ceremonies as representative of the Federal Republic of Germany.

I flew to London on 14 February 1952. The funeral of the King, for whom I felt very great respect, took place on 15 February. On the day of my arrival in London I paid a visit of condolence to Queen Elizabeth II. I saw her once more during my stay in London, on the day of my departure, 19 February, when she received Acheson, Schuman and myself separately in an audience lasting a quarter of an hour. Queen Elizabeth impressed me very much. She had a very natural manner.

After my visit of condolence to the young Queen I drove to Westminster Hall where the late King was lying in state. During the days of mourning in London I was deeply impressed by the ties between the English royal house and the English people which embraced all parts of the population. I was much impressed, too, by the lying in state of the King in Westminster Hall. The Hall is more than eight hundred years old. In its centre stood the coffin with the British flag spread over it. The crown with orb, sceptre, and a cross lay on the coffin. In absolute silence two lines of Englishmen walked through the gigantic hall, to say a last farewell to their King. I do not know how many passed by, but in front of the Hall people were waiting in queues more than two miles long. The Hall, the coffin, and the unending procession of mourners have remained unforgettable to me. The rest of the mourning was very digni-fied, devoid of exaggerated pomp and accompanied by the participation of the entire people. After the mourning ceremonies in London the royal family drove to Windsor by special train with the coffin. Another special train had carried the mourners, including myself, in advance. On both sides of the tracks people were standing for miles and miles, bareheaded, to pay their King their last respects.

The funeral ceremonies had brought the American Secretary of State, Acheson, and the French Foreign Minister, Schuman, to London. There was an urgent need to overcome the obstacles blocking the conclusion of the Agreements.

On 18 and 19 February conferences took place between the Foreign Ministers Eden, Acheson, Schuman and myself. These were among the tensest conferences that until that time I had ever been through. In Paris the National Assembly was meeting as was the Faure cabinet and we never knew what the next hour would bring.

Perhaps the most important question discussed in connection with the system of agreements was the connection between NATO and the European Defence Community.

The French National Assembly had passed a resolution opposing NATO membership for the Federal Republic. The reason given for this resolution was that NATO was a purely defensive organization while we claimed certain territories. Doubts were being expressed lest our membership change the character of NATO.

During the Paris negotiations both the French and Germans had suggested that the organizational link between NATO and the European Defence Community at the political level should be effected by joint sessions of the NATO Council and the Council of Ministers of the EDC. In London we agreed that there were to be mutual consultations on questions concerning the joint affairs of the two organizations. If one of the two Councils, either that of NATO or that of the EDC, decided that it was desirable, there were to be joint sessions. These joint sessions were also to take place when one of the member countries of the North Atlantic Treaty or a member of the EDC should consider the territorial integrity, the political independence or the security of any member, or the existence or integrity of NATO or the EDC to be threatened.

France had asked the United States of America and Great Britain for a general security guarantee in the case that the Federal Republic left the European Defence Community. This demand was also discussed in the London talks. I told Acheson and Eden that I would agree to any guarantee whether of the United States or of Britain that strengthened the EDC and held it together provided, naturally, that such guarantees were not directed unilaterally against the Federal Republic but applied to all members of the EDC.

At the meeting that dealt with this question I had made an explicit statement that we maintained our wish to join NATO. I stressed again that the Federal Republic wanted to achieve the reunification of Germany only by peaceful means and that thus the character of NATO would remain unchanged.

Another question discussed in London was the amount of the defence contributions of individual members. A committee had been formed in Paris, which was generally called the Three Wise Men, to discuss exclusively financial problems of the EDC. Shortly before the meeting of the foreign ministers in London this commission had concluded its work and submitted the result to the foreign ministers. I could not yet finally commit myself in London because the question of the defence contribution had to be judged in the context of the extraordinary social burdens of the Federal Republic and had to be subjected to a thorough examination.

A question that at that time was being much discussed in Germany was the treatment of war criminals. Since the founding of the Federal Republic I had let slip no opportunity to discuss this question with leading foreign personalities. In London we decided to appoint a board consisting of one American, one Frenchman, one Englishman, and three Germans. This board was to be entitled to review all cases to ascertain whether or not a remission of punishment, a reduction of the sentence, or perhaps release on parole was indicated. If the authority came to a unanimous conclusion the power concerned should be obliged to comply with its decision. If the recommendation of this board were by a majority it would not be binding on the power that had to pronounce for release or reduction of the sentence but it could be assumed that in almost all cases in which the board recommended leniency that recommendation would be complied with. The board was also charged with the supervision of the execution of the sentences. It was also to concern itself with the avoidance of unjustified hardship.

During my stay in London I had a long conversation with Schuman on the difficulties that had arisen over the Saar. We did not come to a final solution, but the possibilities of an understanding began to emerge. What united us was the conviction that neither France nor the Federal Republic could make a final decision on the fate of the Saar without the population of the Saar being able to express its will.

There was a very thorough discussion of the question of the build-up of armaments industries in the Federal Republic and of the prohibition or control of the production of weapons and of general security controls in the Federal Republic. The pledges demanded of us seemed to me to go too far and I could not help saying to the foreign ministers: 'We are being asked to promise this or that three or four times as proof of our good intentions. Please do not misunderstand me if I say that it must be a strange partner who on entering the partnership has to declare three times running that he is a decent fellow and has nothing but honest intentions. Surely everybody must be aware that declarations and agreements mean nothing where there is no good will. But if you keep on asking one of the partners for proofs of his good will, it makes a very bad impression.'

I begged the foreign ministers to imagine the actual situation in the Federal Republic. There were at this moment and had been for a number of years heavily armed American and British divisions in the Federal Republic; they would soon be joined by troops of the European Defence Community. On the other side the German police were not even armed. How could one be afraid of people who did not have any arms at all? If there were much more talk about security measures against the Federal Republic I would return there with the feeling that we were really much stronger than I had ever thought. However, what characterized the London talks was the firm determination of all concerned to do everything to promote and achieve the early conclusion of the Agreements.

I was very gratified at the following passage in the final communiqué of the London Conference: 'The four foreign ministers were agreed that the efforts for the reunification of Germany by democratic and peaceful means must be continued.'

Difficulties in Germany before Signature of the Agreements

In the middle of April 1952 I had a message from Dean Acheson expressing his great concern at the dragging pace of the negotiations on the Agreements. He thought that the slow progress of the negotiations was seriously endangering the plan. He addressed an appeal to me just as he did to the foreign ministers of Great Britain and France to make a final great effort together with all governments concerned to finish the different treaties and agreements in time for them to be, if possible, signed at the latest by the middle of May. He drew my attention to the danger provoked by delay in Europe. But he pointed especially to the serious difficulties that would arise in the United States regarding the procedure in Congress as a result of further delay. The funds requested for Mutual Security Aid would be discussed in Congress at the latest in the middle of May. It would be extremely difficult for the United States administration to give persuasive reasons for the adoption of these expenditures as long as the effort for the creation of a European Defence

Community had not come to a successful conclusion. He stated in his message that he was afraid that further vague promises of progress in this field would have a discouraging effect on Congress and would be taken as proof that Europe was unable to make a joint defence effort.

Acheson's warning had its effect and the Agreements were in fact so far advanced in the middle of May that a firm date could be fixed for their signature. At the beginning of May the results of the negotiations on the General Agreement appeared once more to be in jeopardy because the national executive of the FDP in conjunction with the Bundestag group of the FDP and the FDP members of the Foreign Affairs Committee of the Bundestag moved far-reaching amendments on 1 May 1952. The Federal Vice Chancellor, Minister Blücher, who was chairman of the FDP, asked me in a letter of 6 May to consider these very extensive proposed amendments of the FDP. Blücher wrote that the FDP was aware that the important change in the General Agreement which it sought could probably be made only by direct negotiation between me and the three Western foreign ministers. He felt that even if this should mean a temporary delay in the conclusion of negotiations this disadvantage should be accepted in view of the great importance of the Agreements and especially of the General Agreement.

It was quite impossible for me to accede to the demands of the FDP. The negotiations had depended on the great objective being kept in sight whatever blemishes might at first affect the appearance of the agreements.

On the same day I replied to Blücher.

To the Chairman of the Free Democratic Party   Rhöndorf,
Vice Chancellor Blücher   6 May 1952
Bonn

Dear Herr Blücher:

I have received your letter of 6 May with enclosures. I do not want to begin by replying to the detailed demands but would rather comment on the procedure proposed by the FDP which would, I fear, certainly put the conclusion of the Agreements out of the question.

You tell me that on 1 May you gathered under your chairmanship the national executive of the FDP with the executive of the parliamentary group of the FDP and the FDP representatives of the Foreign Affairs Committee for a first discussion of the General Agreement. If I imagine the parliamentary groups of the CDU/CSU and the DP proceeding in like fashion, I estimate that we come to four different bodies numbering about a hundred persons in the aggregate making proposals for amendments in Germany. Imagine, please, the same procedure being adopted in France, in England, in the United States, and you will, I trust, agree with me that it would require years of negotiations to come to any agreement at all. It is surely plain that in such circumstances the door would be opened to indiscretions, intended or otherwise, without let or hindrance, and that Germany would violate the most important obligation of foreign policy negotiations, to observe discretion, in a way that would be extremely detrimental to German interests in the future as well.

Even if no such complicated deliberations take place in the three other countries I have named, these facts remain:

The example of the FDP will be imitated by other parties. Proposals for amendment may agree in this or that respect but not in others, and we shall be left with complete confusion.

My understanding of our procedure has always been – and I believe I said this – that at the meetings held under your chairmanship at the König Museum two expert members of the parliamentary group should attend to the matter under discussion and that then at the cabinet meeting planned for 10, 11 and 12 May, which is to be attended by the chairman and one of these members of each parliamentary group, the question should be answered whether the assent of the majority of the Bundestag for an early ratification is to be rationally expected.

Please do not misunderstand me, dear Herr Blücher, if I say that your action is entirely contrary to all our arrangements and plunges the entire matter into utter confusion. Leaving aside the question of whether the three Western Allies will agree to possible German proposals for amendment – they too have their ideas – it seems to me impossible to bring about an agreed and unified German proposal by this method.

I am convinced that your intentions were of the best, but when I read your letter I almost think that it represents the end of all foreign policy. What consequences this will have for domestic policy I need not describe. The future of German foreign policy is completely jeopardized thereby. I have the impression that many of our colleagues enjoy formulation so much that they forget the facts and the precarious state in which we live.

In conclusion I should like to add something the participants in your discussion had evidently forgotten, that before the defence debate in February of this year the coalition party groups, especially that of the FDP, were informed in detail of the contents of the General Agreement and a large part of the provisions was even read verbatim.

Finally I should like to point out that I gave a detailed report on the General Agreement in the cabinet and that every member of the cabinet received the text of the General Agreement. Nothing has since been changed in the Agreement.

The Bundestag too gave its assent, based on the information on the contents of the General Agreement, in the resolution at the end of the discussion on the defence contribution.

If Germany proposes such amendments now, after the United States, France and Britain have given their assent in Paris in November 1951 as I did too, although the signing remains to be done, confidence in German foreign policy will be completely undermined.

Yours faithfully,
(signed) Adenauer

The Signing of the Agreements

In the middle of May 1952 the Paris negotiations on the EDC treaty and those in Bonn on the Contractual Agreements were as good as concluded and dates were set for the signing of these great treaty systems. At Eden's suggestion it was decided to sign the Contractual Agreements in Bonn on 26 May 1952. On the following day, 27 May 1952, the EDC treaty was to be signed by the foreign ministers of the countries concerned in Paris.

On 23 May 1952 the conclusion of the whole complex of treaties was once more called into question. In France voices of criticism and mistrust against the Federal Republic threatened to jeopardize the result of months of negotiation. On 25 May 1952 the prominent French politician Edouard Herriot, whom I knew well from my time as Oberbürgermeister of Cologne during the Weimar Republic, made a statement that struck me as characteristic of the attitude of many Frenchmen:

> The rearmament of Germany fills me with great anxiety. If we were as convinced that Germany will honour the obligations to which she has subscribed as we are of her will to restore her former greatness we would feel no disquiet. But the obligations agreed on paper are insufficient. With all the powers at my command, I implore our American friends not to drag us into a series of the kind of experiments whose pained and powerless witness I was between the two wars. It is said that the Americans are businessmen. This is not so. They are idealists, with a slightly naïve idealism. To these Americans I address this entreaty: let us not repeat the mistakes into which you drew us before ... Do not forget this relatively recent past.

On 23 May 1952 the French Council of Ministers decided to make the signature and proposal of ratification of the Agreements on the European Defence Community and the Agreements superseding the Occupation Statute dependent on new conditions.

There had been negotiations between the French Government on the one side and the governments of the United States and Great Britain on the other on the guarantee demanded in February 1952 for the eventuality of the secession of one of the members from the EDC. It was the Federal Republic that was meant by this. The declarations given by the United States and Great Britain seemed to be insufficient and the French Council of Ministers was now demanding more precise commitments. Another demand was for an Anglo-American declaration of guarantee against the restoration of an autonomous German Wehrmacht. Another condition was that the Allies should consider

France's overseas military commitments and should embody such consideration in a general declaration. By this it was intended to allay fears expressed in France that one day France might, as a result of overseas commitments such as she had in Indochina and North Africa, find herself in a weaker position than Germany in the context of the European Defence Community.

At the time when the French Council of Ministers took this decision, Robert Schuman was already in Bonn. The Foreign Ministers Acheson and Eden had likewise arrived as early as 23 May 1952. Acheson, Eden, Schuman and I sat down together again in order to discuss and dispel the new difficulties. Schuman had been instructed to submit the French demands to us.

All my efforts to reduce mistrust against us Germans seemed to have had little success. On the other side, however, it was understandable that a mistrust as deep as had grown up against us in France as a result of the history of the last seventy years could not be completely removed in the short span of seven years.

In the negotiations with the foreign ministers I now made some demands as well. Hitherto the entry into force of the General Agreement and the EDC treaty had been linked. In the event that for any reason one of the participating countries were to delay or even reject ratification of the EDC treaty, I needed an assurance that the General Agreement would enter into force at least in part. Under the procedure so far envisaged the Federal Republic was to receive its full sovereignty only at the moment when the EDC treaty had been ratified by all the countries concerned. I requested an assurance that in the case of considerable delay certain provisions of the General Agreement should come into effect earlier. Acheson and Eden were ready to meet my request. Schuman at first refused. He was afraid that if my request were granted new difficulties might arise in the French cabinet. Eventually, however, he too agreed.

I was given a written assurance that in case of a delay of the entry into force of the EDC treaty, a conference of the three occupying powers would be called, in which the Federal Republic would participate, in order to discuss and decide the entry into force of the General Agreement.

The United States and Great Britain made a declaration to the effect that their governments would regard as a threat to their own security any step by anyone endangering the integrity or the unity of the EDC. The United States and Great Britain gave an undertaking to maintain forces in Europe of such strength as might be required for the defence of the NATO area and the safeguarding of the integrity of the EDC. This declaration satisfied the French Government.

The declaration requested on support of French policy in North Africa and Indochina was not given. I was not present at the discussion of this question and only know what I read in the newspapers. At the end of May the *New York Herald Tribune* gave the reasons for the American refusal of such a declaration as follows: Secretary of State Dean Acheson had told the members of the French Government that a satisfactory development in North Africa and Indochina depended primarily on effective measures by France herself. France should expedite the implementation of her reform programme to meet the problems of nationalism in North Africa. She should also hasten measures to organize indigenous combat troops in Indochina. Acheson's reply to the French request that the United States refrain from interference in French North African policies in favour of the Nationalists and support French policy instead was that such support depended on the kind of policy the French were pursuing.

In the evening of 25 May Schuman was informed that the French cabinet regarded the Anglo-American guarantee as sufficient and that now nothing stood in the way of the signing of the treaties. On Monday 26 May at ten o'clock the solemn signature of the 'Convention on Relations between the Three Powers and the Federal Republic of Germany', i.e. the so-called General Agreement, took place in the hall of the Bundesrat. Many guests of honour had been invited from German public life such as the representatives of the parties in the Bundestag and the Ministers President of the *Länder*.

Dr Schumacher had sharply opposed the signing of the Convention in an interview with the United Press Agency on 22 May 1952. He had called the act of signing a 'clumsy triumph of the Allied-clerical coalition over the German people'. He had said, 'Whoever assents to this Convention ceases to be a good German.' There were no representatives of the SPD at the ceremony of signature.

In the afternoon of 26 May Acheson, Eden, Schuman and I flew to Paris where on the morning of the next day, Tuesday 27 May 1952, the treaty on the establishment of the European Defence Community was signed in the Salon de l'Horloge of the Quai d'Orsay by the foreign ministers of Belgium, France, Germany, Holland, Italy, and Luxembourg.

Acheson, Eden and Schuman subsequently signed the security guarantee demanded by France after which an Agreement was signed between the six EDC ministers and Great Britain. In this Agreement Britain declared:

> If at any time, while the United Kingdom is party to the North Atlantic Treaty, any other party to the present Treaty which is at that time a member of the European Defence Community, or the European Defence Forces, should be the object of an armed attack in Europe, the United Kingdom will, in accordance with Article 51 of the United Nations Charter, afford the Party or Forces so attacked all the military and other aid and assistance in its power.

General Reflections

It had been clear to me for many years that a policy of Franco-German reconciliation would encounter great difficulties. One had to accept the likelihood of these difficulties reasserting themselves again and again. Psychological obstacles such as existed between our peoples cannot be overcome from one day to the next. The debate on the defence contribution in the French parliament in February 1952 told this tale with particular clarity.

And yet there are political necessities so compelling that in the long run they must prevail. By the two wars, by revolutions and insurrections subsequent upon them, and especially by the tremendous expansion of the Soviet Union – notably in Europe – the unification of the free peoples of Europe had become a political necessity of the first order. The optimism which I preserved in all my endeavours despite all our difficulties was nothing but faith in the force of this necessity, to which the oscillations of daily politics could make no essential difference. At the heart of European unification, however, lay the problem of Franco-German understanding.

In my opinion the European nation states had a past but no future. This applied in the political and economic as well as in the social sphere. No single European country could guarantee a secure future to its people by its own strength. I regarded the Schuman Plan and the European Defence Community as preliminary steps to a political unification of Europe. In the EDC treaty there was a specific provision for a controlling body, the so-called Parliamentary Assembly – incidentally the same assembly that exercised the parliamentary controlling function in the Coal and Steel Community – to examine the questions arising from the parallelism of diverse existing or future organizations for European cooperation, with a view to securing their coordination in the framework of a federal or confederate structure.

The military aspect was only one dimension of a nascent Europe, or, more rightly at first, Western Europe. If a perfect partnership was to be achieved within Western Europe, one could not stop with defence.

I could not understand the *Ohne-mich* attitude; it was irresponsible and in the last resort hopeless, yet it was widespread in the Federal Republic. I was well aware that there would be no simple and easy decisions for a German politician. I never forgot that the fate of many millions of people was at stake, including the millions in the Soviet zone. But there is one thing a responsible politician cannot do: he cannot simply escape into inactivity only because every action available to him has its drawbacks. For then others will act over the head of this politician and his country, and then the country is certain to be the loser. After twelve years of National Socialism there simply were no perfect solutions for Germany and certainly none for a divided Germany. There was very often only the policy of the lesser evil.

We were a small and very exposed country. By our own strength we could achieve nothing. We must not be a no-man's-land between East and West, for then we would have friends nowhere and a dangerous neighbour in the East. Any refusal by the Federal Republic to make common cause with Europe would have been German isolationism, a dangerous escape into inactivity. There was a cherished political illusion in the Federal Republic in those years: many people believed that America was in any case tied to Europe or even to the Elbe. American patience, however, had its limits. My motto was 'Help yourself and the United States will help you'.

The deeply offensive statements by Dr Schumacher which I have quoted displayed a shocking ignorance of the entire political situation. It was even more shocking that the representatives of the SPD stayed away from the solemn act of signature of the Convention on 26 May in Bonn. What were the Western powers to think of us? Was it worth their trouble to continue to negotiate with Germany? Or were they to share the German spoils with the fourth victorious power, Soviet Russia?

There were those in Germany who thought that for us the choice was either a policy for Europe or a policy for German unity. I considered this 'either/or' a fatal error. Nobody could explain how German unity in freedom was to be achieved without a strong and united Europe. When I say 'in freedom' I mean freedom before, during and above all after all-German elections. No policy is made with wishes alone and even less from weakness. Only when the West was strong might there be a genuine point of departure for peace negotiations to free not only the Soviet zone but all of enslaved Europe east of the iron curtain, and free it peacefully. To take the road that led into the European Community appeared to me the best service we could render the Germans in the Soviet zone.

With the signing of the treaties the Federal Republic was to enter into the community of free peoples. To my mind the process by which the Federal Republic was to be firmly placed in a treaty system created by the free nations for the pursuit of their common goals had a significance for the future of Germany that could not be overestimated. Every German had experienced in his own life, and most of them even on their own bodies, the way in which Germany's relations with the rest of the world and with her neighbours determined the weal or woe of every German citizen.

The signature under the Convention and under the treaty on the EDC meant the turning of a new leaf after the terrible war and post-war period. We Germans would enter a political community in which we shared all rights but also all duties with our partners. The series of agreements that had taken about a year to achieve, which involved four countries in the case of the Convention and six in the case of the treaty on the EDC, probably gave no country the chance to say: it is all as we hoped it would be. The process of give and take is the only way to come to an understanding, to achieve co-operation, and above all to grow together into a community. It had been the guiding idea in our work.

I had negotiated on the Convention with the High Commissioners in more than thirty sessions, often lasting days on end. The hours spent by the experts in negotiations were almost impossible to count. The same applied to the treaty on the EDC. The result represented a tremendous amount of work. Naturally every country concerned had wanted to make its own point of view prevail and to pursue its own interests. At the same time however a readiness to compromise had been alive on all sides. Without this readiness the Agreements could never have been concluded. Everyone had had to yield somewhere. Everyone had renounced this or that desire. The Federal Republic was no exception. It was unthinkable that the system of Agreements could look perfect in the eyes of any single country. The underlying principles were what mattered most.

The representatives of the governments of France, Great Britain, the United States of America and the Federal Republic had signed the Convention in Bonn on 26 May. On 27 May representatives of the governments of France, Italy, the Netherlands, Belgium, Luxembourg and Germany signed the treaty on the European Defence Community in the French Ministry of the Exterior in Paris. The contracting parties were not the same for both sets of Agreements. Nevertheless the Agreements formed an indivisible whole. By the Convention with the three powers the Federal Republic regained its freedom of action in all fields. It was thus put in a position under international law to conclude the treaty on the EDC. It was enabled to enter agreements and alliances.

With the formation of the European Defence Community the Federal Republic achieved a firm link with the Atlantic pact. By joining the EDC the Federal Government would realize one of its aims, the inclusion of Germany in the European community, which in turn had its place in the worldwide structure of treaties the free world had created for the preservation of peace. We were no longer alone. We had ceased being the mere object of the foreign policy of other powers. The full weight of this fact must have struck everyone who, during those May days of historic change, cast his mind back to those days of May 1945 when the extent of the catastrophe became clear to us all. Three years after the signing of the Basic Law of the Federal Republic of Germany in the Bundesrat hall we had regained our freedom of action under international law in the same hall on 26 May 1952. We first used it to sign the treaty on the EDC to help found an enterprise that could in the long run turn the course of German and European history for the better.

At the time of the signing of the Agreements I was perfectly aware that many problems were still unsolved. Germany was still divided, the European communities were confined to Western Europe. I was convinced that the league of the European peoples would attract and appeal to other European countries and would thus become a magnetic field for the reunification of Germany and for the emergence of European unity.

Undoubtedly the treaty on the EDC was the more important of the Agreements signed. It was to give a new shape to the future. The Convention created the necessary preconditions by settling the past. On the way from being an enemy to being a partner of the free world the Convention restored to Germany many freedoms that had been denied us in the period of occupation.

They were freedoms we needed in order to become partners in anything, and so to be able to conclude a European treaty.

It was not without significance that Bonn and Paris were the two sites of signature; more was to be concluded than the post-war phase of the last seven years. A whole epoch was ended, the epoch of enmities and wars between the peoples of the West. France and Germany had been the chief agents and sufferers of this tragic estrangement. The signatures in Bonn and Paris were a symbol of the final turning away from this past.

It was impossible for us whole-heartedly to enjoy a political event as long as Germany was divided. The signature of the Agreements gave us no cause for jubilation let alone for triumph, but we must not allow our political judgment to be confused. The Agreements did not constitute an obstacle to the reunification of Germany. On the contrary I saw in them the only means to bring us closer to German unity in freedom. In the hard world of facts there were only two ways open to the Federal Republic, to go with the West or to go with the Soviets. Anything that lay between was not politics but illusion; for everything that lay between would inflict on us the impotence of isolation and make us a plaything of contending forces. Powerless between the powers we would be booty that was still to be distributed, a magnet for a war.

There was no possibility of going with the Soviets. In league with them one could only become a satellite, a will-less and exploited tool of Moscow's power politics. We saw this everywhere east of the iron curtain, we saw it closest and most clearly in the German Soviet zone. This demonstration sufficed. Germany belongs to the West by tradition and by conviction. The whole of Germany belongs to the West. In this partnership alone lies our future.

There were those who did not regard the way I had indicated as the road to German unity. Nevertheless for the time being there was no other way for us. Sooner or later the Soviets would see that they had to come to terms with the West, that they could not impose their will on it. In such a peaceful understanding lay my hope and in it I saw our chance. It would, however, only be a chance for us if, at the moment of such a general settlement between West and East, we had already proved ourselves the reliable partners of the West. Only then would the West make our interests its own.

It was objected that the exchange of notes with the Soviets of spring 1952 – with which I will deal in great detail in the next volume – gave cause for justified hopes for the early restoration of German unity.

If the Soviets were really prepared to solve the problem of German unity in isolation, there was nothing to stop them; even after the treaties had been signed and even after ratification the door to negotiations with the Soviet Union was in no way slammed shut. I regarded any four-power conversations with the Soviets that had some chance of success as thoroughly desirable and necessary.

The Agreements

In a democracy the government conducts foreign policy negotiations and submits the result to parliament for its decision. It is impossible to let the parliament take part in the negotiations. It is impossible to allow detailed parliamentary discussion of unfinished treaties. Only the principles and general outlines can be debated in parliament, and this is what we had done with the Agreements just concluded. The Bundestag had been able to debate the fundamental elements of the treaty system in all thoroughness. Now, after signature, it was perfectly free to decide whether it would ratify the treaties or not and whether they would enter into force. The Bundestag and the parliaments of the other treaty partners had enough time and all the material to form a judgment, and had unlimited parliamentary sovereignty. To ratify means to say Yes or No in full awareness of the responsibility entailed.

It was unthinkable for every one of the eight parliaments to adopt a number of amendments for the treaties and to charge their governments with renegotiation. It would have meant an unending procedure with no prospect of success. Eight governments, each of whose amendments would have tended in a different direction from the others, could not negotiate with each other at all, let alone achieve results. In the present stage everything depended on the parliaments ratifying the treaties in their entirety or not at all.

I was full of confidence that the German parliament would endorse the treaties by a majority. I trusted the political good sense of the majority of Bundestag deputies. Whoever accepted the basic idea of the treaties would overcome objections to details. The majority of the Bundestag wanted Europe and wanted to put an end to German isolation.

In the treaties we had signed the Western powers had entered into an obligation, confident of the willingness of the Federal Republic for partnership with the West, to work with us for peaceful reunification of Germany. In this respect, too, which for us was of decisive importance, we had become the partners of the West. In the context of the system of treaties just signed there was no longer any danger that the West might come to an understanding with the Soviets at our expense. It was an essential advantage of partnership that negotiations and agreements over our heads were no longer possible.

It was an important step forward that the Convention abolished the Occupation Statute. The High Commissioners were to be replaced by Ambassadors. The Military Security Board and many other Allied control organs would be dissolved. Many restrictions on the German economy, on science and on research were to be removed; the occupation costs once unilaterally imposed became defence costs to be negotiated. Nearly two thirds of our future contribution had in the past been paid on foreign orders without our having any authority to control its use.

The Convention was a kind of provisional peace treaty between the Federal

Republic and the three Western Allies which I hoped would be superseded when the time came by a comprehensive peace treaty between the four Allies and Germany.

The Preamble to the Convention embodied the agreement that it was the common aim of the signatory states – Britain, France, the United States of America, the Federal Republic of Germany – to integrate the Federal Republic within the European Community, itself included in a developing Atlantic Community. The Preamble further declared that the achievement of a fully free and unified Germany through peaceful means and of a freely negotiated peace settlement remained a fundamental and common goal of the signatory states. Article I of the Convention contained the essential provision that the Federal Republic was to have full authority over its internal and external affairs except for some important powers to be retained by the Allies. These powers were clearly enumerated and limited in the Convention and the related Conventions. It was stated that in case of doubt the sovereignty of the Federal Republic should be assumed to take precedence. The retained powers were described in Article II which stated that in view of the international situation the three powers retained the rights heretofore exercised or held by them relating to

(a) the stationing of armed forces in Germany and the protection of their security.
(b) Berlin
(c) Germany as a whole, including the unification of Germany in a peace settlement and

The retention of these rights was in our interest too. The chief reason for it was the desire to avoid giving Russia the opportunity to say that as the three powers had themselves relinquished all contractual obligations entered into with the Russians in regard to these questions, Russia too was therefore quite free in its policy toward the Soviet zone. The retained right relating to Germany as a whole, including reunification, derived from the premise that reunification was only possible by way of negotiations with Soviet Russia as well. That was why the three powers retained the right, in our interest, to negotiate with Soviet Russia with this object in view and with our participation. Paragraph 3 of Article III was especially important containing as it did an undertaking by the three powers to consult with the Federal Republic in negotiations with states with which the Federal Republic maintained no relations in respect of matters directly involving its political interest. I had been very much concerned to get this clause included in the treaty. As long ago as autumn 1951, in my first talks with the High Commissioners on 24 September 1951 after the decisions of the Washington Conference had become known, I had most emphatically demanded consultations.

Article V dealt with a possible state of emergency with regard to the security of the forces stationed in the territory of the Federal Republic. In case of a state of emergency the three powers would be allowed to take measures to maintain or restore order and to safeguard the security of their forces if the Federal Republic and the EDC were unable to deal with the situation. Paragraph 6 of Article V read as follows:

> If the powers do not terminate the state of emergency within thirty days after a request by the Federal Government to do so, the Federal Government may submit a request to the Council of the North Atlantic Treaty Organization to examine the situation and consider whether the state of emergency should be terminated. If the Council concludes that continuance of the state of emergency is no longer justified, the three powers will restore the normal situation as promptly as possible.

This article on the state of emergency did not give the three powers the right to resume full authority.

Article VI provided for the special protection of Berlin.

Article VII was of the greatest importance and hence I should like to reproduce it in part verbatim:

> 1. The Federal Republic and the Three Powers are agreed that an essential aim of their common policy is a peace settlement for the whole of Germany, freely negotiated between Germany and her former enemies, which should lay the foundation for a lasting peace. They further agree that the final determination of the boundaries of Germany must await such a settlement.
>
> 2. Pending the peace settlement, the Federal Republic and the Three Powers will cooperate to achieve, by peaceful means, their common aim of a unified Germany enjoying a liberal-democratic constitution, like that of the Federal Republic, and integrated with the European Community.
>
> 3. In the event of the unification of Germany, the Three Powers will, subject to such adjustments as may be agreed, extend to a unified Germany the rights which the Federal Republic has under the present Convention and the related Conventions and will for their part agree that the rights under the treaties for the formation of an integrated European Community should be similarly extended, upon the assumption by such a unified Germany of the obligations of the Federal Republic toward the Three Powers or to any of them under those conventions and treaties. Except by common consent of all the Signatory States, the Federal Republic will not conclude any agreement or enter into any arrangement which would impair the rights of the Three Powers under those conventions or treaties or lessen the obligations of the Federal Republic thereunder.

This Paragraph 3 of Article VII had been the subject of negotiations as late as the day before signature. Agreement on its final wording had not been reached until noon of the 25th. Before the signing of the Convention the so-called *Bindungsklausel* of Article VII had given rise to considerable doubts.

Article VII had played a great role in the negotiations on the Convention. It concerned the question of what would happen to the treaties in case of German reunification. What would happen on the day when a government was established for the whole of Germany? This question, as Robert Schuman said, caused a certain insecurity. He said that for him the question was this: if, after the entry into force of the treaty, a unified German Government assumed authority in Germany, there would have to be a joint decision whether the area of East Germany was to be included in the defence area and what provisions were to be made for the transition period. There was always uncertainty in political life when new factors came into play. One would have to try to find a solution for this question.

As previously stated, this article was still being discussed on the last day before signature. The final wording says that a reunited Germany can claim the rights embodied in the treaties provided it is prepared to accept the obligations. I thought this text good. By its terms a reunited Germany could not be put in a worse position than the Federal Republic if a government of the whole of Germany was willing to assume the rights and obligations of the treaties.

Article X provided for the review of the terms of the Convention in the event of the reunification of Germany or the creation of a European federation or upon the occurrence of any other event which all of the signatory states recognized to be of a similarly fundamental character.

The treaties did not change the basic principles of the legal position of Berlin. All things considered the position of Berlin was much improved in parts, even if it was not yet possible to give Berlin the status attained by the Federal Republic in the treaties because of the international political situation and Berlin's especially sensitive place in it.

There were a number of related Conventions of which the most voluminous were the so-called Forces Convention and the Convention on the Settlement of Matters arising out of the War and the Occupation.

The related Conventions are very long and I cannot reproduce them in detail. I shall confine myself to selecting and commenting on the most important agreements and provisions.

Let me mention the Forces Convention first. By and large it had been modelled on the agreements with the individual NATO states concerning the presence of foreign troops in their country.

The Forces Convention regulated the requirements arising from the presence of security troops on German soil. It did not relate to EDC forces. Because the entire matter was extraordinarily complicated and there was a desire to gain further experience, a review of the Forces Convention after two years was stipulated. The Convention on the Settlement of Matters arising out of the War and the Occupation followed naturally from the fact that after 1945 first the four-power Allied Control Council and later the three Western Allies had issued a multitude of laws, decrees etc. in the Western zones which could not be nullified in one day without complete chaos. Some transitional settlements were therefore necessary.

Another related Convention was the Finance Convention specifying the financial contribution to be assumed by the Federal Republic for the common defence and regulating the procedural questions connected with it.

The treaty on the EDC was of incomparably greater importance – at the time unfortunately insufficiently recognized by the German public – than the Convention, however important that may have been for us. At that time the treaty was, in my opinion, being viewed too much as a response to the tensions of the moment between East and West. It was regrettable that it was judged mainly as an instrument for defence against possible Soviet aggression. The treaty was primarily intended, quite apart from the problems that had arisen from the defeat and unconditional surrender of Germany, to make a war among the European nations of Western Europe impossible. Its primary purpose was to promote the unification of Europe.

The EDC treaty envisaged the renunciation by the participating countries of their most important sovereign right, namely the raising of their own armed forces, and the transfer of this right to a supranational authority. This would be of the most far-reaching importance for the creation of a united Europe. It was to lead almost automatically to a mutual collaboration of participating countries in economic and foreign policy questions, and hence, together with the Schuman Plan and other projects under discussion, was to lead very soon to a European confederation.

This treaty was an act unique in the long history of Europe which, again and again, convulsed by wars and brought to the brink of the abyss by the last two wars, was to be given permanent peace and a new life.

The Preamble of the treaty stated that the signatory countries were:

anxious to preserve the spiritual and moral values which are the common heritage of their peoples, and convinced that within the common force formed without discrimination between the Member States, national patriotism, far from being weakened, will be consolidated and harmonized in a broader framework; . . . [and recognized] that this is a new and essential step towards the creation of a united Europe . . .

Article 38 of the Treaty imposed definite obligations, with a time limit, on the Assembly and the Council of the European Defence Community as well as on the governments of the member states, intended to lead to the creation of a united Europe.

The Significance of the Treaties

It was an important choice that faced the parliaments after the signing of the treaties in deciding whether or not to ratify. As far as the German parliament was concerned the alternatives seemed to me to be these:

1 To accept the treaties and with them the association with the West.

2 To reject them for the sake of association with the East or the neutralization of Germany.

3 To postpone a decision.

To be in a position to make the right decision meant recognizing the actual situation among us, in the Soviet zone, in Europe, and in the whole world. The connections between the various developments that had led up to the present situation and existing tensions had to be considered. Nor was the problem of Germany a problem all on its own. It was a focal point on the line of tension between East and West. One also had to examine the origins of the present situation and what tendencies were discernible in it that might throw light on future developments. One had to examine the question whether after acccptance of the treaty further peaceful developments, and eventually an acceptable solution of the German problem, could be expected. One had also to be clear about the consequences of rejection whether it were motivated by an intention to neutralize Germany or even to opt for the East. Finally one had to examine conscientiously whether it was possible to postpone the decision and whether such a delay was compatible with German interests. In my opinion a postponement of a decision that was not justified by the facts of the case necessarily amounted to evasion. After the governments of eight countries had by extremely hard work achieved agreement, individual member countries must not procrastinate in the matter of ratification.

Events since 1945 were well known. There were two gigantic power systems. As we had frequently seen, the system led by Soviet Russia had strong tendencies to expansion and aggression whose effects were felt far beyond the frontiers of the Eastern bloc, especially in the territory of the Federal Republic, France and Italy, either disguised or undisguised.

The Western system had found its expression in the North Atlantic Treaty and a series of other defensive pacts and arrangements. Additional protocols connected the North Atlantic Treaty with the European Defence Community whereby the Federal Republic, too, was to be integrated in the security system.

The entry into force of the agreements had the following advantages for the Federal Republic: the Occupation Statute would cease to apply; all economic restrictions would stop; we would receive American support; we would get a defensive alliance with Great Britain. The European federation was to begin in the most sensitive area, the military. European wars would be impossible in future. By being made part of the most comprehensive defence system in history we would obtain the greatest imaginable security. We would cease being the mere object of political and strategic calculations and would help determine action ourselves.

This last point was especially important for us. As long as we were an occupied country, as long as we were not yet part of the Western defence system, we were a no-man's-land between the two big power groups. Just as we were a mere object in diplomatic contests, we would also be mere objects in more serious contests. In other words we would become the theatre of such a conflict with all the terrible consequences that would follow for our people. The present tensions in the world urgently demanded that we should put an end to the state of being suspended. If we became co-actors we could use all our strength to help work for a peaceful solution of tensions.

It was sometimes urged in public discussion that ratification of the two treaties would make reunification with the Soviet zone impossible. I held, on the contrary, that by concluding these treaties we had taken an important step toward the goal expressed almost unanimously by the Bundestag in one of its first sessions in the formula 'reunification of Germany in peace and freedom and in a free Europe'.

It was and is true that reunification in freedom can be brought about only with the consent of the four Allies, that is with Russia's consent as well. To this end I thought it wise to secure the help of at least three of the four great powers as we did in the Convention. Once we had the help of these three powers, I hoped that it would be possible at the right moment to get to the negotiating table with the Russians. No one can have honestly believed that the Soviet Union would spontaneously surrender the Soviet zone. I could therefore not see at all how we were lessening the chances of reunification in freedom by concluding these treaties. A united Germany as the Russians were demanding in their Notes, a neutralized Germany based on the Potsdam Agreement, was impossible for us. We would have to try with the help of the three Western Allies to get Russia to give up this demand. I felt that once she had been convinced that the conclusion of the EDC precluded the success of further attempts to gain control of the Federal Republic by way of the cold war – and first by neutralization – she would respect the new political situation and adjust her policy accordingly. One thing was sure: if we did not sign the treaties, we would not improve the chances of reunification in any way. I knew that the men and women in the Soviet zone shared this view. I knew that they regarded the road taken by us as the only way that might one day lead them too out of their distress.

The question had further been raised whether the military strengthening of the West as a consequence of the treaties might not provoke Russia to change over to a hot war. Here too I thought that the opposite was the case. I was convinced that one cannot restrain a heavily armed totalitarian state by remaining as weak as possible. The history of the last twenty years gave two excellent examples of the point. When Hitler armed, nothing had at first been done by the other European countries or by the United States of America. Because Hitler knew that they were militarily weak, he lashed out the moment he thought he was strong enough to win a quick victory. If, when Hitler began to arm, other countries had increased their defence forces, Hitler would never have dared to go to war.

Events after 1945 were similar. Because Soviet Russia remained highly armed while the other countries disarmed, she made ruthless use of her military superiority by subjecting the countries that are now satellite states. I am convinced that Soviet Russia would not have done this if she had had to fear that the others would intervene to stop her. Every consolidation of the Western power of defence increased the probability that Soviet Russia would not proceed to a hot war.

The Federal Republic could not exist without the support of other countries. Germany's geographical situation is particularly unfavourable from the political point of view. She lies in the middle of Europe and has no protected frontiers. Ever since the 1870s Germany has looked for allies. At first it seemed as if the Three Emperors' League – Germany, Austria and Russia – in the year 1872 might provide allies and security. But Bismarck had soon seen that an alliance founded merely on the monarchist idea would have insufficient cohesion in the long run. Two alliance systems then developed: the Triple Alliance between Germany, Austria-Hungary and Italy in 1882 and the Triple Entente between England, France and Russia. Between 1900 and 1904 the Entente Cordiale was formed between France and Great Britain, and added to the existing Franco-Russian alliance. This development prepared the coming catastrophes.

We now needed allies more than ever to preserve our freedom. By joining the EDC which in its turn was connected with the North Atlantic Treaty, by the conclusion of the defensive agreement with Great Britain and by the security guarantee of the United States, we obtained for our country the greatest possible security. All these alliances and pacts had a purely defensive character which was not only clearly expressed but also inherent in the structure of the whole system. The Western defence system could, it was my firm conviction, safeguard peace and freedom for Europe and ourselves. The tension between East and West existed. The powers of the countries of Europe, taken singly, were paralysed. They were now to be combined for the preservation of peace. The United States and Great Britain supported these endeavours with all their strength. I was convinced that these treaties would serve the cause of liberty, the creation of the new Europe, and the reunification of Germany in peace and freedom.

THE WORLD SITUATION IN THE
SPRING OF 1953

A New President in the United States: Eisenhower Succeeds Truman

Elections had taken place in the United States on 4 November 1952 from which the Republican Party and its Presidential candidate, General Eisenhower, had emerged victorious. The decisive question for us was whether the Eisenhower administration would continue the European policy of the Democratic Party and President Truman.

All were agreed in Europe that without the support of the United States the decline of Europe would be irreversible. There were different schools of thought on the importance of Europe for the United States. These were epitomized in three persons: Taft (Republican), Truman (Democrat), Eisenhower (Republican).

Truman and Eisenhower regarded Europe as more important for the USA than Asia, while Taft spoke for the view that the centre of gravity of American policy should lie in Asia. In the selection of the Republican Presidential candidate the choice had been between General Eisenhower and Senator Taft, the representatives of these opposed political schools of thought. The Eisenhower school had prevailed.

On 6 November 1952 I had a conversation with the American writer Freda Utley on the result of the election in the United States. Mrs Utley asked me for my opinion on the Republican victory. I replied that this was not an easy question to answer; Germany had much cause for gratitude to the Truman administration and its Secretary of State, Acheson. Mrs Utley asked me for my assessment of Eisenhower.

I had met Eisenhower for the first time in June of 1951 when he visited me in his capacity as Supreme Commander of NATO. I met him for a second time on 2 May 1952 on the occasion of his farewell visit as Supreme Commander of NATO in Europe. I was glad that a man who knew European conditions well was to become President of the United States. I had met Dulles, the future Secretary of State, for the first time in 1948. I told Mrs Utley that I was full of confidence in the future administration of the United States of America.

President Eisenhower's assumption of office was an event of great importance not only for the United States but for the whole of the world, and especially for us Europeans. From the period of the war and the time after and his work as Supreme Allied Commander of the NATO forces President Eisenhower knew the situation in Europe and the pressure of Soviet Russia. Because of his character and his experience I was convinced that he would continue and if necessary reinforce the policy initiated and pursued by his predecessor regarding the defence of Europe vis-à-vis the East. Eisenhower's avowal at his inauguration of his intention to protect freedom and peace filled me with sincere joy.

There had been those who before the inauguration of President Eisenhower had expressed the opinion that the new American administration would assume a different attitude towards Soviet Russia and Europe. There were those who believed that the American administration would immediately enter into negotiations for a lessening of tension between Soviet Russia and the United States, and would lose its interest in Europe and thus in the Federal Republic. These prophets were wrong.

The opposite happened: the American interest in the integration of Europe and in the achievement of a treaty on the European Defence Community was expressed even more strongly than in the second half of 1952.

The Visit of Dulles to Bonn in February 1953

The new American Secretary of State, John Foster Dulles, was to visit Europe, and the Federal Republic, in February 1953. I considered this visit very important. Dulles was coming to Europe to learn about conditions here at first hand. His impressions would be extremely important for the shaping of American foreign policy.

The American President and the Secretary of State were in no way obliged to take over the foreign policy of their predecessors *in toto*. This was certainly true of the policy toward Europe and the policy toward Germany was naturally no exception. Not that I expected great changes in American foreign policy; nonetheless, the impressions Dulles would receive during his visit to Europe would have far-reaching significance.

I had come to know President Eisenhower as a man who knew exactly what he wanted. He was, like Truman, not the kind of man who would tomorrow regard something as undesirable that yesterday had appeared necessary.

It seemed to me to be clear that in its European policy the United States would start from the premise that Europe itself must be ready to defend itself and, beyond the military sphere, to create a European political community. I was convinced that on this condition America would continue to be prepared to support Europe and to help in its defence. If this condition was not fulfilled, American policy might indeed change, and this change would certainly not be in favour of the Federal Republic. It was therefore of the greatest importance that the EDC treaty should be ratified as soon as possible by the six countries concerned. If the EDC were to founder the American interest in Europe would be endangered. If we were to be defended on the Elbe, we must behave accordingly. The American interest would be very largely decided by the attitude of the countries of Europe.

First of all President Eisenhower had to be concerned to find a reliable majority in Congress for his foreign policy. The contest inside the Republican Party with the group around Senator Taft who defended the view that the centre of gravity of the United States interest was in Asia, not Europe, had not yet been concluded. Whether and how President Eisenhower would find a majority for his policy depended in high degree on Europe combining for a joint defence policy. Every European hesitation must be grist for the mill of those who gave precedence to the defence of Asia. Whoever wants to insure himself must pay a premium. This went for Europe too. Whoever believed that Europe had an insurance in America without a premium was caught in a fatal error. Europe would either unite or it must in the long run succumb to Soviet Russia. People often asked for an alternative to a European policy. The decline of Europe was and is the true alternative.

During his visit to Europe the American Secretary of State, Dulles, chiefly wanted to collect information on the state of developments in European unification. He had announced this intention very clearly. I wished that he might find time to talk with as many German politicians as possible. I thought this would be useful not only for his own information but also for the information of the Germans he would talk with. A few German illusions, especially among the Social Democrats, needed destroying. If it was only I who said that the Americans would be unwilling to negotiate again in the case of non-ratification of the EDC treaty and the Convention, no one would be prepared to believe me. Dulles would be believed.

The Convention and the EDC treaty still had to have their third reading in the Bundestag. At the time of Dulles's visit to Germany a number of difficulties remained to be overcome in order to get a Bundestag majority for the treaties. I was, however, convinced that this would be possible. I believed that reason and a sense of reality would be stronger than all illusions. Reason and a sense of reality in German foreign policy meant starting from a given world situation and then seeking the best possible place in it for Germany.

Many politicians however took other paths in their thinking. They thought of something very good for Germany without any regard to the world situation.

If a weak country like Germany, which a mere eight years previously had broken down after the most insane of all wars, wanted to pursue a missionary policy of changing the world, this was no more than illusory. The Federal Republic was full of ideas that had nothing to do with reality. Political realism was still our weak point.

Some plans looked roughly like this. Let the Russians and the Americans get together. The Americans stop the war in Korea and leave all Korea to the Communists. In exchange the Russians give up the German Soviet zone and Germany is reunited. Then a national German army is created which will be jointly controlled by the Soviets and the Americans and both these countries will jointly guarantee the neutrality of the united Germany. This is approximately how it looked to neutralist politicians. The entire world situation was to be stood on its head for the sake of a German pipedream. Plans like these, dreamed up at a green table, blocked all access to reality. Neither the Russians nor the Americans had the remotest intention of acting in this way.

The realities looked different. The cold war and the persistent Russian danger were facts. On the Western side the North Atlantic Treaty had been created for mutual protection. There were several beginnings of efforts for closer European cooperation: the Coal and Steel Community, the Defence Community and the Political Community.

In this world situation there was only one possibility that made sense for Germany: to make common cause with the West and to take her place in a free Europe, economically, militarily and politically. It was a policy of pure self-preservation. It was a policy of the smaller risk – and there was no policy without risk.

The divided Germany was unfortunately another given factor of the world situation. But as things stood it simply was a fact that if we did not align ourselves with the West, with Europe, we would not thereby approach by a single step the reunification of Germany in freedom.

Dulles came to Bonn on 5 February 1953. As stated before, I was most concerned that while in Germany he should meet as many German politicians of all parties as possible in order to make the American political attitude unmistakably clear to them.

In my conversations with him Dulles told me of his talks with the representatives of the SPD, Ollenhauer, Carlo Schmid and Wehner. Dulles had been trying to explain the importance of the Convention and the EDC treaty to the Social Democrats. Their chief objection had been, as he reported, that the treaties prevented the reunification of Germany. They were not going to recognize these treaties without a decision of the Constitutional Court nor would the German people, they thought, accept the treaties without such a decision. As an alternative to the EDC they had proposed the formation of a national army in the framework of as comprehensive an alliance as possible.

Dulles had told them that the United States placed the greatest value on a fusion of the French and German armed forces, as it was the only way of keeping these two peoples from ever fighting each other again, and the only way of preventing a resumption of the old European conflicts. The United States would not support a return to the old European situation of nation-states. The success of integration was necessary in order to meet the fatal development that would otherwise ensue. The vision of a European integration had caught the imagination of the American people. If it failed, the old situation of rival and conflicting forces in Europe would return. Even if the present settlement were imperfect and deserved criticism, it was still infinitely better than the catastrophe that would happen if the attempt to integrate failed. Furthermore, German reunification could only be achieved by a policy of strength.

Dulles informed me that he had told the Social Democrats the following on the subject of German unity: he had been concerned with this question since his participation in the Foreign Ministers' Conference in Moscow in 1947 and had as a result of his work on the problems of Austria and Korea special experience in the field of the reunification of divided nations. He knew that a change in the present situation could not be got from the Soviets by discussions, pleas, and verbal displays. The quite decisive point was that West Germany must have the courage for an independent policy. As long as West Germany lacked this and was afraid of impairing Russia's inclination to agree to reunification, reunification would become harder and harder. Indeed such an attitude meant in practice that Soviet Russia, by using its consent to reunification as a bait, virtually controlled the Federal Republic and its policy. There was only one way: Germany must become strong and the Russians' chance of blackmail would cease. All this he, Dulles, had told the gentlemen of the SPD quite clearly.

I was in full agreement with Dulles, and pointed out to him that these views were widely held in the Soviet zone as well. Everything we heard from there, epecially in the statements by refugees, urged a firm policy toward the Russians.

On the ratification of the Convention and the EDC treaty I said that the third reading could begin soon and that I was counting on an even greater majority than in the second reading. Regarding the development of Europe one should not forget, beside the Defence Community, what was being done in Luxembourg in the economic field. The EDC was a part of the comprehensive process of the unification of Europe.

The French had brought up a series of special requests of which however we had so far been told only by word of mouth and in outline. I hoped they were not additional requests that would necessitate a new ratification of the treaty and therefore further delays. This, incidentally, was a hope shared by the other EDC countries.

In my conversation with Dulles I pointed to the special problem facing us in the Federal Republic in its expellees and refugees. Between 1945 and 1952 we had ourselves raised DM 25 billion for this very difficult problem. It was however beyond our strength to resolve it alone, although we were making the greatest efforts. Thus, for instance, the equalization of burdens programme was already halving existing assets. The absorption of refugees was costing DM 3·7 billion a year, of which DM 1·1 billion was beyond our own ability to produce. During the year 1953 we were expecting an additional 250,000 refugees. It was particularly difficult to find a solution in the case of farmers for whom we could not provide enough land. I was not asking for economic aid and as far as possible we wanted to solve our own problems. But I was worried by our lack of capital. If a period of economic difficulties came along this lack would have very serious consequences: our economy would be unable to cope with the unemployed.

The debt negotiations in London were approaching their end. I was hoping that once they were concluded there would be possibilities of our getting credit. I would be very grateful if the administration could use its good offices to get loans for our enterprises. One should not forget that the fight against communism was also taking place on the economic front.

With every year that passed and showed Germany was again rising and giving people hope, the number of those who clung to communism diminished and, incidentally, so did the adherents of the extremist Right. Dulles noted this point.

The EDC was obviously, as everything he said showed, very close to his heart. He stressed that it was of the greatest importance for the EDC to be ratified as quickly as possible. More than nine months had now passed since the signature. In the United States the growing impression that the project was dead had led to discouragement.

The special motive of Dulles's European trip had been to urge action on the EDC. Eisenhower had asked him to go to Europe as quickly as possible in order to breathe a spark of life into the project once more. He drew my attention to American time-tables. There would be an important conference of NATO on 23 April. By that time exact plans would have to be submitted on the defence costs of the United States. Congressional approval was unlikely unless it had previously been made clear that the realization of the European plan was certain.

He did not know the details of the additional French requests. He had however been told categorically by Prime Minister René Mayer that these would not alter the treaties. They merely concerned anticipation of measures that could otherwise not be taken until the treaties had come into force. The best way to forestall an alteration of the treaties was to ratify as quickly as possible. France could not stand alone outside the community. Ratification by the other countries would mean such pressure on France that she would have to ratify herself. He hoped that the Italians were about to ratify in the very near future. He was going to ask the Dutch to do likewise. So long however as no one in Europe concluded ratification there could be no progress.

John McCloy, until recently American High Commissioner, had been succeeded by Professor James Conant, the former President of Harvard, one of the most ancient and venerable American universities. During his talks in Bonn Dulles said that Conant would not have been appointed American representative in Germany had it not been thought that the relations between the United States and Germany would be especially important in the future. Conant was bringing his knowledge, his wisdom, and his strength of character to the task, qualities that were recognized not only in America but in the whole world.

About German reunification, Dulles said that he wished that people in Germany could feel how genuine was the American concern for the fate of the Germans in the East. He said that our brothers and sisters in East Germany did not deserve the fate that had come to them. A way must be found to free them from their fate and to reunite them peacefully with their brothers in the West. He explained that for six years, ever since the Moscow Conference of Foreign Ministers, he had been convinced – and the conviction had grown stronger – that the fragmentation of Germany could be undone again and that Germany must be reunited by international politics. He was completely convinced that the unification of Europe would not mean a delay but on the contrary an acceleration of the reunification of Germany. These two objectives were together two essential tasks of foreign policy and mutually quite compatible. Even if the division of Germany meant nothing more than a weakening of the West, that alone was a crime which would have to be undone. All this showed that Germany could put its confidence in the plan of uniting Europe.

The fact was – and everyone with eyes could see it – that the former Europe, the Europe of contending nations, no longer had a future. The only future for Europe lay in unification and integration. This unification must be possible especially as the culture, civilization, habits of thought and life of Europeans were mutually related. Europe had a great future; but this could be realized only by great men capable of great deeds. The world was fortunate that at this critical moment when its fate was in the balance, Europe had produced a number of wise and vigorous men who were equal to this great historic task.

The Death of Stalin

The death of Stalin surprised the world on 5 March 1953. For some time beforehand there had been those who predicted that his death would bring a general détente. It was, however, very soon clear that this was not the case, and that the new Soviet rulers were restless and unpredictable and therefore especially dangerous.

What direct consequences Stalin's death would have on the course of affairs and on the fate of Germany and Europe could not be clearly seen immediately afterwards. But one thing I thought could be said with certainty: the death of Stalin had certainly not diminished the dangers of the world situation which threatened us Germans particularly. It had further increased instability and with it the danger in which we all found ourselves.

It might be, of course, that Stalin's death would force the rulers of Russia to pay more attention to questions of internal policy. I hoped that the peoples of Europe would use this possible breathing space to build up their defences.

On the great world stage Stalin's disappearance meant an entr'acte. One did not and could not know how things would develop in the East. Vigilance, firmness, a calm and steady continuance of previous policies seemed to me more appropriate than ever at this time of insecurity and uncertainty. No one among us was able to say what was really happening in the Kremlin. Only one thing was sure: the death of Stalin whose person had embodied all authority in Soviet Russia and the satellite countries had created a great gap, a gap which no man and no directorate would be able to fill immediately. Because developments were so uncertain one had to reckon with all possibilities and to be prepared for the good and the bad. I thought that we ought to remember that immediately after the war it was the unsure policy of the West in the face of the Russian advance that had led to the fateful development that followed, and I hoped we had learned that the steady pursuit of a firm policy by the West was the surest road to peace.

The Decisive Criteria of the EDC Treaty

During his first visit to the Federal Republic as American Secretary of State in 1953 Dulles had told me that the United States policy in Europe was determined by American interests and the United States interest lay in a unification and strengthening of Europe.

On 19 March 1953 the Bundestag in its third reading adopted the Convention by a majority of sixty-two and the EDC treaty by a majority of fifty-nine. This was an increased majority compared with the second reading of 6 December 1952. The Bundestag was the first parliament to complete all stages of the ratification of the EDC treaty.

I regarded the EDC as an important instrument of the unification of Europe. A knitting together of European purposes and wills was the real aim of my European policy. The early stages of European integration had already led to a constant exchange of views between the ministers and leading officials of member states in important matters. I was determined to increase contacts of the Federal Government with the governments of the other participating countries so that, while observing their constitutions, members could jointly direct their policies to the needs of creating protection against attack from outside. If the achievement of the EDC and the continuation of the European policy of the Federal Republic were necessary in 1952, they were all the more necessary after the death of Stalin. There was another reason for this policy becoming even more urgent for us: the Federal Republic must at last emerge from the impossible position in which it found itself at the time – we were still under occupation law with all the attendant consequences. We still had industrial restrictions, we were still a mere object of other people's foreign policy. Although the others did not always make us feel this, in view of the signature of the Convention and the EDC treaty by the governments concerned, and consulted us on questions of German relations with Soviet Russia, in the last resort we had no claim to such consultation.

Because of the great instability of the entire political situation all over the globe due to the East-West tensions, every German could have only one wish:

as long as Soviet Russia does not recognize that, despite all her military might she will get nowhere, so long as we cannot live calm and secure, we must do everything to get the necessary protection and the necessary security as quickly as possible. The conclusion and implementation of the treaties would give us the greatest possible security.

An agreement made between six partners cannot fulfil all the wishes or meet all the interests of any one of the contracting parties. It is only by compromise and accommodation that contracts between several participants finally come about. It would be wrong to base one's judgment of an agreement solely on a critique of details and to fail to see the general considerations mentioned before and the features that constituted the essence and importance of the treaty in a world situation such as we were dealing with. My view and verdict was this: We were threatened; we were the object of the foreign policy of others; we were unable to defend ourselves. This state of affairs would change fundamentally and rapidly after ratification of the treaties. Together with the other members of EDC and the NATO forces we would be able to defend ourselves. We would be secure and included in the greatest defence organization mankind had so far created. By ratifying the EDC treaty we helped to lay the foundation, as a free people, for the political and economic unification of Europe and saved Europe from the decay and perdition that threatened it.

In a Note of 11 March 1953 the British Government had declared itself willing to work for an extension of the validity of the North Atlantic Treaty to fifty years, in order to bring it into line with the EDC treaty. The Note had also expressed a British willingness to take a direct part in the work of the EDC by the despatch of a special mission to the Commissariat of the EDC and of a representative to the special sessions of the Council of Ministers. They were to discuss directives for cooperation between the EDC and Great Britain and were to bring about consultations on all matters of common interest. If the EDC treaty had become effective what possibilities of ties between Great Britain and Europe it would have provided!

For all member states as well as for Great Britain the conclusion of the EDC treaty was a matter of vital importance, because all of them, including Great Britain and even the United States, lived under a threat to their security.

These were the big, the truly decisive criteria by which the member countries of the EDC had to decide and to act.

In the Federal Republic it was objected that the treaty would prevent the reunification of Germany. I considered this view wrong. Nobody in the world could believe that Soviet Russia would be prepared to set the Soviet zone free – spontaneously and altruistically – in order that it might freely return to us. The Soviet Union had never paid any attention to the demand for free elections in all of Germany to form a free government. The last Note of the Western Allies on this question remained unanswered. The Soviet Note of 29

436

August 1952 demanded a dictated peace for Germany, based on the Potsdam Agreement. A low standard of living was to be imposed on us as well as controls extending to the smallest details.

It was one of the supreme goals of the policy of the Federal Republic to bring about unification in freedom. At any time the Federal Government would have welcomed promising and proper negotiations by the Western Allies and Soviet Russia in which we should, as a free country, have been entitled to take part. But there was no other way to negotiations with Soviet Russia, there was no other way to the reunification of Germany in conditions of freedom than making the West as strong as possible.

It was the goal of the EDC to create a strong and united Europe. We had to get away from thinking in terms of national states. The last war, the development of weapons technology, and, indeed, of all technology, had created new conditions in the world. There were now two world powers: the United States and Soviet Russia. There was the British Commonwealth whose power was on the decline. The countries of Western Europe to which we belonged were impoverished by wars and weakened politically. They were no longer in a position to save European culture if each country acted by itself. The peoples of Western Europe had to unite politically, economically and culturally. It was the only policy that could enable them to protect the peace, to rebuild Europe, and to make it again a real factor in world politics, in cultural and in economic matters. The EDC treaty was to be decisive for this policy.

The creation of the Council of Europe, the founding of the European Community for Coal and Steel, and the establishment of a European Defence Community were to serve the pacification of Europe. The supranational organizations in particular were to bring the contracting powers so close together through renunciation of sovereignty that wars inside Europe would become impossible. With much care and circumspection a political constitution for Europe was already being worked out. The Federal Republic was involved in this work. It had meanwhile become a member of numerous European organizations. Germany had to become a reliable partner in the nascent community of European peoples.

How many difficulties the free world would have been spared if the European Defence Community had become a reality.

A VISIT OF FRIENDSHIP TO THE
UNITED STATES IN APRIL 1953

First Voyage to America

In 1952 President Truman had invited me to the United States. President Eisenhower repeated this invitation after his inauguration. The first visit of the Chancellor of the Federal Republic of Germany to the United States of America was now fixed for April 1953. It was the first visit of a German head of government to the United States.

I was pleased to accept the invitation. The chief purpose of my visit was further to expand and to strengthen confidence in us and to make the ties of sympathy between the United States and Germany still closer and firmer. A mutual liking and faith in each other's reliability play a decisive role in the relations among peoples.

However, first and foremost I went to the United States in order to take the thanks of the German people for everything the people of the United States had done for Germany after the defeat, and done in a manner so magnanimous that there was no precedent for it in history.

I was full of admiration for the leaders of both parties in that country, among other reasons because of the way they had resisted the danger – after the sudden increase in the power and wealth of the USA in the space of a few decades – of forgetting or overlooking the obligations that power and wealth carry with them. These obligations had been recognized in the United States, first by leading personalities, but then by public opinion at large as well. This awareness of responsibility for other countries after its victory is perhaps one of the greatest merits of the United States.

My visit to Washington took place during an extremely important period for American policy. It was at a time when the Soviet Union was starting a peace offensive. This peace offensive had produced a very insecure political situation. It seemed as though a large part of American public opinion was only too ready to succumb to the blandishments of a détente which for the time being was nothing but a pipedream. American families wanted their sons to come back from Korea. People were tired of war and its tensions.

My visit took place at a time characterized by the uncertainty following Stalin's death. It took place at a time when the Eisenhower administration was deciding its political strategy.

No special programme had been drawn up for the negotiations in the USA and it was not to be expected that precise decisions would be taken as a result of my visit. The new administration was endeavouring to form a general picture of the situation in talks with Great Britain, with France and with us.

I did not go to the United States with the expectation of concluding agreements. The visits of the French Prime Minister, René Mayer, the French Foreign Minister, Bidault, and the British Foreign Secretary, Eden, to Washington shortly before mine had produced no great results and I could not expect that it would be any different in my case. I was hoping for an exchange of views with President Eisenhower and the American administration on general developments in the world and for the chance to discuss in detail certain problems that concerned the two governments especially. I wanted to try to harmonize our views on the political situation and on the position in Europe and thus to facilitate joint political action.

The journey to America began at Le Havre on 2 April 1953. The *United States* was at that time the fastest passenger ship in the world. It was built entirely of firepoof material, mostly light metals. The crossing was extremely stormy. The captain said that after the storm which raged during the first two days of the crossing had calmed down, the waves were still up to 44 feet high. Since the whole ship consisted almost entirely of metal, the din caused by the tremors of the vessel when one of the screws stuck out of the water was indescribable. The journey took five days in all and I had hoped for a little relaxation but there was not much. Nearly all the members of my entourage were seasick and longing for the hour of landing.

We reached New York harbour on 6 April. As we approached the dock, there was a deafening concert of sirens to welcome me. It was indeed a very impressive ceremony of welcome which, I was told, is accorded to very few visitors.

When we had docked many reporters came aboard the *United States* to hear an arrival statement from me. I gave a short press conference aboard the ship and told the journalists that on landing in the United States I felt above all one thing: gratitude to the American people. We Germans thanked them from all our hearts for all the things they had done for us since our defeat. I said:

I believe that it is rare in history that a victor has helped the vanquished in this way. This help has been expressed in many ways, from individual to individual, from organization to organization, by decision of Congress and by measures of your government. The German people have derived courage from all this, we have regained confidence and, above all, we have learned that in the life of nations too, force and egotism are not the only motivating powers.

Those responsible for American politics as well as American public opinion have an exemplary awareness of the fact that power and wealth mean obligations toward others. The American people have not only recognized this obligation, they have acted accordingly. In the history of our times, which contains so many dark chapters, it will be written in golden letters that the United States, true to its tradition and on the basis of its strength, has undertaken the defence of freedom in the world.

During my short time in New York I stayed at the Waldorf Astoria which flew the German flag for the first time since the war.

On the very day of my arrival I called on former President Hoover. I felt an urgent desire to thank this generous man for all the help the German people had received after the war through his work and at his promptings.

President Eisenhower had put his special aircraft *Columbine* at my disposal for the flight from New York to Washington. On the morning of the day after my arrival, 7 April 1953, I flew to Washington. On arrival at the military airfield of Washington I was welcomed by, among others, Vice-President Richard Nixon, Secretary of State John Foster Dulles, Secretary of the Treasury George Humphrey and Secretary of Defence Charles Wilson.

In his address of welcome Nixon described my visit to the United States as a historic moment for the relations between the German and American people. He said that in a park only a stone's throw away from the house in which I was to stay, a statue had been erected to express the gratitude of the American people to Baron von Steuben, the man who gave such powerful and urgently needed help to General Washington and to the young American nation in the days of its war for independence. The American peoples had not forgotten Steuben nor the millions of Germans who came after him and made such a tremendous contribution to the power and the inner strength of the American Republic.

One of the great tragedies of our generation had been that twice within almost a generation our two peoples had been torn asunder by conflict. There was now confidence that we were entering a new era, a new era of peace and friendship between our two peoples, confidence that together we could re-establish the old bonds of friendship which for so long represented the relationship between the German and the American people.

Nixon mentioned the 'truly remarkable recovery' of the Federal Republic and expressed the hope that Germany might soon again achieve a respected and responsible place in the family of nations. He hoped that the fortunate development would continue and that discord and strife would be removed and the foundations laid for a genuine and lasting partnership.

Secretary of State Dulles also made a very remarkable speech of welcome.

He spoke of the encouragement the American people had derived from the fact that the great majority of Germans were ready to link their fate with that of the other free nations of Europe. He said that I had come to Washington at a moment when the representatives of the German people were discussing far-reaching decisions of truly enormous importance. It was not an exaggeration to say that the results of these decisions would not only shape the course of

German history but would also influence the lives of millions of men and women in the whole world. The problems facing the West were great and the time available for their solution was short. The Americans had watched with admiration the big steps taken by the peoples of Europe on their way to political, economic, and military unity. They had witnessed the birth of a new Europe.

During the past eight years the government and people of the USA had stood beside the men and women in Germany who were courageously and successfully attempting to liquidate the inheritance of the past and to build up a new Germany. They were now standing at the threshold of this new Germany, independent and sovereign and yet linked in a genuine partnership with all who love their freedom and love justice and are willing to defend them. Dulles expressed the sincere wish that the Washington talks would promote the common cause and would contribute to the shaping and realization of the new community of free peoples.

As I learned later neither Vice-President Nixon nor Secretary of State Dulles had delivered the prepared texts of their welcoming addresses; both of them had spoken spontaneously and much more warmly.

In my reply I solemnly declared that the German people stood on the side of right and justice for all nations. We would be loyal and zealous partners on the road to freedom and peace on which the United States was leading all nations.

The welcome in Washington was extremely cordial to an extent that 'almost burst the bounds of protocol' as a German paper expressed it in its report.

During my stay in Washington I lived at Blair House, the guest house of the American Government. It is opposite the White House in the centre of Washington and is one of the most famous buildings of the United States. It is closely connected with many important events of American history.

Conversation with President Eisenhower

Soon after my arrival in Washington, on the same morning, I had my first meeting with President Eisenhower at the White House. He received me very warm-heartedly and called me welcome in America.

On the occasion of my visit I had made an offer to send a military hospital with a staff of doctors and nurses for Korea through the Red Cross. I realized, of course, that this was a very modest contribution compared with the sacrifice made by America. Eisenhower began by thanking me for my offer in his own name and that of his cabinet colleagues and the American people. He said that the offer showed that Germany and the United States had common problems that brought them together.

At the beginning of our conversation Eisenhower asked me to feel I was among friends who had the good of a free Germany at heart. Germany and the United States must solve their problems together.

In the course of further statements Eisenhower stressed that the foreign policy of the United States started from the proposition that the countries of Western Europe including Germany must combine in a close federation. Americans were well aware that obstacles to European unity, such as the Saar question, existed and he asked me to talk in greater detail with Secretary of State Dulles. Eisenhower asked me not to misunderstand him. The Americans had no magic remedy for the Saar problem, but they would be glad to be of assistance. He himself was gladly prepared to talk with me about all problems of European unification.

I thanked Eisenhower for his openmindedness and for his interest in the affairs of Europe. Before replying in greater detail to what he had said I assured him that not only the Federal Republic but also the Germans behind the iron curtain stood by the West.

It was my great goal, I continued, to bring about the European Defence Community and the unification of Europe as soon as possible. We Germans endorsed the American policy and would show ourselves to be true and reliable partners. On my arrival at the airport Vice-President Nixon had made me happy when he spoke of the good relations that used to exist between the United States and Germany. It was our desire to restore those relations and if possible to make them even better than they were.

I was very interested to learn what the attitude of the United States was regarding the Soviet peace feelers that had been put out recently.

Eisenhower replied that America was endeavouring like any other people to preserve the peace. But as long as the Soviets wanted only a peace by force they must be stopped by force.

Secretary of State Dulles asked me whether I believed that the Russian peace feelers would have an effect on the attitude of the German people or on the EDC. It was conceivable that some Germans might prefer to wait and see how things developed. He, Dulles, thought that the so-called peace feelers were chiefly a reaction to the constructive policy pursued by the West in Europe and Asia. The obvious conclusion from this was that the policy should continue and that we should not be deflected from it. If the Soviets succeeded in deflecting us from our policy by blandishments we would deserve the misfortunes that would certainly befall us. If, on the other hand, the West stuck to its couse, it could get what it wanted, the reunification of Germany, a State Treaty for Austria, and a peace settlement in Korea and Indochina. It was a communist tactic to recede a bit from time to time in the hope that the other side could be demoralized thereby.

I replied that Americans need have no fear that we in Germany might weaken. The Germans knew the Soviets and their totalitarian ways of thought better than most peoples. Also we knew from our experience during the National Socialist period how a totalitarian state conducts politics. America could rest assured that only a very few people in Germany would welcome a lessening in defence efforts on account of the Soviet peace feelers. Apart from this there was a great similarity between present Russian policy and their policy after the death of Lenin. Then too the Russians had suddenly and temporarily shown themselves more peaceful and conciliatory. I also pointed out that Soviet pressure in the Russian zone of Germany had continued unabated and increased lately especially in Church matters. In my view the Soviet tactics were quite clear. The so-called peace feelers had already been hinted at in an article by Stalin in the periodical *Bolshevik* and in a speech by Malenkov at the Communist Party Conference.

Talks with Secretary of State Dulles

In the afternoon I had another talk with Secretary of State Dulles and Secretary of the Treasury Humphrey and a number of others. Dulles opened the meeting by expressing his satisfaction at the Bundestag's acceptance of the treaties, and at the good prospects of ratification by the Bundesrat. He said he hoped this would facilitate the early entry into force of the EDC. He was somewhat disappointed about the delay of ratification in Italy.

His talks with the French had shown that the main difficulty was the Saar. The Americans found the French thesis that the solution of the Saar question was a precondition for a ratification of the EDC treaty unacceptable on legal grounds. Despite the fact that the American Government could not agree with this French thesis, it was convinced that a solution had to be found before ratification. It would remove the old obstacle. For the rest America was expecting Germany to play the part due to her in an integrated Europe.

I replied that I would very soon make another effort to solve the Saar question. One reason for the lack of progress so far was the change of government in France. The Pinay Government had fallen. The present Prime Minister was René Mayer. Robert Schuman no longer belonged to the cabinet and had been succeeded as Foreign Minister by Bidault. I told Dulles I had nevertheless a feeling that we would soon find a good solution.

I continued that when the EDC treaty was signed all expected it to enter into force in August or September 1952. The delay in ratification in different countries would now postpone the project for another five months, until the autumn. In view of this delay I would welcome it – for the sake of German public opinion – if we could take a few steps forward now. The SPD was engaged in very violent opposition with an eye on the elections in September. These elections also had a great international importance. It was indispensable that the present policy, especially regarding the EDC, should be continued for another four years. It would have been better if the EDC had come into effect before the elections but as this had not happened it was all the more important to dispel any impression among Germans that things had come to a standstill in Europe. There was a clause in the Convention permitting its effectiveness even before all members of EDC had ratified the EDC treaty. I requested an analogous action and the appointment of the American High

Commissioner to the office of Ambassador even now. I did not mean to say that the American High Commission should give up its activity, but there were certain things about which it was easier to talk to an ambassador than to a High Commissioner. It would also be desirable in that case for the German representative in Washington to be given the rank of ambassador. Such a solution had proved possible in the case of Austria. If the Americans granted this request it would impress the Germans very favourably. It would nourish the belief that things were not standing still.

Dulles replied that the United States could do nothing in this respect without consulting the British and French. He himself was in favour of the German suggestion, but it would be better to say nothing about it in public as that might lead to the crystallization of a certain opposition.

Dulles repeated that the United States would look favourably on the German proposal once Germany had done everything possible for ratification and if as much progress as possible could be registered in the Saar question. If the American High Commissioner became Ambassador, the American Government would naturally also welcome a German Ambassador in Washington.

Dulles asked me to describe my views on the Russian situation after the death of Stalin because he assumed that I had information the United States did not have.

I replied that my views on the Russian situation were completely congruent with the President's and those of Dulles himself as far as I had been able to discover. In my opinion the Russian peace feelers were nothing but a sign that the new Soviet leaders needed a lull to settle their internal affairs and therefore wanted to ward off any disturbance that might impinge from outside.

In the Federal Republic we were well informed about events in the Soviet zone and in the satellite countries. There were no indications that Russia had desisted from her intentions. Rearmament was continuing unabated in the Soviet Union, especially along the Western front. There were now seventy divisions in the satellite countries, equipped with the most modern weapons; behind them stood another 140 Russian divisions with several thousand jet planes. Airfields were being built in the Soviet zone for jet planes that could reach Bonn in twenty minutes, Brussels in thirty and Paris in fifty.

In view of this fact there was only one possibility for the West, as I saw it: if the Soviet Union offered something concrete, one should accept it, but for the rest one should continue on the previous course and not be diverted from it. The Federal Republic certainly did not want war, but the danger of war would increase if the West relaxed its rearmament efforts. It would decrease if the West continued to rearm.

I recalled that the Soviet Union had not yet replied to the last Note to the Western powers on free elections in Germany. If the Soviet Union was in earnest about a détente it should permit free elections. Only this would sensibly relax tensions and might actually lead to the reunification of Germany.

In addition I as Federal Chancellor was going to ask the three Western powers through the Allied High Commission to approach the Soviet Union once more about the 300,000 identifiable prisoners of war and deported persons. One should also keep reminding public opinion in the world of these things.

I then turned to the subject of war criminals and commented that it was largely a psychological problem. The American occupation authorities had released the sentenced men in their custody more slowly and hesitantly than the British and French. The chairmen of the soldiers' associations had told me that they would not plead for the release of real war criminals. It would, however, put obstacles in the way of future recruitment if people against whom no war crimes had been proved continued to be held in gaol. For the German defence contingent we would initially need 60,000 to 70,000 volunteers, especially specialists. It would be very difficult to get the best people if nothing had been done by then to improve this situation. The men concerned had expected the establishment of the mixed board envisaged by the treaties, that was to review individual cases, as long ago as last autumn. Now we had to reckon with a delay of a year. It would therefore be useful if the provision for the mixed board could be put in effect ahead of the treaty.

Moreover I asked that the American authorities should be more liberal in their practice of remission. The British and French had made more magnanimous use of their right to remit sentences. America therefore did not have to worry about the other two powers.

Finally I asked that the Spandau cases should also be reviewed once more. I was aware of the difficulties regarding the Russians and I also knew that McCloy had tried to do something in the matter. I did, however, regard it as a moral duty, especially to the old and sick, once more to draw attention to this problem. If the Russians were really concerned to create a better atmosphere now, one could try to get a few concessions on this question. Dulles said that he wanted to think it over and give me an answer the day after.

We then discussed the problem of the financial defence contribution. I expressed the expectation that the conference of ministers in Paris on 17 April would reach an agreement on this question and that the NATO conference of 23 April would then have definite proposals before it.

Dulles replied that the difficulty was that the Germans had so far proposed an amount well below last year's. He must say that in view of the improved economic situation in Germany other countries could not understand a reduction in the defence contribution compared with that of the year before. He did not want to discuss figures with me now but he did want to say that he hoped I would have another look at the problem as soon as I got back to Germany. German financial support was very important for the countries that maintained troops in Germany.

The Americans stressed that the German proposals for a financial defence contribution were being assessed by the same criteria as those of the other countries; there was no discrimination. It was very important for the entire

German contribution to be fixed in time to enable the NATO conference on 23 April to draw up a binding programme. The decisive precondition for the defence contribution was the development of the economy. On the next day, 8 April 1953, I continued the talks with Secretary of State Dulles, again in a larger group. In order to arouse American understanding for the limits of our ability to contribute I went thoroughly into the refugee problem in the Federal Republic.

I stated that this problem had a human, social and economic significance. The world public had so far never adequately appreciated it. The presence of millions of expelled persons and refugees in the Federal Republic made fertile soil for extremism. Those people were very willing to work, but there was a lack of accommodation near the places of work. This had already been recognized in the so-called Sonne Plan* which had proposed an international loan for refugees.

I was told that the American Government could make no concrete proposals before May. Only then would there be a decision in Congress.

I described the equalization of burdens in broad outline and stated that it represented an achievement of unprecedented magnitude on the part of the Federal Republic. We in Germany gave priority to the refugee problem and the German people were determined to go to the limits of the possible in helping themselves.

It was suggested to me during my travels through the United States that I might refer to the equalization of burdens in my speeches. The American administration would certainly keep these facts in mind when approaching Congress with appropriate proposals.

I took the opportunity of a conversation with Dulles to express our thanks for the help given to Berlin, especially because of the unemployment there. The Americans expressed great appreciation of the steadfastness and courage of the inhabitants of Berlin. It was agreed that moral and material support for maintaining the strength of the city was a matter of great importance. I was assured by the Americans that measures of aid were being considered, including an investment programme and other programmes to improve the economic position of Berlin. I also pointed out, however, that the refugees that now arrived in Berlin from the Soviet zone were having to be channelled into the Federal Republic and had to be absorbed there. Moreover one should not let the new refugees make one forget the old. I pointed to the great difficulties faced by the Federal Republic owing to the need to integrate the new flood of refugees from the Soviet zone in addition to the millions of expellees from the Eastern territories of Germany. The Americans recognized the great efforts made in looking after these homeless people and in maintaining the economic and social stability of the Federal Republic. It was also granted that

* Sonne Plan: document worked out by American and German experts, under the chairmanship of Mr Sonne, containing recommendations on the integration of refugees into German economic life; submitted to me on 21 March 1951.

the Federal Republic and Berlin could not bear this burden alone. There was an assurance of help and it was expressly confirmed in the final communiqué.

In the course of the conversation the Americans stressed the importance of the question of East-West trade. It was essential that the American public should not get the impression of less than full cooperation by the Federal Republic on this point. Dulles mentioned the current German shipments of rolling-mill parts to Hungary. The American public and Congress were especially sensitive in the matter of East-West trade and one would have to reckon with cancellation of all foreign aid if a country infringed material portions of the programme drawn up for East-West trade. The importance of the question of East-West trade for German-American relations was urgently underlined. We agreed on joint control of supplies of strategic materials to nations whose policy endangered peace and world security. I gave an assurance that we would, jointly with other trading nations, take additional measures against violation or circumvention of existing strategic controls.

In the course of this conversation Dulles asked the American High Commissioner Conant who was also taking part in the meeting to present the position of the American Government on the subject of war criminals. Conant said that the United States was prepared to put the treaty provisions on the 'Review Board', the mixed committee that was to decide on revision of sentences, into effect as soon as Germany had finally ratified the treaties, that is as soon as the Bundesrat had also endorsed them. If the French or British opposed the suggestion a new reviewing system might be considered for the cases under exclusively American control. Conant asked me for my opinion on a mixed German-American 'Parole Board' such as already existed in Japan.

I stated that I should very much welcome such a committee and would consider it very helpful.

Conant asked that this subject be discussed as little as possible in public in order to avoid mobilizing premature opposition in the British or French camp. As for the Spandau complex, the Americans felt that it should be treated in the context of the Russian peace offensive. This was another subject on which the Russians could demonstrate their good will.

I asked for the mixed German-American 'Parole Board' to be established as soon as possible. It was not a matter of publicity but only a question of releasing from the prisons those who deserved to be released. The British and French, especially the British, were much more generous. I did not think I was betraying a secret in this gathering by saying that the British High Commissioner had assured me that no one temporarily released on grounds of health would be taken back into custody. The Americans could adopt this British system and release people for reasons of health and then simply not let them recover.

Economic questions figured prominently in our discussions in Washington. The relevant part of the final communiqué read:

447

The representatives of both governments exchanged views concerning progress toward the freeing and expansion of world trade and the achievement of currency convertibility. The German representatives expressed particular interest in the reduction of tariffs and customs administrative barriers. For their part, the United States representatives noted President Eisenhower's statement of 7 April that 'the world must achieve an expanding trade, balanced at high levels which will permit each nation to make its full contribution to the progress of the free world's economy and to share fully the benefits of this progress'.

We discussed a number of special problems connected with the normalization of commercial relations between the United States and Germany, including prospects of an increased use of trademarks owned by German nationals before the Second World War. The efforts of the Federal Government to make these trademarks available again to their previous German owners had already met with considerable success. Further progress in this direction, I was assured, would be sympathetically considered by the American administration. I was given an assurance that no further German assets and trademarks would be confiscated or liquidated and that restitution at a later date was under consideration. I expressed my thanks for this assurance and was told that before leaving the United States I would, as a farewell present, receive concrete information on the return of German ships.

After my stay in Washington a statement was simultaneously released in Washington and Bonn announcing the return to the Federal Republic of roughly three hundred and fifty previously German-owned ships. Preparations for the handing over of these ships to the German authorities were to be made by the American High Commissioner in Germany.

On the German side an interest had been expressed in the conclusion of overseas offshore contracts for Germany. On this I was told that as soon as the treaty on the EDC had come into force the same rules would apply to the placing of such contracts in Germany in the framework of EDC as applied in the case of other European countries.

On the subject of closer cultural cooperation between Germany and the United States and the promotion of mutual understanding between the two peoples, there was an exchange of Notes concerning an American-German cultural agreement between Secretary of State Dulles and myself in my capacity as Foreign Minister. This agreement laid down a number of measures intended to promote a better understanding of the intellectual life and social conditions of the two countries. The exchange of teachers, professors and students was to be encouraged by scholarships and privileges of all kinds. The closest possible cooperation was to be achieved between cultural bodies, universities and schools, labour and youth organizations, and agricultural, professional and social associations. Each of the contracting partners was to have the right to establish and maintain institutions in the other country, for

448

instance, cultural and information centres intended to implement the purposes of the cultural agreement. The essential purpose was to strengthen the links between the United States and the Federal Republic by promoting living intellectual contacts and by practical participation in each other's way of life.

My conversations with leading representatives of the new American administration had convinced me that they had recognized the defence of Western Europe as a necessity and intended to meet it by the North Atlantic Treaty Organization which must in turn include a European Defence Community.

Among the achievements of my Washington talks I set the greatest store by the avowal of the American administration that it would work for the reunification of Germany in peace and freedom. The final communiqué declared this to be the common goal and stated that the final reunification of Germany was only possible through West Germany's participation, as a free and equal partner, in the community of the West.

At the end of the conversation I asked that the Saar question be left out of the final communiqué. There were some things which were easier to settle if one did not speak about them. Dulles replied that he had to think about this suggestion. Following the recent visit to Washington of René Mayer, the French Prime Minister, the Saar question had occupied a prominent place in the communiqué and it might lead to misunderstandings if this communiqué did not mention it at all.

We finally agreed on this passage:

The problem of the Saar was discussed and it was agreed that an early agreement should be sought in the common interest.

I had had a comprehensive and frank exchange of opinions in Washington on the world situation in general and American-German relations in particular. There had been full agreement that while no opportunity of achieving a general lessening of tensions should be missed, the free peoples of the West should relax neither their vigilance nor their endeavours to consolidate their unity and to increase their common strength.

A long communiqué was drawn up on our three-day talks in Washington. The text was composed very carefully, every word was considered. The communiqué stressed, at its beginning and at the end, that the conversations had taken place in a spirit of friendship and cooperation and had shown far-reaching agreement on views and goals. At the end there was another explicit mention of the ties of friendship now happily re-established between the two countries by the conversations just concluded. The conclusion of the communiqué read:

The President and the Chancellor are convinced that the conversations just concluded have made a solid contribution to the achievement of common goals of the two countries, in strengthening the ties of friendship now happily re-established and in consolidating the aims and strength of the free world.

The Honorary Degree from Georgetown University

On the day of my arrival in Washington I was made a Doctor of Law *honoris causa* by Georgetown University in a very impressive ceremony.

The President, Edward B. Bunn, S.J., read the text of the citation which stated that it was the challenge of history today 'to find great leaders, men of character and wisdom, who will guide free peoples by persuasion, not by force, by moral ascendancy, not by deceit, by principle, not by opportunism'. I was described in the citation as 'a champion of liberty, a friend of European unity'. President Bunn said: 'Therefore, in virtue of the powers conferred on us by the Congress of the United States, we proudly proclaim Konrad Adenauer Doctor of Law, *honoris causa*.'

The conferment of an honorary doctorate by this old and venerable university immediately after my arrival in the United States impressed me as a signal honour.

In my address at the ceremony I spoke of the struggle going on between the constructive forces of the free world and the destructive forces of atheist totalitarianism. I said that in this decisive struggle, the military defence, economic consolidation, and social progress of the free nations undoubtedly played a great role; but we must have no illusions: military and economic strength alone would not be able to offer resistance to the ever-spreading totalitarian ideology. I said:

> We are in the midst of a decisive spiritual struggle in which universities have a great task to perform. Some educational institutions bear an ample share of responsibility for the false ideologies menacing the peace and freedom of the world through totalitarian systems of different kinds. Many of these destructive theories were taught from academic chairs long before politicians got hold of them, popularized them and made them into totalitarian party ideologies.

I underlined the responsibility resting on institutions of higher learning to do everything by way of scientific research and teaching to disprove false theories endangering the future of the world and to discover and develop the principles best suited to guarantee to human society, as organized in the family, the State, and the comity of nations, healthy and peaceful progress.

Georgetown University consciously based its research and teaching upon Christian humanism. These foundations seemed to me of particular significance in the sphere of international relations. The obligations inherent in the idea of good faith, the recognition of an order based on law and binding upon everyone, the rejection of State omnipotence and narrow state egoism, the affirmation of the solidarity of all men and nations and its concomitant responsibilities, the defence of the *bonum commune* of an international order, the rejection of pernicious race theories, the respect for the dignity and God-given liberty of the individual – all these were ideas which had, to a considerable extent, been formed and developed by Christian thought.

I said that for this reason an institution like Georgetown Unversity was called upon to furnish a decisive contribution to the clarification of the principles on which the comity of nations rests and to draw upon the rich treasures of Christian thought in order to solve, by irreproachable scholarly methods, the difficult problems which modern life posed for us.

Sound ideas were, however, not the only contribution the world expected of a university like Georgetown. Over and above this, it had the task of developing young people into genuine personalities, individuals conscious of their personal responsibilities and able to withstand the temptations of collectivism.

The different totalitarian systems could never have gained control over millions of human beings unless certain tendencies in modern civilization had prepared the ground for subjugation of the masses. In large measure, modern man was no longer conscious of his autonomy or his value as a human being, no longer worked out his own philosophy of life but often for reasons of convenience accepted the ready-made norms offered him by some collective body. This collective, anti-individualist spirit, in diametrical opposition to the very essence of a university, had even invaded the institutions of higher learning. One of their chief tasks was to educate the younger generation to independent thinking and creative work.

In this sphere, too, I concluded, a Christian university today had an imperative task to perform. It was its particular function to educate its students so that they might become mature and independent individuals whose lives rested on the values of religion, the best safeguard against the infiltration of atheist totalitarianism.

Before the National Press Club

On Wednesday, 8 April 1953, the National Press Club gave a luncheon in my honour. On this occasion I communicated to representatives of the American press my thoughts on the situation in the Federal Republic of Germany and the general situation in the world. It is hard to imagine today what it meant in 1953 for a German to be able to speak to this body of the notoriously critical American press.

In my speech I told these journalists that in order to place the constantly changing events of the day in their proper perspective, the events of the last few years must be kept in mind. The following facts I described as so irrefutable and immovable that they had always to be taken into account:

1 The United States had become the most powerful nation on earth. The fundamental principle of its existence was the liberty of the individual.
2 The Soviet Union reached to the heart of Europe and since 1918 had grown very strong militarily and to some extent economically. It was expansionist and had since 1945 greatly extended the territory under its control. By means of a cold war the Soviet Union was seeking to expand that territory

451

still further. The Soviet Union denied personal freedom. It rested on the principles of totalitarian dictatorship.

3 As a consequence of these developments in the United States and the Soviet Union, Great Britain with the Commonwealth no longer had the influence as world power which it had before the two world wars.

4 The countries of continental Europe had suffered extremely heavy losses in the two world wars, politically, economically and militarily. This loss of power was a factor of the greatest importance and one that would influence the history of mankind in one direction or another.

As a man who bore the responsibility of government in the Federal Republic, the country which was, at least in Europe, the prime objective of Soviet policies of expansion and therefore most endangered, I felt it necessary to confront my listeners with these facts in all their gravity. I thought it had to be done in order that the foundations and goals of German policy might be recognized clearly.

The fundamentals of German policy were, I said, these: 'We want freedom. We despise Communism. We want the future of the German people to be associated as closely as possible with the democracies of the West.' I continued:

The United States regards itself as the guardian of freedom by virtue of its historical tradition. America demands of us Europeans that we also use all our might to preserve freedom. And this demand is justified. The European nations, especially the six signatory countries of the European Defence Community, must use all their strength, together with Great Britain, to maintain liberty in Europe.

We in the Federal Republic of Germany see the danger to freedom in all its full significance. We know from our experience of Nazi days what it means to live in bondage. We are prepared to offer our full contribution to the common defence of freedom.

On the subject of Soviet 'peace feelers' I said that one must watch future developments with an open mind but also with caution. One must be careful not to help in a possible attempt to weaken the unity of the West in its stand against Soviet Russia.

In view of the prevailing uncertainty and the precariousness of the whole situation, and particularly in view of the disparity of power relationships in the world, there was only one thing the West could do: it must pursue its policy steadily, consistently, and calmly. This was the right way to preserve peace and liberty and to support Europe in its vitally necessary development, a development that was also in the interests of the United States.

I expressed my conviction that the United States would help Europe to achieve unification. The danger threatening from the East was so great and the European nations were so weakened that, relying solely on their now strength, they could not achieve the goal of European union. I was aware that the nations of Europe who were to form this union would have to relinquish some of their cherished traditions; but times had changed considerably. Progress in the development of European union was so marked that no European statesman could or should evade its necessity. If he did, he would threaten the existence of his own country and of Europe as well. I said:

I do not consider a European union necessary only because of the danger threatening us from the East; I call it good and desirable because it will free new creative forces now shackled by our heritage of fear and distrust. It will open the way for cultural development, for social welfare and for a lasting assurance of peace and freedom . . .

No nation in Europe is able to assure its own military protection or economic development. In the world of today, to insist upon holding high the traditional concepts of nationalism is to surrender Europe.

Every historical epoch has its own tasks. In Europe every single rational argument points toward a united advance at the end of which there will, one day, be the United States of Europe. No one has understood this better than the young people of our continent.

I know that you in the United States of America are impatient at the speed with which we move toward the united Europe. So am I. But nonetheless, we are moving.

I addressed the representatives of the National Press Club for nearly two hours and tried to bring home to my hearers the dangers in which we found ourselves and the road I considered the only right one.

The applause at the end of my speech showed that the audience had listened attentively and agreed with my arguments.

Before the Senate Foreign Relations Committee

One of the most impressive experiences of my trip was a meeting with the Senate Foreign Relations Committee in executive session.

In the foreword to the transcript which was later published on the circumstances of the meeting, Senator Wiley, the chairman of the Foreign Relations Committee, wrote:

During Chancellor Konrad Adenauer's recent visit to the United States, the Foreign Relations Committee extended to him an invitation to meet the members and discuss informally problems of mutual interest in the field of international relations. That meeting took place on the morning of 9 April in executive session, but in view of its importance and its historic nature, it was the opinion of the committee that the record should be made available to the public.

Senator Wiley made a very impressive statement of welcome. He said:

As you know, Mr Chancellor, you are sitting now in the historic room of

453

the Foreign Relations Committee, which under our constitutional system considers all important foreign relations matters . . . As you know, the German people, whom you represent, have made a great contribution to this land of ours. I come from Wisconsin in the Middle West, where one fourth of the people of my state are of German extraction. I believe that is true to a greater or lesser degree of the Senators from other states here today. Some of our ancestors came to the United States in the Revolutionary days; Carl Schurz later made a great contribution during the Civil War, for, as you recall, emigrant Germans and Irish aided in turning the war in favour of the North.

Now, you are here representing the homeland. All America extends to you a welcome . . . On behalf of the Committee, I welcome you, Sir. We feel that your nation and our nation share many common goals. All the Western countries, including some former mortal enemies, are in the same boat now and must pull together, for, as was brought out at the meetings of the Council of Europe, which some of us attended at Strasbourg in 1951, in unity there is strength.

You, as a representative of your nation, and we as representatives of ours, are engaged in a most important enterprise – that of trying to build a stable future. We know something about your background. We know you are a real builder. As Mayor of Cologne, you have helped to build understanding between peoples. You have helped to rub out the misunderstandings between our people and your people, and some of us who have had the privilege of visiting Germany have felt the warmth of that understanding which you have been so instrumental in developing. We are aware that only with understanding can we build a better world, and we recognize you as one of the leaders of that movement to create wider areas of understanding in this world. Without it, the world will go to pieces.

I was deeply impressed by the importance of this hour when, as Chancellor of the Federal Republic of Germany, I was in the room where so many major decisions of foreign policy are settled.

Wiley asked me to speak to the Senators about the Federal Republic and about my impressions in the United States.

I was glad to take this opportunity. On the situation in the Federal Republic I said that we needed two things above all: one had to combine the gift of being realistic in outlook and approach to problems with a certain divination, a certain insight into the way things would probably happen in the future. I thought no good work could be done right at the beginning of the new historical epoch in which we now found ourselves without this gift, this view into the future.

The United States had historically, within a very short period of time, gained such enormous power, such enormous wealth, as involved very serious danger for all concerned. But the people of the United States recognized, as had hardly any other people before, the enormous extent of the responsibility they had to bear as leaders of mankind, and as the protectors of all human ideals.

The impressions I had received in the United States had strengthened my conviction that if Europe did not unite, it would fall to pieces. In view of the magnitude of the United States and the vastness of its means and resources I was convinced that the present political structure of Europe was obsolete.

I was asked to speak about my views on relations with the Soviet Union.

I told the senators that here in the United States people recognized right, justice, faith, but one should not forget that these concepts were unknown in Soviet Russia. Russia used any means she thought would further her purpose. The Soviets were convinced that the end justified the means. I felt that one should not reject any peace moves and peace feelers outright, but they should be watched with caution and also with distrust. The experience with Hitler had shown that a totalitarian state was prepared to discuss and to meet another country only if it knew the other was strong. One should remember Stalin's words on the watchword of the East: wait and see; after all, the West will not succeed in uniting.

On the reunification of Germany I said that this problem was not an isolated one, but a question closely and intimately linked with the question of Europe as such. A neutralized Germany was no solution. With the Soviet bloc on the one hand and on the other the free countries of Western Europe and far away the United States, and between them a neutralized Germany, the following development would probably take place: the influence of Soviet power and Soviet strength would be so great – it could be compared to a magnet which attracts iron – that after some time the Soviet Union would attract all the weakened European countries. The existence of Soviet Russia in the heart of Europe today would finally lead to the other Western European countries coming under the domination of Soviet Russia; and this would mean that Soviet Russia would have achieved one of her essential aims: the mastery of Western Europe.

I concluded with my thanks for the cordial welcome given me in the United States and expressed the hope that in all future foreign policy decisions the senators would be conscious of the immense responsibility resting on their shoulders.

I was particularly struck by a statement by Senator Mansfield, a Democrat from Montana. He said that the American people were very much pleased with German adherence to the EDC and he hoped that the day was not too long distant when Germany could become a member of NATO, when Germany could become unified, when the occupation troops of all powers could be withdrawn and Germans could once again stand on their own feet as members of the common European community.

My first trip to America was one of the many steps on the hard road of a defeated people back into the comity of nations. This path had to be trodden with much patience, with circumspection, and without any overestimate of oneself. One had always to expect setbacks and to some extent deliberate mischief. We had to remember that we still had many opponents and that there were still great psychological obstacles in the way.

What mattered most was leading our country out of its isolation after its complete defeat. I had to do everything I could to win over our opponents of the Second World War as allies and friends. This called for care and subtlety. My chief aim was to lead Germany back as an equal into the European comity of nations and to achieve the integration of Germany in the free world.

The success of my Washington talks lay primarily in the psychological realm which is so difficult to assess. It meant the end of a very unhappy phase of German-American relations. The final communiqué expressly used the word friendship at the beginning and end. This word meant a great deal.

The road we Germans had covered since 1945 had been hard. But much had been achieved in a short span of eight years. This became very clear to me during my visit to the American National Cemetery at Arlington which remains an unforgettable experience.

At the Tomb of the Unknown Soldier at Arlington

I had expressed the intention of laying a wreath at the monument of the unknown soldier at the national cemetery at Arlington.

The American administration made it a very impressive ceremony. The occasion symbolized the end of the years of enmity in a way that was most moving. It showed the world that that epoch was over and that an era of friendship had begun in which the Federal Republic was accepted once more in the circle and company of the free peoples.

Arlington, the national cemetery of the United States, is a little distance from Washington. It lies in a beautiful region in the midst of a large park. My visit there on 8 April 1953 was the climax of my stay in the United States, the symbolic climax of eight years of hard work.

On arriving I was welcomed by an American general. He accompanied me to the tomb. Three American ensigns walked behind us. The middle one carried the German flag. The wide square in front of the tomb was lined by detachments of all branches of the American armed forces. A twenty-one-gun salute thundered across the area as I walked to the tomb with the general, the German flag close behind me. At the tomb, while commands were ringing through the air, I placed a wreath with a ribbon of black, red and gold. It was for the dead of both nations. An American band played the German national anthem. I saw how tears were running down the face of one of my companions, and I, too, was deeply moved. It had been a long and hard road from the total catastrophe of the year 1945 to this moment of the year 1953 when the German national anthem was heard in the national cemetery of the United States.

INDEX

INDEX

Throughout the index the following abbreviations are used: KA for Konrad Adenauer, AHC for Allied High Commissioners, EDC for European Defence Community, FMC for Foreign Ministers' Conference, FR for Federal Republic of Germany, G for Germany or German, *N* for footnote, US for United States of America.

Conferences are listed under the place at which they were held.

459